MATTER, IMAGINATION AND GEOMETRY

This book considers conditions of applicability of mathematics to the study of natural phenomena. The possibility of such an application is one of the fundamental assumptions underlying the enormous theoretical and practical success of modern science. Addressing problems of matter, substance, infinity, number, structure of cognitive faculties, imagination, and of construction of mathematical objects, Dmitri Nikulin examines mathematical (geometrical) objects in their relation to geometrical or intelligible matter and to imagination. The author explores questions in the history of philosophy and science, particularly in late antiquity and early modernity. The focus is on key thinkers Plotinus and Descartes (with the occasional appearance of Plato, Aristotle, Euclid, Proclus, Newton and others), in whom the fundamental presuppositions of ripe antiquity and of early modernity find their definite expression.

Matter, Imagination and Geometry presents one of the first studies to compare the relation of mathematics to physics in ancient (especially Neoplatonic) and early modern science and philosophy.

ASHGATE NEW CRITICAL THINKING IN PHILOSOPHY

The *Ashgate New Critical Thinking in Philosophy* series aims to bring high quality research monograph publishing back into focus for authors, the international library market, and student, academic and research readers. Headed by an international editorial advisory board of acclaimed scholars from across the philosophical spectrum, this new monograph series presents cutting-edge research from established as well as exciting new authors in the field; spans the breadth of philosophy and related disciplinary and interdisciplinary perspectives; and takes contemporary philosophical research into new directions and debate.

Series Editorial Board:

David Cooper, University of Durham, UK
Peter Lipton, University of Cambridge, UK
Sean Sayers, University of Kent at Canterbury, UK
Simon Critchley, University of Essex, UK
Simon Glendinning, University of Reading, UK
Paul Helm, King's College London, UK
David Lamb, University of Birmingham, UK
Stephen Mulhall, University of Oxford, UK
Greg McCulloch, University of Birmingham, UK
Ernest Sosa, Brown University, Rhode Island, USA
John Post, Vanderbilt University, Nashville, USA
Alan Goldman, University of Miami, Florida, USA
Joseph Friggieri, University of Malta, Malta
Graham Priest, University of Queensland, Brisbane, Australia
Moira Gatens, University of Sydney, Australia
Alan Musgrave, University of Otago, New Zealand

Matter, Imagination and Geometry
Ontology, natural philosophy and mathematics in
Plotinus, Proclus and Descartes

DMITRI NIKULIN
New School for Social Research

Ashgate

© Dmitri Nikulin 2002

All rights reserved. No part of this publication may be reproduced, stored in a retrieval system, or transmitted in any form or by any means, electronic, mechanical, photocopying, recording or otherwise without the prior permission of the publisher.

Published by
Ashgate Publishing Limited
Gower House
Croft Road
Aldershot
Hants GU11 3HR
England

Ashgate Publishing Company
131 Main Street
Burlington, VT 05401-5600 USA

Ashgate website: http://www.ashgate.com

British Library Cataloguing in Publication Data
Nikulin, Dmitri
    Matter, imagination and geometry : ontology, natural
    philosophy and mathematics in Plotinus, Proclus and
    Descartes. - (Ashgate new critical thinking in philosophy)
    1. Plotinus 2. Descartes, René, 1596-1650 3. Matter
    4. Mathematics - Philosophy 5. Physics - Philosophy
    6. Ontology
    I. Title
    117

Library of Congress Cataloging-in-Publication Data
Nikulin, D. V. (Dmitri Vladimirovich)
    Matter, imagination and geometry : ontology, natural philosophy and mathematics in
    Plotinus, Proclus and Descartes / Dmitri Nikulin.
       p. cm. -- (Ashgate new critical thinking in philosophy)
    Includes bibliographical references and index.
    ISBN 0-7546-1574-X
    1. Mathematical physics--Philosophy. 2. Science, Ancient. 3. Plotinus. 4. Proclus, ca.
    410-485. 5. Descartes, René, 1596-1650. I. Title. II. Series.

QC20.6 .N54 2001
509--dc21

2001022642

ISBN 0 7546 1574 X

Printed and bound by Athenaeum Press, Ltd.,
Gateshead, Tyne & Wear.

Piae memoriae aviae avique meorum

ὡς τοῦ ἀεὶ ὄντος γνώσεως
ἀλλὰ οὐ τοῦ
ποτέ τι γιγνομένου καὶ ἀπολλυμένου.
εὐομολόγητον, ἔφη· τοῦ γὰρ ἀεὶ ὄντος
ἡ γεωμετρκὴ γνῶσίς ἐστιν

Plato. RP 527b 5-8

Contents

Introduction   ix

PART I: MATTER   1

1.1 The notion of matter   2
    1.1.1 On the notion of matter in Aristotle   2
    1.1.2 Plotinus on matter   6
    1.1.3 Matter and extension in Descartes   12
1.2 Substance: ontology vs. henology   19
    1.2.1 The One and the multitude in Plotinus   20
    1.2.2 Distinction between the One and matter   26
    1.2.3 Substance and attribute in Descartes   28
1.3 Infinity   34
    1.3.1 Infinity in Aristotle and Plotinus   34
    1.3.2 Infinity as perfection: Infini and indéfini   39
    1.3.3 Paradox and infinity   51
    1.3.4 Indefinite divisibility of physical and mathematical entities in Descartes   54
1.4 Substance and essence   58
    1.4.1 Otherness in substance   58
    1.4.2 Essence and existence: Descartes' essentialism   63

PART II: INTELLIGIBLE MATTER AND GEOMETRY   69

2.1 Geometry, arithmetic and physics in antiquity   70
    2.1.1 Foundations of arithmetic in Plotinus   72
    2.1.2 Constitution and the structure of number in Plotinus   81
    2.1.3 Number and magnitude in ancient mathematics: The point   91
    2.1.4 The in(de)finite in mathematical reasoning   95
2.2 Geometry, metaphysics and method in Descartes   103
    2.2.1 Geometry in its relation to physics according to Descartes   113
    2.2.2 Number and magnitude in Descartes   122
2.3 Intermediary   127
    2.3.1 Geometrical objects as intermediary: Proclus vs. Descartes   128
2.4 The notion of intelligible matter   132
    2.4.1 Intelligible matter in Plotinus   135
    2.4.2 Intelligible matter in Proclus   141

PART III: REASON, IMAGINATION AND CONSTRUCTION   145

- 3.1   Reason and the structure of cognitive faculties   146
  - 3.1.1   Intellect-noys in Plotinus   146
  - 3.1.2   Discursive thinking-dianoia   150
  - 3.1.3   Life   152
  - 3.1.4   Mind and its ideas: Descartes   157
- 3.2   Imagination in ancient philosophy   171
  - 3.2.1   Aristotle and Plato on imagination   171
  - 3.2.2   Imagination in Plotinus   175
  - 3.2.3   Main features of imagination in Neoplatonism: Porphyry, Syrianus, Proclus   179
  - 3.2.4   Imagination and intelligible matter   183
- 3.3   Imagination in Descartes   187
  - 3.3.1   Mind, imagination and the infinite   192
  - 3.3.2   Imagination and mathematics according to Descartes   204
- 3.4   Imagination and kinematic construction in geometry   210
  - 3.4.1   Construction and the *verum factum* principle: Cartesian reconstruction of the world   210
  - 3.4.2   Construction in geometry: Kinematic constructibility in Descartes   223
  - 3.4.3   Imagination and geometry: Imagination as constructive   230
  - 3.4.4   Movement in the intellect according to Plotinus   239
  - 3.4.5   Motion and construction in Proclus: Production of a geometrical figure by movement in imagination   245

Conclusion   255

Bibliography   *261*

Index   *283*

Introduction

One of the definite and most important assumptions underlying the enormous theoretical and practical success of modern science is, as is commonly recognized, the mathematization and mechanization of the physical world, based on the possibility of applying mathematics to the study of physical reality, of nature.[1] Early modern scientists constantly return to this theme: Galilei's famous statement in the "Assayer" asserts that science is written in the book of nature in the language of mathematics, the only language that allows one to read this magnificent book.[2] For Kepler, the world—primarily the celestial cosmos, but also the terrestrial one—in its structure and regularity of movements, follows a divine harmonic pattern, exemplified and known primarily through mathematical objects, which are further expressible in proportions and equations of numbers and in regular geometrical solids.[3] In the French Preface to the "Principles of Philosophy", Descartes presents a simile of the tree of knowledge where mechanics, as well as other sciences, appear as branches on the trunk of physics, itself rooted in metaphysics; if, therefore, geometry is also to be recognized as a science, the principles that underlie geometry and mechanics must be taken to be the same.[4] Newton begins his "Principia" with the claim that physics, considered as

---

[1] Cp. Koyré 1968, 12-14; Maier 1938, passim; Duhem 1954, 107 sqq.; Kuhn 1961, 161-193; Burtt 1964, 97-107; Funkenstein 1986, 29-30; Gloy 1996, 98-117 et al. On various senses of the notion of applicability see: Steiner 1998, 16 sqq.

[2] "Philosophy [i.e. science in general] is written in this grand book, the universe, which stands continuously open to our gaze. But the book cannot be understood unless one first learns to comprehend the language and read the letters in which it is composed. It is written in the language of mathematics, and its characters are triangles, circles, and other geometrical figures without which it is humanly impossible to understand a single word of it; without them we would go around as in a dark labyrinth." - Galilei, Assayer (Galilei 1957, 237-238).

[3] See: *Mysterium Cosmographicum and Harmonice Mundi.* –J. Kepler. *Gesammelte Werke*, vols. I (1938) and VI (1940). Cp. Koyré 1973, 127 sqq.

[4] Descartes. Princ., Pref., AT IXB 14-15; Princ. IV 203, AT VIIIA 326. Cp. Gabbey 1993, 311-323. On the historical background of the attempt of Galileo, Beeckman and Descartes to use mathematical description for the study of free fall, see: Gaukroger 1978, 192 sqq.; Schuster 1977, 53 sqq. As Gaukroger argues, unlike Galilei who tries to represent physical objects as mathematical ones, Descartes "wants both to 'mathematize' physics and to 'physicalize' mathematics in one and the same operation. He does not simply want to use mathematics in physics, he wants to *unify* mathematics and physics in certain critical respect" - Gaukroger 1980, 97-98.

mechanics, has to be assimilated to mathematics, considered primarily as geometry.[5]

This seemingly self-evident possibility of the application of mathematics to physics is quite often almost taken for granted. However, as it will be argued, for those ancient scientists and philosophers who follow the Platonic-Pythagorean programme, such an application is not at all evident and is, in fact, impossible.[6] The central question of this book is thus how and why does it become possible for early modern science to apply mathematics and its methods to the description of *rerum natura*.

In contemporary philosophy (and history) of science, which often understands and presents itself as only epistemology and not as natural philosophy, this problem is not among the most commonly discussed: the applicability of mathematics to physics appears frequently to be taken as almost obvious. It is considered grounded either in the structure of physical reality, or in the mind itself. Still, there are a number of attempts to address the problem. The "unreasonable effectiveness of mathematics in the natural sciences", to use the well-known title of Wigner's Courant Lecture, remains for Wigner an utter mystery with no rational explanation. Eventually, he comes to the conclusion that "[t]he miracle of the appropriateness of the language of mathematics for the formulation of the laws of physics is a wonderful gift which we neither understand nor deserve".[7] Recently, Connes similarly argued that the applicability of mathematics to physics is hardly explainable.[8] Steiner takes physics to use formal analogies.[9] However, the question of why physical objects allow for such analogies still remains to be clarified. Separation between mathematics and physics is accepted by Frege, according to whom mathematicians, "instead of investigating the properties a thing really has...don't care about them one iota, but using so-called definitions, ascribe all sorts of properties to a thing that have absolutely no connection with the thing

---

[5] "*Cum veteres* mechanicam (*uti auctor est* Pappus) *in rerum naturalium investigatione maximi fecerint; et recentiores, missis formis substantialibus et qualitatibus occultis, phaenomena naturae ad leges mathematicas revocare aggressi sint... Nam et linearum rectarum et circulorum descriptiones, in quibus* geometria *fundatur, ad* mechanicam *pertinent. Has lineas describere* geometria *non docet, sed postulat.*" - Newton. Princ. Auctoris praefatio ad lectorem (Newton 1972 I, 15).
[6] Cp. Dummett 1991, 301-305.
[7] Wigner 1967, 237.
[8] "The physical world that surrounds us, while not itself the seat of mathematical reality, coheres with it in a definite way that's difficult to explain. Einstein ...said that the most incomprehensible thing about the universe is that it is comprehensible. The thing that's hard to grasp about mathematics is that it governs the organization of natural phenomena. Thanks to mathematics we are able to understand the natural world." - Changeux and Connes 1995, 55-56.
[9] Steiner 1989, 452 sqq.

itself, and then investigate their properties".[10] But if this is the case, it still remains to be seen why the mathematically formulated properties may be ascribed to physical bodies.

Mathematics is taken as the language of physics. Referring to Whewell, Peirce considers geometry to be physical or mechanical geometry.[11] Mathematical entities are to be associated with empirical objects and supposedly describe bodily entities adequately. But why and how is this possible? Why are formal structures applicable to physical objects? Is the mathematical language for describing physical objects discovered in the physical, or is it freely produced and then prescribed to the physical? The "mathematization of physics"[12] in early modern science takes place because spatial, physical characteristics of body are considered to already have intrinsic mathematical properties; these properties may be subsequently observed in both physical bodies and in geometrical entities. Physical characteristics are constituted primarily as *already* geometrical, i.e. as primary qualities, as Galilei and Descartes take them.[13] The underlying presupposition, namely, that the primary physical qualities may be expressed in the language of mathematics is, however, a very strong one and is not immediately self-evident.

The mathematization of physics may become possible either, first, if mathematical concepts somehow arise from physical reality—or, second, if mathematical structures are imposed onto the physical. The first approach is supported by a number of contemporary scholars.[14] Thus, as mentioned to Mach, Münster considers mathematics as making its concepts fit physical objects and their properties, i.e. mathematical objects are to be introduced in such a way that they may conform to the physical world.[15] However, an objection to such an approach might be that in order to be able to portray the relation of mathematics to physics in this way, one already has to presuppose that physical entities must have properties that may be represented in terms of formal mathematical language, which entails a *petitio principii*.

The second way of looking at the role of mathematics in physics, present in many modern thinkers (in particular, in Descartes and in Kant), is constituted by taking physical science as constructed in such a way as to recognize nature in its project, *Entwurf*, as already mathematical.[16] For instance, Manin argues that

---

[10] Frege 1971, 146.
[11] Peirce 1976, 359-362.
[12] Belaval 1950, 489-490.
[13] As Garber notes, "Descartes wants to make *all* of the properties of body geometrical".- Garber 1992, 69. Cp. Locke. Essay, Bk. II, ch. 7.
[14] See: Prosperi 1997, 261-267.
[15] Münster 1994, 205-212.
[16] Kant. Prolegomena § 10-11, 14 sqq.; cp. Heidegger 1993, 362.

mathematics associates its mental constructions with physical abstractions.[17] This, however, presupposes that physical abstractions can already be interpreted as mathematical. But why these abstractions adequately describe physical reality remains not altogether clear.[18] Bohr takes mathematics to study all possible formal structures and therefore to furnish scientists with such structures and notions as may be useful in physics. Obvious objections to this position are, first, that physical reality is already supposed to be in principle mathematizable. And second, even if Bohr is right, nothing guarantees that appropriate mathematical results are actually already established, especially since the number of possible mathematical structures and theories does not appear to be finite.[19] Moreover, it is not immediately clear why the very structuring of the physical *qua* mathematical may take place, since physical objects do not exemplify mathematical precision and cannot be taken properly as geometrical entities.

As an attempt to address the problem of applicability of the "Formalwissenschaft" to the "Realwissenschaft" in this book I will provide a historical reconstruction of two different approaches to the possibility of presenting and describing physical objects in terms of formal mathematical concepts. However, instead of tracing a hypothetical chain of developmental continuity and ruptures in the history of philosophy and science, I have chosen to contrast antiquity and early modernity as represented by two thinkers. Although antiquity and modernity (constituted by a great variety of different, sometimes contrary, theories and opinions) are not uniform historical entities, there still appear to exist certain metaphysical presuppositions that most of the thinkers of a particular epoch share, even if they are mostly unaware of them. In some fundamental presuppositions, which I will try to spell out, antiquity and modernity seem to be very different in their approaches to studying and constituting the physical in terms of the mathematical.[20] Two key thinkers that I am discussing are Plotinus and Descartes (although occasionally Plato, Aristotle, Euclid, Proclus, Newton et al. also appear on stage), in whom, despite all the peculiarities of their own philosophical views, the fundamental presuppositions of ripe antiquity and of early modernity find their expression. Both thinkers are border figures, as it were, because, despite considerable originality of their own views, in both of them

---

[17] Manin 1981, 6 sqq.

[18] As Manin puts it, "a good physicist uses formalism as a poet uses language" (Manin 1981, 5). Mathematical formalism is then to be understood as the language for physics. The poetic language is, however, not only descriptive but, since the language in poetry often says and suggests more than is intended, and, in fact, negates and suspends the language by means of language itself, it may become prescriptive, opening new possibilities for experiencing the world.

[19] Münster 1994, 209.

[20] Cp. Klein 1968, 117-125; Koselleck 1977, 264-299; Nikulin 1993, 203-221.

different philosophical epochs are both separated and connected (ancient and medieval—and medieval and modern respectively, even if these labels might be provisional) with different styles and different understandings of the role philosophy and science play in the knowledge and constitution of the world.[21] The choice of Plotinus might be further justified by the fact that he embraces all three major school traditions of antiquity—Platonic, Aristotelian and Stoic. While necessarily leaving out many important topics, I concentrate on significant distinctions between two thinkers in an attempt to outline those aspects that appear to be important for the discussion of the main problem of the relation of mathematics to physics.

The book consists of three parts. The first one begins with a consideration of the notion of matter, which in Plato and Plotinus is taken as a mere possibility of being. On this reading, matter is indefinite and utterly unlimited, close to non-being—in contrast to matter as substance in Descartes, as a definite subject with a number of attributes, one of which is taken as essential attribute. Preliminary consideration of various "properties" of matter is necessary for the subsequent discussion of the role matter plays in the constitution of both physical and geometrical entities. The Platonic approach to the understanding of substance is further compared to that of Descartes. In the former (represented mostly in Plotinus and also traced in Plato's "Parmenides" and "Republic"), being is introduced not as a primary phenomenon but as a synthetic unity of sameness and otherness, of the one and the many. These themselves, however, have an originating cause, which cannot be considered properly as being. The problem of a possibility of distinction between the cause of being, which itself is not being, and matter, which also is not being, is then addressed. It is also argued that if being in Descartes (for whom the notions of being and substance are at the very center of his thought) is taken in its existential aspect as substance, it turns out to be an ambiguous notion. Being *per se* is rather marked by the attribute of infinity, which appears in the discussion of potential and actual infinity in their relation to being and to the cause of being, through a number of paradoxes and in the problem of infinite divisibility of mathematical entities. A number of auxiliary notions (each playing a role in the subsequent discussion) are also introduced in this part, such as those of various kinds of distinctions, of the one and the many, of the same and the other, of essence and existence.

The second part is dedicated to the discussion of various aspects of the relation of mathematics to physics. Because number is taken as the pattern for the consideration of being and for the constitution of knowledge, the foundations of arithmetic in Plotinus are discussed in the context of the Platonic tradition, partly

---

[21] On the influence of scholasticism on Descartes see: Koyré 1923; Ariew 1992, 58-90; Sorell 1994, 29-45.

known from Aristotle's polemics against it in books M and N of the "Metaphysics". In Plotinus' subtly elaborated doctrine, number is constituted by the principles of sameness and otherness, represented in monad and dyad, which originate number as a synthetic unity of a plurality of henads. Arithmetical entities are then considered in their relation to geometrical objects and later to physical things. In the Platonic approach arithmetical and geometrical objects are taken as epistemologically and ontologically different, since number consists of discrete units, whereas geometrical magnitude is continuous. The possibility of applying geometry to physics in Descartes is grounded in the fact that number (the discrete) and geometrical magnitude (the continuous) are taken to be mutually reducible. Furthermore, no crucial distinction between an object of geometry and an object of physics neither is made (nor can be made) in Descartes, since both belong to the *res extensa*. The notion of the intermediary plays an important role in Platonic ontology as present in Proclus' commentary to the first book of Euclid's "Elements". In this approach, geometrical objects are considered intermediate between ideal objects (notions) and their physical images, being irreducible to any of them. In Descartes, with his rigid dichotomic ontological distinction, there is no room for an intermediary. The equation of geometrical and physical objects in their ontological status further opens a possibility for the application of geometrical methods in physics.

A rather neglected notion of intelligible matter is then discussed, as the specific matter of mathematical objects, first introduced in Aristotle's "Metaphysics". In Plotinus it is considered a substrate of the intelligibles-*noēta*, as an indefinite thinking-*noēsis*. Several arguments are provided in discussing the main features of intelligible matter (such as its affiliation with the irrational) and its relation to physical things. Proclus is primarily interested in considering the role of intelligible matter in constituting geometrical entities: intelligible matter appears here as a geometrical materiality. Such matter may be interpreted as imagination, moreover, it might further be construed as extension, where geometricals may be conceived. It is due to the presence of this geometrical matter in Proclus' and Plotinus' deliberations that geometrical objects are essentially different from physical ones and can neither substitute, nor adequately represent them.

In Cartesian ontology, on the contrary, there is no room for the intelligible matter: only one matter for all the extended things is recognized, that which embraces both physical and geometrical entities. It is due to this non-discrimination of different kinds of matter that it becomes possible to consider the geometrical and the physical in the same terms and to apply the former to the cognition of the latter and thus to implement the whole project of mathematical physics.

The third part of the book discusses the role and the structure of cognitive faculties as involved in consideration and construction of material and geometrical objects. The Plotinian intellect-*noys* with its cosmos of thinkable objects-*noēta*, distinct from the discursive reason-*dianoia*, is next contrasted to the Cartesian mind and its ideas, the mind taken as discursive and as immediately self-accessible, i.e. as fundamentally reflective. Imagination is introduced as a capacity to create mental images, which are different from both the noetic objects and from the images of senses. Imagination can be taken then as a cognitive faculty that both separates and unites the thinkable and the sensible. Moreover, imagination is further related to negativity and to some kind of materiality, which Proclus has to identify with geometrical matter. Imagination then has to be that faculty that primarily represents geometrical objects as divisible, multiple and extended in their own way. Descartes' treatment of imagination is quite different, insofar as imagination is distinguished into mental and corporeal. Contrary to the mind, imagination cannot render the essence of a thing, for imagination is not capable of representing the infinite. Imagination is capable, however, of operating with images of extended things, which further allows to recognize the geometrical and the physical within one matter and extension, the former exemplifying the latter.

In the discussion of the role of construction that follows, it is argued that the imaginary reproduction of the world in Descartes is undertaken according to a model that is constructed as geometrical. Since both geometrical and physical things are considered co-extended, movable and divisible in the same space, the geometrical may be imposed onto the physical. The former thus becomes the pattern for the consideration of the latter, which allows therefore to present mathematical knowledge of the physical material world. In antiquity the imaginary construction is primarily taken to be applicable to geometrical figures in solving problems and not in establishing theoretical knowledge through theorems. Crucial is the connection between intelligible matter and imagination: in Proclus' and Syrianus' interpretation, imagination appears to be geometrical matter, where a geometrical object can be produced by kinematic construction according to the object's noetic form and formative principle, which themselves are already not constructible. The act of imaginary construction, therefore, does not really engender a geometrical figure with all its characteristics, but rather reproduces it in order to facilitate reason in cognition of the properties of the object, now represented in an almost visualizable form, with all its properties, already wholly present in the notion of the object. A brief conclusion summarizes then the main arguments and theses of the book.

In what follows, the references to Descartes' texts are given according to the edition: *Oeuvres de Descartes*. Ed. by Ch. Adam and P. Tannery. Vol. I-XI. Paris, 1974-1986 (2nd ed.), referred to as AT followed by volume and page number. All the translations are from *The Philosophical Writings of Descartes*. Vol. I-III. Translated by J. Cottingham, R. Stoothoff, D. Murdoch (vols. I-II) and by J. Cottingham, R. Stoothoff, D. Murdoch and A. Kenny (vol. III). Cambridge,

1985-1991. References to the Plotinus' "Enneads" are given according to *Plotini opera*. Ed. P. Henry and H. Schwyzer. Vol. I-III. Oxford, 1964-1982; the translations (except when specified) are those of A. H. Armstrong, quoted from Plotinus' *Enneads*. Vol. I-VII. Cambridge (Mass.)-London, 1966-1988. The inner cross-references throughout the text are given to the paragraphs of the book (e.g., 2.4.1).

Parts of the book closely follow my articles reproduced from the following publications by kind permission of the publishers: *Henologische Perspektiven II*. Amsterdam-Atlanta: Rodopi, 1997, p. 49-65 (in 1.2.1); *Hermes* 126 (1998), 326-340 (in 1.2.1); *Dionysius* 16 (1998), 85-113 (in 2.4.1); Le Timée de Platon. Contributions à l'histoire de sa réception. Louvain-Paris: Peeters, 2000, 15-38 (in 3.1.3); and *Méthexis* XI (1998), 85-102 (in 2.1.1).

A number of ideas developed in the book were elaborated when working with Piama Gaidenko. Various aspects of the problems present in the book were discussed with Werner Beierwaltes, John Cleary, Cristina D'Ancona, John Dillon, Alexander Dobrokhotov, Eyólfur Kjalar Emilsson, Michael Frede, Stephen Gersh, Charles Kahn, Paul Kalligas, Karen Gloy, Jens Halfwassen, Heinz Happ, Christoph Horn, Vittorio Hösle, Douglas McGaughey, Christia Mercer, Dominic O'Meara, Yuri Shichalin, Andrew Smith, Thomas Szlezák, Alejandro Vigo and Egil Wyller, to all of whom I am mostly thankful for their thoughtful remarks and suggestions. I am much obliged to my colleagues and to the graduate students of the New School for Social Research, in particular, to Richard Bernstein, Nancy Fraser, Judith Friedlander, Agnes Heller, and Yerri Yovel, who in various ways encouraged me in writing this book. Duane Lacey, Claire Martin, Morgan Meis, Edward Skipton and Sonja Tanner were also helpful in the preparation of the manuscript. I am particularly grateful to Sara Walker Bosworth; this book would not have been possible without her hard work, dedication, and unparalleled commitment as my assistant. Different parts of the book were presented and discussed on various occasions at the New School for Social Research, the University of Notre Dame, Ohio State University, Institute for Philosophy of the Academy of Sciences in Moscow, Columbia University, Istituto italiano per gli studi filosofici in Naples, Novosibirsk University, University of Oslo and Willamette University. I am indebted to the Alexander von Humboldt Foundation for the assistance which gave me the opportunity to stay at the University of Tübingen for a year, where conversations with Hans Krämer were very fruitful. I would also like to express my acknowledgment to the Center for Philosophy of Religion at the University of Notre Dame for the possibility of beginning work on the book and especially my appreciation to Alvin Plantinga, discussions with whom helped me to clarify several central points of the work. Finally, my family—Elena Nikulina, Alexey Nikulin and Anastasiya Nikulina—was always the source of support and inspiration.

PART I
MATTER

1.1 The notion of matter

Addressing the problem of how and why it is possible to apply mathematics to the study and description of the physical or material world implies a discussion of what matter is. Descartes' attitude is that matter is something whose nature is quite self-evident, hence the more we try to trace subtle distinctions within it, the more we obscure the nature and essence of matter. Still, an obvious simplicity of the Cartesian treatment of matter, if thoroughly analyzed, might entail difficulties that render the putative clear and distinct simplicity of matter quite questionable. One of the possible ways to "suspend" the deceptive self-evidence of a notion is to contrast and compare it with another historically "self-evident" treatment of the very same notion. Such a comparison may enable us to see better the implicit presuppositions that made possible the modern concept of matter. In what follows, I will be stressing mostly distinctions between the ancient, mainly Platonic, account of matter, and the modern Cartesian one, in order to be able to trace the consequences of the former in the modern scientific account.

1.1.1 On the notion of matter in Aristotle

In his fundamental investigation of the Aristotelian notion of matter, H. Happ distinguishes two main approaches to the understanding of matter in antiquity: (1) matter as principle, and (2) matter as bulk, mass or bodily stuff.[1] The first interpretation is to be found in Plato (in the Academy and in the later Platonic and Neoplatonic tradition), as well as in Aristotle. If matter is taken as a principle, then, as it will be argued in what follows, it should be fundamentally and inevitably ambiguous in the Platonic interpretation. Indeed, on the one hand, matter may be taken as an ideal principle of otherness and alienation. On the other hand, as non-being, matter is not a principle, but rather mere nothingness, which does not exist in the proper sense and cannot be known. The second understanding of matter, found in the Stoa, prevails in modern philosophy and science, and is influenced by certain features of Aristotle's own account.[2]

---

[1] Cp. Happ 1971, 809 sqq.
[2] SVF II, 325 et al. Cp. Irwin 1988, 88-89. According to Happ, one can discern the following five different reasons that lead to such an understanding of matter: (a) Aristotle himself, treating matter as a substrate, elevates matter-*hylē* into substance-*oysia*. His understanding of matter as substance, however, is limited, whereas for the Stoics matter is substance in the proper sense; it is describable as *ti*, the universal Stoic category, which includes both corporeal entities (the only existing really) and incorporeal (existing only in thought; cp. Chrysippus, frg. 329-335, SVF II 117; Plotinus. Enn. VI.1.25.1 sqq.; Rist 1969, 152-172). (b) When matter becomes substance, form becomes an accident inherent in matter. In Aristotle, form (*eidos*) expresses essential attributes (*ti estin*), while quality (*poion*) expresses accidental attributes, although both are tightly connected. However, when Aristotle speaks of the material constitution of the four elements, the form and the qualitative accidence (*pathos*) become almost disconnected. This tendency is even clearer in the Stoics, who turn essential form into a mere *poion* and place it in matter-*hylē* (Happ 1971, 809-810). (c) In Aristotle's biological treatises, matter is almost unequivocally understood as bodily stuff. (d) Aristotle takes the elementary qualities (warmth, coldness, humidity,

Following mainly Happ's recollection, without going much into the details of the argument, I will first briefly establish the main features of matter as it is portrayed in Aristotle. The notion of matter in Plotinus will then be considered in order to be able to discuss further the notion of intelligible matter, which is crucial for my exegesis and to clarify the main question posed. Aristotle's approach to matter is pluralistic (as is often the case in his writings) in the sense that in discussing certain notions he quite frequently seems to abandon his previous conclusions and starts anew. Such a peculiarity of Aristotle's style might be explained by his intention to investigate various meanings and usages of a single notion, and thereby avoid ambiguity.

Specifically, we find three different "definitions" of matter in Aristotle. (1) Matter is the first (and ultimate) substrate.[3] (2) Matter is *dynamis*, potency and possibility of being.[4] And (3) matter "is" pure indefiniteness, neither this nor that, nor anything particular; as such it has no form and is not any definite thing, it is not a *tode ti*. Substance is characterized for Aristotle by two definite traits: it is separable (*to khōriston*)—that is, it exists independently or apart—and it is a concrete thing (*to tode ti*).[5] Matter is not a substance in any of these two senses. However, matter may be considered a substrate, *hypokeimenon*, as that which underlies all changes in things but itself has no particular form.[6] Plato considers opposites as contrary predicates to be capable of immediate interaction, even if the one ousts the other. Unlike Plato, Aristotle, in order to escape a contradiction, takes opposites to be mediated by and in the substrate or subject, *hypokeimenon*.[7] Matter is then the universal substrate or mediator of opposites, although it is not separable from them.[8] Moreover, matter may be taken as a logical subject.[9] Yet subject itself is considered twofold: either as a definite thing (*tode ti*), or as matter in its relation to actuality.[10] If, then, matter is to be considered a subject, it is only in the second

---

dryness, in Meteor. 378 b 10 sqq.) as bodily and material. (e) Finally, the doctrine of the cosmos as limited implies that the total "amount" of matter, *quantitas materiale*, is preserved as constant (cp. Zeno, frg. 87, SVF I 24-25; Chrysippus, frg. 597, 599, SVF II 184-185; Sambursky 1962, 37-38)—a doctrine that reappears in early modern physics under the guise of the law of preservation of the whole amount of matter in the universe.

[3] Aristotle. Phys. 192a 31 sqq.; cp. Met. 1049a 35-36; 1068b 11; De caelo 293b 14-15.
[4] Aristotle. Met. 1042a 27 sqq.; cp. 1032a 20-22; 1050a 15-16; 1060a 21; Phys. 213a 1-10; Meteor. 378b 34-379a 1.
[5] Aristotle. Met. 1029a 20 sqq.; cp. Phys. 207a 26; De an. 412a 7-8; cp. Happ 1971, 296-297.
[6] Aristotle. Phys. 190a 31 sqq.; De caelo 306b 16-18.
[7] Plato. Phaedo 102d-105c; Aristotle. Anal. Post. 72a 11-14. Cp. Düring 1966, 62; Gaidenko 1980, 258 sqq.
[8] Aristotle. De caelo 286a 25-26; De gen. et corr. 332a 35-332b 1; cp. 329a 30-31; Meteor. 370b 13-15.
[9] Aristotle. Met. 1043a 5-6. See the discussion in: Kung 1978, 140-159; cp. Dancy 1978, 410-412.
[10] Aristotle. Met. 1038b 3-6. Substrate is one of at least four main meanings of substance (*oysia*); and substrate may be further considered either form or matter or that which consists of both of them, see: Cat. 2a 12-13; Met. 999b 13; 1028b 34 sqq.; 1042a 34; 1069b 35-1070a; Phys. 192a 4-7; De an. 412a 6 sqq.

sense, as an indefinite substrate of all things.[11]

Since contrarieties cannot come together immediately without mediation, Aristotle has to support a tripartite scheme and introduce the matter-form-privation (*hylē-eidos-sterēsis*) distinction.[12] Being (form-*energeia*) and non-being (privation) are mediated by the not-yet-being or potential being (*dynamis*) of matter. Matter is to be considered then as accidental non-being, while only privation is non-being par excellence.[13] Since matter only accepts opposites, it itself, as mere potentiality, cannot be opposed to anything. In this particular aspect it is close to substance, which also has nothing opposing it.[14] However, contrary to substance-*oysia*, matter *qua* potentiality and possibility of being (*dynamis* is both *potentia* and *possibilitas*), does not exist separately from a thing.[15] Another obvious difference is that *oysia* is always limited, since form is that which defines and embraces, while matter (as the potentiality of not-yet-being) is close to the infinite and is that which is defined or embraced.[16] As a potentiality, matter is a thing that is not yet there, and therefore cannot be anything definite—as Aristotle states in the third definition. It cannot have any particular contents, but is only displayed in pure relation to form, as the "from which" (*ex hoy*) to the "into which" (*eis ho*).[17] In this sense, matter is a necessary component of the hylomorphic structure.

Since matter is not yet actualized, it shows different qualifications. It does so without violating the principle of non-contradiction, for even if in Aristotle matter may represent the unity of the subject, opposites are always predicated of matter, albeit in different respects. Thus, for instance, the modal meanings that can be ascribed to matter appear to be opposite for two reasons. First, matter is present in the modality of possibility. Matter may always be different exactly because it is potentiality and, as such, may receive any form. A particular thing, *ti*, even if it has a definite essence (and a definition), does not necessarily exist, for a thing may either be or not be. In this sense *ti* is accidental, and the cause of this accidentality is matter.[18] Matter is also accidental, since where matter is, there is no purpose.[19] Second, matter is also the cause of necessity, but in a sense different from purpose as the corresponding material condition, without which a particular thing cannot

---

[11] Cp. Happ 1971, 666.
[12] Aristotle. Met. 1069b 8 sqq.; 1075a 28-34; 1087a 36-1087b 1.
[13] Cp. Aristotle. Phys 192a 4-7.
[14] Aristotle. Cat. 3b 24-25.
[15] Aristotle. Phys. 211b 37-212a 2.
[16] Aristotle. De caelo 312a 12; Phys. 206b 25 sqq.; 209b 5 sqq.
[17] On the "metaphysics of prepositions" see: Plotinus. Enn. VI.6.18.17-19; Proclus. Theol. Plat. II 60.26-61.9 and Theiler 1930, 31-34; Dörrie 1969, 217-228. Cp. also Happ 1971, 784 sqq. and Bussanich 1988, 85-88. Early modern science especially stresses the primacy of relation understood as function to substance, as, for example, in occasionalists and, in particular, in Malebranche. For him truth is only a relation, a "rapport" between either ideas, ideas and things, or things themselves, but not ideas or things as such, Malebranche. *Oeuvres complètes* I 52-53; II 286-287; Funkenstein 1986, 295-296. Cp. Cassirer 1953, passim.
[18] Aristotle. Met. 1027a 13-15.
[19] Aristotle. Meteor. 390a 3-4.

be.[20] For instance, a saw should be made of metal and not from cotton or fur, unless it is produced for some other purpose (e.g., as a work of art).

An important notion in Aristotle's consideration of matter is that of *materia prima* or prime matter. Prime matter is *dynamei sōma aisthēton*, sensually perceptible body in potentiality, itself not constituted of anything else and characterless.[21] Since prime matter itself is body only as pure potentially, it is not body properly speaking, but rather is bodiless and does not exist on its own.[22] Since it is present only potentially, is being *dynamei*, prime matter is preserved and is not any definite thing.[23] Prime matter is not mere nothing, yet it is also not anything particular. It is indefinite but in this indefiniteness it is the material substrate, which is inseparable from the opposites it mediates.[24] Modern philosophy, in particular Neoscholasticism, quite often considers *materia prima* as the first universal substrate of every thing potentially, as matter as such. In Aristotle, however, prime matter is different and distinct from *hylē* as the principle, because prime matter is efficient only in the sublunar world but not in the supralunar ethereal realm. That is to say it is not universal matter, but matter only of a particular (although rather large) class of sublunar physical things. Aristotle insists on the distinction and opposition in the cosmos of prime matter, *prōtē hylē*, to that of *hylē topikē*, or matter of the ethereal region.[25] Why does Aristotle need this distinction, abandoned in modern science, which decisively cancels the distinction between the supra and sublunar world? First of all, because the cosmos for Aristotle is hierarchically structured, so that the most valuable entities—stars representing gods—are situated in the place above the world, in an ontologically and axiologically higher position, which is visibly expressed in their spatial location. The reason is that the stars, even if they are bodily, do not perish, and in moving show perfection through the most perfect (circular) movement, which, unlike the prevalent rectilinear movement of the sublunar realm, never comes to a stop.[26]

---

[20] Aristotle. Phys. 200a 14 sqq.; cp. Met. 1014a 20; 1015a 20 sqq.; Stallmach 1959, 119-125; Happ 1971, 703 sqq.

[21] Aristotle. De gen. et corr. 329a 29-329b 3; Met. 1049a 27; Phys 193a 29. Cp. Dancy 1978, 372-413 (prime matter is "nothing on its own", Ibid., 398), as against S. Cohen 1984, 171-194. Philoponus interprets the notion of prime matter in (Platonic) terms of pure dimensional receptacle: "Prime matter, which is without body, form, or figure before it is filled out, receives the three dimensions and becomes three-dimensional" (trad. I. Mueller). - Philoponus. In Cat. 83.14-15.

[22] Aristotle. De gen. et corr. 332a 17-18.

[23] Aristotle. Met. 1014b 31; 1044a 15 sqq.

[24] Aristotle. De gen. et corr. 332a 1.

[25] Aristotle. De caelo 269b 14-17; cp. Happ 1971, 486-489, 693-698; Algra 1995, passim.

[26] Cp. Proclus. Inst. Phys. II 1-5. Ethereal entities, unlike the sublunar, may also be considered not as temporal but as sempiternal. The sempiternal are those entities that exist always without perishing, but are not eternal in the proper sense (not atemporal), that is, they are never wholly present in one indivisible moment of stable "now", *nunc stans*.

1.1.2 Plotinus on matter

Plotinus, like many thinkers of late Antiquity, humbly presents himself as only a commentator who puts his notes on the margins of the "primary texts" in which the truth is revealed and around which the whole life of a tradition is organized, so that every new written text has the task of being in accordance both with the "primary text" and with the truth itself. Still, providing a systematic interpretation and symphonic concordance of the initially unsystematic and sometimes paradoxical texts, Plotinus at times unwillingly and unintentionally presents an original interpretation and thus secures the further development of the tradition.

In his early treatise II. 4 (12) (specially dedicated to the consideration of matter) and later in III.6 (26), Plotinus gives a comprehensive interpretative exposition of Plato's rather brief account of matter in the "Timaeus" (47e-53c), describing matter in Platonic terms as receptacle and nurse, as the place and seat of form.[27] Plato equally characterizes matter as all-receptive, as mother and nurse of everything, and as that which receives imprints.[28] Matter is considered as that which has nothing of itself, nothing of its own: it neither is nor possesses form, being, formative principle, activity, nor any actuality. Matter is only a pure possibility—a capacity of being—and is neither a subject with predicates (for it cannot properly receive predicates), nor is it anything definite (for it is not defined by itself), nor is a body (for body is matter already defined by form). Matter as such "is" non-being or nothingness: it is that which is not, never was and never will be, a "shadow of non-being", only a receptacle of form, being, quality, figure, division and the like.[29] On the other hand, materiality as alterability is itself governed, in Pythagorean and Platonic tradition, by the *principle* of otherness or duality (called indefinite dyad, *aoristos dyas*, or great-and-small, *mega-mikron*), which itself is purely thinkable.[30]

Plotinus' treatment of matter is Platonic throughout, but also incorporates certain Aristotelian insights (despite the differences in the two notions of matter, which lead Aristotle to criticize Plato sharply).[31] In Plotinus' account, matter has the following main features. (1) Matter is considered non-being (*mē on*), as complete darkness or privation of light. Matter is absolutely different from form (which represents being): it is imagined as something formless (*aneideon ti*

---

[27] Plotinus. Enn. III.6.13.12, 19; cp. III.6.7.1-3; III.6.10.8.

[28] Matter is called by Plato *hypodokhē, tithēnē*, Tim. 49a; *mētēr, pandekhes*, Tim. 51a; *hedra*, Tim. 52b; *khōra*, Tim. 52a; *ekmageion*, Tim. 50c. Cp. Schwyzer 1951, 568; Ashbaugh 1988, 96-136 (consideration of *khōra* as spatiality). In Narbonne's account, the new features of matter introduced by Plotinus are impassibility and inalterability (Narbonne 1994, 41-42; cp. O'Meara 1975, 71 sqq.). Cp. also: Porphyry, frg. 236 Smith = Simplicius. In Phys. 230.34-231.24.

[29] Plato. Tim. 49a-51a; Simplicius. In Phys. 230.34-231.35; cp. Plutarchus. De Is. et Os. 56, 373; Plotinus. Enn. III.6.7.3 sqq.; cp. Porphyry. Sent. 20. Cp. O'Brien 1995, 10-25.

[30] Krämer 1959, 254; Krämer 1971, 296 sqq. Cp. Huffman 1993, 37-53; Philolaus, frg. 1 Huffman.

[31] Cp. Claghorn 1954, 5-19; Szlezák 1979; Hadot 1990, 125-140.

phantazomenē).[32] Therefore, the "is" which plays the role of the copula in predication,[33] may be said about matter only improperly (i.e., about the concept of matter, which is supposed to represent matter). Since matter cannot be properly predicated and represented, the "is" of matter necessarily misrepresents matter and always misses matter as such, matter which, strictly speaking, does not have any notion or concept. The "is" inevitably represents something else, namely, non-being in the form of being. Matter "as such" may be rather vaguely represented as "a kind of unmeasuredness in relation to measure, and unboundedness in relation to limit, and formlessness in relation to creating form (*pros eidopoiētikon*), and perpetual neediness in relation to what is self-sufficient; always undefined, nowhere stable, subject to every sort of influence, insatiate, complete poverty".[34] Since there is nothing proper in matter—nothing to be adequately described, matter as such is indescribable and, as indeterminate, it cannot be really known. In fact, Platonic matter may be even considered a sheer privation of any possibility to change, as otherness removed in its being (which belongs to the otherness *qua* principle). Matter is then just an abstraction of otherness that is brought by privation to such a degree that it cannot be thought at all. That is why we are only able to conceive matter by what Plato calls "spurious reasoning", *logismos nothos*, as if dreaming or imagining.[35]

The "knowledge" of matter is comparable then to seeing darkness in darkness:[36] We see darkness, but not as anything particular or positive, therefore, we see darkness not by seeing, but by a certain "unusual" kind of reasoning. We do not perceive that we see, but rather, we imagine that we see. We are only aware of the act of seeing, but the content of seeing does not come from seeing, for there is nothing out there in the darkness. Darkness is not anything positive, that is why there cannot be any definite image of it. On the other hand, there is something seen as an "object" of such a seeing, so that there is something in such an apprehension of darkness that is not fully explained merely by the act of seeing itself. The "objective contents" of seeing darkness is darkness itself. But since darkness is not anything positive, it "is" only a privation of light or non-being of light as privation. Therefore, the peculiarity of "seeing darkness" or "thinking matter" is that it is not seeing or understanding in the proper sense. Rather, it is a kind of unreasonable reasoning or void imagining. Such thinking is, paradoxically, also not-thinking. One can "see" darkness both with eyes open or with eyes closed.

To compare, in Aristotle one may distinguish three different ways of knowing matter. First, matter is known negatively, as not this and not that, *kat' aphairesin* or *apophasei*: as potentiality that is not yet definite, matter does not have any features that might be firmly established.[37] As it has been pointed out,

---

[32] Plotinus. Enn. II.5. 5.9 sqq., 4.12 sqq.; cp. Plato. RP 382a; Soph. 254d. Cp. Sambursky 1987, 45-46.
[33] Kahn 1973, 85 sqq.
[34] Plotinus. Enn. I.8.3.12-16.
[35] Plato. Tim. 52b ; cp. Plotinus. Enn. II.4.10.11; cp. II.4.12.27-33; III.6.13.46; VI.7.28.11; Eslick 1963, 45-46.
[36] Plotinus. Enn. I.8.4.31.
[37] Aristotle. Met. 1058a 23.

although matter has certain traits of substance or subject, it nevertheless is not a particular, actually existing *oysia*. Second, matter is known analogically, *kat' analogian*.[38] Even if we do not or cannot strictly lay out all the members of proportional relation, we nonetheless can properly describe the relation itself. Analogical knowledge stresses the relational, not the substantial aspect, so that an entity (matter, in particular) is known not as such, but only in its relation to something else. And third, matter is considered by Aristotle as known *kata thesin*, positively, through a number of attributes, although not adequately, for matter is neither known by itself, nor can it be sensually apprehended.[39] Since Plotinus portrays matter negatively, he has to accept only the two first ways of "knowing" matter; that is, the "knowledge" of matter can be either analogical or negative (*aphairesei*).[40]

(2) Matter is that which is left when form is removed, even though the remainder is not anything particular that can be indicated by "positive speech". But what if we also remove or abstract all the "predicates" of matter, like that of mere possibility, what is left then? Not a subject, for matter is not anything definite, but is mere negativity, which, ultimately, cannot be negated. Such a negativity of the non-being of matter is itself necessary and cannot be taken away. In the later treatise "On what are and whence come evils" (Enn. I.8), Plotinus finds it even appropriate to speak about the necessary existence (*hypostasis*) of matter.[41] The mere negativity of matter may be rethought as not only a lack of all definiteness, but rather as a negative potency, the radical evil.[42] For this reason, when Plotinus presents matter as privation in terms of mere negation, he borrows Aristotle's terminology, yet radically redefines the concept itself (*arsis... hē sterēsis*).[43] As J.-M. Narbonne argues, privation in Aristotle is always a *nihil privativum* in relation to something else (to being), because it is privation of something. However, since matter represents for Plotinus the negativity "charged" with the possibility to embody and to represent something definite (even although matter itself is not the source of such an embodiment or definiteness), then, in contrast to Aristotle, Plotinus has to characterize matter as privation in terms of *nihil negativum*.[44] This notion is discussed by Baumgarten, who introduces the notion of being in his ontology as derived from the basic concept of *nihil negativum*, which is absolute, simple, not representing anything positively. On his account, any positivity is inapplicable to it, including the positivity of being a definite subject of speech and

---

[38] Aristotle. Phys. 191a 7-12.
[39] Aristotle. Met. 1036a 8. Cp. Happ 1971, 667.
[40] Plotinus. Enn. I.8.9.1 sqq.; VI.6.3.26 sqq. Cp. Aristotle. Met 1029a 11 sqq.; Simplicius. In Phys. 225, 22 sqq.; Proclus. Theol. Plat. II 37.5-39.26.
[41] Enn. I.8.15.1-3; cp. I.8.7.2-4 and Plato. RP 476a.
[42] Plotinus. Enn. I.8.5. Cp., however, the early Enn. IV.8 (6).6, where Plotinus expresses a much more positive attitude towards matter, not portrayed here as a principle of evil. See also: Schwyzer 1973, 277; Rist 1961, 154-166; Hager 1962, 85-93; Benz 1990, 104 sqq.; O'Brien 1996, 171 sqq.
[43] Plotinus. Enn. II.4.13.22-23; cp. II.4.14; cp. I.8.11.1 sqq.; Aristotle. Phys. 192a 4 sqq.
[44] Plotinus. Enn. II.4.16. Cp. Baumgarten 1963, 3. See also: Courtine 1990, 248-256; Narbonne 1994, 43-49.

cognition. The *nihil negativum* is not a privation of anything that has already existed before. The *nihil privativum* may be arrived at by mere negation or privation, but the *nihil negativum* is precedent to the very attempt of privation, for the *nihil negativum* is nothing. The subsequent negation of nothing, the *non-nihil* gives something, *aliquid*, which is not yet definite and not defined. As a determined object, it is *ens* or being; as not determined, it is *non-ens*, or *nihil privativum*, which represents a mere possibility of being.

As *nihil negativum*, matter (3) is only a potentiality that never becomes actuality: it is always only an "announcement", a "promise" of being (*epaggellomenon*), but not being itself.[45] Matter is thus potentiality, which itself is never actualized but, as Aristotle also argues, is actualized in particular things.[46] Such a potentiality of matter, as it will be argued in more detail in what follows, on the one hand, is displayed not only in bodily matter but also in intelligible matter, which potentially (*dynamei*) is all "real things".[47] On the other hand, the negative potentiality of matter is not capable of producing anything. Hence, it is not the same as the potentiality of the first productive principle (the One).

Matter (4) is unlimited (*to apeiron*) and indefinite and "not yet stable by itself, and is carried about here and there into every form, and since it is altogether adaptable, becomes many by being brought into everything and becoming everything".[48] That is why matter may be properly characterized only in negative terms: it is without quality (*apoios*); it is not body (*asōmatos*); it has no size or magnitude; it is without quantity (*aposon*); and it is shapeless.[49] The argument is preserved by Simplicius quoting Porphyry, who in turn refers to Moderatus: since matter represents pure negativity, Plato calls it a quantity without form or division and without any inherent figure.[50]

Since matter (5) has nothing of itself, everything is brought to it by being, which is form-*eidos*, for matter needs form (*endeēs*) in its pure receptivity.[51] Matter also has "no resistance (*to antikopton*), for it has no activity, but is a shadow, waits passively to endure whatever that which acts upon it wishes".[52] Having nothing of itself, matter (6) cannot be affected and therefore is inalterable, because there is nothing definite in matter that could be subject to change.[53] In matter there is no "self" and since inalterability does not necessarily imply that matter is identically the same, in a sense (paradoxically) it is not even true to claim

---

[45] Plotinus. Enn. II.5.4.3; II.5.5.1-9.
[46] Aristotle. Met. 1088b 1; 1045a 23.
[47] Plotinus. Enn. II.5.5.36.
[48] Plotinus. Enn. II.4.11.40-42; cp. II.4.15.17, 33-34; II.4.16.9-10; I.8.3.13; VI.6.3.3 sqq.
[49] Cp. Plotinus. Enn. II.4.12.34-38; II.4.8.1 sqq.
[50] *Amorphon kai adiaireton kai askhēmatiston* - Simplicius. In Phys. 231.10-11.
[51] Plotinus. Enn. II.4.8.23-24, III.5.9.54-56; VI.5.8.15-22. In contrast to matter, the intellect is unreceptive (*adekton*, Enn. III.6.6.20). Cp. the discussion in: Lee 1979, 79-97 and Wagner 1986, 64 sqq.
[52] Plotinus. Enn. III.6.18.29-31; cp. III.6.7.30.
[53] Plotinus. Enn. III.6.9.34; III.6.10.22; III.6.11.18. Nevertheless, as A.H. Armstrong remarks, in I.8 and in III.6 Plotinus "goes to considerable trouble to show that matter can never really receive form or be changed by it from its own evil nature." - Plotinus. *Enneads* VII, note on pp. 164-165.

that matter is unchangeable, for there is no identity of subject in matter.

(7) Matter cannot possess any inner structure. Because of that, first, bodies lack in their materiality any inner structure and thus are indefinitely divisible (*tmēton gar pan sōma kata pan*).[54] Secondly, matter cannot be destroyed (*anolethron*), for there is simply nothing in it to pass away. Matter, therefore, may be said to endure but not as anything concrete or definite.[55]

Finally, (8) besides the enumerated features of the rather paradoxical description of matter, which is indescribable in the strict sense (for since matter is not anything definite or particular, it cannot have clearly distinguishable and describable traits), a peculiar feature of matter is that it may be described in mutually exclusive, contradictory terms without violating the principle of non-contradiction. Aristotle formulates what he takes to be one of the most fundamental principles of thinking and being as: "It is impossible for the same attribute at once (*hama*) to belong and not to belong to the same thing (*tōi aytōi*) and in the same relation (*kata to ayto*)".[56] Thus, the principle of non-contradiction is violated either when a statement and its negation are both predicated *at once*, which may mean *at the same time* or/ and about *one and the same nature*[57] or/ and it may be either about *the same thing or subject* or/ and *in the same relation* or respect. Now, matter is necessarily characterized in opposite terms: it can be said to be both the same and not the same,[58] both one (in its nature) and double (as represented by two different matters). However, these opposite statements about matter do not violate the principle of non-contradiction, because in matter there is no unity of "togetherness" (*hama*) in the temporal sense, for matter is not in time. Further, there is no "togetherness" in the sense of the unity of nature in matter, for the "nature" of matter may be said to accept opposites but is itself indefinite.[59] Finally, there is no unity or sameness of subject in matter, because, simply, it is not a subject. And fourth, there can be no unity of relation in regards to matter, since there is nothing in matter about which something could be predicated strictly "in one and the same respect".

Thus, since opposite statements may be predicated of matter, it is therefore deeply paradoxical. For example, in Enn. III.6.10.25, Plotinus notes that "existing, for matter, is existing precisely as matter". This "existing as matter" is paradoxical, for, obviously, "existing as matter" means "being different from anything else", which is not matter; in particular, being different and other than being. But still this "being matter" is nothing else than "truly not being". Since matter's "being" consists in non-being, this non-being should be taken, then, as its being, which is again non-being, and so on. In this way there is a resemblance of reflectivity in matter, a kind of empty mirroring, by a mirror which itself does not properly exist. This, however, is not reflectivity in the proper sense, because,

---

[54] Plotinus. Enn. II.4.7.21-22.
[55] Plotinus. Enn. III.6.8.8; cp. III.6.19.14; IV.7.9.11 and Plato. Tim. 52a.
[56] Aristotle. Met. 1005b 19-20; cp. 1011b 16 sqq. Cp. Irwin 1988, 181-183.
[57] *Hama* is taken in the sense of the identity not of time but of nature in what is now called quasi-Aristotelian interpretation", cp. Vincent-Spade 1982, 297-307.
[58] Cp. Plotinus. Enn. III.6.14.29, 35.
[59] Plotinus. Enn. I.8.8.18 sqq.

unlike the intellect which reflects itself *qua* being, matter does not turn upon itself, for, again, there is no identical "self" in it.[60] Because paradox is deeply inherent in matter, it is not by chance that in Enn. III.6 matter is repeatedly characterized in paradoxical, mutually exclusive terms: it "possesses without really possessing"; it "appears to be filled, but contains nothing"; in matter there is "the apparent presence of a kind of image which is not really present"; matter "follows... while not really following"; and it is "static without being stable".[61] Such descriptions of matter, however, are not senseless. For even if matter is not properly a subject, certain statements are false or, at least, make no sense, because matter is inscribed in the whole that is not determined by it. Therefore, matter presents opposite appearances on its surface (*ta enantia... phantazomenon*), but is not affected by them, for they are not really present in matter.[62] Matter may be described then as a "more or less", both deficient and superabundant, although not as two different principles, as Aristotle thinks, but as potentiality capable of embracing opposites and even not as a principle of otherness, but as *nihil negativum*.[63]

In his commentary to Enn. III.6.10.19, Fleet maintains that "matter has no accidental properties".[64] However, when matter is said " not to have accidental properties", this itself is not an accidental property. What, then? Is it an essential property (like that of unlimitedness and inalterabilty)? Obviously not, because, since matter is not a particular subject, it is difficult to argue that it has an essence. It may be even said that matter's essence is to have no particular essence or that its

---

[60] In Enn. III.6.17.35-37 we find a rather enigmatic phrase: "What is nothing of itself can become, by means of something else, the opposite; but when it has become the opposite, it is not the opposite—for if so it would come to a standstill". Taking into account everything that has been said about matter, we may understand this claim as follows: matter, which is nothing, always becomes, through something other than itself, other to itself and then (again) other to that other to itself, and so on, unceasingly, without stop. This means that in matter there is no real reflectivity, no sameness (even as sameness of otherness), for reflectivity presupposes a stop, fixing the reflective as returned back to itself. In fact, only the thinking of the intellect as thinking itself (i.e., its own intelligible objects) is reflective, and nothing else is.
[61] Plotinus. Enn. III.6. 1.36, 7.26, 12.27, 15.31, 7.14. In a sense, matter may be even said to be both generated and not generated, Enn. II.4.5.24-27. Cp. Harder's commentary to II.4: "Die intelligible Materie ist entstanden und zugleich unentstanden. Im vollen Sinne ewig ist sie deshalb nicht, weil sie von den übergeordneten Prinzipien abhängt." - *Plotins Schriften* I, 516. Cp., however, O'Brien's criticism of the thesis of matter's being not generated (this thesis supported in Schwyzer 1973, 266-280), in favor of matter's atemporal (eternal) generation by the soul. For O'Brien, this also should clarify the problem of evil, for matter has to be equally eternally illuminated by the soul, which is always covering matter "with the appearance of form" or goodness. - O'Brien 1981, 108-123. See also the discussion in Narbonne 1993 and Corrigan 1986, 167-181. An interesting argument is provided by Balaudé, who holds that Plotinus advocates an eternal production of matter (and because of that matter exists eternally), although this production is not a real one. – Balaudé 1999, 70-75.
[62] Enn. III.6.7.14 sqq.; cp. VI.3.12.2-6.
[63] Plotinus. Enn. VI.6.3.29; Aristotle. Met. 987b 20 sqq.; 1087b 9 sqq.; Phys. 203a 15-16. Cp. Halfwassen 1992, 366.
[64] Fleet 1995, 199.

essence is elusive. That is why matter cannot be characterized in terms of accidental and essential properties. In fact, every judgement necessarily "misses" matter as its object (as matter itself "misses" its object), because matter is not any particular defined object at all.

If this is the case, then it is proper to speak of matter in terms of otherness. The distinctive characteristic, *idiotēs*, of matter is not form (which is being), but matter "is not something other than what it is; it is not an addition to it but rather consists in its relationship to other things, its being other than they. Other things are not only other but each of them is something as form, but this [matter] would appropriately be called nothing but other, or perhaps, so as not to define it as a unity by the term "other" but to show its indefiniteness by calling it 'others'".[65] That is why when Plotinus introduces the notion of separateness (*to khōris*), which characterizes not the particular individuality of forms but rather the fact that they are all distinct from one another (which may be predicated of every form as its common feature), he says that this separateness consists in otherness (*heterotēti*).[66] Otherness separates not only physical things, but intelligible forms as well.

Otherness is deeply inherent in matter, so that physical matter is always not the same (*oy tayton aei*).[67] Such a statement seems to contradict the previous claim about matter's inalterability. However, otherness as a principle is, as said, different from matter as *nihil negativum*: the former organizes the latter into a particular subject. Since matter is not anything particular by itself, it is not other to anything and thus matter is also always not the same. Further, since the principle of non-contradiction is not strictly applicable to matter, being always other and another is quite compatible with the unchangeability of matter, for it is in being other than it is that matter persists as unchangeable. Even if it is not a substance, matter's "non-essential essence" is to be other to everything else, other to the other, other even to itself. That is why matter is always only a relation, or, rather, is *in* relation to everything else, other than it is.[68] Even if radically other to the existent, matter, never yet definite and defined, is not otherness as such (which is an ideal principle), but otherness as *nihil negativum*.

1.1.3 Matter and extension in Descartes

Physical science studies physical things in their properties and movements. But physical things are material things; therefore, one of the primary concerns of physical science is the study of nature taken as matter—and with all the qualities attributed to matter.[69] Matter is thus crucial for Cartesian scientific investigations. What is matter for Descartes? In the search for clarity, instead of the equivocation of Aristotle's notion of matter (with its three different definitions) and the Platonic subtlety and paradoxality of the notion of matter, Descartes presents matter

---

[65] Plotinus. Enn. II.4.13.24-31.
[66] Plotinus. Enn. IV.4.16.10-11.
[67] Plotinus. Enn. II.4.3.13.
[68] Plotinus. Enn. II.4.16.2-3; III.6.15.6-8; III.6.19.24.
[69] Descartes. The World, AT XI 37.

unequivocally and straightforwardly as extension. Before 1641, when Descartes began considering the possibility of appropriating his philosophy for school teaching and thus tried to present his own terminology consistently and univocally, his terminological usage is, as Garber shows, rather loose.[70] Quite often Descartes uses terms synonymously and interchangeably. This might seem contrary to his own intention to present metaphysics and physics in the clearest and most univocal way, but Descartes is more concerned with clarity of understanding than with a thoroughly elaborated system of notions. The same insight may be put differently, namely that most discussions and quarrels are about words, not thoughts. Thus, Descartes identifies extension and space without much worrying about possible differences between them, since, to him the case appears clear. As Descartes implies, the more we try to elucidate it by drawing distinctions, the more we render it obscure: for example, "by 'extension' we mean whatever has length, breadth and depth, leaving aside the question whether it is a real body or merely a space".[71] In other words, extension is nothing other than three-dimensional *geometrical* space. For this reason, it becomes possible for Descartes to construct his physics as geometrical, because all material nature is already implicitly taken as geometricized (i.e., as immersed into geometrical extension). The main question then (also the main question of this study) is: what makes such a geometrization of the world possible? We will return to it later, when discussing the notion of two matters (see 2.4-2.4.2).

One of the main statements in Descartes that remains unproved, yet is taken for granted as axiomatic—as the most fundamental *factum* about the world—is that the conception or idea of matter in general is not different from the idea of space: for matter the property of occupying space is not an accident, but constitutes its essence.[72] An important feature of space or extension is that it is impenetrable, as Descartes points out in his correspondence with H. More. More argues that space is absolutely penetrable and exercises no resistance whatsoever. Descartes, however, insists that "impenetrability belongs to the essence of extension".[73] The essence of More's polemics against Descartes is that extension implies a spatial location of both material and spiritual substances, with the only difference being that material objects cannot occupy the same place (having the property of resistance to any bodily penetration, *antitypia*), whereas spiritual objects (souls) may be present in one and the same place at the same time.[74] This position is energetically rejected by Descartes solely because it is essential and proper to matter to be extended and to extension to be material, so that when one material part moves, it ousts another part and occupies its position. The presence of two pieces of matter at the same time in the same part of extension would imply the annihilation of one of them. Since space, or extension, is not different from matter, Descartes cannot conceive of bodies and, respectively, parts of space as penetrable without contradicting himself. Likewise, space and corporeal substance

---

[70] See Garber 1992, 65.
[71] Descartes. Reg. 14, AT X 442 sqq.
[72] Descartes. The World, AT XI 36; cp. To ***, June 1645, AT IV 224.
[73] Descartes. To More 15 April 1649, AT V 342; cp. To ***, June 1645, AT IV 224.
[74] Nikulin 1993, 45-52.

are not two different substances, because one can take away each of their qualities, with the exception of extension.[75]

One of the peculiar features of Descartes' approach is his attempt to rehabilitate the corporeal in science. In ancient mathematics the corporeal is regarded mostly as imprecise and fluent, about which there can be no precise mathematical knowledge. For Plato there is no knowledge of bodily things at all, but only of intelligible eternal entities, for that which is in flux and in becoming does not have an identity, but ever changes and thus cannot be grasped by reason, which thinks in definite forms. For Aristotle, physical science is not mathematical because the two have different subjects, which implies a difference in methods of physics and mathematics and their rigid distinction in the hierarchy of sciences. And even if there are some branches of mathematics that are close to physics (optics, harmonics and astronomy), physics is still different from "pure" mathematics because of the mutual irreducibility of the objects of physics and mathematics. On the one hand, numbers, studied by arithmetic, cannot be considered physical entities, because even if physical objects may be numbered, they themselves are not numbers. On the other hand, geometrical entities—a line for instance—may be considered in physical bodies, but not *qua* geometrical and, on the contrary, a physical line may be considered in geometry, but not *qua* physical. The reason why physical and geometrical straight lines are completely different is that the former is never exactly straight, but is in becoming and constantly changes, while the latter is precise and ever unchanging.[76]

From the very beginning Descartes intends to develop a mathematical theory of physical things (i.e., of bodies), or to structure nature as purely mathematical extension. Descartes presents his intention in the form of a simple syllogism: body is matter; matter is space; therefore, body is space.[77] Since there is no real distinction between space and extension, body also is extension. A body or corporeal thing is then merely "that which is extended, or that which contains extension as part of its concept".[78] In the fourteenth rule Descartes argues that the propositions "body possesses extension" and "extension is not body" may both be true without violating the principle of non-contradiction.[79] This is obviously possible only if both are understood in different respects. Indeed, the first proposition refers to an image of imagination, in which it is impossible to distinguish extension from that which is extended (i.e., from body). The second

---

[75] Cp. Descartes. Princ. II 11, AT VIIIA 46.
[76] Plato. Theaet. 151e-154b, RP 522c sqq.; Aristotle. Phys. 194a 7-12; Met. 1026a 6-23; Anal. Post. 75b 12-17; Proclus. Theol. Plat. II 64.5-6. Cp. H. Wagner 1967, 455; Burnyeat 1987, 225 sqq.; Zekl 1990, 83. E. Hussey's treatment of the Aristotelian physics as mathematical is an example of modernization of Aristotle (see Hussey 1991, 213-242).
[77] Cp. Descartes. Princ. II 10, AT VIIIA 45; To More, 15 April 1649, AT V 345. However, as Dicker points out, Descartes' treatment of the notion of body appears to be ambiguous, for upon closer examination one might distinguish two different approaches: each body is a substance and each body is a mode of one single (material) substance (Dicker 1993, 212-217).
[78] Descartes. Seventh Set of Replies, AT VII 519; cp. Princ. II 4-5, AT VIIIA 42-43; To Gibieuf, 19 January 1642, AT III 478.
[79] Descartes. Reg. XIV, AT X 443-445.

proposition, on the contrary, refers to the idea of reason or "pure intellect" and not to that of imagination, which is capable of thinking extension without body. Two important consequences follow: first, that operations of thinking and imagining (which play an important role in the Cartesian physics of the constitution of bodily extension as mathematical, see 3.3.1) are quite different in relation to matter or extension. Second, extension is unintelligible without body and, therefore, according to the definition of three kinds of distinctions Descartes gives in the "Principles", there is also no conceptual distinction between body and extension or matter. It means that there can be only a modal distinction between the two, so that body is only a *mode* of extension, a way of representing the extended substance.

One may say then that the difference between Descartes' and Plotinus' understanding of body is that for the former matter and body are different only quantitatively, insofar as body is a part of matter; whereas for the latter, matter and body are qualitatively different, insofar as body is *not* matter but is matter informed by an intelligible form. More specifically, for Descartes body represents extension *qua* limited, shaped or formed, or is a *part* of extension.[80] Body is "whatever has a determinable shape and a definable location and can occupy a space in such a way as to exclude any other body".[81] In other words, body is fully determined by the following four properties: extension (and, since extension is continuous, also by divisibility[82]), impenetrability, location (and, subsequently, the ability to be moved) and form (or shape).[83] The first and second are properties that body has in common with matter or space, but the third and fourth are its specific properties. It is easy to see that both location and form are due to the fact that body is a particular part of matter or extension. And because extension is impenetrable, as Descartes insists in his polemics with More, the shaped extension has to be movable (as a fish in water).[84] Presented in this way, body obviously satisfies the requirement of being the subject of a mathematically structured physics. For this reason Descartes returns to the notion of body several times: in the "Regulae", we find a different account of bodily features, which are reduced to three, namely, dimension, unity and shape.[85] It is easy to see that both accounts are compatible with each other: insofar as body is extension or matter, it has *dimension*. Insofar as body is a finite part of extension or matter, it has *shape* and *location* (and,

---

[80] Cp. Descartes in a letter to Mislaid: "When we speak of body in general, we mean a determinate part of matter, a part of the quantity of which the universe is composed" (9 February 1645, AT IV 166).
[81] Descartes. Med. II, AT VII 26.
[82] As a part of extension, impenetrable, coherent and continuous, body has no void lacunas and cannot be composed of indivisibles and is thus indefinitely divisible, at least in our imagination (Descartes. To Mersenne, 28 October 1640, AT III 213-214). Extension is to be considered as purely geometrical and, therefore, presents a continuum and does not consist of *quanta* or atoms.
[83] Cp.: "There are certain acts that we call 'corporeal', such as size, shape, motion and all others that cannot be thought of apart from local extension; and we use the term 'body' to refer to the substance in which they inhere." - Descartes. Third Set of Replies, AT VII 176; cp. Princ. I 8, AT VIIIA 7; II 2, AT VIIIA 41; To More, 5 February 1649, AT V 270.
[84] Cp. Descartes. To Elizabeth, 21 May 1643, AT III 665.
[85] Descartes. Reg. 14, AT X 447.

subsequently, is movable). Lastly, insofar as body is continuous and coherent, it has *unity*.

Such an understanding of body allows Descartes to consider body quantitatively, that is, as a purely mathematical or geometrical quantity. Moreover, he is also able to get rid of "occult" qualities and to understand all primary bodily qualities (such as weight, hardness, shape, and so on) only in terms of extension.[86] Furthermore, he can distinguish between primary qualities of bodies (such as those mentioned), which are caused by bodies themselves, and secondary qualities, which are caused only by our sensual apprehension of bodies.[87] On Descartes' account, bodily qualities are modally distinct from extension, because the nature of body consists not in qualities, but solely in extension; or to put it otherwise, all qualities are only modes of extension as substance.[88]

Body can thus be neither thought nor imagined without extension. Because extension may itself be conceived as purely geometrical, the physical body may be understood then as a purely geometrical figure. Consequently, to know the essence of a physical thing or body is to know it in its extension, which is why all bodily features and properties are to be considered as only *geometrical*. The whole world is then constituted by purely geometrical extended entities, and all bodily properties are explainable either in terms of geometrical figures and their properties or in terms of our perception of them. In this way, physics, the science of bodies and their movements, is already structured as a geometrical science. This understanding, which Descartes shares with Galilei, Newton and other seventeenth century scientists, is radically different from any of the ancient accounts of physics. Now we can return to our main question, namely, what makes this new physical science possible as a science mathematically structured.

It is important to note that for Descartes two things or notions are identical if they cannot be differentiated or distinguished: A is B iff A is not different from B. Sameness is introduced as non-difference; identity is understood through non-distinction, as "not different from" and thus through double negation, for distinction itself is a negation.[89] When Descartes proceeds to the systematic

---

[86] Cp. Descartes. To Morin, 13 July 1638, AT II 200; To Mersenne, 20 April 1646, AT IV 401.
[87] Careful and attentive observation of the nature of bodies leads Descartes to conclude that "nothing whatever belongs to the concept of body except the fact that it is something which has length, breadth and depth and is capable of various shapes and motions; moreover, these shapes and motions are merely modes which no power whatever can cause to exist apart from body. But colors, smells, tastes and so on, are, I observed, merely certain sensations which exist in my thought, and are as different from bodies as pain is different from the shape and motion of the weapon which produces it. And lastly, I observed that heaviness and hardness and the power to heat or to attract, or to purge, and all the other qualities which we experience in bodies, consist solely in the motion of bodies, or its absence, and the configuration and situation of their parts." - Descartes. Sixth Set of Replies, AT VII 440.
[88] Descartes. Princ. II 4, AT VIIIA 42; cp. Sixth Set of Replies, AT VII 433.
[89] We find the very same approach in Descartes' understanding of number: number is not different from the thing numbered (The World, AT XI 36), or there is only a conceptual distinction between quantity or number and the thing that has quantity or number (Princ. II 8, AT VIIIA 44-45).

formulation and presentation of his approach in the "Principles", he has to specify the notion of difference or distinction itself. Every attempt to distinguish and delineate any two different entities and their properties inevitably leads to a discussion of the notion of distinction. In defining matter as not different from extension, Descartes introduces the distinction as non-distinction, which is noteworthy since Descartes' primary intention is to escape negativity's uncertainty—which for him is only a privation (*nihil privativum*)—in favor of the clarity of positive being and understanding. It appears to be fundamental for Descartes and for modern thinkers (who base their considerations in the tradition of Enlightenment) to consider philosophy a *scientia*, that is, a possibly all-embracing systematic account, accessible to reason, so that the more general and universal a statement is about the nature of the material world or human understanding, the simpler and clearer the underlying principles should appear to the mind.

The two main kinds of distinctions commonly accepted in scholasticism are *real* distinctions, which occur between thing and thing, and *mental* (or *conceptual*) distinctions, which, as Suarez puts it, are not between things as they exist in themselves but only as they exist in our mind. Mental distinction is itself twofold: it is either *distinctio rationis ratiocinantis*, conceptual distinction, which has no foundation in reality, or *distinctio rationis ratiocinatae*, which has its foundation in reality, is "prior to the discriminating operation of the mind" and requires the intellect only to recognize such a distinction, but not to constitute it.[90] However, for certain philosophical and theological purposes, these two kinds of distinctions are not enough. The famous third kind is *formal* distinction, introduced by Duns Scotus primarily to explain the difference between the divine attributes while still preserving the unity of God (Scotus also uses the notion of formal distinction in order to distinguish between the universal nature and *quidditas*—"thisness"—of a finite created thing). Two objects, according to Scotus, are formally distinct if they correspond to two different (non-identical) notions that are not merely mental concepts. Formal distinction does not thus presuppose a real distinction of subjects (i.e., that they be two different really existing things).[91] Many scholastic writers reject the notion of formal distinction: Ockham, John of Gent, and Cajetan deny any necessity for a third, intermediary distinction. Suarez, who also rejects the notion of formal distinction as excessively equivocal, argues that there should be an intermediary distinction between real and mental (or conceptual) distinctions, which in the "Metaphysical disputations" he calls modal: a distinction "in between" real and mental. Mode is that which affects quantity and determines "its state and manner of existing, without adding to it a proper new entity, but merely modifying a pre-existing entity".[92] Modal distinction is then the distinction between a mode and the thing modified or between modes.[93]

---

[90] Suarez. Disp. met. VII.1.1, 1.4.
[91] Duns Scotus. In I Sent. dist. 2 qu. 7; Opus ox. I. 8. 4; Suarez. Disp. met. VII. 1. 13. Cp. Copleston 1990, 222-223.
[92] Suarez. Disp. met. VII.1.17; cp. VI.1.9.
[93] Although, unlike for Descartes, for Suarez there can be only mental distinction between the modes, Suarez. Disp. met. VII.1.18-26.

In his early period, Descartes, in attempting to render things known as clear and univocal as possible, tries to escape distinctions within the distinctions themselves. This however, leads to confusion. When Caterus asks Descartes to explain further the difference between soul and body in terms of formal distinction, Descartes erroneously identifies formal distinction with modal distinction.[94] The probable source of Descartes' later theory of distinction is Suarez: trying to systematize his own philosophy, Descartes *volens nolens* has to follow the pattern of scholastic presentation. In particular, he finds Suarez' tripartite distinction appropriate for his own purpose. Descartes distinguishes three kinds of distinctions: real, modal, and conceptual. The *real* distinction is between two or more substances. The *modal* distinction is either between a mode and its substance or between two modes of the same substance. The *conceptual* distinction is between an attribute and a substance "without which the substance is unintelligible", or between two such attributes of the same substance.[95]

Thus, when Descartes says "there is no real distinction" (e.g., between corporeal substance and space) or "there is no conceptual distinction" (e.g., between a number and a thing numbered), it means that there is no difference between two subjects either in reality or in our ideas, which eventually makes them essentially the same—both as real things or as concepts of the mind. But as is quite often the case in philosophy, an attempt to put one's thought in the traditional, already quite elaborated philosophical language, hides the original thought more than reveals it. Or at the very least, the standard usage becomes modified. Among the three kinds, the notion of modal distinction seems especially congenial to Descartes, because of his revision of the notion of "mode" as a loose notion that somehow represents or shows the essence of a thing.[96] In the "Principles" Descartes states that "by *mode*...we understand exactly the same as what is elsewhere meant by an *attribute* or *quality*. But we employ the term *mode* when we are thinking of a substance as being affected or modified; when the modification enables the substance to be designated as a substance of such a kind, we use the term *quality*; and finally, when we are simply thinking in a more general way of what is in a substance, we use the term *attribute*".[97] There is, however, no

---

[94] First Set of Objections and Replies, AT VII 100, 120; Descartes himself recognizes that he does not draw difference between conceptual and modal distinctions in the "Meditations", Princ. I 62, AT VIIIA 30.

[95] Descartes. Princ. I 60-62, AT VIIIA 28-30; cp. To ***, 1645 or 1646, AT IV 350.

[96] Wells 1965, 1-22.

[97] Princ. I 56, AT VIIIA 26. Cp.: "...I make a distinction between modes, strictly so called, and attributes, without which the things whose attributes they are cannot be; or between the modes of things themselves and the modes of thinking. ...Thus shape and motion are modes, in the strict sense, of corporeal substance; because the same body can exist at one time with one shape and at the other with another, now in motion and now at rest, whereas, conversely, neither this shape nor this motion can exist without this body. Thus love, hatred, affirmation, doubt, and so on are true modes in the mind. But existence, duration, size, number and all universals are not, it seems to me, modes in the strict sense; nor in this sense are justice, mercy, and so on modes in God. They are referred to by a broader term and called attributes, or modes of thinking, because we do indeed understand the essence of a thing in one way when we conceive it in abstraction from whether it exists or not, and in a

univocality in Descartes' usage, for all three notions (mode, quality and attribute) may be used almost interchangeably, especially when the three are related to the case when substance is modified or changed—when the attribute or quality is modified.[98] The notion of "mode" seems further to be congenial to Descartes, since there is no way for him to know, and thus to compare, substances directly. Therefore, the mind is able to compare substances only through modes, understood either as essential or as accidental attributes, which do not exist independently and separately, but express their "vehicles" (their subjects) in the most adequate way. Following the distinction Descartes has made, how can the relation between matter and extension then be characterized? Obviously, their distinction is not real, for they are not two different substances. Nor are they modally distinct, for neither is to be considered only a mode, expressing the other as substance. Therefore, they have to be understood as only conceptually distinct, if each is taken as the essential attribute of the other considered as substance (i.e., "extension is material" and "matter is extended"). The subject (substance) is, however, one and the same in both cases, univocally understandable and positively expressible, unlike the elusive negativity of matter in the Platonic tradition.

1.2 Substance: ontology vs. henology

Comparing the two approaches to the treatment of geometrical and physical entities, one might say that Descartes thinks and develops his philosophy and science within an ontological framework, departing from the initial presupposition that whatever simply and necessarily *is*, without detriment and change, is the primary reality that causes everything that does not exist necessarily. Plotinus, on the contrary, thinks within the henological (Greek *hen*, "one") framework, which posits the cause and source even for being, the source which is not being itself and is thereby primary to being. In order to be able to give an account and to appreciate fully the difference between the ancient and modern approaches to science, let us first briefly characterize the henological and then the ontological positions by their fundaments, considering Plotinus and Descartes as their two representatives. Of course, henology and ontology do not represent two complete and closed systems, for within each of the two approaches there exists a significant number of variations (in fact, every thinker always proposes his or her own variant of the whole, which could hardly be ever fully thematized), but there definitely are clearly distinguishable "family resemblances" that make the two fundamentally non-isomorphic and incompatible with each other. Gilson puts it nicely: "In the

---

different way when we consider it as existing; but the thing itself cannot be outside our thought without its existence, or without its duration or size, and so on." - To ***, 1645 or 1646, AT IV 348-349. Cp. Gaukroger 1995, 366-367.

[98] As Garber puts it, "the term 'mode', *modus* in Latin, means quite simply 'way'; it is a perfect term to choose to express the fact that all accidents are *ways* of something being extended or being a thinking thing, *ways* of expressing the essence of a thing. In emphasizing the necessity of a link between essence and accident, attribute and mode, Descartes is saying something his teachers would not have, and thus departures from their terminology" - Garber 1992, 69. Cp. Wolfson 1969 I, 71-72.

doctrine of Being the inferior *is* only because of the being of the superior. On the contrary, in the doctrine of the One the general principle is that the inferior *is* only because of that which the superior is not. In fact, the superior ever gives only that which it itself does not have, because, in order to be able to give it, the superior has to be above it."[99]

1.2.1 The One and the multitude in Plotinus

The starting (or "launching", as Porphyry puts it) point for Plotinus is the One, which is not being (*ho mē on estin*). The problem posed by the One draws all of his attention—his intellectual and physical forces—and, in fact, Plotinus comes to define the entirety of his life and philosophy as an attempt to grasp this One and escape "in solitude to the solitary" in an invincible desire to become one.[100] Henology thus precedes and underlies ontology. Plotinus implicitly accepts the following axiomatic statements about the One.

I. There is the principle (*arkhē, aitia, pēgē* or *rhiza*) of everything existent. This principle is the highest possible good, *agathon*, so that nothing can be better or greater than it.[101]

II. Everything which is perfect (*teleia*), necessarily *produces* or *gives*.[102]

III. That which gives is better than that which is given.[103]

IV. A unified simple whole is better and more perfect than that which is complex, compound and composite; it takes precedence over all the parts as distinctions and differences which can be discerned in it only afterwards.

These four axioms underlie and determine the specific way of exposition and specific features of Plotinus' system. First of all, they entail (1) that there is only one (*monon*) principle, *the* principle, the One.[104] Evidently, if there were two of them, they would have formed a complex system, which (according to axiom IV) is not as good as a unique single principle. Therefore, as principles they could not represent the good. The good and the One are thus identical. The one good or the good One is the One-good, is absolutely one and the same, so that the good as *different* from or *not identical* with the One, in fact, can only be discerned in a secondary way. This One-good (2) has not come to be (*mēde gegone*),[105] since otherwise there would have to be something better according to axiom IV, (in other words, the One would not be perfectly "one"). This "not-coming-to-being" of the

---

[99] Gilson 1948, 42.
[100] Plotinus. Enn. VI. 9. 5. 30; VI.9.11.51.
[101] Plotinus. Enn. VI.9.9.1-2; VI.8.8.9. Cp. Steel 1989, 69-84, Bussanich 1988, 207-208 and Siegmann 1990, 142 sqq.
[102] Plotinus. Enn. V.1.6.38.
[103] Plotinus. Enn. VI.7.17.5.
[104] Plotinus. Enn. V.1.7.20. On various readings of the relation of monism and dualism in Platonism see: Halfwassen 1997, 1-21. Among the Neoplatonists, Iamblichus was later the first to postulate two Ones, the One allowing no participation and being completely ineffable, *pantelōs arrhēton*, and the One simply, precedent to all duality, *ho haplōs hen*, see Dillon in: Iamblichus 1973, 29-33.
[105] Plotinus. Enn. VI.8.7.35.

One presupposes that it is beyond all temporal characteristics or duration of any kind and gives or produces, first, the monadic "now" of eternity and, then, time and temporal duration.[106]

This further implies (3) that the One produces eternally—it is neither in a certain fixed moment or moments of time, nor in each moment of time, because it is not in time at all. The One is the infinite, the "unspeakably great" potency of all, *dynamis pantōn*, which never becomes that all. It, in other words, is ever transcendent to being and to anything that participates in being and is absent from anything other than itself (only a certain "trace" of the One is in everything as the uniqueness of its individuality).[107] The One (4) is absolutely simple, without any parts whatsoever.[108] For if there were several parts in it, then only one of them, according to (1) and axiom I (in fact, as it is easy to see, axiom I and (1) are mutually convertible) and axiom III, would be the best, and hence, according to axiom II, would be the generator of the other parts. Moreover, it is only the One that is absolutely simple, indissoluble and without any addition. Therefore (5), everything other is complex—it is itself *and* something else.[109] Particularly, it means that for each and every "*ayto*", for every substance (be it real or hypothetical), its essence differs from its existence. The only and unique exception is the One "itself", where no such distinction can be made. In this sense, which is crucial for the henological approach, the One identical to itself as "*ayto*" is *not* being, *oyde to on*.[110] At this point Plotinus turns to Plato's "Parmenides", which is so important for constituting the whole of his system. The "Parmenides" is the starting point for Plotinus, around which the whole of his henology is based. Plotinus' henology, as has been discussed, subsumes ontology with its distinction of dual intelligible principles of the same and other—or of oneness and duality—which subsequently form the realm of being and underlie human subjectivity.

The One of the first hypothesis of Plato's "Parmenides", considered beyond any otherness or many, can be grasped neither by sensation, nor imagination, nor thought. It cannot even be (unlike the One considered together with the multiple) the one-many of the second hypothesis, which really comes into being, is being itself and is first to be thought.[111] If that which is after the One, the

---

[106] Cp. Plotinus. Enn. III.7.3.36 et al. See also: Pines, Samburksy 1987, passim; Galpérine 1980, 325-341; Hoffmann 1980, 307-323.
[107] Plotinus. Enn. III.8.10.1; IV.8.6.11; V.1.7.10; VI.8.20.38 sqq. See: Nikulin 2000, 15-38.
[108] Plotinus. Enn. V.4.1.5.
[109] The One "is something which has its place high above everything, this which alone is free in truth, because it is not enslaved to itself, but is only itself and really itself, while every other thing is itself and something else" (Plotinus. Enn. VI.8.21.30-33).
[110] Plotinus. Enn. VI.9.2.47, cp. VI.9.3.37-38. Plotinus constantly refers to the famous passage in Plato's "Republic", although stressing it much more energetically: "the good itself is not essence but transcends essence (*epekeina tēs oysias*) in dignity and power" (RP 509b; cp. Plotinus. Enn. VI.8.9.28, VI.9.11.42 et al.). There is nothing above the One, *mēden esti to hyperkeimenon* (Enn. VI.7.22.20-21). *Hyperkeimenon*, "superstratum", the source of being which precedes the being, is an obvious opposition to the Aristotelian *hypokeimenon* as underlying substratum of an existing substance.
[111] Plato. Parm. 137c-142a; 142b-157b. Cp. Wyller 1960, 81 sqq.

intellect-*noys*, is the one and unique being, it should somehow contain the very form of multiplicity. Thus, although the intellect as being is one (the one-being), it is not altogether simple, but contains a (finite, according to Plotinus) number of forms of things. The oneness-*hen* is not therefore altogether identical with being-*on* in intellect, but both form a primary multiplicity as forms of otherness or duality.

This implies (6) that the One is absolutely different from everything that is, in particular, from the intellect: it is neither the collection of forms, nor thinking.[112] Moreover, it itself is not thinkable. Paradoxically, it is not even thinkable that the One or the good is not thinkable, because the very concept of "not being thinkable" is itself thinkable. Thinking serves the purpose of overcoming the state of partiality, incompleteness and being split; it gathers many into one. For this reason the One cannot be thought; it is neither incomplete, nor deficient, nor does it need anything.[113] Therefore (7), the One is not knowable in its essence, which (as not different from its existence) can be represented to us only negatively, as not-essence (of anything else) or as above essence, which coincides with non-existence.[114] The One is also (8) before all things (*pro toytōn*), since it precedes being, just as being precedes and is separate from becoming.[115] Consequently (9), the One is absolutely different from everything that is, or somehow participates in being, and is even different from the non-being of matter (i.e., not only from the intellect and being, but also from becoming; from the distinction into positive and negative, and so on; and from all that can be thought, imagined, sensually apprehended, uttered or predicated). But since the One or the good is the first, the cause of bringing forth all the other things, it is in a sense all these things, still being absolutely different from them.[116] So finally (10), we have to conclude that, after all, it is extremely difficult to speak about the One and it is only in this unique case that we have to make use of a peculiar way of negative expression, traditionally called the *via negativa* or apophatic approach.

Where being is presented not as simply existing by itself as an act of itself, but as caused, one faces an ambiguity of thinking and speaking about that which is neither speakable nor thinkable.[117] The appropriate language is found in the *via negativa*.[118] Such a language is a peculiar way of speaking about non-being and the actually infinite in "the audacity to think the unthinkable", in the words of Funkenstein[119]—a specific way of putting statements in negative form about that which cannot be formulated in an ordinary way and which escapes adequate expression in terms of the usual predicative structure (cp. above, (6)). Ordinary

---

[112] Plotinus. Enn. III.9.9.1; V.3.14.19; V.4.2.3; V.7.35.43 et al.
[113] Plotinus. Enn. V.3.10.47.
[114] Cp. Gregory Palamas. Triads III.ii.5; Capita 150, 132-145.
[115] Plotinus. Enn. VI.9.5.38; VI.9.11.35.
[116] Plotinus. Enn. VI.8.21.24; VI.9.3.40. Cp. Lloyd 1976, 146-156.
[117] Cp. Parmenides' warning against the danger of reasoning about the non-existent (Plato. Soph. 236e-237b).
[118] Cp. Armstrong 1940, 29-47; Hadot 1968, I 278-283; Beierwaltes 1985, 104-107; Guérard 1985, 331-354.
[119] Funkenstein 1986, 15.

language presupposes that the subject-predicate dichotomy refers to finite definite subjects and is exemplified in logical structures. The *via positiva* or kataphatic way consists in enumerating attributes or predicates of a considered subject that appear to be either essential or accidental to it. But since the primary principle in henology is supposed to be beyond being and actually infinite, it is not immediately clear how it can be grasped or spoken of. The apophatic way is not merely a negation or abstention from judgement, as it would be in skepticism, but a specific way of expressing definite statements in negative terms, as not this and not that, as not such-and-such, of speaking about that which cannot be ordinarily described. The One that cannot be grasped *per se* is revealed through negation, which thus (re)presents the not representable.

For this reason Plotinus repeatedly claims that every way of "expressing about the One" (not "expressing the One") is inadequate.[120] Therefore, it is more appropriate to understand the One negatively: it is neither intellect, nor discursive reasoning, nor substance, nor relation or *logos* of any kind, nor form, nor limit, is non-dual and not many.[121] That is why the One is pre-reflective and, being *the* Good, it is primarily the good for the other or, rather, is above goodness.[122] Furthermore, since nothing can be properly predicated about the One and there is not yet an other, in relation to which the cause might be distinguished from the caused and the foundation from the founded, it is only *in some way*, "as if" (*hoion*), relative to our perception and thinking, that the One can be considered the cause of itself and subsisting by itself; thus equally it may be taken as not self-foundational, a *not sub-stantia, anypotheton*.[123] The One defines everything, while not itself being defined by the defined.

Mere negation, however, is not an adequate way of expressing the One, which transcends all negation, as well as all affirmation. Since the negated in the *via negativa* still remains properly inaccessible (as beyond being and infinite), negation, as Proclus argues, is not privative but primarily productive: negation does not affect the negated (the One), but also does not establish anything really opposite to the negated. Thus, to negate the non-being of the One is to affirm being, although being is not really opposite to the One, which has no opposites and cannot be thought in terms of opposites. To negate the multiplicity of the One is not only to affirm unity (which is not strictly applicable to the One), but also to make multiplicity (as otherness or duality) exist.[124] Similarly, the negation of the finite amounts to the acknowledgment of the infinite, but also, simultaneously, to

---

[120] Gerson 1994, 15-16.
[121] Cp. Plotinus. Enn. V.3.14.4-8: *kai gar legomen ho mē estin: ho de estin, oy legomen.*
[122] Plotinus. Enn. VI.7.13.34; VI.7.17.15, 42; VI.8.13.52; VI.7.41.28-29.
[123] Plotinus. Enn VI.8.11.32-33 (*eph' haytoy gar kai hyphestēke, prin allo*); VI.8.14.35-42; cp. Plato. RP 510b. On the notion of the *causa sui* in Plotinus see: Beierwaltes 1999, 191-225. Narbonne, who argues that both in Plotinus (who is historically the first to introduce the notion) and in Descartes, *causa sui* implies insurmountable difficulties in understanding the One and God, who should rather be considered as subsisting (in Plotinus, beyond being) *a se*, understood as *sine causa*, without cause. - Narbonne 1993a, 177-195.
[124] Proclus. Theol. Plat. II 37.5-39.5, 63. 8-17; cp. In Parm. VI 1074.15 sqq. Cp. Steel 1999, 351-368.

the affirmation of the finite.

Technically, the notion of negation is expressed either by the term *apophasis* or by *aphairesis*. The former means "abstraction" or "taking away" and is used by Albinus to characterize the way a conception is formed by removing certain attributes.[125] The latter means negation in a logical proposition and is used by Aristotle. Negation, as *aphairesis* is opposed by Aristotle to privation, *sterēsis*: privation occurs in affirmative propositions and expresses the lack of a certain quality that might be present but is not there. Negation, contrarily, stands in negative propositions and is such that the opposite to negation can never be affirmed of the subject.[126] In Plotinus it is possible to distinguish a tendency of reserving the *aphairesis* for the properly apophatic context, while using the term *apophasis* for discussing examples put in Aristotelian language.[127] However, both terms may also be used very much interchangeably and, as Wolfson argues, they are equivalent in the context of *via negativa*.[128] Thus, the notion of *aphairesis* rather exemplifies that which can never be characterized by any positive predicates, the *nihil negativum*, while *sterēsis* primarily refers to the *nihil privativum*.

The most congenial way of conceiving "about the One" (again, not "conceiving the One") is then negating negation itself, applying the generative procedure of negation to negation itself. The *negatio negationis* plays such an important role not only in late Platonic thought (in Iamblichus, Proclus and Damascius, in Dionysius the Areopagite), but also in Philo, Nicholas of Cusa, in Newton and in Hegel.[129] It is only when negativity reflectively applies or turns to itself, even if not being anything substantial, that it can give way to that which cannot be positively defined, although without really grasping the subject to which the double negation is applied.

Plotinus claims the One to be "other than all the things which come after it" (*pantōn heteron tōn met' ayto*), a *non-aliud*, non-striving towards anything other than itself, a non-striving even to itself.[130] But it is also correct to say that the One is not non-being, *oyk esti mē einai*.[131] Since the One is not in being but produces it, it may be said to be not-being, yet since it is not a lifeless privation of being, it is also not non-being. But the *negatio negationis* cannot pertain to the One itself (of the first hypothesis of the "Parmenides"), but the double negation is valid only in representing reflectively the One in the multiplicity (duality) of thinking of

---

[125] Alcinous (Albinus). Didask. 10.5.
[126] Aristotle. Met. 1004a 14-16; 1056a 15-16.
[127] Plotinus. Enn. VI.1.9.33-38; VI.3.27.19; VI.7.36.7; VI.8.11.34.
[128] Wolfson 1973 I, 119-121. Cp. Wolfson 1957, 145-156.
[129] Cp. Beierwaltes 1965, 395-398.
[130] Plotinus. Enn. V.4.1.6; VI.8.10.25-26. Cp. Cusanus. *De li non-aliud* 6 sqq. In a sense, the very inability not to speak or not to think about the One is a certain modal reproduction of the structure of double negation as "not possible not to". And, of course, it is also not by chance that this basic structure is to be found in the expression of freedom that is the rational freedom of the intellect, which "could be said to have freedom and anything in its power, when it does not have it in its power *not to act*" (Enn. VI.8.4.6-7; italics added). See: O'Meara 1992, 343-349.
[131] Plotinus. Enn. VI.7.12.18; cp. VI.5.1.23-24.

the one-being of the intellect (of the second hypothesis of the "Parmenides").

Besides the *via negationis*, the other way of representing the One is analogy, *via analogiae*.[132] When a considered subject cannot be grasped directly, one can nevertheless know the relation in which it stands to other things (in case of the One, the relation of participation of being in its cause, as the light to the sun). This way of approaching the One is mathematical, because it is structured as a proportion.[133] In such a proportion one of the terms, the source of being, is expressed analogically in its relation to a known term through the relation of the other two terms, which are known as well. In this way the term in question may still not be known *per se*, but only through the relation of the other to it.

Thus, although the One is the first and prior to the multitude in any of its representations, nevertheless it is not the first for us in our considerations, because of its simplicity that surpasses all simplicity. In fact, everything simple considered as such by our mind, is not simple, but has the structure of the "one-being" of the second hypothesis of the "Parmenides". If we conceive X as simple and say: X is simple, then S = "being simple" is already thought in an elementary complex structure, that of duality, of X—S. If we say "simple (i.e., being simple) is Y", then, again, S* = "being simple", which now is understood as the subject, is conceived not as simple, but through the other, i.e. through its predicate in S*—Y. Thus, it may be argued once again that (by analogy) simplicity, which is discursively thought in any of the above two cases, may be thought only insofar as it participates in a simplicity that does not allow duality of the kind "one-being". However, everything that cannot be conceived under this pattern is not properly thought in discursive logical analysis.

We have to begin with something other, namely, with the many that is not the One itself, but ensues the One, totally different from it and depends on it.[134] This primary otherness cannot be taken just as pure otherness or difference from everything else, as otherwise nothing could be fixed in being or thought (in particular, the first otherness itself). Therefore, the first otherness, as it has been argued, should be different from mere privation, although through the procedure of double negation it should arrive at the other of the otherness as something positive, that is, as the same.[135] Thus, the first point of departure for us is not the absolute unity of the One, but the dual unity of sameness-otherness, or one-being. That otherness (*thateron, heterotēs*) is already in duality, without which nothing can be

---

[132] Cp. Plato. RP 506d-509c; Plotinus. Enn. VI.7.36.7-9; Proclus. Theol. Plat. II 39.6-26; cp. Damascius. De princ. I 42.11 sqq. The third way, *via eminentiae*, consists in raising from a concept exemplified in particular subjects to the concept in itself, e.g. from contemplation of the beautiful in bodies to the beauty in souls, then in sciences and finally—to the understanding of the beauty as such, cp. Plato. Symp. 210a-e; Alcinous. Didask. 10.6. This method is not, however, applicable in henology, for the One does not have a rationally apprehensible concept. See also commentary by Dillon ap. Alcinous. Didask., p. 109-110.
[133] Cp. Euclid. Elem. VII, def. 20.
[134] Cp. Plotinus. Enn. VI.7.8.18; Halfwassen 1992, 75-81.
[135] For this reason, the same and the other of Plato's "Sophist" (254d sqq.) are mutually inseparable in the list of five categories, applicable, according to Plotinus, to the noetic world (cp. Enn. VI.2.8).

understood or exist. It is to be considered together with sameness (*tayton*) as the two main principles constituting being and intellect.[136] These two principles may be further identified with the one as oneness-*hen* (*tayton*) and the many as duality-*aoristos dyas* (*thateron, polla*) of the Platonic tradition.[137] Otherness (the dyad) together and inseparable from sameness, both constitute in their interaction the whole sphere of the intellect, which is being in and through multiplicity, defined by the initial form of the duality of *hen-on*. The multiplicity in being, in the intellect, may then be considered as shaped through the interaction of the two principles of oneness (sameness) and the dyad (otherness), interpreted by the Pythagoreans as the active limiting principle (*horizon*) and as the passive limited one (*horiston kai horizomenon*).[138] Only the One is beyond otherness, since the One precedes all possible distinctions, while everything the other participates in, as it occurs through otherness, involves the many.[139] The many is profoundly ambiguous: as otherness, it appears as both the ideal thinkable principle of multitude, and as a multiplicity of not being it is represented as matter.

1.2.2 Distinction between the One and matter

One of the main problems that arises in the henological approach is the relation of the source of being to the absolute negativity of matter: is there any difference between them, and if so, in what sense, since both cannot be properly described. Matter is the most distant from the One as the absolute lack of goodness and being, but, paradoxically, it appears to be the closest to the One. The reason is that, first, both appear to be unlimited potency-*dynamis* and, second, neither belongs to the sphere of being. There are a number of "predicates" that both the One and matter seem to have in common (although it is impossible to ascribe any predicates to them properly). Thus, both the One and matter may be characterized negatively; both—and only they—may be characterized as *nihil negativum*. Both are formless, *aneideon*, without any image; in(de)finite, *apeiron*; cannot be spoken of; and are mere potentiality.[140]

Remarkably, even when Plotinus enters the shaky ground of considering non-being, he cannot completely fail to distinguish the One from matter. If we say

---

[136] Cp. Plotinus. Enn. III.7.3.8-11.
[137] J. Rist argues that the dyad should not be identified with the many as such, because the former is the generative principle of the latter (Rist 1962, 99-107). The problem here is whether the dyad and otherness are mutually substitutive or if one of them is logically prior. I am inclined to think that although *dyas* and *heterotēs* in most cases are synonymous in the Enneads, nevertheless *heterotēs* is more fundamental as a principle, because the first distinction of duality (and, further, of multiplicity) becomes possible only when the first otherness is brought forward as a distinction from the non-distinction of the One.
[138] Cp. Kallikratidos, 103.11 Thesleff; Iamblichus. Theolog. Arithm. 7,19; 9,6; Pythagoras. Hier. log. 164.24 Thesleff; Anon. Alexandri 234.18-20 Theslesff. On the role and dialectic of *hen* and *aoristos dyas* see: Hösle 1984, 459 sqq.
[139] So, there can be no thinking in the intellect without otherness, that is, without at least a virtual doubling of *noēsis-noēta*, cp. Plotinus. Enn. VI.9.6.42-43; VI.9.8.25.
[140] Plotinus. Enn. VI.7.33.21; III.6.7.7 sqq.; II.5.4.12; VI.7.32.15; II.4.15.10; VI.7.38.11-12; III.6.15.28.

that matter cannot be identical with the One, this judgement is itself paradoxically untrue in relation to the One itself, for it cannot be put in terms of the S—P structure, since the One and matter are not any particular subjects. In fact, it is not even correct to say "both", because, prior to any otherness, only the One "is". If there is a fundamental difference between the two, it cannot be brought in by matter, for, as it has been said, the difference of matter is constituted only negatively (i.e., to everything else), so that it is only the One that ultimately may be the cause of such a difference. There are at least four points of distinction between the One and matter.

(1) The difference is already there in terms of difference itself. Matter differs from everything and in its non-being is radically other to being.[141] Since there is no "self" in matter, it cannot be, in its radical otherness, anything in itself. Here we encounter an inevitable paradox: matter, as absolute otherness, has to be different from and other not only to any particular thing or entity, but to itself as otherness. Matter does not arrive or return back to itself through double negation, exactly because "pure" otherness in matter is not anything definite—it is not an ideal principle, rather it is nothing (unlike in the principle of otherness, *aoristos dyas*). Matter, unlike the One, is not "not non-being" as the One, but still remains non-being. The One, on the contrary, while being absolutely different from everything else, is introduced by double negation, as "not other than itself", remaining "itself by itself".[142]

(2) The One is the good *per se* and is the first and the ultimate in the order of procession and causation. Since the One is the first and beyond being, everything that comes after the One is different from the One, and is not the good. Since being comes second and necessarily consists of an admixture of multiplicity, being is not as good as the One. Matter is after the first and is itself the last in the existing or in the order of procession. Since being is not the good as such, in a certain sense being may even be ascribed to matter.[143] The notion of matter is extremely ambiguous: it is nothing of the existent and, as said, does not properly exist—it "is" non-being. On the other hand, since some shadow or image of being is brought to everything that is after the One, being may be ascribed also to matter. However, the presence of the being of matter is rather metaphorical, or so faint that matter, the last, may be conceived also as closest to the One. This is an important conclusion for henology, because it leads first to the recognition of the above mentioned purely thinkable principle of otherness, or of materiality, and second to the recognition of matter of a special kind, namely, of intelligible matter (see 2.4).

(3) Next, the One is the good, the source of light, as it were, while matter is darkness as privation of light and is even said to be evil.[144] The distinction between matter (as evil) and the One lies in that there is evil neither in that which is above being, nor in the intellect. And if evil "is", it "exists" among non-existent

---

[141] Plotinus. Enn. I.8.3.6-9.
[142] *Oy gar estin allo haytoy to agathon,* Plotinus. Enn. V.6.5.11-12; *ayto pros hayto menei,* Enn. V.3.10.51.
[143] Plotinus. Enn. I.8.7.17-23; VI.8.8.9; I.8.7.12. In Enn. V.8.7.22 matter is called *eidos ti eskhaton*.
[144] Plotinus. Enn. VI.8.8.9; I.8.7.12; II.4.5.7-9.

things, in matter as a sort of form of non-existence.[145] As otherness, matter is not any particular evil, but rather the "basis" of evil as privation of goodness. In the One *qua* the good there is no evil at all, because there is neither deficiency in it, nor anything contrary to it. The One is other to being, because it is incomparably better than being and is, so to say, "before" or "above" being, while matter is incomparably worse than anything else and is "after" or "beneath" being—it is absolute deficiency, *elleipsis*, different from otherness as the principle.[146]

(4) Lastly, potentiality of matter is not the same as potentiality of the One. As the infinite potency of everything, the One is ever transcendent to everything and thus never becomes anything itself. The One is therefore always absent in its presence. The One is the overwhelming power to produce being, a unique source of all, an absolute richness and fullness. Quite to the contrary, matter, as negative potency that is never actualized, is always present in everything, even in intelligible objects. Plotinus has to ascribe to matter a certain negative potentiality, incapable of any production but as if bothering that which is in being, inexhaustible because there is simply nothing in matter to be exhausted, an absolute poverty and emptiness.[147] It is only a "promise" and is ever present through its absence.

1.2.3 *Substance and attribute in Descartes*

Let us now turn to the ontological description represented in and by Descartes as opposed to the henological one. Cartesian ontology is based on the notion of substance. Descartes seems to be less interested in precise definitions of terms and subtle distinctions he might use; rather, he is more concerned with a clear and simple explanation and description of certain phenomena, which he supposes to be accessible and understandable to every reasonable human being. For this purpose he uses the inherited scholastic Aristotelian language, rather than inventing his own, inevitably rethinking much of its contents.[148]

However, when asked about the notion of substance, in the objections to the "Meditations", Descartes needs to provide explanations. The definition of substance he gives in the second set of replies to the "Meditations" stresses that substance is the *subject* in which its perceivable attributes reside, which is the Aristotelian usage of the term, since for Aristotle substance-*oysia* is primarily the

---

[145] *Eidos ti toy mē ontos,* Plotinus. Enn. I.8.3.1-6; cp. Corrigan, O'Cleirigh 1987, 576-577.
[146] Plotinus. Enn. I.8.5.5; cp. I.8.6.21; VI.7.23.6-8.
[147] Plotinus. Enn. II.5.4.3 sqq.; I.8.14.35-36; VI.7.27.11. As Plotinus puts it, the many does not come from the many, i.e., it does not engender itself and, therefore, matter does not come from itself, but from the One (Plotinus. Enn. V.3.16.12-13).
[148] Cp. Gilson 1979, 275-281. As Descartes argues, it is better to accept a provisional, already existing building (of the general principles, morals, language etc.) which one already has at hand, than to construct a new one based solely on rationally verifiable presuppositions (cp. Disc. III, AT VI 22; see also: Peperzak 1995, 133-155). But every language is charged with historical connotations and has its immanent structure and logic. Language thus resists our intentions to transform it and usually says either what we do not intend or more than we want to say.

subject that cannot be further predicated of anything else.[149] Descartes also agrees with Aristotle that all attributes are attributes of substance(s) and cannot exist apart and independent from them. There is "more reality" in a substance than in an attribute or mode, because if accidents existed independently, they would have been substances and not accidents, by their very definition and notion.[150] These attributes are not, however, all equal but express the substance as their subject differently. Essential attributes are true and adequate expressions of underlying substance(s), which are thinking, in the case of the mind; extension, in the case of matter and body; and ultimate perfection (infinity), in the case of God.[151]

Descartes considers it possible for the attributes to be subordinated to each other, so that "there is no awkwardness in saying that an accident is the subject of another accident, just as we say that quantity is the subject of other accidents".[152] Attributes thus may form a kind of ladder, so that one attribute may appear as a subject of another attribute. Descartes does not, however, go as far as to say that the difference between substance and attribute is only relative (i.e., depends only on the point of view of their consideration), because that would have made attributes real, or existing without substance, which Descartes rejects.

The allegedly obvious clarity and simplicity of Descartes' account of extended substance as matter, and thought as mind, is not as simple as it appears. Even the most fundamental distinction between a finite substance and its essential attribute is not as univocal as Descartes would like it to be. Indeed, extension and thought may be considered not only as two created substances, but simultaneously also as two essential attributes of these same substances. Descartes has to recognize that "it seems necessary that the mind should always be actually engaged in thinking; because thought constitutes its essence, just as extension constitutes the essence of a body. Thought is not conceived as an attribute that can be present or absent like the division of parts, or motion, in a body".[153] In other words, thought (as well as the extension) appears to be *both* substance and the substantial (essential) attribute.[154] Perhaps, this equivocation might be overcome by

---

[149] Descartes. Second Set of Replies, AT VII 161. Cp. Aristotle. Cat. 2a 12-13; Met. 1028a 10 sqq.; Phys. 190a 36-190b 1. See: Frede 1987, 72-80. An obvious distinction between Aristotelian and Cartesian accounts of substance and matter is that for Aristotle nothing is opposite to substance (Cat. 3b 25). Even if in Aristotle matter may be treated as substance, it nonetheless has no opposite. And more so in Plato and Plotinus: since matter "is" non-being and is not a real subject, there can be no real opposition to being and to any subject. In Descartes matter as substance is opposite to mind as the other substance; and matter as finite substance is opposed to God as the infinite substance.

[150] Cp. Descartes. Third Set of Replies, AT VII 185; Sixth Set of Replies, AT VII 434.

[151] Descartes. Second Set of Replies, AT VII 161-162, 165; Fifth Set of Replies, AT VII 385; Princ. I 53, AT VIIIA 25; To Arnauld, 29 July 1648, AT V 221.

[152] Descartes. To Mersenne for Hobbes, 21 April 1641, AT III 355. Cp. Grene 1985, 88-108; Marion 1992, 129-131.

[153] Descartes. For [Arnauld], 4 June 1648, AT V 192; cp. Princ. I 63-64, AT VIIIA 30-31; Comments on a Certain Broadsheet, AT VIIIB 348-349.

[154] In scholastic terminology that follows Aristotle and Porphyry's *Eisagoge*, *proprium* is an accident that is not essential, but found only in this particular species—as writing or laughing are proper only to humans, even if they might not essentially characterize humans.

introducing certain distinctions (like that between thinking and the objects of thinking, see 3.1.1), but Descartes does not do so, despite providing some hints in this direction.[155] Obviously, Descartes tries to avoid distorting the clarity and simplicity of the attentive mind, which intuits reality as consisting simply of two finite created substances—*res extensa* and *res cogitans*—and one infinite creating thinking substance. Descartes rejects the possibility of a mistake or misunderstanding, since the natural light of reason, the light that secures the truth of the clear and distinct cogitation or perception,[156] is itself grounded in the truth of the infinite thinking. The process of questioning stops in the self-exhaustion of doubt in the act of the "cogito", the clarity and certainty of which is itself provided and supported by the natural light. However, the truth of the infinite thinking is exemplified for Descartes by the finite mind, which departs from the starting point of absolute certitude of self-awareness, initially without any content. But the finite mind is itself grounded in the infinite one. This is not however, a vicious circle, because the finite *res extensa* is secured in its being by the infinite one, or ontologically, whereas the infinite thinking is secured as known for us by the finite one, or epistemologically. The objection that the notion of the infinite substance is introduced by Descartes simply *ad hoc*—primarily in order to justify the existence of the two created substances, which support thinking and extension—is left unanswered and so is potentially destructive for the whole Cartesian project of justifying the existence of God.[157]

An important question then is why there is only one essential attribute. A possible answer might be that, as they are introduced by Descartes, essential attributes separate all that is considered substance into non intersecting classes of equivalence.[158] If R designates a two-place relation, then it is the relation of equivalence iff it is: (1) reflective: xRx, (2) symmetrical: xRy iff yRx, and (3) transitive: (xRy & yRz) entails xRz. Obviously, in the case of Descartes, if T = "possesses (the attribute of) thinking, equally as" and E = "possesses (the attribute of) extension, equally as", then the whole reality is separated (by these two relations of equivalence T and E) into two non-intersecting classes of *res cogitans* and *res extensa*. Moreover, T and E are merely relations, but at the same time, as said, they may also be considered finite substances themselves, thinking and extension as such. Perfection, the distinctive "attribute" of God, can also be

---

Such accidents are called *accidentia propria* (cp. Aristotle. Topics 102 a 17 sqq.). As Garber argues, in order to explain all bodily properties as geometrical, Descartes wants to make all accidents intimately connected with their substance or subject, that is, to be its *propria* or *accidentia propria* (Garber 1992, 68). If essential attributes may be equivocally taken as substances and attributes of these substances, and if Descartes wants to preserve his already rather loose ontology, then essential attributes should somehow differ from all other attributes, qualities or modes, which are then to be considered *propria* or *accidentia propria* of these substances, subordinated to essential attributes and understood solely through them.
[155] See: Descartes. For [Arnauld], 29 July 1648, AT V 221.
[156] Descartes. Princ. I 45, AT VIIIA 21-22.
[157] Cp. Descartes. Med. III, AT VII 34 sqq.
[158] Cp. Spinoza, Ethics I, Prop. 2: "Two substances having different attributes have nothing in common with one another".

considered in this way with the only difference being that there is only one member that belongs to the whole class, one single infinite substance that satisfies all three conditions, which once again shows that God may be considered substance in a different sense.

Thus, the first aspect of the notion of substance in Descartes is that it is *subject* with attributes that discloses its subject univocally (although the unequivocal difference between various kinds of attributes and modes is not itself established univocally). The mind is required to find an appropriate attribute that makes one substance different from another. The second aspect of the notion of substance is that of *existence*: substance is that which exists by itself, it is "without aid of any other substance".[159] If substance exists due only to itself, it does not depend on anything else other than itself and, therefore, thirdly, is *independent*. Thus, there are three aspects of understanding substance in Descartes (also to be found in scholasticism):[160] substance may be taken as subject, substance exists only due to itself and substance is independent.

Strictly speaking, that substance depends in its existence only on itself, applies only to the infinite not created and creating substance or God, for only God does not depend on any other thing.[161] "By the word 'God'", says Descartes, "I understand a substance that is infinite, eternal, immutable, independent, supremely intelligent, supremely powerful, and which created both myself and everything else (if anything else there be) that exists".[162] This makes the notion of substance equivocal, so that Descartes has to specify that *the* substance is God and the other two—finite mind and body—are substances only in a limited sense, as dependent on nothing else but *the* substance, for they need "only the concurrence of God in order to exist".[163] Thus, in the proper sense, there is only one substance, the infinite perfect thinking: as non-created it does not really depend on anything else but itself—and, further, there are two derivative or created substances, the one spiritual (mind), the other material (body). In Picot's French edition of the "Principles" we find the following explanation: "In the case of other things, some are of such a nature that they cannot exist without other things, while some need only the ordinary concurrence of God in order to exist. We make the distinction by calling the latter 'substances' and the former 'qualities' or 'attributes' of those substances".[164] This, again, makes the two finite substances (essential) attributes

---

[159] Descartes. Fourth Set of Replies, AT VII 226. Cp. substance is "nothing other than a thing which exists in such a way as to depend on no other thing for its existence", Princ. I 5, AT VIIIA 24.
[160] A possible source Descartes might have in mind is the manual of Eustachius, which was known to Descartes. In Eustachius' presentation, substance "is defined as a being in and of itself; an accident is being in another. ...the subject of an accident is substance". Eustachius a Sancto Paulo. *Summa Philosophiae Quadripartita* [1609]. Cambridge, 1648. P. 52; cp. P.41 sqq.
[161] Cp. Markie 1994, 63-87.
[162] Descartes. Med. III, AT VII 45.
[163] Descartes. Princ. I 52, AT VIIIA 25. Cp. Spinoza. Principles of the Philosophy of Descartes, Part I, def. 5-8 and Bourdin's classification of substances, rejected by Descartes, Seventh Set of Objections, AT VII 506, 520.
[164] Descartes. Princ. I 51, AT VIIIA 24; cp. To Regis, May 1641, AT III 372.

and renders the whole ontological project of Descartes doubtful, since the notion of substance is not univocal and is used in different senses in the case of God and in the case of finite mind and body. The notion of substance, however, becomes instrumentally useful and important for the unequivocal distinction between mind and body. Or, put otherwise, Descartes is much more interested in the essential than in the existential dimension of being and cognition (cp. 1.4.2).[165]

There further arises a difficult question for Descartes: does substance necessarily exist? Or otherwise, does the notion of substance necessarily include that of existence? Obviously, the answer in the case of the created substances is 'no', for it is easily conceivable that God did not create anything, for the opposite would ascribe limits to his power (cp. 1.3.2; 1.3.4). But does it necessarily pertain to God *qua* substance to exist? God, as Descartes argues on several occasions, exists necessarily, which also secures the necessity of all other truths, even though it is not necessary that God created them, for this would have diminished his infinite power. But the notion of existence does not appear to be necessarily included in the notion of substance, because of the equivocality of the latter. The second Cartesian definition says simply that *if* substance exists, it does not need anything else to exist. It is worth noting that Spinoza challenges such a conclusion in Proposition 7 of Part I of "Ethics", maintaining that "It pertains to the nature of a substance to exist", because since substance cannot be produced by anything else, it has to be *causa sui* (i.e., that whose essence necessarily involves existence). Descartes also has to accept that God is the *causa sui*, which follows straight from his second definition of substance. Spinoza's proposition, however, is only true if God is considered in such a way that the notion of *causa sui* expresses his essence, that is, represents God essentially. But for Descartes, although God does necessarily exist and we are able to know that God *is*, it is impossible for a finite mind to know *what* God is, that is, to know him in his essence (see 1.4.3). Therefore, the finite mind cannot have any clear and distinct vision or understanding of *how* God causes his own (necessary) existence. In this sense the subsistence of substance[166] is only necessary in the infinite substance, whereas in the finite one it is only possible.[167] For this reason, the attribute of infinite/ finite, even if not explicitly recognized essential by Descartes, plays an exceptionally important role in his ontology.

The crucial distinction between the not-produced infinite substance, or God, and the created finite substances of mind and matter in Descartes, is that God does not need anything else to preserve himself as necessarily existing, whereas mind and matter—since they are not substances in the proper sense (i.e., since neither exists only due to itself)—need something else in order to exist. To put it otherwise, only the infinite substance is pure actuality with no passivity at all: it is acting only and does not involve being acted upon, because being acted upon

---

[165] Similarly, Spinoza stresses exactly the essential, and not existential, aspect in the definition of substance in his "Ethics" Part I, def. 3: "By substance I understand what is in itself and conceived through itself, that is, that whose concept does not require the concept of another thing, from which it must be formed".

[166] By definition, "*subsistentia est existentia substantiae*", Baumgarten 1963, § 58.

[167] Cp. Descartes. To ***, 1645 or 1646, AT IV 349.

means dependence on something else and thus is improper to substance. Because of that, the divine mind has to be taken as pure thinking (which later in the "Principles" is assumed by Descartes not to be really distinct from the will) with no sense-perception whatsoever, since sense-perception also implies "being acted upon".[168] Thus, the only *res* that exists due to itself is the infinite substance or God. If limited substances existed due to themselves, they would have been infinite substances, which is not the case (see 1.3.2). And if they existed due to some other thing, different from substance in the proper sense, that other thing would need also to be caused by something else, so that there would inevitably arise either a circle of causation or an infinite regress. Therefore, substances in the limited sense (i.e., mind and body) should be caused in their existence by *the* unique substance, which exists only due to itself or, in traditional theological language, should be created by God. Since finite substances are continually existing (which is not rationally deduced, but simply stated by Descartes as a fact of consciousness), they need to be constantly created or preserved in their existence, which is taken as an axiom: "It is a greater thing to create or to preserve a substance than to create or to preserve the attributes or properties of that substance. However, it is not a greater thing to create something than to preserve".[169] Every finite existence is thus a production of the infinite mind, who knows a thing insofar as it produces that thing (see 3.4.1). God, however, is the cause not only of *coming into being*, but also of the *being* of the two substances and of all things, as Descartes tells Gassendi.[170] That is, even if Descartes still formally discerns between being and becoming, the way he presents causation by the infinite substance makes such a distinction eventually obsolete, because recreation takes place at every moment, in which coming to be and being cannot be distinguished.

Although the idea of substance can be produced (deduced) by our mind, substance as such cannot be produced by the finite mind or subject. A peculiar feature of the Cartesian approach is that the "I" is considered a substance, "*an immaterial substance* with no bodily element".[171] It is no longer the case that the

---

[168] Descartes. Princ. I 23, AT VIIIA 13-14.

[169] Descartes. Second Set of Replies, AT VII 166; cp. Disc. V, AT VI 45; Med. Synopsis, AT VIII 14; To De Beaune, 30 April 1639, AT II 543. As Descartes puts it, "there is no doubt that if God withdrew his concurrence, everything which he has created would immediately go to nothing; because all things were nothing until God created them and lent them his concurrence. This does not mean that they should not be called substances, because when we call a created substance self-sufficient we do not rule out the divine concurrence which it needs in order to subsist. We mean only that it is a kind of thing that can exist without any other created thing; and this is something that cannot be said about the modes of things, like shape and number" (To Hyperaspistes, AT III 429). Or: "God continues to preserve it [matter] in the same way that he created it" (The World VII, AT XI 37, cp. 44). To be preserved is to be recreated at every moment of time. This removes the two substances from time, in a sense, since their existence does not causally follow from their own existence in the immediate past and does not entail the existence in the immediate future, but wholly depends only on the concurrence of God.

[170] Descartes. Fifth Set of Replies, AT VII 369.

[171] Descartes. To Colvius, 14 November 1640, AT III 247; cp. Med., Synopsis, AT VII 14; Med. III, AT VII 45.

ego is only operational and depends in its activity on the intellect, independent of myself. Quite to the contrary, the self-evident truth of the *sum* testifies that the *ego* becomes a substance and not only a sign of something else that surpasses the *ego* and is considered as real objectivity, as that which is capable of production or, at least, of reproduction: the essence of a thing may be reproduced by the finite subjectivity, although the existence of that thing in Descartes still depends on the infinite substance.

At this point the Aristotelian and scholastic "subject" becomes "object" and the "subject" turns into the modern *ego*. How does this become possible? Descartes' answer is simple: because I myself am a substance. I am a thinking substance, which is the source of ideas, for, according to Descartes, nothing besides my thoughts is fully within my power. This claim is obviously contestable, since merely wishing to have a thought that might correspond to or express an unknown property of a thing (e.g., a geometrical object) may not yet be sufficient actually to have such a thought. Only an image of imagination appears to be fully within my power (see 3.2.1-3.2.3).

Such an understanding of the *ego* makes it co-demiurgic, as it were, for even if the *ego* is the instance that, due to its finitude, does not really create, at least it recognizes the creation of finite substances. For this reason, recognition becomes extremely important for modernity and, in a sense, is a substitution for creation, because to create a personal identity is to make others recognize it as such.

To illustrate how the deduction works, Descartes shows how the idea of substance (as well as that of duration and number) is produced from the idea of myself: "For example, I think that a stone is a substance, or is a thing capable of existing independently, and I also think that I am a substance. Admittedly I conceive of myself as a thing that thinks and is not extended, whereas I conceive of the stone as a thing that is extended and does not think, so that the two conceptions differ enormously; but they seem to agree with respect to the classification 'substance'."[172] But, as Descartes argues further, it is impossible for the *ego* to be the source of the idea of God, not because God is the thinking substance, but because God is considered to be *infinite* substance. In other words, the only idea that cannot be generated or produced by subjectivity or the *ego* is that of actual infinity,[173] because *ego* is a finite thinking substance. Therefore, it is not substance, but infinity that appears to be the primary not deducible entity and which thus becomes a kind of *a priori* structure, both epistemologically and ontologically.

1.3 Infinity

1.3.1 Infinity in Aristotle and Plotinus

As it has been shown in the previous discussion, the notion of matter was considered in the Platonic tradition as radical otherness and as lack of all form and

---

[172] Descartes. Med. II, AT VII 44-46.
[173] Descartes. Med. III, AT VII 45-46.Cp. the criticism of Gassendi, Fifth Set of Objections, AT VII 293.

limit, as indefinite (1.1.2).[174] The notion of the infinite, which is of importance also for Descartes, was then introduced. Let us now turn to a consideration of infinity, again pointing out mostly the differences in its appropriation by *les anciens et les modernes*, leaving aside the task of a historical examination of the notion through the Middle ages.

The famous "definition" of the infinite in Aristotle is: "it is not that beyond which there is nothing, but that which always has something beyond."[175] This is potential infinity. The infinite is thus primarily introduced through the notion of possibility—of the elusive not-yet-being—and for that reason one can hardly rely on thinking-*noēsis* in discussing the infinite. On such an account, the infinite is that which always allows for consideration of a quantity surpassing any fixed amount. On the contrary, that for which it is not possible to take or consider anything surpassing, is a whole and complete (*holon de kai teleion*); it is organized and structured by the pattern of *telos*—purpose and end. The end, however, is also the limit of a thing, that is, it delimits it in its existence and definition, so that that which has neither end nor limit has thereby no definition in the strict sense—it is incomplete, unknowable and properly not existing.[176] Therefore, substance as complete and, in this sense, as indivisible has to be limited and therefore cannot be infinite.[177]

The ancient *horror infiniti* thus appears to be fully justified within the ontological representation of substance through limit.[178] Further, if the infinite is to be accepted at all, there can be no *telos* in it and, because of that, no infinite as actually and wholly existing. On the contrary, if modernity, and Descartes in particular, dismisses any teleology in science,[179] then, as it will be argued, the only way in which *telos* can be preserved is by placing it within substance understood as a complete whole, the substance that can only be a complete infinite and thus is

---

[174] Cp. Aristotle. Phys. 209b 11.

[175] *Oy gar hoy meden exo, all' hoy aei ti exo esti, toyto apeiron estin.*- Aristotle. Phys. 207a 1-2. See also: Heath 1949, 102-113; Hintikka 1973, 114-134, Kouromenos 1995, 9 sqq.

[176] Aristotle. Phys. 207a 7 sqq.

[177] Cp. Aristotle. Met. 1066b 6.

[178] The finite, at least until Plotinus, has ontological, epistemological and axiological priority (cp. Heimsoeth 1994, 82-85). Aristotle objects to introducing an object that is not and cannot in principle be fully understood through and by reason, which operates only in terms of finite determinations and limits. His attitude is that of prudence: once we admit something we are not able to know, we open the possibility for contradiction and thus for the destruction of being and thought, and should be prepared for unexpected consequences. But once actual infinity is accepted, the psychological attitude towards it can only be ambiguous. On the one hand, infinity as an infinite whole produces feelings corresponding to the sublime: feelings of awe and dread (cp. Pascal 1950, 94-96 (§199-202); Moore 1990, 76). On the other hand, if the infinite is actual, it is to be existent or it has to be God. That is why, as Descartes puts it, "the consideration of an object which has no limits to its perfections fills us with satisfaction and assurance" (Descartes. Princ. I 19, AT VIIIA 12 (addition to the French edition); cp. Spinoza, Ethics Part I, def. 2, 6, 8 and Props. 8, 11, 13, 15, 21-26; Bennett 1984). Infinity thus is psychologically perceived with a kind of joy rooted in fear.

[179] Schramm 1985, 25-30.

inaccessible to finite reasoning. The infinite, as preserved in early modernity, appears to be a necessary and most characteristic trait of substance, although, due to its inaccessibility, the infinite substance must be left outside the consideration of science and can only pertain to metaphysics.

The infinite, as Aristotle holds, should exist in a way.[180] But even then the being (*einai*) of the infinite is not itself infinite.[181] The very existence or form of being of the infinite is not existence in the proper sense (i.e., the infinite does not exist as complete and as actual). The infinite in such a case is not a substance, one of the main features of which, as it has been argued, is separate and independent existence.[182] The infinite, however, does not exist separately as a complete infinite, or else each of its parts would equally be infinite. This is impossible since there can be no *logos*, no relation of essence of such an entity to any of its hypothetical parts. The infinite also cannot exist as an actually infinite quantity, because such a quantity can neither be gone through nor grasped. It also cannot be a body, for according to its definition, body is that which is limited by finite planes, which obviously is not the case in the infinite.[183] The infinite then can only be that which either cannot be transgressed, or has no limit. It is only *potential*—it is ever becoming another and yet another, always different from its present state (*aei allo kai allo; aei heteron kai heteron*) in which the process of addition or division never ends.[184] There is an important distinction in the way the infinite is present in number (*plēthos*), divisible into non-continuous parts, that is, in units and in magnitude (*megethos*), itself divisible into continuous, further divisible parts. Such a distinction represents the infinite in respect to addition and division, *kata prosthesin* and *kata diairesin* (cp. 2.1.3; 2.2.2).[185]

Since the infinite is present in Aristotle primarily as sheer potentiality, it appears to be close to matter (cp. 1.1.2), because whatever exists and can be known, is limited and limiting and thus is that which embraces, whereas matter and infinity never embrace but are only embraced (*oy periekhei alla periekhetai*).[186] In this respect Aristotle is close to Plato, who represents matter as lacking any immanent limit. Still, there is also an important difference between the two, namely, that Plato and the Pythagoreans consider the infinite not as an accident but in itself (*kath' hayto*), as an independent entity.[187]

As it has been mentioned, Plato considers infinity as "great and small" in

---

[180] Aristotle gives us five reasons for the existence of the infinite: the infinity of time; the infinity of division of a magnitude; the persistence of coming-to-be and of perishing; the fact that the limited is always bordered by something limited; and the fact that thinking does not stop. Aristotle. Phys. 203b 15 sqq.
[181] Aristotle. Met. 994b 26-27.
[182] Aristotle. Phys. 207b 27 sqq. et al.
[183] Aristotle. Met. 1066b 11 sqq. (which is a later compilation from Phys. III 4-8). Cp. also: Phys. 204 a 9 sqq.
[184] Aristotle. Met. 994a17-18; 1048b 15-18; 1066a 35-38; Phys. 204 a 2-5; Phys. 206a 23-30.
[185] Aristotle. Phys. 206a 15 sqq; esp. 206b 16-18; cp. Met. 1020a 9-11; Phys. 261b 27 sqq. Cp. Nikulin 1996, 51-53.
[186] Aristotle. Phys. 207a 25; 208a 1-2.
[187] As reported by Aristotle in Phys. 203a 5.

its relation primarily to matter. Aristotle reports that Plato recognizes two infinities, in great and in small (*dya ta apeira, to mega kai to mikron*).[188] There are no direct indications, either in the texts of the dialogues of Plato, or in the doxographic tradition, that Plato had an elaborated doctrine of two infinities. Rather, both *apeira* should refer to one indefiniteness-*aoristos dyas* which, due to its indefiniteness cannot be presented through an exact definition or *logos*, but instead as "more or less" and, therefore, as great and small. However, the reference to the infinite as great and small may also be taken as both the above mentioned distinction of number and magnitude in respect to division, and the distinction of physical and intelligible matter (see 2.4; 2.4.1).

Aristotle considers infinity, *apeiria* or *aoristia*, as potential infinity, which implies a lack of limit, form and definiteness, and thus an imperfection. The attitude towards infinity changes, however, in antiquity—particularly in Plotinus, for whom infinity is primarily actual. Thus, Proclus proves theorems about the infinite using the *reductio ad absurdum*, where he tacitly presupposes that the infinite should be taken as complete and as an independent subject.[189] It is not my intention here to trace possible reasons for the change in attitude towards infinity; for the purpose of the book it is enough to establish the distinction.

For Plato, and especially for the later Platonic thinkers, infinity is a notion of major interest.[190] Since infinity still represents non-being, however, it cannot be positively defined—it has no proper *logos*. Plotinus' approach to infinity is characterized by the following: (a) infinity is perfection, and (b) infinity implies non-being, because being is a defined form and is exemplified through the communication of limit and the unlimited, of sameness and otherness. From this perspective, Plotinus is radically different both from Aristotle, for whom infinity as potential infinity (i.e., as lack of determination) is a sign of imperfection, and from Descartes and medieval scholastics, for whom being is perfection and *the* being (God) is infinite. Infinity as such does not, however, become a special object of his consideration (and so, in Plotinus there is no special treatise dedicated to the infinite), although it constantly reappears under various guises. The infinite permeates the whole of the cosmos and its intelligible pattern; it is present everywhere, although differently. In Plotinus infinity appears in three ways: (1) in the One, (2) in the intellect-*noys* and (3) in matter.[191] Since each of the three is considered in due place (see 1.1.2; 1.2.1; 3.1.1), the infinite in Plotinus will not be discussed in much detail. For our purpose it is sufficient to note (1) that the infinite in the One is present through and as absence of form and as non-being, for the One is not being but its transcendent principle. At the same time the infinity of the One is the actually infinite generative or productive power. The One is infinite in its creative potency or power-*dynamis*, which precedes and is beyond being, and can neither be extinguished nor diminished and thus presents, in modern usage, actual infinity. Unlike potential infinity (which is primarily defined through a *relation*,

---

[188] Aristotle. Phys. 203a 15; cp. Met. 987b 25, 988a 25.
[189] Proclus. Inst. phys. II 11-13.
[190] Cp. de Vogel 1959, 21-39.
[191] Plotinus. Enn. I.8.3.13; III.8.8.46; VI.1.1.2; VI.9.6.10 et al. Cp. Sleeman, Pollet 1980, 117-120; Sweeney 1992, 167-222.

and is in a constant flux and becoming and is able either of ever growing or of ever decreasing), actual infinity, according to Cantor's definition, is that which does not change, but at the same time is greater than any finite magnitude. Cantor makes a further important distinction, not made before him, namely, into transfinite infinity, which is actual infinity capable of increasing (e.g., transfinite ordinal and cardinal numbers), and absolute infinity, not capable of any change.[192] In what follows, when speaking of actual infinity, we will be referring to absolute actual infinity.

(2) In the intellect-*noys*, which is primarily characterized by measure and limit within its objects of contemplation,[193] the infinite still appears in a number of ways. First, it is present as infinite intelligible matter, the archetype for physical matter (see 2.4.1). Second, it is present in the infinity that ideal archetypes bring into physical and geometrical entities, which all may be said to participate in being, but may be represented in their relations-*logoi* to each other in an infinite number of ways. Third, the infinite is present in the infinite power of the intellect of contemplating intelligible objects within *noys*.[194] The infinite power may be ascribed to the intellect-*noys* insofar as it produces its objects. Infinity is present in the intellect even though it is represented as thinking definite and defined forms.[195] This defined infinity appears in ideal numbers and forms as one of two principles, that of indefiniteness, of otherness, *aoristos dyas* (cp. 1.2.1; 1.2.2; 1.3.1), itself bound in a synthesis of the one-many of intellect.[196] Actual infinity, rejected by Aristotle, is accepted by Plotinus and becomes a sort of empty object for the intellect, which takes part in infinity, even if it is unable to think it directly, since every act of thought is presented in finite terms and notions.

As *apeiron* or *apeiria*, infinity is to be found both in the One and in matter, for neither is, strictly speaking, *in* being but they are "whence" and "into what" being as definite is originated. Thus finally, (3) the infinite in matter is matter "itself" as lacking all definition and being, as destitute of any power to produce, as always present through its actual absence, even though it cannot in principle be withdrawn from the structure of the whole.[197] This infinity is a "total falling away" (*apostasis panteles*) from the One. It can only be indefinite—great and small (*mega kai smikron*)—and in this way it may be regarded *both* as

---

[192] Cantor 1985, 288-293. At another point, Cantor discerns between transfinite actual infinity *in abstracto seu in natura naturata* and *in concreto*, that is, in the form of transfinite ordinal numbers, which he equates with Platonic ideal numbers, *arithmoi noētoi* or *arithmoi eidētikoi* (Cantor 1985, 264; cp. 2.1.1).

[193] Cp. Emilsson 1995, 21-41.

[194] Plotinus. Enn. II.4.15.17-21; V.4.2.4-7; V.7.3.22; V.8.9.24-28; VI.2.21.7 sqq.; VI.2.22.15 sqq.; VI.4.14.5-7. Cp. Plato. Parm. 144b-c; Phil.16e.

[195] As Plotinus says, the intellect-*noys*, infinite in its life, is to be defined when looking at and striving towards the One, which itself has no limit, *horon oyk ekhontos*, Enn. VI.7.17.14-16.

[196] Plotinus. Enn. VI.7.14.11-12; Simplicius. In Phys. 151.6-11; 453.25-31.

[197] Thus, even if one makes a distinction, as Heimsoeth does, between the infinite of the One and the infinite of matter (Heimsoeth 1994, 88), one cannot represent this distinction as a distinction between actual and potential infinity, but rather between that of immense power of production of being and of absolute powerlessness.

opposites considered at once, and as not opposites.[198] Matter represents another type of the infinite that is closer to potential infinity, which allows no exact measure or counting, where nothing can be discerned, a boundless indefiniteness, *apeiron*.[199] This infinity appears to be imperfection and even evil. It is rather an extreme degeneration of potential infinity. However, here one also has to distinguish two different cases: (3a) matter as the ultimate and utterly indefinite receptacle—as the non-being that underlies all being. And (3b) matter of intelligibles (see 2.4), which is of the utmost interest for us and which itself does not lack being altogether, for it appears in and for the intellect. Obviously, the cases match each other and make pairs of the infinite in non-being (1) and (3a) and of the infinite in being (2) and (3b). In the first pair infinity appears without any inner structure whatsoever; while in the One it is the infinity of superabundance, in matter it is that of absolute deficiency and lack of all delimitation.[200] Besides, the first element within each pair presupposes a productive aspect, whereas the second element has a receptive aspect.

One can thus clearly discern different kinds of infinity in later Greek philosophy, particularly, in Plotinus. Even if they are not distinct as infinities with different cardinal and ordinal numbers (cardinal numbers in set theory express the entire "number" of elements in a set; ordinal numbers determine the position (order) of a set in a certain list of sets), they nonetheless already represent different types of infinity. We find a more systematic and elaborated classification of inifnities in Proclus, who discerns at least three kinds of infinity: the superabundant One, the eternity of the whole of the cosmos (*to pan*, which has its paradigm within the intellect), and the infinity of the infinite divisibility—that of continuous magnitudes and matter.[201]

1.3.2 Infinity as perfection: Infini and indéfini

As we have seen, substance for Descartes is characterized by the following features: independence, self-reliance and being a subject of predication. The human mind as a finite substance cannot produce substance: not *the* substance in the proper sense (God), nor limited substances; neither itself in its existence, nor matter. However, the *notion* of substance can be produced by the finite human subjectivity, insofar as it itself is considered (or, rather, considers itself) a substance. The only exclusion, a notion that cannot be engendered by the *ego*, is that of infinity.[202] *The* substance is distinct from finite substances of mind and body not in that it exists but in that it is *infinite*. Why is this the case? Descartes mostly stresses the essential aspect of substance; *the* substance, which for him is God, should be radically different from limited substances. Since, further, finitude of mind and body is considered a limitation (i.e., a lack of perfection), the radical

---

[198] Cp. Plotinus. Enn. VI.6.1.1-2; VI.6.3.28-33.
[199] Plotinus. Enn. II.4.15.1 sqq.
[200] Cp. Plotinus. Enn. I.8.3.13.
[201] Proclus. Elem. theol. 92-96; Theol. Plat. II 26.8-28.13; In Eucl. 6.7-7.1. I am grateful to E. Kutasch for drawing my attention to these quotations.
[202] Descartes. Med. III, AT VII 45 sqq.

difference of substance in the proper sense is its lack of perfection. Put otherwise, *the* substance should not be deficient, especially in that which marks two substances of mind and body, namely, their finitude. Therefore, *the* substance should be infinite.

Infinity is thus understood not as a lack of being, but as positive, that is, as actual and complete.[203] Independence of *the* substance thus primarily involves not being (for finite substances also exist, albeit not necessarily), but infinity.[204] As Descartes writes in one of his last letters, "By 'infinite substance' I mean a substance which has actually infinite, immense, true and real perfections. This is not an accident added to the notion of substance, but the very essence of substance taken absolutely and bounded by no defects; these defects, in respect of substance, are accidents; but infinity or infinitude is not. It should be observed that I never use the word 'infinite' to signify the mere lack of limits (which is something negative, for which I have used the term 'indefinite') but to signify a real thing, which is incomparably greater than all those which are in some way limited".[205] Infinity therefore is not a privation of limit; it is not a *nihil privativum*, but an actual perfection—which is not Descartes' invention by any means, but a commonplace in scholasticism from at least the middle of the twelfth century.[206]

Infinity is thus taken by Descartes, who relies on (even if rejecting) the scholastic tradition, as the sign of being that exists due only to itself and which is the highest perfection: infinity is divine.[207] The very way we form the idea of utter perfection is very important for understanding infinity. On the one hand, perfection may be considered an abstraction from imperfection, by consecutively negating the limitations that constitute the imperfection as a lack of a certain quality. However, if one seeks ultimate perfection in this way (i.e., that of which greater cannot be conceived), nothing guarantees in advance that such perfection may be finally achieved in a finite number of steps of negating an imperfection. A hypothetical ultimate perfection (e.g., omniscience—infinite actual knowledge) may be only indefinitely approximated by the finite mind and thus remains inaccessible and unknown in its essence to the finite mind. On the other hand, if one begins with the presupposition of perfection as infinite, so that imperfection is simply considered a limitation of this initial actual perfection, then perfection is preserved and also leaves a possibility of a rational proof of the necessity of existence of *the*

---

[203] Descartes. Sixth Set of Replies, AT VII 231-232.

[204] Cp. Descartes. To Mersenne, 28 October 1640, AT III 191.

[205] Descartes. To Clerselier, 23 April 1649, AT V 355-356.

[206] Cp. Gregory of Nyssa and John Damascene ("Deus est incircumscriptus, increatus, infinitus." - De fide orthod. I, 8 (PG 94, 808C). Later Thomas Aquinas, Bonaventure, Robert Fishacre, Albert the Great, Henry of Ghent assert that actual infinity as perfection belongs only to the essence of God *qua* infinite being and to nothing else. See: Sweeney 1992, 167, 289 sqq.; cp. Gilson 1979, 142-150. As Suarez argues in his "Disputationes Metaphysicae" quoted by Caterus, "every limitation proceeds from some cause; therefore if something is limited and finite this is because its cause was either unable or unwilling to endow it with more greatness or perfection; and hence if something derives its existence from itself, and not from some cause, it is indeed unlimited and infinite". - Descartes. First Set of Objections, AT VII 95.

[207] Cp. Locke. Essay, Bk. II, ch. XXIII, 36.

substance.[208] Descartes univocally maintains the second approach, choosing as his starting point that an ultimate perfection cannot come from an imperfection, independence from dependence, existence from privation, and in general, something from nothing.[209]

The infinite as primary and positive becomes the distinctive mark of true substance. Clearly, if infinity is taken as perfection, then, since perfection is an actual entity (that is, it is precedent to the lack of perfection or to imperfection), infinity should be anterior both to finite and to potential infinity (i.e., to the not actualized whole).[210] "[I]t is false", says Descartes, "that the infinite is understood through the negation of a boundary or limit; on the contrary, all limitation implies a negation of the finite."[211] Or also: "it is quite true that we do not understand the infinite by the negation of limitation; and one cannot infer that, because limitation involves the negation of infinity, the negation of the limitation involves knowledge of the infinite. What makes the infinite different from the finite is something real and positive; but the limitation which makes the finite different from the infinite is non-being or the negation of being. That which is not cannot bring us to the knowledge of that which is; on the contrary, the negation of a thing has to be perceived on the basis of knowledge of the thing itself".[212] Infinity thus becomes a kind of *a priori* for all considerations, both metaphysical and mathematical (e.g., the infinite is a necessary presupposition in the projective geometry of Desargues, cp. 2.1.4).

The notion of *the* substance, or God, is characterized by Descartes and introduced primarily through the notion of perfection: "The substance which we understand to be supremely perfect, and in which we conceive absolutely nothing that implies any defect or limitation in that perfection, is called God."[213] Further, since infinity as a complete whole represents such a perfection (God cannot be infinite in the sense of lack of completeness), and since perfection precedes to an imperfection as privation, then the very notion of infinity cannot be invented by the finite cogitation. No wonder then that the proof of the existence of God essentially involves the notion of actual infinity. The idea is unique and different from all other ideas insofar as it cannot be produced or invented by the finite mind, because the idea of the infinite substance has more objectivity than the idea of a finite substance, since the idea of a finite substance has more objectivity or objective reality than that of a mode or an accident. I have an idea of substance because I myself am a thinking substance; yet I am a finite substance and if I have an idea of an infinite substance, it is only because it is precedent to me and proceeds from some other, infinite substance: being finite, I (the finite mind) cannot produce the

---

[208] As Henrich notes, unlike Anselm who considers God to be *ens perfectissimum*, Descartes presupposes in his proof rather the notion of *ens necessarium* (Henrich 1960, 11 sqq.).
[209] Descartes. Discourse IV, AT VI 34-35, 38.
[210] Descartes. Conversation with Burman, AT V 153. Cp. also Third Set of Objections, AT VII 185.
[211] Descartes. Fifth Set of Replies, AT VII 365.
[212] Descartes. To Hyperaspistes, August 1641, AT III 427.
[213] Descartes. Second Set of Replies, AT VII 162. Only God is "actually infinite, so that nothing can be added to his perfection".- Med. III, AT VII 47.

idea of the infinite. Therefore, the notion of actual infinity should be in some way inherent in the finite mind.[214]

The divine essence is such that, first, in it the notions of the attributes of infinity, perfection, being, reality, self-causation, and inexhaustible power may be all considered as tautological expressions of this essence.[215] Infinity is then the most adequate expression of all other attributes because the divine perfection is expressed primarily in terms of what might be called *omni*-attributes, which are to be considered actually infinite: omniscience, omnipotence, omnipresence, and so on.[216] What is the difference between all these attributes? The distinction between the *omni*-attributes cannot be real since all the attributes refer to one single substance. In such a case, the distinction might be either modal or conceptual (mental, cp. 1.1.3). A modal distinction can be either between a substance and its mode, or between two substances. Since we are dealing with attributes (even if they are of a special—infinite—character), the distinction cannot be modal. The distinction must be conceptual, since it is only within the finite mind that there is a difference between the *omni*-attributes. And furthermore, the divine essence should necessarily include existence. Therefore, if the notion of actual infinity cannot be thought away by the finite mind, the infinite essence is necessary and thus should exist.

Now, why does Descartes associate the infinite with being and not, like Plato and Plotinus, with non-being or beyond-being? Obviously, Descartes follows the Aristotelian tradition (represented, e.g., in Aquinas), which identifies God with being as *actus purus*, pure activity and actuality outside all potentiality. Thus the divine infinite creative power is not the mere possibility of generation but rather is the already actualized divine capacity and ability of producing finite things. It is important to note that the actual divine infinity is not exclusive of the finite—it entails and presupposes the existence of the finite (of finite substances, things and their attributes and modes).[217] Unlike in the Platonic tradition, the difference

---

[214] Descartes. Med. III, AT VI 40, 45; First Set of Replies, AT VII 116-117; Second Set of Replies, AT VII 135-136; Third Set of Replies, AT VII 188; Princ. I 18, AT VIIIA 11-12. As Levinas explains, "the idea of infinity is exceptional in that its *ideatum* surpasses its idea, whereas for the things the total coincidence of their "objective" and "formal" realities is not precluded; we could conceivably have accounted for all the ideas, other than that of Infinity, by ourselves. ...The distance that separates *ideatum* and idea here constitutes the content of the *ideatum* itself. Infinity is characteristic of a transcendent being as transcendent; the infinity is the absolutely other. The transcendent is the sole *ideatum* of which there can be only an idea in us; it is infinitely removed from its idea, that is, exterior, because it is infinite". - Levinas 1969, 48-49. Cp. Peperzak 1993, 80 sqq.

[215] Descartes. Med. IV, AT VII 56-62; First Set of Replies, AT VII 109-110; Fourth Set of Replies, AT VII 236; Sixth Set of Replies, AT VII 435; To Elizabeth, 6 October 1645, AT IV 314; 3 November 1645, AT IV 332; To Chanut, 1 February 1647, AT IV 608-609; To More, 15 April 1649, AT V 343.

[216] "[O]ur understanding tells us that there is in God an absolute immensity, simplicity and unity which embraces all other attributes and has no copy in us." - Descartes. Second Set of Replies, AT VII 137. Cp. Med. I, AT VII 21; Princ. I 5, AT VIIIA 6; Princ. I 22, AT VIIIA 13; Princ. II 36, AT VIIIA 61. Cp. also: Proclus. Theol. Plat. I 59.2 sqq.

[217] Cp. Descartes. Second Set of Objections, AT VII 125.

between being and its principle is not that the latter is transcendent to the former but that the principle of being is itself infinite being and because of that, necessary being is included in its essence. As Descartes points out in one of his later letters, the very notion of a principle may be taken in two different senses. On the one hand, principle may be considered epistemologically—it may mean "a common notion so clear and so general that it can serve as a principle for proving the existence of all the beings, or entities, to be discovered later". The Aristotelian principle of non-contradiction (*impossibile est idem simul esse et non esse*) exemplifies such a principle. On the other hand, principle may be taken ontologically—as a "*being* whose existence is known to us better than that of any other, so that it can serve as a principle for discovering them".[218] The example of principle thus understood is the soul because, as Descartes insists, its existence is best known to us through the conscience of the *cogito*.

A difficult problem arises, however, when Descartes speaks about God as describable by *omni*-predicates. The problem is that the finite mind can only know that these *omni*-attributes *are*, and not, because of their infinity, *what* they are. In the same way, the finite mind knows (finds in itself) the idea or notion of infinity, although the finite mind remains ignorant of what infinity is. Because of the finitude of human reason, the difference between these *omni*-predicates is beyond the grasp of finite cogitation. It is not clear—and Descartes does not provide a univocal answer—how it can happen that the infinite substance is one and yet there are many of its *omni*-attributes, each of which essentially expresses the substance and are not really different from it. Perhaps, it might be argued that there should be an essential unity of the *omni*-attributes, insofar as they all are actually infinite. The problem at hand is not solved this way, however, but just substituted by the problem of knowledge of the actually infinite.

Thus, Descartes does not consider the infinite to be a negation of the finite or limited or indefinite extension of the finite. On the contrary, the infinite is taken as primary, so that its negation enables the finite mind, first, to understand finite things as negations and limitations of the infinite and, second, to operate somehow with the notion of the infinite itself.

The problem is thus that if one accepts, as Descartes does, the actually infinite as the ultimate perfection and source of all finite truths and things and as the ontological starting point (although epistemologically the starting point is the finite self-awareness of the *ego*), then one chooses a principle that, although it is being, is incomprehensible insofar as it is actually infinite. This infinite substance is God for Descartes, "*vn estre infini & incomprehensible*".[219] The price for preserving an absolute difference and otherness between the creator and the created

---

[218] Descartes. To Clerselier, June or July 1646, AT IV 444-445.
[219] Descartes. To Mersenne, 6 May 1630, AT I 150. Cp. Med. IV, AT VII 53 sqq.; First Set of Replies, AT VII 107 sqq.; Second Set of Replies, AT VII 163; "...we must begin with knowledge of God, and our knowledge of all other things must then be subordinated to this single initial piece of knowledge".- Sixth Set of Replies, AT VII 430. Cp. Beyssade 1993, 85-94.

is the inability of finite thinking to know the essence of infinite thinking.[220] "At the place where I speak of infinity", as Descartes writes to Mersenne, "it is a good idea to insert, as you say, 'the infinite *qua* infinite can in no way be comprehended by us'".[221] Thereby there is something in the ontological picture of the world that is not, and in principle cannot be, fully transparent to finite thinking. Since in God there is no real distinction between will and reason, infinite thinking sets certain purposes of and for the world that, as Descartes stresses, cannot be known by the finite mind.[222]

Even if the actually infinite cannot be fully known to the finite mind, the mind is able and, according to Descartes, has to know the infinite in a certain way. As we have seen, the presence of the very notion or idea of the infinite is the starting point of the Cartesian proof of the existence of God in the Third "Meditation". That is, since the idea of the actually infinite cannot be produced by the finite mind, this idea, which is also the idea of God as infinite substance, has to be "*imprinted on the human mind in such a way* that everyone has within himself the power to know him".[223] The infinite is thus rationally and indisputably known to the finite mind in its existence—that the infinite *is*. Why is the finite mind capable of having any firm knowledge about the infinite at all? Because both the finite mind and the infinite substance are cointensive, as it were, for each is *res cogitans*, although they are not coextensive in their greatness. The finite mind cannot embrace and encompass the infinite all at once.[224] Because of that the infinite, which actually surpasses any limited magnitude, can never be reached by gradually expanding the finite in any number of steps, for in doing this the finite will always remain finite.[225]

The infinite surpasses any finite limits. Hence, even if it is known in its existence that it *is*, it cannot be known in its essence *what* it is. In recognizing this, Descartes follows many medieval theologians who stress the incomprehensibility of the divine essence.[226] Modern mathematics, which operates with the notion of actual infinity, has elaborated a procedure that putatively allows for knowledge about infinity by establishing a one-to-one correspondence between two infinite sets. If we consider a set to be (actually) infinite, it may be known in its properties if we find another equally infinite set and establish a univocal relation (a bijection) between each member of the two sets (e.g., between two sets of integers and all

---

[220] "The Cartesian notion of the idea of the Infinite designates a relation with a being that maintains its total exteriority with respect to him who thinks it." - Levinas 1969, 50.

[221] Descartes. To Mersenne, 31 December 1640, AT III 273. Cp. To Mersenne, 11 October 1638, AT II 383; To Mersenne, 28 January 1641. AT III 293; To Hyperaspistes, August 1641, AT III 430.

[222] Descartes. Fifth Set of Replies, AT VII 375; Princ. III 2, AT VIIIA 80.

[223] Descartes. To Mesland, May 1645, AT IV 187-188; cp. To Regius, 24 May 1640, AT III 64.

[224] Descartes. First Set of Replies, AT VII 114. Cp. Med. III, AT VII 47; To Mersenne, 6 May 1620, AT I 150; To Mersenne, 21 January 1641, AT III 284; To Hyperaspistes, August 1641, AT III 430; To Clerselier, 23 April 1649, AT V 35—356; Princ. I 18, AT 11-12.

[225] Cp. Descartes. Third Set of Replies, AT VII 188.

[226] As Aquinas argues, God is not known to the human mind in his essence, although it may be proven that God's existence is demonstrable. -Summa theol. I, qu. 2, art. 2.

integer odd numbers, if both sets are considered actually infinite—as a relation described by a simple formula, "$n\to 2n+1$"). Such a procedure is central in, for example, set theory.[227] However, what we are really able to know in this case is only a *relation* between two elements of different infinite sets, which is always a *finite* relation. We are thus able to handle the infinite without yet knowing what it is.

If there is anything in principle unknown to the finite mind, it might entail one of two different epistemological positions. The first is that of sheer skepticism, which claims that there is ultimately no true and firm knowledge, but only opinion, which more or less corresponds to the experienced state of affairs. This is definitely not Descartes' approach since he stresses the certainty of self-awareness and of scientific, especially mathematical, truths. The other position is that, although the infinite (God) as such is not known to the (radically finite) human mind, there is nevertheless true knowledge, presentable in a simple and clear way and accessible to every finite mind. Such true (scientific) knowledge is possible however only within the realm of finite thinking and of finite essences. How does the infinite, which supposedly originates the finite, have to be thought? There is something in Descartes' account that we are able to know and say with certainty even about the infinite: that it is, for instance, a perfection, that it necessarily exists and that its essence involves existence. But the infinite (infinite thinking and infinite being) is not and cannot be thought in its entirety by a simple single act of understanding of the human mind—its concept is necessary but inadequate.

In other words, there is a certain negativity necessarily present in every relation of finite thinking to the infinite, which cannot be known *qua* infinite. As Descartes puts it, "I distinguish between the formal concept of the infinite, or 'infinity', and the thing which is infinite. In the case of infinity, even if we understand it to be positive in the highest degree, nevertheless our way of understanding it is negative, because it depends on our not noticing any limitation in the thing. But in the case of the thing itself which is infinite, although our understanding is positive, it is not adequate, that is to say, we do not have a complete grasp of everything in it that is capable of being understood".[228]

Thus, it may be the case that if a finite entity has a potentially infinite number of properties (like those of a triangle), they all are either *not yet* known to the finite mind, but will be once discovered in the future, or the scientific research might fail to discover them, so that they remain hidden from humankind as a collective bearer of the total knowledge of properties of finite things and mathematical objects. However, even if one rejects the utterly skeptical position, one has to recognize that in actual infinity there is something that cannot be known *in principle*, but is merely a "sheer article of faith and cannot be known by the natural light".[229] There is an insurmountable distinction in knowledge of the idea of the infinite by the finite mind and by the infinite mind, namely, in the way the infinite is present to the mind: "[T]he idea of the infinite, if it is to be a true idea,

---

[227] Cantor 1883, 8-14; Brumbaugh 1982, 104-113.
[228] Descartes. First Set of Replies, AT VII 113; cp. Second Set of Replies, AT VII 152.
[229] Descartes. To Mersenne, 31 December 1640, AT III 274.

cannot be grasped at all, since the impossibility of being grasped is contained in the formal definition of the infinite. Nonetheless, it is evident that the idea which we have of the infinite does not merely represent one part of it, but represents the infinite in its entirety. The manner of representation, however, is the manner appropriate to a human idea; and undoubtedly God, or some other intelligent nature more perfect than a human mind, could have a much more perfect, i.e. more accurate and distinct, idea."[230] Even if certain elements of the *via negativa* are clearly present in Descartes, he is still mostly interested in studying the realm of finite properties and propositions, for which he quite often uses the kataphatic approach.

There is a perplexing question, however, that is not satisfactorily answered by Descartes. Namely, since in God infinity embraces and permeates all other attributes, we know that infinity *is*. But in the case of the infinite substance, or God, existence is necessarily included in essence or even may be said to coincide with it. Therefore, on the one hand, if we know the existence as necessary, we also know the essence. On the other hand, we cannot know the divine essence because of its infinity. One has to state then that either the essence-existence distinction is insufficient and obsolete in the case of the infinite substance (for even if we know that such an existence is necessary, we cannot perceive the infinite essence), or that we are aware of the infinite essence, but not fully—we are not able to grasp any quantitative differentiations within it. Hence the Cartesian distinction between "to know" and "to grasp".

The Cartesian claim about knowledge of the infinite has often been a target of criticism. One of the immediate and obvious objections raised by Gassendi is that if one cannot grasp the infinite, then one cannot have any concept or idea of it.[231] Descartes' reply is that although we cannot grasp the infinite as such, we can understand the "true and complete idea of the infinite in its entirety", which consists in understanding that the infinite is and that it is—negatively—that which is not bounded by any limits. The vulnerability of his claim forces Descartes to introduce a further distinction, that between *understanding* and *grasping* reason. The finite mind necessarily knows that God is infinite, but cannot grasp, *how* he is infinite. In like manner, the mind knows that infinity *is*—the finite mind understands it, but cannot grasp, or, moreover, know *what* it is. The difference between understanding and grasping the infinite becomes clear in the example of how do we know the vastness of a mountain if we stand close to it and cannot see it all at once. Although physically we cannot embrace the mountain (i.e. *grasp* it), we can touch it and in this way *understand* it: "To grasp something is to embrace it in one's thought; to know something, it is sufficient to touch it with one's thought."[232] In the case of the infinite (of infinite perfection), the finite mind

---

[230] Descartes. Fifth Set of Replies, AT VII 367-368.
[231] Descartes. Fifth Set of Objections, AT VII 294 sqq.
[232] Descartes. To Mersenne, 26 May 1630, AT I 152. Cp.: "Since the word 'grasp' implies some limitation, a finite mind cannot grasp God, who is infinite. But that does not prevent him having a perception of God, just as one can touch a mountain without being able to put one's arms round it". - Appendix to the Fifth Set of Objections and Replies: AT IXA 210. See also Med. III, AT VII 46, 52.

cannot grasp the *how* of it, because of the immensity of its object, it can only grasp that it *is*. This is because God understands—and thus produces—all things in a single mental act, in which the divine infinite intellect actually does grasp the infinite, whereas the finite mind can only approach—and thus understand—it.[233] Understanding is expressed in terms of the "clear and distinct" idea of the infinite (of God), which simply tells us that there should be the most perfect being (and infinity is considered to be perfection), which is not just a figment of the imagination.

It is important to emphasize this distinction within the infinite, between the "is" and the "what" or the "how". To know, to understand, the "what" is to observe an object or a state of affairs that is independent of the activity of the observing mind. To know, to grasp, the "how" it happens is to be able to reproduce the actual object or state of affairs. The understanding-grasping distinction has to do then with knowing as (re)production (see 3.4.1): only if the mind is capable of producing or reproducing an object, is it able to know that object. From Descartes' point of view, a mistake to be avoided is that the finite mind thinks that it is capable of "completely mastering" the infinite and to comprehend or grasp its properties: "I have never written about the infinite except to submit myself to it, and not to determine what it is or is not."[234] That we are not able to fully grasp the infinite (i.e., that we are radically finite), shows that Descartes still firmly retains the distinction between the (infinite) creator and the (finite) creature. The finite, the human mind in Descartes, can already assume the role of infinite subjectivity, which produces all meanings within itself and the world while retaining its position of finitude. Why is this the case? The mental operation of "to know", which understands the "is", is reserved for the finite human mind, which is thus involved only in an "as-if"-production of essences. On the contrary, the mental operation of "to grasp", which understands the "what" and the "how" of finite things, of mathematical objects, and also of the infinite substance, is reserved solely for the infinite, divine mind, which produces all essences.

The distinction between knowing and grasping corresponds also to the distinction between objective and formal concepts. If the finite mind has an objective concept of a thing that it both knows and grasps, then the objective being of that concept is contained formally in its cause. But if the finite mind only knows and does not grasp its object, then the objective being of that thing's concept is contained in its cause not formally, but eminently, that is, in a higher form.[235]

The distinction between "grasping" and "knowing", however, implies difficulties not explicitly mentioned by Descartes. First, the understanding-grasping distinction should imply a differentiation of mental capacities, namely, of

---

[233] Descartes. Conversation with Burman, AT V 154, 165-166. "Although we do not fully grasp these [divine] perfections", says Descartes, "since it is in the nature of an infinite being not to be fully grasped by us, who are finite, nonetheless we are able to understand them more clearly and distinctly than any corporeal things. This is because they permeate our thought to a greater extent, being simpler and unobscured by any limitations". - Princ. I 19, AT VIIIA 12.
[234] Descartes. To Mersenne, 28 January 1641, AT III 293.
[235] Cp. To Mersenne, March 1642, AT III 545.

immediate grasping (e.g., of the truth of a proposition) and of discursive reasoning (which arrives at the truth of a proposition in a number of logically justifiable steps). Descartes, in leveling all mental faculties into one single and simple awareness of cogitation, does not, however, make such a distinction (cp. 3.1.1; 3.1.2). Second, if there is something principally unknowable (not graspable) in the infinite, then what sense does it make to say that the infinite is being and only in this single case does essence necessarily involve existence? For it might be the case that the actually infinite, although perhaps being the source and generator of finite being, itself is not being, or, at least, that the difference between finite and infinite being is such that it does not make any sense to call the infinite "being". For, again, only "being"—the existence of the infinite—is known to the finite mind as necessary; "being-something"—the essence of the infinite—is not grasped. In this way, clearly, Descartes paves the way to expelling any objective teleology from the realm of finite essences and substances, because being is now identified not with the notion of limit, as is the case in Plato and Aristotle, but with the lack of limit and its suspension, with the actually infinite.

Descartes retains and stresses the distinction between understanding and grasping throughout his writings, from his early letters up to the "Principles of Philosophy".[236] The distinction is important not only for Descartes' theology and metaphysics, but also for his physics and geometry. Since every finite *res* is considered to be produced or created by the infinite substance, it implies that not only physical, or materially extended bodies are created, but also truths and objective concepts of things. The knowing-grasping distinction then becomes both very convenient and important: it is only the infinite creating substance or God that our finite mind is unable to grasp, although the mind is able to understand certain fundamental truths about the infinite. But in cognition of finite substances and truths, the act of knowing coincides with that of grasping, except that the act of cognition is to be understood as reached through a chain of discursive logical cogitations. Descartes thus places a possible incomprehensibility not in the sphere of the finite (as it is the case with Plato and the Platonic thinkers, for whom the realm of finite physical things is that of the ever-fluent and thus not properly understandable and not thinkable becoming), but only in the actually infinite. Finite objects, both physical bodies and geometrical entities, become accessible to true and adequate cognition.

Since actual infinity expresses for Descartes the essence of the infinite substance, it is to be found only in God. What can then be said about matter and spatial extension? Is it possible to conceive that the infinite substance, which is infinite in its productive power, can equally produce infinite substance(s)? Plotinus' answer to the question of whether this infinite power is capable of producing an equally infinite effect is "yes", because the intellect-*noys* is equally infinite in its contemplative ability. Descartes' answer is "no", for he considers the infinite intellect to be God. Furthermore, since Descartes accepts only two finite, created substances, the human mind must be finite, because whatever it thinks, it should think in terms of finite determinations—as limited (which is also the

---

[236] Cp. Descartes. To Mersenne, 15 April 1630, AT I 145-146.

Aristotelian argument). What about the second finite substance, the *res extensa*? Aristotle, as we have seen, equally argues that it cannot be infinite, for the infinite excludes limit, concept, definition or *logos,* and further, it cannot be known and is not capable of existing. Descartes does not accept this argument: his attitude towards the quantity of the extension of matter is quite ambiguous. For him to say that matter is finite in extension is to diminish the infinite productive power of the infinite substance by putting limitations on it. On the one hand, Descartes reproduces a traditional theological prohibition on putting the first (divine) cause and its effect on the same axiological and ontological level. Or, to put it in theological terms, there is an insurmountable difference between the creator and the created. God is absolutely transcendent both to the world and to the human mind. On the other hand, if one considered the effect(s) of the infinite cause to be only finite, it would impose external limitations on the infinite creative power. To say, thus, that matter is actually infinite is equally to diminish, or to put limits onto, the infinite power by supposing that there is no real distinction between that power and its effect, no real transcendence of the infinite.[237] Descartes' solution is to consider matter *indefinite* in extension.[238]

Descartes' argument is this: matter is nothing but space or mere extension. Now, let us suppose that the amount of matter is finite. In this case, there should be empty space beyond certain limits. But one can only conceive this empty space *qua* space (i.e., as three-dimensional and therefore as extended). However, the extended is matter. Therefore, by *reductio ad absurdum*, the premise is false, q.e.d.[239] An important implicit premise in the argument is that the supposed extra-mundane extension is *imagined.* The imaginary space is, however, equally extended; it is not only imaginary but real substance—namely, matter or extension. Imagination thus appears in Descartes to be performatively self-contradictory, although it essentially is involved in Descartes' consideration of matter and extension. The importance of imagination for knowing matter is considered in what follows in more detail (see 3.2.4; 3.3).

In other words, the entire amount of matter or extension in the world can be neither actually infinite, nor can it be finite. The only logical possibility left is to conceive matter or extension as *indefinitely* great or as potentially infinite. Such a position involves abstaining from judgement about the "real" extension of matter, which may be known to the infinite mind but is concealed from the finite mind: "For our part, in the case of anything in which, from some point of view, we are unable to discover a limit, we shall avoid asserting that it is infinite, and instead regard it as indefinite".[240]

---

[237] Descartes. To Chanut, 1 February 1647.
[238] "[T]he existence of actually infinite *quantity* was thought by many to involve paradox, and the assertion of an infinite *world* had brought upon many more than one philosopher the censure of theologians. The Aristotelians avoided the problem by denying reality to infinite extracosmic space; More by supposing infinite space to be God; Descartes by holding that the world is *indefinite* in size." - Des Chene 1996, 386; cp. McGuire 1983, 69-112.
[239] Descartes. To Chanut, 6 June 1647, AT V 52; cp. Princ. II 21, AT VIIIA 52; To Elizabeth, 15 September 1645, AT IV 292; To More 15 April 1649, AT V 345.
[240] Descartes. Princ. I 26, AT VIIIA 15; cp. The World, AT XI 31-32; Disc. IV, AT VI 36;

The difference between the infinite and the indefinite, *infini* and *indéfini*, has a number of implications, which appear to be the following. (1) One can easily identify different types of infinity, implied in the infini/ indéfini distinction: the infinite represents actual infinity, whereas the indefinite corresponds to potential infinity. (2) The notion of the infinite is reserved only for the substance or God, in whom "not only do we fail to recognize any limits in any respect, but our understanding positively tells us that there are none".[241] In other words, we *know* (about) the infinite, although we do not *grasp* it. That which we conceive is either finite or indefinite.[242] As for the world or matter as a whole, not only do we not grasp it, but we do not even know it clearly and "positively", in the sense of knowing no limits to it, as is the case with God. Descartes is thus ambiguous in his usage of negative description: the infinite for him is negativity, which is taken as an utmost positivity (the infinite positively, i.e., it actually has no bounds), while the indefinite is negative only privatively; it is *nihil privativum* as embodied in the positivity of the extended substance—in matter.

(3) The Cartesian argument for accepting the indefinite essentially refers to imagination (see 3.3.1). At this point we need only mention that the mental ability to go beyond any given limits without grasping or embracing the whole is the distinctive trait of imagination, "for no matter where we imagine the boundaries to be, there are always some indefinitely extended spaces beyond them, which we not only imagine but also perceive to be imaginable in a true fashion, that is, real".[243] The immediate corollary is that for Descartes there can be no plurality or infinity of worlds.[244] Why is this the case? Imagination is able to extend and to go beyond any given limits, to the *indefinite*, although its object is finite at any particular moment, so that reason interprets (knows) the imaginable as material, for matter is nothing but extension. For Descartes, the indefinite is not a sign of an imperfection of the infinite power, but rather of our own finitude, and is further an indication of the conflict between the finite understanding of the mind and the ability of imagination to go beyond any limits.[245]

(4) It is also important to note that Descartes, unlike Aristotle, insists that no intermediary structures, no mediation between opposites (namely, between *res extensa* and *res cogitans*) is necessary (see 2.3.1). The intermediary, although expelled from ontology by Descartes, appears under another guise of the indefinite, which plays the role of mediator between actual infinity and the finite, so that every limited *res* participates both in the finite (as a particular limited subject) and

---

To Chanut, 6 June 1647, AT V 51-52. "The reason why I say that the world is indeterminate, or indefinite", writes Descartes, "is that I can discover no limits in it; but I would not dare to call it infinite, because I perceive that God is greater than the world, not in extension ... but in perfection." - To More, 15 April 1649, AT V 273.

[241] Descartes. Princ. I 27, AT VIIIA 15. Descartes' distinction of *infini/ indéfini* appears to parallel Cusanus' distinction of negative and privative infinity, De docta ignor. 91-97, 135-135 et al. Cp. also: Locke, Essay, Bk. II, ch. XVII, §1.

[242] Descartes. Conversation with Burman, 16 April 1648, AT V 154.

[243] Descartes. Princ. II 21, AT VIIIA 52.

[244] See: Koyré 1957.

[245] Descartes. Med. III, AT VII 47; cp. Princ. III 1, AT VIIIA 80.

in the indefinite (as part of the world).

(5) The situation of radical finitude, when the finite mind is incapable of grasping the infinite thinking all at once and has only to increase gradually its knowledge, is the sign of imperfection for Descartes. Cognition moves as if within a circle, which it tries to approximate by a polygon with an ever increasing number of sides that, despite all its efforts, can never truly become a circle. That is why one has to invent and apply a method of cognition—a special procedure that should enable the finite mind to gradually increase its knowledge, whereas the infinite intellect knows and grasps (or at least is supposed to grasp) the variety of links and connections within the indefinite all at once. The indefinite thus expresses the *attitude* of the finite mind to the actual infinity. (6) Both Descartes and the ancient philosophers agree that matter is indefinite, although in different respects: for Descartes it is indefinite in extension; for Aristotle and Plotinus it is indefinite in its very existence, since matter "is" primarily non-being. Finally (7), the notion of the indefinite may be applicable to three entities: first, to the extension of imaginary space, which can hardly be distinguished from the real space. Second, to the set of integers, for whatever large number n we may choose, there is always a bigger one, $n+1$ (cp. 2.1.2; 2.1.4). And third, the indefinite as potentially infinite applies to the divisibility of continuous magnitude, which is always divisible in any of its parts. In all three cases, the presence of actual infinity is denied, because Descartes reserves the notion of *infini* for God only, while the finite mind is only able to recognize a limit within that which is capable of increase or decrease.[246] It is worth noting that the delimitation of these three spheres of the indefinite fits exactly the ancient (both Pythagorean-Platonic and Aristotelian) distinction of the subject-matters of physics, arithmetic and geometry.[247]

Important questions that arise in the discussion of infinity are how the infinite is present, first, in the functioning of mental faculties (namely, will and imagination), and second, in mathematical entities (namely, geometrical figures and numbers). These questions are considered in due place (see 2.1.3; 3.3.1), after the notions of cognitive faculties and mathematical entities are introduced.

1.3.3 Paradox and infinity

As it has been argued, the consideration of matter in Plotinus is inherently paradoxical (1.1.2). The not finite One too appears to be paradoxical. On the one hand, it is impossible to speak about it using the ordinary logical distinction between subject and predicates, since the One is beyond any definition in finite terms: the One is not any particular subject and is prior to all predicates, hence nothing can be predicated of it.[248] It is not the case, however, that we cannot speak about the One at all or express it in any way. The most important constitutive fact about ourselves, argues Plotinus, is that we are *unable not to speak* about the One,

---

[246] Descartes. First Set of Replies, AT VII 112-113.
[247] Cp. Nikulin 1996, 66-69.
[248] Plotinus. Enn. III.8.10.28-35; VI.8.14.30. In other words, the One is really not expressible, cannot be spoken of or written, *oyde rhēton, oyde grapton*, as Plato puts it in Ep. VII, 341c. Cp. Plotinus. Enn. V.3.13.1, V.5.6.24, VI.8.8.6.

just as we are unable not to strive towards the good. It is exactly this aspiration towards the One as the good that precedes all other aspirations (e.g., to any particular good or that which appears to be good). This aspiration appears to be a *sui generis* transcendental condition for the possibility of all other particular aspirations—the first fundamental aspiration, which itself is an expression of the One's presence preceding all presence.[249]

In such a case it is important to distinguish between "speaking about the One" (possible "knowledge about") and "speaking the One" ("knowledge of", which is above the capacities of reasoning of the finite mind).[250] "Speaking the One" does not follow logical laws, in particular, the principle of non-contradiction, since nothing can be predicated about the One. "Speaking the One" is then inevitably paradoxical. For instance, if we say "the One is not predicable", this itself is a self-denying or self-negating, unpredicable predication. In other words, contradictory propositions are false in "speaking the One", which itself is self-contradictory. At the same time, each statement should be true in "speaking about One". But of course being both false and true is not possible from the point of view of discursive logical thinking.

An example of such paired statements or propositions can be: (a) the One is one; (b) the One is not one. On the one hand, (a) holds because the One is the only and unique principle of being. On the other hand, the One cannot be predicated and is altogether beyond oneness, therefore the One is not one, (b). *Both* statements (a) and (b) are true in "speaking about the One", but since they contradict each other, they cannot *both* be true. Another example is: (c) the One is "itself" (*ayto*), and (d) the One is not "itself".[251] The first, (c), may be said of the One as that which only "is" without any addition, to which no predicate may be added. The second, (d), appears to be true as well, since the One, the most self-sufficient (*aytarkestaton*), is prior to every possible identification, since the act of identification requires a distinction of that which is identified, and this distinction should obviously precede all identification (namely, identification to itself).[252] Therefore, the One has to be prior to any distinction, and thus is not an identity—it is not sameness, paired and opposed to otherness, but is rather the source of identity beyond all identity and therefore cannot be conceived even as non-identical before the act of identification.

Why does a paradox appear in Plotinus? There seems to be two different reasons. First, consideration of non-being follows the pattern of consideration of the existent and thus always opens a possibility for paradox.[253] Second, a paradoxical situation is implied by the notion of actual infinity (rejected by

---

[249] Plotinus. Enn. VI.7.22.18.
[250] "We do indeed say something about it (*legomen ti peri aytoy*), but we certainly do not speak it (*oy mēn ayto legomen*), and we have neither knowledge nor thought of it."-Plotinus. Enn. V.3.14.1-3. Cp. Gerson 1994, 15-16.
[251] Cp. Plotinus. Enn. VI.8.9.35 sqq.
[252] Plotinus. Enn. V.4.1.13. Another example might be: the One is beyond active actuality of energy (*epekeina energeias*, Enn. VI.7.17.10; cp. VI.8.20.14), but also is primal actuality (*energeia*) itself (Enn. VI.8.20.9 sqq.).
[253] Cp. Plato. Soph. 237a.

Aristotle, which allows him to stress the primary role of the principle of non-contradiction in ontology and epistemology). The first reason we do not find in Descartes, for whom non-being is simply an imperfection. The second, however, is definitely present in the Cartesian system, since God is taken to be actually infinite.

Thus, acceptance of the actually infinite appears to involve paradox. There are a number of paradoxes implicit in the notions of the infinitely big, the infinitely small, the one and the many. The cost for the introduction and acceptance of the infinite in mathematics is paradox.[254] Let us confine ourselves here to the paradox of infinite power. If the finite mind in Descartes can clearly (and distinctly) understand a thing (mental or physical), that thing might be created— that is, it might exist. This statement, however, is loaded with paradox, because, while everything appears to be possible for the infinite power, a thing that involves conceptual contradiction, or is unintelligible, is said to be impossible, even for God.[255] How is it possible then to combine the notion of infinite power (which is governed by the equally infinite will, not really distinct from the infinite thinking) with the principle of non-contradiction? If everything is supposed to be possible for the infinite power, it can or could make the contradictories join without mediation, as is supposed by Nicholas of Cusa or Hegel. The paradox is concealed in the following statement: "God cannot have been determined to make it true that contradictories cannot be true together, and therefore that he could have done the opposite."[256] It is contradictory that God could not have created such a world where the principle of non-contradiction would have been invalid. But then, since it is possible for the infinite power to suspend, as it were, the principle of non-contradiction, it is also possible to cancel the contradiction that it could not have created such a world where the principle of non-contradiction would have been invalid. To put it otherwise, infinite power (which is not really distinct from infinite thinking) is capable of conceptual contradiction. Or, simply, if there is actual infinity, contradictories and opposites may immediately come together, without being mediated by a substrate or *hypokeimenon*; and this is precisely the moment at which the paradox appears.

An obvious example of a paradox of actual infinity is that God cannot deprive himself of his own infinite power, as well as of his own existence. In other words, being actually infinite, God cannot choose not to be infinite, omnipotent, necessarily existent and supremely perfect.[257] The contradiction of infinite power

---

[254] Cp. Russell 1970, 56-58. Russell's paradox produced a shock among mathematicians, logicians and philosophers of science, enabling a number of them (intuitionists or constructivists) to drop the idea of actual infinity and to accept only the notion of potential infinity—that which is in a process of becoming or is being constructed. - See: Weyl 1949, 33-66; Abian 1965, 32 sqq.; Moore 1990, 115; Brouwer 1992, 30. The paradox was first reported by Russell in a letter to Frege in 1895. Cp. Cavalieri 1966, 651-653 who already envisages a possibility of building mathematics without using the notion of the actually infinite.
[255] Descartes. To Regius, June 1642, AT III 567. Cp. To Regis, January 1642: AT III 492: "But what is done cannot be undone".
[256] Descartes. To [Mesland], 2 May 1644, AT IV 118.
[257] Descartes. Princ. II 20, AT VIIIA 51-52; cp. Princ. I 60, AT VIIIA 29; To ***, March 1642, AT V 546; For [Arnauld], 29 July 1648, AT V 224; cp. To [Beeckman], 17 October

is, of course, known well before Descartes, for instance, in the scholastic question of whether God could have created a stone that he himself would not have been able to lift. It is interesting to note that for Origen, who is still an ancient thinker in his rejection of actual infinity, the divine power cannot be infinite, because then it could not know itself.[258]

How does Descartes solve the paradox of the actually infinite power, which turns out to be self-contradictory? Two observations need to be made here. First, for the actually infinite, free (i.e., not determined by anything external to it) will to will (*vouloir*) something as necessary is different from willing it necessarily, or to be necessitated to will it.[259] Second, as it has been already mentioned, since there is an unparalleled qualitative difference between the finite and the actually infinite, the former cannot grasp the latter. Descartes simply dismisses the paradox of infinity by stressing the finitude of the human mind, which in principle is unable to grasp the infinite. The source of the paradox is the following discrepancy: "[S]ince we are finite, it would be absurd for us to determine anything concerning the infinite; for this would be to attempt to limit it and grasp it. So we shall not bother to reply to those who ask if half an infinite line would itself be infinite, or whether an infinite number is odd or even, and so on. It seems that nobody has any business to think about such matters unless he regards his own mind as infinite."[260] In other words, the principle of non-contradiction is only valid for the finite mind. In the infinite, where there is an ungraspable "single activity, entirely simple and entirely pure",[261] the actual coexistence of the opposites might be understood but not grasped by the finite mind.

1.3.4 Indefinite divisibility of physical and mathematical entities in Descartes

Paradox appears further in the consideration of materiality and continuity. As it has been argued, the notion of matter implies a paradox for Plotinus, for matter is no thing, it has no identity and no order whatsoever. There is only a lack of all possible organization or junction, primarily exemplified in the infinite divisibility of the continuum. In the continuum one cannot discover or recognize any stable form or inner structure, but whatever form is associated with it in a geometrical figure or physical body can always be split further and has *partes extra partes*.

1630, AT I 165; Conversation with Burman, 16 April 1648, AT V 160. " 'God does not have the faculty of taking away from himself his own existence.' Now by a 'faculty' we normally mean some perfection; yet it would be an imperfection in God to be able to take away existence from himself. So to forestall any quibbling, I would prefer to put it as follows: 'it is a contradiction that God should take away from himself his own existence; or be able to lose it in some other way.'" - To ***, March 1642, AT V 546). Another paradox is that for God it is impossible not to know himself. Cp. 2 Tim. 2:13; Cusanus, Apologia doctae ignor., 8; Dionysius. De div. Nom. 8, 6.

[258] Origen. De princ. II, 9.
[259] Descartes. To [Mesland], 2 May 1644, AT IV 118.
[260] Descartes. Princ. I 26, AT VIIIA 14-15. Cp.: "[W]hat basis have we for judging whether one infinity can be greater than another or not? It would no longer be infinity if we could grasp it." - To Mersenne, 15 April 1630, AT I 146-147.
[261] Descartes. To [Mesland], 2 May 1644, AT IV 119.

Every extended magnitude, which becomes the subject-matter of science, is associated with matter. And even if matter is not a continuum *per se*, it always appears in continuous magnitudes, both physical and geometrical. In fact, in appearing thus matter hides, since it is not a particular subject. Nevertheless, it is possible to discern two different, albeit tightly connected, aspects of matter as appearing in and through continuous magnitudes, which may be discerned in Plotinus' treatment of matter. First, since matter is not a particular subject and thus has no inner organization or any inherent structure, opposites may both be predicated of it simultaneously. Second, since there is no form or limit in matter at which the cognition could stop, every continuous entity may be always further divisible. The insurmountable gap between the discrete and the continuous is further represented in the distinction between number and magnitude, which is one of the main reasons for the rigid distinction between arithmetic and geometry in ancient mathematics from Aristotle to Proclus (cp. 2.1.3).[262]

That opposites may both be predicated of matter is not, however, accepted by Descartes, for whom matter represents finite or indefinite being and therefore is a particular subject. But even then, while matter is thought of by Descartes as a continuous magnitude, one cannot say that it is altogether free of paradox. As Descartes argues, the actually infinite being or God cannot deprive himself of his own infinite power, and even if we imagine that God chose to make a particle of matter indivisible for us, he could not have deprived himself of infinite power, so that it would still be within that power to divide the particle further in principle.[263] We are able thus to imagine a situation where the infinite power makes a finite part of matter indivisible, but we are not able to think that the infinite power is unable to divide that particle *ad infinitum*.

Although in his early years Descartes seemed to accept, along with Beeckman, the idea of atomism, in his later treatises he most definitely rejects the idea from the methodological point of view. Conceiving of bodies or parts of matter as not infinitely divisible involves a *contradictio in adiecto*, for the very notion of extension is that of the continuum or infinitely divisible quantity.[264] It means that there are, and can be, no atoms, because their very notion is self-contradictory. Every body has to be continuous and infinitely divisible.[265] Indeed, it is always possible to conceive—in fact, to imagine—that a fixed part of matter may be further divided, since matter, on Descartes' account, is pure extension and

---

[262] Consequently, the one and the many are present in different ways in the discrete and in the continuous: the discrete (number as a set of discrete units) cannot be infinitely divisible, because the "lower" limit of division is an indivisible unit, *monas*. The (quantitative) number, however, can be increased by repetitive addition of the unit. On the other hand, continuous magnitude, be it geometrical or physical, cannot increase at all, because otherwise it would turn into another magnitude. That is why the "upper" limit of a magnitude is magnitude itself as a whole. Still, it can be divided infinitely at any particular limit, simply because there is no limit in the continuous (cp. Aristotle. Phys. 232a 24-25).
[263] Descartes. Princ. II 20, AT VIIIA 51-52; cp. To More, 5 February 1649, AT V 273.
[264] Descartes. Second Set of Replies, AT VII 163; cp. To Mersenne, 28 October 1640, AT III 191-192.
[265] Descartes. To Vorstius, 19 June 1643, AT III 686.

extension is continuous—it is always divisible into further parts. In this way the notion of infinite divisibility is connected with that of contradiction; both are necessarily implied by the notion of matter.

The question that immediately arises is whether matter is infinitely or indefinitely divisible. In other words, if we take a body or a particle of matter, is it already divided into an actually infinite number of parts or is it merely potentially divisible? Here again we encounter Descartes' rigid separation between the actual infinity of God, which cannot be grasped by the finite mind, and the potential infinity or "indefinity", which is accessible (knowable) to the human mind. Even if one might conceive of a finite continuous magnitude (without contradiction) divided into an actually infinite number of parts, it would be conceivable only for the equally actually infinite mind. Descartes thus implicitly establishes a methodological prohibition on the infinitesimals as actually existing, representing the infinite in small. The finite mind then has to grasp the finite objects, even if it may in principle never come to a stop in considering ever smaller and smaller parts of a body—the infinitesimals or particles of extension which, if considered, should be taken in the process of ever becoming less and less, smaller than any given (however small) finite magnitude $\varepsilon > 0$. Descartes claims that "the principle that a series cannot go on for ever (*non datur progressus in infinitum*) is commonly accepted. I do not accept that principle; on the contrary, I think that in the division of the parts of matter there really is an endless series (*datur revera talis progressus in divisione partium materiae*)".[266] But even thus Descartes has to deny an indefinite regress in thinking, since the very act of thinking is a limitation and definition of its object as different from other subjects. That is why there cannot be an infinite regress in ideas: the finite discursive thinking must, after a number of steps, finally stop.[267] Thus, matter or body must be only indefinitely, rather than infinitely, divisible.[268] Again, as in the case of knowing the infinite, we only perceive (know) the truth of the indefinite divisibility of matter, but we do not and cannot grasp it, because of the definiteness of finite thinking.

Discussing Descartes' stance against atomism, Garber argues that "basic to atomists, both ancients and seventeenth century, was a distinction between two different sorts of atomism, mathematical (or conceptual) and physical".[269] The distinction is that in dividing the physical continuous magnitude one has to stop at a certain point when the further division is no longer possible for physical reasons (e.g., because we do not possess enough power to continue the division). But mathematical division is still considered possible in principle, because logically there is no reason for not performing another dichotomic step. As Garber goes on to argue, Aristotle does not distinguish between conceptual and physical divisibility, whereas Descartes does, at least in the 1640s. This, however, does not really seem to be the case with Descartes. Attempting to present his natural

---

[266] Descartes. To [Mesland], 2 May 1644; AT IV 133; cp. To Gibieuf, 19 January 1642, AT III 477.
[267] Descartes. To Clerselier, 23 April 1649, AT V 355; cp. Med. III, AT VII 42.
[268] Descartes. Disc. IV, AT VI 36. Cp. Princ. I 26, AT VIIIA 15; Princ. II 34, AT VIIIA 59-60; Princ. III 46, AT VIIIA 100; Princ. IV 201, AT VIIIA 324-325.
[269] Garber 1992, 123. Cp. Gassendi. *Opera Omnia* I, 263 sqq.; Jones 1981, 286-287.

philosophy as simply and unambiguously as possible, he simplifies the problem of the continuum and criticizes Fromondus' distinction, which explicitly presupposes every body or part of matter (every physical atom) to be continuous and thus divisible into infinity (i.e., indefinitely).[270] Since physical and mathematical (geometrical) objects are considered in(de)finitely divisible in one and the same extension, there is no sufficient ground for discerning between the two cases; moreover, geometrical entities may also be considered moving (cp. 3.4.2). Therefore, the distinction between physical and mathematical divisibility is not that between "real" and "mental" divisibility. The distinction, as it follows from Descartes' argument, is between the potentially infinite, or indefinite divisibility for the finite mind (which is *both* applicable to physical and mathematical entities), and the infinite as complete and (possibly) accessible only to the infinite mind of God.

We find another interesting example of the consideration of the divisibility of continuum in early Newton. In his notebooks from the time of his studies at Trinity College, Newton sketches a theory of indivisibles or atoms, equally applicable to both physical and mathematical objects.[271] He considers four different hypotheses of the possible structure of prime matter, which is continuous and underlies all physical things. The hypotheses themselves are originally suggested by W. Charleton and suggest that prime matter—pure continuous extension—either (1) consists of mathematical points; (2) consists of mathematical points together with extended divisible parts; (3) is a whole indivisible entity; or (4) consists of indivisible atoms.[272] Newton provides arguments to show that the first three hypotheses cannot be valid and that only the last one holds. He illustrates his position by a construction showing that the atomic structure of the continuum or "prime matter" does not differ in physical and geometrical entities.[273] He introduces entities called "ciphers", provided with the following features: they are without magnitude and are such that one "cipher" cannot be identified with another (i.e., as if it has a repulsive force which prevents two such entities from merging). If two such "ciphers" are posited, then, by way of construction, they form an indivisible entity, a unit or an atom which at the same time may be considered as the indivisible basis of number, of geometrical magnitude and of physical body. The structure of the mathematical and the physical continuum appears to be the same in both mathematical and physical objects. A strong presupposition in Newton (as also in Descartes) is that both mathematical and physical objects may share the same measure or unit and that both may be referred to the same kind of extension. This is impossible both for Aristotle and for later ancient thinkers—in particular, for Plotinus and Proclus—but becomes a fundamental presupposition for the successful development of the new mathematical science (see 2.1.3; 2.2.2).

A possible objection supporting a difference in the indefinite divisibility of physical objects and mathematical objects might be that the former are divisible in matter, whereas the latter are so only in imagination. Such an objection,

---

[270] Cp. Descartes. To Plempius for Fromondus, 3 October 1637, AT I 422.
[271] McGuire, Tamny 1983, 336 sqq.; cp. Cavalieri 1966, 654 sqq.; Nikulin 1993, 113-118.
[272] Charleton 1966, 23, 85, 95.
[273] McGuire, Tamny 1983, 420.

however, is not applicable to Descartes, who explicitly states that all indefinite or innumerable physical particles of matter are imaginable and, moreover, divisible in imagination.[274] Both physical and mathematical entities are then divisible in imagination and are primarily subjects of and to imagination: this, as discussed later (see 3.3.1), is a crucial position in Descartes, which becomes revolutionary in the new scientific programme of the mathematical investigation of the world.

1.4 Substance and essence

1.4.1 Otherness in substance

An important aspect of the Cartesian treatment of the notion of substance is its introduction not through the notion of substance, but primarily through the notion of the other—by the *negatio negationis*. As a subject existing by and through itself, substance is *nothing other* than that which depends on *no other thing* in order to exist. Substance is primarily understood as *not other*. Descartes thus constantly struggles with otherness in an attempt to reject it. Such a rejection takes place in obtaining certitude by means of radical doubt, when Descartes expels everything he can in order to arrive at a simple truth of "cogito ergo sum".[275] Thus, (a) the absolute or unconditioned other for mind and matter is the not-created substance or God. The conditioned otherness, (b) for the mind is that which is not the *cogito*— that which is not thinking and can be understood only as the "outer", as that which is unable to think. The other to the mind, which is both complementary to and exclusive of the mind, is matter (body) and *vice versa*, so that the mind may be conceived as existing without the body, and the body without the mind.[276] Since the two created substances are conditionally other to each other and thus are different, they are independent of one another and therefore can exist without and apart from each other. That is why the real distinction of the two finite substances is constituted not so much by unconditioned otherness (a), but by the conditioned one (b), which determines the corresponding essential attribute, opposite to the attribute of the other substance: the other to the thinking substance is matter; the other to matter is thought (we do not find otherness functioning this way in Plotinus, for whom matter also represents otherness, but never is taken as a substance, even in a limited sense).

One might say that otherness in its (b)-aspect is epistemologically primary by way of cognition (e.g., when the *ego* starts in cognition with getting rid of everything that is other to itself), for the infinite, as it has been argued (1.3.2), is not known in its essence. Moreover, the two finite substances, thinking and extension, are complementary and thereby ontologically equivalent (for both are equally supported in their existence by the infinite substance). But epistemologically, thinking is prior, because extension is justified as not-thinking

---

[274] Descartes. To Mersenne, 28 October 1640, AT III 213-214; Princ. II 34, AT VIIIA.
[275] Descartes. Med. I, AT VII 17 sqq.; Disc. IV, AT VI 32; Princ. I 10, AT VIIIA 8.
[276] Descartes. Second Set of Replies, AT VII 169-170; cp. Fourth Set of Replies, AT VII 219; Seventh Set of Replies, AT VII 484; To [De Launay], 22 July 1641, AT III 421; To Regis, June 1642, AT III 567.

(which Descartes claims to be immediately and clearly perceivable), even though it is not immediately self-evident whether everything that is not-extension is thinking, for thinking is already necessarily involved in the very act of distinction.

Thought and extension are thus mutually complementary but also mutually ontologically and epistemologically exclusive.[277] Ontologically, otherness in its (a)-aspect is prior, for only God *qua* substance strictly and primarily *is*. Descartes is more interested, however, in clear and distinct cognition—in the epistemological, (b)-aspect of otherness, and not so much in the fabulous hypothesizing about being as such. That is, if something is a substance and is not extended, then it is self-evidently thinking, and *vice versa*. As Descartes writes to Pollot, "you agree that thought is an attribute of a substance which contains no extension, and conversely that extension is an attribute of a substance that contains no thought. So you must also agree that a thinking substance is distinct from an extended substance. For the only criterion enabling us to know that one substance differs from another is that we understand one apart from the other".[278] With no active principle in it, matter is merely a *moles quiescens*. Matter, then, is the pure "outside". This becomes one of the main theses underlying not only Cartesian physics and metaphysics, but also modern science. It is worth noting that being, understood as spatially located existence, is first found in Aquinas.[279] In Descartes, any physical thing may be known by means of a strict science, primarily by mathematics, but only to the extent that this thing does not have any inner activity itself. A thing may be an object of scientific consideration only insofar as it is fully spatially (i.e., materially) expressed. Only a purely material thing without any subjectivity or soul, having no "inner" side, may be scientifically studied and known. Every "inside" might render a thing unpredictable or as violating the mathematical laws of physical interaction. In other words, mind and matter are distinct as pure "inside" and "outside". It is in this way that the distinction between subject and object is understood in modernity, where "object" substitutes that which for Aristotle was "subject". Although Spinoza tries to overcome this distinction by considering "subject" and "object" as mind (thinking) and body (extension) as just two different attributes of the same substance,[280] the dichotomy is quite definite and becomes one of the *differentia specifica* of modernity.

The question of why there are only two finite substances remains unsatisfactorily answered by Descartes, except by an appeal to the clarity of understanding only two substances of mind and body. In an attempt to answer this question, Spinoza postulates a single infinite substance having an infinite number of attributes of which we are able to know and conceive of only two. The problem remains unsolved, however, for it is still not clear why only two, and not more or fewer, finite attributes (or, respectively, substances) are known to us. A satisfactory answer to this question might be given if one took into account the "inner"-"outer" dichotomy. Descartes gets rid of any intermediary entities that do not fit either "in" or "out", because of his intention to render the structure of the world-*corpus* and

---

[277] Cp. Descartes. Princ. I 48, AT VIIIA 23; I 63, AT VIIIA 30-31.
[278] Descartes. To Pollot, 6 October 1642, AT III 567.
[279] Nijenhuis 1994, 1-14.
[280] Spinoza. Ethics Part II, Props. 1, 2; cp. Part I, Prop. 11.

thinking-*mens* as simple and univocal as possible.[281] This appears to be the case because simplicity is a precondition for clarity, and clarity is a precondition for truth. Descartes cannot accept only one finite substance, since otherwise he would have either to acknowledge that the world is cosubstantial with God (which he tries to avoid as pantheism) or to recognize that there is no (free) rational cognizant agent in the world, which is unacceptable for him as well.

In the case of only two substances, Descartes needs to describe only one single relation between them, whereas in the case of three substance there would already be three different relationships to explain, for four substances—six relationships, for five substances—ten relationships, and so on (in general, in the case of n substances one has to describe $R=n(n-1)/2$ different relationships). Even in the case of a single relation (that of the mind/ body) the problem is already complex, so that one might expect enormous difficulties (comparable to the problem of many bodies in classical dynamics) as the number n grows, for R grows not linearly but in the order of n^2. Obviously, the simplest case is when only two substances are recognized ($n=2$, $R=1$). Still, in order to realize this seemingly rather arbitrary construction, Descartes has to expel all entities from the mind and from the world that might mediate between the two substances, thus leaving no room for a possibility of distinguishing between the specifically physical and the specifically geometrical, or also between the intelligible and the discursive in thinking (see 3.1.1-3.1.2).

As it has been argued (1.1.2), the main approach to understanding matter in the Platonic tradition (and to some extent in Aristotle), with all its subtle distinctions and various disagreements, is taking matter as *not* substance. Matter therefore does not actually exist and can neither be properly known nor adequately described.[282] This means, first, that matter is not a definite subject; thus, there does not exist any particular, finite set of predicates that could fully characterize matter. Second, matter cannot be said properly to exist (maybe only as a pure potentiality); and so it cannot be characterized by any "positive speech". Finally, matter is not independent; hence it cannot by itself produce or engender anything existent.

Descartes explicitly rejects such an understanding of matter.[283] For him, matter as finite substance is understood univocally, because, unlike mind, matter cannot be co-substantial with the infinite thinking substance, God. On the other hand, matter possesses all the features of substance in a limited sense, namely, it is a subject with a number of predicates; it is independent; and its subsistence is due to no other cause but the concurrence of the infinite substance. Being a substance, matter may be adequately *known* in its idea and thus, adequately *described*.[284]

---

[281] Following Descartes' exposition, Spinoza mentions the ambiguity of the term "soul": "I speak here of mind (*mens*) rather than of soul (*anima*) because the word *soul* is equivocal and is often used for a corporeal thing". Principles of the Philosophy of Descartes, Part I, def. 6.

[282] Cp. "*materia non est substantia rei... ipsum esse non est proprius actus materiae, sed substantiae totius.*" - Thomas Aquinas. Summa contra gent. II 54.

[283] Cp. Descartes. The World, AT XI 33. See also: Gilson 1979, 169-175.

[284] Cp. Descartes. To Gibieuf, 19 January 1642, AT III 475; Discourse V, AT VI 42-43. Since matter is taken as a limited substance by Descartes, and the limited substance does not

Since matter is taken as substance, the question of how matter is known can be reformulated as the question of how substance is known. Two closely related main themes determine the cognition of substance in Descartes. First, substance is not known immediately in itself but only through its attributes. Second, substance can only be thought, but neither imagined nor sensually apprehended.

That substance is not known immediately follows from the mentioned general principle that attributes do not exist independently, that is, apart from a substance as their vehicle subject. The subject has to be known in its *act* through a number of modes or accidents, ultimately reducible to one essential attribute.[285] The very term "act"—besides its traditional scholastic meaning of *actus*, which translates Aristotelian *energeia*—receives a new meaning in Descartes, that of *representation* (which may lead to knowledge) through action (of a noun—through a verb), because it is in acting that we know, produce or reproduce things (see 3.4.1-3.4.2). Substance, in Descartes' own words, is *revealed* only through its accidents, which play the role of mediators, and thus make cognition possible.[286] Revelation has easily recognizable religious connotations in the case of the infinite substance or God, whose essence is not grasped and is not known immediately in itself, besides its acts and attributes, one of which—thought—is co-intensive with the human mind, although not coextensive, since the human mind is finite. The

---

necessarily exist due only to itself, and the world (the nature) is matter, a problem that arises is that of the objectivity of the (outer) world. To note, this problem is specifically a modern one: we do not find it in antiquity, because matter is not considered something necessarily existent, and if it is considered to be such (in the Stoics), it simply is there, and does not need any further justification or speculation about the fact of its presence—only about its properties. Descartes, however, has to prove the objective existence of the outer material world (Med. VI, AT VII 71 sqq.). Peculiar to Descartes' argument is that for him everything that may be clearly and distinctly conceived by the mind—such is the power of reason as thinking substance co-intensive and co-substantial with the divine—*may* be created by (or is possible for) God. The argument consists then in demonstrating that in case of matter or bodies their possible existence is necessary as being supported by God. In particular, bodies or matter in general exist because the ideas we have of them can neither be produced by ourselves, nor can such ideas of external extended bodies be present without bodies being real, just be infused in our mind by God, for God is not a deceiver, and deceiving is an imperfection, incompatible with the highest possible perfection, which is necessarily comprised in the essence of God (cp. Princ. I 29, AT VIII A 16; II 1, AT VIIIA 40-41). As Descartes writes in a letter to Hyperaspistes, "I proved the existence of material things not from the fact that we have ideas of them but from the fact that these ideas come to us in such a way as to make us aware that they are not produced by ourselves but come from elsewhere" (To Hyperaspistes, August 1641, AT III 428-429).

[285] "We do not have immediate knowledge of substances, as I have noted elsewhere. We know them only by perceiving certain forms or attributes which must inhere in something if they are to exist; and we call the thing in which they inhere a 'substance'. But if we subsequently wanted to strip the substance of the attributes through which we know it, we would be destroying our entire knowledge of it." - Descartes. Fourth Set of Replies, AT VII 222. Cp. Third Set of Replies, AT VII 175-176; Princ. I 52, AT VIIIA 24-25; Princ. I 65, AT VIIIA 32.

[286] Descartes. Appendix to the Fifth Set of Replies, AT IXA 216.

unknowability of substance is further stressed by Locke and Kant, for whom substance *per se* is an unknown "*x*", which is known only phenomenally, through its accidents and modes, remaining ever closed and hermetic in itself.[287] This thesis appears to be initially rooted in the notion of absolute an unbridgeable transcendence of the creator to the created. This makes knowledge of substance both negative and positive, both *kat' aphairesin* and *kata thesin*. Indeed, substance is known negatively insofar as its essence remains directly inaccessible. But substance is known positively insofar as its attributes represent or "reveal" it adequately to the finite mind. In particular, matter is known for Descartes both negatively, as not thought, and positively, as extension. In this respect, Descartes comes close to the above discussed position of Aristotle in the knowledge of matter, although for Aristotle positive knowledge of matter is not altogether certain. At the same time, Descartes differs from Plato, for whom knowledge of matter as not-substance is negative *par excellence* and cannot be revealed by any attribute, because, strictly speaking, matter has no attributes.

Suppose, however, we abstract all attributes, accidents and modes from a substance. Is there then anything left? Is there a substance beyond its attributes? This question can be hardly univocally answered by Descartes, because in the case of infinite substance, attributes reveal it in a rather specific sense, so that the essence remains not fully accessible even through the essential attribute (see 1.3.3). And in the case of finite substance, if it is stripped of its essential attribute(s), there is nothing left that would allow the identification of the substance (respectively, as mind or body). There is literally *nothing* left, especially since the essential attribute may also be taken as infinite substance itself.

Still, cognition of two substances is not symmetrical: the *res extensa* is known through the *res cogitans* and not vice versa, because every attribute is represented in the mind. Further, it is possible to think that there exists no body, but it is not possible to think that there exists no thought; this would be performatively self-contradictory since it is thought that performs the operations of both just "thinking" and of "thinking that something is the case" (in parallel to "being" and "being something"). We know, says Descartes, "more attributes in the case of our mind than we do in the case of anything else. For no matter how many attributes we recognize in any given thing, we can always list a corresponding number of attributes in the mind which it has in virtue of knowing the attributes of the thing; and hence the nature of the mind is the one we know best of all".[288] And since every attribute is represented in thought, and we—the finite mind(s)—are essentially the thinking substance, we know that which is represented in thought better than that which is in body. In other words, we know body not because we have body or are in body, but because the attribute of extension is also represented in thought (from this point of view, there is no primacy of my own body for me as different from any other body, that is, the *ego* rationally—not sensually—knows its own body as the other's body). This is the reason why knowledge of substance through attribute(s) or modes of substance (in particular, knowledge of matter) is

---

[287] Locke. Essay, Bk. I, ch.4, § 19; Kant. Critique of Pure Reason B 298 et al.
[288] Descartes. Fifth Set of Replies, AT VII 360.

accessible to the reason or mind only—to the thought, and not to the imagination or senses, which may distort or misrepresent an attribute or mode (cp. 3.1.4).[289]

1.4.2 Essence and existence: Descartes' essentialism

A further distinction important for the discussion is that of *essence* and *existence*, which goes back to Aristotle, for whom *to be* is not the same as *to be something*.[290] Thus, to be *a point* is not the same as for a point *to be*. "Being something" implies the notion of essence, which indicates *what* something is, *quid sit*; and "to be" implies the notion of existence, which indicates that something *is*, *an sit*. In its most general sense, essence is and shows "that which" or "what" something is. Summing up scholastic discussions around the notion of essence, Zubiri presents essence as "that which responds to the name or to the question 'what' something is, its *quid* or *ti*".[291] The "what" comprises all the properties and attributes (further

---

[289] Descartes. Fifth Set of Replies, AT VII 364; Princ. I 11, AT VIIIA 8-9. To note, an immediate consequence for physics of the Cartesian notion of matter is the impossibility of the vacuum. In rejecting the very notion of the vacuum as self-contradictory, Descartes appears to follow Aristotle, who denies the void as either only a privation (*sterēsis*), or non-being (*mē on*), or a place where nothing is (Phys. 213a 12 sqq.). The reasons for denying the possibility of the void are, however, very different for both thinkers. Aristotle mainly proves the impossibility of void from various absurdities and contradictions for movements of bodies in a vacuum. But Descartes has a completely different theory of motion based on the notion of inertia and does not thus require the notions of a mover, moving thing and a medium for movement. The argument for the non-existence of the void from movement does not play any important role in Descartes (cp. however To Mersenne, 15 November 1638, AT II 440). Descartes' main reason is much more evident and simple: "void" extension is substance, and, therefore, not nothing, that is, "the existence of vacuum involves a contradiction, because we have the same idea of matter as we have of space" (To [the Marquess of Newcastle], October 1645, AT IV 329; cp. Princ. II 16, AT VIIIA 50). The imperceivable matter is called *matiere subtile*, which we do not immediately apprehend, but which still has the same extensional substantiality as perceivable bodily matter. Thus, if one makes a thought experiment and imagines that the air has been removed from a certain place (a room or vessel), the result would be that the walls of the room (or of the vessel, for example) would have immediately joined each other, for there would have been no matter left—that is, no extension between them (To Plempius for Fromondus, 3 October 1637, AT I 417; To Mersenne, 9 January 1639, AT II 482).

[290] Cp. Aristotle. Anal. Post. 92b 4 sqq. See also: MacIntyre 1967, 58-62; Wippel 1982, 385 sqq.

[291] Zubiri 1980, 51. See also: Owens 1963, 140-143; Irwin 1988, 211 sqq.; Witt 1989, 101 sqq. Cp. Locke. Essay, Bk. III, ch. III, § 15. The distinction between essence and existence is also common in scholasticism, in particular, it is maintained by Aquinas (De ente et essentia 5), Eckhart (Opus Tripartitum, Prologue), Nicholas of Cusa (De coniecturis I 5), Suarez (Disp. met. XXXI. 1 sqq.) and others. Cp. Gilson 1979, 103-106; Copleston 1990, 280, 318. One might also make further distinctions here, for example, of the existential sense of the 'is': (1) as applied to a general notion or universal ("number is") and (2) as applied to a particular ("this book is"). In the essential sense, one may further distinguish (1.1) the definitional usage of the 'is' in the case of a general notion ("a flower is a plant"); (1.2.) the tautological usage of the "is" in the case of a general notion ("a tree is a tree"); (2.1.) the definitional usage in the case of a particular ((a) "this flower is a plant"; (b) "this

distinguished into essential and accidental). In Aristotle, however, essence is considered only a moment of substance. Only natural entities, *physei onta*, have essence, only they are considered substances as proper subjects of predication. Of those predicates some are expressed by *logos* or definition as disclosing the subject as it is in itself, *kath' hayto* (i.e., essentially), and some show the subject in a number of accidental properties, *kata symbebēkos*.[292] The essence/ existence distinction is taken not as *physei*—not as a real difference within a thing, for a thing is not a "sum" of essence and existence—but only in the way of expression or predication, *legomenon*, as mental distinction. Historically, only toward the end of the fourteenth century and culminating in Descartes does essence become separate from substance and opposed to existence. This is due to the idea of the creation of all things, material bodies and thinking souls, so that they have their existence only because, and insofar as, they are subsumed to divine causation. In fact, the *res*, as Descartes uses it, is much closer to the notion of essence than to that of substance, because, in the case of finite substance, be it mind or matter, the notion of *res* mainly expresses the "what" it is. If essence is considered as not really separate from substance, as is the case in Aristotle, then essence is the correlate of the definition of a thing not only as conceived in the mind, but as real, as *to ti ēn einai*.[293] If, on the other hand, essence is taken in its opposition to existence, as merely a "notion" that refers to thinking or conceiving, as opposed to the reality of a thing, then, as it will be argued, essence is taken as a concept, which may be further distinguished into formal and objective.

An immediate consequence of the essence-existence distinction is that every definite particular thing has its essence, while it might not necessarily exist. Existence, however, is not considered just an accident of essence—essence has being through the act of existence. In other words, in the finite (created) substances and things, essence does not necessarily presuppose existence. But is there a case where existence is, or might be, considered necessary? Is there any instance where essence necessarily presupposes existence (i.e., is there anything that is not able not to exist)? The only instance where essence and existence are identical is the infinite substance, or substance in the proper sense—God; it is only God who necessarily exists of himself and because of himself, who is *actus purus*.[294] Only God's essence consists solely in being. Such a conclusion, fundamental for medieval Aristotelian theology, does not hold in the Platonic account, because the first principle is considered not as pure being but as the source of being, which is not being itself. It should be noted, however, that the essence that consists solely in being—i.e., that is *esse*, existence *per se*—is not a "being-of" some thing and therefore cannot be thought, because it has no other definitive specifications, except for just "to be", but not "be something", and hence it is nothing. Thus, pure being *is*, but is unthinkable in *what* it is.

---

flower is flower" (as genus)) and (2.2) the tautological usage of a particular ("this tree is this tree").

[292] Cp. Aristotle. Met. 1025a 30-32; Top. 102b 4-7.
[293] Aristotle. Met. 1029b 11 sqq.
[294] Cp. Thomas Aquinas. Summa theol. I, qu. 3, art. 1-3.

In a sense, Descartes does not even really need the aforementioned notion of substance: the weight of the distinction lies rather in the difference between the not created or infinite substance (which does not need anything besides itself) and the created or finite one. Following the Thomistic distinction, Descartes might argue that in the created finite substances essence is different from existence, since it is possible to conceive an essence of something (for instance, of a book or of a horse) without necessarily presupposing that it exists at the same time; the only instance in which essence is not different from existence is God, for his essence is to be.[295] Yet since the notion of substance is not univocal; the truth that it belongs to the essence of God to exist does not follow for Descartes from the fact that God is substance. It is not the objectivity of substance but human subjectivity that secures the truth "God does necessarily exist" or "subsistence of the infinite substance is necessary".

The *essentia-existentia* distinction is wholeheartedly supported by Descartes, for whom divine essence necessarily contains existence (i.e., God cannot not exist). [296] For any system of modal logic, "not possible not to" is identical to "necessary", $\sim \Diamond \sim p = \Box p$. In other words, there is no real distinction in God between essence and existence, because he is the only substance that exists due to itself. No real distinction can then also be traced between essence and perfection, essence and infinity, essence and power.[297] On various occasions Descartes uses "the regular theological idiom" that "it belongs to God's essence to exist" and that "apart from God, there is nothing else of which I am capable of thinking such that existence belongs to its essence".[298]

For Descartes, not only thought, but also extension or matter represent being or substance. But why does matter exist not necessarily, or why does matter's essence not include existence? An obvious answer would be that since the infinite substance is pure thinking and thought, and thought is complementary to extension, the infinite substance is not extended. And since, further, it is only in the infinite substance that existence belongs to essence, matter does not necessarily exist. Matter, on this account, is substance in a limited sense, as dependent in its existence on *the* substance, which solely necessarily includes existence into essence. One might consider Spinoza's inclusion of matter as extension into the unique substance or God as an attempt to overcome this difficulty. Then, it is not thinking *qua* substance that exists necessarily, but only thinking *qua infinite*, that thinking whose essence necessarily includes existence. Only the existence of finite (or created) substances, whose essence does not necessarily presuppose existence, or whose existence is contingent, depends wholly on the concurrence of the infinite

---

[295] Cp. also Spinoza. Ethics Part I, Props. 7, 24.
[296] Descartes uses this principle stating that "it is not possible that God does not exist, since existence is contained in the concept of God—and not just possible or contingent existence, as in the ideas of all other things, but absolutely necessary and actual existence".-Comments on a Certain Broadsheet, AT VIIIB 361.
[297] Descartes. To More, 15 April 1649, AT V 343.
[298] Descartes. Med. V, AT VII 68-69. The French version of the "Meditations" stresses that existence *necessarily* belongs to the divine essence. Cp. Fifth Set of Replies, AT VII 369; Hyperaspistes, August 1641, AT III 433.

substance. For this reason, the notion of essence cannot univocally belong both to the infinite substance and to finite substances.[299] That is why Descartes has to specify in the second set of replies to the "Meditations" that "we notice that necessary existence is contained in our concept of God (*however inadequate that concept may be*)".[300] Even if we, *qua* finite thinking substance, have an adequate conception of the infinite substance, we cannot escape the conclusion that the existence of this infinite substance is necessary and not merely contingent or accidental.

One might make two further observations at this point. The first is that the notions of essence and existence, even if not directly derived from, are always exemplified by language use. This is stressed by Ockham, who presents the difference between essence and existence as that between two *vocabula*, a noun (*res*) and a verb (*esse*): the one (essence) signifies as a noun (*nominaliter*), the other (existence) as a verb (*verbaliter*).[301] The second observation is that mathematicians, as Arnauld mentions, following Aristotle, have to consider essence only, and not existence.[302] The definition of a finite thing clarifies its essence but not its existence.[303] This is also true in cases that involve objects of scientific knowledge, whose essence still can be defined even if they are not actually present *qua* existent.

Comparing Plotinus and Descartes in regards to the essence-existence distinction, we can say that for Plotinus (and for Plato) it is only in the real being or intellect that essence is not really distinct from existence: thinking and being are the same (see 3.1.1). The first principle in henology is, however, beyond being and is not accessible for intellection of any kind—it is outside existence and, strictly speaking, does not have an essence. And matter has neither existence nor essence and is not a substance at all. For Descartes, who supports the ontological approach, on the contrary, the principle and cause of finite substance and of every thing is pure being, in which essence necessarily implies existence. What is beyond the grasp of the human finite mind (whose essence does not already include existence), is not the beyond-being, but the infinite (see 1.3.3). And matter is a finite substance whose existence is accidental to it (because matter is or exists only insofar as it is constantly recreated by the necessarily existing substance), and whose essence is to be extension, in which bodies may be considered as geometrically expressed entities.

---

[299] As Descartes writes, "existence is contained in the idea or concept of every single thing, since we cannot conceive of anything except as existing. Possible or contingent existence is contained in the concept of a limited thing, whereas necessary and perfect existence is contained in the concept of a supremely perfect being", Second Set of Replies, AT VII 165-166; cp. First Set of Replies, AT VII 118; Sixth Set of Replies, AT VII 433.
[300] Descartes. Second Set of Replies, AT VII 152; italics added.
[301] Ockham. Summa logicae III, 2, ch. 27 ("*Utrum esse rei et essentia rei sint duo extra animam distincta inter se*"). Cp. Plato. Soph. 261d-262e. Ockham does not, however, recognize a real distinction between essence and existence.
[302] Fourth Set of Objections, AT VII 212 sqq.
[303] Aristotle. Met. 1030b 14 sqq., Anal. Post. 72a 18-24; 76b 7 sqq. " A definition is a phrase (saying) indicating the essence of something, *esti d' horos men logos ho to ti ēn einai sēmainōn*" - Top. 101b 37-102a 17. Cp. Barnes 1993, 100-101; Szabó 1994, 355-356.

The existence of a finite thing is that "counterpart" of it in the essence/ existence distinction that is individual and contingent. Therefore, knowledge and thinking of universal (i.e., not contingent) truths must start for Descartes not with existence (*an est*), but with essence (*quid est*).[304] It does not mean, however, that existence is of no concern for Descartes. Existence is the realm of the divine providence, of constant care and of recreative support. Finite existence is produced by God and is that which makes essence real or "embodied". But Descartes is more interested in the study of the essence of existence. For this reason, his position may be called essentialism. Essence is essence of a thing that either does exist or can exist. Since essence, even if it shows a really existing thing, does not necessarily entail existence but remains in the realm of concepts or "ideas", essence, as it is known to and by the finite mind, is primarily connected with potentiality or possibility. It is not by chance that contemporary philosophy, which owes much to Descartes, abandons to a great extent the consideration of necessary existence and is more interested in possibility, in possible worlds, in modal logic, and so on. Since a finite thing as a substance may have an essence without really existing, to know a thing, is to know it as necessary only in its essence (e.g., mathematical entities), and not in its existence. That is why even if essence is referred to as potential existence, it is known as necessary in its concept.[305] Such knowledge is firm and sure, and its paradigmatic example is the conception of mathematical objects. Even if both necessary essence and contingent existence of a thing are supposed to be produced by the infinite essence of God, this essence of a finite thing "is nothing other than eternal truths" and therefore has to precede existence.[306]

What does guarantee then that in the last instance the cognition of essences is neither futile nor just invented by the finite mind? The warrant can only be the unique essence in which existence is necessarily included: God, who conceives all things in their essences from eternity, who supports these things in existence by (re)creating them and who, by providing the *lumen naturale* to the finite mind, makes the cognition certain, excluding any error.[307]

The connection of essence and existence is then established by the principle that the essence which is clearly and distinctly perceived, may be also brought into existence by God.[308] Put otherwise, the link between essence and

---

[304] Descartes. First Set of Replies, AT VII 108.
[305] Such a potentiality of existence is not a probability, although the idea that probability may represent strict knowledge arises for the first time in early modernity, as, for example, in Pascal's elaboration of the theory of probability.
[306] Descartes. To [Mersenne], 27 May 1630, AT I, 152. Later Descartes contends that "we do indeed understand the essence of a thing in one way when we consider it in abstraction from whether it exists or not, and in a different way when we consider it as existing; but the thing itself cannot be outside our thought without its existence", To ***, 1645 or 1646, AT IV 349. He does not explain, however, what constitutes this difference. The distinction remains obsolete, a part of a confused discussion, as Descartes himself recognizes (Ibid., AT IV 350).
[307] Descartes. Med. IV, AT VII 58.
[308] As Descartes says, "It seems very clear to me that possible existence is contained in everything which we clearly understand, because from the fact that we clearly understand

existence in the case of finite substances is ontologically secured by the infinite thinking, but epistemologically—by the finite one. Such a structure, first, allows Descartes to prove the existence of God from the mere act of *cogito*, where the *cogito* is itself secured in its thinking (i.e., in its essence and existence) by God. This kind of circle is not a logical one, for the first in the order of knowing (essence) is not necessarily the first in the order of being (existence). And second, the claim that Descartes' metaphysics is epistemology *par excellence* is too much a simplification, for his metaphysics starts with knowing God and soul through the *ego*, but the very possibility and essence of the *ego* is secured by the necessary existence of that which is sought to be proven.[309]

Now, what does Descartes' essentialism have to do with the notion of matter? For Descartes, as for most contemporary philosophers, artificial (or human-made) bodily things have essence exactly in the same way as natural (or God-made) things. There is no sufficient ground for distinguishing them, since both artificial and natural things are finite and are thought to have essence as *made* or *produced* (see 3.4.1). Making or producing a thing according to its pattern gives a thing its existence. The only difference between natural and artificial might be that for natural things the pattern has to preexist in the infinite mind, whereas for artificial things—in the finite mind. The distinction between *tekhnē*, which constructs the artifacts, and *epistēmē*, which knows *physis* or natural facts—that which cannot be otherwise—thus becomes obsolete.[310] For this reason, the whole of the extended physical or bodily world might be considered produced, or at least reproduced in the imagination. There is no need for "real" existence—only an *as if*-existence, imaginable and imaginary. If this is the case, then existence, as contingent, may not be preserved through different mental operations involved in cognition. Existence could be mentally (imaginary) recreated. Since it is the necessity of essence, and not the contingency of existence, that is known and is the content of truth, essence is the ontological and epistemological ground of the truth of all things and, therefore, it is only the essence of things and finite substances (both of *res extensa* and of *res cogitans*) that are then invariant in all possible transformations of things.

---

something it follows that it can be created by God," To Mersenne, 31 December 1640, AT III 273-274; cp. Med. V, AT VII 70; Med. VI, AT VII 78; Fourth Set of Objections, AT VII 219. "For when we come to know God, we are certain that he can bring about anything of which we have a distinct understanding", Princ. I 60, AT VIIIA 28.

[309] "And when I consider the fact that I have doubts, or that I am a thing that is incomplete and dependent, then there arises in me a clear and distinct idea of a being who is independent, that is, an idea of God. And from the mere fact that there is such an idea within me, or that I who possess this idea exist, I clearly infer that God also exists, and that every single moment of my entire existence depends on him." – Descartes. Med. IV, AT VII 53.

[310] Cp. Nikulin 1996, 64-67.

PART II
INTELLIGIBLE MATTER AND GEOMETRY

2.1 Geometry, arithmetic and physics in antiquity

Mathematics for the ancient Weltanschauung is an example of science that exercises an utmost precision of knowledge-*epistēmē* about that which cannot be otherwise.[1] In mathematics, arithmetic is distinguished from geometry. In various classifications geometry comes second to arithmetic, because, rather than considering merely the thinkable number, geometry considers the figure, which (even if unchangeable in its properties) is not only thinkable but also quasi-corporeal as extended.[2] Put otherwise, the subject matter of geometry displays less precision than that of arithmetic, and the more precise is better known.[3] As the fundamental ontological structure and the pattern of being, number is a matter of great importance in the Academy, as well as in the later Pythagoreans and Neoplatonists.[4] Number is taken as the pattern by which being is both constituted and considered; number exists separately from things and can therefore only be thought—this is why knowledge-*epistēmē* is based on number and structured by it.[5]

Indeed, numbers reveal some remarkable properties that, once established, are forever valid. Thus, for instance, in 1909 David Hilbert proved that for every integer n there exists an integer m such that every integer is a sum of m n-th powers, which is a generalization of a 1770 hypothesis of Edward Waring: namely, that each positive integer is a sum of 9 cubes ($n=3$, $m=9$) and of 19 fourth powers ($n=4$, $m=19$).[6] This noteworthy result presents a remarkable constancy and immutability in and of numbers, which makes them the best representatives of being as that which does not change. Mathematics is, in turn, different from physics insofar as the subject matter of the former is not found in the world of becoming. Mathematics has to do with the *mathēmata*—objects of strict

---

[1] Cp. Aristotle. Met. 1026a 6 sqq.; 1064b 1-10; Anatolius. Ap. Heron. Def. 164.9-18. Mathematics in particular, as arithmetic, differs from the logistic as a practical art of counting and solving mathematical problems (this difference is especially stressed by Plato and the Neoplatonists). See: Klein 1968, 10-25; Gaidenko 1980, 18-20; Fowler 1987, 108-117. According to Plutarch, Archimedes regarded mathematics an incomparably more dignified science than any of its applications, of which he did not condescend to write about. - Plutarch. Vita Marcelli 14.4; 17.4.
[2] Archytas. Thesleff 1965, 6.12-15; Proclus. In Eucl. 35.21 sqq.
[3] Cp. Plato. Meno 81a sqq.; Phaedo 73a-77b; Phil. 56c sqq.; Aristotle. Anal. Post. 87a 31-37; Met. 1078a 28-30; Themistius. In de an.12. 10-12. 27. See also: Fowler 1987, 8-25; Englisch 1994, 91-96.
[4] Plato. Phil 16c-19a; Phaedo 101c-106b; Aristotle. Met. 1080a 14 sqq.; frg. 2, Peri thagatoy, Ross = Alexander Aphrod. In Met. 55.20 sqq.; Theophrastus. Met. 6a 15-6b 17; Simplicius. In Phys. 453.25-454.19. Cp. A. Wilson 1995, 367-387.
[5] Philolaos B4, B11 DK; Plato. Theaet. 185c-d, 195c-196b.
[6] Another example is Vinogradov's estimation of the number I_N of the representations of a positive odd number N as a sum of three primes: $N=p_1+p_2+p_3$, given by the expression: $I_N=RS+O(N^2 n^{-c})$, where $A=O(B)$ denotes that the ratio $|A|/B$ does not exceed a certain constant, $n=\ln N$; h and c are arbitrary constants bigger than 3; $R=N^2(1+8)/(2n^3)$ where lim $8=0$ when $N\to\infty$; $t=Nn^{-3h}$, $0<a\leq q$; $0<q\leq t$; $(a,q)=1$; $p=f(q)$; and for $q=1$ to ∞: $S=\Gamma:(q)/p^3 \Gamma e^{2\pi i(a/q)N}$ (Vinogradov 1985, 129-132; cp. 101-123).

knowledge that, once discovered, may be not only systematically structured but also taught.

But is it at all possible to apply mathematics to the study of physical objects? Plato unequivocally denies any possibility of such an application because of the mentioned rigid distinction between the stable being exemplified in numbers (and, to a lesser degree, in geometricals, which are already connected with movement (see 3.4.3-3.4.5)) and becoming, which is represented in physical things.[7] And even if in the "Timaeus" Plato develops a physical theory based on a consideration of four elements (i.e., physical elementary bodies, which themselves are taken as regular geometrical bodies), he, first, presents his theory as a just *mythos*, as a *possible* and *probable* account of the constitution of things (*eikos*, 48d).[8] Second, only the elements themselves (fire, air, water and earth) are constituted *qua* geometrical; the geometrical itself is not grounded in any possible experience but rather is postulated. All other physical objects are constituted by elements as their primary compounds. But bodies are *not* already geometrical and their structure and pattern of behavior cannot be mathematically or geometrically described, because combinations of primary bodies (i.e., of elements) produces an infinite multitude of things (*poikilia apeira*, 57d), the subject matter of mere opinion or probable account. A possible exception can only be the regular (circular) movement of stars; stars, however, represent gods and are bodies of a special kind. And third, what is never explained by Plato is why and how ideal geometrical entities—triangles of two kinds—constitute the properly physical characteristics in elements, not accountable in terms of pure geometry (e.g., weight).

Aristotle develops his physics as a strict but not mathematical science, structured not numerically but qualitatively. Every physical object on this account may be taken as the primary substance considered as a subject with a variety of predicates and a number of properties. When properties are abstracted from their subject, they may be arranged and studied analytically, by means of logic. In his critique of the Platonic account of number in the Met. M Aristotle's aim is to challenge the Platonic notion of the independence and precedence of number *qua* being from and to physical things. Aristotle's alternative is to accept the mere logical precedence of number. For that reason, he has to concede that the general propositions of mathematics may be applicable to physical things not *qua* physical but only insofar as they are magnitudes, only insofar as they are movable subjects with certain predicates that may be subjects of syllogism, calculation and representation in a geometrical scheme.[9] Physical objects themselves, however, cannot be properly studied by means of mathematics—they cannot themselves be *mathēmata*. In order to become objects of a strict science, physical things should

---

[7] Cp. *ho men arithmos hestōtōn, to de megethos en kinēsei*, "number is of static things, but magnitude is in movement". - Plotinus. Enn. VI.2.13.30. It is interesting to note that even the contemporary theory of numbers, a very developed and sophisticated theory, finds almost no applications in physics (see: Manin 1981, 98-99).

[8] Plato. Tim. 47e-61c.

[9] See: Aristotle. Met. 1077b 18-23; 1078a 14-17; Phys. 231b 19 sqq. Cp. Dijksterhuis 1961, 68-72.

therefore cease to be physical things: they should be lost *qua* physical and be substituted by objects that represent properties abstracted from the physical things—by their geometrical representatives. Only thought in (or, rather, into) a geometrical object, may these properties be studied mathematically.

Aristotle's operation of abstraction (*aphairein* or separation, *khōrizein*) involved in the substitution of a physical thing by a geometrical entity[10] is, however, not itself completely univocal and for that reason the legitimacy of abstraction may be called into doubt. First, it appears to refer not to the thinking of the intellect or physical perception, but to discursive thinking and especially to imagination (for more details see 3.1.1; 3.1.2; 3.2.1). Second, Frege's critique of abstraction is applicable to Aristotle's consideration. When abstracting, discursive reason (or imagination) obtains "from each object a *something* wholly deprived of content; but the *something* obtained from one object is different from the *something* obtained from another object—though it is not easy to say how".[11] In his critique of the Platonic approach, Aristotle does not provide a definitive answer to the above two difficulties; thus, the ontological status of the relation of abstracted properties or qualities as mediating between physicals and geometricals remains unclear. It is clear, however, that the abstracted mental (imaginable) substitutions of physical entities are themselves *not* physical things and that ontologically they need not have anything in common with physical objects, except for being extended and having a certain shape. But one cannot ignore the fundamental fact that a physical surface can never be measured with absolute precision, whereas a geometrical surface can be measured precisely. Obviously, there might be different theoretical accounts of this fundamental distinction. In spite of his criticism, Aristotle takes a way that turns out to be fundamentally compatible with the Platonic treatment of mathematical (arithmetical and geometrical) and physical objects, a way that later is followed and substantially developed by Proclus—namely, the consideration of geometrical objects as connected with, and immersed in, a different (not physical) spatiality or materiality.

2.1.1 Foundations of arithmetic in Plotinus

Plotinus' treatise VI.6 [34] "On Numbers" (*Peri arithmōn*) of the Enneads is dedicated to considering the place and the ontological status of number in the whole structure of being and thinking, number as mediating between the original unity of the One and the multiplicity of the infinite. Plotinus dedicates the Enn. V.5.4-5 (a part of the "Großschrift", Enn. III.8; V.8; V.5; II.9), which immediately precedes the Enn. VI.6, to the consideration of the One in its relation to number, outlining the main questions on the structure of the number, as if postponing their solution to a later point.

In the Enn. VI.6 we do not find, however, any discussion specially dedicated to the problem of the constitution of number as such. The question remains explicitly unresolved: Plotinus does not address it in either the Enn. V.5 or

---

[10] Aristotle. Phys. 193b 31sqq. Cp. Simplicius. In Phys. 290.27-30.
[11] Frege 1967, 85.

in VI.6, thus leaving the problem without a definitive answer. Here we will attempt to reconstruct the constitution, derivation and construction of number in Plotinus in its various representations, referring to the hints Plotinus provides in his texts. The "foundations of arithmetic" are understood in the Fregean sense, as a comprehensive study of number in its different aspects and in its specific constitution *qua* number.[12]

Plotinus discerns between what he calls essential or substantial number (*oysiōdēs arithmos*) and quantitative or monadic number (*monadikos, toy posoy*).[13] In this distinction Plotinus follows Plato, who, in his later years (as reported by Aristotle and later Greek authors) made a distinction between the so-called "ideal" and "mathematical" numbers and was even inclined to reduce the forms-*eidē* to ideal numbers.[14] The quantitative number is the image (*eidōlon*) of the essential number through participation (*metokhē, metalēpsis*).[15] The quantitative number is that which provides quantity (i.e., is that by which things are numbered and counted). The essential number always provides existence (*ho to einai aei parekhōn*).[16] In the act of numbering, the quantitative number constitutes quantity in the numbered as the realization or actualization of the essential number. Krämer and Szlezák point out that the distinction between these two types of number comes back to Plato and the early Academic discussions, traces of which are preserved in Aristotle's criticism of ideal (essential) and mathematical (quantitative) numbers in Met. M 6-9.[17]

Essential number in Plotinus is introduced as contemplated primarily in or "over" (*epitheōroymenos*) the forms-*eidē*.[18] In order to fit the essential number, as the ordering principle, into the structure of being, Plotinus has to split being (*oysia, to einai*) into being proper (*on*) and beings (*onta*) (i.e., to discern between being as

---

[12] Frege 1986, 66 sqq. Plotinus himself uses the term *arithmetikē* quite rarely, in Enn. VI.3.16.20; I.3.6.3 and III.1.3.26, when referring to the science of numbers within the Pythagorean distinction of various sciences.
[13] Plotinus. Enn. V.5.4.17 sqq.; VI.6.9.34-35; 16.26; cp. VI.6.10.25 sqq. and commentary of R. Beutler and W. Theiler *ad loc.*: Plotinus 1956 (1964), III 450-451. The term *oysiōdēs* is used neither by Plato nor by Aristotle, cp. Plotinus 1980, 199. See also a detailed and precise exposition of Plotinus' number theory in: Horn 1995, 149 sqq. and the distinction of the "epitheoretical" (existing due only to the activity of our thinking) and "accidental" numbers (Ibid., 201-220). Cp. Trouillard 1983, 227-234.
[14] This distinction is, however, rejected by Xenocrates, cp. Aristotle. Met.1080b 11-14; 1083b 1-2; 1090b 32 sqq.; Syrianus. In Met. 186.30-36. Cp. Aristotle. Met. 1083a 17-20; 1090a 3-6; frg. 11, Peri philosophias, Ross = Syrianus. In Met. 159.33-160.5; frg. 4 Peri ideon, Ross = Alexander Aphrod. In Met. 85.18 sqq. See also: Wedberg 1955, 64-84, 116-122; Annas 1976, 62-73. Cp. Burkert 1972, 15-28.
[15] Plotinus. Enn. V.5.4.3; V.5.5.11-12.
[16] Plotinus. Enn. V.5.4.18.
[17] Cp. Aristotle. Met. 987b 22; 1080a 12 sqq.; Phys. 209b 34; Test. Plat.56-65 Gaiser. See also: Krämer 1964, 305 sqq.; Th. A. Szlezák 1979, 90 sqq.; Cleary 1995, 346-365. For Aristotle, who in his usage follows Plato, Xenocrates and Speusippus, essential number coincides with the ideal (*eidētikos*) and quantitative number with the mathematical. Cp. Syrianus. In Met. 45.33-46.6 and commentary to: Plotinus 1980, 170-171.
[18] Plotinus. Enn. VI.6.9.35-36.

one and as many).[19] This distinction is not, however, itself the real one, for being remains a synthetic conjunction of the dual unity of *hen-on* or *hen-polla*, which appears as the structure of all-unity within *noys* (*homoy en heni panta*).[20] Plotinus faces the choice of presenting the being of *noys* either as the duality of thinking-*noēsis*, which thinks itself as thought-*noēta*, or as the triad of being, intellect and life.[21] The difficulty that arises here is how to understand the being-beings distinction. Thus, in the case of the *noēsis-noēta* division, the former appears to be the *on*, while the latter seems to represent the *onta*. On the other hand, the being-*on* is prior to the intellect-*noys* and the thinking-*noēsis* is already a multiplicity bound into a unity, the *hen on* of the second hypothesis of the "Parmenides". Now, in the triad of being, intellect and life *qua* living being, the last term represents the *cosmos noētos* of all the forms in which the intellect fulfills its being—it thinks itself as the *noēta*.[22] Since, however, every object of thought, *noēton*, is an instance of being, life as the living being has to be identified with the *onta*. But if the beings-*onta* represent the aspect of multiplicity within the *noēsis*, they have to be identified either with the intellect *qua* thinking or even with being, because *noēsis* represents being as the first produced by and after the One.

Comparing the *on-onta* and the *on-noys-zōion* partition schemes, one might argue that the *onta* are represented as *noys* in the activity and actuality of thinking thinking itself[23] and thus split into the numerical multiplicity of the *zōion*. Plotinus seems to be aware of the difficulty of establishing a direct correspondence between ontological systems based on double and triple distinctions (into which the notion of number then has to be inscribed). He does not explicitly resolve the difficulty, even if he does provide some hints, in particular, by introducing the distinction of four terms (*on-onta-noys-zōion*, which he states in the form of the rhetorical question) that might resolve the problem of making a correspondence between the two- and the three-term ontological systems into a sort of synthesis of the two and the three in the four.[24] Such a task would be important (although it is a subject of special discussion) both from the systematic and from the exegetic points of view. The dyad of the opposed principles is mainly used by Plato, whereas the triad of the principles (where one mediates the other two) is employed by Aristotle (although Plato is aware of the possibility of mediation between the opposites).[25]

Plotinus formulates four hypotheses of possible relations between number and the forms-*eidē*: the former may be either after, together with, or independent of, the latter. In the last case number may be also conceived either before or after

---

[19] Plotinus. Enn. V.5.5.22.
[20] Enn. VI.6.7.4; cp. Anaxagoras B1. See also Parm. 143a, 144e. Cp. also Wagner 1985, 280-285; Halfwassen 1992, 56-57.
[21] Plotinus. Enn. V.1.4.30-34; V.9.7.6 sqq.; VI.6.8.15-22; 9.27-31; 15.2-3; 18.31-33; III.9.6. The term "life" comes back to Plato's Tim. 30c-31b, 39e and Soph. 248e-249a. Cp. Hadot 1960, 105-141.
[22] Cp. Plotinus. Enn. V.9.9.1-8 et al. Cp. Plato. Tim. 39e. On the historical background of the term '*cosmos noētos*' in Plotinus see: Runia 1999, 165-168.
[23] *Noēsis* is considered as the actuality of the *noys*, Plotinus. Enn. V.4.2.3-4; cp. 3.1.1.
[24] Plotinus. Enn. VI.6.9.29-31.
[25] Cp. Test. Plat. 44a Gaiser.

the forms.[26] Plotinus argues (not without a certain ambiguity) in favor of the independence of (essential) number as existing before beings and forms: number is already present in the intellect and in the living being as the principle of being itself.[27] Thus, if we stage a thought experiment in which we create something, we have to know precisely beforehand how many things are to be produced. In this way, number has to precede beings.[28] As the structuring and already structured principle, number is inseparable from being, which is split by thinking-*noēsis* into the united multiplicity of life according to essential number, the living being, which itself is a collection of archetypes, forms-*eidē*, or the cosmos of intelligible objects-*noēta* (in the Enn. VI.6.15.16 number is qualified as *noy energeiai*). In the Enn. VI.6.8 Plotinus changes the hierarchical being-life-intellect order of the Enn. III.9.1 to being-intellect-life. This is already noticed by Proclus, who resolves the difficulty by referring life to two different intellects: the higher one and the lower one.[29] This is present in a rather complicated system of hypostases, absent in Plotinus.[30] I would, however, argue that the order of being-intellect-life should be preserved. Within the one-being, the unity, the image of the One, is the ontological precondition of the possibility of being-*on*, because being cannot be thought or considered as not one. Furthermore, being-*on* is itself the ontological precondition of the possibility of thinking-*noēsis*. In order to think at all, thinking primarily has to be; thinking is the precondition of the possibility of life. Life as the cosmos of beings or intelligible objects-*noēta* needs to presuppose thinking, which thinks itself in and as these particular forms. In other words, even before something is thought as a noetic object-*noēton*, there should be an act of thinking, *noēsis*. Before the act of thinking there should simply *be* something—the *on*. Before being there should be unity; without unity being is impossible.[31] The order of being-life-intellect may be then preserved only in the sense that life mediates being and thinking—thinking as one-being is realized in the plurality of the objects of thought—in the living being.

The *logos* or the proportional relation between various representations of being is therefore established in the following way: unity relates to being as (essential) number to beings, or, unity relates to (essential) number as being to beings.[32] Essential number is then said to be *in* (*en*) being, *with* (*meta*) being and *before* (*pro*) the being*s* which have their foundation, source, root and principle (*basis, pēgē, rhiza, arkhē*) in the essential number, while the principle of being

---

[26] Plotinus. Enn. VI.6.4.1 sqq.
[27] Plotinus. Enn. VI.6.9.38 sqq.; *to de on genomenon arithmos*, VI.6.15.29 et sqq. Cp. Sextus Empiricus. Adv. Math. X 258; Krämer 1964, 301-302; Pépin 1979, 199-200. Proclus misunderstands VI.6.9.23-24 when he concludes "*to prōtiston on pro tōn arithmōn*", Theol. Plat. I 50.15-19.
[28] Cp. Plotinus. Enn. VI.6.9.14 sqq.
[29] Proclus. In Tim. I 427.6-20.
[30] Cp. Henry 1938, 228.
[31] Cp. *oyden gar on, ho mē hen*, Plotinus. Enn. VI.6.13.50-51.
[32] Plotinus. Enn. VI.6.9.29; 39-40. Cp. Plotinus 1980, 74, 186.

itself is the One, which is the source of being, and is transcendent to being.[33] The essential number, which exists in and with being, and is before intellect and life, only becomes fully developed and expressed in all of its powers on the level of life.[34] In Krämer's concise formulation, the second hypostasis of Plotinus in its triple unity is nothing else but (essential) number thinking itself.[35]

Plotinus begins his consideration of number by implicitly accepting the following fundamental Platonic postulates: first, the absolute superiority of the producing unconditioned unity of the One to the indefinite unlimitedness of non-being and, second, the one-being as soaring between the One and the absolute unlimited privation of unity and being. This enables Plotinus to present a row of oppositions where the first element in every pair is ontologically and axiologically prior to the second one, the former being "closer" to unity, participating in a higher degree in the unique principle of being that itself is beyond being. The latter stands further from it, in its multiplicity and dissipation, tending to the absolute non-being, destitute of any productive capacity. In relation to being (usually considered as the second hypostasis), opposites are to be considered contraries. But related to the One and to the absolute privative non-being, opposites are not contraries, because neither the One nor the *mē on* are subjects of which anything may be properly predicated. The "Pythagorean" opposites are thus the one-unity itself, the truly and really one, which is beautiful, possesses itself and does not participate in the many, as opposed to the many participating in the unique one, the other that stays away or falls away from the unity, the pure "outside", base and disorderly, present as matter and the unlimited.[36]

The problem of the constitution of number arises then as an important and legitimate question for Plotinus; a question that is tightly connected with the constitution of being as thinking. Since number as constitutive for being mediates between unity and multiplicity,[37] number itself should be brought forward by unity and multiplicity. But how? Plotinus does not give a direct answer to the question but gives a number of indirect indications and provides a henological and ontological system within which the problem of the constitution of number can be solved.

In the Enn. V.5.4.20 sqq. Plotinus further requires that the following be postulated.
(a) Before being there "is" the One as the principle of number and being, the "bare One", *hen psilon*.[38]

---

[33] Plotinus. Enn. VI.6.9.36-39. On the "metaphysics of prepositions" cp. Plotinus. Enn. VI.6.18.17-19; Proclus. Theol. Plat. II 60.22-61.9 and the commentary of H. D. Saffrey and L. G. Westerink *ad loc.* (p. 117); Simplicius. In Phys. 10.35-11.3.
[34] Plotinus. Enn. VI.6.15.8 sqq.; VI.6.16.48.
[35] "Sichselbstdenkende Zahl" - Krämer 1964, 304.
[36] Cp.: *hen, alēthōs hen, to mē metokhēi hen, katharōs hen, ontōs hen, oy kath' allo hen, hayto, to endon, ekhei heayto, kalon* as opposed to *ta alla hen, polla onta metokhēi henos hen, oy to katharōs hen, allo, apostasis toy henos, to exō, apollymenon, aiskhrōn, akosmon, hylē, apeira.* - Plotinus. Enn. V.5.4.1 sqq.; VI.6.1.10 sqq. Cp. also: Aristotle. Met. 986a 21 sqq.
[37] Cp. Plotinus. Enn. VI.7.13.9; Plato. Phil. 16c sqq.
[38] Plotinus. Enn. VI.6.11.19.

(b) The essential number is ontologically prior to, and causes the existence of, the quantitative number by participation.
(c) There are two principles that constitute essential numbers, the monad *(monas)* and the dyad *(dyas)*, the former being the principle of sameness, the latter the principle of otherness.
(d) In number, units may be discerned.

First of all, for the sake of clarity and non-ambiguity of argumentation we have to lay out a number of terminological distinctions. In what follows, the One *(hen)* refers to the One as the unique principle of being, which itself is beyond being. The monad *(monas)* refers to the one as the first principle in being; and the henad *(henas)* or unit—to the unity within number. The later Pythagoreans tended to distinguish one-*hen* as an ideal principle from *monas* as a numeric unit.[39] The notion of henad plays an important role in Proclus (who seems to borrow it from Iamblichus), where a number of equal henads represents the first plurality of being after the One.[40] Plotinus himself does not make any strict distinction between these terms, using them rather loosely and interchangeably.[41]

The fundamental problem that arises from postulate (c) is the ontological status of the two principles of number and the way these principles constituted themselves. The monad is to be taken as the first and the simplest undifferentiated unity of being when being is engendered by the One, *ontōs hen*.[42] Such a unity is not different from pure being-*on*, which itself is not different from the yet not determinate thinking-*noēsis*. The one *being* is however already the *one* being, *hen on*, and as such already necessarily presupposes multiplicity, first appearing as a simple dyad, which, together with the monad, constitute the two principles of number and being *within* being.[43]

But how is the dyad constituted? First of all, the essential dyad cannot be said to be a collection of two units for the simple reason that before the dyad, there is no multiplicity or duality. Two different units cannot arise. Therefore, the dyad should be taken as one whole. The dyad may be defined simply as that which is not the monad, the *other* to it. But where does this other come from? How does the *hen on* evolve into *polla onta*? The consecutive acts that engender the dyad may be represented in the following way (the succession here should be understood as logical and ontological and not temporal). When being is brought forward by the

---

[39] Cp. Anon. Photii 237.17 sqq., Thesleff. Cp. Iamblichus. In Nicom. 11.1-26.
[40] Proclus. Elem. theol. 6, 113-165; Theol. Plat. III 11.29-17.12. See also: Dillon 1993, 48-54.
[41] See: Plotinus. Enn. VI.6.4.4; 5.6; 5.37-38; 9.33; 10.3-4; 10.19 *(to hen kata tēn monada)*; 11.16-23; 12.1 *(to hen kai monas)*. Cp. Plato. Phil. 15a; Theon. Expos. rer. math. 21.14-16; *monas, kath' hēn hekaston tōn ontōn hen legetai* - Euclid. Elem. VII, def. 1. See also: Syrianus. In Met. 183.24-25; Proclus. In Parm. IV 880.30-38. Anonymous Photii ascribes to the Pythagoreans the usage of *monas* for the intelligible and *hen*—for numbers (Thesleff 1965, 237.17-19). Here the terms are used in the sense of Iamblichus, for whom *hen* refers to the One productive of being, while *monas*—to the produced (being), *monas ek toy henos*, De myst. VIII 2, 262.3-5. Cp. Frege 1986, 44 sqq.; Dummett 1991, 82-83.
[42] Plotinus. Enn. III.8.9.2-5.
[43] Cp.: *hen on, all' oyk on, eita hen*, Enn. VI.6.13.52-53. See also: Plato. Parm. 142d, 143a, 144e; Pépin 1979, 203-204.

One, there is nothing else in being besides the yet undifferentiated being itself, which is nothing else but the monad, the ideal principle of number. Plotinus argues that logically the monad may be said to be before being, because "one" may be predicated of being and of beings in noetic forms.[44] At the same time, since in the *hen on* conjunction each of the two terms may in turn be considered as subject and the other as predicate, it may also be said that "being" is predicated of the one monad (contrary to Aristotle).[45]

Every act of thinking however, is the thinking of something. Thus, the being, which at first is nothing else but thinking-*noēsis*, strives to grasp that which has produced it (i.e., the One, which, as beyond being, cannot be properly thought). In order that the *noēsis* could be a complete whole able to think itself as complete and completed—that is, as self-thinking—one has to presuppose a sort of movement of and from the being as one and the same. The final definiteness and sameness of the *noys* could be obtained as self-thinking and not as the initial indefinite thinking without objects-*noēta*. As Plotinus puts it, the perfect unity of the monad and that of the One is paralyzed by fear of departing from this unity. Every smallest stirring already brings forward the other and thus the two.[46] The movement away from the unity of the one in being is not, however, proper to the monad as such but appears only in the falling away (*apostasis*) from that unity.[47] Such a movement is teleologically directed towards its end, which is the thinking thinking itself through the forms—the collection of intelligible objects-*noēta*.

The primary movement and the otherness appear thus as inseparable and constitutive of the dyad, whereas rest and sameness characterize the monad.[48] This first movement is then pure otherness-*heterotēs*, which forever separates (*kekhōristhai*) the *noys* from the One.[49] The fundamental principle Plotinus has in mind here is that "everything seeks not another but itself".[50] The pure otherness or bare negativity is therefore nothing else but the essential (ideal) dyad, which enables the thinking to return to itself to its sameness of self-thinking through the otherness of the multitude of intelligible objects. The one simple undifferentiated thinking-*noēsis* sees itself as one in an object of vision and therefore not as one as thinking *and* thought (which then turns out to be triple as that which thinks, that which is thought and the act of thinking itself or the knower, the known and the knowledge, *ho epistēmōn, to epistēton, hē epistēmē*).[51]

---

[44] Plotinus. Enn. VI.6.5.35-38. On predication in Plotinus see: Vigo 1999, 119-127.
[45] Aristotle. Cat. 2a 11-14.
[46] Plotinus. Enn. V.5.4.8-11.
[47] Plotinus. Enn. VI.6.1.2.
[48] Cp. Aristotle. Met 1004b 29: *stasis toy henos, kinēsis de toy plēthoys*; see also 988a 14-15; 992b 7-8; 1066a 7-16; 1084a 35; 1091b 13-1092a 8; Theiler 1964, 106-107; Rist 1971, 77-87. Rist argues that the notion of otherness as movement away from the transcendent One is incompatible with the union of the soul with the One and that Plotinus should have defined otherness as finite being, which he did not do. This argument is not valid, however, in the case of the monad, the dyad and numbers, for while they keep their unity through participation, they do so without ever uniting with the One.
[49] Plotinus. Enn. V.1.6.53; VI.4.11.9-10.
[50] *Hekaston gar oyk allo, all' hayto zētei.* - Plotinus. Enn. VI.6.1.10-11.
[51] Plotinus. Enn. V.4.2.4-7; VI.6.15.20.

Thus, the dyad as pure otherness makes being of the initial thinking-*noēsis* leave its state of sameness and unreflective identity. When *noēsis* necessarily misses the only object worth thinking or seeing (cp. the postulate (a)), the source of thinking and being (i.e., the One, of which it yet has an indefinite image),[52] then thinking can only turn to itself and think itself, since at that point there is nothing else to be thought. Thinking is itself *not other* to itself, *oyk allo*. The "not other" is nothing else but one—it is the monad in being. But the act of constituting the one-monad requires the *other* which is the dyad. The otherness, represented in the form of the indefinite dyad, *aoristos dyas*, is the principle of indefiniteness. The in(de)finite as such is not pure *apeiria*, which by itself is absolutely indefinite (in fact, there is neither "self" nor "itself" in it), and may be said to be embracing opposites and contraries at the same time, to be both moving and at rest, big and small, *mega kai smikron* (cp. the postulate (c)).[53]

Therefore, the constitution of being necessarily has to presuppose *two* principles in being and not only one (the postulate (c)).[54] The second principle, that of the otherness, the dyad, may be said to be posterior to the monad.[55] At the same time, the dyad may be also considered prior to the monad, because the sameness of the monad is first realized as the negation of the otherness, as *oyk allo*.[56] The dyad itself is thus *to allo* and *to heteron*, it is first merely as an indefinite other, *to allo*, but when the monad comes forth, the dyad is the other to it, *to heteron*. It is in this sense that the monad is both prior and posterior to the dyad, although differently.[57]

Constitution of the dyad as the otherness-*heterotēs* that separates being from its origin presupposes then not only the duality of same and other, rest and movement, but involves a more complicated structure of the triplicity through going out, turning back and, finally, staying in unity.[58] In the Enn. V.1 [10] "On

---

[52] Cp. Lloyd 1987, 155-186, *contra* Bussanich 1988, 123-124 and Emilsson 1999, 286-287.
[53] Plotinus. Enn. VI.6.3.28 sqq. Cp. Aristotle. Met. 987b 26; 1089a 35-36; 1091a 3-5; Test. Plat. 22B, 23B, 27B, 30, 48B, 50 Gaiser; Sextus Empiricus. Adv. Math. X 261, 274 sqq. *Aoristos dyas* may be both considered the other, *heteron* (Aristotle. Met. 1087b 26; cp. Plato. Parm. 158c) and multitude, *plēthos* (Aristotle. Met. 1085b 10). Cp. Theiler 1964, 95, 108.
[54] Cp.: *ek de tēs aoristoy dyados kai toy henos ta eidē kai hoi arithmoi: toyto gar ho noys*, V.4.2.6; cp. Merlan 1964, 45-47; Szlezák 1979, 58; Plato. Tim. 35 a; Aristotle. Met. 1081a 14. In Enn. V.1.5.13 sqq. Plotinus argues that number determines the structure of the intellect and is constituted by the monad and the dyad; the dyad is indefinite (*aoristos*), a sort of substrate (*hypokeimenon*). Numenius deduced the soul from the monad and the dyad; cp. Xenocrates, frg. 60 Heinze = 165-187 Isnardi Parente; Enn. VI.6.16.45; Aristotle. De an. 404b 27-28.
[55] Plotinus. Enn. V.5.4.24-25; cp. *plēthos henos hysteron*, III.8.9.3-4; Aristotle. Met. 1083b 23-24.
[56] Plotinus. Enn. VI.6.13.9-11.
[57] Cp. Aristotle. Met. 1084b 29-30.
[58] Plotinus. Enn. VI.6.3.7-9. The order of procession-returning-staying is different from that of Proclus' *proodos-monē-epistrophē* (In Tim. I 87.28-30; 211.28-212.1; 274.25-30; II 215. 22-24; III 18.1-2; In RP I 88.11-16; I 140.2 et al.). Perhaps, it is not by chance that the structure of the Plotinian Enn. VI.6. is itself triadic (two chapters in the beginning and two chapters at the end are dedicated to the consideration of number and infinity (Enn. VI.6.2-3; 17-18), while the middle chapters (Enn. VI.6.4-16) consider the constitution of number and

the Three Primary Hypostases" Plotinus argues that in returning to the One the being-intellect sees. This seeing (*horasis*) is the intellect itself. The initial act of seeing or of contemplation can be compared to the yet unlimited and indefinite (*aoristos*) thinking, as if thinking "unintelligently" (*anoētōs*).[59] Such a thinking does not yet think itself unless it thinks in definite forms-*noēta*. As if in movement, thinking comes out of the One (which in itself has no limit), then returns back to itself (without having really left itself), and finally stays in fullness in itself as both the same and the other, thus acquiring limit, boundary and form (*horon, peras, eidos*).[60] One can also understand in this sense the process (again, logical and not temporal) of unfolding the unity of being into the unified "colored" multiplicity within the same being, now unwrapped according to the essential number. Such a multiplicity is present as *on-onta* in thinking-*noēsis*, thinking itself as the forms-*noēta*. This process may be then synthetically represented through four terms, namely, as the initial simple unity of being, as the unfolding of beings, as the intellect moving in itself, and finally as the living being of the noetic cosmos.[61]

Since otherness is constitutive of the intellect itself, it is present in the most fundamental acts of intellection, namely, in distinguishing between two different things. The very act of counting may be regarded as the simplest and the originative for distinguishing primary units, equal in all respects except for being different numerically (i.e., as discerned within the essential number). These acts of simple intuition, which are non-discursive and non-logical, are called *epibolai* by Plotinus.[62] Such acts that establish the primary form of otherness as dyad, or movement within the intellect, are an elementary simple pointing to the other, recognition of the other, as "this is this and that is that", *tode tode, tode tode*.[63] The otherness-dyad establishes the other element in every pair, so that for every pair only sameness is needed. This states the identity of each element and its opposition to the other element. In other words, otherness does not itself need otherness but only sameness, so that the intellect does not need to go into infinity; two primary principles are enough within the realm of being.

---

its relation to the being of intellect): the very structure of the treatise appears to imitate the original infinity of the One, the multiple unity of *hen-polla* of the being-intellect and the unlimited dyad.

[59] Plotinus. Enn. V.1.7.5-6; VI.7.16.14. Cp. D'Ancona 1999, 237 sqq.

[60] Plotinus. Enn. VI.7.16.14 sqq.; 17.14-21.

[61] *To men on arithmos hēnōmenos, ta de onta exelēligmenos arithmos, noys de arithmos en heaytōi kinoymenos, to de zōion arithmos periekhōn.* - Plotinus. Enn. VI.6.9.29-31.

[62] It is worth noting that the term *epibolē* is of the Stoic origin. When Plotinus argues that in order to think a particular object, for instance, one horse, one already has to be in the position to recur to the notion of the "one", he asks whether the monad precedes being and number precedes beings in cogitation, in intuitive act of the intellect or also in reality, *tēi epinoiai kai tēi epibolēi ē kai tēi hypostasei* (Plotinus. Enn. VI.6.9.13-14), he uses three terms, the first of which, "*epinoia*" is the term of Plato which is not found in Aristotle, "*epibolē*" is used by the Stoics and is absent in Plato and Aristotle and "*hypostasis*" is used only by Aristotle and is absent in Plato, see: Plotinus 1980, 197, 200-201.

[63] Plotinus. Enn. VI.3.18.12 sqq.

2.1.2 Constitution and the structure of number in Plotinus

Let us now turn to the question of how essential or ideal numbers are formed. The monad and the dyad as such are not yet numbers, but the ideal principles of numbers. The first essential number appears to be the number two.[64]

If pure otherness as *aoristos dyas* is the principle of indefiniteness, then, after Plato, it may be said to be great and small, *mega kai mikron, polla kai oliga* or *hyperokhē kai elleipsis* (not as two different opposed principles but as one), it should have an inclination to abandon the stable identity of the monad.[65] This inclination, however, is prevented from going into absolute unlimitedness by the limiting potency of the monad. Being as exemplified in thinking becomes thus other than it is. At this point there is no exact measure yet; becoming—through the first movement—becomes "bigger" than the being initially is. Two is then originated: the initial is taken as the monad and the originated as the dyad. The difference constitutes that henad, which makes two numerically different from the monad. The increasing (as leaving the state of identity) may then be taken as doubling and the decreasing (as coming back to the initial state) may be regarded as dividing into halves.[66] Both operations originate the number two and are mutually convertible, even if addition as increasing by way of construction is logically prior to division as decreasing.[67]

Plotinus seems to reject this way of deducing the first number (the two), denying that the number two is either an addition (coming together or union, *synodos*) or division (splitting, *skhisis*). Otherwise the number would have been reduced to merely a relation, *to pros ti* or *skhesis*. Yet this relation has to be a relation of something which is already there, that is, of being split according to the form of number.[68] Simply bringing together two units will not give two, because the dyad should already be there in order that two units might be thought, predicated, and exist *qua* two.[69] Moreover, the dyad (*hē dyas*) and the two as the first essential number (*ta dyo*) are not in relation as entities of equal ontological status. The dyad through its presence (*paroysiai*) determines the two as the first number; both are connected through participation.

In rejecting the hypothesis that takes number to be posterior to the forms, Plotinus argues that from the analysis of predication one can establish the logical

---

[64] Cp. Plotinus. Enn. VI.6.5.4. See also: Alexander. In Met. 56.31-32 Hayduck; Simplicius. In Phys. 454.28 Diehl.
[65] Cp. Plotinus. Enn. VI.3.28.10; VI.4.2.30-31.
[66] Cp. Alexander. In Met. 56.5-33; Porphyry as quoted by Simplicius (In Phys. 454.9-16). See also: Plato. Phaedr. 96e-97b (does the number two come from the addition of two units or from the division of one unit?) and Prot. 356e-357b; Gorg. 451a-454a; Aristotle. Met. 986a 21-26; 1081b 14-15; 1085 b 7; Sextus Empiricus. Hyp. pyrrh. III 164-167; Plotinus. Enn. V.1.5.4 sqq. Cp. Becker 1938, 464 sqq.; Wedberg 1955; Markovic 1965, 308-318; Szabó 1994, 357-359.
[67] Cp. Aristotle's report that the infinite by addition and by division is the same in Plato: Phys. 206b 3-16 = Test. Plat. 24.
[68] The double and the half, *to diplasion kai to hēmisy* is an example of relation, *skhesis*, Plotinus. Enn. VI.1.6.4. Cp. Aristotle. Met. 1020b 26-27.
[69] Plotinus. Enn. VI.6.14.15 sqq.

and ontological priority of being one. If one utters "one man", the "one" (which is one in being—the monad) is already predicated of man.[70] The same argument appears in the second hypothesis of the "Parmenides": being can only be one-being, *hen on*. Although being is one, nevertheless it always already involves the form of pure duality in the primary compound or *synthesis* of two components, of *hen-on*, for being presupposes that it is one, and one, if thought and predicated, is in being.[71] Since the essential number, according to Plotinus, is *in* being,[72] it defines the structure of being and, since being is the synthetic *hen on*, the very form of the number two is thereby established. Still, since being is unity (of thinking-*noēsis*) in multiplicity (of the thought-*noēta*), the one as monad should be prior to being, which (in regard to the monad) is the "falsely or spuriously one". Plotinus puts it as follows: "And if the one is like an element of a compound (*hōs stoikheion de synthetoy*), there must be beforehand a one which is one in itself, that it may be compounded with another; then, if it is compounded with another which has become one through it, it will make that other spuriously (*pseydōs*) one, by making it two."[73]

Therefore, by the way of production being is constituted by the monad and the dyad, and is structured according to the number two. The very way of production of the first essential number involves that the unit that may be discerned within that number—the henad—should be posterior to the number. In its very form, the number is prior to its units, which may only be discerned in a secondary way (the postulate (d)).[74] Every henad of the two and the number two itself are both one (insofar as they participate in the monad) but differently: the unity of the former is similar to that of a house which is one in virtue of its continuity (*to synekhes hen*, although the henad is not continuous but discrete; its unity is that of one subject). The unity of the latter may be compared to that of an army that is one substantially or quantitatively.[75] In other words, strictly speaking, number does not consist of henads nor is it counted by them, although when henads are discerned within a number, the number may be said to comprise these henads. For this reason Plotinus has to disagree with Aristotle that the henad may be regarded as matter of number.[76] The matter of the essential number is rather a multiplicity of the dyad, bounded by the form of the monad.

In the philosophical and arithmetical consideration of number within the Platonic-Pythagorean tradition, number is defined as a limited magnitude. It is a magnitude made up of units, or—as a concrete multitude—a *plēthos* of discrete and indivisible monads, a synthetic collection, a unity of units, a *systēma*, both

---

[70] Plotinus. Enn. VI.6.5.29 sqq. Cp. Plato. Phil. 15a.
[71] Plato. Parm. 142b sqq.
[72] Plotinus. Enn. VI.6.15.24.
[73] Plotinus. Enn. VI.6.5.43-46, trans. Armstrong.
[74] As Aristotle recalls, for Plato two is also prior to its units: Met. 1084b 36-37; cp. 1085a 6-7.
[75] Plotinus. Enn. V.5.4.29-33.
[76] Cp. Aristotle. Met. 1084b 5-6.

united in, and limited by, these units.[77] Such a definition, however, is ambiguous and has to be further clarified; it is not immediately clear, first, whether this definition applies to essential or to quantitative numbers and, second, whether such a distinction is implied at all in the definition.

It is important to note that even if the notion of number plays a key role both in Platonic ontology and science as the most fundamental characteristic of being, the notion of number has to be *defined*, in order to demonstrate its connection with being and its place in the whole ontological picture. In other words, number is considered through something else, something more fundamental and primary. In contemporary mathematics different kinds of number—such as negative, rational, irrational (algebraic and transcendental), complex and quaternions—are all defined constructively from the notion of natural numbers, which are mostly considered elementary and "self-evident" and thus not properly definable but simply postulated. Thus, for example, Hilbert takes natural numbers as the result of the process of calculation (Abzählung) (i.e., of a fundamental intuition of succession).[78]

Plotinus is not unaware of the traditional definition of number but he has to define it in a more precise and subtle way, in order to be in a position to include all the fruitful distinctions he has made. Thus, in order to discuss properly the structure of the number, one has to be able first to discern the constitutive element of the number. The difficulty that arises here is that the number itself, as Plotinus argues, is prior to the thinking that thinks itself in particular forms, or as already structured according to the number.[79] This difficulty may be resolved by accepting a unity in number, the henad, one by participation in the monad or through the presence (*paroysiai*) of the monad.[80] Such a distinction resolves a seeming paradox and explains how and why the one is both prior and posterior to the dyad and to the number two: the one is prior to the dyad as the One and as monad; and the one is posterior to the dyad as henad.[81]

---

[77] *Arithmos plēthos hōrismenon* or *peperasmenon*, Aristotle. Met. 1020a 13; *monadōn plēthos*, Euclid. Elem. VII, def.2; *arithmos esti plēthos hōrismenon ē monadōn systēma ē posotētos khyma ek monadōn sygkeimenon*, Nicomachus. Introd. I 7.1; *monadōn systēma*, Thales ap. Iamblichus. In Nicom. 10.8-9; *plēthos hōrismenon*, Eudoxus ap. Iamblichus. In Nicom. 10.16-20; *systēma monadōn*, Theon. Expos. rer. math. 18.3. Cp. later definitions of number in Proclus, such as: *plēthos hōrismenon*, Theol. Plat. II 16.15; *plēthos diakekrimenon*, Theol. Plat. IV 81.6; *finita autem multitudo numerus*, In Parm. VII, 56.9-10 and in Boethius: *numerus est unitatum collectio, vel quantitatis acervus ex unitatibus profusus*, Inst. arithm. I 3. See also: Becker 1957, 44-47; Szabó 1964, 115-121; Klein 1968, 46-60; Burkert 1972, Mohr 1981, 620-627; Cantor 1985, 270-272; Stein 1995, 334-342.
[78] Hilbert 1990, 1: "Der Begriff der ganzen Zahl ist der einfachste und wichtigste Begriff in der Mathematik."
[79] Cp. O'Meara 1975, 79-82.
[80] Plotinus. Enn. VI.6.5.49; VI.6.14.27-28. On the one as the principle of numbers see: Cleary 1995, 365-377. As Cleary mentions, Aristotle is somewhat ambiguous (Met. 1052b 14-20; cp. 1088a 6-8: *oyk esti to hen arithmos ...all' arkhē [toy arithmoy] kai to metron hen*) on whether the essence of the unity is being indivisible (so Aquinas and Cleary) or being the first measure of a number (Ross). - Cleary 1995, 369.
[81] Plotinus. Enn. V.5.4.11, 24.

The One and the monad preceding the henad can also be seen from the fact that there are many henads participating in one monad that is common (*koinon*) to them, and which itself participates in the One.[82] As absolutely transcendent to being, the One cannot be equal to other units (to the monad and the henads), so as to be one of them.[83] The multiplicity of the henads (*plēthos henadōn*) can be proved by a *reductio ad absurdum*.[84] If there is only one monad, it should be joined or associated with the one being, *hen on* either (1) in the aspect of being-*on* or (2) in the aspect of the one-*hen*. The (1) is impossible, because (a) either the units that are distinguished in number have only the same name but ontologically are not the same (*oy syntakhthēsontai*) and, therefore, are equivocally (*homōnymōs*) said to be henads; thus there are no units in number at all. Or (b) number will consist of unlike units (*ex anomoiōn monadōn*), which Plotinus implicitly rejects, because every distinction between the henads is superfluous. If the henads were all different, there would have to be an additional explanation of how the first principles of the monad and the dyad constitute this difference. But even if henads are all identical, there is still a non-identity represented in them as a multitude. There are many henads within each essential number. Such a multitude differs, however, from the multitude of the one-many of the *noys*, where all the intelligible objects (*noēta*) are different as representing various forms. Henads, on the contrary, form a set of equals, intrinsically indiscernible, because the distinction is extrinsic to them, and is brought by the essential number as setting a definite number of the henads. If the henads of the essential number two are absolutely the same and equal *per se*, how can it be said at all that there are two henads, that is, that they are different as different numerically? The only explanation is to presuppose the number two as that form which allows the duplicity of the henads. Otherwise, it could not be said that there are two henads. Different henads may be thought then as forming not a consequential but rather a coexistential order. In other words, henads, unlike the forms-*eidē*, do not have individual "faces". Their distinction comes from what defines them as a set (i.e., as such and such number of henads). The (2) is impossible as well, for in order to be one, the one which *is*, the monad needs only the unique One and no other one, in particular, no henad. The primary duality of the *hen on* turns out to be enough for generating all the rich variety of numbers and the forms within being. However, one should note that although the henad is not individualized, it is not divisible, because the henad is defined solely by the essential number as the principle of individuation of the henad.[85] For if the henad were divisible, it would have defined another number (e.g., if one henad composed of two henads of the number two would have been divided into two henads, there would have been three henads— they would have referred to the number three and not to the number two).

---

[82] Cp. Plotinus. Enn. VI.6.11.7; 5.31.
[83] Plotinus. Enn. V.5.4.14-15.
[84] Plotinus. Enn. VI.6.11.10 sqq.
[85] Cp.: *ameriston kai adiaireton to hen hōs hen*. - Theon. Expos. rer. math. 18.15. A privileged position of the henad is shown by the fact that the henad is preserved not only in the operation of division, but also in that of multiplication: multiplied by itself an indefinite number of times, it still remains a henad. - Theon. Expos. rer. math. 19.10-11.

Part II: Intelligible Matter and Geometry

Now that the first number, two, and the henad are deduced, we need to see how the other essential numbers are constituted in Plotinus. Essential numbers appear to be produced by the monad and the dyad as well.[86] Since there inevitably is otherness in being, in the form of *hen on* or *hen polla* and the dyad as otherness is connected with movement,[87] Plotinus finds an original way of describing the deduction of the essential numbers by means of kinematic production, or by movement (cp. 3.4.4). If the nature of being "generates in a kind of succession (*ephexēs*), or rather has generated, or does not stand still at one thing of those which it has generated, but makes a kind of continuous one, when it draws [a line] (*perigrapsasa*) and stops more quickly in its outgoing it generates the lesser numbers, but when it moves further, not in other things but in its very own movements, it brings the greater numbers into existence; and so it would fit the particular multiplicities and each particular being to the particular numbers, knowing that, if each particular being was not fitted to each particular number, it could not exist at all or would get away and be something else by becoming innumerable and irrational".[88]

We see the following main points in the description of Plotinus. (1) Essential number results from a stop (or consecutive stops) of and within intelligible movement. These stops do not form a temporal succession, for time appears only with the soul.[89] Therefore, the stops can only establish a logical sequence, so that (2) all the numbers are *already* there, *already* having been moved. Plotinus finds it more appropriate to describe essential numbers, even if produced by movement, not temporarily—for this movement is not temporal—but rather in quasi-spatial terms.[90] (3) The non-temporal kinematic production of the numbers is also presented by Plotinus as the multiplication of being-*on* into beings-*onta*, when being is split (*skhizetai*) according to the potencies of the essential number, which, as the first and true number, is then the principle and the source of the existence of beings.[91] Things thus may be numbered only because of the existence of essential numbers, which form the ontological precondition for numbering and are not simply an abstraction from the things numbered.

Most important is that (4) the kinematic production of geometrical entities, later used by Proclus,[92] is already present in Plotinus (similar to the kinematic generation of numbers, which are, however, ontologically prior to

---

[86] Plotinus. Enn. V.5.5.2-4. Cp. Iamblichus. De comm. math. sci. 18.3 sqq. Festa: *ek de tēs syntheseōs toy henos kai tēs toy plēthoys aitias hylēs hyphistatai men ho arithmos*.
[87] Cp. Plotinus. Enn. II.4.5.28 sqq.: otherness as the intelligible matter is the first movement.
[88] Plotinus. Enn. VI.6.11.24-33; cp. V.5.4.8-10; the closest passage in Plato might be Phil. 24d, although Plato does not speak about the kinematic generation of either arithmetic or geometrical entities.
[89] Plotinus. Enn. III.7.11.
[90] Cp. Plotinus' explication of the ubiquity of the One: it is everywhere, "for there is nowhere where it is not" (*pōs oyn ex henos plēthos; hoti pantakhoy: oy gar estin hopoy oy*, Plotinus. Enn. III.9.4.1-2).
[91] *Arkhē oyn kai pēgē hypostaseōs tois oysin ho arithmos ho prōtos kai alēthēs*, Plotinus. Enn. VI.6.15.29-35.
[92] Proclus describes drawing of a line by uniform movement or flowing (*tōi rhysin einai*) of a point: Proclus. In Eucl. 185.8-15; cp. 51.21.

geometricals, cp. 3.4.4-3.4.5). This production, used for drawing geometrical figures, is extended by Plotinus to the sphere of discrete entities. It proves to be very fruitful, for later Plotinus returns to kinematic production in discussing the nature of quantity. The "expansion" (*epektasis*) of the discrete number serves the paradigmatic example for prolongation of the continuous into the distance (*eis to porrō*). "So there is a quantum (*poson*) when the unit (*to hen*, i.e. the henad) moves forward, and also when the point (*to sēmeion*) does.[93] But if either of them comes to a stop quickly in its progress, one is many and the other is large."[94]

Finally, (5) one can easily recognize the *proodos-epistrophē-monē* sequence in the very description of the constitution of essential numbers, used in describing the constitution of the dyad. Original movement constitutes the moment of *proodos*. The stop in movement, as the beginning of turning to itself, corresponds to the *epistrophē* as a definite number. The "recognition" of a particular quantitative determination of a number, in which all of its posteriorly discernible "parts" or henads are gathered into a unity of being this particular number, embodies the *monē* moment of the kinematic constitution of numbers.[95]

In the "Metaphysics" M 6, Aristotle considers three hypotheses of possible relations of the units within number: a unit may be either incompatible with any other unit (*asymblētos*) within any number; compatible with any other unit; or finally, it may be compatible with the unit(s) within this particular number but incompatible with the units within any other number.[96] Following Aristotle, Plotinus poses similar questions (which he leaves without an explicit answer) in relation to the constitution of numbers. How are two units of the dyad different? How is the dyad one? Are the two units equal within the dyad?[97]

First of all, we need to address the question of the relation of henads to number. Is the essential number a multitude consisting of indivisible henads that define it? The answer has to be "no", just as in the case of the number two. As Plotinus argues, the essential number does *not* consist of henads but precedes them as a unity (as a chorus or an army may be said to precede its parts).[98] This can be clearly seen from the way numbers are kinematically constituted. Each number is to be considered not as a set or collection of so many henads. Rather, it is the successor of the previous essential number, through performing another step within intelligible movement. It makes no sense to try to determine the "length" of each step or even to ask if they are all of equal "length", for there is no unit of length as yet, so that every new movement brings forth another number by simply presenting it as different from the previous one. Since every successor in numbers differs

---

[93] The difference between a henad and a point being that the point is the unit which has position (cp. *hē gar stigmē monas esti thesin ekhoysa*, Aristotle. De an. 409a 6; Met. 1016b 24-26; *monas proslaboysa thesin*, Proclus. In Eucl. 95.22), i.e. the point exists in the continuous, where otherness is present not as the *aoristos dyas* but as matter.
[94] Plotinus. Enn. VI.3.12.9-14.
[95] *Ta panta merē pros hen*. - Plotinus. Enn. VI.6.1.19-20.
[96] Aristotle. Met. 1080a 15 sqq. Aristotle consecutively rejects all the hypotheses in order to show the inconsistency of the Academic teaching of number.
[97] Plotinus. Enn. V.5.4.27-29. Cp. Szlezák 1979, 91-92.
[98] Cp. Plotinus. Enn. VI.6.5.38 sqq.

Part II: Intelligible Matter and Geometry

from the predecessor by one unit or henad, every step constitutes a difference of one henad. And since the steps are discrete, the henads are also discrete, or indivisible. Divisibility in the essential number exists only as its divisibility into a particular multitude of its units-henads, and not as the divisibility of its constituents.

Essential number is thus determined as an ordinal, that is, by and from the order of its production—recurrently defined by the previous number plus one more step. A similar procedure was perhaps meant in the ancient Academy, in particular, by the late Plato, for whom, as Aristotle explains, quantitative numbers are constituted as counted (1+1=2, 2+1=3, etc.), while the essential numbers are simply presented (as 1, then 2, then 3 etc.), that is, essential numbers are constituted as the structured wholes that do not consist of units.[99] The units or the henads may be discerned, then, in essential numbers—as in the number two—only in a secondary way. Since the number three is kinematically constituted after the number two, in which two henads can be discerned, one can consider three henads in the number three; in the number four, constituted after the number three, one can discern four henads, and so on. Three objections arise, however. First, the kinematic production is not itself a temporal process. Second, the logical sequence that establishes the set of essential numbers exists only within discursive dianoetic thinking absent in the intellect-*noys*. Third, the notion of succession presupposes number as its own precondition. Because of that, it cannot be properly said that essential numbers are established in succession after each other; rather, they are established as *already* existing or generated, as coexisting and as forming one set of numbers, which itself determines the multiplicity of beings-*onta* and, subsequently, the structure of intelligible objects-*noēta*.[100] As already produced, the essential numbers (and the henads in them) may be considered not as following each other, but as simply coexisting.

Now, are henads in essential numbers comparable to each other or are they all different within one number and within different numbers? Since henads are separated from each other by a "unit of movement" (which is discrete and of no length), by way of their constitution and distinction they are not different, but are all equal. But what is the principle of the individuation of henads? As in the case of the essential number two, discussed above, all henads within any essential number are alike, having no individuality. This principle of individuation can only be, then, the number as a whole precedent to particular henads. In other words, seven henads are all exactly alike; they are discernible only because of the essential number "seven", which is a precondition for the possibility of considering exactly seven henads, all of them being different, *qua* seven henads, and all of them being alike, *qua* henads. The essential number can only establish a numerical distinction between henads, but there is no specific distinction between them. It means that henads must be comparable to each other within one number. But are they comparable to the henads of another number, for example, in five and ten?[101] There is no definitive answer in Plotinus' text. In fact, henads within different numbers

---

[99] Aristotle. Met. 1080a 30-35, *contra* Allen 1970, 30-34.
[100] Cp. Plotinus. Enn. VI.6.10.1-4. Cp. also 3.4.4.
[101] Plotinus. Enn. V.5.4.33-35.

may be said to be both comparable and incomparable, although in different senses. On the one hand, henads may be said to be comparable, first, insofar as they all are discernible in the same way from the essential number (as the pure form of a particular multitude of henads) and, second, insofar as a henad may be considered as constituted in and by another step in the kinematic production of numbers. Therefore, insofar as henads are considered constituted not one by one, but as a particular multitude within which they coexist as a system of henads (of the number seven, eight, and so on), they may be considered different in different numbers, because each number defines a different multitude of henads.[102]

And finally, is the total number of essential numbers limited?[103] Plotinus often uses ten as an example (in the Enn. VI.6. term *deka/dekas* is mentioned forty-five times) but, again, he gives no clear indication of whether the number of numbers is limited by a particular number (perhaps, escaping the discussion of the number of number(s)). If we take into consideration the above argument about the constitution of number in Plotinus, it is possible to claim that such a number has to be limited. Indeed, the essential number cannot go to infinity, but has to stop, for number as the multiple unity is both limiting and limited. The infinite number cannot therefore exist: number is unlimited only in the sense that it is not measured, but is itself the measure for being.[104] "The infinite struggles with number".[105] Moreover, since number defines and measures the multitude of forms and the number of the forms-*eidē* is limited, the number of essential numbers cannot be unlimited, because the infinite may define the finite only as the actual infinity of the power of the One, as *dynamis pantōn*,[106] and not as a potentially infinite—even if numerable, like the potentially infinite row of natural numbers— which is more dimly established in being than the limit, by which being is first introduced.

Let us at last turn to the question of how quantitative numbers are constituted. Since beings-*onta* are generated and organized according to the essential number, and things are further determined by the forms through participation, things are organized and separated (i.e., can be counted) according to number.[107] The quantitative numbers are also organized under the paradigm of essential numbers. The quantitative numbers are numbering (*arithmoyntes*) insofar as they are applicable to the things that always change (although the numbering

---

[102] Similarly, the late Plato took the units or henads within an ideal (essential) number to be comparable to each other, whereas the units of different numbers as incomparable. - Gaiser 1963, 537-538.

[103] Plato, for instance, limits the number of the ideal numbers to ten only. See Aristotle. Phys. 206 b 32-33; Met. 1073 a 19-21; 1084 a 12, 24-25. Cp., however, Becker's suggestion (not much confirmed in the original texts) to interpret the first ten numbers not as numbers properly but rather as digits, in which case they may represent (once they are put in a certain order in diairetic subdivisions) an infinite number of ideas and ideal numbers - Becker 1963, 119-124.

[104] Plotinus. Enn. VI.6.2.1 sqq.; 17.1 sqq., esp. 18.5-6. Cp. Plato. Parm. 144a sqq.; Aristotle. Met. 1083b 36-1084a 8; Phys. 203b 23-24.

[105] *To gar apeiron makhetai tōi arithmōi*, Plotinus. Enn. VI.6.17.3.

[106] Plotinus. Enn. III.8.10.1,V.4.1.36 et al.

[107] *Kai entaytha meta arithmōn hē genesis hekastois*. - Plotinus. Enn. VI.6.15.29-36.

number cannot properly grasp the becoming, which always escapes any definitive limitation). Essential numbers, on the contrary, are numbered (*arithmētoi*), because they always already are and are exempt from any change. Essential numbers are numbered in the sense that they are not the ultimate measure but rather are themselves measured through the transcendent measure of the One, which alone is not measured by anything.[108] The One is thus the measure of measure for being—the One provides the unity for measure, both for the monad, which imitates the One, and for the henad, which participates in the monad. The One itself, as absolutely transcendent, is incommensurable with everything else and radically other even to otherness.

Plotinus uses, although reverses, the terminology of Aristotle, probably because in Aristotle time is the numbered, and not the numbering number. It is to be noted that although Aristotle is critical of Plato and the Pythagoreans in their treatment of number, he himself discerns at least three different kinds of number, at the very end of his discussion of the notion of time.[109] First, there is the number numbered, that of a group of things (ten horses). Next, there is the numbering, or quantitative, number, which allows the discernment of a group as constituted by ten things. This number itself consists of a definite number of units (e.g., of ten) and may be situated in a row of succession (after the number nine); that is, it is a member of the set of natural numbers. And lastly, there is the number by itself, which does not stand in a relation of precedence to (or of following) other numbers, and is a kind of paradigmatic number for the numbering number.[110] Aristotle presents a lengthy discussion of whether units within a number of this kind are mutually commensurable or not. He discusses the so-called "combinable" (*symblētoi*) numbers, reportedly developed by Plato. Units are said to be "combinable" in a number if they constitute only this particular number and cannot enter any other number.[111] This is the paradigm for numbering numbers, for example, ten as such, which already is not a member of a succession or sequence, but is a discrete indivisible principle, indissoluble into simple monadic units and unrelated to other such principles through the operation of addition or doubling the unit. Thus, for example, five and seven would not differ by two units, since they would not be resolved into units as their parts, but would be two different ideal paradigms for quantitative numbers 5 and 7.

It is not altogether clear, however, whether these ideal numbers form a finite set (for example, in the case of ten: the decade is the completion of the set of numbers[112]). It would seem that there should be a finite set of them, since the number of the forms-ideas is finite, according to Plotinus, and the all-in-one structure of the forms repeats that of the ideal numbers (cp. 3.1.1). In any case, numbers form a set of discrete entities, which are identical as produced from and by the unity-one, *monas*, and dyad, *aoristos dyas*, but different numerically. This Platonic teaching dates back at least to Xenocrates and his followers in the

---

[108] *Metron, oy metroymenon.* - Plotinus. Enn. V.5.4.13-14.
[109] Aristotle. Phys. 224a 2 sqq.; Met. 991a 4.
[110] Cp. Aristotle. Met. 1092b 20.
[111] Aristotle. Met. 1080a 11 sqq.
[112] Cp. Aristotle. Phys. 206b 33; Speusippus, frg. 4 Lang.

Academy, for whom, as Plutarch reports, "nothing but the generation of number is signified by the mixture of the indivisible and divisible being, the one being indivisible and multiplicity divisible and number being the product of these when the one bounds multiplicity and inserts a limit in infinitude, which they call indefinite dyad too".[113] Most importantly, ideal numbers represent the paradigmatic structure for organizing being and the intelligible forms as the one-many, where one and dyad are not separate, but are kept as synthesis, structured under the pattern of ideal numbers as a composite unity which, in turn, becomes a paradigm for the functioning and understanding of the geometrical and to some extent, of the physical world.

It is interesting to note that when Peano elaborates his axiomatization of arithmetic, he introduces three fundamental, further indefinable notions: zero, integer number and the successor of an integer (i.e., the operation of addition, "+").[114] Obviously, the notion of the follower, which substitutes the operation of adding another unit, corresponds to the operation of the indefinite dyad. For methodological reasons, Greek mathematics does not have a notion of zero, 0, for, first, zero would have been a sign (a something) of and for nothing and in this way would have substantivized non-being or matter. The not-being is represented differently in arithmetic, for instance, in Plotinus it is the unit, 1, the one in numbers, the transcendent basis of being of and in numbers and thus is not itself being (Peano himself mentions that the unit is not considered a number by the Pythagoreans). However, the unit does not represent the non-being of matter, but the beyond-being of the One. And second, zero does not have any place in the genetic account of the constitution of both essential and quantitative numbers: zero is redundant. Zero is thus alien to the system of natural numbers as understood within the Platonic-Pythagorean tradition, further elaborated in Plotinus. It is not by chance then that Peano has to introduce zero separately from all other numbers. Were zero not present in his reconstruction of arithmetic, the system of axioms would have been considerably simpler.

For Plotinus, however, the essential number is out of reach of any temporality, and even if a succession in the generation of essential numbers could be established, this succession would again be purely logical. As it has been argued, all essential numbers may be considered coexisting.[115] The quantitative number exists by participation in the essential number. The essential number, as already numbered, is then the pure actuality of number, fully unwrapped as number in the living being or the intelligible cosmos. Actuality in being and thinking precedes potentiality (this general principle of Aristotle[116] is valid for Plotinus for every representation of being, but not for the One, which, as the infinite *dynamis pantōn*, is never actualized). Therefore, the purely quantitative numbering number

---

[113] Plutarch. De an. procr. in Tim. 1012d-f; cp. Plat. quaest. 1002a: "unity does not produce number unless it comes into contact with the unlimited dyad".
[114] Peano 1990, 27.
[115] Plotinus. Enn. VI.6.15.37 sqq.; Aristotle. Phys. 219b 5-9. Cp. Amado 1953, 423-425; Plotinus 1980, 187.
[116] Aristotle, Met. 1049b 5 sqq.

(*katharōs poson*) has to have an admixture of potentiality.[117] The quantitative number, even if it may be considered as (potentially) existing before the act of counting, has yet to be fully actualized in the very act of numbering.[118] Therefore, the quantitative number may be presented in the form of 1+1+1, and so on (i.e., as numbering). For this reason, the quantitative number may already be referred to the discursive logical process and so grasped by the *dianoia* as well.

Do the quantitative henads, the units of the quantitative number that may be considered as participating in the essential henad (which itself participates in the monad), constitute quantitative number? Or are they discerned in it only in a secondary way, as in the case of essential numbers? Even if presented as counted, as produced by the consecutive addition of the quantitative henads, the quantitative or mathematical number is not really engendered in the act of counting. It does already exist potentially as a unity, for instance, as a chorus consisting of nine people already comprises this number, even if not yet counted. The quantitative number is only actualized as definite for discursive thinking through a number of the added quantitative henads.[119] In other words, the quantitative number, as numbering, properly exists in the discursive dianoetic activity of counting. Until the number of men in this particular chorus is actually numbered, we do not yet know it as counted, it is not yet "ordered together into one", although potentially it is already there.[120] For this reason the quantitative number precedes its henads, but as a potential and not actual entity, unlike the essential number.

2.1.3 Number and magnitude in ancient mathematics: The point

An important distinction that practically vanishes in modern mathematics and physics (in particular, in Descartes) is that between number and magnitude (geometrical figure)—the subject matters of two different sciences, arithmetic and geometry, and the distinction that constitutes a major starting point for ancient science.[121] Although Euclid describes in his general theory of proportions in book V of the "Elements" (usually attributed to Eudoxus) certain procedures applicable both to numbers and magnitudes, he nevertheless makes a careful distinction between magnitudes and numbers as such. Three arithmetical books, VII-IX, are dedicated to the consideration of properties of numbers; numbers may have a ratio, *logos*, to each other, just as geometrical magnitudes of equal dimension may have a ratio. The former, however, belong to a different genus and can never be substituted by the latter. Number and magnitude are never confounded terminologically: in Euclid the former is referred to as *poson* and the latter—as

---

[117] Plotinus. Enn. VI.6.16.18.
[118] Cp.: *energeis poson*, Plotinus. Enn. VI.6.16.51. To note, Plotinus is the first to use the verb *energeō* as transitive, Schwyzer 1951, 525.
[119] Cp. Plotinus. Enn. VI.6.16.28 sqq.
[120] Plotinus. Enn. VI.6.16.34; cp. VI.6.13.20.
[121] Plato. RP 525a-527c; Theaet. 198a-d. Cp. Plotinus. Enn. VI.3.13.23-24; Proclus. In Eucl. 60.9-12.

pēlikon: the former is discrete, the latter is continuous.[122]

Thus, numbers and magnitudes are distinct insofar as number is a *multitude* (*plēthos*) consisting of indivisible units, whereas geometrical magnitudes are continuous and, therefore, infinitely divisible, even if both are derivable from the same principles of the one and the dyad.[123] The geometrical entity is a continuous *magnitude, megethos*. As Proclus notes, numbers are also purer and more immaterial (*aylotheroi kai katharōteroi*) than magnitudes (cp. 2.1.1; 2.4).[124] The only important exclusion is the partless point, which plays the same role in magnitudes as the monad or henad in numbers. Both the point and the monad (henad) are representatives of the generative principle in their genus and both appear as the limit and indivisible basis: the point—of a line, the monad (henad)—of a number.[125] Among all the geometrical entities, it is the point that represents limit in the most adequate way, while line, plane and solid participate more in the unlimited. In general, the more dimensions a geometrical figure has and the more complicated motions it requires for its construction, the more it takes part in the unlimited.[126] Because of this privileged position of the point, Plato and Xenocrates (according to the reports of Aristotle and later commentators) have to "struggle" with the point in their attempt to introduce the "indivisible line" as the elementary, atomic constituent of the continuous magnitude, as a synthesis of the same (*hen*) and the other (*aoristos dyas*) in the realm of the geometrical (cp. 1.1.2; 1.2.1; 2.1.1).[127] As Proclus writes, the point has a certain similarity with the One: as the One, the point has no parts, and as the One itself of the first hypothesis of the "Parmenides", it presents a problem for cognition.[128] Such an analogy is also traceable in Plotinus: the point as partless is comparable to the One, whereas the

---

[122] Cp. Nicomachus. Introd. arithm. I 2.5; Iamblichus. In Nicom. 8.3-5; Proclus. In Eucl. 35.21-36.5. It is worth noting, however, that Euclid gives the definition of relation-*logos* only in book V, where he considers relations between magnitudes (Elem. V, def. III). But book VII, where the theory of proportions in numbers is discussed, does not provide a definition of *logos* specifically for numbers. This might mean that the relation between numbers has to be considered in the same way as that between magnitudes. See: Gardies 1984, 111-125. Although, even if there is a parallelism in the consideration of relations in magnitudes and of numbers, it does not yet make both kinds of entities similar and interchangeable.

[123] Cp. Aristotle. Met. 1085b 20-34.

[124] Proclus. In Eucl. 95.23-25; cp. Szabó 1978, 304-307.

[125] Cp. Aristotle. De an. 427a 9-14; Themistius. In De an. 86.18-86.27; Plotinus. Enn. IV.7.6.10-15; Proclus. In Eucl. 85.2 sqq.

[126] Proclus. In Eucl. 87.21 sqq.

[127] Aristotle criticizes Plato for introducing the "indivisible lines" (*atomoi grammai*) or "indivisible magnitudes" (*atoma megethē*) and for rejecting the indivisible, the point, as the limit of the divisible, because even indivisible lines, *qua* lines, should have limits, which have to be not lines but points, themselves indivisible. - Aristotle. Met. 992a 20-23; [Aristotle]. De lineis insec. 968a 1 sqq.; Xenocrates, frg. 123-124 Isnardi-Parente. Cp. Heath 1956, I 156. Other reasons for accepting "indivisible lines" might be attempts, first, to solve Zeno's paradoxes and the problem of continuum in general and second, to solve the problem of incommensurability in the sphere of the geometrical, since the "indivisible line" would be a common measure of any two lines.

[128] Proclus. In Eucl. 104.5-6.

circle (a self-contained and perfect figure) is comparable to the intellect and the line—to sense-perception.[129]

In Euclid's definition, "a point is that which has no part".[130] Another, earlier definition comes back to the Pythagoreans: the point is the "unit to which position is added".[131] The point—the simplest, indivisible and partless—is taken as *the* limit of the line, just as the unit itself is not a number but the indivisible principle of the number.[132] In a sense, the point may be taken as infinite, because it has no limit by itself or is limitless. If, however, infinity is taken as potential infinity, there is no need for a point to be either infinite or finite, because the property of being infinite simply is not applicable to the point (as it is not applicable to the notion of property itself).[133]

There is no room here for discussing the differences in the above three definitions. What is important for the present aim is to note that the point (*stigmē, sēmeion*) (1) is unique among geometrical entities, insofar as it is the only geometrical object that is completely indivisible since it has no parts.[134] As indivisible, the point (2) is *the* limiting principle (*arkhē*) in geometry, in the same way as the unit as henad is the principle of number and thus of arithmetic.[135] And the point is (3) the geometrical representative of the noetic entity, of the monad (and henad), which may be understood as embodied in intelligible matter and visualizable in imagination ("the point is a monad to which position is added").[136] Just as arithmetic is considered by ancient mathematicians to be prior to geometry, because the object of the former is simpler than that of the latter and number is divisible only in finite discrete units, whereas extended geometrical figure is infinitely divisible (a number consists of units or henads, whereas a line does not consist of points).[137] In like manner, the unit-henad is prior to the point, because although both are partless, unit has no position in extension, while the point does and is thus connected with (intelligible geometrical) materiality (see 2.4, 3.4.5).

Another important distinction between numbers and geometricals lies in their relation to infinity. As Aristotle argues, they are different in respect to increasing and decreasing: (quantitative) number may be potentially infinitely

---

[129] Cp. D'Ancona 1999, 252-259.
[130] *Sēmeion estin, hoy meros oythen.* - Euclid. Elem. I, def. I.
[131] *Monas proslaboysa thesin.* Proclus. In Eucl. 59.18-20; 95.22; cp. Aristotle. De an. 409a 6; Met. 1016b 24-26.
[132] *To peras tēs grammēs stigmē,* Plotinus. Enn. VI.3.14.14; cp. Euclid. Elem. I, def. 3; Aristotle. Met. 1090b 5-7; cp. Heath 1956, I 155-157.
[133] Cp. Aristotle. Phys. 202b 33-34.
[134] In Descartes, on the contrary, no geometrical figure or number has any privileged position and all are equal in their worth and value. It is to be noted that in modern discussions there is a tendency to modernize Ancient mathematics, in particular, to interpret Proclus in the sense of Descartes, to find in Proclus' Euclid commentary a "geometrical algebra", cp. Van der Waerden 1983, 78. For the discussion and refutation of this thesis see: Unguru 1976, 67-114; Schmitz 1997, 126-132.
[135] Proclus. In Eucl. 59.19-20; cp. 85.2 sqq.; Aristotle. Met. 1014b 7-8; 1016b 24-26; 1085b 33-34.
[136] Proclus. In Eucl. 59.17-19; 205.15.
[137] Aristotle. Phys. 215b 19-20; Proclus. In Eucl. 59.7 sqq. Cp. M. White 1992, 8 sqq.

increased through addition, but not divided, since the numerical unit or henad is indivisible. On the contrary, geometrical magnitude, being continuous, may be indefinitely divided, but not increased—for the simple reason that it would then turn into another, different quantity.[138] In other words, each of the two has its peculiar generic limit: in the case of number it is the limit "from below", the henad as the indivisible basis of the sameness in number, whereas for magnitude the limit "from 'above' is the magnitude itself as a whole".[139] As Iamblichus puts it in his commentary to Nicomachus' "Introduction to arithmetic", "the continuous and unified should be called magnitude, and the juxtaposed and discrete should be called multitude".[140]

Lastly, number and magnitude differ insofar as any two (mathematical) numbers are commensurable (*symmetra*), for their common measure is the unit and their ratio is expressible (*rhētos*) through a ratio of two integers.[141] Geometrical magnitudes, on the contrary, may be incommensurable (the side and the diagonal of a square, for example),[142] which is another reason for considering arithmetic to be prior to geometry. Commensurable magnitudes, as Euclid demonstrates, have the same ratio to one another as a number has to another number.[143] On the contrary, incommensurable geometrical magnitudes have no such measure, that is, their relation cannot be expressed (*alogos*), since there is a certain irrationality, something inexpressible (*arrhēton*), in the last instance coming from non-being or matter.

In order to be able to incorporate incommensurable geometrical magnitudes into science, Euclid has to redefine the notion of ratio and extend it to continuous magnitudes, that is, to incorporate the irrationality of *pēlikon*, rather than *poson*, discrete multitude. In order to do that, Euclid introduces ratio or *logos* as a "relation in respect of size (*hē kata pēlikotēta poia skhesis*) between two magnitudes of the same kind" in book V of the "Elements".[144] Incommensurable magnitudes are said to have a ratio, when multiplied they may exceed each other.[145] The ratio is to be distinguished from proportion (*analogia*), which is established among a number of magnitudes.[146] Such a definition of ratio enables

---

[138] Aristotle. Phys. 207a 33 sqq. Cp. Anaxagoras B3 DK, ap. Simplicius. In Phys. 164.16-20 (here, however, Anaxagoras seems to argue that a magnitude may be equally potentially infinitely decreased (divided) and increased). See also: Prantl 1987, 493; Gaidenko 1980, 318-320.

[139] It is this insurmountable distinction of number and geometrical magnitude that Aristotle obviously has in mind when saying that Plato discerns two infinities, which correspond to the infinity of addition in numbers and to the infinity of division in magnitudes—although Plato himself does not make such a distinction.

[140] "...[T]o men synekhes kai henōmenon kaloit' an megethos, to de parakeimenon kai diēirēmenon plēthos". - Iamblichus. In Nicom. 7.8-10. See also: Euclid. Elem. VII, def. 2; Aristotle. Met. 1020a 9-13.

[141] Euclid. Elem. X, def. 1.

[142] Cp. e.g. Proclus. In Eucl. 6.19-21; Heath 1956, I 351 sqq.

[143] Euclid. Elem. X, prop. 5.

[144] Euclid. Elem. V, def. 3; cp. Stein 1995, 334 sqq.

[145] Euclid. Elem. V, def. 4.

[146] Euclid. Elem. V, def. 6; cp. Aristotle. NE 1131a 30 sqq. Cp. Patzig 1960-1961, 204-205.

Euclid, first, to establish a relation between incommensurable entities and, second, to exclude infinitely big and infinitely small magnitudes (thus, for example, an angle of a triangle cannot have a ratio to an angle constituted by two tangent circles).

Important is the fact that irrationality under the guise of incommensurability may be observed only within geometrical magnitudes and not within (quantitative) numbers, each two of which are always in proportion, are commensurable as m/n and have a common measure in the numerical unit as the quantitative henad. The incommensurability may be exemplified only in extended geometrical magnitudes, which thus may be considered immersed in a specific extension that exemplifies the presence of geometrical matter (cp. 2.4). *Qua* geometrical, this matter embodies eternal objects, that is, objects whose properties do not change, but, *qua* matter, it brings irrationality, present through incommensurability and the potentially infinite (indefinite) divisibility of geometrical extended objects.

2.1.4 The in(de)finite in mathematical reasoning

The Cartesian concept of the indefinite as opposed to the infinite (1.3.2) is significant for the current discussion, insofar as the concept is applicable not only within the realm of physical things but in geometrical figures as well. The reason for this is obvious: one can always extend or enlarge a geometrical figure. The problem is then whether a particular geometrical figure, when related to the infinite or to the indefinite (e.g., when indefinitely extended), still preserves all of its properties and its form. For the infinite is something that cannot be apprehended or grasped by the finite mind.

As it has been said, the notion of the indefinite corresponds to the notion of potential infinity. If a geometrical figure is indefinitely extended, then at every step of its potentially infinite growth it will still remain the same figure with the same relations between its different elements: a circle will still be a circle, an ellipse will retain the same relation between its two main components, an isosceles triangle will keep the ratio of its sides, and so on. And since in geometrical objects, unlike in physical things, we are mostly not interested in measuring a "real" length of a line but rather in proportional relations of various elements, an indefinitely (i.e., potentially infinitely extended) geometrical figure will by no means be different in all of its properties from the initial figure, except for the relative size of two figures, expressed by a finite number. In other words, the indefinite figure, which is finite at each step but is capable of being ever further extended, does not qualitatively differ from a figure taken as the initial one: they both belong to the same species.

The case appears to be more complicated once not only the indefinite (potentially infinite), but also the infinite is admitted into modern mathematics, making it radically different from Greek mathematics and physics, which abstain from accepting actual infinity.[147] When the notion of an actually infinite mathematical object (a geometrical figure or number) is accepted, the finite mind

---

[147] Archimedes. Opera II, 242-290.

inevitably encounters a number of paradoxes (see 1.3.4). For instance, if one considers an infinitely extended circle, one can say that in infinity the circle becomes a straight line: "in geometry the concept of the arc of an indefinitely large circle is customarily extended to the concept of a straight line; or the concept of a rectilinear polygon with an indefinite number of sides is extended to that of a circle."[148] That in the infinite the properties of geometrical figures may radically change and show a fundamental affinity between various geometrical figures, hidden in the finite, is one of the main ideas of the projective geometry of Desargues.[149] In this case the finite mind can only conceive that a polygon *is* (becomes) a circle (or that the arc becomes a straight line) in the infinite, but *how* it happens still cannot be conceived. Or, another example (one that induced the new non-Euclidean geometry of Lobachevsky-Bolyai) is the famous fifth postulate of Euclid, which, in an alternative reading, states that two parallel lines never intersect when indefinitely extended, however they do intersect in an actually infinitely-distanced point.[150] The example of parallel lines intersecting "in infinity" may be explained through lines intersecting in a point at a finite distance, for example when Desargues explains an obscured species through another species that is more clear, and not vice versa.[151]

Ancient geometry, on the contrary, studies its objects insofar as they are limited, because the infinite cannot be properly known. Thus, for instance, every surface (*epipedon*) has to be taken only as limited (*peperasmenon*).[152] Modern geometry begins, as Descartes shows in his treatment of the *infini*, with the infinite (or possibly indefinite) line, plane or solid and only then considers their limitations as particular physical or geometrical objects. In this way even a geometrical figure may be considered as indefinitely increasing or decreasing if this takes place in and by means of the imagination (cp. 3.4.2). Nevertheless, the actually infinite in geometrical objects is absolutely transcendent to the indefinite increasing or decreasing, insofar as the former can—and in fact does—change the properties of a figure, while the latter does not.

A problem that arises here is how a finite figure (however large) relates to its infinite extension. The polygon differs from the circle in its properties and way

---

[148] Descartes. Fourth Set of Replies, AT VII 239.
[149] Desargues 1987, 142. Cp. Gray 1994, 897-907; Field 1997, 192-205.
[150] The fifth postulate is formulated by Euclid himself as: "That, if a straight line falling on two straight lines makes the interior angles on the same side less than two right angles, the two straight lines, if produced indefinitely, meet on that side on which are the angles less than the two straight angles". - Euclid. Elem. I, 202-220. Cp. Proclus. In Eucl. 386.24-373.2. Proclus, however, considers only three of Euclid's first postulates ("old", i.e., known already in the time of Plato, Archytas and Eudoxus) to be real postulates, excluding the fourth and the fifth. In the later developed Riemann geometry it is possible to draw an infinite number of straight lines through a given point, parallel to a given line (when the point does not lie on the line), that is, all the drawn lines do not intersect the given line. Cp. Gray 1994 877-886. Lobachevsky 1902, 5 sqq.; Riemann 1923, 1-20; Hilbert 1950, 11-12; Bolyai 1987, 14 sqq.
[151] Descartes. To [Desargues], [19 June 1639], AT II 554-556. Cp. Desargues 1864 I, 104 and also Newton on the infinite lines - McGuire 1983, 69 sqq.
[152] Plotinus, Enn. VI.3.14.28-29.

of construction; the circle differs from the straight line; the hyperbole indefinitely approximates its asymptote but never actually reaches it, and so on. The difference between the *infini* and the *indéfini* still remains insurmountable, because the finite reason can understand what happens when a geometrical object "becomes" infinite. Or, in terms of Descartes, reason can understand how a concept of a polygon is "extended" to the concept of circle, but it cannot grasp how the geometrical object "becomes" infinite; an absolute limit or an abyss between the potentially and the actually infinite cannot be overcome. Finite reason can efficiently operate with the notion of the infinite and know it (the "is"), but it cannot apprehend or grasp what actually happens in the infinite (the "how" of the passage from the potentially infinite to the actually infinite) (cp. 1.3.2). The infinite can then be explained analogically through the finite (a physical or geometrical object clearly graspable by reason and easily imaginable), but the question of why this is possible at all remains unanswered. Taking into account, however, what has already been said about the ontological and axiological precedence of the infinite in Descartes, one might argue that the procedure of the "extension" of a figure up to its limit, where the figure quite often turns into another genus (a polygon into a circle, a circle into a straight line, and so on), is itself justified only insofar as a kind of *a priori* infinite structure or entity has to be presupposed (the *infini*). Because the infinite is already there, it itself is not, and cannot be, constructed, although it allows a particular figure to be understood as a limitation of its infinite limit. Acceptance of the infinite thus becomes a necessary presupposition for the justification of contemporary science, in particular, of mathematics.

An obvious difference between geometrical figures and numbers is that the set of all integer numbers is well ordered; there is a rule that determines for every two numbers which of the two is prior to the other, whereas there is no such ordering within figures. Nevertheless, the infinite is represented both in geometrical objects and in numbers. Much of what has been said about geometrical figures in respect to the infinite is also true in the case of numbers. For instance, $\lim 1/n = 0$ when $n \to \infty$ (n is a natural number), although zero is never actually attended. Even if the infinite in mathematical objects is not immediately accessible or graspable, the finite mind is nevertheless able to draw certain conclusions about it.[153]

In the Second Set of Objections to the "Meditations", compiled by Mersenne, an objection is raised against the Cartesian proof of the existence of God, namely, that our mind has neither an idea of God, nor an idea of an infinite number, and that even if the idea of the infinite were to exist in the mind, it would not mean that the infinite as such does exist. Therefore, the idea of infinity can only be a construction of the finite mind and does not represent anything really existing. As Mersenne states, "Even if there were just one degree of heat or light, I could always imagine further degrees and continue the process of addition up to infinity. In the same way, I can surely take a given degree of being, which I

---

[153] Cp. Dirichlet 1889, I 357-380; Bromwich 1926, 26 sqq. Descartes mentions in his letter an infinite series of numbers, 15/16, 31/32, 63/64, 127/128, 255/256 *et sic in infinitum*, which express the "resistance of air" and whose limit is 1 (although never actually attended), - To Mersenne, 18 December 1629, AT I 93.

perceive within myself, and add on a further degree, and thus construct the idea of a perfect being from all the degrees which are capable of being added on."[154] The question whether the infinite does really exist or whether it is only a construction of the finite mind thus becomes crucial for the Cartesian proof of the existence of God. If the infinite is just an extension of the finite, considered in it highest possible degree, then nothing guarantees that the infinite does, or has to, really exist, independently of operations of the finite mind. But if the infinite is a kind of *a priori* structure, a particular limitation of which forms finite notions and representations (particularly, of a finite number or geometrical figure), without which they are neither thinkable nor possible as having a number of properties and attributes, then the infinite has to be accepted as the primary reality.

If God does exist as the infinite thinking substance, if he supports and constantly recreates the finite substances, then, because he is utterly perfect and thus actually infinite, infinity must also be present in mathematical—arithmetical and geometrical—objects. Descartes' argument is the following: "Now in my thought or intellect I can somehow come upon a perfection that is above me; thus I notice that, when I count, I cannot reach the largest number, and hence I recognize that there is something in the process of counting which exceeds my powers. And I contend that from this alone it necessarily follows, not that an infinite number exists, nor indeed that it is a contradictory notion, as you say, but that I have the power of conceiving that there is a thinkable number which is larger than any number that I can ever think of, and hence that this power is something which I have received not from myself but from some other being which is more perfect than I am."[155]

The supposedly largest number cannot be reached by the procedure that the finite mind resorts to—namely, counting. In other words, natural numbers form a potentially infinite set. That there is at least one potentially infinite ordered set (of natural numbers) is described in contemporary mathematics by the axiom of infinity: there exists at least one set Z such that, first, 0 belongs to Z; second, if x belongs to Z, then the set $\{x\}$ also belongs to Z. Then $\{0\}$, $\{0, \{0\}\}$, $\{0, \{0, \{0\}\}\}$, etc., all belong to Z. Now, we may simply consider $\{0\}=1$, $\{0, 1\}=2$, $\{0, 1,...n-1\}=n$, and all the natural number described this way will belong to Z and will also be different from each other. The natural order among them is then also easily established by the operation "+1", which signifies the passage from n-1 to n.[156] Every integer may be exceeded by adding another unit to it. It means that there is no largest number and no actually infinite number accessible to the finite mind.

Now, if we accept the notion of an actually infinite entity (infinitely large

---

[154] Mersenne. Second Set of Objections, AT VII 123-124.

[155] Descartes. Second Set of Replies, AT VII 139. Later Descartes explains it to Burman: "I know God exists and I have proved it. And at the same time, I notice that when I count I can never reach a highest number, but there is always a number that can be thought of which is greater than any number that I can think of. It follows that the power of conceiving of this is something I do not derive from myself, but must have received from some entity more perfect than myself. And this entity is God, whose existence I have proved by means of the arguments already adduced". - Conversation with Burman, AT V 157.

[156] Cp. Dedekind 1911, passim and the axioms of Peano - Peano 1990, 27-32.

or infinitely small, as in the case of infinitesimals), two approaches are possible, both accepted in modern mathematics. First, the actually infinite can be regarded as inexistent as such, so that we are always thinking in finite terms. Even if infinity cannot be grasped as such, it nevertheless appears, for instance, in the approximation of a particular quantity through a number of iterative steps. For example, the notion of infinity is essentially involved in the definition of the limit of a sequence: if a series a_n has A as its limit, then for any number $\varepsilon>0$ there exists an integer N such that $|a_n-A|<\varepsilon$ for all n>N. The notions of the largest number or of infinitesimals thus relate to potential infinity. This is the approach of Cauchy and of the classical analysis. The other approach is present in contemporary non-standard analysis, which takes the infinitely large number and infinitesimals to be actually existing: the transfinite infinite number "follows" any large natural number and the infinitesimal is considered to be a fixed quantity, less than any smallest quantity one might choose (although Cantor himself rejects the possibility of the existence of actually infinitely small magnitudes).[157]

In the above passage Descartes may be seen as anticipating Cantor's theory. It seems, rather, that Descartes simply tries to extend his approach to infinity (by stressing the precedence of the infinite to the finite) to natural numbers, so that every number might be regarded as a particular limitation of the initial number, which has to be then *a priori* presupposed as a condition of the possibility of finite numbers. The finite mind can neither think (grasp) nor reach the infinite number. In this respect, the infinite number does not exist for the finite mind. But the fact that it is capable of thinking about (capable of knowing) the infinite number and of continuing the process of counting, has to imply that there is something that makes the potentially infinite counting possible and which is perfect in a higher degree. Such a perfection can only be for Descartes actual infinity. The infinite can be neither merely imaginable nor something that may be derived from the contents of the finite mind. Therefore, there should be an infinite (transfinite) number in God, who is considered to be infinite thinking (it is not by chance that in his later years Cantor tried to justify his theory by referring to Plato).[158] The infinite number has thus to be accepted on the ground that also appears in Descartes' ontological proof. At least, the ability of the human mind to recur to the infinite in mathematics can be explained only if there is an *a priori* entity, which is itself infinite. That infinite entity may exist then only if God, being actually infinite and perfect, exists. The infinite number may not necessarily be a number in the usual sense: in fact, Descartes does not accept the infinite *qua* number. But in God the infinite represents the highest possible—the actually infinite—degree of perfection, which, however, is always considered through the finite and the limited by the finite mind. In the infinite mind this infinite number

---

[157] Cantor 1985, 294-295; Robinson 1966, 57 sqq., 279-282; cp. Frege 1969, 76-80; Gödel 1990, II 311. Leibniz is at times hesitant about which of the two approaches to choose, for at times he takes the infinitesimal to be in the process of becoming and sometimes—as already a complete entity, see: Nikulin 1993, 167-169.

[158] Cantor 1985, 247, 264. Cantor himself considered an infinite set as actually infinite and in this sense as a whole unity—as the Platonic *eidos* or *idea*—and referred to potential infinity as *apeiron*. Cp. Dauben 1979, 170.

may not be represented as number—it need not formally, but only eminently be number in and for the infinite thinking. Such an infinite number makes possible then all mathematical procedures that involve the infinite and are thus rejected by ancient mathematics. Therefore although Descartes recognizes that infinite knowledge and power are contained formally in the idea of God, infinite number and length can only be eminently in this idea.[159]

In the "Parmenides" Plato mentions an "infinite number" (*apeiros arithmos*) understood by Parmenides as quantitatively infinite, that is, the set of natural numbers is considered potentially infinite, so that, once a number is given, one can always consider a bigger one.[160] The notion of the "infinite number" generated, however, a number of commentaries in the later Platonic tradition, which, as we saw in Plotinus, already accepts the notion of actual infinity. Along with Plato, Plotinus too considers the "number of the infinite".[161] The number, as a form of numbering and also as numbered, has to be definite and thus limited, both in the intelligible and as referring to particular things, since otherwise nothing could be thought in its definiteness. In this respect the intelligible line—the notion of line, which makes geometrical lines of any length possible—is to be posterior to the number and may be said to be infinite or, rather, indefinite, in the sense that the limit is not thought in the definition of a line (*en tōi logōi tēs aytogrammēs oyk eni prosnooymenon peras*). The infinite, *apeiria*, according to this argument, cannot limit or define, but may only be limited or defined; it can only appear as a sort of matter that always escapes limiting and defining (*to peras kai horos kai logos*). Plotinus' conclusion is that if number may be said to be infinite, it is only in the negative sense, namely, that number is not limited and not defined by anything else.[162]

Damascius argues that the infinite has to be necessarily present in number, although not as actually infinite but as a lack of any limits for further division. But even if any concrete positive integer is taken by Damascius as finite, because it is limited by its own form of being this particular number, there should be an infinite number without qualification (*haplōs*). As does Descartes, Damascius claims this number to be inaccessible to finite human understanding, grasped only by the intellect—by pure being, which in thinking itself must necessarily employ the notion of the actually infinite, which, in turn, points to the source of being, to the infinite One.[163]

The question that arises in Descartes is whether the set of numbers (e.g., of natural numbers) exists as a whole, as actually infinite or only as potentially infinite, where it is always possible to extend a list of numbers or to produce a bigger number. Descartes sometimes speaks about the infinite immensity (*l'immensité infinie*) of numbers, without specifying how he understands it.[164]

---

[159] Descartes. Second Set of Replies, AT VII 137.
[160] Plato. Parm. 144a. Cp. Aristotle. Phys. 203b 24, 206a 11; Proclus. In Eucl. 6.15-17.
[161] Plotinus. Enn. VI.6.2.1 sqq.
[162] Plotinus. Enn. VI.6.3.2, 9-12; VI.6.17.4-18; VI.6.18.1-12; Plotinus 1980, 190-194. Cp. Aristotle. Met. 1028b 24-26.
[163] Damascius. De princ., 200.
[164] Descartes. To Frenicle, 9 January 1639, AT II 474.

From what has been said, it would appear that for the finite mind the set of numbers is only potentially infinite: it is always possible to make another step, but at each particular moment the finite mind thinks a number or an ensemble of numbers as only finite. For and in the infinite intellect, however, the set of numbers might be thought and understood as complete, so that even if there is no actually infinite number as a formal concept, there is an infinite power and thinking that knows and grasps the whole immensity of numbers eminently and all at once.

In other words, numbers, when thought, may be considered as produced or constructed by the finite mind, although on Descartes' account it has to be only a *re*production or an *as if* construction, for the whole immensity of numbers is already there in and for the infinite mind (cp. 3.4.1-3.4.2). The infinite substance is then the only instance that may be said to really produce the numbers, although not in a discursive process of counting, but in a single act of comprehension and a simple intuition of the divine mind, inaccessible and not graspable by the finite mind. The insurmountable difference between the finite and the infinite intellects, constantly stressed by Descartes, necessitates an acceptance of the scientific approach or *method*. Indeed, if one happens to discover or guess a certain property of numbers (e.g., the Fermat theorem), it does not yet suffice that this property holds for any finite (however large) number of numbers, which may be proven directly (calculated). Nothing guarantees that, beginning at a certain point, the property in question is invalid. The finitude of our mind plays a crucial role here: we cannot see or grasp *all* numbers simply by verifying all the possible cases to be sure that the discussed property really holds. Such a procedure, as Descartes writes in a letter to Frenicle, is available only to the infinite mind, which can simply and immediately *see* in a single act that the property holds.[165] The finite mind, which cannot immediately enumerate all the possible cases, has to *prove* a theorem, that is, to establish, in a finite number of steps of discursive thinking, that the property is valid for all the members of an infinite set or class.

Thus, we encounter once again the fundamental difference between knowing and grasping: the former is referred to the finite discursive reason, while the latter—to the infinite non-discursive intellect (cp. 3.1.1; 3.1.2). It is important to note that the two are rigidly separated in Descartes and in modern philosophy, because of the insurmountable distinction between the creator and the created, between the infinite and the finite. The notions of the infinite and of production are indeed tightly connected. Thus, Hilbert considers transfinite or infinite objects of mathematics to be nothing but constructions of the human mind, freely created; the only requirement is to avoid contradictions. Kronecker, as well as the constructivists and the intuitionists, rejects the notion of actual infinity (and, on this ground, also Cantor's theory, where different infinities are treated as finite numbers), because, first, the acceptance of actual infinity leads to paradoxes and, second, from the point of view of the constructivists, unlike that of the formalists, a mathematical object exists not if it is free of contradiction, but if one can describe the way this object is (or may be) constructed (see 3.4.1).

The appropriate way for the finite mind to know the actually infinite in discursive reasoning and proofs is to establish a one-to-one correspondence

---

[165] Descartes. To Frenicle, 9 January 1639, AT II 474.

between two sets or subsets of a set: if it is possible to find such a correspondence, two sets have the same cardinal number or "number" of members, even if the number is infinite. Besides, as Descartes notices, there can be enormously long numbers, so that the span of an entire human life would be insufficient to write them down. However, one can conveniently refer to them as *a*, *b*, *c*, etc., and in this way express them, which further enables the remarkable development of algebraic methods in Fermat, Descartes and their contemporaries. This operation corresponds exactly to the contemporary notion of the abstraction of potential realizability in mathematics and logic, which, in order to represent an infinite object, presupposes the performance of a finite number of operations or steps. However, if it is practically impossible to write (to construct) an entity (a long word or a number written by a substantially large number of signs) to imply the performance of a large number of consecutive operations, one may abstract from the actual realization of the task and simply denote that entity by a sign. Actual infinity is retained by Descartes only for the infinite intellect, while everything accessible to the finite mind is displayed by the potentially infinite or by its abstraction through a finite sign.

An evident analogy for such a conclusion is that the finite mind can know but cannot grasp such a long number in the entirety of its digits (even if it is a finite number, such as an irrational—algebraic or transcendental—number, which cannot be written either by a finite or by a periodic decimal expansion). The same is true, as has been argued, in the case of actual divine infinity: one can possibly know it in its existence, but not in its essence. In the case of number, the finite mind may not be able to grasp a substantially large number *a* in its entirety (the number may not be readable by the finite mind or by a computer within a certain substantially large period of time), but we are able to know (i.e., prove) what it is in its properties. The very same procedure is then applicable to the ordinal and cardinal transfinite numbers, ω and $\aleph_0$,[166] so that the finite mind is able to know that this infinite number *is*, because there is an idea of it in the finite mind (namely, it is thinkable that there is a number "after" all the natural numbers or a number that expresses the number of all possible subsets of the set of natural numbers), but not to know *what* it is—and therefore to be unable to grasp the infinite number—because of the essential finitude of the human mind. In the very same way as it is known that the infinite *is* but it is not grasped *what* it is, one might conclude that there should be (an) infinite mathematical object(s), by limitation of which one conceives finite mathematical objects with their properties.

Actual infinity is thus not an extension of the finite or of the potentially infinite. There is a principal and insurmountable difference between the two. By adding another element, even a potentially infinite number of times, we will never achieve the actually infinite, the infinite as a whole. Actual infinity cannot be presented as potential infinity added or even multiplied a (even infinite) number of times. As Descartes says, "I readily and freely confess that the idea which we have of the divine intellect, for example, does not differ from that which we have of our own intellect, except in so far as the idea of an infinite number differs from the

---

[166] Cp. Cantor 1883, 32 sqq.; Abian 1965, 316 sqq.; Jech 1978, 42-52.

idea of a number raised to the second or fourth power".[167] The impossibility of arriving at actual infinity by simply indefinitely extending the finite (perfections), underlies, as it has been said, the Cartesian proof of the existence of God, because there is no mental operation that might produce the infinite and its very notion out and from the finite. Or, put otherwise, actual infinity can neither be constructed nor understood by means of construction (cp. 3.4.1).

2.2 Geometry, metaphysics and method in Descartes

Mathematics plays a major role in Descartes' considerations, which seem to fully support the Platonic claim that mathematics is the clearest and the most certain science that sets the standard and is itself an example of strict and correct reasoning, indispensable for searching for the truth. Thus, in geometry, as Descartes says, "we seek only exactitude (*iustesse*) of reasoning".[168] Exactitude is the main requirement for scientific investigations. Exactitude is *justice*, "iustesse", of reasoning, which in particular implies that, first, in our reason there should be a capacity of discriminating the just or exact from the unjust or inexact. Being finite, reason is unable to immediately apprehend or "see" the truth in its entirety; instead, it should limit itself to pronouncing a correct judgement. The capacity of judgement becomes, together with taste, one of the most important faculties of reason in modernity. Judgement presupposes not only correct reasoning but also a personal stand: even if a finite subjectivity sincerely, *sine ira et studio,* tries to sentence a fact to truth, it nevertheless cannot get rid of itself, of its own presence and necessary involvement in judgement. As the addition to the French edition of the "Principles" runs, "[a]bsolute certainty arises when we believe that it is wholly impossible that something should be otherwise than we judge it to be".[169]

Every judgement has thus a flavor of taste and subjectivity. On the other hand, exactitude as *iustesse* of reasoning presupposes law, *ius*, which is to be found both in geometrical and in natural things. The notion of *ius*—either *ius civile, ius naturale, ius divinum,* or in any other form—is not descriptive but essentially *prescriptive*. *Ius* prescribes the conditions of fulfillment of truth, both in social matters and in nature. In a very similar manner, Descartes prescribes truth and exactitude as law to geometrical and physical things (see 3.4.1; 3.4.2). If truth, not only in moral, social and political questions but also in science, whose purpose is to investigate the objective world of physical things and mathematical entities, is the subject of taste, then it can hardly be other than prescriptive. Indeed, taste, even if it is a most intimate capacity of individual reasoning, is itself the subject of public opinion, tradition and fashion, which may change throughout history and prescribe to much extent what should be judged and considered beautiful, elegant,

---

[167] Descartes. Second Set of Replies, AT VII 137. As an example one might mention the operation of the Cartesian multiplication of two sets: for two sets X and Y, X×Y is the set of all pairs of {x, y} where x belongs X and y belongs to Y. The result of the multiplication of two finite sets will also be a finite set and of two potentially infinite sets will also be a potentially, not actually, infinite set.
[168] Descartes. Geometry II, AT VI 389.
[169] Descartes. Princ. IV 206, AT VIIIA 328.

good and true. The alleged exactitude and precision as *justice* of reason are to be prescribed, produced or constructed and are thus imposed onto extended—both geometrical and physical—reality.

Descartes' task, then, is to find an adequate description or method that would fit this ideal of exactitude, clarity and distinctness—which becomes a methodological demand—and would eliminate all possible ambiguity and equivocation in scientific description (see 3.3.1).[170] Because of the certainty of mathematics and because the most certain and unequivocal results known in the history of science belong to mathematical knowledge, the description (or, rather, the *prescription*), which may fit the ideal of exactitude as *iustesse*, has to be mathematical. If Descartes criticizes ancient mathematicians—Euclid, Pappus, Apollonius—it is for being unable to elaborate fully the true method or language of science, since ancient mathematics confines itself to studying mathematical objects only and does not extend to any other kinds of objects (in particular, to physical things). Thus, mathematics is to be considered the science that provides the method for all other sciences or the pattern on which the universal method may be constructed. If not fully equivalent to mathematics, a pure non-empirical ideal for the method as *mathesis* may at least be found in the mathematical practice of solving problems,[171] in the practice of both arithmetic and geometry, which "alone are concerned with an object so pure and simple that they make no assumptions that experience might render uncertain; they consist entirely in deducing conclusions by means of rational arguments".[172]

At the same time, the ultimate truth Descartes wants to establish and to ground is not that of mathematics, but of metaphysics—of the existence of God and the soul.[173] This truth is then supposed to provide an ultimate foundation for all other possible truths. Ontologically it has to be the first, although in the order of consideration (i.e., logically and epistemologically), it is not the first, for metaphysical truth is originally demonstrated from the subjective certainty of the self-awareness of the *cogito*.[174] A certain circularity arises in Descartes' considerations. On the one hand, a possibility of establishing the necessity of being of the not created thinking substance is rooted in the certainty of the subjective judgement of the *ego*. On the other hand, the certainty of the *cogito ergo sum* is itself possible only because of the necessity of being of the infinite not created thinking substance, which produces the finite thinking substance, the *ego* itself, capable of knowing and understanding the very source and cause of its finite existence.[175] Such a circle, however, is not vicious, because a proposition, in the Cartesian account, may be considered true if it is grounded *both* in the divine mind, which produces and guarantees the necessity of its truth, and in the human mind,

---

[170] Funkenstein 1986, 28 sqq. Cp. Aristotle. Met. 1003a 21 sqq.
[171] Lachterman 1989, 141 sqq.
[172] Descartes. Reg. II, AT X 364-365.
[173] Descartes. Med. III, AT VII 34 sqq.
[174] For interpretation of the *cogito* as initially non-representative, non-intentional and non-reflective, see M. Henry 1993, 40-51. For a criticism of such interpretation, see Marion 1993, 52-74.
[175] Cp. Descartes. To Mersenne, 15 April 1630, AT I 145.

which, through the *lumen naturale*, discursively justifies the statement as necessary, that is, proves it. A similar circle can also be seen in the relation of mathematics to metaphysics. If mathematics is the rational science *par excellence*, which sets a canon for metaphysical considerations, then mathematics has to be considered as logically and epistemologically prior. But since metaphysics has to provide a foundation for mathematics, metaphysics should be ontologically prior. That is why Descartes has to claim that "the proofs in metaphysics are more certain than those in mathematics".[176]

The finite mind has to start in its subjective evidence with essence and only then arrive at the recognition of existence as necessarily presumed in the unique essence of the infinite substance (cp. 1.3.2). Because of its finitude, the human mind cannot start with direct comprehension of the supposedly infinite divine mind, the source of all possible truths. The quest of the finite mind can only be realized through a chain of simple and evident steps in reasoning, by means of which one can reach or tie together premises and conclusion.[177] These steps are aimed at the understanding and the demonstration of already not immediately evident truths (metaphysical, mathematical and physical). But if the finite mind gradually, first through reflective understanding of itself and then by justifying the necessary truths, comes to the understanding of the infinite mind, this infinite has to be presupposed as a necessary transcendental condition for the possibility of such knowledge.

Where should the finite mind look for the paradigm of its discursive search for truth? Not among extended things, although not because they are ever fluent and thus are subject only to opinion-*doxa* and not to knowledge, as Plato takes them to be, but because extended things can be imagined as non-existent in a reductive act of doubt. Therefore, they do not belong to the realm of primary evidence and to the truth of the *cogito*.[178] Descartes presupposes the existence of only two finite substances, hence the paradigm is to be found among objects of thought. Every finite object bears a trace of its infinite productive cause, considered the source of truth, so every finite *res* has to exemplify a certain order and regularity, and mathematical (geometrical) objects are most suitable as a model for it. Since, however, metaphysics is to be considered the ground and foundation of both mathematics and physics, metaphysical arguments should display at least the same, or even more, certainty than mathematical proofs. It is

---

[176] Descartes. Conversation with Burman, AT V 177; cp. Med. Synopsis AT VII 15 and: "The principal aim of my metaphysics is to show which are the things that can be distinctly conceived...". - Descartes. To Mersenne, 30 September 1640, AT III 192. Descartes' claim is contested by Gassendi (Fifth Set of Objections, AT VII 327-328), to which Descartes replies that the metaphysical knowledge, primarily, of the existence of God, "is prior in the order of knowledge and more evident and more certain" (Fifth Set of Replies, AT VII 384). Such a knowledge is not, however, easily established: thus, in his letter to Huygens, Descartes complains that there are more people who introduce philosophical notions into mathematics than, on the contrary, those who use certainty and evidence of the mathematical demonstrations in metaphysics (To Huygens, 1 November 1635, AT I 331-332).
[177] Descartes. Disc. II, AT VI 19.
[178] Descartes. Med. I, AT VII 17 sqq.

even *in suo genere* an epistemological obligation to employ one's reason to know metaphysical truths—about God and ourselves—and only "along that road", *par cete voye*, can foundations of physics be discovered.[179]

The program of catalogical ordering of all knowledge, that method which should be indiscriminately applicable both to the extended and the thinkable, structures knowledge as logical, since it has to be established by means of rational argumentation and in a finite number of deductive steps. It first implies that every predicate is analytically contained in its subject, so each step of discursive reasoning provides a mere tautology on both sides of the equation. Second, every knowledge has to be presented in the form of a proposition that is sentenced to be either true or false. This program of sheer logicism, seemingly attractive for providing a foundation of science, fails, however, with the discovery of the incompleteness of formal axiomatic systems.

If mathematics is considered the model for the method of scientific description, then it should be applicable not only to mathematical problems, but also to every problem that can be put in the mathematical form.[180] Mathematics as the pattern for the method is neither the algebra "of the moderns", nor the geometry "of the ancients", for both are just two particular sciences, the former studying relations of numbers understood as signs, the latter studying figures and their properties. One of the purposes of the method is liberation from "greatly tiring the imagination" of the ancient geometrical analysis of figures and from the pure formality of algebra.[181]

Indeed, if any investigation that has to be exact is about things that allow of *order* and *measure*, then, as Descartes argues in the Rule IV, there should be a "general science which explains all the points which can be raised concerning order and measure", a true *mathesis* (*vera mathesis*) that has to be superior to all sciences in utility and simplicity (*vtilitate et simplicitate*), for "it covers all they deal with, and more besides".[182] It thus is the pure form of mathematical investigation that becomes an attractive model for the construction of the universal *mathesis*. Still, the *mathesis universalis* differs from ordinary mathematics, as Descartes himself recognizes in the "Regulae", because the *mathesis* "should contain the primary rudiments of human reason and extend to the discovery of truths in any field whatever".[183] In a later letter to Hogelande, Descartes defines *mathesis* (the project of which appears yet in Proclus and in early modernity in Van Roomen) as "the ability to resolve all problems, and moreover to discover by one's own industry everything that can be discovered by the human mind in this

---

[179] Descartes. To Mersenne, 15 April 1630, AT I 144. In another letter, Descartes claims that the arguments for the existence of God "are clearer in themselves than any demonstrations of geometers". - To Mersenne, 27 February 1637, AT I 350. Cp. also: Discourse I, AT VI 7; Med. V, AT VII 65. Cp., however, Clarke 1982, 83-87, who argues that Descartes does not manage to provide a univocal depiction of the way physics is to be derived from metaphysics.
[180] Descartes. Discourse III, AT VI 29.
[181] Descartes. Discourse II, AT VI 17-18.
[182] Descartes. Reg. IV, AT X 376-378, cp. Reg. XIV, AT X 451; Discourse II, AT VI 17 sqq.; cp. Geometry I, AT VI 368.
[183] Descartes. Reg. IV, AT X 374.

science".[184] As Van de Pitte argues at length, *mathesis universalis* should not be understood and translated as "universal mathematics", although in Descartes' times, *mathesis* ordinarily meant "mathematical science". Namely, if it is supposed that (a) every discipline that considers objects in terms of order and measure as related to quantity of whatever kind may be called *mathematica*, (b) order and measure are distinct from the principles of order and measure and (c) the principles of order and measure are logically prior to order and measure, then one can make the following distinctions in Descartes. (One may generalize (b) and (c) as requiring in general that the principles of a science belong to a metascience, that metascience does not constitute a part of a science and that metascience be logically prior to the corresponding science.) If this is the case, then, first, one has to distinguish *mathesis* (*prima mathesis*) from mathematics, and second, *mathesis*—from *mathesis universalis*: *mathesis* contains the principles that make mathematics a science, both principles of validity and of discovery (or learning) in the *mathematica*. The latter is to be taken as constituting the principles of all sciences as *mathematicae* (i.e., the science of *method* or universal methodology). Moreover, *mathesis universalis* has to present certain procedure(s) by which the universal methodology has to be applicable in every particular science.[185] "By a 'method'", writes Descartes in the "Regulae", "I mean reliable rules which are easy to apply, and such that if one follows them exactly, one will never take what is false to be true or fruitlessly expend one's mental efforts, but will gradually and constantly increase one's knowledge (*scientiam*) till one arrives at a true understanding of everything within one's capacity".[186] These procedures or rules are not, however, explicitly formulated in the "Regulae"; later in the "Discourse" Descartes provides a small number of simple rules, but it remains not altogether clear whether they should be taken as the rules of the *mathesis universalis*.[187] There is, however, no obvious reason to identify the method suggested in the "Discourse" with the *mathesis universalis* of the "Regulae".

The ideal of *the* method based on the simple and easy study of relations or proportions is present throughout the corpus of Descartes' texts, from the "Discourse" published in 1637 to the conversation with Burman in 1648:

---

[184] Descartes. To Hogelande, 8 February 1640, AT XII Suppl. 2.

[185] Van de Pitte 1979, 154-174. Cp. Crapulli 1969; Schuster 1980, 41-96; Lachterman 1986, 435-458 and Sepper 1996, 144-152. For the historical background of the "universal mathematics" and the difficulties involved in the realization of the project see: Schuster 1977, 160 sqq., 459 sqq. Sepper tends to see all mathematics in Descartes as reducible to knowledge of proportions and presents *mathesis universalis* as "the science of concretely imagined proportional relations" (Op. cit., 192). However, if there is a distinction between the science of order and measure and the science of the principles to which the former applies, then the two do not appear to be discerned in Sepper's presentation. Van de Pitte in his interpretation seems to follow Van Roomen, who distinguishes *mathesis* into *specialis* and *universalis* and the latter into *logistice* and *prima mathesis*, which for Van de Pitte is "the essential core of basic principles" of mathematics.

[186] Descartes. Reg. IV, AT X 371-372.

[187] The rules are: clearness and distinctness of the premises; dividing problems into simplest "atomic" parts; following order in procession from simple to complex; and making enumerations. - Descartes. Discourse II, AT VI 20. Cp. Garber 1992, 31 sqq.

mathematics *qua* the exemplary method or pure form of reasoning is indispensable both as a prerequisite for accustoming the mind to searching for and recognizing the truth—and as the specimen for new discoveries (although later Descartes gradually abandons his interest in a universal methodology of science).[188] That mathematics is the most exact of all sciences is no novelty.[189] New is Descartes' attempt to abstract mathematics as the method and the presumably correct form of reasoning from the content of mathematics; that is, to liberate mathematics as the instrument, as the *organon* of every—even physical—investigation, from mathematics as a concrete science, rooted in a particular practice. In doing so, he tries to "upgrade", as it were, this new mathematically structured science into a universal science that would operate with pure forms of description. Since, however, the content of description is left out (the described object may be of any kind, both mental and extended; and if extended, both geometrical and physical), description turns into prescription: in describing a phenomenon (e.g., a physical one) Descartes implicitly imposes the very structures of description upon the described. Description thus turns into a construction (see 3.4.1).

The Cartesian consideration of mathematics as providing a method, or even *the* method, applicable to both metaphysics and physics has an interesting structure. If one recalls Aristotle's triad of the three exact theoretical sciences—metaphysics (or first philosophy), mathematics and physics,[190] one can easily recognize all three in Descartes' project of the method, where *mathesis* plays the role of the science mediating in cognition between the other two, similar to that of mathematics in Aristotle. The discursiveness of *mathesis* fits well the subjectivity of the *ego*-point, epistemologically prior but ontologically posterior to the subjectivity of the divine-point, to which metaphysics corresponds. In a sense, *mathesis universalis* for Descartes is a (or even *the*) method of discursive overcoming of human finitude, which appears in the unavoidable discursiveness of thinking. *Mathesis* mediates between metaphysics, which has to reveal the necessity of existence of the infinite thinking substance, and physics, which refers to the finite (or indefinite) extended substance. If this is the case, then if one also takes into consideration that mathematics is considered detached from its contents, then mathematics *qua* discursive method of reasoning may be applicable to every extended entity without discrimination, be it physical or geometrical (see 2.2.1). Even if Descartes, as it will be argued (2.3.1), tends to expel intermediary structures, they nevertheless return and appear unexpectedly under various guises,

---

[188] Descartes. Conversation with Burman, AT V 176-177. Cp. Preface to the French Edition of the "Principles", AT IXB 14; To Beeckman, 26 March 1619, AT X 156-157. In Reg. XIV, AT X 447 Descartes mentions three characteristics which describe differences in proportion: dimension, unity and figure (shape).
[189] Cp. Plato. RP 517b sqq.
[190] Aristotle. Met. 1003a 21 sqq.; 1026a 6-32. Aristotle calls the first philosophy theology (*theologikē*, 1026a 18-19). However, in books Γ and E of "Metaphysics", evidently composed prior to Z, H and Θ, there appears a certain discrepancy between considering the first philosophy, *prōtē philosophia*, as, on the one hand, the only discipline that considers being as such, the discipline that thus has to be regarded as *the* science. On the other hand, the first philosophy is taken as just one of the three theoretical disciplines. See the discussion in: Patzig 1960-1961, 185-205.

in particular, under the guise of mathematics *qua* the formal method.

Mathesis thus has to determine the order of reasoning for both metaphysics and physics, while the standard of precision should come from metaphysics. Therefore, *mathesis* is epistemologically the first—it is prior in the order of cognition. Without application of the method, the whole of logical analytic truths might only be supposed to have been known all at once only in a momentary grasp in one single point of the putative *panopticum*, attainable only to the infinite divine intellect. Such a point represents the limit of the potentially infinite striving of cognition of the finite mind, which at every particular moment possesses only finite knowledge—that is, the knowledge expressible in a finite number of (presumably true) propositions, achievable by the method and capable of being increased in their number.

As the universal methodology, *mathesis universalis* should be then applicable to every *mathematica*, which considers as its objects everything falling under the categories of order and measure, which are to be taken as common characteristics of all sciences.[191] In particular, this very method also has to be applicable to physical science, which studies physical bodies. Descartes thus makes a very strong presupposition about the realm of physical objects, namely, that it has to be the subject of order and measure: corporeal nature is the subject matter of pure *mathesis* (*purae Matheseos objectum*), as he puts it in the "Meditations".[192] However, as it has been pointed out, Descartes takes this presupposition for granted, without really justifying it.

It is also important to note that if the *mathesis universalis* is to be the universal science of principles for every science and, further, if for Descartes all sciences borrow their principles from philosophy (in the "Discourse"), or that metaphysics as first philosophy contains "the principles of knowledge" (in the "Principles"), then the *mathesis universalis* is to replace first philosophy itself.[193] Or, put otherwise, first philosophy has to be conceived as *methodology*—the approach that we find at the core of consideration of science in modernity, from Neokantianism to critical rationalism.

Furthermore, the *mathesis universalis* appears to be different from the *more geometrico* method, insofar as the former is to consider the principles of the universal application of order and measure (the method commonly searched for in early modern philosophy), while the latter, already well elaborated and firmly established in antiquity, considers deduction of a consistent set of propositions obtained from a set of primary principles (definitions, axioms and postulates). A paradigmatic example of the method that starts with definitions, postulates and axioms and then goes on to proving theorems and solving problems, is presented by Euclid's "Elements" (mathematics *more geometrico*)[194] and in theoretical philosophy by Proclus' "Elements of Theology" (metaphysics *more geometrico*)

---

[191] Cp. Mittelstraß 1978, 177-192.
[192] Descartes. Med. VI, AT VII 74. Cp. Reg. XII, AT X 412.
[193] Descartes. Disc. II, AT VI 21-22; Princ. Preface to the French edition, AT IXB 14. For a discussion of the problems involved in the Cartesian project of method and an argument that Descartes might fail to produce the intended method, see: Schuster 1993, 195-223.
[194] Cp. Heath 1953, clxxxii-clxxxiii.

and in his "Institutio Physica". Descartes applies the same method of reasoning to metaphysics, namely, to the demonstration of the existence of God and of the difference between soul and body, of which he gives an example in his second set of replies to the objections raised to the "Meditations".[195] The "Meditations" themselves are not, however, written in the "geometrical fashion" (which is a reproach of one of Descartes' objectors).[196] The reason is that the best suitable genre for a consideration beginning with subjective evidence has to be not *mathesis,* but rather confession. *Confessio* (found already in Augustine) initially has the double meaning of proclaiming the greatness of being as the primary cause for existing truths and things—and of recognition of human fault and guilt. In Descartes' very personal description of his way to truth (in the "Meditations" and, in a sense, in the second part of the Fourth "Rule"),[197] the notion of confession is philosophically redefined as the way of knowing the infinite substance through knowing the self, the finite thinking substance, as the recognition of Descartes' own "epistemological sin", which consists in having taken for granted that which has been transmitted through the previous (scholastic) tradition. Because of that, Descartes rejects the incontestability of tradition as non-critical and unquestioned, as authoritative and not genuine, as contingent and therefore not true, because the traditional (school) knowledge is not reconstructed from the immediate evidence of the self, of the finite subjectivity.

In modern philosophy the "geometrical method" of argumentation finds its most notable application in the "Ethics" of Spinoza, who uses the *more geometrico* method for the purposes of philosophy which studies not only the divine but also—to an even greater extent—the finite subjectivity, in his exposition and discussion of the affects (Parts II-V). Spinoza achieves a remarkably original synthesis, for none of the ancient philosophers has ever attempted to write ethics under the pattern of geometry: since ethics has to do with more or less contingent human actions, none of the ancient philosophers sees any possibility to understand and to structure ethics as a strict science. Ethics has to have its own measure of exactitude that stands far away from that of geometry and metaphysics.[198] In a certain sense, Spinoza's "Ethics" may also be considered a confession, as an attempt to understand and to order the effects of finite subjectivity through knowledge of the infinite. For these reasons the *more geometrico* exposition has a rather decent place in Descartes' "Meditations" and appears only in marginal replies to the objections and notes to the main text: on the one hand, as the tribute to the (scholastic) tradition of philosophizing and, on the other, as an attempt to persuade opponents who do not adopt the Cartesian confessional position of the first person singular by their own means.

Reproached for refusing to set out in the "Meditations" "the entire argument in geometrical fashion, starting from a number of definitions, postulates

---

[195] Descartes. Second Set of Replies, AT VII 160-170.
[196] Descartes. Second Set of Replies, AT VII 128.
[197] Descartes. Reg. IVB, AT X 374.16 sqq. Many contemporary philosophical treatises might be considered a *confessio,* for example, Heidegger's *Sein und Zeit.*
[198] Cp. Aristotle. NE 1094b 12 sqq.

Part II: Intelligible Matter and Geometry 111

and axioms",[199] Descartes replies that such a method would amount to using the synthetic method, preferred by ancient mathematicians and logicians, who start with the commonly accepted principles and premises and arrive at a proven conclusion that then is necessary, that is, cannot be otherwise and thus represents knowledge.[200] By opposing *synthesis* to *analysis* in the "Meditations", Descartes highlights an important difference between his own approach and that of the ancient mathematicians. According to him, the ancients used only synthesis, which "demonstrates the conclusion clearly and employs a long series of definitions, postulates, axioms, theorems and problems, so that if anyone denies one of the conclusions it can be shown at once that it is contained in what has gone before, and hence the reader however argumentative or stubborn he may be, is compelled to give his assent." Descartes himself, on the contrary, uses analysis, which proceeds from the epistemologically prior, more evident and simple, "so that if the reader is willing to follow it and give sufficient attention to all points, he will make the thing his own and understand it just as perfectly as if he had discovered it for himself," as a truth anew, as freely (re)constructed by the finite mind (cp. 3.4.2).[201] Synthesis, as Proclus points out, goes from premises to conclusion, "the method of proceeding from things better known to things we seek to know", whereas analysis (also widely used in ancient mathematics to establish the correctness of the premises as hypotheses, assuming the conclusion as a given) goes in the opposite direction, from conclusion to premises.[202]

Indeed, Descartes needs the analytic method insofar as in his metaphysics he begins with the end ("first for us but last in the order of being", to paraphrase Aristotle), with the *cogito*, arriving at the first principles ("last for us but first in the order of being"), that is, God as the infinite substance and being and the soul. In a sense, presenting *in nuce* the transcendental method of the later critical philosophy, Descartes uses analysis to establish the possibility of the antecedent by analyzing the structure and the very possibility of the consequent, coming back to the starting point, demonstrating it as necessary. And in his geometry too he takes advantage of the analytic method of analyzing a given geometrical entity presented through an algebraic formula or equation to arrive at the first elementary constituents.[203]

In antiquity, the method of synthesis was yet reportedly taught by Plato Leodamas.[204] Referring to Porphyry, Proclus explains that all mathematical proofs proceed either from initial principles or aim at attaining initial principles, which themselves may be either self-evident axioms or already established results. Proofs, which ascend to starting-points, are either destructive or affirmative. The

---

[199] Mersenne. Second Set of Objections, AT VII 128.
[200] Cp. Aristotle. Anal. Post. 71b 37 sqq., who argues that those who aim at gaining knowledge by proof should adhere to the first principles as the most reliable.
[201] Descartes. Second Set of Replies, AT VII 155-156. See also: Curley 1986, 153-176. As Mittelstraß points out, the theoretical purpose of analysis in Descartes is not primarily that of foundation, but of demonstration. - Mittelstraß 1978, 184-187.
[202] Proclus. In Eucl. 8.4-8.6; cp. 43.18-21; 69.16-19. Cp. also: Aristotle. Anal. Post. 71b 9-72b 4.
[203] See: Katasonov 1999, 88-100.
[204] Proclus. In Eucl. 211.17-23; Diog. Laert. III 24. Initially, the analysis was applicable to geometrical figures, see: Hintikka, Remes 1974, 31 sqq.

destruction of the starting point is the *reductio ad absurdum*, because it denies the starting point by showing the impossibility of the conclusions that follow. Affirmation of the starting point is analysis as a method "which traces the desired result back to an acknowledged principle." Synthesis is exactly the reverse, proceeding from the principles in order to establish a conclusion.[205] Analysis—assuming an entity or a conclusion as a given, and arriving at undissolvable and thus "atomic" (not further analyzable) first principles—is also, despite Descartes' claim, widely used in ancient mathematics, for instance, by Pappus.[206]

The Cartesian opposition of synthesis to analysis might also stress a difference between "les anciens et les modernes" in the use of the geometrical method. In antiquity the *more geometrico* method is used for the systematic (synthetic) presentation and rearrangement of discovered properties and theorems, so that one can univocally demonstrate a necessary connection between them. Such a rearrangement may reveal a whole cosmos of intelligible entities, which are independent of our cognitive actions, but are structured in such a way that every entity or proposition is connected with every other into a system (cp. 3.1.1). Since every entity and every statement in such a system—represented in Euclid in a distilled way—is eventually connected with every other entity and statement (even if not immediately but through a mediation of other entities), then any entity or statement may be taken as the starting point, although some are preferred due to their compelling evidence. But within such a system, the analytic and synthetic approach have to be convertible (i.e., a statement can be proven, as Euclid often does, both analytically and synthetically). The distinction between analysis and synthesis arises only for, and within, finite discursive thinking, which is unable to grasp the system of entities and propositions in their entirety and thus proceeds step by step either from principles (synthetically) or ascending to them (analytically).

Modern science and mathematics in particular, as represented in Descartes, does not start with an explicit calling into question the very existence of

---

[205] Proclus. In Eucl. 242.14-16; 245.10-15; 255.8-256.8 et al.

[206] "Now analysis is the method of taking that which is sought as though it were admitted and passing from it through its consequences in order to something which is admitted as a result of synthesis; for in analysis we suppose that which is sought to be already done, and we inquire what it is from which this comes about, and again what is the antecedent cause of the latter, and so on until, by retracing our steps, we light upon something already known or ranking as a first principle; and such a method we call analysis, as being a reverse solution. But in synthesis, proceeding in the opposite way, we suppose to be already done that which was last reached in analysis, and arranging in their natural order as consequents what were formerly antecedents and linking them one with another, we finally arrive at the construction of what is sought; and this we call synthesis." Pappus. Collectio VII, Preface 1-3, 634.3-636.30 Hultsch (trans. I. Thomas). See also: Mugler 1958, 57-58, 400-402; Szabó 1994, 341-345; Schmitz 1997, 108-126. Cp. a MSS addition to Euclid. Elem. XIII 1 (Heath 1953, III 442): "Analysis is the assumption of that which is sought as if it were admitted [and the arrival] by means of its consequences at something admitted to be true. Synthesis is an assumption of that which is admitted [and the arrival] by means of its consequences at something admitted to be true."

the system of mathematical entities and truths as independent from the activity of the finite mind, because such a system can still be supposed to exist as given in the divine infinite intellect. Nevertheless, the finite mind is capable of considering necessary truths and mathematical objects themselves as its own analytic constructions. Still, the necessity of a truth exemplified through the finite mind is possible for Descartes only because the finite *res cogitans* is rooted in, and lives from, the infinite *res cogitans*. Once the connection between the finite and the infinite subjectivity becomes loose, the infinite subject (in Descartes, still the analytic starting point that needs to be arrived at) becomes itself only a hypothetical construction and a backward projection of the finite subject (in Descartes, still the result that makes the whole of metaphysical and mathematical analysis possible), and truth has to be considered a production of the finite mind. As contemporary intuitivism or constructivism puts it, an object (of mathematics) may be considered as freely engendered by the finite mind, in *statu nascendi*, rendered and defined in a more precise way at every consecutive step (cp. 3.4.2). The *more geometrico* method thus loses its importance and survives only in contemporary mathematics itself, presenting more of a systematization of the obtained results, rather than presenting the innermost "objective" structure of a mathematical science.

2.2.1 Geometry in its relation to physics according to Descartes

That geometry and, in general, mathematics, may and even has to be applicable to physical objects is one of the most important methodological demands of modern physics. As mentioned, for Galilei the book of nature is written in mathematical language, where words are lines, circles and triangles. Descartes writes to Mersenne that "sizes, shapes, positions and motions are my formal object..., and the physical objects I explain are my material object. The principles or premises from which I derive these conclusions are only the axioms on which geometers base their demonstrations".[207] Another formulation of the program of the mathematization of the physical is as follows: "The only principles which I accept, or require, in physics are those of geometry and pure mathematics; these principles explain all natural phenomena, and enable us to provide quite certain demonstrations regarding them. ...I recognize no matter in corporeal things apart from that which the geometers call quantity, and take as the object of their demonstrations, i.e. that to which every kind of division, shape and motion is applicable. ...And since all natural phenomena can be explained in this way, as will become clear in what follows, I do not think that any other principles are either admissible or desirable in physics".[208]

For Kepler too the world can be known by means of mathematics.[209] Still, Kepler considers geometry and numerical proportions as primarily applicable to

---

[207] Descartes. To Mersenne, end of 1637, AT I 476; cp. To Vorstius, 19 June 1643, AT III 686.
[208] Descartes. Princ. II 64, AT VIIIA 78-79. Cp. Dijksterhuis 1961, 404-409.
[209] Even in studying and presenting a *new* astronomy, Kepler qualifies himself primarily as a "mathematician". –*Astronomia nova*, Kepler 1992, 35 ("Dedicatory letter").

the study of astronomy, and thus, to celestial mechanics, more than to the terrestrial mechanics: "I believe that both sciences [astronomy and physics] are so closely bound with one another that neither can achieve perfection without the other".[210] The reason for such a claim might be, on the one hand, the influence of the Platonic-Pythagorean tradition on Kepler (in particular, of Proclus)[211] and, on the other hand, that the celestial might be taken to represent, in accordance with the same tradition, the ontologically "higher" or "more valuable" world, whose harmonious and beautiful geometrical architecture, describable in mathematical language, is to disclose the utter perfection of its architect. The terrestrial, however, is not altogether excluded from the realm where mathematically conceived mechanics might be applicable, and for the following reasons. First, Kepler does not already support the Peripatetic distinction of the supra- and sublunar world. Second, he ascribes the regularity in both "ordered shapes of plants and of numerical constants" to the same cause—supreme divine reason.[212] Third, Kepler does explicitly apply mathematics to the study of optics, music and meteorology. Nevertheless, all these three disciplines may still be considered as connecting the earthly to the heavenly, since optics studies light, the "subtlest matter", as it were, which, from antiquity on is taken as generated in and coming directly from "above", from the celestial region.[213] Meteorology equally connects

---

[210] Cit. ap.: Caspar 1959, 135. Maestlin, Kepler's teacher in Tübingen, still rejects the very possibility of application of physics to astronomy: "Existimo autem...à causis physicis abstinendum esse, et Astronomica astronomicè, per causas et hypotheses astronomicas, non physicas esse tractanda. Calculus enim fundamenta Astronomica ex Geometria et Arithmetica, suis videlicet alis, postulat, non coniectures physicas, quae lectorem magis perturbant, quam informant". (Letter to Kepler of 21 September 1616, ap. Kepler. *Gesammelte Werke*, vol. XVII (1955), 187; cp. Koyré 1973, 462). And even in Kepler's own "New Astronomy" ("Astronomia nova, Aitiologētos, seu physica coelestis" (1609)) we still find a distinction made between a geometrical and a physical explanation of celestial phenomena, in particular, of the movement of Mars, whose correct distances from the Sun are demonstrated geometrically ("in their nature, quality and quantity"), in opposition to a physical account "from the corrected motive causes" (cp. chs. 56-57). Non-mechanical teleological explanation of the movement of planets still plays an important role in Kepler: in the "Epitome Astronomiae Copernicanae", the rotation of the planets around the Sun is explained mechanistically, whereas Earth's rotation around its axis—by referring to an alleged earth soul (cp. Caspar 1959, 293 sqq.).

[211] See: *Somnium*, Kepler's note 37, where he praises Porphyry (Kepler 1967, 51). The idea of five regular (Platonic) solids Kepler took from Proclus' commentary to the first book of Euclid's "Elements" (see Proclus. In Eucl. 70.24 et al.; cp. Euclid. Elem., bk. XIII and Plato. Tim. 53 c sqq.), to which Kepler explicitly refers a number of times (e.g., Kepler 1965, 10; 37 et al.). Cp. Caspar 1959, 44, 380-381.

[212] Kepler 1966, 32-33.

[213] See: *Astronomia Pars Optica* and *Dioptrice*-Kepler. *Gesammelte Werke*, vol. II (1939) and vol. IV (1941). *Dioptrice* is written as a "mathematical book", as Kepler calls it in the Introduction, and contains definitions, axioms, problems, and propositions, i.e. copies the *more geometrico* way of exposition. Descartes, Newton, Hooke and Snel all dedicated much of their effort to the study of optics, conceived primarily as geometrical optics. Newton, himself author of the "Opticks", studied, as a young man, Kepler's "Dioptrice". Descartes famously compares the mind's power to know truth clearly and distinctly to a "natural light"

Part II: Intelligible Matter and Geometry 115

"heaven" and "earth", taking its object of study from the "border" region, as it were, so that these objects exemplify a great deal of geometrical regularity, which, for instance, can be seen in the hexagonal form of snow-flakes.[214] Finally, music is to present or reflect the divine celestial harmony, established by the creator of the cosmos, the harmony thus describable in mathematical proportions and discernible through regular geometrical solids.[215] The genuine synthesis of the celestial and terrestrial mechanics is eventually achieved only in Newton.[216]

"Toute ma Physique n'est autre chose que Géométrie"—"my entire physics is nothing but geometry"—is the often cited *credo* and a brief formulation of the Cartesian program.[217] Descartes then has to postulate that the corporeal nature be the subject of pure mathematics.[218] In order to be able to explain the movement and the inner structure of a material physical object, one has to apply certain formal instrumentarium of "sizes, shapes, positions and movements", which are considered to be shared both by geometrical figures and by physical bodies. This last assumption constitutes the main implicit hypothetical premise in Descartes' considerations, which cannot find immediate support in sensual experience.

Descartes still retains, however, certain traces of the ancient distinction and hierarchy of sciences and of geometrical problems according to the simplicity of the lines involved in construction.[219] Nevertheless, he considers the construction and study by means of mathematics (geometry and algebra) self-evidently possible not only for physics, but also for optics and music.[220] Sizes, shapes, positions and

---

within the soul. It is not by chance, then, that the full title of Descartes' treatise on the world runs "Le Monde...ou le Traité de la Lumière" (1664) (AT XI 3 sqq.). It is also important to point out that the first published work of Descartes, the "Discourse on Method" (1637) is printed as accompanied by three essays: on *optics* ("La Dioptrique"), *meteorology* and *geometry* (ΛT VI 81 sqq.).

[214] *Strena seu De Nive Sexangula*.-Kepler 1611. It is interesting to note that Descartes in his "Meteorologia" (1635), as well as R. Hooke in the "Micrographia" (1665) also turned to the study of snow-flakes, cp. Kepler 1966, 48-49.

[215] See: *Harmonice Mundi* (1619), esp. bk. III-Kepler. *Gesammelte Werke*, vol. VI (1940). It is worth noting that Kepler read Vincenzo Galilei's "Dialogo della musica antica e moderna".

[216] Cp. Koyré 1973, 364.

[217] "...I have decided to give up only abstract geometry, that is to say, the investigation of problems which function merely as mental exercises. My aim is to have more time to devote to another sort of geometry where the problems have to do with the explanation of natural phenomena. If he cares to think about what I wrote about salt, snow, rainbows, etc., he will see that *my entire physics is nothing but geometry*". - Descartes. To Mersenne, 27 July 1638, AT II 268, italics added.

[218] Descartes. Med. VI, AT VII 74.

[219] Cp. Descartes. To Mersenne, 15 April 1630, AT I 139; To Mersenne, 31 March 1638, AT II 91. In the "Regulae" Descartes formally discerns between arithmetic and geometry, further considering algebra as a sort of arithmetic, *Arithmeticae genus quoddam*. - Reg. IV, AT X 373.

[220] Descartes. Geometry II, AT VI 424, 430 sqq. Cp. Optics II, AT VI 93 sqq.; To Mersenne, 18 December 1629, AT I 93. Des Chene notes that in Descartes music and optics

motions may be studied and described by means of mathematics and are ascribable to extended entities of any kind. Extended entities are either physical bodies or geometrical figures; therefore, both may be studied by means of mathematics.

Geometrization of the physical has to presuppose that, first, the methods of geometry and physics have no crucial distinction and, second, that geometrical objects are not crucially different from physical bodies.[221] The first presupposition is consecutively rejected by ancient science, in particular, by Aristotle in his physics and also by Plato in his understanding of geometry as a preparation for the contemplation of being, as a science which provides exact knowledge-*epistēmē* only about ideal, and not physical, objects.[222]

Yet in Aristotle we find a claim that physical natural bodies also have surfaces and volumes that are studied by mathematics—namely, by geometry—and that theorems of arithmetic should be applicable to sensible things (cp. 2.1).[223] Still, the physical line is studied by geometry not as physical but as geometrical; namely, through the procedure of mental (or, rather, imaginable) abstraction, line, surface, and volume are separated and studied as purely geometrical objects (for arithmeticians and geometers consider as separate—i.e., as substance—that which, according to Aristotle, does not exist separately),[224] while the physical body still keeps its imprecision and is not studied by the means and methods of mathematics.

What, then, is the object of geometry for Descartes? In the "Discourse on the Method" it is "a continuous body, or a space indefinitely extended in length, breadth and height or depth, and divisible into different parts which may have various shapes and sizes, and may be moved or transposed in every way: for all this is assumed by geometers in their object of study".[225] The implicit argument involved here is: geometry studies space; space is body; body is matter; therefore, geometry studies matter. Such a conclusion obviously renders impossible and superfluous the Aristotelian distinction of the geometrical as abstractable from matter as opposed to the bodily as always immersed in matter. It is thus primarily extension that becomes the subject-matter of geometry. Since extension is not different from matter, the object studied by geometry has to be matter, which is a very important implication that has far-reaching consequences for modern science. Since, further, according to Descartes, to know extension in its nature is primarily to think it, the geometrical truths are not to be based in sensory experience, but

---

are "middle mathematics", "neither wholly physical nor wholly mathematical" (Des Chene 1996, 116-117).
[221] A further distinction between presenting a physical problem geometrically and reducing a physical problem to a geometrical one (Gaukroger 1978, 184; 192 sqq.) appears to be unnecessary: in order to present a physical problem geometrically, one already has to presuppose the possibility of the geometrization of the physical, and thus the possibility of the reduction of the physical to the geometrical.
[222] Plato. RP 526d-527c; Aristotle. Phys. 184b 25 sqq.
[223] Aristotle. Phys. 193b 23-194a 13; Met. 1090a 14-15.
[224] Cp. Aristotle. Met. 1078a 21-23.
[225] Descartes. Discourse V, AT VI 36.

merely in thinking: "We come to know them [geometrical truths] by the power of our own native intelligence, without any sensory experience."[226]

In the distinction between the *method* and the *object*, the former has to appeal to relation or proportion which belongs to the *res cogitans*; the latter—to continuous body which is *res extensa*. The duality of method and object as applicable to both physical and mathematical (geometrical) refers to the duality of proportion (relation) and extension as applicable to both physicals and geometricals.[227] The very application of mathematics to physics becomes possible because the new method of *mathesis* considers only a relation and not the substance itself. Relation (*pros ti*) and proportion (*analogia*) thus become prior to substance-*oysia*.[228] Descartes has to make, however, a concession in recognizing a distinction between geometrical and physical principles insofar as the latter "are not abstracted from all sensible matter, as in geometry, but applied to various observational data which are known by the senses and indubitable".[229] Such a concession does not affect the program of the mathematization of the world, because the physical principles are not applied to the physical reality *qua* physical and sensible, but *qua* already implicitly taken as geometrical.

The object of geometry is characterized by two main features: first, it is extended and, second, it is (unlike in Aristotle) movable.[230] The first feature presupposes further distinction, insofar as: (1) the geometrical object may be taken only as continuous body without further specifications, i.e. not as qualitatively different from the space it occupies; (2) the occupied space may be indefinitely extended, as in the case of a straight line or parabola, and (3) such space is indefinitely divisible. But considered under these three further specifications, an object of geometry does not principally differ from an object of physical science, for both share the aforementioned features. In other words, since physical bodies are primarily understood in terms of mere extension, i.e. as spatial, one of the main presuppositions of Descartes is that geometrical and physical bodies are to be referred to one and the same space or one and the same matter as the corporeal substance of three dimensions, because, simply, there is no other space or matter.[231]

---

[226] Descartes. To Voetius, May 1643, AT VIIIB 166-167.

[227] Cp.: "This identification [of mathematics and physics] is effected by a two-fold 'reduction' in which the objects of mathematics are constructed purely as proportions that can be represented symbolically as figures and line segments and in which the objects of physics are construed as extensions, all other physical properties being treatable in terms of extension". - Gaukroger 1980, 98.

[228] Proclus argues that proportion cannot be the basis or bond (*syndesmos*) of mathematics (In Eucl. 43.22-23). Cp. Plato. RP 534e.

[229] Descartes. To Mersenne, End of 1637, AT I 476.

[230] For Aristotle, mathematics studies entities that do not exist independently (*oy khōrista*) and are immovable (*akinēta*), whereas physics studies things existing independently and not immovable and first philosophy (metaphysics) considers entities existing independently and immovable. - Aristotle. Met. 1026a 13-16.

[231] Descartes. The World, AT XI 17; cp. Princ. III 46, AT VIIIA 100-101.

Geometrical objects do not merely substitute physical objects and adequately express their properties—geometrical entities are even better and more preferable objects of study. Indeed, if physical things are to be treated as "the objects of geometry made real",[232] then physical things have the same *essence*, although they differ in their *existence*, insofar as the existence of geometricals is only possible, even if necessary, whereas the existence of the physicals is real, even if contingent (cp. 1.4.3).[233] The "real" physical things may be conceived as produced by the infinite thinking, whereas the "possible" geometrical objects are products of finite thinking (see 3.4.1; 3.4.2). That is why, in studying properties of physical bodies as exemplified in their geometrical substituents, one may fully ignore the question whether the object of investigation does really exist or not: one is interested solely in essence and not in existence.[234]

The Cartesian approach immediately becomes an object of criticism for Gassendi, who points out that "material things are subject-matter of applied, not pure, mathematics, and the subject-matter of pure mathematics—including the point, the line, the surface, and the indivisible figures which are composed of these elements and yet remain indivisible—cannot exist in reality".[235] Such a criticism, legitimate within the framework of Aristotelian physics (even if Gassendi himself is critical of Aristotle), does not hit its target, however, because in the Cartesian approach geometrical representatives of physical reality have the same essential, but not existential, status—since geometricals exist only virtually, not as "substances but as boundaries within which a substance [i.e., physical body] is contained".[236] This is an important point, because in this way qualities of physical bodies may be considered merely in terms of relations and functions.

Descartes thus considers it possible to study physical and geometrical entities in the same way, insofar as both are extended. There are, however, not only close similarities between geometricals and physicals, but also differences that cannot be ignored. An objection that arises against the assumption that geometry is applicable to the physical world is that sizes, shapes and positions belong both to geometrical objects and to physical bodies. Nothing guarantees *a priori* that these features belong to both kinds of objects in one and the same respect. And in fact, sizes, shapes and positions belong, strictly speaking, only to geometrical figures in which they may be exemplified with exactitude and precision.

For Plato there is a insurmountable distinction between being and that which only participates in being but is not being itself, and because of that a physical figure, a physical circle for example, is always imprecise and participates

---

[232] Garber 1992, 63.
[233] Descartes. Conversation with Burman, 16 April 1648, AT V 160.
[234] Cp. Descartes' addition to the very end of the Fifth Meditation of the French edition: "...[A]nd also concerning things which belong to corporeal nature in so far as it can serve as the object of geometrical demonstrations which have no concern with whether that object exists" - Med. V, AT VII 71. Cp. Med. VI, AT VII 80.
[235] Gassendi. Fifth Set of Objections, AT VII 328-329.
[236] Descartes. Fifth Set of Replies, AT VII 380-381.

in straightness, whereas the geometrical circle itself is perfect.[237] Descartes is aware of this problem and recognizes in his "Geometry" that geometrical figures are perfect in their shapes, without any flaw, while physical bodies always distort these shapes: "For although we cannot include in Geometry any lines that are like cords—that is to say, sometimes straight and sometimes curved [i.e., analogous to physical imprecise lines]—because the ratios between straight and curved lines are unknown, and even, I believe, unknowable to men, so that we cannot thereby reach any exact and assured conclusions: nevertheless, because we use cords in these constructions only to determine straight lines whose length we know exactly, we must not entirely reject them."[238] Acknowledging a difference between a geometrical line which is perfectly straight and a physical line which is irregular and consists of wavy curves, Descartes encounters a difficulty that he is not able to resolve. Geometrical figures have to be wholly corporeal and thus lose their unique role as the link between the intelligible and the physical (see 2.3; 2.3.1),[239] but there is no satisfactory explanation of why geometricals have to be precise, while the equally extended physical bodies, which represent geometricals, are imprecise.

The finite mind is then able to conceive a physical line as geometrical because of the idea of the geometrical line which precedes the physical line and corresponds to it, so that the former makes possible conceiving of the latter: "I could not conceive of an imperfect triangle unless there were in me the idea of a perfect one, since the former is the negation of the later. Thus, when I see a triangle, I have a conception of a perfect triangle, and it is by comparison with this that I subsequently realize that what I am seeing is imperfect".[240] But even if geometricals appear thus to be a kind of *a priori* form, which enable consideration of physical things as objects of a strict, mathematically structured science—even then one cannot argue that geometricals have to be considered as naturally existing, insofar as they may be constructed by the mind (see 3.4.2-3.4.3).

Descartes' approach entails, however, a difficulty. Indeed, physical lines are curvy and imprecise, while geometrical lines are perfect; and physical bodies are a production of the infinite mind, whereas geometrical entities, since they are merely possible, can be conceived as produced by the finite mind. This might point to a flaw of the infinite divine construction of the world, construction that still admits imprecision in physical lines. On the contrary, whatever the finite human may produce (e.g., a geometrical line) might be conceived as perfect and irreproachable (cp. 3.4.1). Such a conclusion would then contradict Descartes' position that infinity is incomparably better than the infinite (cp. 1.3.2). In order to get rid of this aporia, one has to substitute physical objects by their geometrical representations and make these latter the only objects of scientific investigation. This is quite an acceptable conclusion for Descartes, because on the one hand, one cannot study the imprecise and distorted by means of mathematics. On the other

---

[237] Plato. Ep. VII, 343a-b.
[238] Descartes. Geometry II, AT VI 412. Cp. Malebranche 1997, 255.
[239] Descartes Fifth Set of Replies, AT VII 385.
[240] Descartes. Conversation with Burman, 16 April 1648, AT V 161-162. Cp.: "We could not recognize the geometrical triangle from the diagram on the paper unless our mind already possessed the idea of it from some other source." - Fifth Set of Replies, AT VII 382.

hand, in the Cartesian world there is no room for matter as non-being, matter which might escape cognition or is a principle of otherness and distortion.

In other words, one first has to know the geometrical figure in order to be able to discern further its presence in the physical body, which, however, represents the geometrical figure only and always as distorted. The peculiarity of the Cartesian approach is that one cannot take the geometrical figure as an *a priori* of the possibility of geometrization of the physical, because the figure itself is not a given and objectively independent of the finite mind. For the finite mind the figure is only possible and therefore may and in fact has first to be constructed or reproduced by the mind (cp. 3.4.2) and only after that be considered as the prescriptive pattern for the corresponding physical thing. At the same time, Descartes describes the physical, as we have seen, in purely geometrical terms of sizes, shapes and positions, which seems to be in contradiction with his initial assumption. Sensual data from physical bodies may be then considered indubitable only if the physical bodies are taken as something other than they are, as representing "wavy curves"—i.e., as merely geometrical figures. Thus, with Descartes modern physics does not investigate physical bodies as such, but only their "ideal" or idealized geometrical representations. The "real" irregular physical bodies simply are not at all considered as objects of science when, for example, a moving body is substituted by the "material point"—i.e., by a geometrical point allotted with bodily properties. In this way, Descartes tacitly expels proper physical bodies and substitutes them with geometrical entities. Therefore, physical things can become legitimate objects of physical science only when, and if, they are expelled and lost *qua* physical or, rather, equated with the geometricals.

In addition to reducing physics to mere geometry, Descartes supports the program of further reducing physics to mechanics.[241] This approach eventually prevails in modern science. Physics has to be developed as mechanics through the mediation of mathematics: "[T]he mechanics now current is nothing but a part of the true physics which, not being welcomed by supporters of the common sort of philosophy, took refuge with the mathematicians."[242]

Why is Descartes able to consider mechanics, taken in antiquity as only an imitation of nature,[243] as a strict science? It seems that the incorporation of mechanics into physics becomes possible for two reasons. First, both sciences consider natural laws, which are (or have to be) subject to one single method.[244] Second, mechanics and physics both study objects that may be expressed solely in terms of "sizes, shapes, positions and movements". But sizes, shapes and positions may be ascribed, as we have seen, to both geometrical and physical objects *qua* extended, and, moreover, *qua* movable. Since ("real") physical entities may be adequately represented by ("possible") geometrical ones and since geometrical objects are describable in the same terms as mechanical objects are, nothing prevents the physical things from being considered exactly in the same way as the mechanical objects. Therefore, by confining the object of science to merely

---

[241] See: Descartes. To [De Beaune], 30 April 1639, AT II 542. Cp. Gabbey 1993, 311-323.
[242] Descartes. To Plempius for Fromondus, 3 October 1637, AT I 421.
[243] Cp. Isnardi Parente 1966.
[244] Descartes. Discourse V, AT VI 54.

extended thing, the science of the external world (physics) may be rethought as an essentially mathematical (geometrical) *and* mechanical enterprise.

Two immediate consequences of the mechanization of physical science by means of geometry are, first, that the whole of the universe is considered nothing but a huge machine (a clock) and its creator an infinite mechanical engineer who preserves the mechanism in its motion.[245] The other consequence is that there is no ground left for drawing any essential differences between the natural and the artificial, i.e. every object of study may be considered as constructed: a natural thing may be considered as made by the infinite designer, while that thing's geometrical representative—as constructed by a finite maker. The whole of matter—all the extended things in their entirety—is then structured as a mechanism.[246] Body has to be nothing but mechanism—there is no room for any inner principle of animation and movement.[247]

But although there is no essential difference between an artificial human-made and the divine-made machine, there is still a distinction between them, which again has to do with the superiority of the infinite over the finite. Namely, the construction of the infinite engineer has to be incomparably better than that of the finite maker. This is why a human-made machine can never be arranged in its parts in such a way as to, first, be able to use words (i.e., to be capable of speech) and, second, to be able to react in all possible situations, since they can never be foreseen in their entirety.[248] And even if an artificial machine may be given any number of organs, it still will only be an automaton—it will be lacking the universal non-physical "organ" of reason,[249] such a machine will always be less perfect than a natural one.

This new attitude towards the mechanization of the physical can be seen even in the way of drawing and designing instruments and machines. Ancient engineers do not know any precise schemes of mechanisms, always presenting them in the form of rough and approximate sketches with no exact sizes and proportions, as shown, for instance, in the treatises on poliorcetics, or the art of besieging towns.[250] Quite on the contrary, modern constructors present machines through and as geometrical figures. If in Leonardo da Vinci machines are drawn as pictures, this is because he considers art and drawing to become the most precise of all sciences, so that what the eye sees is not just approximation, but the real, precise and exact object: the eye no longer sees a deceptive fluent appearance, but the essence itself, insofar as the eye fixes, draws, depicts and prescribes that essence through appearance.

---

[245] "God is the primary cause of motion; and he always preserves the same quantity of motion in the universe." - Descartes. Princ. II 36, AT VIIIA 61; cp. To More, August 1649, AT V 404.
[246] Cp. Descartes. To ***, March 1642, AT III 546.
[247] Descartes. Treatise on Man, AT XI 120; Description of the Human Body, AT XI 226 sqq.; Passions I 6, AT XI 331; I 16, AT XI 341-342.
[248] Cp. Séris 1993, 177-192.
[249] Descartes. Disc. V, AT VI 55-56.
[250] Cp. Apollodorus, Poliorc. 139 sqq.; Vegetius, Epitoma rei milit., IV; Philo of Byzantium. Pneum. 1974, 73-79 et passim.

It is not by chance then that Descartes shows considerable interest in mechanical inventions, especially in his earlier years when he also devises his project of the universal science as method.[251] Since mathematics can be practically applied to the construction of instruments, machines and automata, in Descartes the descriptions and drawings of machines are not paintings, but geometrically constructed figures.[252]

2.2.2 Number and magnitude in Descartes

Every finite truth for Descartes has to be established through the forms of correct reasoning but not through substantial forms of any kind. Substantial forms are to be dismissed, hence within the very objects of the scientific investigation, it is primarily relation to the others which matters. As it has been said, this makes the application of one and the same method to both physical and geometrical objects possible. Moreover, geometrical figures can themselves be represented through algebraic equations, because, once the substantial forms in figures are ignored, their properties are expressible solely in terms of proportions and then can be marked by signs of any kind (e.g., by letters).[253] This is not a novelty, of course, since Euclid uses a theory of proportions extensively in the V and VI books of his "Elements", in order to describe geometricals and their mutual relations. The Cartesian approach is different, however, in presenting geometrical entities as numerical functions, which implicitly presupposes the identification of number and magnitude. For Descartes the identification of number and magnitude, of the discrete and the continuous, is a matter of methodological importance. It is not by chance that in modern mathematics the continuum is taken as a whole entity, as a discrete unit and not as an unlimited potentiality where the mind is able to discern the parts. Even if Cantor posits the cardinal number of the continuum to be greater than that of the set of natural numbers, he nevertheless considers the continuum to be an independent entity characterized by a particular number. If the intuitionist indivisibility of the continuum is accepted—according to Brouwer, the continuum can be split only into the whole and an empty set—the specific difference between the discrete and the continuous is removed.[254] The identification of number and magnitude is possible because of the dispelling of the once insurmountable distinction between the discrete (number) and the continuous (magnitude). Because

---

[251] Cp. Descartes' description of a machine for polishing lenses in purely geometrical terms, of a "Chariot-Chaise", pulley and other mechanical advises - Descartes. To Ferrier, 12 November 1629, AT I 53-74; To Ville-Bressieu, Summer 1631, AT I 214; To Huygens, 5 October 1637, AT I 435 sqq.

[252] Descartes. To Hogelande, 8 February 1640, AT III 724; cp. To Mersenne, 15 May 1634, AT I 293 et al.

[253] "Arithmetization (or algebraization) of geometry" and "geometrization of arithmetic (and algebra)" both take place in Descartes' "Geometry". See: Boyer 1959, 390-393; Belaval 1960; Lachterman 1989, 143. An important shift in early modern mathematics (due to the works of François Viète) is substitution not only of given magnitudes and entities by a letter or sign—but also introduction of a *variable* (Viète 1983, 5), i.e. of a magnitude considered in a process of becoming (e.g., in the process of a kinematic construction, cp. 3.4.2).

[254] Brouwer 1981, 85-87.

of this, it becomes possible to consider the extended geometrical (and, correspondingly, the physicals) by means of studying mere relations between them, i.e., by means of functions.

Descartes seems to be uninterested in number as such: number for him is not substance, and thus he does not discuss the notion of number in detail. Number is not a main attribute either, for it is both applicable, as well as other universals, such as being, substance, duration, truth, perfection, order etc., to everything conceivable, to both *res cogitans* and *res extensa*.[255] Number is then just a mode of thinking. It is therefore rethought as stripped of its substantial status that it had in the Platonic-Pythagorean tradition, because it is not a separate ideal entity, but is present in the things extended insofar as it is a mode of thought under which the mind conceives of things numbered.[256] Very much like later mathematicians (for instance, Hilbert), Descartes considers number as a mental abstraction of the counted subject, which places number together with the notions of duration and order.

There is, however, an ambiguity in the Cartesian notion of number, since, on the one hand, Descartes tends to portray number as applied in counting the extended things. On the other hand, number appears just a way of ordering things not only in reason but also in the imagination.[257] Since there is only a modal distinction between number and the thing numbered, there can only be a modal difference between the number and the numbered (cp. 1.1.3). Number is thus only a mode of thought—it belongs only to thinking. In order to be able to get rid of the above ambiguity, Descartes has to postulate only the conceptual (mental), and not the real, distinction between the number and the thing numbered, as, for example, the number ten is not really distinct from a continuous quantity of ten feet long.[258] In the same way, in the case of other universals there should be no difference between truth and a true thing, between perfection and a perfect thing etc.[259]

Descartes' treatment of the notion of number reveals an interesting and important structure. First, as we know, Descartes accepts the possibility of deducing the categories, like the notion of substance, merely from individual thinking (cp. 1.2.3). In a like manner, the notion of number can also be deduced from the mind's activity of counting thoughts, which is tightly connected with the notion of duration: "With regard to the clear and distinct elements in my ideas of corporeal things, it appears that I could have borrowed some of these from my idea of myself, namely substance, duration, number and anything else of this kind. ...Again, I perceive that I now exist, and remember that I have existed for some time; moreover, I have various thoughts which I can count; it is in these ways that I acquire the ideas of duration and number which I can then transfer to other things".[260] In a very similar way, Brouwer, together with Kant, deduces

---

[255] Descartes. To Elizabeth, 21 May 1643, AT III 665.
[256] Descartes. Princ. I 55, AT VIIIA 26; Princ. I 58, AT VIIIA 27; cp. To Hyperaspistes, AT III 429.
[257] Descartes. Reg. XIV AT X 446.
[258] Descartes. Princ. II 8, AT VIIIA 44-45; cp. The World, AT XI 36.
[259] Descartes. To Clerselier, 23 April 1649, AT V 355.
[260] Descartes. Med. III, AT VII 44-45.

mathematics as pure ("intuitive") mental activity, essentially languageless, from the perception of the movement of time which gives the pure form of otherness or duality.[261]

Second, the idea of number is contained formally—neither objectively nor eminently—in the mind, which means that number neither exists as an objective ideal structure, nor is present in the things themselves. Number is then not a mental abstraction of and from extended things but, on the contrary, being formed from and by counting the thoughts, it is *imposed* onto things numbered. Put otherwise, the fact that number may be discerned in things (as ten feet, ten horses) means that the number numbered in the things can be counted only insofar as there is the number numbering, which is a mode of thought, itself produced by the activity of the mind. It means that number in things is a sheer construction of the mind (see 3.4.1). It is only because the mind first forms the concept of number introspectively, from self-observation (from the succession of thoughts or cogitations of all sorts), that it is capable of counting order and measure in the extended things and of revealing laws in the extended—both in physical and in geometrical entities.

When Descartes explains his method in the "Regulae", he presupposes that all entities of the same genus—which may either be continuous or discrete—are to be referred to one of the two categories, either of order or of measure (*ad ordinem, vel ad mensuram*). Order appears to correspond to the discrete entities, whereas measure to the continuous objects. However, the problems that involve measure can be further reduced to the problems involving order, or at least order and measure are to be mutually reducible.[262] The *more geometrico* method is equally applicable to both continuous and discrete quantities without discrimination,[263] because both are either extended or considered solely in terms of relation. In the "Regulae" Descartes describes a calculus, defining four arithmetic operations—addition, subtraction, multiplication and division—which are to be applicable to geometrical objects and which allow treatment of these objects in the same way as numbers would be treated.[264] In solving algebraic equations, Descartes resorts to the use of geometrical bodies[265] and, respectively, geometrical problems are presented in terms of algebraic equations in his "Geometry". In particular, such an approach enables Descartes to get rid of the ancient classification of problems and their hierarchy (problems solved by means of only a rule and compass, by means of conic sections and by means of more complex lines).[266] Once mathematical entities—numbers and extended magnitudes—are considered as even if not properly identical, but at least mutually convertible, the ancient distinction between them becomes redundant. The reason that number and magnitude can be treated on an equal basis is that, in the last instance, the ontological status of the subject-matter of the strict science does not matter: it

---

[261] Cp. Brouwer 1981, 4-5.
[262] Descartes. Reg. XIV, AT X 451.
[263] Descartes. To Beeckman, 26 March 1619, AT X 156-157.
[264] Descartes. Reg. XVII, AT X 461 sqq.
[265] Descartes. To Stampioen, [End of 1633], AT I 276-277.
[266] Cp. Geminus' classification of lines, ap. Proclus. In Eucl. 111.1 sqq.

should only be subject to order and measure, so that the content of pure mathematics is to be limited to the study of relations or proportions only.[267] In ancient mathematics such a position is definitely rejected by Proclus, for whom mathematics cannot have proportion (*analogia*) as its nexus (*syndesmos*), because the entire mathematics is to be ultimately based rather on the notion of form and substance.[268] Ancient mathematics can never ignore the difference between arithmetic and geometry, because, first, both mathematical disciplines are rooted in the activity of different cognitive faculties (namely, in the discursive reason and in the discursive reason plus imagination, 3.1-3.2) and, second, because their objects differ ontologically (2.3-2.3.1).

The non-discrimination of number and magnitude is realized through the Cartesian system of coordinates, where to every number a geometrical figure (e.g., a line) corresponds, and, on the contrary, every geometrical figure is univocally expressed in terms of number.[269] Even if already in antiquity, especially in the Pythagoreans, we find examples of the representation of geometricals in terms of numbers, this does not abolish the fundamental difference between discrete number and continuous magnitude. Pythagorean representation of integer numbers through geometrical entities is further extended in modern mathematics to rational and to real numbers (including also irrational numbers).[270] The Cartesian procedure of equating numbers with geometrical magnitudes "lowers" the status of number, bringing it down to the physical world, whereas the Platonic-Pythagorean representation of numbers by figures still recognizes the insurmountable difference between numbers, discrete ideal entities, and continuous figures, which display an irreducible otherness, due to their presence in matter. Such a representation is twofold: first, it merely symbolically represents numbers in terms of geometricals, which can only be taken as limited, for the unlimited cannot be measured and cannot be in any relation or proportion to anything else.[271] Unit represents point, dyad—line, triad—plane and tetrad—solid. And second, the identification of number and magnitude is in principle impossible for ancient mathematics because of the incommensurability of geometrical lines (e.g., of the diagonal and the side of a square). The theory of proportion (*analogia*) goes back at least to the Pythagoreans who distinguished various—arithmetic, geometric and harmonic— proportions as means between numbers.[272] The theory of proportion is further elaborated after the discovery of incommensurability by Eudoxus, who establishes

---

[267] Cp. Descartes. Reg. VI, AT X 384-385; Discourse II, AT VII 19 sqq.
[268] Proclus. In Eucl. 43.22-44.7.
[269] Bronstein, Semendyaev 1980, 685.
[270] Thus, Dedekind begins his lectures on differential and integral calculus with the statement: "Wir können jede ganze Zahl bildlich oder geometrisch darstellen" (Dedekind 1985, 23). The unique role of number is still recognized by some contemporary mathematicians; for example, Dirichlet claims that every mathematical proposition is ultimately reducible to a proposition about natural numbers (Dedekind 1911, XI and 7-9), and Russell and Whitehead try to reduce all mathematics to logic, whose forms have to represent numbers.
[271] See: Plato. Tim. 53c-54b; Aristotle. Met. 985b 24 sqq.; Aristotle. De caelo 268a 7-13; De an. 404b 18-24. Cp. Nicomachus. Introd. arithm. II 6.4; Plotinus. Enn. VI.3.14.28-29.
[272] Cp. Iamblichus. In Nicom. 118.19 sqq.

his theory of proportion, systematized by Euclid in Book V of the "Elements". In this theory, *logos* may not only mean a relation of two commensurables (as in Proposition 5 of Book X of the "Elements"), but also, as definition 3 of Book V of "Elements" states, there may be a relation (*skhesis*) between any two magnitudes of the same genus in respect of the size. From the very definition of proportion thus introduced, it follows that since number and magnitude belong to different genera, there can be no proper *logos* between them. Besides, ancient mathematics does not know the irrational number that may represent a relation of incommensurable entities. Even if ancient thinkers have to accept otherness in numbers as intelligible matter (see 2.4), numbers themselves are always commensurable with each other, since the numerical unit is their common ground and measure (cp. 2.1.1).[273]

Formally, Descartes retains the ancient distinction between arithmetical number and geometrical figure. Still, they are treated on an equal basis when substituted by algebraic signs—a, b, c, etc.—which are considered purely formally, as subject to the new formal calculus, to mathematical operations, the signs that may be further arranged in a proper order. Rejecting any generic difference between number and magnitude, as well as the difference between the discrete and the continuous, Descartes still has to recognize their specific difference, making a formal distinction between numbers and geometricals. Solving a geometrical problem can be then reduced to solving an algebraic equation, or a number of equations.[274] Descartes' intention to relate possibly close geometrical objects to numbers amounts to an introduction of the analogues and substitutes of the numerical unit and of four operations and equations into geometry,[275] while Euclid, on the contrary, presents arithmetic operations in terms of geometry. The attraction of the algebraic method proposed by Descartes lies in its simplicity and brevity.[276] Moreover, since every value may in principle be ascribed to any sign, the formal signs can represent and be substituted by variables, they need not have a fixed value.[277] In this way the idea of function as operating not with a fixed object but with a variable is introduced into mathematics. Thus, for instance, a line in the Cartesian geometry can be considered as not fixed but as successively taking an *infinite number of different values*, i.e., is described by a *variable*.[278] The whole cosmos, modeled after the pattern of mathematical objects, is then also desubstantialized and reduced to a great number of relations.

We see thus that, first, the same rules and procedures (the same algebraic calculus) are applicable to both numbers and geometrical magnitudes. Second, although numbers are themselves applicable to both *res cogitans* and *res extensa*, the numbers *qua* modes of thinking belong to the thinking thing—numbers are not bodies and are not extended. However, a problem arises: namely, if numbers and

---

[273] See: Proclus. In Eucl. 60.6-9.
[274] Descartes. Geometry III, AT VI 444 sqq.
[275] Descartes. Geometry I, AT VI 369-373; cp. 385.
[276] Descartes. Geometry I, AT VI 376, 383.
[277] "[O]ften one has no need so to trace these lines on paper, and it suffices to designate them by certain letters, one for each." - Descartes. Geometry I, AT VI 371 sq.
[278] Descartes. Geometry I, AT VI 385; cp. 411.

geometricals can be treated in the same (algebraic) terms, do the geometrical figures belong to thinking or to extended substance? Consideration of the geometrical figure is necessarily ambiguous, for, obviously, geometrical figures can be described both in terms of signs—either as fixed or variable—and in terms of shape. The first may be considered a mode of *res cogitans*, the second is a mode of *res extensa*. The notion or idea of the geometrical is only thought, and thought is complementary to the extended. Therefore, the notion of a figure as represented and substituted by a sign cannot be corporeal. Geometrical figure itself *qua* extended must be corporeal, present in the same extension as physical things, which, as we have seen, becomes a most important precondition for applying the former to studying and describing the latter.[279]

2.3 Intermediary

One can find a number of interesting and fruitful attempts in contemporary scholarship to present Aristotle's views on mathematics in a consistent and systematic way.[280] Somewhat simplifying, one might say that in his scientific orientation Plato is a mathematician, whereas Aristotle is primarily a physicist. There is no science of moving and becoming for Plato, and for Aristotle there is primarily a science of the things of nature, which live and move on their own. In fact, much of what Aristotle tells us about mathematics is his paraphrasing of Plato and the Academic doctrines. Much of what is known about the oral tradition of Plato and the Academy is also preserved by Aristotle.[281] And because the critical attitude of Aristotle towards his teacher is well known, we have good reasons not to consider his evidence of Plato's teaching uncritical.

As we know, one of the main points of Aristotle's criticism of Plato is the critique of the Platonic method of bringing opposites together without any mediation, an example of which is to be found in the "Parmenides'" one-being relation.[282] According to Aristotle, the immediate joining of opposites violates the principle of non-contradiction (see 1.1.1). Therefore, one has to look for the third, for the substrate, the mediator or the intermediate, *metaxy* or *meson*, which acquires, receives and mediates the opposites. Such a mediator is to be found in every kind of object, be it physical or mathematical. Since Aristotle is sensitive to the problem of mediation, of the third, an important place in his consideration of the Platonic doctrines, as transmitted in the "Physics", belongs to the discussion of intermediary entities. In Aristotle's testimony, Plato "states that besides sensible things (*ta aistheta*) and forms (*eidē*) there exist, as something intermediary, mathematical objects (*ta mathēmatika*) which are different from the sensible things insofar as they are eternal and immovable, and they differ from the forms insofar

---

[279] As Descartes notes to Gassendi, "although geometrical figures are wholly corporeal, this does not entail that the ideas by means of which we understand them should be thought of as corporeal (unless they fall under the imagination)". - Descartes. Fifth Set of Replies, AT VII 385. Cp. Princ. I 65, AT VIIIA 32; cp. Princ. I, AT VIIIA 27.
[280] See, for instance: Annas 1976, 26-41 and especially Cleary 1995.
[281] Cp. Krämer 1959; 1971; Gaiser 1962, passim.
[282] Plato. Parm. 135d sqq.

as there are many similar things, whereas every form is unique".[283]

Aristotle himself does not, however, accept mathematical intermediate entities, because he refuses to take the mathematicals as existing separately from things and independently of them.[284] The main objections that Aristotle raises against the existence of Plato's intermediate mathematical entities are the following: if one accepts the intermediary as existing separately, one has to recognize entities like an intermediate heaven prior to the visible one, and the same would be true of every other physical object. This would lead to the duplication of all physical objects and to the subsequent duplication of the sciences, which Aristotle takes to be absurd. If, on the contrary, intermediate entities exist in bodies, then, first, nothing prevents the consideration of ideal forms as existing in physical things as well; second, two bodies would occupy the same place; and third, the intermediates would not be immovable.[285] However, even if Aristotle does not accept mathematical intermediates, he clearly sees the problem of the relation of geometrical entities and their exemplification in the physical. Namely, a geometrical circle is perfectly round and a geometrical line is perfectly straight and, as Protagoras points out, the one may touch the other in a single point, whereas in the physical representatives of circle and line the same properties can never be found (this, as we have seen, is also a problem for Descartes).[286] This is a serious difficulty which needs to be addressed, if one wishes to explain how mathematical structures are present in physical things. Aristotle, for whom physics is not geometrically structured, leaves the question open and the problem unsolved. Now, what precisely are these intermediate entities?

2.3.1 Geometrical objects as intermediary: Proclus vs. Descartes

One of our most important sources of knowledge about ancient Greek mathematics is Proclus' commentary to the first book of Euclid's "Elements", which begins with the following programmatic statement: "Mathematical being necessarily belongs neither among the first nor among the last and least and simple of the kinds of being, but occupies the middle ground between the partless realities (*ameristōn...hyposthaseōn*)—simple (*haplōn*), not composite (*asynthetōn*), and indivisible (*adiairetōn*)—and divisible things characterized by every variety of composition and differentiation. The unchangeable (*aei kata tayta ekhon*), stable (*monimon*), and incontrovertible (*anelegkton*) character of the propositions about it shows that it is superior to the kinds of things that move about in matter. But discursiveness of [mathematical] procedure, its dealing with its subjects as extended, and its setting up of different prior principles for different objects—these give to mathematical being a rank below that indivisible nature that is completely grounded in itself".[287]

---

[283] Aristotle. Met. 987b 15-18; cp. 992b 17; 995b 17-18; 1028b 20-28. Cp. Plato. Phil. 17a. See also: Breton 1969, 137 sqq.
[284] Cp. Pritchard 1995, 156-157.
[285] Aristotle. Met. 997b 2 sqq.
[286] Aristotle. Met. 998a 1-5.
[287] Proclus. In Eucl. 3.1-14. See also: Hartmann 1909; Bastid 1969.

Similar considerations of mathematical or geometrical entities as intermediary between the ideal notions and the physical things are also found in Iamblichus' "De communi mathematica scientia".[288] The very distinction of several kinds of entities that differ in their ontological status is originally grounded in the notion of a hierarchical structure of being and of cosmos, which may be clearly seen in Plato and Aristotle.[289] The order of being finds its correspondence in the order of knowing. However, unlike Descartes, Plato maintains that being as such, the ideal being, is not immediately given to the introspective observation of the finite discursive mind, but is the task and the purpose to be accomplished. At the same time, the source of being, which is transcendent to being and thus is not being itself but generates being, cannot be given in any possible act of contemplation or mental experience.

The whole Platonic ontology (to which corresponds a specific order of cognition, see 3.1.1; 3.1.2) is not as simplistic as it is sometimes presented, as the dichotomy of separately existing ideas opposed to physical bodily things. Further acceptance of the intermediate mathematical entities makes the ideal and the physical not only distinct and separate, but also connected through the mathematical. The intermediary effectively allows for the explanation of the generic difference between things and their notions (or, rather, of notions and their things) and their connection.

The notion of the intermediary also plays an important role in the structure of cognitive faculties (see 3.2.2; 3.2.3). Thus, the soul within the Platonic tradition is considered intermediate between the demiurgical intellect-*noys* and its product, the cosmos.[290] A passage from the first chapter of book Λ of Aristotle's "Metaphysics" (the earliest in the collection), where Aristotle mentions three different kinds of substances, drew much attention from Neoplatonic commentators from Dexippus to Simplicius, who interpreted the text as hinting at a third order of entities, mathematical or psychic ones, intermediate between noetic and physical objects.[291] The universal soul-*psykhē*, on the one hand, participates in the eternal and unchangeable, in being of the intellect. On the other hand, since the produced and the caused is considered secondary, worse and weaker than the producer and the cause, and the soul itself is considered produced by the intellect, the soul is present to the physical, to the becoming. Thus, the two realms of being and becoming are not only separated, but are also connected through the soul which itself is neither pure being (because of that its thinking is discursive), nor mere becoming (because of that the soul does not perish with the dissolution of its physical vehicle). The intermediateness of the soul consists in that, first, it shapes and molds particular things; second, that it governs the movement and running of the whole cosmos of particular living bodies;[292] and third, that it exemplifies the discursive faculty of reasoning, *dianoia*, which already is unable, due to its relative

---

[288] Iamblichus. De comm. math. sci. 9.4 sqq. Both Iamblichus and Proclus might originally have the same source for their mathematical commentaries. See: Mueller 1987, 334-348.
[289] Plato. RP 511b-e; Aristotle. Met. 986b 14 sqq.
[290] Plato. Tim. 34b sqq.; Phaedr. 245c sqq.; Plutarch. De an. procr. in Tim. 1014a sqq.
[291] Aristotle. Met. 1069a 30 sqq. Cp. Dalsgaard Larsen 1972, 256.
[292] Cp. Aristotle. De an. 432a 15-435a 10.

weakness in contemplation and remoteness from the first principle(s), to grasp being in a simultaneous act of encompassing mental comprehension, which is characteristic of the *noys*.

Let us first turn to the ontological aspect of the intermediateness of the mathematicals *qua* geometricals. The geometrical figures, as Plato, Proclus and Iamblichus present them, are to be situated between the ideal entities and the physical things. The former are characterized as generative, indivisible, partless, simple, not composite, unitary, undivided and stable. The latter are generated, divisible, composite, differentiated, have parts, are complex and movable. One may reduce the whole list of various attributes to three main ones, which may be taken then as fundamental characteristics in distinguishing between the realms of the ideal and the physical. These attributes are: 1. generative/ generated, 2. divisible/ indivisible and 3. stable/ movable. Intelligibles are generative (as archetypes of the existent), indivisible (for every intelligible object is itself a unique "face" of being) and stable (for they do not change). Physical things or bodies, on the contrary, are generated (for a body is said to be existent by participating in being, i.e. in its archetype), divisible (for they are material magnitudes, spatially extended) and capable of being moved (the movement, which may be taken not only as locomotion, but also as alteration, expresses their inability not to change and not to be always the same).[293] If geometrical objects are intermediary, they also have to relate to the three pairs of opposite attributes. Proclus describes the peculiarity of geometricals in the following way: they are similar to intelligibles and, consequently, are dissimilar to bodies insofar as the theoretical considerations of the objects of geometry are unchangeable, stable and indisputable. On the other hand, geometricals are also similar to material bodies and dissimilar to intelligibles insofar as consideration of their properties has to be presented discursively, in a logical form. Moreover, geometricals themselves are also extended.

The conclusion Proclus reaches is: "Mathematical objects, and in general all the objects of the understanding, have an intermediate position. They go beyond the objects of intellect in being divisible, but they surpass sensible things in being devoid of [physical] matter. They are inferior to the former in simplicity yet superior to the latter in precision, reflecting intelligible reality more clearly than do perceptible things. Nevertheless they are only images, imitating in their divided fashion the indivisible and in their multiform fashion the uniform patterns of being. In short, they stand in the vestibule of the primary forms, announcing their unitary and undivided and generative reality, but have not risen above the particularity and compositeness of ideas and the reality that belongs to likenesses; nor have they yet escaped from the soul's varied and discursive ways of thinking and attained conformity with the absolute and simple modes of knowing which are free from all traces of matter. Let this be our understanding, for the present, of the intermediate status of mathematical genera and species, as lying between absolutely indivisible

---

[293] Aristotle. Phys. 200b 13 sqq.; 225a 2 sqq. For Plato the only possible regular—circular—bodily motion is not that of physical things on Earth, but only of the celestial bodies, which are not ordinary bodies capable of decay, for they are gods. Cp. Blumenberg 1987, 300-302.

realities and the divisible things that come to be in the world of matter."[294]

From an epistemological perspective, there are three different cognitive mental capacities which correspond to intelligibles, geometricals and bodies; namely, intellect-*noys*, discursive reasoning (or understanding-*dianoia*), and mere opinion-*doxa*. A more detailed discussion of the structure of cognitive faculties in their relation to the objects of science follows in the next chapter (3.1). Here we need only to note that the intellect is as if in "touch" with being, i.e., thinks being without any mediation, because there is no mediation between the intellect as thinking and its intelligible object.[295] Intellect itself always *is*—i.e., is being—as Plotinus, together with Parmenides, takes it to be.

Now, how can geometricals be properly characterized in terms of the three pairs of attributes? First of all, neither of the opposite attributes within every pair is exceptionally applicable to the geometrical entities, because they share certain properties both with intelligible objects and with bodies. It cannot also be the case that neither of the paired attributes is applicable to the geometrical, exactly for the same reason. The only possibility left is that *both* of the opposite main attributes should be applicable to geometrical objects. But in order to avoid contradiction, the attributes should be applicable in different respects, since the identity of subject and of time is present in every geometrical entity (cp. 1.1.2). Thus, (1) geometricals are generated insofar as they are produced under the pattern of an intelligible object or *eidos*, but they also can be taken as generative, as patterns for construction and distinguishing physical figures—points, lines, planes etc. (cp. 3.4.2-3.4.3). The geometricals (2) are divisible insofar as in every figure there may be distinguished various parts (except for a point which is has certain privileged position among geometricals, since it represents the monad, the indivisible basis of number as pure being and the monad itself represents the first principle of being (cp. 2.1.3). Geometricals are however indivisible in their form, once every figure is considered as such in its identity (as a circle, an ellipse, etc.), i.e. as a species. And lastly, (3) the geometricals, on the one hand, may be considered stable, since they are conceived in a single act of reasoning (and of imagination) and never change. But on the other hand, movement may be also applicable to geometrical entities, because geometrical it may be conceived as drawn by a movement of another geometrical figure (a solid—by movement of a line and a line—by movement of a point, 3.4.2).

One of the main peculiar features of modernity is expelling of all kinds of the intermediary in ontological and epistemological structures. Put in mutually exclusive and complimentary terms of either/ or—either mind, or body, either the one or the other—they lack any mediation and thus become absolutely disconnected. Thus, once the notion of the soul as mediating between the intellect and the body is abandoned, the mind-body problem becomes an exemplary riddle for modern philosophy, amounting to the mystery of the embodiment of the soul. In fact, it is the disembodied finite *ego* or subjectivity that becomes the mediator between being and non-being, between the infinite and the finite. As Descartes puts it, "I realize that I am, as it were, something intermediate between God and

---

[294] Proclus. In Eucl. 4.18-5.14, trans. G.M. Morrow. Cp. O'Meara 1989, 173-175.
[295] Cp. Proclus. In Eucl. 4.2-3.

nothingness, or between supreme being and non-being."[296] The *ego* is not however an intermediary, for, as the complementary to the body, it is—it has to be—disconnected from the body. Rather, the finite subjectivity puts itself in the center, driving out *the* being to the margins of cognitive activity which becomes thus self-(*ego*)-centered.

And by reducing of the object of scientific study to merely extended object, which is not different from the geometrical object in its fundamental characteristics (shape, extension, movability), Descartes also paradoxically expels geometricals as intermediary entities. Intermediary structures simply cannot have any place in the world where every entity is assigned either to the *res cogitans* or to the *res extensa*. The starting point of subjectivity that expels everything which is not thinking but is external (extended—physical or geometrical), does not leave any room for mediation. Descartes thus makes the most decisive step in the geometrization of the physical: by abandoning the intermediary, i.e., by the very construction, he abolishes every possibility of making a crucial distinction between the physical and the geometrical.

2.4 The notion of intelligible matter

The problem of matter is one of the central and most fundamental problems in Plotinus, since it is intimately present in all the other constituents of his philosophy. As it will be argued in what follows, matter is not only present to physical bodily things, but also to thinkable objects, under the guise of the so-called intelligible, or noetic, matter. Not only in Plotinus' earlier reflections but throughout the whole body of his work the notion of intelligible matter plays an important role and thus constitutes one of the intrinsic components in his philosophy, in particular, in his consideration of mathematical objects. Moreover, bodily matter and intelligible matter appear to be necessarily connected as different but at the same time as inseparable; the notion of matter, if thoroughly analyzed, necessarily entails the notion of the intelligible matter.

In the Ennead II.4.2-5 Plotinus gives a developed account of intelligible matter, *hylē noētē*.[297] Some philosophers maintain, says Plotinus, the existence of "another, prior, kind [of mater] in the intelligible world (*en tois noētois*) which underlies the forms there and the incorporeal substances".[298] Plato does not have any univocal and elaborated notion of intelligible matter. One might see an analog of the *hylē noētē* in Plato's consideration of the four elements in the "Timaeus": since they are considered material but at the same time mathematically structured, each element is represented by a regular polyhedron. A weakness of the "plausible myth" of the "Timaeus", as it has already been mentioned, is that Plato does not provide any clear account of how such a combination of geometrical entities might

---

[296] Descartes. Med. IV, AT 54.
[297] In the edition of the "Enneads" the treatise II. 4 appears under the title "On Matter"; its other title, "On the Two Kinds of Matter", we find in Porphyry's *Vita Plotini* 4. 45; 24, 46. Both titles, however, do not belong to Plotinus himself and reflect the school's usage, cp. Schwyzer 1951, col. 487.
[298] Plotinus. Enn. II.4.1.14-18.

also have, or obtain, physical properties (e.g., weight), nor of how the utterly unformed matter-*khōra* differs from the formed and structured matter of the elements.[299] The very notion of *hylē noētē* appears first in Aristotle, occurring three times in the "Metaphysics".[300] In the "Metaphysics" Z 11, 1036b 35-1037a 4 and in H 6, 1045a 34 Aristotle contrasts sensual (bodily) matter to intelligible matter (*esti gar hē hylē hē men aisthētē hē de noētē*). And in Z 10, 1035a 9 sqq., he stresses the unknowability of matter as such (*agnōstos*, cp. 1.1.1) and describes intelligible matter as present "in sensible things not *qua* sensible, e.g. the objects of mathematics".[301] Aristotle does not, however, elaborate the notion of intelligible matter thoroughly, so that this notion does not play any important role in his philosophy.

Joachim suggests that the already mentioned Aristotelian distinction between *prōtē hylē* and *hylē topikē* (see 1.1.1) parallels that of physical and geometrical (intelligible) matter.[302] Still, even if in a certain respect *hylē topikē* is similar to intelligible matter, insofar as both heavenly bodies and geometrical objects may be considered synthetic entities constituted by form within matter, there are, nevertheless, two important distinctions between the two. First, geometrical entities, unlike celestial bodies, first, do not move themselves (they are not in constant circular motion) unless imagined as moved. And second, geometrical objects are not sensually perceivable, but are thought and imagined.

In the contemporary discussion we find an interpretation of the concept of intelligible matter as an "oddity in Aristotle's thought", as an attempt to solve a problem raised by abstraction—to avoid the substantialization of qualities as the forms without matter, qualities as abstracted from the matter of physical things. Therefore, Aristotle is supposed to introduce *ad hoc* a matter of special kind, in order to associate with it the abstracted qualities.[303] This is not, however, a particularly convincing explanation, because even if Aristotle might avoid substantialization of qualities by relating them to a special non-physical kind of matter, nevertheless nothing prevents that these qualities be further, once again, abstracted from intelligible matter. In such a case one would need to introduce the third kind of matter in order to inform in it the qualities abstracted from the second kind of matter (i.e., from intelligible matter), and so on *ad infinitum*. The whole structure of the underlying argument would repeat that of the third man argument,[304] which Aristotle himself rejects, because thinking has always to be performed in finite and definite terms, i.e., can never go into infinity.

That intelligible matter is not just an "oddity", and that it was a concept that might be discussed yet in the ancient Academy, is indicated by the fact that

---

[299] Plato. Tim. 31b-34a; 53a sqq.
[300] Aristotle. Met. 1035a 9 sqq.; 1036b 35-1037a 4; 1045a 34-36. Cp. Pritchard 1995, 157-158.
[301] It is worth recalling that the books Z and H are among the latest and central in "Metaphysics" according to the chronology of Düring, where Aristotle expresses his mature doctrine of substance.
[302] Joachim 1982, xxxiv.
[303] Annas 1976, 33.
[304] Cp. Plato. Parm. 132d-133a; Aristotle. Met. 990b 18; 1079a 14.

Speusippus reserves one matter, *hylē*, for numbers, and the other for geometrical objects.[305] Xenocrates considers geometrical entities to be constituted by matter and number: line—by the dyad, plane—by the triad, solid—by the tetrad.[306] It is not immediately clear from Aristotle's report whether the matter Xenocrates has in mind is different from the matter of physical things. However, since the distinction between geometricals and physicals plays a crucial role in Platonism, one might argue that the matter as formed by number into a geometrical entity has to be different from that of physical bodies. Later Calcidius uses the term *intelligibilis silva*.[307]

The notion of intelligible matter appears to be neither superfluous nor accidental, as Szlezák demonstrates in an informative and detailed discussion of the notion of *hylē noētē* in Plotinus in its relation to Aristotle's considerations.[308] In Met. 1045a 36, intelligible matter is depicted as the generic constituent of a geometrical figure, as, for example, "plane figure" in: "circle is a plane figure." Still, the three descriptions in Aristotle are too brief to present the notion of intelligible matter in full. Alexander of Aphrodisias further interprets the *hylē noētē* as pure extension (*diastasis*).[309] This is also the understanding of H. Happ.[310] Such an extension has to be different from a system of places, because place, as Aristotle argues, both defines a body as the immovable outer limit and spatially separates the body from all the other bodies. Mathematical (geometrical) objects are not in a place, for one cannot argue that they are separated in the same way as physical bodies are.[311] In this sense, intelligible matter as *diastasis* is closer to the modern Newtonian (pre-Einsteinian) notion of the uniform extension, unrelated to bodies that might be put into it. Rist, however, challenges this interpretation and agrees with Ross that intelligible matter is the generic element, or constituent, in both species and individuals. Rist concludes that Plotinus appropriates the Aristotelian notion of intelligible matter found in the relation between genus and species, and turns it into the relation between "the first effluence from the One [which is] the base of form and form itself".[312]

First of all, it is important to notice that in all the examples referred to by Aristotle, it is geometrical figures that instantiate intelligible matter.[313] More precisely, intelligible matter is associated with the following notions: (1)

---

[305] Ap. Iamblichus. Comm. math. sci. 17.13 sqq.; cp. Merlan 1953, 88 sqq.; Theiler 1964, 98.
[306] Aristotle. Met. 1090b 22-24. See also: Plutarchus. De E 390e; Krämer 1964, 302-303.
[307] Calcidius. In Tim. 283.10.
[308] Szlezák 1979, 72-85.
[309] Alexander Aphrodisiensis. In Met. 510.3.
[310] Happ interprets *hylē noētē* as "reine Ausdehnung", *diastasis* or *diastēma* (Op. cit. P. 29, 581 sqq., 639-649). Happ mentions two different meanings of intelligible matter, *hylē noētē*: 1. as pure extension of geometrical figures, 2. as genus in opposition to *differentia specifica*.
[311] Aristotle. Met. 1092a 18-20; Phys. 208a 28 sqq. Cp. Zekl 1990, 91-92.
[312] Ross 1953, 199; Rist 1962, 106-107.
[313] In Mueller's interpretation, geometrical objects in Aristotle are compounds of properties abstracted from physical things and of intelligible matter (Mueller 1970, 156-171). Aristotle does not, however, provide an exact account of the way properties are exemplified in the *hylē noētē*.

irrationality (there is something in it that cannot be apprehended), (2) mathematical objects and (3) certain extension. If, as it will be argued, intelligible matter is also to be associated with the *plenum* of geometrical figures, then—although the Ross-Rist hypothesis still remains valid—the Alexander-Happ hypothesis cannot be rejected either. Moreover, both accounts are not incompatible insofar as intelligible matter may be understood as the generic element of the geometrical (mathematical) species as existing in the geometrical extension (of course, in such a case the "genus" in the Ross-Rist hypothesis should be restricted to geometrical objects only).

2.4.1 Intelligible matter in Plotinus

Why does Plotinus need the notion of intelligible matter at all? A plausible answer is that he tries to incorporate the Aristotelian notion, never found in Plato, in his own considerations. Plotinus discusses the *hylē noētē* mainly in his early treatise II. 4 [12]. In the treatises of the middle period II. 5 [25] "On What Exists Potentially and What Actually" and III. 6 [26] "On the Impassibility of Things Without Body", there are occasional references to *hylē noētē* and no mention of it at all in the late I. 8 [51] "On What Are and Whence Come Evils". It is only in the immediately precedent III. 5 [50] "On Love" that intelligible matter reappears in chapter six to characterize an important distinction and difference between *daimones* (spirits) as intermediate between gods and humans. Still, as it seems, the notion of intelligible matter is not likely to be introduced by Plotinus only for exegetic purposes—namely, for the reconciliation of the Platonic and Aristotelian views on matter—but it represents an important intrinsic component in Plotinus' philosophical considerations.

What role does intelligible matter play in the "Enneads"? In Enn. II.4.2.1-2 Plotinus sketches a program of investigation of intelligible matter: we have to find out whether intelligible matter (a) exists (*ei estin*), (b) what it is (*tis oysa*) and (c) how it exists (*pōs estin*). All three points should be mutually connected, for the question of existence entails the question of essence, and the question of essence presupposes discussing the question of the mode of existence, i.e., the way essence is represented in being. Plotinus presents several arguments in support of his view that intelligible matter is a necessary constituent of everything that is.

(A) Does intelligible matter exist? It should exist, and (1) the *mimetic* argument supports this claim.[314] If there is an intelligible order or cosmos "there", in the intelligible (*kosmos noētos*), and if this bodily cosmos is an imitation (*mimēma*) of the intelligible cosmos, and if physical cosmos has matter, then there should be matter "there" too as a paradigm of this bodily matter. Moreover, form cannot really be form without being imposed on something that differs from it.

This brings us to (2) the argument of substrate or *hypokeimenon*.[315] Intelligible matter should also exist, because we assume that the forms-*eidē*

---

[314] Plotinus. Enn. II.4.4.8-11. Cp. Nikulin 1998, 85-113.
[315] Cp. Aristotle. Phys. 192a 31.

exist.[316] And if the forms exist, there should be something common to all of them, but also something individual, by which the forms differ from each other. This individual difference in form is called shape (*morphē*); if there is shape, there should be that which is shaped *qua* forms. Therefore, there should be matter that receives this shape—this is intelligible matter. From this point of view, intelligible matter is a non-physical substrate, *hypokeimenon* of the forms.[317] In other words, shape is a peculiar characteristic in and of the forms, the source of individuation, while intelligible matter is that which is *common* to all of them as the undifferentiated substrate of the intelligible, representing the aspect of *unity* of and in the forms.[318] But although this substrate is *in* the intelligible, it is *not* being as such, for being is a synthetic unity which arises as the result of the (re)turning of the not yet differentiated thinking of the intellect to its source, to the superabundant unity (which is not even really a unity) of the One.

(3) Next comes the argument from *parts*.[319] "There", in the intelligible, everything is partless (*ameres*), but, in a way, the forms may also be said to have parts. Intelligible matter is then to be understood as that single shapeless *plenum* where many shapes (*morphai*) of the forms are "cut out", or embodied: "But if intelligible reality is at once many and partless, then the many existing in one are in matter which is that one, and they are its shapes; conceive this unity as varied and of many shapes".[320] Intelligible matter is then an indefinite and undefined source of unity in the forms, a potentiality of and for the multiple definiteness of being. Nevertheless, intelligible matter is "one" in a peculiar sense, as the basis for duality, itself non-dual.

(4) Matter is also present as a "*ladder*". That which is hypostatically and hierarchically "higher" can be considered a form of the "lower", which is thus "matter" to the "higher"; the whole structure thus reminds a ladder. The intelligible matter is closer to being, for it constitutes a moment *in* being. It therefore should be in a "higher" position to the "lower", or bodily, matter. Such a structure is commonly present in Plotinus: that which has more potentiality is matter to what has more actuality.[321] The not defined and formless, says Plotinus, should not necessarily be rejected, for it offers itself to that which is before it and better: such is the soul to the intellect and to *logos*, the rational formative principle.[322] Likewise, the soul may be considered as matter to the intellect. "[W]e must assume that soul is matter to the first reality [i.e., to the intellect] which makes it and is afterwards given shape and perfected."[323] At this point it is important to note that intelligible matter may be associated not only with the intellect but also with the soul; this will be crucial in the discussion of the relation between intelligible matter

---

[316] Plotinus. Enn. II.4.4.2-8; cp. Enn. V.9.3-4.
[317] Cp. Aristotle. Phys. 192a 31; Met. 1024b 8-9.
[318] See: Armstrong 1940, 67-68.
[319] Plotinus. Enn. II.4.4.11-20.
[320] Plotinus. Enn. II.4.4.14-16.
[321] Plotinus. Enn. III.9.5.3.
[322] Plotinus. Enn. II.4.3.1-4.
[323] Plotinus. Enn. V. 9. 4. 10-12; cp. V.1.3.12-14, 21-23; I.2.2.21-23; V.8.3.9; VI.3.16.14-15.

and imagination (3.2.4).

(B) Consideration of the *hylē noētē* as a shapeless unity embracing many shapes brings us to the answer to the question of what intelligible matter is (*tis oysa*). Intelligible matter may be presented (5) as the indefinite dyad, *aoristos dyas* (cp. 1.2.1). The dyad is the primary source and principle of potentiality, of multiplicity, of indefiniteness and of receiving opposites.[324] It plays an important role in the (logical, not temporal) "process" of constituting the intellect-*noys*. The dyad, which represents the not yet definite and not defined thinking of the second hypostasis of the "Parmenides", tends to "offer itself" back to its source, the One which is beyond being and any determination.[325] Therefore, the dyad (which itself is *not* multitude, but the potentiality of multitude) necessarily "misses" the One and can only grasp it as not one but as multiplicity and plurality instead. The dyad, then, in "looking" towards that which cannot be seen (for that reason it is comparable to "seeing in the darkness"[326]), and in returning back to the One, engenders the whole multiplicity of the forms. When the dyad appears as the first being, as the first existing—i.e., as indefinite thinking—this indefinite thinking has no particular defined object yet, in the form of which it might think itself. The only object of indefinite thinking at this stage (of course not in a temporal process) can only be its source, the One, which is not in being, and for that reason cannot be thought.[327] The not yet definite thinking then necessarily has to "miss" its object and to represent it in a number of concrete forms, which thus become the objects of thought, or the intelligible objects (see 3.1.1). Thinking thus becomes definite, for now it thinks itself in the forms of itself which it itself has produced. As the dyad, thinking receives thus a double definition, as it were, both from the source of being and from the multitude of the thinkable forms. Such a structure forms a complete system, so that nothing can be either added or removed from it.[328]

The primary (intelligible) indefiniteness of "seeing"-thinking is thus informed through this arisen multitude of the forms. For this reason, intelligible matter is not different from indefinite thinking as a mere capacity of seeing (or, rather, the intention of seeing) that which as such cannot be seen. That is why the dyad represents the material aspect of the intellect and thus may be considered intelligible matter, because before the act of turning back and "looking" at the One and subsequent (again: not temporal) determination by the noetic forms, it is indefinite.[329] Strictly speaking, the dyad may be considered intelligible matter only

---

[324] Cp. Aristotle. Phys. 203a 15-16, Met. 987b 21-35; Proclus. In Tim. II 153.19-25 = Numenius. Test. 31 Leemans; Themistius. In De an. 12.13-27; Plotinus. Enn. VI.3.12.2-6; VI.6.3.29.

[325] Plotinus. Enn. III.8.11. Cp. Iamblichus. Theolog. arithm. 7.19. See also: Armstrong 1967, 241.

[326] Cp. Plotinus. Enn. I.8.4.31.

[327] Cp. Lloyd 1987, 177 et passim.

[328] Descartes is close to asserting such a structure when he states: "Truth is indivisible, so the slightest thing which is added or taken away falsifies it" (To Mersenne, March 1642, AT III 545).

[329] Plotinus. Enn. V. 1. 7; V. 3. 11; V. 4. 2. Cp. Plato. Phil. 23c sqq.; Aristotle. Met. 987b 20 ff.; Diog. Laert. VIII 25. Cp.: "Why must there be a principle above the *noys*, Plotinus asks

at the second step, after the rise of the noetic objects (see 3.1.1 3, constitution of the intellect), of which it may really be said to be matter. Therefore, the dyad as intelligible matter should be associated with a certain contemplative capacity, which is unconscious, for there is no determination of conscious reflective thinking yet. This contemplative ability to stare at the complete darkness will be later discussed as an irrational construction of imagination (cp. 3.2.2).

As it has been argued, in its elusive nature—which cannot be fully grasped in and by reasoning—matter, as pure otherness, appears to be present in everything to which the multitude in some way is also present (cp. 1.1.2). For Plotinus, otherness separates everything that may be considered different, primarily, generically different. Otherness distinguishes not only different bodily things, but also intelligible objects. Therefore, otherness has to be understood as the dyad, as the first produced, as other to the One, as the basis of and for being. Since thinking always presupposes distinction and distinguishing, the dyad as prime otherness should necessarily be present in thought, in particular, in thought about the good: "[W]hen what is other than the good thinks it, it does so by being 'like the good' and having a resemblance to the good, and it thinks it as good and as desired by itself, and as if it had a mental image (*phantasia*) of the Good".[330]

Sameness in matter is present in a very peculiar way, namely, in being always the source of difference. Intelligible matter is always the same and always retains the same form implemented in it; it is always identical but in its identity it, as the dyad, is the basis of otherness, of multiplicity, of not coincidence with itself, since it primarily represents something other (a mathematical object). One might even say that bodily matter is the otherness that is always the same to itself, while intelligible matter is the sameness that is always other to itself. Thus, on the one hand, intelligible matter as the dyad may be recognized as the principle (of multitude, but not the multitude itself), but on the other hand, matter as pure nothingness or otherness is different to everything else, for it is incompatible with any end, *peras*. Physical matter and intelligible matter are still one and the same matter as negativity, but in a sense they also oppose each other, since intelligible matter appears as the principle of multiplicity in the forms, which itself is a unity, which unites the forms in the structure of all-unity as unity-in-diversity (see 3.1.1).

This duality of otherness is insurmountable, for its main purpose is always pointing at and referring to something else. In matter it is present, on the one hand, as pure otherness, as mere privation of anything definite, as a possibility of embodiment of form. On the other hand, it appears to be the principle of multiplicity, first as duality and then as the one-many of the intellect. That is why matter is present both at the very beginning (in the primary being) and at the very end.[331]

Intelligible matter as the dyad, then, is also a substrate. The dyad is neither being, which in the first place is represented in and *qua* intelligible forms, nor is it non-being (as bodily matter "is" non-being), because it is different from

---

in Enn. V. 4.2.8-9. Because the activity of *noys* which is thinking, is *aoristos* and receives its determination only from its object (the intelligible)." - Merlan 1964, 45.

[330] Plotinus. Enn. V.6.5.12-15. Cp. Plato. RP 509a.

[331] Cp. Happ 1971, 193-195.

the One, which alone is beyond being. Intelligible matter is then a necessary "substrate" for the forms (being), which is "prior" to being. The intellect is then a synthesis of thinking and thought and is constituted as the unity of thinking, which engenders, but also is itself defined by, the objects of thought.[332]

And lastly (6), intelligible matter is to be considered a *potentiality* of being because *hylē noētē* is to be defined both by the One and by the forms. As Rist argues, Plotinus simply associates Aristotelian intelligible matter with the Platonic indefinite dyad.[333] In this very sense, intelligible matter parallels matter in general as mere potentiality.

(C) Consideration of intelligible matter as dyad, as the principle of multiplicity, helps answer the last question of Plotinus: *how* does intelligible matter exist. Indeed, the very way the dyad is introduced—as being closer to the One than anything else and thus as intimately related to the ultimate source of everything existent—presents intelligible matter as the potentiality of and for real beings, as the possibility of their subsistence and embodiment as the forms-*eidē*.

Is intelligible matter produced? Recently, there were a number of discussions concerning this question, inspired by O'Brien, who supports the thesis of the generation of matter, and by Schwyzer, who rejects the thesis.[334] Due to its inherent ambiguity and paradoxality, in a certain sense matter may be considered as produced, insofar as it comes next to the One and is also at a later point reconstituted by the creative potency of the soul.[335] But, on the other hand, matter may also be said to be not produced, because, first, it comes not in time and, second, matter as pure indefiniteness, unless and until it is defined, is not a substance or being in the proper sense and, therefore, cannot be said to be produced.[336] Similarly the noetic objects are engendered when the originally produced indefinite—and in this sense material—primary thinking turns to thinking its own origin. Because of that noetic objects may also be considered as "originated in so far as they have a beginning, but not originated because they have not a beginning in time; they always proceed from something else, not as always coming into being, like the universe, but as always existing, like the universe there [in the intelligible]. For otherness 'there' exists always (*hē heterotēs hē ekei aei*), which produces [intelligible] matter; for this is the principle of matter, this and the primary movement (*hē kinēsis hē prōtē*). For this reason movement, too, was called otherness, because movement and otherness sprang forth (*exephysan*) together. The movement and the otherness which came from the first are undefined, and need the first to define them; and they are defined when they turn back to it. But before the turning, matter, too, was undefined and the other and not yet good, but unilluminated from the first. For if light comes from the first, then that which receives the light, before it receives it has everlastingly no light; but it has light as

---

[332] Cp. O'Meara 1995, 62-65.
[333] Rist 1962, 104.
[334] See the discussion in: O'Brien 1971, 113-146; 1981, 108-123; Schwyzer 1973, 266-280; Corrigan, O'Cleirigh 1987, 577-578; Narbonne 1993, 133 sqq.
[335] Plotinus. Enn. III.4.1.9-12. Cp. Corrigan 1986, 167-181.
[336] Cp. Plotinus. Enn. IV. 8.6.18-23.

other that itself, since the light comes to it from something else".[337]

This description, first, fits the description of the intelligible matter *qua* dyad perfectly well: before turning back to the One matter is indefinite, i.e. is not yet defined and therefore "is" non existing. Matter receives definition and quasi-existence only through its epistrophic relation, through turning back to its source, which is prior and better than matter. Second, when receiving a definition through the movement towards the origin and the good, the ever-existing (and, therefore, not produced) radical otherness, (other to everything, even to itself) finds its realization in and as intelligible matter, which may be said to be produced in its identity *qua* intelligible matter.[338] That is why matter originally is not defined and thus does not properly exist.

In the late treatise, "On What Are and Whence Come Evils" (I.8 [51]), we can hardly find any traces of intelligible matter, and every attempt of "reading it out" of the text would be interpretative, even if justified. It seems that for Plotinus one cannot speak about two *different* matters. First, matter is not any definite subject with a number of distinctive predicates by which it differs from another subject or entity. Intelligible matter is not a form (for, as dyad, it still has to be shaped by being, which is different from itself), and bodily matter is not mere nothing as "zero" potentiality, but is a certain negative capacity, a *nihil negativum*. Second, before the whole structure of intelligible objects arise, there is no principle of distinction, so that one cannot distinguish anything. Therefore, intelligible matter cannot be different from bodily matter at this stage. Do they become, perhaps, distinct at a later stage (although, again, not in time) when the intelligible noetic being arises? The appearance of the objects of thought does not, however, change anything in the nature of matter nor in the relation of intelligible matter to bodily matter. Therefore, the two cannot be said to be really different. That is why Plotinus has to state that matter "must not be composite, but simple and one thing in its nature".[339] Matter "keeps (*phylattei*) its own nature".[340] Does this mean that there is no distinction between the two matters?

The two matters cannot be considered as identically the same. For, first, unless the ideal forms arise, there is no way to judge about sameness—there is no principle of sameness either in the not yet formed matter, nor even in the One, which is beyond sameness and otherness. We might speak about the nature of matter, but this nature can only be taken as the source of becoming. In other words, the "nature" of matter does not express any identity. Quite on the contrary, its identity consists in being always non-identical. The second point of distinction of the two matters is thus explained by Plotinus: "[I]n the intelligible world the

---

[337] Plotinus. Enn. II.4.5.24-37. Cp. Aristotle. Phys. 201b 19-28 = Testimonia Platonica 55A Gaiser. See also: Narbonne 1993, 281.

[338] At this point Plotinus brings a new component to his discussion—namely, primary movement—which obviously is in reference to Plato's account of five *megista genē*: being, motion, rest, sameness and otherness. Plato. Soph. 254d sqq. Plotinus often refers to this place in "Sophist" throughout the "Enneads" (Enn. III.7.3.9-11; V.1.4.35-36; V.3.15.40; VI.2.7.30; VI.7.39.4-6 et al.). Cp. O'Brien 1991, 24-25.

[339] Plotinus. Enn. II.4.8.13-14.

[340] Plotinus. Enn. III.6.18.19; cp. III.6.10.18 and 11.36.

composite being (*syntheton*) is differently constituted, not like bodies: since forming principles, too, are composite, and by their actuality make composite the nature which is active toward the production of form...The matter, too, of the things that came into being is always receiving different the forms, but the matter of eternal things is always the same and always has the same form. With matter here, it is pretty well exactly the other way round; for here it is all things in turn and only one thing at each particular time; so nothing lasts because one thing pushes out another; so it is not the same for ever".[341] The composition of the intelligible may be thus understood as that of peculiarity (shape) and universality (the intelligible matter). This universality is, however, differently constituted in bodies, since intelligible matter can be understood as the same (*tayton*) as receiving the same form. In other words, the defined form is the source of identity in the *hylē noētē*, while bodily matter is unable to retain anything firmly and constantly.

The two matters are rather in proportion to each other: the relation of intelligible matter as an "*as if*" form of bodily matter is similar to the relation (or proportion) of the form (*eidos*) to bodily matter as *khōra* (cp. 1.1.2). Still, intelligible matter is not a form in the proper sense, because it is only the potentiality of and for the forms. Therefore, one has to somewhat paradoxically conclude that one cannot treat "matter" as one single subject, but one also cannot say that it really differs from itself in the distinction between intelligible and bodily matter. Thus matter should be recognized as fundamentally ambiguous. Ambiguity may even be found in intelligible matter, insofar as intelligible matter—as it will be argued in what follows—is represented not only through the indefinite dyad but also through imagination (3.2.4), which is itself double, insofar as it is positioned and directed toward both the intelligible and the sensual.

2.4.2 Intelligible matter in Proclus

Let us now turn to Proclus' reflections on the notion of intelligible matter. Proclus begins his commentary to the "Elements" of Euclid with a prologue that consists of two parts. The first part describes geometricals solely in terms of discursive reasoning; their closeness to intelligibles consists in an immateriality (*aylia*), which they share with the forms-*eidē*. However, in the second part of the prologue Proclus turns to the discussion of intelligible matter as primarily present in geometrical objects very much in the same way as Plotinus does.[342] At the same time, Proclus introduces a necessary counterpart of intelligible matter: imagination-*phantasia* (see 3.2.3). There may be a historical reason for not mentioning intelligible matter in the first part of the prologue, because it appears that in the first part Proclus exposes the Pythagorean point of view, whereas in the second part he turns to the consideration of the Platonic position, as influenced by the Stoics with their interest in imagination.

To what genus of entities should this intelligible, or geometrical, matter (*geōmetrikē hylē*) belong? On the one hand, geometrical figures cannot pertain to the realm of sensible things and thus be associated with physical matter, because,

---

[341] Plotinus. Enn. II.4.3.5-13.
[342] Proclus. In Eucl. 49.5 sqq.

first, geometry "emancipates us from sensible things, converts us to the realm of bodiless existence, habituates us to the sight of intelligibles, and prepares us for activity in accordance with the intellect".[343] Second, a point without parts and a line without width do not exist as physical things or physical figures in matter, where point has parts and line has width. And third, physical things are always "more or less" precise, since they are embodied in physical matter, which distorts everything put in it, while geometricals are always the same, perfectly precise and uniform in their shape (cp. 3.4.3).[344]

On the other hand, geometrical entities cannot be completely outside certain matter, because, first, they would have been completely indivisible. On the contrary, one can discern various parts in figures, enlarge and diminish them and one can make figures touch each other. All these properties can be explained only if one presupposes a certain quasi-material "receptacle" that makes geometrical entities divisible and extended.[345] Second, there is only one intelligible circle, or the notion of the circle, whereas there are many (a potentially infinite number of) geometrical circles.[346] Therefore, geometrical objects should first and foremost be associated with intelligible or geometrical matter, and so Proclus' claim that the intermediate geometrical entities are immaterial means only that they are not immersed into physical matter. The doctrine of intelligible matter is referred by Proclus directly to the Aristotelian two matters (which are explicitly mentioned),[347] and is paralleled in Plotinus and, perhaps, in Porphyry as well, who also wrote a commentary to Euclid and whom Proclus mentions in his commentary.[348] Proclus might be referring to the not preserved commentary on Euclid's "Elements" by Porphyry, who was much interested in incorporating Stoic notions into Platonic philosophy. Iamblichus might also be referring to Porphyry's commentary in his "De communi mathematica scientia".[349]

Since intelligible matter is understood by Proclus as geometrical *par excellence*, he criticizes Plotinus for bringing matter into the intelligible. However, as it will argued in more detail in what follows (3.2.4), Proclus' approach, linking intelligible matter to imagination, may be reconciled with that of Plotinus. First, intelligible matter understood as the indefinite dyad may be considered present not only in geometrical entities, but in arithmeticals as well—i.e., in numbers. In numbers *hylē noētē* appears through the multiplicity of numbers and through their distinction from each other (cp. 2.1.1-2.1.2; 2.4.1), i.e., as the principle of otherness and individuation in numbers. And second, the intelligible realm for Proclus is separated from the geometrical, because the intelligible is constituted primarily by the limit, whereas matter is utterly unlimited.[350] Limit for Proclus is

---

[343] Proclus. In Eucl. 49.9-12.
[344] Proclus. In Eucl. 49.12-24.
[345] Proclus. In Eucl. 49.27-50.2. As Happ argues, *hylē noētē* of geometry is to be taken as pure extensio – Happ 1971, 127.
[346] Proclus. In Eucl. 54.5-13.
[347] Proclus. In Eucl. 51.15-17.
[348] Proclus. In Eucl. 255.12-256.8 et al. Cp. Mueller 1987, 334-348.
[349] Iamblichus. De comm. math. sci. 12.18 sqq.; cp. Syrianus. In Met. 101.22-103.12.
[350] Proclus. Theol. Plat. III 40.10-41.15.

related to the unlimited as substance is related to pure potency, *dynamis*. He further distinguishes two potencies, the one of the productive principle, which has to be associated with the One (cp. 1.2.1), the other of pure receptivity, which has to be linked to matter.[351] Since Proclus does not accept any potentiality in the intelligible, all matter should be excluded from there. But since the intelligible is constituted for him by both principles of the limit and the unlimited, being has to exemplify a certain potency, which is the infinite potency of unceasing thinking and production; although, this potency of being is not potentiality and in this way is different from the potentiality of coming to be.[352]

An obvious conclusion from the previous discussion of physical and intelligible matter is that no concept of intelligible or geometrical matter would make any sense for Descartes, who simply leaves no room for any such kind of matter in his considerations.[353] The reasons for this are quite obvious. First, there is no matter other than extension for Descartes, and extension is the essential attribute of bodies. Descartes has to postulate a hypothetical "matiere subtile" instead of a vacuum in order to explain what is "left" in a closed tube or vessel after the air has been pumped off (see 1.4.2); this is the only way to save his two-substance approach. The supposed "matiere subtile" then can only be of the same kind as physical matter; there is no geometrical matter. Since body and mind are mutually exclusive and complementary, there can be no matter related to the mind and to mental objects of whatever kind. The difficulty of where to put geometrical objects *qua* extended—to the *res extensa* or *res cogitans*—remains unsolved by Descartes. Moreover, methodologically it can hardly be solved within the framework of Cartesianism. The second reason for not accepting intelligible matter as the specific matter of the mathematical, or at least of geometrical entities, is that the infinite for Descartes is *actually* infinite. Because of that, the idea of the infinite is by no means a negative or privative idea, as darkness is privation of light or rest is

---

[351] Proclus: In Alc. 122.8-10: *dittē gar hē dynamis, hē men toy poioyntos, hē de toy paskhontos.* Cp. Theol Plat. III, 34.8-11, 40.12-20.

[352] Proclus. Elem. theol. 85-86, 90; Theol. Plat. III 30.15 sqq.; cp. Plato. Soph. 247d-e. Originally, the two principles were introduced by the Pythagoreans as the constitutive principles of the *cosmos*, later rethought by the Platonists as the intelligible, noetic cosmos. As Philolaus puts it, "Nature in the world-order was fitted together both out of things which are unlimited (*ex apeirōn*) and out of things which are limited (*peiranontōn*), both the world-order as a whole and all the things in it." - Philolaus, frg.1 Huffman.

[353] Although Toletus, following Aquinas, distinguishes sensible matter from intelligible matter (In Phys. I, ch. 1, qu. 3). He presents sensible matter as substance with elementary qualities (heat, cold, wetness, dryness), while intelligible matter is taken as a quantity considered in mathematics, which studies figures and forms as they occur in quantity. The proportional relation between the two matters is: figure relates to quantity as form relates to matter. See: Des Chene 1996, 116-117. In modernity, Malebranche assumes the existence of "intelligible extension" in God, the divine idea of extension, in and through which the finite human mind apprehends ideas of extended things and figures.
– Malebranche 1997, 626-627.

privation of movement.[354] And because Descartes understands God in terms of pure being, as *the* substance, everything in the infinite divine mind has to be actual. Evidently, there is no place then for the indefinite potency of intelligible matter within the infinite mind. Consequently, geometrical objects as intermediary are to be rejected and expelled by Descartes, and the distinction between the geometrical and the bodily has to be banished. Physical straight lines are still curvy; therefore Descartes has to exclude them from scientific considerations and substitute them with their geometrical representatives. Geometricals thus cease to be intermediates, because the specifically physical, as changing and becoming always other, is left out. Geometrical entities replace physical things and thus become *the* objects of scientific study and investigation. It is exactly for this reason that it becomes possible to study bodies as geometrical objects and to apply mathematical rules and procedures to physics.

---

[354] Descartes. Med. III, AT VII 45. Since an idea always represents a "thing", there can be no idea of nothing, whether nothing is taken as something positive or merely as privation - Descartes. Conversation with Burman, AT V 153.

PART III
REASON, IMAGINATION AND CONSTRUCTION

3.1 Reason and the structure of cognitive faculties

3.1.1 Intellect-noys in Plotinus

The notion of intelligible matter has been discussed in its connection with intelligible and geometrical objects. Now we have to examine the role intelligible matter plays in cognition and in the structure of reason. Reason as intellect-*noys* plays a major role in Platonic philosophy and in mathematical considerations, which are taken primarily not as constructive, but rather as discovering certain properties constituted by the intellect.

The main features of the intellect or reason in the Platonic tradition can be presented in the following way. Intellect is understood primarily as identical with being. Only *noys* really *is*, is being as ideal paradigmatic activity and actuality; and, vice versa, that which is exists without any change or detriment—is *noys*. Being and thinking, as Parmenides puts it in his famous maxim, are the same.[1]

How is being constituted? First of all, being is not a primary given, but is constituted or produced by the interaction of the one and the many, or sameness and otherness. Hence, being is, on the one hand, definite (only the definite form enables us to understand a thing in its identity, as both unique and different from everything else) and, on the other hand, limited. Therefore, to characterize the first principle as "infinite being", as Descartes does, would be a *contradictio in adiecto*, for the infinite is not being and being is not infinite. Not only is being limited but it is also always represented as many equally independent beings or intelligibles, each of which is truly one and unique. Contrary to Descartes, for Plato and Plotinus only that which is (non-discursively) thought properly *is*; and that which is, is and can be thought. Because of this, neither matter nor anything material can represent being or substance.

Qua being, intellect can be characterized as the first *energeia*, the real activity and perfect actuality without any diminishing—as that which really is and is the first to be.[2] Intellect can be defined as that which always necessarily and properly *is* or exists, *esti monon*. Only the *noys* is unable to not be. As pure actuality, being is not affected and, as pure activity, cannot have an end, *telos*, outside of itself and not from itself. That is why the intellect is always *already* there, not searching but already having the *is* and the *what* of itself in itself, so that nothing can be added to it. Being is then the end of striving, *ephesis*, of all other things that "struggle" for being, as it were, defined in their existence by being and in their notions by the *noys*.[3] Similarly, thinking of the *noys* is the end of all mental cognitive processes. Because of the identity of intellect and being, not only the intellect's *is*, but also its *what* have to be always the same, so that the *noys* cannot be properly described in terms of "will be" or "was" but only the "*always* is". The

---

[1] Parmenides B3 DK. The B3 fragment is the keystone for Plotinus, who explicitly mentions it at least seven times in the "Enneads" (Enn. I.4.10.6; III.5.7.51; III.8.8.8; V.1.8.17-18; V.4.2.44; V.6.6.22-23; V.9.5.29-30; VI.7.41.18). The same is also true for Iamblichus, Porphyry, Proclus and Damascius.
[2] Plotinus. Enn. VI.7.13.1 sqq. Cp. Themistius. In de an. 106.
[3] Plotinus. Enn. III.7.4.17 sqq.

intellect thus presupposes eternity as "always", not as an unlimited duration, but as a single gatheredness.[4]

The intellect is not simple but represents multiplicity bound into one, the *noys* is itself caused, or engendered, by the unity without multiplicity—by the One, which is not itself being (see 2.1.1).[5] The cause of being has thus to be transcendent to being; i.e., itself is not being as such or being of any kind. However, even if the intellect is not the first and the ultimate principle but is non-temporarily engendered, it nevertheless has to be taken as the *generative* principle of existence of particular thinkable entities, insofar as it contains their archetypes or notions.[6] Understanding being as engendered is opposite to the later medieval and modern understanding of being as a pure (divine) act which exists from itself and due only to itself, i.e., as having no origin (for a more detailed argument see 1.2.1). In other words, for Plotinus, that which *is*, is only a trace (*ikhnos*) of the unique cause of being, the One. The produced has therefore to be thought as one-many.[7] The central point of such a consideration is the identification of the one-many of the second hypothesis of the "Parmenides" with the intellect. Although it is drawn in the conclusion, this one-many is already implicitly presupposed in the premises as an *a priori* condition of the validity of the whole argument, because otherwise, following the first "Parmenides" hypothesis, we could not have argued about the one *per se* at all. Being-intellect is thus the first other to the One, but also, on the contrary, the One is the first and absolute other to the intellect. For that reason, in order to be able to draw any conclusions about the One at all, we have to start with otherness as not-sameness or with the principle of the many in the synthesis of the one-many. The primary duality of the opposition of being to its cause, which itself is not being but a unity, establishes the pure form of the many.[8]

---

[4] Cp. Plato. Tim. 37e sqq. As Plotinus puts it, the intellect is *"to 'estin' aei, kai oydamoy to mellon—esti gar kai tote—oyde to parelēlythos—oy gar ti ekei parelēlythen—all' enestēken aei,"* Enn. V.1.4.22-24. Since the intellect is already fully there, no "will be" can be added to it, or otherwise the intellect would have "fallen from the seat of being" (*to errein ek tēs toy einai hedras*, Plotinus. Enn. III.7.4.19-20). Cp. Enn. V.8.3.11.

[5] See: Bussanich 1988, 58 et passim; Emilsson 1999, 283-289. On various occasions Plotinus reiterates that the One is the potency of all, *dynamis pantōn* - Enn. III.8.10.1, IV.8.6.11, V.1.7.10, V.4.1.36, VI.4.1.25, VI.7.32.31, VI.8.20.38, VI.9.6.8 et al.

[6] Plato. RP 509b; Tim.29e-31b.

[7] Plotinus. Enn. V.3.15.7-12; VI.7.17.39. The One is identified by Plotinus with the one, or oneness, *hen* of the I. Hypothesis of the "Parmenides"; the intellect—with one-many, *hen polla* of the second hypothesis and the soul—with one *and* many, *hen kai polla* of the third hypothesis, Plato. Parm. 157b-159b.

[8] Plotinus. Enn. V.3.15.40-45. This casts light upon double negation as a way of conceiving the inconceivable. The ascension to the One, *anagogē eis hen* (Enn. III. 8. 10. 20, V. 5. 4. 1 et al.) goes from dispersion and division to unity. But this "henological reduction" (Halfwassen 1992, 53 sqq.) through *negatio negationis* is a movement in reverse to that, say, in Hegel, from thesis through the negativity of antithesis to synthesis. Quite to the contrary, in Plotinus we see ascension from the intellect to the One as a dissolution of the composite synthesis of the one-many and of the whole system of all-unity (which is ultimately production of the One, not of the intellect itself) to the simplest non-dual thesis or, rather, un-thesis.

Pure otherness, however, is also represented through intelligible matter (2.4.1-2.4.2). Being thus exemplifies not only identity, but also primary radical otherness; in this respect being appears to be very close to intelligible matter.

Qua being, the intellect cannot be mere potentiality, which is not limited, and as such has to exemplify unity. This unity is not, however, the unity disconnected from multiplicity, because pure otherness or unity, as Plato argues in the first hypothesis of the "Parmenides," is not thinkable and not apprehensible in any way. The intellect then has to be dual in its unity (*diploys*—while only the One is simple, *haploys*), as both the activity of thinking and the actuality of the noetic cosmos of thinkable objects. Being-*noys* thus inherently embraces multitude and for that reason thinking and thought can be distinguished in it; that is, the thinking that thinks itself in the form of intelligible objects. Since the intellect is not absolutely simple but is inescapably and fundamentally dual, it is to be understood as constituted by the one and the many, or by the one and the dyad, as abundance (*hyperbolē*) and deficiency (*elleipsis*), or as sameness (*taytotēs*) and otherness (*heterotēs*). Along with Plato, Plotinus takes being to be primarily represented in and through the structure of the one-being, *hen-on*, of the second hypothesis of the "Parmenides".[9] This primordial simplest conjunction already contains the form of the two or duplicity; not only sameness, but otherness as well, and not only one, but also many. The form of duplicity is exemplified by the distinction of *one* and *being* in the conjunction of *one-being* of the second "Parmenides" hypothesis. However, this initial, virtual opposition of one to being (in the apprehension of the "one is") is possible only because the unity without multiplicity precedes the unity in multiplicity (the One precedes being-intellect).

This one-being ("the one which is") is nothing else but intellect-*noys*, which thinks itself in its otherness and sameness together, *heteron kai tayton*.[10] Sameness in being means that the intellect always *is* and, as thinking thinking itself, is always the same. Otherness in being-intellect is represented as inherent plurality. This otherness appears in three different ways: first, within the intellect itself, being and thinking are virtually—not really—the other to each other. Second, every particular object of thought is different from, and other to, every other object of thought. And third, the intellect in its integrity of being as one-many is the other to its source, which cannot be understood in terms of multitude and being.

The distinction between the thought (*noēsis* or *nooyn*) and the thinkable (*ta noēta* or *nooymenon*, a unique complete system of ideal archetypes or paradigms of things) can already be found in Plato and Aristotle and is elaborated in much detail in later ancient philosophy.[11] In the intellect we have to distinguish thinking and thought, which are not actually separated, but represent two different aspects of being or intellect. The intellect is thus thinking that thinks itself in the

---

[9] Cp. Plotinus. Enn. V.1.3 sqq.
[10] Plotinus. Enn. V.3.15.40.
[11] Plato. Tim 29d sqq.; Aristotle. De an. 429a 10 sqq.; Cp. Plotinus. Enn. II.4.4.8; III.3.5.17; III.8.11.36; IV.7.10.35; IV.8.3.8; V.1.4.31-34; V.4.2.12; V.8.1.1; V.9.9.7; VI.7.13.1; Proclus. Theol. Plat. IV.6 sqq.

forms of its own objects, which are, however, first produced in an attempt to think the pure unity, properly unthinkable (see 2.1.1). All thinkable objects are without detriment, so that the intellect thinks everything it has, and there is nothing in the *noys* that it does not think. Self-thinking of the intellect seeks nothing, but rather already *has* everything in itself in the way that it constantly uses (thinks) what it has.[12] The intellect is then one bounded multiple unity, where thinking thinks itself in the objects of thought and where every such object is actually communicating with every other one. This structure of multiple unity, *hen polla*, is known from Plato's "Parmenides" (144e) and is realized through the communication-*koinōnia* of the intelligible forms, where each form-*eidos* is independent but at the same time actually—not potentially—reflects and contains all the other forms.[13] In the intelligible realm, *kosmos noētos*, every constituting element expresses every other, so that such a constituent is both individual (for it has, or rather is, a particular *eidos*) and universal (for all the other constituents actually communicate according to the principle of *koinōnia*). *Koinōnia* is the principle of organization of the intelligible sphere where, as Plotinus puts it, the whole "has not been put together out of its parts, but has produced its parts itself, in order that it may truly be a whole (*pan*) in this way too".[14] Every thinkable object is single and individual and at the same time actually contains the totality of all other forms, which are thus bound in their plurality. *Koinōnia* represents the holistic structure of communication within the intellect, where every intelligible object keeps its individual identity (as *eidos*), and at the same time is present to every other intelligible object and every other intelligible object is present to it. Such all-unity is a structure where each is in each, and also each actually contains the whole without mixing with it. The intellect as a whole may be then compared to a multi-colored sphere, every part of which is transparent to every other, reflecting and actually containing every other part in itself.[15]

The structure of all-unity is not imaginable, but may be present only in thought. For example, if we understand something (e.g., a theorem), we appear to be in communication with all other objects of thought (other relevant theorems referring to the same object or a number of similar objects), so that it is possible to restore a whole (mathematical) system from a single act of understanding (from one single theorem). If we conceive a number of conclusions of theorems within a mathematical theory, we may understand them by first grasping the sequence of deductions and demonstrations. But if we might also conceive an inner connection of various theorems not by means of accepted logical or formal procedures, but by metamathematical means—by immediately (i.e. not mediated by a discursive

---

[12] Cp. Blumenthal 1971, 100-111.
[13] Plato. Soph. 254b-c, 257a; RP 476a.
[14] Plotinus. Enn. III.7.4.8-11.
[15] Cp. Plato. Parm. 144b sqq.; Soph. 256b, 257c-d. See also: Dodds 1928, 129-142; Darrell Jackson 1967, 315-327. Plotinus. Enn. V.8.4.7-12; VI.7.14.12; VI.7.15.25. Cp.: "Truth is indivisible, so the slightest thing which is added or taken away falsifies it". (Descartes. To Mersenne, March 1642, AT III 544).

rational justification) intuiting their inner connection into one (presumably consistent) theory—that would represent the mathematical theory as a whole.

Thinking-*noēsis* aims at thinking intelligible objects-*noēta*, which are not really different from thinking and which arise, as we have seen (1.2.1), as inevitable misrepresentations in an attempt of the *noys* to grasp its own origin or source, which is not being and thus is not properly thinkable. The intellect then inevitably strives towards, without ever really gaining it, that unity which does not presuppose any dual opposition. Such a striving presents an important moment in the *noys* as constituted by constant reflection where the object of thinking is the *noys* itself as the other—as not itself, i.e., as one without the other. Therefore, the intellect necessarily conceives something other than the pure One (of the first "Parmenides" hypothesis); namely, that unity which is present as one among many (the one of the second hypothesis). Rather, the many of the intellect appears to be *in* (*en*), *around* (*peri*), *after* (*meta*) and *towards* (*pros*) the One.[16]

The intellect is not, however, simply an opposition of two different counterparts as subject and object but is the first real *synthesis* of the inseparable duality of oneness and otherness, a complex unity or a simplex. It is a unity in diversity.[17] The image Plotinus uses here is that of an army or of a chorus where the whole is maintained only through, and in accordance with, each of its constitutive elements, but is still not reducible to any of them.[18] The intellect is thus both divisible and indivisible. It is a complete system (in this sense it is indivisible) of the whole of ideal archetypes, each of which is distinct from every other (and in this sense the *noys* is divisible): the intellect is one ordered unity, *hen syntetagmenos*.[19]

Such a system of communicating ideal (noetic) objects, distinct without separation, is itself the ideal form and paradigm for the whole physical cosmos. Physical things, however, are mutually exclusive (and the terms and expressions of such an exclusiveness are time and space), and the ideal (mathematical) description cannot adequately fit physical reality, because thinking of the intellect has to do with those objects which always are and thus cannot be otherwise, unlike physical things, which constantly change, are "more or less", divisible, moving, and are subject to only (possibly right) opinion-*doxa*.[20]

3.1.2 Discursive thinking-dianoia

The inability of an individual thinking to always preserve its actual states is present in an unavoidable partiality of discursive thinking, *dianoia*. Although Plato tends to use this term generally as "thinking", in the later Platonic tradition discursive thinking-*dianoia* is taken as reasoning that follows a certain order, as questioning and answering about right and wrong, as if running (*discurrere*) from

---

[16] Plotinus. Enn. III. 8. 6-7; V.3.10.51; V.3.11.1-15; VI.5.4.17; VI.5.6.1-4. See also: Plato. Phil. 14c.
[17] Plotinus. Enn. V.4.2.9; VI.9.2.29 sqq.
[18] Plotinus. Enn. VI.9.1.5.
[19] Plotinus. Enn. VI.8.17.14; VI.9.5.16.
[20] Plato. Meno 97b sqq. et al.

one object or its property to another, as Plato himself argues in the "Theaetetus".[21] Unlike thinking of the *noys*, *dianoia* is always incomplete and only partial. It cannot embrace the whole of thinking in the structure of all-unity, but has to represent itself as *judgement* in a strictly ordered number of statements, deducing one from another. In doing so, discursive thinking always presupposes a fundamental duality of indemonstrable first principles (e.g., axioms) and formal rules of deduction, which have to be preserved and followed at all times and in all steps of an argument. For instance, thinking as exemplified in scientific procedures is only discursive and thus is unable to represent the whole ordered unity of thought in its entirety where every thinkable object is actually present to, and in, every other object, so that logical or mathematical thinking has to gradually move from one proposition to another, thus developing appropriate demonstrations (i.e., rational justifications), and thus constructing a system (as Euclid does in his "Elements"). *Dianoia* then primarily operates, on the one hand, in logical and mathematical kind of justification of a true conclusion. On the other hand, discursive thinking always has to be mediated by signs and cannot immediately proceed from one object of thinking to another. Presence of otherness is thus even stronger in the discursive *dianoia*, where unity of the intellect is split, so that it becomes virtually impossible for thinking to retain the whole of the noetic cosmos of thought in its pluralistic unity.[22]

Still, unlike mere opinion-*doxa*, *dianoia* can provide a strict and invariable knowledge-*epistēmē*. Discursive reasoning-*dianoia* is situated as if between *doxa* and *noys*. *Dianoia* is similar to *doxa* insofar as it presents its considerations in an ordered manner, as Descartes also describes it in the "Rules for the Direction of the Mind". But for Platonic thinkers discursiveness is a sign of detriment, for it expresses the inability to immediately grasp a single object in its notion, as well as the whole of the object's infinite set of properties and relations to other objects. As Proclus puts it, *dianoia* "traverses and unfolds the measureless content of *noys* by making articulate its concentrated intellectual insight, and then gathers together again the things it has distinguished and refers them back to *noys*".[23] Syrianus considers *dianoia* in his commentary to Aristotle's "Metaphysics" in a similar way. Referring to Plato, Syrianus distinguishes three layers of being—the *strata* of the intelligible, the discursive and the sensual—which at the same time correspond to the structure of cognitive faculties (in particular, this implies that there is no real difference between the order of being and the order of cognition).[24]

Discursive reasoning starts with particular objects (e.g., with geometrical figures or any of their constituents), analyzes their properties in their mutual connection, and presents them through a synthetic conclusion formulated as a theorem or a number of justified or proven statements. Because of that, *dianoia*

---

[21] Plato. Theaet. 189d-190a; RP 533e-534c; cp. Soph 260e, 263d-e and Aristotle. Met.1025b 3 sqq.; De an. 431a 1 sqq.
[22] Cp. Plotinus. Enn IV.3.19.25 sqq.
[23] Proclus. In Eucl. 4.11-14.
[24] *Noētēn, dianoētēn, aisthētēn taxin tōn ontōn*, Syrianus. In Met. 4.5-6; 82.1 sqq. et al.

(together with the imagination, which assists *dianoia* in visualizing, i.e., in a clearer representation of its object, see 3.2.4), is fundamental for scientific reasoning. Science, as Proclus suggests, "as a whole has two parts: in one it occupies itself with immediate premises, while in the other it treats systematically the things that can be demonstrated or constructed from these first principles, or in general are consequences of them".[25]

3.1.3 Life

Late ancient thinkers appear to be perceptive to the problem of mediation (cp. 1.1.1), aspiring to disclose mediating structure(s) in *noys* and being, which might also help to get rid of the rigid dichotomy of thinking and thought. Since intellect and being are the same, and thus are one, there is no real distinction between them; only a mental distinction might be made. However, such a distinction is produced by the intellect in order to understand itself; this very distinction may only arise through a reflective procedure of *noys* thinking itself as an object of thought. In order to overcome duality in thinking, one might recognize a more complex structure within thinking, which involves not only duality but also triplicity. In every act of identification, A=B (or even A=A), three terms are involved: two terms of the equation and then the act of identification itself. This structure is present even in an attempt of thinking the unthinkable. The One, the source and principle of every identification, *aytos par' haytoy aytos*, "itself is itself from itself", as Plotinus puts it, without being properly any particular subject.[26] In other words, there should be a third that mediates the other two without being really distinct from both of them, because, as said, there is no real distinction between being and intellect.

An appropriate way of presenting mediating structures in the intelligible and in being may be found in Plato's "Sophist", where Plato argues that there are five main ontological categories, or *genera* (*genē*): being-*oysia*, rest, movement, sameness and otherness.[27] As it has already been mentioned (3.1.1), categories of being, sameness and otherness are associated with the intellect-*noys*. Categories of rest and movement are also applicable to it, although not in the same way as to physical bodies: namely, the intellect may be rather metaphorically described as unmoving movement, so that all the intelligible objects remain in constant actual connection with each other without being changed, according to the principle of *koinōnia*, or all-unity.[28]

Stable movement may thus be taken as mediating, as if constantly bringing thinking to being in the forms of thinkable objects, and uniting these forms through sameness without depriving them of their multiplicity and difference. The unity in the plurality of the intellect is realized through the interaction of sameness and otherness, and is a kind of movement that forever remains at rest. The intellect, then, does not cease to be one while preserving its

---

[25] Proclus. In Eucl. 200.23-201.3.
[26] Plotinus. Enn. VI.8.20.19.
[27] Plato. Soph. 254d-257b; cp. Plotinus. Enn. VI.2.7-8.
[28] Gersh 1973; Plotinus. Enn. VI.9.5.14-15.

plurality of forms while representing otherness. The mediating "third", which preserves the identity of being and intellect, is *life*—primarily exemplified through the good of, and for, the intellect, which is to be one (both to *be* one and to be *one*; *to hen to en tōi onti*). And the good for being is "its activity towards the Good; but this is life; but this is movement".[29] Thus, there is not only the inseparable duality of being-intellect, but also the triplicity of being-life-intellect—a distinction much elaborated in late ancient philosophy (in particular, in Proclus).[30] It is life, connected with the movement within thinking, that appears to be the inherent principle of the communication between intellect and being, thinking and thought, unity and plurality.[31] It is life that, according to Aristotle, is the perfect activity and actuality of the intellect.[32]

This "first life" (*prōtē zōē*) can be only modally distinct from being and thinking. The life of the intellect can be considered as mediating between thinking-*noēsis* and its objects-*noēta*. It is primarily due to life that communication takes place within the intellect—the communication that makes thinking seem as if moving from one object to another without having really moved, always already being present to every object of thought, thinking all of them at once: the life of the intellect is then at rest, *en stasei*.[33] It is such communication that subtly balances sameness and otherness (which "*wakes* the intellect to life") within the *noys*.[34] And it is due to the presence of otherness through the mediation of movement that the intellect incorporates its multitude into a perfect identity constituted by sameness and rest.[35] Because of the indissoluble unity of the one-many within the intellect, life, as mediating in stable movement, is proper to the intellect only. This unity is already disrupted in the thinking-*dianoia* that forever attempts to recollect wholeness out of single parts by the consequent gluing together of the whole of the *noēta*.

Thus, without movement or "journeying" there is no life and, consequently, no communication-*koinōnia*, no thinking, and no system of noetic "living beings" in the all-unity of the intellect.[36] As *kinēsis*, life is constituted by both principles of sameness (insofar as it is in the unchanging being) and of otherness (insofar as it goes to different objects, always remaining where it is): "there in the intelligible, through which [the movement goes], the life is the same, but because it is always other, not the same".[37] This connection of life with some kind of movement can be seen even in physical things, among which only those capable of self-movement are alive and, in the Aristotelian sense, belong to nature, as the source of motion.[38]

---

[29] Plotinus. Enn. VI.2.17.25-30.
[30] Cp. Proclus. Theol. Plat. IV 6.16 sqq. et al.
[31] Cp. Plato. RP 521a; Plutarch. De an. procr. in Tim. 1012d-f.
[32] *Noy energeia zōē,* Aristotle. Met. 1072b 7.
[33] Plotinus. Enn. III.7.11.45-46.
[34] Cp. Plotinus. Enn. VI.7.13.11.
[35] Cp.: *oyden estin aytoy, ho ti mē allo*, Plotinus. Enn. VI.7.13.55.
[36] *Pasa de dia zōēs hē poreia kai dia zōiōn pasa*, Plotinus. Enn. VI.7.13.44-45.
[37] Plotinus. Enn. VI.7.13.46-47; cp. Plato. Soph. 255a-b.
[38] Cp. Plato. Phaedr. 245c-246a; Tim. 37d; Aristotle. De an. 434a 23 sqq.; Phys. 200b 13.

If we recall the distinction between being and being-something, as *existentia* and *essentia*, we may say that in the intellect, "to be intellect" already tautologically includes "to be" (this is unlike a physical thing—for instance, "to be a stone" does not necessarily imply "to be"). In other words, the intellect always *is*, and this "*is*" is not temporal but eternal. The intellect is unable not to be: it *is* insofar as it thinks, and it thinks insofar as it *is*. That *noys* constantly thinks itself in the forms of itself, and that it is as if movement at rest, means that the intellect is alive. One can say then that the intellect is life, because life cannot be separated from it, as the essence of the intellect cannot be separated from its existence. The life of the intellect expresses this inability of separating being from being-intellect and their constant connection without ignoring their distinction through the movement at rest. This movement seems to "split" the intellect, always reflexively returning the intellect to itself without delay, in the "already" (*ēdē*) of eternity. The source or the giver (*khorēgos*) of life for the intellect is the One, which itself does not have life, however, as it does not have being or thinking.[39]

Understanding life as a kind of *kinēsis* is only possible under two main implicit presuppositions. First, life as the intellectual movement makes sense only within the system of the ever communicating *noēsis* and *noēta*; only within the intellect, which is the "hearth" of being and incessant active actuality, existing all together, with "abiding life and a thought whose activity is not directed towards what is coming but what is here already, or rather 'here already and always here already', and the always present, and it is a thought thinking in itself and not outside. In its thinking, then, there is activity and motion, and in its thinking itself, substance and being".[40] And second, within the five Platonic *genera*, life as movement is not opposed to rest, but rather represents a condition of the possibility of the unchanging (and thus eternal) being of the intellect in reflective communication with itself.[41] Life, as a specific movement, is not a movement from something not yet present in being toward its actualization. On the contrary, everything is *already* there in being as thinking, actualizing each other and itself through the other. A good illustration here would be Schelling's example of a child who lives in the not yet developed fullness of life and, although being yet unable to give an account (*logos*) of what she herself and her world are, already possesses the fulfillment of the as yet unevolved life that is already present in her.[42]

We may say thus that life is an incessant intellectual activity, free of all potentiality, a restful movement "from", "around" and "to" being, a movement of thinking that thinks itself in the intelligible forms, communicating according to the principle of all-unity, the condition for communication of *noēta* brought into oneness by *noēsis*. But although life essentially is mediation between the unity of being and *noys*, it allows further distinctions. First of all, (1) life is *in* (*en*) the one of being, of the intellectual and intelligible nature; it is *from* (*ex*) it and *with* (*syn*)

---

[39] Plotinus. Enn. I.6.7.11; I.8.2.6; III.8.9.38-39; V.5.10.12; VI.7.23.19-20; VI.9.9.1-2, 50; cp. Plato. RP 509b.
[40] Plotinus. Enn. VI.2.8.7-13.
[41] Cp. Plotinus. Enn. III.7.3.7 sqq.
[42] See: Gadamer 1970, 349.

it.[43] Next (2), as it has been already mentioned, life is a movement of a specific kind, namely, it is an intellectual movement, *kinēsis noera*, which, unlike the subsequent movement of the soul, which represents time, is without parts; it is present all together and remains as if at rest.[44] This life is (3) always the "selfsame" or self-identical (*hōsaytōs*) and (4) remains the same in the same (*taytotēs, menontos, en tōi aytōi*). As such, life (5) is present, as Plotinus puts it, in "compressing the otherness in the intelligible objects, and seeing the unceasingness and self-identity of their activity, and that it is never other and is not a thinking of life that goes from one thing to another".[45] In the case of life that evolves in and through a succession, we may make a distinction between the time *of* something (i.e. a life span) and the time *for* something, of which there is always a greater shortage the less time *of* it (human life, for example) is left. On the contrary, in eternity such a distinction as eternity *of* and eternity *for* makes no sense, because both refer to the intellect in which, due to the reflective teleological structure of thinking, "of" and "for" fully coincide. This life of the intellect (6) can only be without expansion, extension or interval (*adiastatos*), because there is no sequence in it. Again, in this respect, life as movement differs from rest: the distinction consists in that although the notion of rest is presupposed in the notion of substance, the notion of rest (unlike the notion of movement) does not entail the notion of the dynamic unity of being and intellect.[46]

From (1) and (6) it follows, as it is easy to see, (7) that there are no separate parts within life, but rather it is present altogether and cannot be extinguished.[47] Life represents (8) the partless completion (*telos ameres*) of the intellect, due to which the intellect forever finds its end, which is not different from itself; it gathers itself into a unity of thinking that thinks itself. Such a perfect completion (according to (6), it is comparable to extension) is similar to a point that is always the same and has not yet begun moving, thus producing a line.[48]

Since life remains the same, it (9) only *is*, *esti monon*, being full without any dissipation whatsoever; it does not change and is deficient in nothing.[49] This eternal *is* (10) is not a substrate or substance (which corresponds to rest), but rather is a perfect activity that makes being manifest not by way of demonstration, but by simply showing or displaying itself as that which *is*. And that which is, shows itself as true. The truthfulness of being is thus not a paradigm-image correspondence, but

---

[43] Plotinus. Enn. III.7.4.2; cp. III.7.11.61-62; VI.9.9.15-16.
[44] Plotinus. Enn. III.7.11.50. Plotinus clearly makes a distinction between *noētos* and *noeros*—intelligible belonging to the sphere of the objects of thought and intellectual belonging to thinking itself. The life of the intellect is thus intellectual and not intelligible. That is why Armstrong's translation "intelligible motion" is somewhat misleading in the present case.
[45] Plotinus. Enn. III.7.3.12-15.
[46] Plotinus. Enn. III.7.2.32-34; cp. III.7.3.15; III.7.13.63.
[47] Life is primarily a holistic structure, in which "not now this, and then again that, but all things [are] at once (*hama ta panta*), and not now some things and then again others." - Plotinus. Enn. III.7.3.16-19, 37; III.7.11.55; V.3.15.21-22. Cp. Anaxagoras DK B1.
[48] Plotinus. Enn. III.7.3.19-20.
[49] *Oyk endees*, Plotinus. Enn. III.7.3.23, 34-35; III.7.4.15; III.7.6.37.

the presence of being through a noetic object. Every noetic object, however, *is* in its communication with the others; and in its "simply-being" or "being-there", every intelligible object is what it is and as it is—and is thus true, since in the intellect there is no real distinction between being and being-something (or thinking and its object).[50] Such a representation of being through the activity of its life means that ontologically, being is never non-being; epistemologically, being cannot be known as non-being (because non-being is not anything that might be positively known or expressed, and therefore cannot be known in principle); and modally, being cannot not be, or be otherwise than it is.

Since life always is and is not changed, it (11) always *already* (*ēdē*) exists in its completion; it is already eternal (*ēdē aidion*).[51] This "already", which is often taken to be the central characteristic of the intellect in Neoplatonism, expresses the pure actuality of the intellect, in which there is nothing that might change into something else, because everything is already present there as it is. It also means that when we think or understand something discursively, we neither construct nor engender the object of thought by the act of thinking, but rather discover that which is already there in the intelligible sphere of the *noys*.[52]

From (7), (9) and (11) it follows that (12) life can have neither future nor past, neither "before", nor "after", for it cannot acquire anything that it would not already have.[53] So it can neither become, nor be, otherwise than it is now. The "is" of being may mean that being always *is* and that it *always* is, or is gathered and has neither extension nor duration, which could make any intrinsic distinction. For that reason being is indifferent, or without difference (*adiaphorōs*). Life, in order to represent being, has then to "follow" it in these two aspects of one and the same "always is": life also always *is* and *always* is—it is fully in the present, or, again, life is without any extension, detriment and change. In other words, the life of the intellect is eternity.[54] In its present, life (13) which governs the communication

---

[50] Plotinus. Enn. III.7.3.24-25; III.7.4.11-14; cp. III.7.6.12-14.
[51] Plotinus. Enn. III.7.5.4; cp. also I.5.2.12-13; III.7.3.26-28; VI.2.8.9-10; VI.7.1.49 sqq.
[52] Plotinus. Enn. II.5.3.1-7; VI.6.18.4.
[53] Cp. Plotinus. Enn. IV.3.25.14-17.
[54] *En tōi paronti aei*, Plotinus. Enn. III.7.5.21-23, 29-33; III.7.6.7-8, 14; cp. I.5.7.15-16. Plato. Tim. 37d. It is to be noted that Plotinus does not say that the eternal life is "now" or is in "now", as *nunc stans*. The text of the treatise "On Eternity and Time" can be interpreted in this sense, but for Plotinus himself the "now" is rather a negative characteristic of the eternal (e.g., it will become "nothing that it would not be now", Enn. III.7.3.28-29). Plotinus often uses "now" negatively as "not now", *oy nyn, mē nyn* (Enn. III.7.3.17, 30). Criticizing Aristotle's concept of time, he uses the notion of "now" in the way Aristotle does, i.e., as the limit within time at which "before" stops and "after" begins. The "now" thus primarily characterizes time for Plotinus, not eternity (Enn. III.7.9.65; cp. IV.3.13.21; VI.1.5.16; VI.3.19.22-23). The life as a stable movement is rather in the "present" than in the "now". The "now" is even once opposed to the eternity of *aei* (Enn. IV.3.8.33-34). Quite often "now" does not have any special technical meaning in the "Enneads" (cp. *Lexicon Plotinianum*, col. 715-716). The *nunc stans* of Augustine, of Themistius (In de an. 110.20 sqq.), and of the later scholastic tradition, the "all at once" (*simul*) of Boethius (De consol. 5. 6), originate in Plotinus, but it would be misleading to present Plotinus himself as an advocate of the view of eternity as "standing now".

within the intelligible cosmos, displays the same structure of the one-many; i.e., although life is without parts, it is constituted through multiplicity bound into unity.[55] And finally, (14) because of the infinite potency of the *noys*, life is infinite and represents the infinite, *to apeiron*, of intelligible objects, not as a lack of limit, but as infinite in *dynamis*, in its power of unification and production.[56]

3.1.4 Mind and its ideas: Descartes

One of the immediately noticeable differences in Descartes' consideration of the mind as compared with the Platonic approach is the considerable simplification of the structure of the mental. Throughout all of his writings Descartes rigidly opposes the mental to the material, the mind to the body. Yet, as it will be argued in what follows, he leaves no room for the proper distinction between the discursive and the non-discursive in the mind and for the intermediary in thinking. Reason is taken by Descartes as mind or soul, *mens sive anima*, without stressing an important distinction between the two.[57] The mind is simply a finite thinking substance and thus has to be characterized by its main attribute—thinking (see 1.2.3). However, the human mind is radically finite (cp. 1.3.2), so if there is any image or likeness of the divine infinite mind in the human, it is not so much in the finite mind but in the *will*, which is not limited, and, as freedom of choice, resembles the divine not *qua* substance but *qua* in(de)finite.[58] In every act of thinking, the mind keeps its substantial sameness; moreover, it is the same mind that is present in all mental operations—in perception, remembering, discursive thinking and intellection.

In the "Regulae" Descartes presents the mind as *ingenium*, which acquires knowledge about the mental and the extended (in particular, about geometricals) through two elementary operations of *intuitus* and *deductio*. The former proceeds only from the light of reason and is the "conception (*conceptum*) of a clear and attentive mind, which is so easy and distinct that there can be no room for doubt about what we are understanding". The latter implies "the inference of something as following necessarily from some other propositions which we know with certainty".[59] The *intuitus* shows clear and self-evident truths (and decides what is to be taken as the starting points, as the simple natures, be they common, intellectual or material—such as corporeal nature, extension, shape, etc.).[60] The *deductio* resembles a "movement or sequence" (*motus sive successio*) and allows one to apprehend with certainty an operation of discursive thinking in a chain of deductions, to know necessary true conclusions from the known by the *intuitus*. Still, despite the *intuitus-deductio* distinction, the finite mind for Descartes is to be

---

[55] *Ek pollōn*, Plotinus. Enn. III.7.5.22.
[56] Plotinus. Enn. III.7.5.23-24; III.7.11.54. Cp. Plato. Tim. 37d, 38b-c.
[57] Descartes uses the terms *mens, animus, intellectus* and *ratio* as synonyms (Med. II, AT VII 27). Cp. Cottingham 1992, 236 sqq. Equation of soul with mind can, however, be already found in John Damascene (De fide orthod. Bk. II, cap. 27).
[58] Descartes. Med. IV, AT VII 57.
[59] Descartes. Reg. III, AT X 368 sqq.
[60] Descartes. Reg. XII, AT X 418 sqq. Cp. Marion 1992, 115-139.

considered uniform and essentially discursive (in the "Regulae" Descartes also uses the terms *enumeratio* and *inductio* to designate operations of discursive thinking). Non-discursivity can be presupposed only as a privileged feature of the infinite mind in "a single identical and perfectly simple act by means of which he [God] simultaneously understands, wills and accomplishes everything".[61] Some traces of non-discursivity in the finite mind may be seen in the concept of the *intuitus*, which is an act rather then a process.[62] But even if it is the immediate apprehension of the mind, the *intuitus* is different from the noetic non-discursive conceiving of a *noēton* by the *noys*, insofar as the *intuitus* is involved in apprehension not of noetic objects, but rather of the simplest propositions: for example, that the thinking mind intuits that it exists, that it thinks (*vnusquisque animo potest intueri, se existere, se cogitare*); that the triangle is limited by only three lines; that the sphere is limited by one plane, and so on.[63] Another atavistic *noys*-like feature of the mind is that the mind, like the *noys*, is fundamentally reflective; every act of thinking is always accompanied by immediate awareness of that very act. But, unlike the *noys*, the mind does not grasp its object fully in all its different aspects. The difference between the two is that in the mind immediate awareness is contentless; it consists in a simple apprehension of the act of thinking, *cogito*, as actually being there or taking place: "We cannot fail constantly to experience within ourselves that we are thinking."[64] On the contrary, the *noys* thinks itself only insofar as it thinks the *noēta*, which are not really different from the *noēsis* (see 3.1.1). It means that Descartes expels the intellect-*noys* as precedent to, and distinct from, the *dianoia*, reducing the mind to only discursive reasoning (in a similar way, Hobbes takes thinking to be only ratiocination, i.e., discursive logical computation).[65]

Since, further, for Descartes, as for the majority of later philosophers, *the* substance is God and is infinite (i.e., is supremely perfect), there is no, and there can be no, principle or *arkhē* of the mind other than the mind itself. Because of that there is a spark of the divine within the finite mind.[66] The human mind and the divine mind differ only extensively (as the finite from the infinite) and not intensively. The divine mind produces the human mind; the human mind conceives the divine mind in its existence, although still missing its (infinite) essence.

From the early "Regulae" till the late "Principles" Descartes still retains a distinction between different faculties within the mind: intellect (reason),

---

[61] Descartes. Princ. I 23, AT VIIIA 14.

[62] A *sui generis* non-discursive intuitive understanding (an "illumination of the mind") is reserved by Descartes (who obviously follows Aquinas in this point) to the "beatific vision", which can only be an act of divine grace and is not accessible in our present state, where we can only cognize by means of discursive reasoning - Descartes. To [Silhon], March or April 1648, AT V 136-137. Traces of the Platonic distinction between the non-discursive intellect (divine *ratio*, the cause of mathematical regularity within the cosmos) and the discursive reasoning (human *ratiocinatio*) are to be found also in Kepler's "The Six-cornered Snowflake"-Kepler 1966, 32-33.

[63] Descartes. Reg. III, AT X 368.

[64] Descartes. Sixth Set of Replies, AT VII 427.

[65] Th. Hobbes. De corpore I 1 2.

[66] Descartes. Reg. IV, AT X 373.

imagination, memory, sense-perception, and will (the role of the will as an active faculty of mind is especially stressed in the later treatises). But if the mind is taken simply and only as thought, then everything referable to thinking is mind in some way: "Thinking is to be identified...not merely with understanding, willing and imagining, but also with sensory awareness."[67] The distinction of the faculties of the mind is more a tribute to the tradition and is 'horizontal' rather than 'vertical': different faculties are not so much hierarchically structured or ordered, but represent different cognitive functions of the same mind. The modern tendency towards homogenization of the mind is manifest in Descartes, in that various mental faculties are easily reducible to "kinds of thought", functions or modes of the same finite created thinking substance.[68] Mind is hence a progression of thinking, and it is one and the same mind-substance that can be presented as different mental faculties in different cognitive roles. We can thus say that in Descartes the mind is discursive: there are no single acts of thought not inscribed into a continuous succession of thinking-*cogitatio*.[69]

The mind has to be able to apply itself not only to itself but also to the external world, effectively judging other things, having "the power of judging well and of distinguishing the true from the false... it is not enough to have a good mind; the main thing is to apply it well".[70] This constitutes the modern "turn" towards understanding the mind as judgement *par excellence*, judgement that both unifies and separates spheres of being and of nature—the turn towards accepting the phenomenon of taste as expressing the subjective autonomy of individual judgement.

Striving to secure the clarity and distinctness of cognition, Descartes establishes two complementary substances, which should be as simple in their inner structure as possible. This simplicity is rendered by the acceptance of only one single attribute of thinking or of extension, which makes both substances innerly homogeneous (and for that reason all sorts of "substantial forms" or "occult qualities" are expelled) and mutually incompatible. In this case, however, the mind loses the radically other to itself within itself, so subtly presented and preserved in the Platonic theory of the *noys*. The only other to the mind is matter. In Descartes' simple dichotomic distinction there is no room left for any otherness within the

---

[67] Descartes. Princ. I 9, AT VIIIA 7. Cp. Reg. VIII, AT X 395-396; XII, AT X 410-411.
[68] Descartes. Description of the Human Body, AT XI 224; cp. Princ. I 65, AT VIIIA 32.
[69] In Med. II, AT VII 29 Descartes equates *cogitare* with *sentire*. In its most general sense, *cogitatio* in Descartes may be taken as a somehow organized thought. Sepper draws an interesting parallel between Descartes' terms *cogitatio*, *meditatio* and *contemplatio* and those used in the St. Victor school - Sepper 1996, 128, 257 sqq. In Descartes, cogitation is explained as "the directed action of what, when undirected, is an aimless agitation of thought", and meditation as a prolonged, intense and recursive act of thought, whereas contemplation is explained as a final understanding and knowledge of truth (Ibid., 262, 272).
[70] Descartes. Disc. I, AT VI 2. Cp. Aristotle who argues that *using* (*khrēsis*) is preferable to just *having* (*hexis*) and that the latter is for the sake of the former which is thus the actuality and the purpose of the *hexis*, MM 1184b 15-17. Descartes, however (as Kenny points out), is unable to distinguish between a mere not yet realized capacity of acquiring something (knowledge) and the non-exercise of the already acquired *hexis* (Kenny 1987, 103).

mind—in particular, there is no room for the notion of intelligible matter, which plays such an important role in ancient mathematical considerations (2.4-2.4.2). The other to the mind is thus fully externalized and ousted from the mind. This other is matter, not God, which explains why Descartes does not accept any principle or *arkhē* beyond being or thinking. Mind literally becomes anarchic. What is most important for the consideration of geometrical and mathematical entities is that the loss of any inner, "ideal" otherness within the mind leads to the impossibility of finding any appropriate place for matter in the intelligible, which might be other to the mind but still be within the mind.

Let us now turn to a brief discussion of the Cartesian understanding of the notion of idea in contrast to the Platonic "idea". In the Platonic tradition, idea—*idea* or *eidos*—is an intelligible archetype not only of physical things (of a stone, of a horse), but also of intermediate geometrical figures (of a circle, of a line).[71] In this respect the Platonic idea is independent of both physical and geometrical entities. Such an archetype is a member of the communicative system of the *noēta*, which are actually present to each other in the structure of *koinōnia*. Idea is primarily the subject of understanding of the *noys* but may also be accessible to discursive reasoning-*dianoia* through a number of demonstrable propositions or arguments. Idea is responsible for both the being of a thing and, as the limit-*peras* of that thing which fully defines it, allows for knowledge of the thing.

The Cartesian use of the term "idea", as Kenny, Ariew and Grene argue, is both new and not altogether unequivocal. It is new for at least two reasons. First, for Descartes, unlike for the scholastic thinkers, an idea is not an archetype of things in the divine mind.[72] Second, unlike in the seventeenth century literary usage, an idea is not an image derived from senses or imagination. It is equivocal because Descartes does not have a thoroughly and systematically elaborated consistent theory of ideas; he confines himself to occasional descriptions (e.g., in the "Meditations" and in the replies to the objections raised to them) and metaphors, which may appear incompatible, incoherent or too loose at best. It is rather difficult to draw a clear and unambiguous picture of the mind's relation to ideas in Descartes, of ideas in relation to thoughts, and of the distinction between idea as an act of thought, as an exercise of a concept and as an occurrence of an experience.[73]

As Descartes states in his later letter to Mersenne, "idea" is "in *general* everything which is in our mind when we conceive something, no matter how we conceive it".[74] In other words, idea is everything that is in the mind properly, every mental content of any kind of cogitation and cogitation of any kind. Such an understanding of idea represents the Cartesian tendency toward the homogenization of substance and the abolition of distinct mental cognitive structures. An idea may originally be caused by senses or imagination, but once it is processed in the mind-reason, it is different from an image in the senses or in

---

[71] Plato. Tim. 28a, 35a; Phil. 16d; RP 486d-e, 505a; Parm. 129a et al.
[72] Cp. Descartes. Third Set of Replies, AT VII 181.
[73] Kenny 1987 96-116; Ariew, Grene 1995, 87-106.
[74] Descartes. To Mersenne, July 1641, AT III 392-393; cp. Third Set of Replies, AT VII 185; Fifth Set of Replies, AT VII 366. Cp. Yolton 1981, 208-224.

imagination, since the mind is to be understood as autonomous and possibly free from imagination and the senses. And although Descartes does not reject ideas in the infinite mind, an idea is to be considered in the first place in the *finite*, in "our" mind: an idea always, and only, is in the *mind* and is *in* the mind, *nunquam est extra intellectum*.[75]

Still, already in this "definition" there arises an ambiguity: is an idea, as "everything which is in our mind when we conceive something", an object of thought or is it an act or mental state?[76] This question will be addressed in the subsequent discussion of formal and objective. Here we only need to note that on different occasions Descartes appears to support different approaches: at times ideas are presented as the acts, operations or modes of thought, and at times ideas are taken as objects of thought or of operations of thinking. (Thus, for example, in a note to the Latin edition of the "Discourse", "idea" denotes any thinkable thing, insofar as it is represented by an object in the mind.)[77]

Although there is a certain ambiguity in Descartes' treatment of the notion of an idea, it is still possible to discern several distinctive traits in his considerations. First, every idea represents something: "[T]here can be no ideas which are not as it were of things."[78] An idea thus is a mental representation and, insofar as a particular object is represented in the mind, be it mental or physical, it has to have an idea. The Platonic idea is being and is paradigm either of a thing that exists, or of a thing that is thought. The thing is also an image of that idea. A thing is thus not being, but rather an image or representation of being. On the contrary, the Cartesian idea, as it is portrayed in the "Meditations", represents a thing. Therefore, such idea is itself being, insofar as it belongs to the thinking substance, but it also represents being. Because of that, ideas for Descartes primarily express the essence, and not existence, of a thing (see 1.4.3).

Such a notion of idea allows Descartes to ascribe an idea to every thing—to every mental and physical object—as its representation, which allows for the possibility of the *strict* knowledge of physical things, because physics, the science of them, has to study their ideas as mental representations. It is therefore possible to restructure physics as a mathematical science only if it is possible to treat these images of physical things by means of mathematics. The latter becomes possible once mathematics comes to interpret any representations—in particular, ideas of physical things—by means of proportional relations with no distinction of

---

[75] Descartes. First Set of Replies, AT VII 102.
[76] Kenny 1987, 99-101. Cp. a distinction made by V. Chappel and supported by N. Jolley, that between idea as an act (idea$_m$) and idea as an object (content) of thought (idea$_o$). - Chappel 1986, 177-198; Jolley 1990, 12 sqq.
[77] "*Nota hoc in loco et ubique in sequentibus nomen ideae generaliter sumi pro omni re cogitata, quatenus habet tantum esse quoddam objectivum in intellectu.*" - Descartes. Disc. IV, AT VI 34. Cp. Med. Preface, AT VII 8; Med. III, AT VII 40; Second Set of Replies, AT VII 160. Cp. also: Spinoza, Ethics II, def. 3.
[78] "*...Nullae ideae nisi tanquam rerum esse possunt*" - Descartes. Med. III, AT VII 44. Cp.: since "our ideas cannot receive their forms or their being except from external objects or from ourselves, they cannot represent any reality or perfection which is not either in those objects or in ourselves" .- Descartes. To [Vatier], 22 February 1638, AT I 561.

number and magnitude, put in the form of meaningful propositions, which may then form a scientific theory.

But, second, an idea is not to be taken as an image, despite Descartes' own rather perplexing remark in the Third "Meditation", which seems to equate an idea as thought with an image of a thing. When Hobbes criticizes this ambiguity, however, Descartes restates that "idea" refers to "whatever is immediately perceived by the mind", explaining that an idea has to be distinguished from an image—if by image one means a corporeal image in imagination.[79] This thesis is further explicitly presented in a letter to Mersenne: "[W]hatever we conceive without an image is an idea of the pure mind, and whatever we conceive with an image is an idea of the imagination."[80] Thus, for example, ideas of common notions are also not immediate images of things.[81] And even if, as it will be argued, an idea may be accompanied by a mental or corporeal image of imagination, an idea cannot be equated with them, for the mind-reason has to be kept different from the imagination and from the corporeal (see 3.3).

And third, in the definitions in the Second Set of Replies to the "Meditations", Descartes makes a distinction between thought and idea. Thought is any mental state, act or content that the mind is immediately aware of, but this immediate awareness is possible only because there is an idea that is the *form* of that thought. It is through the immediate perception of this idea that the mind is aware of that thought.[82] Thus, the idea as form organizes thinking in its mental content and in its acts of cogitation in such a way that the mind is immediately aware of itself, i.e., of its content and its cogitation. In other words, mind is *reflective* through the idea. Such an understanding of the notion of idea is implied in Descartes' consideration of the mind, in which every act of cogitation (i.e., of thinking, imagining, sense-perception and even of will as determined and guided by an idea of reason) has to be accompanied by an immediate awareness of that very act.[83]

Descartes makes a famous distinction between three kinds of ideas: innate ("my understanding of what a thing is, what truth is, and what thought is"), adventitious (which come from outside objects, of sensations) and those invented by me (fictitious ideas of imaginable entities, such as sirens and hippogriffs).[84] Of

---

[79] "Some of my thoughts are as it were the images of things, and it is only in these cases that the term 'idea' is strictly appropriate—for example, when I think of a man, or a chimera, or the sky, or an angel, or God". Descartes. Med. III, AT VII 37. Cp. Treatise on Man, AT XI 176-177. See also Second Set of Replies, AT VII 160-161 and Passions I 35, AT XI 355.
[80] Descartes. To Mersenne, July 1641, AT III 395.
[81] Descartes. Conversation with Burman, AT V 153.
[82] Descartes. Second Set of Replies, AT VII 160. Cp. "I am taking the word 'idea' to refer immediately to whatever is immediately perceived by the mind". - Third Set of Replies, AT VII 181.
[83] Cp. Descartes. Med. II, AT VII 33 and To Mersenne, 28 January 1641, AT III 295.
[84] Descartes. Med. III, AT VII 37-38. Gassendi, however, raises a legitimate objection to such a division, arguing that adventitious and fictitious ideas should not be different, because both come from the combination of sensual images, "for the idea of a chimera is simply the idea of the head of a lion, the body of a goat and the tail of a serpent, out of

particular importance is the notion of the innate idea, which, first, allows one to understand what a thing or a thought is, and second, is derived from man's own nature—it does not come from an outer stimulus.[85] Examples of innate ideas for Descartes are ideas of God, of a triangle, or of geometrical truths.[86] The innateness of an idea does not signify its self-evidence, however. An innate idea is self-evident only once "attended" by the mind, only when actually thought—for it can happen that a person, even having an idea of God or of a geometrical truth, will never actually think it. Thus the innate idea is close to *hexis*, which is not simply a possibility of doing or understanding something, but is a capacity to realize a notion as self-evident in the presence of clear and attentive thinking. It is in this sense that one has to take Descartes' claim in the "Comments on a Certain Broadsheet" that innate ideas are not distinct from the mind's own faculty of thinking.[87] Because of that, the mind does require innate ideas to be distinct from its own thinking. As ideas in *general*, they are not to be understood as divine archetypes. Innate ideas thus have no other source than myself, the finite mind. That is why for Descartes "when we say that an idea is innate in us, we do not mean that it is always there before us. This would mean that no idea was innate. We simply mean that we have within ourselves the faculty of summoning up (*facultas eliciendi*) the idea".[88] But the ability of the finite mind to produce innate ideas is still not unrestricted. The mind is not really producing innate ideas but rather is activating them as actual and clear in thinking, because the finite mind is itself produced by God or the infinite mind.[89] Therefore, the infinite mind produces the finite mind capable of awakening the ideas, which in this sense are innate. The innate ideas then show the essence of that which is. It is for this reason that innate ideas, as Descartes tells Mersenne, involve neither affirmation nor negation.[90] They presuppose no judgement but simply show what *is* there and *what* it is essentially (thought, thing, truth), without a reference to that which is external to the mind (in particular, to the non-mental).

In his late "Comments on a Certain Broadsheet" Descartes goes even further, arguing that even an adventitious idea is in some sense innate, because any idea of an external object is not in any way similar in the mind to the thing thought (it is the image of imagination that may resemble the thing imagined and thought, cp. 3.3), and thus the idea in the mind is different from the image of the corresponding sense-perception. If thinking is informed through external stimuli ("corporeal motions"), then these ideas are adventitious; if it is informed by internal mental stimuli (when the object comes only from the thinking itself), then

---

which the mind puts together one idea, although the individual elements are adventitious". - P. Gassendi. Fifth Set of Objections, AT VII 279-280.
[85] Descartes. Med. III, AT VII 38. Cp. Cottingham 1986, 144-149.
[86] Descartes. Fifth Set of Replies, AT VII 381-382; Comments on a Certain Broadsheet, AT VIIIB 360; To Hyperaspistes, August 1641, AT III 424.
[87] Descartes. Comments on a Certain Broadsheet, AT VIIIB 357.
[88] Descartes. Third Set of Replies, AT VII 189.
[89] Descartes. Second Set of Replies, AT VII 133.
[90] Descartes. To Mersenne, 22 July 1641, AT III 417-418.

the ideas are properly innate.[91] Such an understanding of innateness opens a possibility of understanding the mind as constructing and producing its own ideas (cp. 3.4.1), which in Descartes is still limited to the infinite mind, which, as said, creates the finite mind. The finite mind is then capable of "summoning up" innate ideas.[92]

The innateness of ideas has three different meanings. First, that the idea refers to the realm of intelligible objects, which are independent from finite thinking, and which define a particular thing in its notion and existence.[93] Second, innateness may mean the physiological existence of certain mental structures, accompanying every human at least from the moment of her physical appearance into the world. Even if the mind does not recognize these structures at first, gradually they become clear and explicit to the mind through the mind's awareness of its own mental experience. And third, innateness may mean that the mind knows certain notions as innate (e.g., of finite substance) insofar as the mind itself brings and imposes its own structures unto the known (in particular, unto physical things), and knows them insofar as it constructs them. Plato and Plotinus accept innateness in the first sense, and Descartes (as later Kant) only in the third sense.

One might say, perhaps, that from the Platonic perspective, innate ideas may be considered ideas of the intellect; ideas invented by me—as images of imagination; and, lastly, adventitious ideas—as sensual perceptions. Still, there are important points of difference between the Cartesian and the Platonic understanding of innate ideas. First, in Plato, Plotinus and Proclus, every idea is innate, for adventitious and fictitious ideas are not ideas in the proper sense; they are not *eidē*. Even if Descartes might take adventitious ideas to be innate, he does so in a very different way, as explained above. Thus, not every idea is properly innate for him. Second, unlike in Plotinus, in Descartes there is no consistent and elaborated description of the process of the constitution of innate ideas by and within thinking. And finally, in Plato and Plotinus innate idea is a *noēton*, an object of thought, different from, and originally constituted by, the *noēsis* (see 3.1.1). In Descartes innate idea is rather a *hexis* and therefore is not really distinct from the mind as the faculty of thinking, so that the "objectivity" of innate ideas is produced by the "subjectivity".[94] "Summoned up" by finite subjectivity, innate ideas are not themselves being *strictu sensu*, but are an "objective" representation of being, merely signs of being.

An important distinction that still plays its role in seventeenth century philosophy, particularly in Descartes, is the scholastic distinction between formal and objective concepts or ideas. We find a clear and concise definition of the two in Goclenius' widely read "Lexicon philosophicum": "The formal concept is that which we form concerning something apprehended by the intellect. The objective concept is the thing which is conceived insofar as it is the object of our formal

---

[91] Descartes. Comments on a Certain Broadsheet, AT VIIIB 358-359. Cp. Kenny 1987, 103-105.
[92] Cp. Descartes. Princ. I 58-59, AT VIIIA 27-28.
[93] Cp. Plato. Meno 81b-86b et al.
[94] Cp. Descartes. Comments on a Certain Broadsheet, AT VIIIB 366.

concept."[95] Originally, the objective-formal distinction arises from the distinction between the conceived, *res cogitata* (objective) and the conception, *res cogitans* (formal). Descartes takes a concept or an idea to be "objective" when it represents a thing through its attribute to the mind as "the being of the thing which is represented by an idea, insofar as it exists in the idea. ...For whatever we perceive as being in the objects of our ideas exists objectively in the ideas themselves".[96] "Objective" is thus the content of thinking, whereas "formal" is the act of thinking or conception.[97]

Of course, an idea or concept[98] may have an objective reality insofar as it has a formal reality in the finite mind, e.g. a fictitious idea (or factitious, *a me ipso facta*). However, in some cases the objective reality of an idea cannot be produced by the formal act of the finite mind. This claim is of central importance for Descartes, for such are sensual ideas and especially innate ideas—in particular, ideas of God and infinity. In other words, in the finite mind, the formal reality of an idea cannot in many cases be the cause of the objective reality of that idea. For this reason Descartes insists that "the objective reality of our ideas needs a cause which contains this reality not merely objectively but formally or eminently".[99] This cause is the infinite mind, in which—and only in which—formal and objective do fully coincide in all cases, because the infinite mind knows things insofar as it always produces those things. But how can Descartes justify his claim,

---

[95] Goclenius 1613, 428 (trans. Ariew and Grene). For parallels in scholasticism see: Gilson 1979, 86-90.
[96] Descartes. Second Set of Replies, AT VII 161.
[97] In Gassendi's formulation, formal reality "applies to the idea itself not as it represents something but as an entity in its own right".- Fifth Set of Objections, AT VII 285. Spinoza, after Descartes, provides the following definition: "Things are said to be in the objects of ideas *formally*, when they are the same in the objects as they are in our perceptions" (Principles of the Philosophy of Descartes, Part I, def. 4).
[98] As Kenny argues, the terms "idea" and "concept" are to be distinguished in Descartes. - Kenny 1987, 108-109. However, Kenny seems to modernize Descartes in this point, taking the notion of concept in a contemporary sense, as a notion that discloses what a thing is, whereas both scholastic and seventeenth century usage of the *conceptus* is rather loose, meaning both an act of conceiving and a thing conceived, i.e., used both formally and objectively. Cp. Goclenius 1613, 427; Ariew, Grene 1995, 99-100. See also: Leibniz, New Essays, 119.
[99] Descartes. Second Set of Replies, AT VII 165. Cp.: "All the reality or perfection which is present in an idea merely objectively must be present in its cause either formally or eminently" (Second Set of Replies, AT VII 135). In Descartes' definition (where he follows the traditional scholastic *via eminentiae*, which comes back to Plato and is put by Alcinous in his "Handbook of Platonism", Didask. 10.5-6.), "something is said to exist *eminently* in an object when, although it does not exactly correspond to our perceptions of it, its greatness is such that it can fill the role of that which does so correspond" (Second Set of Replies, AT VII 161). Or, in Spinoza's paraphrase, things are said to be in the objects eminently, "when they are not actually such as we perceive them, but are of such force that they can be substituted for things as we actually perceive them. Notice that when I say a cause contains the perfections of its effect *eminently*, I mean that the cause contains the perfections of its effect more excellently than the effect itself" (Principles of the Philosophy of Descartes, Part I, def. 4). Cp. Rovane 1994, 89 sqq.

then, that it is possible to originate the very notion of substance simply from within the finite mind (1.4.1)? When Descartes says that the finite mind is able to produce the idea of substance, this only means that the essence of substance as an objective idea has to be posited as different (and, in finite things, separated) from existence. The example of an entity that cannot be produced in this way is the idea or concept of ultimate perfection, which refers to that unique instance where existence is included or coincides with the essence (which itself is a perfection), or in which the formal and objective coincide. Descartes thus still restricts the ability of the finite mind to produce ideas as the content of its own cogitation (cp. 3.4.1). For him the finite mind is a finite thinking substance not emancipated from the infinite substance, which therefore cannot be considered merely hypothetical.[100]

Now, we need to make several observations. (1) Matter has an objective concept for Descartes revealing matter's essence—i.e., being extended. And this concept cannot be produced by the finite mind because the objective concept of matter is perceived, as Descartes insists, clearly and distinctly (and independently of the mind's possible intentions), and such a perception cannot be false.

(2) The objective concept consists of (a system of) all the independent and non-contradictory properties or attributes (whose consistency cannot be proven within that system of the finite discursive mind).[101] Objective concepts as such do not produce, or necessarily imply, either a formal concept or existence and as such are merely possible, unless they are formally conceived.

(3) The distinction between formal and objective concepts resembles the Platonic distinction between thinking and objects of thought—*noēsis* and *noēta*. Descartes, however, understands the objective concept as only "ideal," i.e., as being *in mente* and not *in re*, as having only mental reality; depending on the mind as opposed to the "external" reality of either the *res corporea* or the infinite thinking. Even if in the *noēsis-noēta* distinction thinking is logically anterior to the objects of thought, both are not really different and both may be said to really exist (cp. 3.1.4). The same is true for Descartes only in the infinite intellect, where formal concepts (such as "thinking") coincide with the objective.

(4) Because of the distinction between the objective (conceived) and the formal (conception) in the idea, another definition of the notion of idea becomes possible as "the thing which is thought of in so far as it has objective being in the intellect".[102] But Descartes also further introduces the notion of the "materiality" of the idea as the operation, *operatio*, of the mind.[103] The notion of the materiality of ideas does not imply, however, any concept of intelligible matter, since Descartes insists that ideas cannot correlate to materiality in the proper sense: the former represent the *res cogitans*, the latter represent the *res extensa*. In his reply to Arnauld, Descartes supports the scholastic distinction that "ideas are forms of a kind, and are not composed of any matter, when we think of them as representing something we are taking them not materially (*materialiter*) but formally (*formaliter*). If, however, we were considering them not as representing this or that

---

[100] Unlike Laplace's "je n'avais pas besoin de cette hypothèse" to Napoleon.
[101] Zubiri 1980, 88 sqq. Cp. Gödel 1986, I 147 sqq.; Moore 1990, 172 sqq.
[102] Descartes. First Set of Replies, AT VII 102.
[103] Descartes. Med. Preface, AT VII 8.

but simply as operations of the intellect, then it could be said that we were taking them materially".[104] There is no further clear explanation by Descartes of the relation between formality and materiality in ideas. The difference between the two appears to be the following: formality consists in thinking-something, whereas materiality is just an unspecified thinking. Still, both the material and the formal in thinking are opposed to the objective or the conceived.

There is thus no room in Descartes for any distinction between intelligible and bodily matter, the former exemplified in the ideas as objects of and for thinking, the latter represented in physical things. But if we recall that for Plotinus materiality in thinking is its indefiniteness (2.4.1), while for Descartes materiality consists in the operation of the mind-reason, taken only as an unspecified activity of thinking, we might discover an interesting and surprising parallel between the Platonic (Plotinian) and Cartesian accounts of materiality in thinking, of which Descartes is not aware and which is not elaborated any further and does not play a major role in his philosophy.

(5) Lastly, essence is considered an objective concept, for it shows what a thing is as represented to the mind. The categorization of essence as objective affects the understanding of reflectivity. Thus, for Plotinus and Proclus only the intellect-*noys* is being. It simply *is* and insofar as it is, it is thinking; and it is thinking that thinks itself through the *noēta*, since there is nothing else that really is. Being and thinking are (is) thus the same and represent pure actuality, as Parmenides puts it.[105] As it has been noted, for Descartes being and thinking, objective and formal, can coincide only in the infinite mind. In the case of the finite mind there is a discrepancy between being and thinking; because, although mind in Descartes as substance is being, it is only *a* being, for it is opposed to the being of another finite (extended) substance, and possibly to another minds and to the being of the infinite thinking substance. In the finite mind, on the contrary, being does not coincide with thinking, insofar as in innate and in adventitious ideas the objective is not included in the formal. Because of this non-coincidence of being and thinking in the finite mind, Descartes has to negate the immediacy of being; the expression of such negation is radical doubt. Since, however, being has to be mediated in its representation by an objective concept, being should be expressed in thinking and speaking. The very immediacy of the act of *cogito* is then in fact not immediate, but is arrived at only through the mediation of thinking itself: the *sum* is not produced by the *cogito*, but the former is the presupposition of the possibility of the latter.

Furthermore, for Plato, Plotinus and Proclus the principle of being and of intellect is itself beyond being and thus is not being (cp. 1.2.1). For Descartes the principle of all things is pure being and infinite intellect, which already and always is. Descartes thus needs no initial indefinite thinking, which in its desperate

---

[104] Descartes. Fourth Set of Replies, AT VII 232-233. Cp.: "I regard the difference between the soul and its ideas as the same as that between a piece of wax and the various shapes it can take." - Descartes. To [Mislaid], 2 May 1644, AT IV 113. Cp. Aristotle. De an. 429b 24 sqq. See also: Chappell 1986, 177-184.
[105] Parmenides B3 DK; Parmenides, frg. II Tarán; Clement. Strom. II 440.12; Plotinus. Enn. I.4.10.6; III.8.8.8; V.1.8.17; V.9.5.29.

attempt to think the unthinkable source of being and thinking, constitutes the *kosmos noētos*. Descartes therefore does not leave any room for an initial indefinite dyad or intelligible matter, especially as specifically associated with geometrical entities as an extension in which geometricals might be considered irreducibly different from corporeal things (see 2.4). For Descartes both material and geometrical objects appear to be placed and considered in one and the same (material) extension, which is the most important precondition for the possibility of the application of mathematics to physics.

The necessity to speak about or to express being as mediated by thinking has a number of important implications in Descartes. First of all, the mind as thinking has to pass a *judgement* about its object. Judgement thus becomes one of the central concerns for modern philosophy, understood by Kant as the only mediator between the theoretical and the practical, between necessity and freedom. As Hannah Arendt argues, in the form of taste, judgement becomes the distinctive feature of modernity.[106] As such, judgement is already ambiguous, being both an operation of the mind and a (new) mind's faculty. Every finite mind has to express its own judgement. On the one hand, this makes such a judgement almost autonomous and universally valuable (for the finite mind is recognized, among the other minds, as equal in its right and ability to produce and express its judgement). On the other hand, as taste, judgement is only individual and subjective and cannot pretend to be universal. Another implication is that, unlike sense-perception, which just tells us what it perceives, judgement is supposed to be either true or false. Ideas *per se* are not false (clear ideas are true, cp. 1.2.3), falsity appears only in judgement. For Descartes a clear idea—as opposed to the confused idea or to an idea that represents a non-thing as thing—is an idea which, due to the natural light of reason, corresponds to its object, which implies the adequation concept of truth.[107] Thus, in the Third "Meditation" Descartes argues that in itself and by itself an idea cannot be false—only judgement can be *strictu sensu* false in combining ideas in a way that corresponds or does not correspond to a thing.[108] Falsity thus does not exist in ideas, but in judgement only, which has to pronounce its verdict, i.e. has to put ideas in a right order, reconstructing this order in correspondence or adequation to the order of the things. Moreover, the mind may also will to judge, and error occurs when the will surpasses the limits of reason.[109] The truth of things is thus no longer in the things themselves, but only in their mental representation, which may either be correct (adequate) or not: the truth then has to be "tasted" in judgement, and it has to be properly presented, i.e., in a refined judgement.

Further, a thing has to be thought in its objective concept, and so has to be judged by the mind. Until then a thing simply is, but is not yet thought. When it is thought, it is thought as something—as having an essence. But once it is actually

---

[106] Arendt 1978, 111 sqq.
[107] Descartes. Med. III, AT VII 43; cp. Second Set of Replies, AT VII 147-148; Fourth Set of Replies, AT VII 233.
[108] Descartes. Med. III, AT VII 37; Princ. I 13, AT VIIIA 9. Cp. the criticism of Arnauld and Descartes' reply: Fourth Set of Objections, AT VII 206; Fourth Set of Replies, AT VII 233.
[109] Cp. Williams 1978, 163-183.

thought, it has to be expressed or a judgement has to be uttered. The pragmatic dimension thus receives particular attention.[110] Lastly, there is a remarkable parallel between thinking and reflectivity on one hand, and the duality of existence and essence on the other (cp. 1.4.2). *To be* (existentially) is not the same as *to be something* (essentially). Similarly, *to think* differs from *to think something*. The distinction between thinking and thinking-something parallels the distinction between thinking as the activity of the mind, and thinking as reflectivity and judgement. Within the finite mind such a distinction is exemplified in that the thinking thing (the mind) can have as its object, as the thing thought, not only the "external" material thing, but also the "internal" thinking thing, i.e. itself. Obviously, "to be" matches "to think", and "to be something" corresponds to "to think something". "To be something" is realized by the mind as the essence of a thing through the objective concept of that thing. And the objective concept is that which makes the mind think that thing as something (i.e. as definite), which means that the "being" of the mind is to think, and the "essence" of the mind is to think something.

An important implicit presupposition behind the Cartesian understanding of idea is the reflectivity of the mind. The mind for Descartes has to be reflective—aware of itself and of its contents. Indeed, for the finite mind perceiving or thinking is always accompanied by perception of perceiving or by thought of thinking. In the distinction between thought and idea, the thought, *cogitatio*, is everything "we are immediately (*immediate*) aware of".[111] Or also: "By the term 'thought' I understand everything which we are aware of as happening within us, in so far as we have awareness of it."[112] Descartes thus presupposes that there is a thing of which there is a thought as an act of thinking—distinguished as the objective and the formal. (The Cartesian mind differs from the *noys*, which is also reflective, in that reflectivity of the mind does not presuppose communication-*koinōnia* of, and within, noetic objects, cp. 3.1.1.) If the thing that is thought is itself material, the idea or representation of such a thing still belongs to the mind. If the thing that is thought is itself mental (e.g., a universal), its representation in thinking is mental as well.

To the formal-objective distinction one might still add a third moment, that of immediate mental perception, whereby the mind is aware of its formal act in which it thinks its "objective" content. In fact, such a distinction would well fit the distinction between thought and idea, where thought designates any mental state, act or content of which the mind is immediately aware, and the idea is the form of thought, through which the mind is aware of that thought. Still, such immediate mental perception (*perceptio* as *cogitatio*), as well as any reflectivity, is not immediately implied in the formal-objective distinction, because if in an act of thinking the mind thinks something, nothing yet guarantees that the mind should thereby think itself. Immediate mental perception can hardly be characterized in terms of either formal or objective concepts, because it represents both an act (of

---

[110] In the Wittgensteinian question: "How can I think this or that as expressed in my perception, feeling or thinking by means of language?" – Cp. Wittgenstein 1967, passim.
[111] Descartes. Second Set of Replies, AT VII 160. Cp. Med. II, AT VII 33.
[112] Descartes. Princ. I 9, AT VIIIA 7.

awareness of itself) and a content (of awareness of *itself*).

These three constituents—formal, objective and immediate mental perception—might be taken as constituting three stages in the reflectivity of the mind, namely, the "I think", the "I think something" and the "I think that I think". Each consecutive stage may be understood as implied by the precedent one, but is not fully describable by it. The act of *cogito* may then be analyzed and put in terms of these three subsequent stages, which constitute three successive logical (not temporary) steps in the reflective procedure of the mind. These stages cannot be reduced to one another, but rather are exemplified in their synthetic unity through the apparent simplicity of the mind's self-awareness.

To note, one might attempt to distinguish a fourth moment in the reflective procedure, namely, that of the "I think that I think something". But in fact, as it is easy to see, this last moment in reflective thinking arises simply as an application of the pure intentional form of thinking ("I think something") to the immediate perception taken in its general form ("I think that X"; when X is the idea of the self—i.e., "I think"—then we have a particular case of the mentioned reflective mental immediate perception, i.e., "I think that I think"). Obviously, the result of such an application will be the "I think that I think something", which thus is not an independent moment in thinking, but is derivable from the three mentioned moments.

On this account, the very act of the self-awareness of the *cogito* has to be tripartite, rather than one elementary, undissolvable act of consciousness—although the composite nature of self-consciousness may remain unnoticed—because the three constituents of self-perception are exemplified not in a temporal, but only in a logical, sequence. Once again we encounter one of the fundamental presuppositions of modern philosophy; namely, that the mind's understanding and knowledge of something (of an external thing and also of itself) presupposes at the same time that the mind—through the described reflective procedure—also understands and knows its own state and content. Until the contemporary radical criticism of self-transparency of consciousness (with its precursors in Leibniz, Schelling and E. Hartmann),[113] the "I" is regarded as only discursive, self-transparent thought, which in thinking thinks itself and also knows itself. The very fact of thinking, the conclusion "cogito ergo sum", is possible only because of the reflectivity of thinking, which always turns to itself and through this constant turning justifies itself and the metaphysical truth(s). Without such structure of reflectivity the *cogito* could not even have been thought, expressed or uttered, because the "I" would have been simply unaware of the fact that it actually thinks. But such self-evidence of *cogito*—which, under the guise of clearness, also becomes the distinctive mark of truth—is in fact a complex reflective self-awareness of thought.

Reflectivity may also be considered essential for distinguishing between the two created substances (cp. 1.1.3; 1.2.3; 1.4.1). Descartes does not provide an argument to explain why extension and thought (and nothing else) have to be the

---

[113] Cp. Leibniz's theory of small unnoticeable perceptions (Monadology, э 19-24 et al.) and E. Hartmann 1869.

main attributes, and why there are only two attributes and not more, except for referring to an alleged self-evidence of such a distinction. It might be considered to be the case simply because God wills to create such a world where only thought and extension are the main attributes of the created substances. Such an answer, however, is insufficient for Descartes, because of his explicit rejection of the blind will: the creative will then has to follow the divine mind or reason.[114] Instead of positing two different essential features of two substances, one might confine oneself to one single feature, that of reflectivity. The relative complexity and heterogeneity of thought and extension as attributes might then be substituted by the attributes of the reflectivity of the mind and the non-reflectivity of the body: that which is reflective is thought or mind, and that which is not reflective is body or matter.

Such a distinction might still be ambiguous, since reflectivity may either be considered in the not created (in the infinite mind), or in the created (in the finite mind). Moreover, when the finite mind reflectively turns to itself, nothing prevents it from considering itself as the creator of all its mental content and objective ideas instead of receiving it from the other to the mind—from the infinite mind or from the extended world. In other words, mind always envisages a possibility of solipsism, or of viewing itself as the creator of itself (i.e., as thinking which constitutes itself in thinking and by thinking itself). Reflectivity thus may be reconsidered as the mark of creativity and the ability to produce not only things but also truth in the form of true propositions.

3.2 Imagination in ancient philosophy

3.2.1 Aristotle and Plato on imagination

An important question we now need to address is a possible connection or affinity of geometrical entities with the *hylē noētē* and with imagination. We will begin with a discussion of Plato and Aristotle, and then turn to a more elaborated account of imagination in Plotinus and Proclus. In recent years the notion of imagination in ancient philosophy received much attention—which parallels contemporary interest in imagination in general—in the discussion in the works of H. J. Blumenthal, I. Chitchaline, J. Dillon, E. Emilsson, M. Nussbaum, M. Schofield, G. Watson, M. Wedin and others.

Plato is the first in Greek literature to use the term *phantasia* (in "Republic" 382e), although in the dialogues he uses it only occasionally and does not present any consistent theory of it.[115] Still, it appears that in the "Philebus" he speaks about the imagination without mentioning it by name.[116] Here Plato presents the soul as a "painter" in its capacity (1) to create mental images (*eikonas*) of whatever kind after the "inscriptions" within the soul's memory. Since,

---

[114] Cp. Descartes. Discourse III, AT VI 28. Facing this very problem, Spinoza posits an infinite number of attributes belonging to one single substance, God, only two of which can be and are known to us (Spinoza, Ethics II, Prop. 1 sq.).
[115] Watson 1994, 4766, 4771; cp. Plato. Theaet. 152c, 161e.
[116] Plato. Phil. 38a-40e. Cp. Schofield 1978, 99.

however, image is always weaker and worse than its paradigm, the capacity of creating images (2) brings distortion into its products and (3) separates and thus distinguishes them from images of sense-perception (those of vision or of any other sense). These mental (imaginary) images (4) refer not only to the past and present but may also be projected into the anticipated future. Lastly, (5) imagination, as the capacity of producing and as if contemplating mental representations, is connected with both sense-perception and with reason in its capacity to form opinion, further expressible by speech.[117]

In the "Sophist" Plato takes *phantasia* to be a mixture of sensation and opinion (*symmeixis aisthēseōs kai doxēs*), where opinion is the end, termination and completion of the discursive reasoning of the soul, of its inner discussion with itself.[118] Imagination is thus connected to, and at the same time separated from, sensation and thinking and is neither of them—as if occupying a middle position between the two. Imagination is thus connected with opinion, which is also an intermediate faculty (*hē metaxy dynamis*) aimed at grasping that which is between being and utter non-being.[119] Important is that even though opinion may be false in its content, when it is falsely related to a thing (i.e., in a way in which this thing does not exist), the very act of having opinion can never be false, because if a person has an opinion of having an opinion, she really has an opinion that she is unable not to have.[120] The same may be said about imagining as appropriation of an image: an image may refer to a non-existent, or not properly existent, thing (e.g., a physical thing), but the act of image-making itself cannot be called into doubt. If we now recall the Cartesian *cogito*, we will discover a striking similarity between its self-evidence and that of the opinion-making of *dianoia* and of image-making.

Aristotle mentions the notion of *phantasia* more frequently than does Plato, and dedicates several pages to it in the "De anima" III.3.[121] Scholars differ considerably, however, in interpreting what Aristotle does indeed say. Thus, Schofield takes imagination in Aristotle to stand for all kinds of abnormal, pathological or "non-paradigmatic sensory experiences".[122] Wedin, on the contrary, argues that *phantasia* in Aristotle is not a faculty at all, but "subserves full faculties in the sense that images [of the imagination] are the devices by which such faculties (re)present the objects toward which they are directed".[123] Both approaches seem to be extreme in the interpretation of the notion of imagination. One might rather follow C. de Vogel, who suggests that *phantasia* is a necessary and normal constituent in cognition.[124]

---

[117] Cp. Plato. Soph. 236c. See: Emilsson 1988, 107-111.
[118] Plato. Soph. 263d-264b.
[119] Plato. RP 476d-480a, esp. 479c-d.
[120] Plato. Phil. 40c.
[121] Aristotle. De an. 427b 14 sqq. See also: Bernadete 1975, 611-622; Todd 1981, 49-59; Watson 1988, 14-34; A. White 1990, 7-13.
[122] Schofield 1978, 101-106.
[123] Wedin 1988, 24.
[124] Cit. ap. Schofield 1978, 105.

For our present purpose we will only briefly recollect the conclusions of Aristotle's argument.[125] First of all (1), *phantasia* is an ability to produce images or "representations" different both from images of senses and from objects of thought.[126] The term itself comes from *phainesthai*, "to appear", so that the faculty has to do only with phenomena and not with essences. That is why (2) imagination may be false (and is mostly so)[127] and (3) it is capable of negativity, and has to do with the unreal, with a certain irrationality or "as if-ness"—as in the case when we look at a picture portraying something awful. We might be frightened, but our emotional state is "suspended", as it were, because we understand that the frightening exists only "as if", in the imagination.[128] Still, *phantasia* does not seem to be a faculty (*dynamis*) specifically defined by its own object and by a proper activity, but is rather a state (*hexis*), or even a movement, that arises and follows the activity of sense-perception.[129]

As such, *phantasia* (4) differs from all other faculties that provide images to the soul. It is different from sensation (*aisthēsis*) and from discursive thinking (*dianoia*), as well as from mere opinion (*doxa*) and from strict knowledge (*epistēmē*). Imagination (5) does not arise without sense-perception, but the supposition or discursive combination of judgements (*hypolēpsis*) and discursive thinking itself are both impossible without imagination, which provides the "material" for interpretation by thinking.[130] In other words, imagination relates both to sense-perception and to discursive thinking. Also, Aristotle seems to suggest that imagination cannot happen without a body, which might explain why imagination (6) is present in most animals.[131]

A further important distinction is that between productive and reproductive imagination.[132] The latter only reproduces or "paints" an image, *phantasma*, of a thing after the thing has gone. Clearly, this after-picturing can be very lively, producing bright and vivid images. It inevitably distorts its image, however, because it reproduces the image of a thing always only more or less precisely, never exactly portraying the thing. Reproductive imagination is always an after-representation, for it becomes effective only after its object has been removed.[133] Aristotle obviously acknowledges this kind of imagination—which operates mostly when the sensible object is gone—as an ability of keeping images of sense-perception, especially of seeing (in this sense, imagination is *as if* mental visualization). Reproductive imagination is also able to act in the presence of a thing, however. It either reconstructs the properties of a thing in bringing that thing

---

[125] Aristotle. De an. 427b 14-429a 8.
[126] Aristotle. De an. 428a 1-2.
[127] Cp. Aristotle. Met. 1024b 24-1025a 6; 1062b 43.
[128] Aristotle. De an. 427b 22-24.
[129] Aristotle. De an. 429a 1-2; cp. Met. 1022b 4-5.
[130] Cp. Aristotle. De an. 403a 8 sqq.; 431a 15-17; De mem. 449b 31 sqq.
[131] Aristotle. De an. 403a 8-10; cp. 428a 9-11; Met. 980b 25-27; De motu anim. 700a 6 sqq.
[132] Cp. I. Kant. Critique of Pure Reason A 115 sqq., B 151-152; Anthropology, § 28, where *facultas imaginandi* is divided into *exhibitio originaria* and *exhibitio derivativa*.
[133] As Wittgenstein remarks, "while I am looking at an object, I cannot imagine it". - Wittgenstein 1967, 109 (§ 621).

to completion (e.g., when we see only the front of a book, we add in the imagination the hind part of it, bringing the book to a three-dimensional imaginable unity), or the reproductive imagination projects and extrapolates a thing with its properties into a future situation. Aristotle in fact presupposes the reproductive imagination when mentioning a mnemonic technique based on the creation of images.[134] Still, the notion of productive imagination does not yet have its full recognition and consideration in Aristotle.[135] In any case, (7) Aristotle's account leaves room for a distinction between productive and reproductive imagination. The notion of productive imagination appears first in Philostratus, as a capacity to produce images of true reality, of being, as opposed to mere imitation, *mimēsis*, of bodily things.[136]

Productivity of imagination presupposes a capacity of making changes in the visualized or represented object. This further implies a certain plasticity and mobility of imagination. Indeed, imagination (8) is said to be a *movement* that results from the activity of sense-perception.[137] But imagination is also (9) the only faculty that can act completely at will, whereas the senses transmit what they have and discursive thinking has to follow necessity in combining its objects in the right succession.

In what follows, "phantasia" will be rendered as "imagination", although, of course, there are important differences between ancient and modern notions of imagination. Thus, for instance, imagination in Plato and Aristotle is never taken in the transcendental sense,[138] as it appears in Kant, because ancient thinkers never raise the question about *a priori* formal structures in their epistemological investigations, which might render experience possible and valid without simultaneously asking about the ontological status of these structures. Historically, as Watson argues, *phantasia* turns into creative or productive imagination due to the Stoic influence on later Neoplatonism. According to Sextus Empiricus, humans differ from animals not because the former have imagination—for animals have imagination too—but because humans have imagination that allows for transition and composition.[139]

Although Plato and Aristotle may vary on a number of points in their accounts of imagination, there nevertheless appears a remarkable similarity in both approaches. We have to agree with Dillon, who takes the Aristotelian treatment of

---

[134] Aristotle. De an. 427b 18-20.
[135] An important question that is left open here is to what extent does the imagination affect our actions and activity: thus, image-making is for Aristotle active in dreaming, but we cannot act when asleep, cp. Aristotle. De insomn. 460b 15-461b 5; NE 1098b 31-1099a 3. Nevertheless, quite often in acting we (and even animals) follow imagination - Aristotle. De an. 429a 4-6.
[136] Philostratus. Vita Apol. VI 19; cp. Watson 1994, 4766-4769.
[137] Aristotle. De an. 428b 30-429a 1; cp. Aquinas 1951, 396.
[138] Against Dillon 1986, 57-58.
[139] *Ti metabatikēi kai synthetikēi* - Sextus Emp. Adv. Math. VIII 276. *Phantasia* becomes *imaginatio* for the first time in Augustine and in Boethius and is later developed by Aquinas and by Dante into an intermediate active faculty securing the way to the divine - Watson 1994, 4790 sqq.

imagination to be an elaboration of Plato's account.[140] Plato's position is developed in more detail by the later tradition, in particular, by the Neoplatonists.[141] Summarizing the previous discussion, it is important to stress the following traits of imagination, which will be important in the subsequent considerations: (A) the unique creative ability or spontaneity of imagination; (B) the intermediate position of imagination "between" sense-perception and discursive thinking; (C) an affinity with negativity—the presence in the imagination of an admixture of the irrational; (D) its relation to a certain (quasi)extension through the capacity of representing physical and ideal objects; and (E) its connection with some kind of movement ((E) will be considered, in 3.4.3 and 3.4.5).

3.2.2 Imagination in Plotinus

Various aspects of the notion of imagination in Plotinus are discussed in the works of Blumenthal, Emilsson, Warren and Watson. One can discern the following major points in Plotinus' interpretation of imagination. First of all, (A) imagination can be broadly understood in the Aristotelian vein as an ability to produce psychic images-*phantasmata*.[142] The notion of *phantasia* is used in the "Enneads" rather broadly as an ability—again, not as a distinct faculty—to represent objects of whatever kind as mental or psychic images. But, as a capacity of representation, imagination is not just a passive reflecting or mirroring, for imagination forms its images (*phantasiai*) quite unlike impressions on the wax that receives them. Criticizing the Gnostics, Plotinus argues that the soul can create "through imagination (*dia phantasias*) and, still more, through rational activity".[143] Imagination is thus considered not only as productive, but also as reproductive, insofar as it is taken as possessing (or, rather, itself being) an active potency, independent of the images it produces, because of the general principle that image does not affect its origin.[144]

(B) Most importantly, imagination for Plotinus, as for Plato, has an intermediate position between the sensible and the thinkable. Imagination, to which otherness is present as irrationality, is to be strictly separated from the intelligible. Imagination may be taken then as a mirroring, a projection of the intellectual act (*noēma*, cp. 3.1.1), rather than as an act of the intellection itself.[145] In other words, imagination in its "upper" end meets the intelligible not immediately, but at best through the discursive reasoning. Because of such intermediateness, Plotinus has to distinguish two imaginations (*phantastika*) or rather, two different aspects of the same psychic ability. In Enn. IV.3.31.2 sqq., Plotinus explicitly discerns two imaginations corresponding to the higher and the

---

[140] Dillon 1986, 55.
[141] Plato never uses the term "phantasia" in his early dialogues, so it very well might be that the notion of imagination receives much attention in the Academy toward the end of Plato's life and Aristotle himself benefits from this discussion.
[142] Cp. Plotinus 1995, 73.
[143] *Toy logizesthai*, Plotinus. Enn. II.9.11.22; cp. II.6.3.29.
[144] Cp. Fleet 1995, 248, 266; Moutsopoulos 1976, 11-22.
[145] Dillon 1986, 56-57; Plotinus. Enn. IV.3.30.5-6.

lower levels in the soul which, when undisturbed, allows the two imaginations to be in accord. The higher imagination then subsumes the lower one and both produce one mental image.[146] Two imaginations correspond to two souls: the higher disembodied one, and the lower soul connected to the body. This latter soul keeps remembrances acquired in the imagination.[147] The two souls are not really different, however, but rather express a modal distinction within the soul in its dual relation to the sensible and the thinkable. The higher, "primary" imagination (*prōtē phantasia*) represents the opinion-*doxa* and, as Dillon argues, may be taken as a capacity to synthesize and reproduce the data of sense-perception. The other, lower imagination is "uncriticized, indeterminate or indistinct (*anepikritos*)".[148]

The two imaginations are usually indiscernible, for when the highest soul governs, then "the image becomes one, as if a shadow followed by the other and as if a little light slipped in under the great one; but when there is a war and disharmony between them, the other image becomes manifest by itself, but we do not notice in general the duality of the souls".[149] This duality is overwhelmed by the image of the lower imagination, which resembles a double reflection. The image of the lower imagination makes the image of the higher imagination dim and almost invisible (which is why the difference between the two imaginations usually is not noticed). The lower imagination is then almost completely unaware that the image of the higher imagination itself reflects and visualizes a noetic object. It does not mean, however, that the two imaginations are completely separate, the one belonging merely to the intelligible, the other to the sensual. Plotinus argues that this cannot be the case, "for in this way there will be two living things with nothing at all in common with each other".[150] There thus would have been two different and separate souls, or two different cognitive faculties, that would have nothing to do with each other. The difference between the two imaginations may also be considered modal, brought in not by the difference of their objects but by the hierarchical difference in the whole ontological structure (which in the last instance comes back to the henological difference between the superabundant One and the indefinite dyad). The "intermediateness" of imagination, then, consists not in that the imagination is in "between" the intelligible and the sensual, but that it reaches both "here" and "there". This reflects an insurmountable ambiguity in the imagination, in regard to both its object (intelligible and sensual) and the ontological reality with which it is associated (the higher and the lower soul).[151]

---

[146] Blumenthal 1976, 51-55; 1971, 92-93; Warren 1966, 284.

[147] Plotinus. Enn. IV.3.31.1 sqq. Cp. the also a note of A. H. Armstrong in: Plotinus. *Enneads* VII, 234-235.

[148] Plotinus. Enn. III.6.4.19-21.

[149] Plotinus. Enn. IV.3.31.9-13. Cp. Watson 1994, 4795.

[150] Plotinus. Enn. IV.3.31.6-9.

[151] Cp. Warren 1966, 277-285. Warren argues that the faculty of imagination is double: "When the sensitive and rational functions are combined into one soul, a new conceptual imagination performs a function analogous to that of sensible imagination" - Warren 1966, 278. Regarding the two kinds of imagination, which correspond to two different levels of the soul, Blumenthal suggests that one kind is between sense-perception and reason and the other is subsensitive (Blumenthal 1971, 89-95; 1976, 51-55). See, however, the convincing criticism of Emilsson 1988, 108.

What position does imagination occupy in respect to sense-perception and reasoning? In his analysis of sense-perception, Emilsson stresses the connection of sensual perception and imagination in Plotinus.[152] The argument is that imagination is the terminating point of perceptions or *phantasmata*, as representations of things that arise in the soul as the result of sense-perception; in this respect Plotinus appears to be close to Aristotle.[153] Imagination and perception thus are connected, although they appear to have different objects. If imagination were to be considered only as the function of sense-perception, however, it would be rather difficult to account for the unity of a "synthesized" image of sense-perception, recollected from a multiplicity of disrupted and disconnected sense-data. For even if sense-perception and imagination meet in an act of perception, they are different in that imagination, unlike sense-perception, does not have to directly refer to physical objects. In producing its objects-*phantasmata*, imagination begins with non-physical data transmitted by senses and not with the physical objects themselves. Imagination, even when considered as the lower imagination, should thus be different from, and "higher" to, sense-perception—that is, closer to the dianoetic interpretative discursive reasoning of the soul. Emilsson suggests another hypothesis of imagination as conscious awareness, for instance, the act of reading when reading.[154] Still, as it has been argued, reflectivity in the awareness of thinking while actually thinking is proper primarily to the thinking of the intellect (3.1.1).

Thus, to be intermediate, imagination has to be a "bridge" that both separates and unites sense-perception and reasoning, as the soul mediates between the domains of the sensible and the intelligible, being also a "bridge" between the two.[155] Imagination is then as if on the border-line (*methorion*) between the sensible and the intelligible.[156] On its "upper side" imagination meets discursive reasoning to which it transmits the *phantasmata*, and on its "lower side" it meets and absorbs the data of sense-perception.[157] Therefore, Plotinus' claim that "the imaging part [of the soul] has a sort of intelligence"[158] can be fully justified.

Another argument in favor of situating imagination as intermediate may be recovered from Enn. VI.8.2.17, where imagination, linked here with experiences of the body, is said to be compelling.[159] On the one hand, a compelling force is primarily associated with the necessity of matter. On the other hand, since freedom is determined by a closeness of thinking to the One and thus emerges through ascension to the good, the intellect is mostly free. But the intellect is free "when it does not have it in its power not to act".[160] However compelling it may

---

[152] Emilsson 1988, 107-112.
[153] Plotinus. Enn. IV.3.29; IV.3.30; IV.8.8; IV.4.20.17-18.
[154] Emilsson 1988, 112. See Plotinus. Enn. I.4.10.19-22; II.9.1.34-36.
[155] Cp. Plotinus. Enn. IV.6.3.5-7; Watson 1994, 4796.
[156] Plotinus. Enn. IV.4.3.11; cp. V.3.9.28-36.
[157] Although, it is sense-perception that already begins the interpretive work: perceptions for Plotinus are judgements (*kriseis*). Cp. Emilsson 1988, 121-125.
[158] *Phantastikon hoion noeron*, Plotinus. Enn. IV.3.23.33.
[159] Plotinus. Enn. VI.8.3.7-16.
[160] Plotinus. Enn. VI.8.4.4 sqq.; VI.8.4.6-7.

seem, freedom consists in the voluntary act of choosing to pursue the good and therefore in freely accepting the necessity not to act in a contrary way. This "not able not to" is, however, radically different from the simple necessity of the "not able" of matter.

Imagination thus may be compared to a two-sided mirror that reflects in its images-*phantasmata* both sensual things and intelligible objects.[161] What *phantasmata* share in common with physical things is that objects of the imagination are visualized by the imagination, first, as extended and, second, as divisible. *Phantasmata* are also similar to intelligible objects insofar as both are stable and exemplify unchanging properties (at least, unless imagination voluntarily brings change into its image).

Although the teaching of two imaginations is not thoroughly elaborated in Plotinus, the very reason for introducing it seems to be dual: on the one hand, to stress even more the intermediateness of the imagination as capable of reflecting both intellectual acts (in their processed form of discursive cogitations, *logoi*) and acts of sensual perception, while still preserving a rigid distinction between the sensual and the thinkable. On the other hand, the doctrine of two imaginations (which may be interpreted as two "sides" of one and the same mirror) helps to explain why imagination may conceive both perfect geometrical figures and arbitrary images, to which no intelligible form corresponds, no discursive account (*logos*) and no sensual object. The former can be taken as contained within the higher imagination, and the latter as processed by the lower imagination, being closer to the sensible. This is another reason for taking geometrical objects to be separate from numbers, because geometrical entities are imaginable, whereas numbers are only thinkable (cp. 2.1.1).

(C) The mirroring of imagination is still of a very peculiar kind, for *phantasia* represents physical objects in a non-physical form and intelligible objects as visualizable through an image, which the *noēta* do not have. Products of imagination are thus ambiguous and ontologically different from both sensual and intelligible objects. This distinguishes *phantasia* from every other faculty. The imagination is unable to adequately reproduce both kinds of objects, but always needs to reconstruct them as *not* what they are (imaginary representation of a circle is neither a physical circle, nor the circle's ideal notion). The imagination thus inevitably misrepresents its object, either grasping it in an integral image, or representing it in a succession, i.e., as being constructed part by part (3.4.3). Such immanent misrepresentation or inalienable negativity is due to the imagination's connection with the irrational, *alogon*, which comes "from a stroke of something irrational from outside".[162] Images of imagination are themselves vague and unclear; they are *amydrai phantasiai*, described exactly in the same terms as Plato characterizes matter, *khalepon kai amydron eidos*.[163] Once again we encounter the fundamental ambiguity in imagination. On the one hand, it may reproduce and

---

[161] Plotinus. Enn. IV.3.30; cp. I.4.10.7 sqq. Blumenthal 1971, 88; Watson 1988. The image of mirror may come back to Plato's Tim. 71b-d.
[162] *Phantasia de plēlgēi alogoy exōthen*, Plotinus. Enn. I.8.15.18-19. Another reading adopted by Henry and Schwyzer is that imagination *is* itself a stroke (*plēgē*).
[163] Plato. Tim. 49a; Plotinus. Enn. I.8.14.5.

construct its images in an unrestrained way, at will, and subsequently can put its images in arbitrary associations by connecting, disconnecting and distorting them. On the other hand, there is a certain irrationality or "darkness" within *phantasia*, which cannot be controlled. This is why when describing inner detachment, the exhortation of the higher part of the soul to the state of pure being and thinking, Plotinus argues that it should not only be detached from everything bodily, but from the imagination as well.[164] Imagination is then compelling and compelled in that it receives the shape of and for its images from something else: either from physical bodies (e.g., the head of a man, the tail of a horse, in the image of a centaur) or from intelligibles (e.g., the form of a circle). Imagination thus has certain features both of the intelligible and of the material, but at the same time *phantasia* belongs to neither of them exclusively, because imagination has features that are altogether alien to both intellection and matter.

(D) Imagination represents its objects as quasi-extended images, connected with a kind of *plenum* where psychic images are present as embodied and as quasi-extended. Intelligible matter was introduced as the indefinite dyad of the not yet formed intellection-*noēsis* which, in a desperate attempt to grasp its originating principle and cause, (mis)represents it as a multitude of forms (cp. 2.4.1). In a sense, the originating principle, which is beyond being, can only be imagined, but not really thought. That is why when Plotinus speaks about the One in Enn. VI. 8, he proposes an imaginary experiment: in thinking about the One, "we first assume a space and place (*khōran kai topon*), a kind of vast emptiness (*khaos*), and then, when the space is already there, we bring this nature into that place which has come to be or is in our imagination, and bringing it into this kind of place we inquire in this way as if into whence and how it came here, and as if it was a stranger we have asked about its presence and, in a way, its substance, really just as if we thought that it had been thrown up from some depth or down from some height".[165] In its very notion, imagination cannot be separated from some kind of materiality and extension. And in fact, as it will be argued in what follows, intelligible matter in Plotinus appears to be necessarily connected with imagination (see 3.2.4). Thus, the distinctive features of imagination that may be discovered in Plotinus are its creativity, intermediateness, negativity and affinity to extension.

3.2.3 Main features of imagination in Neoplatonism: Porphyry, Syrianus, Proclus

Neoplatonists further develop an original theory of imagination. As Watson puts it, "the Neoplatonist treatment of *phantasia* is governed by two contrasting attitudes to it: 1) a suspicion that it is dangerous and to be avoided because of the deceits of the body, and 2) an acceptance of it in the (Aristotelian) understanding of it as a middle between sense and intellect, and even a welcoming of it as a possible help to a glimpse of a higher world".[166]

The features of imagination that we have seen in Plotinus may also be

---

[164] Plotinus. Enn. V.5.6.17-19.
[165] Plotinus. Enn. VI.8.11.15-22.
[166] Watson 1994, 4792. In Neoplatonic considerations of imagination the Stoic influence is traceable.

discovered as elaborated more explicitly in later Neoplatonic thinkers. Thus, (A) imagination is taken as an ability to produce images; according to Proclus it is a thinking capable of producing images, in and through which it tends to know intelligible objects.[167] Important to note is that imagination is also considered a necessary constituent in the production of speech (the so-called *phantasia lektikē* or *semantikē*), which we will have to leave here without further discussion.[168] Ideal objects-*noēta* are represented as partless in thinking-*noēsis*, whereas imagination takes them in the form of an image in which one can already discern parts.[169] Imagination is capable of both reproducing and producing images according to data that may come either from sense-perception or from purely thinkable objects. In the former case, imagination recollects the form of various multiple sensual data and presents them to the further judgement of reasoning-*dianoia*. In the latter case, representation moves in the opposite direction, as it were, from intelligible objects-*noēta* to their discursive representation in the *dianoia*, and then to the activity of imagination. It is on the basis of images formed in the imagination that we may further apply and recognize them in physical things, as in the case of the construction of a mechanism or building a house.

Imagination (B) is to be understood as intermediary, as "between" sense-perception and discursive logical reasoning.[170] Images or products of imagination, *phantasmata*, have, on the one hand, certain features common with both physical things (they have parts, are visualizable and divisible) and with intelligible objects (both display identical non-changing properties).[171] On the other hand, *phantasmata* are themselves neither purely physical, nor purely intelligible. As the content of imagination, they cannot be reduced to the content of discursive thinking. In *phantasmata* there is always some kind of materiality or quasi-spatiality, which is lacking in the objects of discursive thinking. *Phantasmata* do not come to be, unless caused voluntarily by, and in, the imagination. *Phantasmata* are quasi-extended: they appear to be extended, but not in the same way as physical things are, i.e., images of imagination are not spatial. They are also multiple, so that one and the same object (intelligible or physical) can be represented by an unlimited number of different images of imagination.

The intermediateness of imagination is explicitly stressed by Proclus when he argues in the commentary to Plato's "Alcibiades" that the intellect-*noys* is precedent to discursive reasoning-*dianoia*, and that discursive reasoning is itself precedent to the imagination-*phantasia* and opinion-*doxa*.[172] The notion of imagination as double (which is already found in Plotinus' doctrine of two

---

[167] *Phantasia noēsis oysa morphōtikē noētōn ethelei gnōsis einai tinōn*, Proclus. In RP I 235.18-19.

[168] Proclus. In Crat. 19.8 sqq.; Syrianus. In Met. 9.22; 163.21; Simplicius. In de an. 142.24; Watson 1988, 133.

[169] Syrianus. In Met. 98.26 sqq.

[170] Porphyry. Sent. 43; Proclus. In Tim. III 286.29 sqq. Sometimes Proclus hesitates whether it is imagination-*phantasia* or opinion-*doxa* that is to be considered immediately adjacent to sense-perception. See: Blumenthal 1975 144-146; Blumenthal 1999, 324.

[171] Cp. Proclus. In Eucl. 51.17-20.

[172] Proclus. In Alc. 140.18-20.

imaginations) is very much in accord with Aristotle—for him imagination is always connected with both reasoning and sensation.[173] As also (Pseudo-) Philoponus reports, Plutarch of Athens "considers the imagination to be double, and that its upper boundary, which is to say its originative principle is the [lower] boundary of the discursive intellect (*dianoētikoy*), while its other boundary is the upper limit of the senses".[174]

Here we need to note, however, that imagination is not the only faculty to be considered intermediate. Discursive reasoning-*dianoia*, as Plato argues, is intermediate (*metaxy*) between intellect-*noys* and opinion-*doxa*, and is necessarily involved in the understanding and consideration of geometrical entities.[175] Thus, in Plato we may see a distinction that is not ternary but rather quaternary, that of four hierarchically ordered mental faculties: intellect-*noys*, discursive reasoning-*dianoia*, imagination-*phantasia* and sense-perception-*aisthēsis* (cp. 3.1.2). This requires the consideration of *phantasia* as a proper mental faculty and not just as an ability of being moved by another object (namely, that of sense-perception), as in Aristotle. Objects of these four faculties are respectively *noēta, dianoēta (logoi), phantasmata* and *aisthēta*.[176] Obviously, two of these four mental faculties, discursive reasoning and imagination, can be taken as intermediate, although, first, reasoning has to be understood as a faculty "higher" than that of the imagination—i.e., as presenting being in a more adequate way. *Dianoia* binds the notions-*logoi* (for example, of geometrical entities) logically and discursively, whereas *phantasia* represents them as if visualizing in a quasi-extended shape. As intermediate, both discursive reasoning and imagination are involved in understanding and knowing geometrical entities (and not physical things). Namely, *phantasia* seems to visually represent and construct the geometrical figure in a certain *plenum*, according to the notion-*logos* of discursive thinking. The *logos* itself, however, is a representation of the ideal form-*noēton* of that figure within the intellect-*noys*. And second, both discursive reasoning and imagination can obviously be taken as terminal faculties in two triadic sequences of mental structures, namely, in *noys-dianoia-phantasia* and in *dianoia-phantasia-aisthēsis*. The first triad represents rather the material aspect of the imagination, in which it submits entities-*phantasmata* (in particular, of geometrical figures) for interpretations and proofs of discursive reasoning, which borrows the form-*eidos* of the objects in question from the intellect-*noys*. The second triad may be said to represent the formal and formative aspect of imagination, in which it is taken as capable of constructing and reconstructing its objects, in particular, presenting geometrical figures as produced by movement (see 3.4.5).

Imagination is thus ambiguous in a certain sense, because it reflects in itself both physical and intelligible objects, both uniting and separating them.

---

[173] Cp. Aristotle. De an. 433b 29; 434a 5-7.
[174] Philoponus. In de an. 515, 12-15.
[175] Plato. RP 511b-e. *Eikasia* ("conjecture" or imitation) might be considered similar to imagination. Still, *eikasia*, a notion not elaborated at length in Plato, seems to refer rather to the sphere of sensual images and imitations and, being followed by the opinion-*doxa*, is not an intermediate faculty connected to discursive thinking.
[176] Cp. Syrianus. In Met. 24.4; 38.9-10; 82.1.

Imagination unites sensation and thinking, insofar as it transmits the form of sense-data to discursive reasoning. Yet it also separates both, insofar as the form processed by discursive reasoning is purely intelligible and not imaginable—hence the already mentioned metaphor of the imagination as a (double-sided) mirror that reflects and thus both unites and separates the physical and the intelligible.[177]

The mirroring of the imagination inevitably implies negativity and misrepresentation (for although the imaginary circle is perfect, it is generically different from its paradigm-*eidos*, which is neither visualizable nor circular). This is because of the admixture of otherness, which does not allow *phantasmata* to be simple and communicating as intelligible objects-*noēta*. In other words, (C) there is negativity or irrationality (*ta aloga*) in the imagination.[178] Imagination, as Plutarch says, is that which prevents the human mind from being active, from always thinking; imagination brings passivity into thinking and splits or "extends" it into a visualized image-*phantasma*.[179] Thinking should thus stay away from imagination.[180] Thinking of a merely intelligible form (*to noeron*) lacks a visualizable image.[181] As Iamblichus puts it, the power of imagination (*hē phantastikē dynamis*) is sleeping when intelligible life is perfectly active.[182]

Imagination thus appears to veil the intelligible.[183] It depicts an invisible, and only thinkable, form-*eidos* in an imaginable shape. Since imagination reveals *eidos* as visualizable, however, *phantasia* simultaneously conceals the ideal form of what it currently represents.[184] In this sense, the imagination inevitably misrepresents that which it has to convey, and appears to be able to produce the not (yet) existent. As Synesius, influenced by the Neoplatonic philosophy, states: imagination takes being (*ta onta*) away from existence (*einai*) and brings in non-being.[185] Images of imagination, *phantasmata* or simulacra, in E. des Places' translation, always tend to represent intelligible objects but always inevitably miss them. Imagination visually represents these objects with all of their properties (for instance, an imaginable circle contains and displays all the properties included in the ideal notion or the form of the circle), but at the same time also necessarily presents them inadequately, admixing otherness and thus inevitably representing noetic objects in the way they are not (as extended, divisible, and so on).

If imagination represents a partless ideal object (*idea* or *eidos* or *noēton*) (D) as quasi-extended or quasi-spatial, then *phantasia* has to be connected with some kind of extension in which such an object can be considered—that is, visualized as having parts and a recognizable shape or image. Since *phantasmata*,

---

[177] Cp. Proclus. In Eucl. 121.5-6; Iamblichus. De myst. 94.4; De comm. math. sci. 28.7.
[178] Cp. Philoponus. In de an. 515.9-11; Proclus. In Tim. I 247.10 sqq.; 269.7-9; Watson 1988, 119.
[179] Plutarch ap. Philoponus. In de an. 541.20 sqq.
[180] Proclus. In Parm. 1020.8 sqq.
[181] Iamblichus. De myst. 107.11-12. Cp., however, *hai noēseis oyk aney phantasias*, Porphyry. Sent. 16.
[182] Iamblichus. De myst. 287.1-3; cp. 250.14.
[183] Porphyry. Sent. 47; Iamblichus. De myst. 246.13-14.
[184] Iamblichus. De myst. 167.16; cp. 173.5.
[185] Synesius. De insomniis, 1316c. See also: Chitchaline 1993.

as constructed and reconstructed by imagination, do not exist as physical things, such "extension" may be understood as connected with intelligible, and not physical, matter. In his commentary to the "Alcibiades" Proclus argues that "what sense-perception ascertains in a manner immersed in matter, exists in a more immaterial manner in the imagination"[186] (cp. 3.2.4).

In the Neoplatonic tradition after Plotinus—in Porphyry, Iamblichus, Syrianus, Proclus and Simplicius—we find the teaching of a quasi-material pneumatic "vehicle" (*okhēma*) of the soul.[187] The notion of this non-physical body is referred back to Plato and especially to Aristotle. As Dodds points out, for Aristotle *pneyma* is "the seat of the nutritive and sensitive soul and the physiological condition of *phantasia*", and, as Aristotle himself explains, it is analogous to the "quintessentia"—the "fifth element", which constitutes the stars (the divine bodies).[188] In Porphyry and Proclus there are a number of hints of a possible connection of *phantasia* to *pneyma*, or soul's pneumatic "vehicle". Even though Porphyry avoids a direct identification of imagination with *pneyma*, he still asserts that impressions of imagination, themselves received from the (sensual) affection, are further brought on to *pneyma*.[189] In his commentary to "Timaeus", Proclus conceives *phantasia* to even be some kind of perception-*aisthēsis* whose external activity is sense-perception and whose internal activity is imagination, which looks at the images in *pneyma*.[190] Proclus thus takes the intermediateness of imagination to be that *phantasia* unites rather than separates sense-perception and mental processing of sensual images. On another occasion, Proclus assigns to imagination the function of *sensus communis* (cp. 3.3).[191] However, even if the imagination is to be conceived as connected to some kind of material or quasi-material substrate, the purported relation of *phantasia* to *pneyma* and *okhēma* is left without a detailed discussion and is not elaborated into a consistent theory.

3.2.4 Imagination and intelligible matter

Imagination thus has an affinity with some kind of extension; objects of imagination therefore appear to be similar to physical things, insofar as the former are divisible and imaginable as extended. Still, *phantasmata* are fundamentally different from physical things, insofar as the latter are in constant change—they incessantly appear and perish. Objects of imagination can also be considered engendered, but only in the sense of being constructed, part by part, by means of another imaginable object in and by the imagination (see 3.4.3). *Phantasmata*, especially geometrical figures as imagined, differ from physical bodily things insofar as geometricals do not really perish unless they are either no longer

---

[186] Proclus. In Alc. 199.5 sqq.
[187] See: Dodds ap. Proclus 1963, 313-321; Finamore 1985. There is an even further distinction into two different vehicles of a higher and lower soul, Blumenthal 1999, 326.
[188] Cp. Plato. Phaedo 113d, Phaedr. 247b, Tim. 41e et al. and Aristotle. De gen. Anim. 736b 27 sqq. Dodds ap. Proclus 1963, 315-316.
[189] Porphyry. Sent. 29. See also: Smith 1974, 152 sqq.
[190] Proclus. In Tim. III 286.20-28.
[191] See: Blumenthal 1999, 324-328.

retained by the imagination (not actually imagined) or they are transformed by the imagination into different imaginable object(s). Moreover, geometrical, imaginable objects, unlike their bodily images (e.g., a circle drawn on paper), exemplify non-changing properties of the corresponding intelligible object (the idea or notion of the circle) of a purely thinkable form, *noēton* or *eidos*.[192]

As it has been argued, intelligible matter has to be understood as both otherness and multiplicity within the intelligible, and also as geometrical matter, where geometrical entities exist (see 2.4.1; 2.4.2). Geometricals are not to be found in the physical world, so that their divisibility, multiplicity (even in those belonging to the same species) and quasi-extension differ from the divisibility and multiplicity in and of physical bodies. Therefore, the divisibility of geometrical objects cannot be sensually perceived. Nor can they be understood by the intellect, which considers geometricals as indivisible intelligible objects, i.e. as noetic forms. As visualizable and quasi-extended, geometricals are also not apprehensible by discursive reasoning, because *dianoia* considers geometrical objects without paying attention to their divisibility and quasi-extension. The reason for this is that the main purpose of discursive reasoning is, on the one hand, to construct arguments or proofs (e.g., of theorems), or to provide logically valid and justifiable passages from one established statement to another, putting them in a systematic order. Thus, it can only be imagination that can present geometrical objects as divisible and extended (with the only exception being the point, see 2.1.3)—as considered in intelligible or geometrical matter. Discursive thinking tends to overcome, however, the multiplicity of the visualizable extension of imaginable geometricals, bringing them back to the unity of their rational notions-*logoi*, unimaginable and unextended in any way (as Syrianus argues, the mathematical—geometrical—object primarily exists in the dianoetic reason and is structured under the pattern of the *logos*).[193] The originality of Proclus' approach consists not only in his equation of *phantasia* with the matter of geometrical objects, *hylē geōmetrikē*, but also (since imagination can be affected and, as a special kind of matter, can embody form and formative principle) in taking imagination to be the "passive intellect" (*noys pathētikos*), introduced by Aristotle as the material component of thinking, informed by the active and productive intellect, *noys poiētikos* (see 3.4.5).[194]

In what follows, it will be shown that intelligible matter, as it appears in Plotinus, is also necessarily connected with the imagination. This would mean that geometry, as a science and as a practice (in particular, as the kinematic imaginary

---

[192] See Plato. RP 510d sqq.
[193] Syrianus. In Met. 85.4-5; Proclus. In Eucl. 55.6 sqq.; cp. Plato. RP. 511a-b. Morrow notes that Nikolai Hartmann "sees Proclus in this passage anticipating Descartes' analytic geometry" (Morrow 1992, 45; see Hartmann 1909, 35). But even if Descartes tries to reduce geometry to arithmetic (more precisely, to algebra, where signs may be substituted by numbers), he nevertheless does not get rid of the imagination but, on the contrary, introduces it even into the sphere of arithmetic, which in ancient mathematics is out of reach of the imagination.
[194] Aristotle. De an. 430a 10-25; Proclus. In Eucl. 52.3; 56.17-18; In RP II 107.14-29; In Tim. I 244.20-21; III 158.8-10 et al.; cp. Porphyry. Sent. 16; 43.

production of a geometrical figure, see 3.4.3), is grounded not only in discursive reason, but in the imagination as well.

Imaginable matter appears in the intellect's attempts to think that which cannot be properly thought, namely, the source of being and of thinking (cp. 2.4.1; 3.1.1). When (A) we attempt to think the One, as Plotinus has argued, we cannot think it otherwise than imagining it put into a certain place. This place cannot be real (for it is not yet defined, because the One is not yet definite for thinking, and place defines that of which, and for which, it is the place)[195] but it also cannot be altogether unreal (for, as intelligible extension or indefinite dyad, it represents pure, and yet undefined, thinking-*noēsis*, which constitutes being). It can therefore be only an *imaginary* place, an "as-if" place ("as-ifness" is also an important feature of intelligible matter). Since thinking about the primary source of being involves non-being, imagination is appropriate here, because it can embody (visualize or imagine) both being (thinking thinking its own source) and non-being (the beyond-being). All things other than the One or the good—primarily intelligible objects-*noēta*—"are satisfied with themselves by their participation in or imagination of the Good".[196] Participation-*metoysia* in the good or the One may be considered then as providing form-*noēton*, while intelligible matter comes in as *phantasia*, as a kind of imaginary place.

Next, (B) this imaginable place can be characterized in the same terms as Plato's *khōra*—as the sheer possibility of the embodiment of a physical thing.[197] This imaginary "place", however, primarily belongs not to the physical but to the noetic realm, and so is not merely a privative non-being, but also somehow represents being. Furthermore, (C) the imaginary "place" of the beyond-being (of the One) is not a place in a proper sense, but only an "as-if" place. But since place is distinct from that of which it is the place, conceiving the One as if in a place already presupposes duality. Imaginary place can first be considered as the place for extended non-physical, or geometrical, entities. This place can be then taken as quasi-spatial, as a *plenum* in which continuous, divisible and extended objects can be embodied. This imaginary place is close in its characteristics (which are vague and improperly defined) to Plato's *khōra* and thus also to matter, which has no proper notion (1.1.2). This imaginary place, however, is only a possibility or pure potentiality of extension; it is the material component of a geometrical object, as it were. As Plotinus argues, matter as such "is not contained in the definition of the three-dimensionality, nor three-dimensionality in the definition of matter".[198] Empty space is not extension (neither should it necessarily be extended), but the extended may be put into space as an empty and non-qualified receptacle. A scientific theory of place, which becomes space in modern science, becomes possible only when the imaginary "as-if" status of the receptacle is abandoned, so that the space is considered already intrinsically measured, the real space of and for being.[199] The other, complementary formal component that constitutes the

---

[195] Cp. Aristotle. Phys. 209b 1 sqq.
[196] Plotinus. Enn. VI.8.13.46.
[197] Plato. Tim. 52a.
[198] Plotinus. Enn. VI.1.26.24-25; cp. VI.27.36.51.
[199] See: Nikulin 1993.

particular identity of a geometrical object, measurable and extended (i.e., one-, two- or three-dimensional), is the ideal form, the *noēton*.

Imaginary place is then the *locus* where forms or intelligible objects may be considered embodied and apprehended as extended without really being extended. Such place is not anything that might have an essence or might be a substance; it is only a capacity to acquire form which, however different, is both present in bodily spatiality and in imaginary quasi-spatiality. The imaginary extension is not in any way organized: it is, as Armstrong notes, close to chaos, which Plotinus takes, "as Aristotle does, as the empty space or place which things occupy".[200] Alexander's interpretation of intelligible matter as *diastasis* (2.4) also suggests a striking similarity between imagination and *hylē noētē*.

(D) The ambiguity of imagination, which makes Plotinus acknowledge two *phantasias* (see 3.2.2), parallels the distinction between intelligible and bodily matter. Finally, the ability to retain images within the imagination and to visualize them as quasi-extended is connected with the faculty of memory, which represents that very perception in the form of a remembrance or a retained image.[201] In the case of a geometrical figure, it is, however, both memory and discursive reasoning that are involved in the apprehension of an image provided by perception, since the faculty of imagination is itself involved in the operation of discursive reasoning.[202]

As we have seen, even the intellect is not free from a certain— intelligible—materiality, exemplified through the initial indefiniteness, *aoristos dyas*, of the not yet defined thinking-*noēsis*, which intends to think its own origin. An analysis of the features of imagination—its creativity, its intermediate position between the sensual and the thinkable, its connection with inalienable irrationality and its quasi-spatial character—may now unveil the relation of intelligible matter to imagination. Indeed, all of the above-mentioned features of the imagination are equally applicable to intelligible matter as well.

First of all, one might ascribe a certain creativity to intelligible matter, insofar as indefinite thinking *qua aoristos dyas*, in its striving towards the source of being, brings forth the (finite, according to Plotinus) multitude of forms. The One is beyond any possible representation, however, and the dyad, as mere potentiality of being, is undefined. The creativity of intelligible matter is then only illusory or imaginary. Imagination creates its objects within itself, but only *as if*, because it makes visualizable—as *phantasmata*—that which already *is* as an object of thinking. Second, irrationality is also found in intelligible matter, because, as primary indefinite potency, *hylē noētē* is alogical before it is determined in concrete noetic forms. Third, intelligible matter is also intermediary—it is "in between" pure being (noetic forms) and mere non-being (bodily matter). And last, intelligible matter is "plenum" and *khōra* as an empty, not a definite "place" for the embodiment of intelligible objects-*noēta* and geometrical figures.

In other words, imagination and intelligible matter have much in common. Such a conclusion is supported by a passage from the treatise "On the

---

[200] Plotinus. *Enneads* VII, 1988, 262-263. Cp. Hesiod. Theog. 116; Aristotle. Phys. 208b 31-33.
[201] Plotinus. Enn. IV.3.25 sqq; esp. IV.3.29.26-28.
[202] Cp. Aristotle. De an. 431a 17; Themistius. In de an., ad. loc.

Part III: Reason, Imagination and Construction 187

Impassibility of Things Without Body" (Enn. III.6), where Plotinus speaks about imagination as matter to the soul: "in the soul the mental picture (*eidōlon*) is imagination, while the nature of the soul is not phatasmal [i.e. not of the nature of the image, *oyk eidōloy*]; and although the imagination in many ways seems to lead the soul and take it wherever it wants to, the soul none the less uses it as if it [the imagination] was matter or something like it (*analogon*)."²⁰³ Imagination is thus located between the intelligible and the bodily. Similar to intelligible matter, imagination acquires and embodies images. At the same time, this similarity does not yet make both identical, because *hylē noētē* represents the fundamental otherness within thinking-*noēsis*—it represents *noēsis* as indefinite—while the imagination is secondary to *noys*, only reflecting *noys* and imitating the *noēsis* in its thinking of the *noēta* in a visualizable, or inadequate, form.

3.3 Imagination in Descartes

It is not easy to establish a univocal sense in which Descartes uses the notion of imagination. He does not elaborate any single consistent theory of imagination. Moreover, his treatment of imagination appears to be different in different writings, which is why Descartes' considerations of imagination need interpretation. In the "Discourse", Descartes defines imagination by its activity and by its object, as a specific "way of thinking specially suited to material things".²⁰⁴ In the "Meditations", he presents imagination as an ability to visualize inwardly, to contemplate, to adequately grasp "the shape or image of a corporeal thing" and "an application of the cognitive faculty to a body that is intimately present to it".²⁰⁵ The activity of imagination consists in the apprehension, perception, copying and formation of images of corporeal figures; these figures can be both physical things and geometrical figures, since they are not different in the way they are present to the imagination. In a more narrow sense, imagination is involved in the process of transmitting and submitting sensory perceptions to the mind. The scheme of this process is appropriated by Descartes from Aristotle: sense-data are transmitted to, and coordinated in, the "common sense" and are further interpreted by imagination.²⁰⁶ Imagination is thus a faculty or a mode of thinking involved in

---

²⁰³ Plotinus. Enn. III.6.15.16-22.
²⁰⁴ Descartes. Disc. IV, AT VI 37. See also: Roy 1944. Klein argues that Descartes' concept of imagination is Stoic in origin. - Klein 1968, 198-199.
²⁰⁵ "...*Nihil aliud est imaginari quàm rei corporeae figuram, seu imaginem, contemplari.*" - Descartes. Med. II, AT VII 28; Med. VI, AT VII 71-72; To Mersenne, 25 December 1639, AT II 622. Cp. Williams 1973, 26-45.
²⁰⁶ Cp. Aristotle. De an. 425a 13-b 11; 427b 11 sqq. See Gilson 1979, 137-140. In Aristotle the notion of "common sense" (*aisthēsis koinē, sensus communis*) is mentioned only a few times (De an. 425a 27; De mem. 450a 10; Part. anim. 686a 31; cp. De somno 454b 25-27; De an. 426b 12 sqq. and Themistius. In de an. 84.35 sqq.) and designates the common nature, which is inherent in all particular senses but exemplified differently in them. Due to the *sensus communis*, one is able to perceive the so-called "common sensibles" (size, number, unity, duration, rest and movement); to perceive "incidental sensibles" (De an. 418a 21, e.g.: "the white thing's being the son of Diares"); to perceive that one perceives; to

processing images of extended things.[207]

What is the relation of imagination to corporeal substance? On the one hand, imagination appears to belong properly to the mind as one of its modes, which allows for conception of the corporeal (although imagination does not have a special organ). Imagination appears then to be a part of thinking-cogitation, which in a restricted sense may be taken as sensory perception (in this sense, *sentire* is nothing else but *cogitare*).[208] As Descartes writes to Gibieuf of 1642, "I do not see any difficulty in understanding on the one hand that the faculties of imagination and sensation belong to the soul, because they are species of thoughts, and on the other hand that they belong to the soul only in so far as it is joined to the body, because they are kinds of thoughts without which one can conceive the soul in all its purity."[209] Imagination is thus present to the finite mind because it is connected to the body: imagination is "proper" to humans yet it belongs to the mind not as thinking, but rather as embodied. In a sense, it is a *sui generis* purpose of imagination to represent the corporeal and the extended to the not extended. Because of that, although imagination, on the account of the "Meditations", belongs to the mind and cannot be understood without it, the mind as a thinking thing has to be understood without and besides the imagination. The power of imagining (*vis imaginandi*) differs from the power of understanding (*vis intelligendi*) and does not constitute human essence (as the finite thinking substance).[210] The (subjective) finite mind, the "I", is thus not imagination. Since, however, it is the imagination (now taken as a mental capacity) that helps the finite mind to get rid of the body and then of the imagination itself, such a reduction itself becomes possible only because of the imagination. I am therefore defined by imagination; in a sense, negatively I *am* imagination. "What else am I?" asks Descartes, "I will use my imagination".[211] In other words, in order to show that imagination does not belong to my essence, I have to use that very imagination. Therefore, it is primarily imagination that has the power of self-negation. Such a conclusion is in agreement with Descartes' essentialism, for it is easier to say *what* I am (or, negatively, what I am *not*) than to establish an existential or ontological status of the I *am*.

On the other hand, imagination appears to be connected not only to the mental but also immersed in the corporeal, because imagination conceives corporeal images—images of extended things—and further brings them to the

---

discern between the objects of two senses; and to give an account of why senses are all inactive at the same time during sleep (cp. Ross 1949, 139-142).

[207] Cp. Tye 1991, 33-60.
[208] Descartes. Med. VI AT VII 29.
[209] Descartes. To Gibieuf, 19 January 1642, AT III 479. Since an idea is taken by Descartes to be a mental image of whatever kind, he has to stress specifically in his objection to Gassendi: "you restrict the term 'idea' to images in the imagination, whereas I extend it to cover any object of thought" .- Descartes. Fifth Set of Replies, AT VI 366. Cp. Roy 1944, 9-55; Williams 1978, 231; Cottingham 1986, 126; Sepper 1996, 253-254.
[210] Descartes. Med. VI AT VII 73, 78.
[211] In the French edition of the "Meditations" it is also added to this place: "to see if I am something more" .- Med. II, AT VII 27.

consideration of the discursive faculty of the mind-reason. This is why Descartes distinguishes between *imaginatio (facultas imaginandi)* as mental imagination, and *phantasia* as corporeal imagination (although he still finds it difficult to explain in general the connection and the interaction between the extended and the non-extended). Corporeal imagination is "a genuine part of the body" and represents corporeal images (corporeal ideas, which are physiological events), which, being extended and thus material, are not ideas properly. The mental imagination is a faculty of the mind that acts on images of the corporeal imagination and produces non-extended images submitted to the discursive mind-reason, already capable of thinking ideas without images.[212]

Among the early notes of Descartes preserved by Leibniz, we find a brief one, stating that "just as imagination employs figures to conceive of bodies, so, in order to frame ideas of spiritual things, the intellect makes use of certain bodies which are perceived through the senses...".[213] This statement should not be overemphasized; Descartes does not develop it in other texts.[214] Still, it clearly suggests that, on the one hand, the imagination as corporeal connects bodies to figures, by which one can reliably understand geometrical figures. On the other hand, intellect as *ingenium* is taken to include the mental imagination, connecting bodies, or rather their images, to the *spiritualia*-ideas. What arises here is the question (discussed in 3.3.1) of how we should understand the ontological status of geometrical objects and their relation to bodies, mental entities and the mental imagination.

If imagination primarily aims at representing the corporeal, as well as the possible affections connected to it, and there is a further distinction between mental and corporeal imagination, then how does the mind-reason conceive of the corporeal (extended or material) through imagination? First of all, in the "Regulae" corporeal imagination-*phantasia* is portrayed, "along with the ideas existing in it, as being nothing but a *real body* with a *real extension* and shape".[215] On the account of the "Treatise on Man", imagination as corporeal is located, together

---

[212] Cp. Descartes. Reg. XII, AT X 414; Med. IV, AT VII 57; Second Set of Replies, AT VII 160-161; Third Set of Replies, AT VII 181. The distinction between *imaginatio* and *phantasia* is supported by Fóti and Sepper against Marion (see: Fóti 1986, 635; Sepper 1989, 387-389; Sepper 1996, 272, 402). Marion argues that imagination in Descartes may be understood "de manière purement mécanique", because images-*phantasmata* are spatially transmitted.- Marion 1981, 124-126. On the notion of corporeal ideas, which Descartes uses in his earlier works to denote corporeal sense-impressions, see: E. Michael; F. S. Michael 1989, 33 sqq.

[213] "*Vt imaginatio vtitur figuris ad corpora concipienda, ita intellectus vtitur quibusdam corporibus sensibilibus ad spiritualia figuranda...*" - Descartes. Cogitationes Privatae, AT X 217. Cp. Fóti 1986, 632-633; Sepper 1989, 381; Sepper 1996, 46 sqq.

[214] From this note Sepper deduces a hierarchy of geometrical figures-bodies-spiritual entities (Sepper 1996, 117-118). Nothing in Descartes' other writings, however, suggests that physical bodies might be conceived in any way intermediate between physical and mental objects.

[215] Descartes. Reg. XIV, AT X 441, italics added; cp. Comments on a Certain Broadsheet, AT VIIIB 364. As Joachim puts it, "the *phantasia* is a genuine part of the body and *phantasmata* are bodily changes in it." - Joachim 1957, 23.

with common sense, in the brain, in the pineal gland. Unlike the intellectual or mental imagination (which forms non-corporeal, and thus not extended, images of extended things that further allow the mind-reason to recognize or to form the corresponding ideas), the corporeal imagination operates within corporeal images or phantasms, which serve as the material for further recognition and interpretation by the mental imagination.[216]

Corporeal images, also called corporeal forms or figures, are indispensable to the discursive mind in understanding the extended. Corporeal forms for Descartes are "not only things which somehow represent the position of the edges and surfaces of objects, but also anything which…can give soul occasion to perceive movement, size, distance, colors, sounds, smells and other such qualities".[217] As Descartes also explains to Gassendi, "the powers of understanding and imagining do not differ merely in degree but are two quite different kinds of mental operation. For in understanding the mind employs only itself, while in imagination it contemplates a corporeal form".[218]

But is the mind-reason able to apprehend ideas without images? The earlier Descartes is not always unambiguous in his use of the term "idea", as we see, for example, in his reference to "the simple ideas in the human imagination out of which all human thoughts are compounded".[219] In the "Regulae", however, he uses the notion of "idea" in a more restricted sense, referring to the content of the corporeal imagination, an image or a "look" of a corporeal thing.[220] Later, in the "Meditations", Descartes suggests that even if the mind-reason thinks of spiritual things—such as the ideas of substance and of God—without images, the ideas of extended material things are accompanied by images, although not corporeal but mental (cp. 3.1.4).[221] Thus, in the "Meditations" we find a succession of, first, the extended corporeal images or forms of the corporeal imagination, which are figures and represent an extended object, projected from the external sense organs and from inner parts of the brain onto the surface of the pineal gland, that part of the body where corporeal is transmitted, affects and is affected by the mental (this affection is mutual).[222] Second come the images of mental imagination, which are formed according to corporeal images (in fact, Descartes does not exclude a possibility of forming the corporeal images under the pattern of

---

[216] See: Beck 1952, 219; Sepper 1996, 272.
[217] Descartes. Treatise on Man, AT XI 176; cp. Ibid., 202.
[218] Descartes. Fifth Set of Replies, AT VII 385.
[219] Descartes. To Mersenne, 18 December 1629, AT I 81.
[220] Sepper even argues that in Descartes there is no thinking without phantasms. This might be true only in Descartes' earlier writings, e.g. in the "Regulae" where, as Sepper himself recognizes, the mind-reason (intellect) and imagination operate yet in concord, whereas in the "Meditations" there is a sharp divide between the two. - Sepper 1996, 7, 97, 242, 245, 266. Cp. Kenny 1987, 106-107.
[221] Descartes. Second Set of Replies, AT VII 139; cp. Ibid., AT VII 160-161; Med. III, AT VII 37; "…by 'idea' I do not just mean the images depicted in the [corporeal] imagination (*fantaisie*); indeed, in so far as these images are in the corporeal imagination, I do not use that term for them at all". - To Mersenne, July 1641, AT III 392. Cp. also: Princ. I 73, AT VIIIA 37.
[222] Descartes. Reg. XII, AT X 415.

mental images). And, third, there are the ideas of the mind-reason, in terms of which the mind interprets and understands figures (both physical and geometrical) and which correspond not to corporeal but to mental images, because ideas have no affinity to extended corporeal images. The images of mental imagination act as if they are playing the role of intermediary between images of the corporeal imagination and ideas of the mind—but only *as if*, since images of mental imagination are in no way ontologically commensurable with those of the corporeal imagination.[223] The corporeal and the mental are still separated from each other and the mechanism of their interaction—in particular, of the corporeal and the mental imagination—is neither clearly explained, nor firmly established, because the communication between mind and body amounts in Descartes to the unresolved problem of embodiment and interaction of the spiritual and the corporeal.

Historical development and changes in the Cartesian understanding of the notion of imagination are traced in a detailed and comprehensive study by Sepper. According to him, Descartes does not use the notion of *imaginatio* in any special technical sense in his early writings (between 1618 and 1621, mostly scattered through a number of brief notes, for example in "Cogitationes privatae" and "Musicae Compendium"), even if it is of central importance. Instead, he uses the notion of imagination to refer to various processes of visualizing and constructing (including auditory synthesizing): for example, the division of a continuous magnitude, the bringing of parts of a song into a unity, the visualization of geometrical constructions, and so on.[224] Mental imagination is taken here as belonging to the cognitive power and is primarily discursive, involved in the discovery of propositions and in the consideration of order and proportions, or in visualizing processes of geometric construction. Later in the "Regulae"—where imagination is portrayed as belonging to the mind-*ingenium*—Descartes, partly under the influence of Beeckman, presents imagination as figurative, applicable to recognition and to the conception of images of memory, of geometrical figures (taken, at the end of the "Regulae", to be of the dimension not higher than two), and of corporeal images involved in geometrical algebra. The consecutive diminution of the cognitive role of imagination in Descartes' later works (particularly in the "Meditations") characterizes a shift in the Cartesian understanding of imagination. As Sepper argues, imagination is initially split into bodily (image-making) and mental or intellectual (poetic-cognitive), of which the latter is further considered two-fold: as producing and conceiving mathematical images of corporeal things (assigned partly to the body and partly to the intellect), and as cognizing in the intellectual synthesis of thinking. Beginning with 1637, any uniform and unique theory of imagination can hardly be traced. There is a sharper distinction and dissociation between an image of a figure present in a sense-organ and in the corporeal imagination and the idea of that figure in the mind. An

---

[223] Due to the non-distinction of corporeal and mental imagination, Gaukroger's attempt to portray imagination in Descartes as intermediate between the intellect (reason) and the corporeal world (imagination is to represent then abstract algebraic entities as geometrical magnitudes) is unconvincing. - Gaukroger 1992, 109-111.
[224] Descartes. Compendium Musicae, AT X 89 sqq.

inability to explain neither infinity nor the physiology of perception (both appear to be beyond the representative capacity of imagination) illustrates some problems now encountered by Descartes' earlier account of the imagination. Moreover, the mental imagination of the "Passions" seems to be driven more by the will than by the mind-intellect. Imaginings appear here among the perceptions of the soul dependent mostly on the activity of volition. Thus, the development of the notion of imagination in Descartes appears to be from the *imaginatio* of the "Regulae"—as a hypostasis of the *vis cognoscens* involved in discursive apprehension of proportional relations—to the *facultas* opposed to, and separate from, the intellect (in the "Meditations"), active and spontaneous under the guise of volition.[225]

In what follows, we will concentrate on a discussion of the Cartesian treatment of imagination without focusing on the changes in Descartes' understanding of imagination throughout his writings. Our primary interests are the ontological status of imagination; the possibility of it being intermediate; its relation to infinity; and its connection to geometrical objects. Concerning the last case, we will also discuss the difference between corporeal and geometrical representation in corporeal and mental imagination, and the way in which the imagination relates the geometrical to the physical.

3.3.1 Mind, imagination and the infinite

Imagination is thus twofold for Descartes, appearing as mental and corporeal.[226] In order to explain different mental faculties in a univocal manner, in the "Regulae"—where mind is taken as *ingenium*—Descartes further introduces a notion of cognitive power, *vis cognoscens*. This "power is sometimes passive,

---

[225] Sepper 1989, 382-383, 397-401; Sepper 1996, 6, 28-46, 102-113, 208, 244, 254, 276 et al.; see also: Fóti 1986, 635, 641-642. Sepper is reluctant, however, to draw conclusions about any possible immanent logic of development of the Cartesian notion of imagination, mostly providing factual descriptions and their possible interpretations, while Fóti stresses the partiality and incompleteness of such development. Cp. A. White 1990, 20-24; Gaukroger 1995, 124. Descartes. Passions I 19-20, AT XI 343-344.

[226] Similarly, memory also appears to be distinguished into mental and corporeal: on the one hand, memory (placed by Descartes in the pineal gland or *conarium*) is a corporeal capacity of keeping and preserving corporeal images of past events, although not all of them, for many are lost (To Mersenne, 1 April 1640, AT III 47). These images are of the same nature as the images of imagination and are stored in the "folds" of the brain, which "are not unlike the folds which remain in this paper after it has once been folded" (To Meyssonnier, 29 January 1640, AT III 20; cp. To Mersenne, 11 June 1640, AT III 84; 6 August 1640, AT III 143-144). Memory preserves images of external objects, as well as ideas of internal passions, which come from the "common sense" (Treatise on Man, AT XI 177-178; Discourse V, AT VI 55). But on the other hand, as in the case with imagination, Descartes has to recognize memory also as a mental capacity: "As for memory, I think that the memory of material things depends on the traces which remain in the brain after an image has been imprinted on it; and that memory of intellectual things depends on some other traces which remain in the mind itself". - Descartes. To [Mesland], 2 May 1644, AT IV 114; cp. To [Arnauld], 4 June 1649, AT V 192-193.

sometimes active; sometimes resembling the seal, sometimes the wax...It is one and the same power: when applying itself along with imagination to the 'common' sense, it is said to see, touch etc.; when addressing itself to the imagination alone, in so far as the latter is invested with various figures (*figuris*), it is said to remember; when applying itself to the imagination in order to form new figures, it is said to imagine or conceive (*imaginari vel concipere*); and lastly, when it acts on its own, it is said to understand. ...According to its different functions, then, the same power is called either pure intellect, or imagination, or memory, or sense-perception".[227] An act of the mental imagination, which forms mental images, thus has to be understood as an application of one universal spiritual power to the corporeal imagination, where extended figures are located.

Cognitive power is not really different from thought—Descartes stresses its incorporeality (*neque enim in rebus corporeis aliquid omnino huic simile invenitur*). Cognitive power thinks or understands only when acting by itself. But then it is hard to draw a real distinction between cognitive power and the mind-*ingenium*. Cognitive power has to be taken rather as a unique determinant in, and of, cognition, different from the other faculties—such as sense-perception, memory and imagination, which are thus the determined. Consequently, reason as cognitive power should be, on the one hand, different from the other three faculties, because it assumes different "functions" in these faculties. Yet on the other hand, reason also cannot differ from them, because it is in these "functions" that this same mind, as cognitive power, is variously represented as referring to the body (in particular, as corporeal imagination), displaying itself either as reason properly, or as imagination, memory, or the senses. Obviously, Descartes' intention is to explain, or rather deduce, various faculties involved in cognition from one single simple (and not yet differentiated) thinking as applied to the *sensus communis*, to the corporeal imagination and to itself, operating "on its own". Only in the latter case the mind-*ingenium* is the mind *simpliciter*, whereas in the operation of all the other faculties—sensation, memory and imagination—the corporeal imagination is essentially involved as the material aspect of these faculties or mental capacities. Descartes does not abandon this position even later, portraying imagination as one of the different modes of thinking, *façons de penser*, together with understanding, willing and sensation (*vouloir, entendre, imaginer, sentir*), and arguing in the "Principles" that together with sensation and will, imagination is intelligible only in the mind.[228]

What is the relation between the mind as reason, and mental imagination? First of all, they have to be firmly separated: even if the imagination may be considered a *façon de penser*, it is to be strictly distinguished from the mind as reason in the proper sense, *intellectio ab imaginatione secernitur*.[229] Why? Because even if reason and imagination may affect each other, the mind-reason thinks, whereas the imagination depicts.[230] Mental imagination, a faculty of the mind, is

---

[227] Descartes. Reg. XII, AT X 415-416.
[228] Descartes. To Mersenne, end of May 1637, AT I 366; Princ. I 53, AT VIIIA 25.
[229] Descartes. Med. Synopsis, AT VII 15.
[230] "*Nam cum intellectus moveri possit ab imaginatione, vel contra agere in illam*". - Descartes. Reg. XII, AT X 416.

responsible for transforming corporeal images of the corporeal imagination into mental images, representing the former for being further processed in the ideas by reason. It is only by reason that the mind can know that extension exists and that it is an extended substance, but extension in its representation can be pictured only in, and by, the imagination. Reason can think (in particular, can think itself) by referring to images, but it can also think and understand *without* them (which is especially stressed in the "Meditations"). Reason is therefore to be considered superior to the imagination. Because imagination primarily refers to the corporeal, it may assist reason when representing the extended—the corporeal and the mathematical—but impedes reason when it is thinking about the not extended.[231]

A major difference between reason and mental imagination is that imagination can represent images that do not exist in reality.[232] Imagination hides and clothes thought with visual and visualizable shapes, as if veiling the understanding in, and by, innumerable bodily images.[233] And even if the objects of imagination may be considered not real, the imagination itself still cannot be considered not real. Imagination represents negativity in picturing the not real and thus may embody the "falsehood and uncertainty" and become an obstacle for truth, and therefore has to be eliminated or suspended even as mental.[234] In the "Meditations", where Descartes seems to be preoccupied with the necessity to delimit imagination and describe it more closely, he argues that through introspection ("I find in myself", *invenio in me*) one has to recognize the faculty of imagination, together with sense-perception (*facultates imaginandi et sentiendi*), as "special modes of cogitation" (*modis cogitandi*). As Descartes explains to Burman, imagination is thus considered parallel to sensation but is different from sensation in that in sense-perception images are imprinted by external objects, whereas in the imagination they are imprinted by the mind itself without the presence of external

---

[231] Cp. Descartes. Reg. XIV, AT X 440-441.

[232] Descartes. To Elizabeth, May or June 1645, AT IV 218-219.

[233] Descartes. [To Silhon], March or April 1648, AT V 137. In his early notes Descartes claims that truth is more accessible to poets through imagination: "It may seem surprising to find weighty judgements in the writings of the poets rather than the philosophers. The reason is that the poets were driven to write by enthusiasm and the force of imagination. We have within us the sparks of knowledge, as in a flint: philosophers extract them through reason (*ratio*), but poets force them out through the sharp blows of the imagination, so that they shine more brightly". - Descartes. Cogitationes Privatae, AT X 217. The difference between reason and imagination is, however, already recognized and established.

[234] Although it is not imagination, but reason *qua* judgement that is primarily responsible for error. In the "Meditations" and the "Principles" it is will that is the primary source and cause of error through non-coincidence of the scope of will implied in the judgement with the scope of reason. This happens because the will can easily extend onto that which is not clearly perceived—it is will that is primarily infinite or, rather, indefinite—and thus can cause error. - Descartes. To Mersenne, 27 February 1637, AT I 350; The Search for Truth, AT X 508; Reg. XIV 442-444; Med. IV, AT VII 56-58; Princ. I 34-35, AT VIIIA 18. Cp.: imagination which is "the part of the mind that most helps mathematics, is more of a hindrance than a help in metaphysical speculation". - Descartes. To Mersenne, 25 December 1639, AT II 622.

objects.[235] Does this mean that imagination is only reproductive, or may it also be considered productive? Later in the "Principles", the will begins to play a much more important role as an active principle in cognition, whereas understanding, imagination and sense-perception are presented as passive perceptions of the intellect. Here Descartes appears to introduce just another dichotomy within the imagination: not only mental/ corporeal, but also mental/ volitional imagination. In the latter distinction, imagination as a mode of perception in a broader sense appears to be receptive and reproductive, whereas imagination linked to the acts of will is active—spontaneous and productive.[236]

As it has been stated, imagination cannot be understood outside of the cognitive activity of the mind-reason, but reason can be understood without imagination. Reason, as pure intellection, is opposed to imagination and sense-perception, insofar as intellection is independent of the body.[237] Moreover, reason is able to think that which imagination cannot represent. The preservation of a clear image in the imagination requires a peculiar *effort* (*contentio*), which may be above the capacity of the imagination—an effort not required for discursive understanding.[238] This constitutes another major difference between mind as *intellectio pura* and mental *imaginatio*. Imagination is thus limited cognitively but not productively, since it may always imagine a magnitude bigger and larger than the one given.

A further important distinction between mind-reason and mental imagination is exemplified in sleeping: when "we are asleep and are aware that we are dreaming, we need imagination in order to dream, but to be aware that we are dreaming we need only the intellect".[239] Reason is thus always aware of something. In particular, reason is aware of itself and of its present state, which means that reason is fundamentally reflective, whereas the imagination is not: every act of thinking and of thinking something is, and always has to be, accompanied by the awareness of thinking. On the contrary, in an act of imagining, the imagination should not necessarily be aware of imagining; moreover, it is reason that can assure such an awareness. And even when in the later works of Descartes the will assumes the role of the leading active mental faculty, it is reason that is aware of willing. Every act of will is always necessarily accompanied by rational perception—by the understanding of the fact of willing—and thus it is still the mind-reason that is primarily reflective.[240]

Escaping ambiguity, according to Funkenstein, appears to be one of the major intentions of early modern science and philosophy, which aspire to present most complex problems in an understandable fashion, to assist others in using the

---

[235] Descartes. Med. VI, AT VII 78; Conversation with Burman, AT V 162-163; cp. Princ. I 32, AT VIIIA 17.
[236] Descartes. Princ. I 32-33, AT VIIIA 17-18; cp. Med. IV, AT VII 56-57.
[237] Cp. Rozemond 1993, 97-114.
[238] Cp. Descartes. Med. VI, AT VII 72 and the discussion of the impossibility of imagining the chiliagon in what follows.
[239] Descartes. Fifth Set of Replies, AT VII 358-359.
[240] "For it is certain that we cannot will anything without thereby perceiving that we are willing it." - Descartes. Passions I 19, AT XI 343.

faculty of reason (cp. 2.2), and to avoid ambiguous perceptions and thoughts.[241] In Plotinus imagination is marked by profound ambiguity (3.2.2). But Descartes too cannot altogether escape ambiguity in his treatment of imagination, which appears as both corporeal and as mental, as the image-making power.[242]

The Cartesian mind is fundamentally discursive. It moves from one single clear idea to another, and in this way arrives at a propositional truth that may not be immediately self-evident. The discursive mind grasps the truth of such axiomatic statements as "the whole is greater than its part" or "if equal magnitudes are added to the equals, the result is equal". The mental activity that appears to be reflective may be, however, either discursive or non-discursive. Discursive reflectivity is that of the discursive mind, and non-discursive reflectivity is that involved in one single act of thinking. In Descartes such an act may further be either the act of *cogito* or the immediate clear understanding of an idea—the idea that can also be visualized in and by the corporeal imagination and then conceived by the mental imagination. In the act of *cogito*, the mind is immediately aware of itself without any image. The mind thus can think itself in the pure awareness of *cogito*. But imagination is not immediately reflective, for it cannot imagine itself. On the contrary, the imagination can imagine itself only in and through an object of imagination—i.e., itself imagining an image, but not itself as a capacity of imagining. In other words, imagination is not reflective for Descartes, which constitutes another important distinction between understanding and imagination. Here, however, Descartes agrees with Aristotle and the Neoplatonists, for whom imagination is not reflective either: reflectivity is the privilege of the intellect-*noys* only. The crucial point of difference is that for Plotinus and the Neoplatonic philosophers, imagination is a border faculty; it is "between" senses and thinking, reflecting both but itself lacking the gift of reflectivity due to the irrationality and negativity involved in imagination (3.2.2; 3.2.3). In a sense, for Descartes imagination may be also considered a medium of representation for the intellect and a power standing between sense-perception and understanding.[243] But even then imagination is not really a border faculty because, first, Descartes reserves the possibility of thinking without images of imagination and, second, imagination in Descartes is split into corporeal and mental without a clear elucidation of the

---

[241] Funkenstein 1986, 28 sqq. Cp. Owens 1963, 111 sqq.

[242] There also is a certain ambiguity in the fact that—unlike in Aristotle, for whom imagination is proper to most animals (De an. 428a 9-11)—for Descartes imagination is not present in animals (To Gibieuf, 19 January 1642, AT III 479); animals are not supposed to have souls. However, on another occasion Descartes does ascribe imagination to them, as in the experiment with a hen: drawing lines right in front of its eyes prevents the activity of hen's imagination to such an extent that it becomes immobile (To Mersenne, 2 November 1646, AT IV 555).

[243] Cp. Fóti 1986, 636; Sepper 1996, 2, 119-120. An interesting problem raised by Sepper is whether the activity of imagination may take place without the objects of imagination. Since imagination is not reflective, it cannot have an immediate awareness of itself without images, whereas reason knows itself primarily in an act of reflective thinking. Therefore, reason does not appear to be able to notice the activity of the mental imagination in the absence of the objects of imagination.

Part III: Reason, Imagination and Construction 197

mechanism of their interaction.

The essence of a thing is accessible to reason alone and not to the mental imagination, as Descartes argues in the Second "Meditation": in a piece of wax the imagination may only vaguely grasp an "immeasurable number" of different figures and shapes possibly implemented in that piece, or even produced by the imagination itself.[244] Why is this the case? Descartes argues that the potentially infinite number of possible figures contained in a piece of wax cannot possibly be clearly discernible all at once; they cannot be visualizable by the imagination, which can represent only a finite number of features within an object or a finite number of objects. Since any piece of extension can assume an indefinitely great number of forms and the imagination is unable to grasp the infinite, *infini*, then extension in general can be imagined only vaguely (or only in the simplest cases, when an extended piece has small number of visualizable features). The nature or essence of extension, as it has already been pointed out, can only be thought: "bodies are not strictly perceived by the senses or the faculty of imagination but by intellect alone, and...this perception derives not from their being touched or seen but from their being understood".[245] Extension can be easily perceived by the imagination, but the imagination is unable to represent extension as such. Imagination can only display a particular species of magnitude, not "in isolation from subjects" (from shaped figures), but only extension or magnitude *in concrete*—as limited, and thus as specifically determined.[246] In examining a body, reason can only be supported by the evidence of imagination.[247] Since imagination does not reveal (it rather conceals) the essence of the extended, the imaginable visualization of an extended—physical or geometrical—body does not yet prove anything about it, for the strict proof is reserved for reason alone, although imagination may provide useful support and evidence for reason (for example, in a geometrical proof). This means that extended entities, both physical and geometrical, are represented equally and in the same imagination, and are to be further reduced to their non-imaginable form in the mind as reason. Descartes insists that knowledge arises only when the mind is separated and freed from the imagination, that understanding and imagination are not to be confused, and that "the powers of understanding and imagining do not differ merely in degree but are two quite different kinds of mental operation. For in understanding, the mind employs only itself, while in imagination it contemplates a corporeal form".[248] Thus, since the essence of matter is extension, and extension can be represented in an infinite number of ways (and yet is the same extension), neither the infinite nor the extension can be known in their essence to the imagination, but to the mind alone.

Imagination thus does not "see" the true essence of a thing not only

---

[244] Descartes. Med. II, AT VII 30-31. Cp. Hobbes' and Gassendi's objections: Third Set of Objections, AT VII 178-179; Fifth Set of Objections, AT VII 272.
[245] Descartes. Med. II, AT VII 34; cp. Med. V, AT VII 63; Fifth Set of Objections, AT VII 267 and Optics VI, AT VI 132.
[246] Descartes. Reg. XIV, AT X 441-443.
[247] Descartes. Reg. XII, AT X 416-417.
[248] Descartes. Fifth Set of Replies, AT VII 365; cp. Med. III, AT VII 52-53.

because that essence is purely intelligible, but because imagination (both sensual and mental) cannot run through *all* the possible modifications (or modes) of it. Imagination fails to represent not only the infinite, but even the indefinite. Imagination differs from sense-perception insofar as the former is limited "from above" in its ability to clearly depict a large number of bodily features (for example, a thousand sides of a polygon or a great number of particles), whereas the latter is limited "from below", insofar as the senses fail to grasp the smallest particles of matter, which, as Descartes argues against Henry More, are imperceptible.[249]

Another distinction between the mind and the imagination is that only the mind has access to the infinite (although only to its existence, not its essence: in thinking that the actually infinite *is*, not *what* it is) and to the essence of two finite substances. Imagination, on the contrary, has no access to adequate understanding of either thought or matter, because it is unable to embrace the infinite (or even the indefinite) variety of possible modifications, and thus it is unable to grasp the essence of a substance. This cognitive opposition of reason to imagination is further illustrated by Descartes in the separation of an image of a material thing in imagination, an image that depicts a phenomenon as distinct from an idea in the mind-reason—the idea that depicts the essence of a thing.[250]

Of what kind is the distinction between the mind and the imagination—is it real, conceptual or modal? First, obviously there is a real distinction between (a) reason (as *res cogitans*) and corporeal imagination (as *res extensa*), which is a trivial case of the distinction between mind and body (brain). There is, however, no real distinction between (b) reason and mental imagination (which is a mode of the cognitive power), since both belong to the *ingenium* and thus to the *res cogitans*. Second, modal distinction is obviously applicable only in the case of (b), so that there is a modal distinction between the mind as reason properly and the mind as cognitive power operating as mental imagination (between two modes of cognitive power). Descartes compares imagination to seeing an image (of a geometrical figure or a body), while reason understands an image without any "seeing" of its shape. In particular, the modal distinction between reason and imagination (as a mode of cognitive power) consists in that the former is discursive, whereas the latter is not or may not be, for imagination is not only capable of the quasi-visual production of its object in a process, but also of visualizing its object as a whole in one single act. And finally, a conceptual distinction is not applicable in this case, since only reason, as thinking, is the substantial attribute, whereas imagination cannot be taken as an attribute.

As it has been pointed out, substance as such can be known for Descartes by reason only (1.4.2) and cannot be known by imagination. Since, further, God is *the* substance, he cannot be known by imagination, or, is unimaginable. Descartes by all means wants to escape the conclusion that the idea of God might be just imaginary, i.e., voluntarily invented by any productive faculty of the mind.[251] Since

---

[249] Descartes. To More, 5 February 1649, AT V 268.
[250] Descartes. Second Set of Replies, AT VII 139.
[251] Descartes. Fourth Set of Objections [of P. Petit], AT VII 206 sqq.; cp. To Mersenne, 27 May 1638, AT II 144.

God and the soul are purely intelligible, they cannot be objects that might correspond to images of the corporeal imagination.[252] When polemicizing with Descartes, Henry More introduces the doctrine of spiritual extension (an extension proper to God, angels and souls), trying to overcome the Cartesian dichotomy of the extended and the not extended, and substituting it with the dichotomy of the divisible (body) and the not divisible (thought).[253] Such a new distinction would make thinking imaginable, however, which is the reason why Descartes (for whom imagination *qua* corporeal is a hindrance to knowledge of truth) rejects More's hypothesis without hesitation: "God is not imaginable or distinguishable into parts that are measurable and have shape."[254] In regard to the divine, only feeling or "passion" can be imagined, which is ultimately a corporeal affection—that of love caused by attraction to the sublime.[255] Even the finite mind cannot understand *what* the infinite is in its perfections, because the mind cannot grasp and reproduce them as actually infinite. The actually infinite substance remains inaccessible to the imagination, which can only represent the indefinite expansion of an ever greater and greater perfection of the mind and of extension as *indéfini* (see 1.3.3).

Since, further, God is the thinking substance, everything corporeal and material should be alien to it: "We recognize", insists Descartes, "that God does not possess any corporeal imagination."[256] Corporeal imagination-*phantasia* thus can have no place in the infinite substance. But the supposed all-embracing divine intellect can also have no lack in perfection exercised in thinking and thus all faculties that may be discovered in thinking should be present in the infinite thinking as actually infinite, without being really distinct. Upon examining our finite mind we find, first, the faculty of imagination in ourselves; second, that this faculty is finite; and third, that the finite is the limitation of the infinite and not vice versa (cp. 1.3.2). Therefore, as Descartes concludes in the Fourth Meditation, there should exist an infinite mental imagination (and memory) in God, in the infinite mind,[257] which cannot be just a hypothetical projection of the finite mental imagination onto the infinite—but the infinite mental imagination should be a (ontological and epistemological) precondition for the possibility of the existence of the finite imagination.

An obvious problem that arises at this point is that the finite imagination implies a connection of the finite mind to the finite body. There is no body or extension present in the infinite mind, as Descartes argues against H. More, and therefore infinite imagination can only express the fact that there is an indefinite

---

[252] Descartes. Third Set of Replies, AT VII 183.
[253] See Nikulin 1993, 45-58.
[254] Descartes. To More, 5 February 1649, AT V 270-272. Cp.: "il n'y a rien en Dieu qui soit imaginable." - Descartes. To Chanut, 1 February 1647, AT IV 607.
[255] For Descartes, God arouses love and "although we cannot imagine anything in God, who is the object of our love, we can imagine our love itself, which consists in our wanting to unite ourselves with some object. That is, we can consider ourselves in relation to God as a minute part of all the immensity of the created universe". - Descartes. To Chanut, 1 February 1647, AT IV 609-610.
[256] Descartes. Third Set of Replies, AT VII 181.
[257] Descartes. Med. IV, AT VII 57.

extension that may be conceived in, and by, the infinite mind. In the finite mind the mental imagination may either interpret images of the corporeal imagination or produce images itself (for example, of geometrical figures) that are not corporeal and thus not extended. Obviously, in the infinite mind the first possibility is missing, since there is no corporeal imagination associated with it. This means that for Descartes the infinite mind can only know images of the corporeal (of the physical and geometrical) *not* as corporeal and extended (for, because of mutual complementarity and exclusion of the material and the mental, there is no way to represent corporeal images *qua* extended to the mind), but rather as produced, as thought without a corporeal image—not as described, but as prescribed for extended entities, thus constructed into the world of the *res extensa*.

The notion of infinity appears to be not only tightly interwoven into the ontological structures in Descartes (see 1.3.2; 1.3.3), but also involved in the differentiation of various faculties of the mind. Thus, in the "Principles" Descartes accepts two different modes of thinking: perception of the intellect and operation of the will. An important difference between intellect and will in the finite mind is that the former is limited, whereas the latter is not, for we can easily "extend our will beyond what we clearly perceive".[258] In the divine mind there are no real distinctions, hence one cannot suppose a real or even a modal difference between various faculties and mental operations within the infinite intellect; for example, between reasoning (where also knowing and grasping are not different) and willing in God—just as one cannot suppose such a difference between the divine infinite *omni*-attributes (cp. 1.3.2).[259]

If everything in the world is caused by the infinite substance, which is pure thinking, then also nothing can happen without the infinite will, because it is not really distinct from the infinite mind.[260] Only the divine will can be considered really infinite (*infini*) for Descartes, whereas the human will is only potentially infinite (*indefini*), always able, unlike the finite reason, to surpass any given limits or borders. It is in its ability to go beyond any limits that the will appears to be similar to imagination: imagination is the only mental ability or faculty that may operate at will. Not only physical things but also necessary truths are to be considered caused by the infinite mind-will, not because of their inner consistency or adequation to certain facts, but because God wills them as necessary (which is not the same as God necessarily willing them, for this would impose limitations on him: God is understood as actually infinite and destitute of any inner immanent limitations, cp. 1.3.4).[261] A problem then is whether necessary truths may be, or could have been, different from what they are, as known by the finite mind *qua* necessary. It appears that for Descartes the rule of modal logic, $\Box p = p$ (cp. 1.4.3), is valid only for the finite thinking that operates within the sphere of the *lumen naturale intelligibile*, where knowing is (or may be) different from grasping (cp. 1.3.3). However, in the case of the infinite intellect, where there is no real

---

[258] Descartes. Princ. I 35, AT VIIIA 18.
[259] Descartes. Princ. I 23, AT VIIIA 14.
[260] Cp. Descartes. To Elizabeth, 6 October 1645, AT IV 314; To [Mesland], 2 May 1644, AT IV 118-119.
[261] Descartes. To [Mesland], 2 May 1644, AT IV 118-119.

distinction between will and intellection, nothing prevents that physical, logical and mathematical truths be established (willed or thought) otherwise. As Descartes puts it, eternal truths "are possible only because God knows them as true or possible. They are not known as true by God in any way that would imply that they are true independently of him. ...In God willing and knowing are a single thing in such a way that by the very fact of willing something he knows it and it is only for this reason that such a thing is true".[262]

Still, due to its actual infinity, the divine intellect cannot be grasped (it can only be known that it *is*, not *what* it is) either by the finite mind or by the finite imagination.[263] One can therefore only affirm that if the finite mind understands something clearly, this very thing is possible for the infinite mind, because, as Descartes argues, everything that is clearly perceivable for the finite mind is possible for God, that is, it may be created by him (see 1.4.3). The possibility of being true is expressed then as "it cannot be thought otherwise" (e.g., that 2+2=4), or through a logical necessity linked to the sphere of finite essence, that is, the essence that does not necessarily presuppose or include existence. The situation changes once no real distinction between essence and existence can be made, such as in the actually infinite. Here, first, mere logical consistency (as presented to the finite mind) implies real being or existence (as included in the infinite essence). Second, if the finite mind does not understand a thing (especially, if it does not grasp that thing), this does not yet mean that this thing is impossible for the infinite thinking—but only that this thing is not within the grasp of the finite mind.[264]

In modernity the notion of actual infinity is accepted into science and philosophy, and not only the new physical universe but also the whole social world is constructed from the point of view of the hypothetical, all-embracing and calculating divine intellect.[265] Since the finite mind cannot discursively embrace

---

[262] "*Ex hoc ipso quod aliquid velit, ideò cognoscit, & ideò tantum talis res est verá*" - Descartes. To Mersenne, 6 May 1630, AT I 149. In his letters to Mersenne, Descartes also mentions several times the notion of "eternal truths", *verités eternelles*, which does not appear in the "Regulae" and seems to be originally introduced in the exchange by Mersenne (To Mersenne, 15 April 1630, AT I 145). Mathematical truths are examples of eternal truths; eternal truths are established (*establies*) by God and are known by him as true and possible, but are not independent of him. - To Mersenne, 6 May 1630, AT I 149-150, To Mersenne, 27 May 1630, AT I 151-153; To Mersenne, 27 May 1630, AT II 138. See also the discussion in: Hatfield 1993, 259-287. But are eternal truths innate? There is no clear answer in Descartes to this question; however, eternal truths appear to be distinct from innate ideas in at least three respects. Unlike innate ideas, eternal truths are, first, established by the infinite mind, not the finite mind. Second, an eternal truth is considered an actual object of thinking rather than a *hexis*. And third, eternal truths are supposed to be caused by God in the same way as things are, that is, through efficient causation, whereas (as it has been mentioned) innate ideas are not directly caused by the infinite mind.
[263] Descartes. Conversation with Burman, 16 April 1648, AT V 154; cp. Med. III, AT VII 46.
[264] Descartes. To Mersenne, 15 April 1630, AT I 146. For Descartes God could render invalid even the most evident mathematical truths. See the discussion in: Funkenstein 1975, 186-199.
[265] Cp. Moore 1990, 75 sqq.

actual infinity, the mind as non-discursive intellect becomes itself either obsolete or merely hypothetical, which is why reasoning is understood only as discursive, in terms of a logically elaborated and structured argument.

Among all the faculties of the mind, it is the will that represents the infinite *par excellence* (see 3.1.4). The mind as discursive reason cannot grasp the infinite as such but is able to know that the infinite is or exists: the conception of the mind is an operation that can only discursively run from one idea to another and thus can be stretched over the indefinite, without ever really grasping the actually infinite—for example, the whole of "the extension of the imaginary space, or the set of numbers, or the divisibility of the parts of quantity".[266] But even if the mind is always able to move discursively further, it necessarily has to stop at a certain point, in order to grasp its object as definite and to arrive at a demonstration of an argument in a finite number of steps, for otherwise the argument cannot prove anything. For Descartes, imagination can visually represent or grasp only a finite and limited number of elements, whereas reason is able to think any number, however large, and even actual infinity, without grasping it (see 1.3.3).[267] The Cartesian insistence on the extension of matter as indefinite is justified by the fact that imagination can always reach any fixed limits and transgress them. Important is that (mental) imagination may represent its objects at will. Being connected to the will, imagination is thus also capable of expressing the indefinite or the potentially infinite in its own way. An imaginary overstepping of any fixed limits (involved also in the Cartesian *cogito*-procedure) can be considered double: on the one hand, as surpassing any limits in an increasing (imaginary) growth, for example, in imagining the world of an ever larger and larger size. On the other hand, such overstepping can be taken as dividing, as in the case of an extended physical or geometrical entity that may always be split further into as many parts as one may *will* to imagine, so that the very process of division may, in principle, never stop but always be carried further. In other words, both imaginable addition and imaginable division are potentially infinite.[268]

If the argument of the indefiniteness of the extension of matter is grounded in the (volitional) ability of imagination to go beyond any fixed limits, it does not yet imply that the imagination creates matter, but only that the activity of imagination is such that it makes sure that there are no limits to matter. The implicit presupposition behind this argument is that only the infinite, *infini*, can, and in fact necessarily does, create. Imagination, however, is indefinite; that is, it is always limited, although it is capable of voluntary overcoming its current definite contents. The imagination is thus unable to grasp the infinite in its entirety. As Descartes writes in a letter to Mersenne, "You ask whether there would be real space, as there is now, if God had created nothing. At first this question seems to be beyond the capacity of the human mind, like *infinity*, so that it would be unreasonable to discuss it; but in fact I think that it is merely beyond the capacity of our *imagination*, like the questions of the existence of God and of the human

---

[266] Descartes. First Set of Replies, AT VII 113.
[267] Descartes. Med. II, AT VII 30-31; First Set of Replies, AT VII 113; cp. Reg. XIV, AT X 449; The World, AT XI 31-32.
[268] Cp. Descartes. To Mersenne, 5 October 1637, AT I 453.

soul."[269] Imagination thus does not, and cannot really, create a real extended thing, but it can produce it only as imaginable; imagination can only *as if* create. And vice versa, if the infinite does not really and necessarily create, it is only imaginary.[270]

Extending into the indefinite, imagination is nevertheless always kept within finite boundaries, for the following reasons. First, every image of imagination, even if vague, is limited. And second, in order to know the truth, the mind should primarily keep the imagination severely restrained: "our imagination is tightly and narrowly limited, while our mind has hardly any limits, there are very few things, even corporeal things, which we can imagine, even though we are capable of conceiving them."[271] This is not simply a methodological rule that needs no further explanations. Descartes has to impose rigid limits on the imagination because it can properly imagine only a finite number of factors, and the finite is considered inferior to the actually infinite. This can be clearly demonstrated in an imaginable experiment described in the Sixth "Meditation", which displays the difference between understanding and imagination. We are capable of understanding equally well both a triangle and a chiliagon, since we are able to understand clearly the rule of their construction and the number of their sides. However, the triangle is easily imaginable, and the chiliagon is not, or at least only vaguely: "When I imagine a triangle, for example, I do not merely understand that it is a figure bounded by three lines, but at the same time I also see lines with my mind's eye as if they were present before me; and this is what I call imagining. But if I want to think of a chiliagon, although I understand that it is a figure consisting of a thousand sides just as well as I understand the triangle to be a three-sided figure, I do not in the same way imagine the thousand sides or see them as if they were present before me. It is true that since I am in the habit of imagining something whenever I think of a corporeal thing, I may construct in my mind a confused representation of some figure; but it is clear that this is not a chiliagon. ...I notice quite clearly that imagination requires a peculiar effort of mind which is not required for understanding; this additional effort of mind clearly shows the difference between imagination and pure understanding."[272]

When the mind introspectively investigates itself, it arrives at an apodictic certainty, finding its own limitations and the limitations of the faculties associated with itself (in particular, of imagination). The inability to represent clearly and to retain the image of the chiliagon with all its thousand sides in the imagination, demonstrates that imagination as a representational mental faculty is limited not in its power of overstepping limits but in its ability to visualize a large number of features in one single act, requiring a peculiar "effort" of mental gathering or attention.[273] Imagination is denied the knowledge of truth and reality, not because

---

[269] Descartes. To Mersenne, 27 May 1638, AT II 138, italics added.
[270] Descartes. Second Set of Replies, AT VII 141-142, which is the second of three arguments proving that the infinite does not exclude the existence of finite things.
[271] Descartes. To Mersenne, July 1641, AT III 395.
[272] Descartes. Med. VI, AT VII 72-73. Cp. Locke. Essay, Bk. II, ch. 29, § 13.
[273] In the same way as in the "Meditations" imagination, unlike reason, is considered incapable of grasping all possible forms that may be implemented in a piece of wax, in the

it is a constructive faculty, but because it is incapable of grasping the infinite in any of its forms, as neither actual nor potential. The ideal of philosophy as a strict (perhaps the strictest) science implies that philosophy is to be considered a rational enterprise independent of sense-perception and imagination. Indeed, imagination, first, is able to deliberately and voluntarily represent the non-existent as existent. And second, it can conceive the extended—not in its essence (which can only be thought), but by representing the extended through an image. The extended is not different from the corporeal, but the corporeal only obscures and as if veils for Descartes the clear and distinct primary notions and the (self-)evidence of truth. Therefore, those who strive to know the truth of metaphysics should "withdraw their minds from corporeal things, so far as is possible".[274]

One might further conjecture that since for the infinite divine mind there can be no real distinction between reason and imagination, and a mind only has to think and not imagine, the infinite mind would need no "mental effort" for representing any object, even an object with an actually infinite number of parts, such as the world as a whole. Imagination can represent the extension of the world as *indefini*, not in its multiple different features, but only as capable of ever further increasing. Imagination is thus capable of overcoming any fixed limits but is limited in its ability to represent and to retain a considerably large number of distinct features in an image, whereas the mind is virtually unlimited in its ability to discursively connect ideas together.[275]

3.3.2 Imagination and mathematics according to Descartes

One of the major presuppositions of early modern science is that every corporeal object can be considered within a mathematically formulated empirical theory (cp. 2.2.1). How and why is this possible in Descartes? For him, the geometrical figure

---

"Geometry" the imagination appears to be incapable of grasping all possible curves, ordered from simplest to most complex. - Hyppolite 1952, 170. Descartes further explains the chiliagon example to Burman: "Since my mind can easily form and depict three lines in the brain, it can easily go on to contemplate them, and thus imagine a triangle, pentagon, etc. It cannot, however, trace out and form a thousand lines in the brain [i.e., in the corporeal imagination] except in a confused manner, and this is why it does not imagine a chiliagon distinctly, but only in a confused manner". - Descartes. Conversation with Burman, AT V 162-163.
[274] Descartes. Second Set of Replies, AT VII 157.
[275] Cp. Descartes' explication of the chiliagon example to Gassendi: "[W]e have a clear understanding of the whole figure, even though we cannot imagine it in its entirety all at once". - Descartes. Fifth Set of Replies, AT VII 384; cp. Fifth Set of Objections, AT VII 329-330. Descartes insists on abandoning the realm of the incertitude of the sensual and the imaginary and on considering only the order, measure and mutual relations of objects of whatever nature by means of *mathesis* (see 2.2). Such a method (even though this project is abandoned in the later writings, but it is never rejected) comprises long chains of elementary "atomic" reasonings secured through *intuitus* and *deductio* and applies a small number of algorithmic rules for joining simple thinkable entities. The *mathesis* is then to be structured according to discursive reasoning only and not according to the imagination, which might cause an aberration and misrepresentation of its object, as is the case with the chiliagon.

is extended (except for the point) and has properties that do not change over time and can be expressed mathematically, that is, by means of numbers (for example, through a function). Numbers can themselves be represented and are imaginable as either sets of units or as magnitudes.[276] As has been argued (2.2; 2.2.1), Descartes cannot univocally decide to which of the two substances the geometrical figure should belong. Indeed, as extended, the geometrical figure should belong to the *res extensa*; but as thinkable, it should belong to the *res cogitans*. Since geometrical figures may be present to the corporeal imagination, which is a physical thing, they can thus preserve and exemplify all their unchangeable properties in the physical world. Every corporeal image of imagination corresponds to its mental image and to its idea. But, unlike the mental image, the corporeal image is extended and, as extended, is material. The imagination, which yet in the "Regulae" plays a crucial role in figuring mathematical objects, is capable of visualizing numbers and ratios and comparing them immediately through their imaginable representations (for example, 1/2 and 1/3); that is, without any further calculation, almost assuming the immediate non-discursive capacity of the intuition of the *noys*. In doing so, mental imagination "displays more distinctly" its objects than any other faculty. Every mathematical problem can then be put in terms of proportions, subsequently expressed in terms of equations, finally presented through extended geometrical figures.[277] In the "Regulae", geometrical constructions correspond to algebraic operations, and algebraic signs (letters) and geometrical figures univocally represent each other. Hence, numerical discrete entities and extended geometrical figures are rendered fully mutually convertible. Algebra and arithmetic thus may be reduced to geometry; in this reduction imagination plays a decisive role. As Sepper argues, in the "Regulae" and even in the "Cogitationes privatae", Descartes substitutes mathematics by mathetics, that is, by the universal *mathesis*: an analysis of proportional relations between objects of any kind based on an analogy between different levels of being. In particular, a physical object can be represented through a geometrical one in the imagination, and then that can be represented through an algebraically studied proportion. Thus, for example, various colors might be (and some have to be) represented through various geometrical figures and then those would be further analyzed in terms of pure proportions.[278]

Such a reduction methodologically plays an auxiliary role, namely, making the solution of mathematical problems easier. The mind-reason can, and should, be aided in its conclusions by the imagination, but not fully substituted by it, because imagination is only able to visualize concrete, finite and limited objects (particularly,in the number of features displayed) and therefore cannot ascend to universal conclusions and formulations of theorems, which are the end of scientific investigation. There are a number of difficulties implied in such a project. First, the imagination may easily be able to figure or represent a difference in proportion between, for example, 1/2 and 1/10, yet it is not at all evident whether it is capable of doing the same in the case of 1/999 and 1/1000, since the imagination is

---

[276] Descartes. Reg. XIV, AT X 445-446.
[277] Descartes. Reg. XIV, AT X 440-443.
[278] Sepper 1989, 396-397; Sepper 1996, 100 sqq. et passim. Cp. Descartes. Reg. XII, AT X 412 sqq.

incapable of representing and retaining a substantially large number of features in one single act. Also, if there is an "analogical structure of reality" in Descartes, as Sepper assumes, there should further be rather strong implicit presuppositions that will make the "how" and "why" of such an analogy possible. In particular, there should be, second, an implicit identification of the discrete (number and algebraic signs) with the continuous (geometrical figures) in their fundamental properties (see 2.2.2). And third, geometrical figures are precise, whereas physical things (which geometricals presumably represent) are not, which is recognized by Descartes himself. If this is the case, the "how" and the "why" of the representation of the physical by the geometrical remains to be further elucidated. Then, it would seem, unless the implicit presuppositions of the analogical proportional mathetical approach are clarified, the whole Cartesian project remains questionable.

Geometrical objects are imaginable and extended, i.e. are represented as extended corporeal images in the corporeal imagination (which reproduce the form of geometrical figures) and also as non-extended mental images in the mental imagination. That geometrical figure, be it a line, square or cube, is primarily represented to the imagination, is one of the starting points for Descartes, established already in the "Regulae": "If we are to imagine something and are to make use, not of the pure intellect, but of the intellect aided by images depicted in the imagination, then nothing can be ascribed to magnitudes in *general* which cannot also be ascribed to any species of magnitude".[279] Geometrical figure as extended (not in its notion or rule of construction) is a particular species of magnitude and is a subject of the corporeal imagination, any geometrical figure is "*wholly corporeal*" (*omnino corporeae*)[280] and thus material, belonging to the same substance as any physical object. It is because of that the activity of imagination consists, as it has been pointed out, in contemplation of an image of a corporeal thing (in the "Regulae"), a particular way of figuring material things (in the "Discourse", see 3.3).

How should one consider the relation between geometry and imagination? One might say with Descartes that imagination conceives bodies by means of, and through, geometrical figures. Everything extended is corporeal and everything corporeal is imaginable, that is, is representable to the corporeal imagination and then to the mental imagination. Still, not all objects of mathematics have to be conceived as corporeal, for example, a purely discursive order or sequence of true statements does not (see 2.2).[281] However, this order or sequence, which is

---

[279] Descartes. Reg. XIV, AT X 440-441, 456; cp. Reg. XII, AT X 413 sqq. Cp. Boutroux 1900. To Elizabeth, Descartes writes: "Metaphysical thoughts, which exercise the pure intellect, help to familiarize us with the notion of the soul; and the study of mathematics, which exercises mainly the imagination in the consideration of shapes and motions, accustoms us to form very distinct notions of body." - To Elizabeth, 28 June 1643, AT III 692.
[280] Descartes. Fifth Set of Replies, AT VII 385.
[281] Cp.: "...[T]he only order which I could follow was that normally employed by geometers, namely to set out all the premisses on which a desired proposition depends, before drawing any conclusions about it." - Descartes. Med. Synopsis, AT VII 13.

comprehended primarily by the mind as discursive reasoning, itself may also be imagined, because this sequence can be represented either by a sequence of discrete units (for example, points) or by a continuous magnitude (for example, a line with a clear order of its parts). But since every object of mathematics can be imagined, and everything imaginable can be related to the corporeal, then, in a sense, everything that is an object of mathematics can be also considered corporeal.

What is, further, the relation between the geometrical figure as thought and the figure as extended? As we have seen, for Plato arithmetic is based in the activity of the intellect-*noys*, whereas geometry—in that of the intermediate discursive reasoning-*dianoia*, supported by imagination (see 2.1).[282] The distinction between number and magnitude plays an important role in ancient mathematics: numbers are entities of a higher ontological status than geometricals, because numbers are only thought; they are unimaginable and lack specific corporeality, associated with geometrical entities.[283] Extension, according to Descartes, is primarily thought in its essence. Likewise, the geometrical figure has "a determinate essence or nature or form which is immutable and eternal and not invented by me or dependent on my mind".[284] Therefore, a figure has a number of demonstrable properties that in the first place are thought, but, as Descartes wants to establish in the "Regulae", can also be geometrically and imaginably represented. That a geometrical figure is imaginable, fits Descartes' essentialism well, since a figure should not necessarily exist but may only be imagined: it may only *as if* exist. The geometrical figure is not, however, essentially extended, since its intrinsic properties in principle can be conceived as clear and distinct and presented by non-extended entities, for example, numbers or proportions. Thus, the essentially geometrical figure is only thought and thus belongs to the *res cogitans*.[285] This means that the essence of mathematical entities (both arithmetic and geometrical) is determinate and unchangeable, and is only thinkable and not imaginable. In the last instance, it is determined by the infinite thinking substance. But existentially a mathematical entity is only possible. In other words, essence cannot be attributed to a mathematical entity by the finite mind, but existence can be ascribed to a mathematical object by a spontaneous voluntary act of imagination, which may represent an entity (a geometrical figure or a number

---

[282] Plato. RP 511d; cp. 522c-527c.
[283] Proclus. In Eucl. 48.9-13.
[284] Descartes. Med. V, AT VII 64.
[285] As Descartes explains to Burman, "an entity is said to be 'fictitious' ...when it is merely our supposition that it exists. Thus, all the demonstrations of mathematicians deal with true entities and objects, and the complete and entire object of mathematics and everything it deals with is a true and real entity. This object has a true and real nature, just as much as the object of physics itself. The only difference is that physics considers its object not just as a true and real entity, but also as something actually and specifically existing. Mathematics, on the other hand, considers its object merely as possible, i.e. as something which does not actually exist in space but is capable of doing so. It must be stressed at this point that we are talking of clear perception, not of imagination. ...As to whether our perceptions are clear or not, this is something we know perfectly well from our own inner awareness". - Descartes. Conversation with Burman, 16 April 1648, AT V 160.

through a geometrical figure) as merely *as if* existing, or as existing as *imaginary*.

Imagination for Descartes has corporeal things as its objects (which may have a semblance to a physical extended body): "nothing falls within the scope of the imagination without being in some way extended."[286] The geometrical object as extended, and thus as corporeal, is present in four ways: in the physical world, in the corporeal imagination, in the mental imagination and in reason. The first and second are corporeal and extended; the third and fourth are mental and not extended. But which one is the genuine geometrical figure? Descartes does not provide a clear answer to this question. However, if the geometrical figure is to be understood not simply as a collection of properties present in the mental imagination and thought by reason, but also as having an inalienable spatial component that, as representing a substance (namely, matter as extension), cannot be reduced to any general thinkable term or number of synthetic properties, then the geometrical figure has to be present either in physical matter or in the corporeal imagination.

Further, both the physical image and the image in the corporeal imagination belong, on the one hand, to the realm of the extended and therefore are of equal ontological status. On the other hand, geometrical lines and figures are perfect and cannot be adequately represented or depicted in the physical world, as Descartes himself recognizes (see 2.2.1). As extended, geometricals cannot be adequately presented in the physical realm, but only *recognized* as "semblances" of physical things. The same geometricals, however, are also formed as corporeal in the corporeal imagination, and as such can be imposed unto the extended physical things or constructed into the world of bodies, as it were. In this case, geometrical entities can be understood as imagined in the physical, and because of that they can be recognized as unchanging imaginary patterns of changing physical things. Geometricals in the corporeal imagination can be understood themselves as produced by, and in, the imagination under the pattern of a thinkable figure. Imagination can further recognize these forms in corporeal things, in fact substituting the "more or less" of the physical by precise mental images or ideas brought into the physical. Imagination as corporeal appears thus to be the instantiating center that transmits the non-corporeal form into the corporeal image, and then constructs it into the physical world. Imagination is not intermediate in Descartes, as is the case in Plato, Plotinus and Proclus, because geometrical images of the corporeal imagination are corporeal as well, coinciding with the images of geometrical objects as imposed onto physical bodies. In order to remain in compliance with his own rigid ontological dichotomy, Descartes must expel, or rather, not recognize, any intermediary structures, both in ontology (intelligible matter and geometrical objects) and in epistemology (imagination and discursive reason as intermediate faculties, cp. 2.3.1). It is this simplification that enables Descartes to put geometricals (*qua* extended) and physical bodies into *one and the same extension*, and thus to be able to apply all the rules and theorems of the geometrical to the physical.

---

[286] Descartes. To More, 5 February 1649, AT V 270. Cp. Fifth Set of Replies, AT VII 387.

And although Descartes makes a distinction a between perfect geometrical figure (perceived by the corporeal imagination) and its physical representation, which is an approximation of that figure (perceived by the senses), nevertheless, both are extended; therefore, they are to be present in one and the same space or extension. Because of this, the former may represent the latter, allowing for the possibility of constructing a mathematical empirical science. Besides, one has to distinguish between imagined, extended, perfect geometrical figures (accessible to the corporeal imagination) and geometrical figures as a collection of purely thinkable properties and relations, expressible, describable and formalizable mathematically, also known to the mind or cognitive power as reason.

There are thus two important presuppositions that make the precise scientific study of imprecise physical bodies possible. The first has just been mentioned: physical things and geometrical objects are co-extended, as it were, since there is only one uniform extension, *res extensa*.[287] Geometrical figures, on the one hand, are distinctly discernible as extended and as represented in the corporeal imagination.[288] On the other hand, they can be adequately represented through, and by, various figures and, more specifically, through proportions that are primarily thought.[289] Second, by presenting the physical through the geometrical, Descartes further reduces geometrical problems to algebraic equations (the roots of which are either real or imaginary, that is, expressed by complex numbers),[290] thus introducing pure algebraic form into mathematics, which itself becomes possible because of the non-discrimination of numbers and magnitudes (cp. 2.1.3; 2.2.2).

The application of algebraic methods to the study of geometrical figures further implies that a geometrical figure can be considered either an extended figure in the corporeal imagination, or an ideal figure conceived by the mind (mental imagination and reason). The corporeal imagination receives its images from the senses, and only then are these images transmitted for the interpretation and analysis of the mental imagination and then of reason. One might perhaps say that the "ideal" figure is simply abstracted from the "extended" figure, which itself is abstracted from a corporeal physical imitation (or a drawing) of that figure. In geometry objects are considered extended, the extended is material, and the material is corporeal. Therefore, geometry has to conceive various shapes and forms of the corporeal (although not the corporeality or extension as such, which is the subject matter of reason). But geometrical figures have properties that are to be understood as precise and numerically expressible, and for that reason geometrical figures have rather to be considered produced under the pattern of reason and in reason, and only then imposed onto (and not abstracted from) the physical. The

---

[287] Descartes. Reg. XIV, AT X 438 sqq.; cp. Gäbe 1983, 654-660.

[288] "Even though the mind is united to the whole body, it does not follow that it is extended throughout the body, since it is not its nature to be extended, but only to think. Nor does it understand extension by means of an extended semblance which is present within it (although it does *imagine* extension by turning to a corporeal semblance which is extended, as I have explained)." - Descartes. Fifth Set of Replies, AT VII 389.

[289] Descartes. Discourse II, AT VI 20.

[290] Descartes. Geometry III, AT VI 453-454.

physical then, as co-extended with the geometrical, has to be subdued to the geometrical and thus structured as mathematical (see 3.4.1).

3.4 Imagination and kinematic construction in geometry

3.4.1 Construction and the verum factum *principle: Cartesian reconstruction of the world*

Let us once again turn to our main question, namely, why and how physical changing things can be known and described in the new science by means of mathematics, which is a *thayma* of the new science. A previously obtained answer is that mathematical physics of early modern science becomes possible for Descartes because of the expulsion of intermediate structures, which would both separate and connect the physical and the mathematical (the geometrical), making them still mutually irreducible. In particular, there is no room left for intelligible matter either in ontology or in epistemology (see 2.3.1; 2.4.2). Because of that, both physical and mathematical objects (the latter being adequately represented as, and in, geometricals) are put into one and the same extension or space. Therefore, both are considered co-substantial—so, first, geometrical entities can adequately represent physical objects and, second, both are studied exactly in the same way, by the same procedures of reason supported by imagination. Since the world is *res extensa*, it can be conceived as substituted, and adequately represented, in its entirety and in each of its extended parts by geometrical figures.

It is now possible to reconsider the main problem from a slightly different perspective. Both ordinary experience and the tradition of ancient physics reject the possibility of description of the physical in terms of the mathematical. The former teaches us that it is simply impossible to measure exactly (that is, to express in a number) the real parameters of a physical magnitude, such as its size, position, or impulse; for every measurement is performed with some degree of precision. This material "more or less" of physical measurement can never coincide with the formal exactitude of mathematical identification, first, because of the imprecision of measurement itself (measuring instruments are physical things themselves). And second, a physical thing never coincides with its geometrical substitute. For example, one cannot exactly measure breadth of a table, for it is never precise: the limits of a table are never perfectly straight lines, round circles, and so on. They are never properly geometrical, but rather as if "shifting" around some quantity and never coinciding with it. And ancient physics is either not considered science, as strict *epistēmē*, at all (as is the case in Plato, for whom everything physical is essentially unknowable becoming) or is considered science in a very different way, as not mathematical but qualitative, as in Aristotle or the Stoics (see 2.1).[291] It might be objected, however, that in the "Timaeus" Plato describes the constitution of physical things with four elements (fire, air, water and earth). Every element is itself constituted as a regular geometrical polyhedron by a number of primary triangles (of which there are two different kinds; the number of

---

[291] See: Sambursky 1959.

triangles is different for each element).[292] In this way, geometrical triangles make up geometrical bodies, which further compose elements (ordered "by form and number")[293] that, in turn, constitute physical things. To this it may be replied that geometricals, which represent being, are strictly separated in Plato from physical things, which are not in being but in a constant flow and change. A difficulty in Plato's interpretation and representation of physical things in the "Timaeus" results from the fact that although Plato recognizes an essential difference between mathematical objects (numbers and geometricals) and physical things (the former can represent the latter only symbolically at best), in the "Timaeus" he does not give any consistent account of geometricals as intermediary (cp. 2.3; 2.3.1). The four elements might be further interpreted as intermediate between being (represented through geometricals) and becoming (represented through physical bodies). However, Plato unequivocally says that the elements are themselves bodies. The elements thus appear as equivocal centauric entities that, *qua* elementary constituents presenting the ground structures of the cosmos, somehow bring together the immutability of the mathematical with the changeability and the properties of the physical (for example, they have weight), being "maximally" mathematical and "minimally" material, as it were. Thus, the elements might be considered as combining both mathematical and physical properties. However, *how* such a combination takes place remains unclear and can hardly be elucidated in Plato's own terms. The Pythagorean project of mathematizing the cosmos thus remains not fully realized in Plato, who has to recognize that there is a radical otherness, present through matter, that prevents number from really becoming everything, and prevents the complete mathematization of the world.[294]

The "project of modernity" finds its expression in the works of Descartes not only because of the establishing of the existence of the infinite subjectivity (which subsequently produces the finite subjectivity, finally coming to the recognition of the infinite subjectivity and of itself), but rather because of certain implicitly accepted principles that underlie modernity. Beyond the claim made above, another reason for the possibility of applying exact mathematical reasoning to overtly inexact and fluent physical things is the constructiveness of subjectivity, discussed by a number of contemporary writers (Löwith, Blumenberg, Funkenstein, Lachterman, Gaidenko, Hösle et al.).[295] According to the *verum factum* principle, subjectivity knows its object to the extent that, and only insofar as, it produces this very object and the means for knowing it. According to this principle, the *verum* and the *factum* are mutually convertible (*verum et factum convertuntur*), and the paradigmatic example of it is found in the construction of geometrical problems.[296]

---

[292] Plato. Tim. 53c-57d.
[293] Plato. Tim. 53b.
[294] Cp.: Gaidenko 1980, 163 sqq.; Funkenstein 1986, 31-35.
[295] See: Blumenberg 1966, 175; Löwith 1971, 157-188; Funkenstein 1986, 12, 290 sqq. et passim; Gaidenko 1987, 319-328; Lachterman 1989, 8-24; Hösle 1990, 45; Nikulin 1996, 38-47, 94-102.
[296] Vico 1982, 50 sqq.

The *verum factum* principle can be traced back at least to Nicholas of Cusa and is also present in Descartes. Moreover, the constructivist approach can be seen in many early modern thinkers whose philosophical positions are quite distinct from those of Descartes. Thus, from a very different perspective of the rejection of any "innate ideas" or principles, the *verum factum* principle is supported by Locke, who presents most of the variegated and multiple contents of the mind as "complex ideas", produced or constructed (out of the elementary "bricks" of "simple ideas") through, and by, the activity of the mind itself.[297] In Hobbes the human mind (understood as the pure ability to calculate) has demonstrative knowledge only insofar as it itself produces this knowledge.[298] Knowing is thus realized as doing, *praxis*, so that "truth" and "construction" are synonyms for Hobbes. In a word (that of Leibniz), *mens facit phenomena*.[299]

For Kepler, the world is already ordered in such a way that mathematical laws are applicable to it, describing its structure and movements. The universe is conceived as produced *qua* geometrical by its creator, whose goodness is therefore expressible in terms of the regularity of mathematical proportions and figures. Kepler accepts the ancient Platonic-Pythagorean idea of God the creator being a geometer, so that the divine ratio embraces geometrical archetypes, due to which the ideas of mathematical objects (e.g., of regular solids) are not invented by the finite mind, but are rather discovered: "Geometry, being part of the divine mind from the time immemorial, from before the origin of things, being God Himself (for what is not God that was not God Himself), has supplied God with the models for the creation of the world and has been transferred to man together with the image of God. Geometry was not received inside through the eyes."[300] It is because Kepler takes the world and the soul (the mind) to be created in God's image—the former being corporeal, the latter incorporeal, *mundus est imago Dei corporea, animus est imago Dei incorporea*—that the two exemplify features of remarkable (mathematical) regularity, which is primarily the regularity of geometry: "Geometry is one of the reasons to call man an image of God."[301] What is modern in Kepler's approach, however, is that the *ego*, which looks for a mathematical explanation of the phenomena of the world, takes part not only in a re-creation, but rather in a mathematical co-creation of the world: "There is nothing I want to find out and long to know with greater urgency than this: I can find God, whom I can almost grasp with my own hands in looking at the universe, also in myself."[302] It is therefore the mind (the divine mind, but also the human mind, insofar as it is able to discover the divine mathematical design) that becomes the source of order in the

---

[297] Locke. Essay, Bk. II, chs. II, XXIII et passim.
[298] Hobbes. English Works VII, 183 sqq.
[299] Cit. ap. Lachterman 1989, XIII.
[300] Kepler. *Harmonice mundi*, Bk. IV, ch. I - Kepler. *Gesammelte Werke*, Vol. VI, 223 (cit. ap. Caspar 1959, 271).
[301] Cit. ap. Caspar 1959, 93. Cp.: "To God there are, in the whole material world, material laws, figures and relations of special excellency and of the most appropriate order".
- Kepler. Letter to Herwart, 9 or 10 April 1599, cit. ap. Baumgardt 1952, 50.
[302] Kepler, letter to Peter Heinrich von Strahlendorf, 23 October, 1613. Cit. ap. Baumgardt 1952, 114-115.

world, which turns out to be mathematized: "The mind is the source of orderliness. Nothing arranged by the mind is out of order and confused unless the mind, using its own judgement, has given free rein to instrumental causes different from itself."[303] The remarkable mathematical regularity of the physical arises thus as a mind's construction into the world.

In contemporary science, and particularly in mathematics, the properties of an object are quite often introduced through the construction of that object, as is the case with irrational numbers in Dedekind; with the foundation of mathematics in Lorenzens; or in Brouwer and intuitionists—for whom existence is identified with constructibility and truth—with actual construction. (In this sense intuitionists are genuine Cartesians, since they reduce theorems to solving—that is, constructing—problems.)[304]

In "The Ethics of Geometry", Lachterman, with good reasons, stresses the continuity between Descartes and Kant; both implement the principle of construction, which plays an exceptional role for them. (The leading role of construction explains also the interest of modernity in potentiality as possibility: it is implicitly presupposed that everything can be put in quantitative terms only.) Most clearly and consistently the constructionist approach is represented in Kant, whose solution to the problem of the applicability of mathematics to physics is that mathematical structures are *a priori* structures of subjectivity, or of the finite mind (in particular, of its sense-perception), which puts or constructs them into the physical phenomenal world in which the mind subsequently cognizes and recognizes these very structures. In other words, what the mind describes as (scientifically) known in the world is that which the mind itself prescribes to the known, both in terms of its contents and its structure, that is, in terms of the notions the mind applies to the known.[305]

In ancient *Weltanschauung* the *verum factum* principle has a rather limited application—it is mostly accepted in geometry (see 3.4.3). In the "Republic" Plato also subordinates opinion (*pistis*) based on the production or construction of a thing (for example, of a flute) to the knowledge (*epistēmē*) based on the use of that thing. Only he who uses the thing (*ho khrōmenos*) is able to disclose the thing's structure and purpose, which (even if realized by the maker) represent the *eidos* and *telos* of the thing not produced by the finite mind.[306] Descartes accepts the *verum factum* principle in his "Geometry": in order to really understand a proof of a theorem or a solution of a problem one has to produce, or

---

[303] Kepler's note XIX to the Somnium - Kepler 1967, 157.
[304] Dedekind 1912, 12-17; Weyl 1949, 50-54 et al. See also: Becker 1954, 393-398; Dummett 1977. Descartes in his "Geometry" solves problems and does not prove theorems; cp. Viète 1968, 320 sqq.
[305] Cp. Kant. Prolegomena A 34; Critique of Pure Reason B 41; A 128-130; B 168-169 et al. As Gaukroger argues, the project of mathematical physics is rendered possible through a shift in the explanatory structures in physical science, which in early modernity (in particular, in Galileo) are conceived as determined by mathematics, that is, by its proof structure, which is reciprocally defined by its system of concepts (Gaukroger 1978, 182-229). The explanation in physics is thus already to be constructed as mathematical.
[306] Plato. RP 601d-602a.

at least reproduce, the proof or the solution: "I have not demonstrated here most of what I have said, because the demonstrations seem to me so simple that, provided you take the pains to see methodologically whether I have been mistaken, they will present themselves to you; and it will be of much more value to you to learn them this way than by reading them."[307] As Descartes later explains to Hogelande, "I generally distinguish two aspects of mathematics, the historical and the scientific. By 'history' I understand everything which has been discovered already and is contained in books. By 'science' I mean the skill to solve every problem, and thus to discover by one's own efforts everything capable of being discovered in that science by means of our native human intelligence".[308] Thus, one might say that knowledge is scientific (that is, demonstrable as strict) only if it is scientific (that is, demonstrable as reproducible).

One needs to make a distinction, however, between understanding as production and understanding as reproduction. If we speak about artificial things, then understanding of such artifacts can be obtained by both production and reproduction. A master produces a thing that he constructs under certain preconceived pattern(s) and rules. Nevertheless, he realizes and understands his own intended project only as he advances in implementing it. The product that arises in the end bears a similarity to the original project and design, insofar as it is made according to the original plan. Yet the final product is also quite dissimilar from the intended, insofar as the produced discloses features that originally were wrapped up and hidden from the finite demiurgic mind. Now, when looking at the work, we might understand certain inner principles involved in it by reproducing or copying it, either physically or in the imagination. However, in the case of entities supposed to exist by themselves, one might say that our task as mathematicians is not to produce, but only to reproduce their hidden properties in order to understand them—only to disclose, and not to invent—the properties that are thus only reconstructed by us.

The constructor of physical things—those existing *physei*—can be only the divine infinite intellect for Descartes. It is this intellect that produces the soul, the whole world and all their properties, and prescribes their laws. As the infinite mind (and thus omniscient), God has all concepts of things formally. That is, on the one hand, he has these concepts from eternity, on the other hand, he knows things insofar as he creates them. In other words, first, for the creator it is the same to know and to produce. Second, things in their concepts should be known by the divine mind not discursively, as the finite mind knows them, but in an intuitive momentary grasp, because to know is to create and the creation is momentary. Third, the infinite mind has to know every idea quite differently, not only essentially, as the finite mind does, but in the highest degree—that is, eminently.[309] The finite mind that constructs its object always has to "look" at the eternal paradigm of a thing or of a geometrical object, the paradigm which itself is not produced by the finite subjectivity.[310] However, since finite subjectivity itself has

---

[307] Descartes. Geometry III, AT VI 464.
[308] Descartes. To Hogelande, 8 February 1640, AT III 722-723.
[309] Descartes. Med. IV, AT VII 79; Second Set of Replies, AT VII 135, 161-169 et al.
[310] Cp. Plato RP 507 b-c; Tim. 28c-29a.

constructive capacity, it can eventually substitute the infinite mind by the sovereign constructive finite *ego*. One of the reasons for such a substitution, which cannot be discussed here, appears to be that in the Western Aristotelian theological tradition, God is equated with being and with the infinite intellect and is no longer considered, as in the Platonic tradition, the superabundant cause of being which is not being itself.[311] And if the source of being is considered to belong to being itself, and, further, being can be thought in an act of self-reflection of finite subjectivity, then a distinction between the objective source of thought and the reflecting thought itself becomes not immediately self-evident. The finite subjectivity finds itself in a position to produce contents of its own thinking and in this way to determine itself, being autonomous.

As it has already been stressed, only the opposition of finite and infinite still separates the two thinking substances for Descartes, which still allows him to recognize the "innateness" of some ideas of which the *ego* cannot be the cause.[312] Since, however, finite human subjectivity is considered essentially capable of construction, capable of overcoming any "naturally" prescribed limits and borders, it eventually comes to understand and establish itself in overriding the veto of actual infinity. For the finite subjectivity, which understands itself as *the* being, as the (re)productive thinking substance, infinite subjectivity simply become obsolete, as well as the distinction between the non-created and the created subjectivity. The paradox that thinking creates itself in reflectively turning upon itself—in thinking itself when the *ego* reflectively constitutes itself—can be solved only by assigning the status of *the* substance to thinking, the substance that indeed needs nothing except itself in order to exist. Subjectivity becomes substantial as the source of everything and of itself. Objectivity becomes superfluous.

Descartes, however, still wants to retain the objectivity of the divine subjectivity (that is, its full independence of the finite subjectivity or the mind). On the contrary, it is the finite subjectivity that is independent from the infinite one for Descartes. Such subordination can be seen in the preservation of at least one category of ideas (innate, see 3.1.4) independent from the productive activity, desires and intentions of the finite mind. The independent existence of substances, assured and supported by the introspection of the *ego* in the *cogito*, is not yet cancelled by complete autonomy of the finite subjectivity. In Descartes, the production of the world is still ascribed to its incessant recreation by the divine intellect. But since the human mind is co-substantial with the divine—for both belong to the *res cogitans*—the only division left is that between the infinite and the finite, which may be understood as creative and recreative, constructive and reconstructive respectively. The distinction between the infinite and the finite is still insurmountable in Descartes, but is eventually overcome due to the potentially unlimited constructive capacity of the human mind, which is capable of bracketing the actually infinite—either by putting it outside the set of objects of reasonable consideration, or by constructing the infinite (as in modern mathematical constructivism, as an abstraction of finitude) and thereby overcoming the absolute

---

[311] Cp. Proclus. Theol. Plat. II 30.22-26.
[312] Cp. Descartes. Med. III, AT VII 38 sqq.

transcendence of the infinite to being and thinking (cp. 1.3.2). Since in the mind, both infinite and finite, there is a productive capacity represented by the mental imagination, not only the form but also the content of reasoning may be considered subjectively prescribed and regulated, and therefore constructed by the mind itself. Descartes' famous claim is: "Nothing lies within our power except our thoughts."[313] Even though originally this claim means that it is easier to master oneself rather than to change the (independent of finite subjectivity) rules and laws of the world, nevertheless, when the mind eventually becomes independent of the divine, subjective reason is then considered autarchic and demiurgic. Finite human reason becomes thus emancipated from the infinite intellect. Descartes does in fact violate a principle he himself has declared: it is not the finite that is understood as a limitation of the infinite (cp. 1.3.2), but on the contrary, the infinite is implicitly considered a projection and an extension of the finite.

The finite being (which in fact is not being any more than being without existence is, only a pure essence reducible to the reflective self-consciousness) brings forward a number of options for how the world and the self will appear. If these options are all produced, in the last instance, willingly or unwillingly, consciously or unconsciously, by the finite subjectivity, there is no sufficient ground to prefer one option to the other. The situation seems rather paradoxical: all mutually exclusive options are initially produced by the finite subjectivity, which then itself has to decide which one to choose. Since there appears to be no sufficient ground for such a choice (except a voluntary or random one), the choice becomes completely "free"—that is, contingent. The number of options is either finite or potentially infinite, if a new one can always be introduced. The "I" has to consider then that it is entirely up to itself to decide which choice is the right one, in which of the empty boxes to put a check-mark, which particular identity to choose.

Because of this, any objective teleology becomes redundant, being deliberately wiped out by Descartes and by most modern thinkers. Since the world is merely a *res extensa*, it has no purposes by and for itself.[314] Every purpose or *telos* may be given to it only by its creator or constructor, by the infinite *res cogitans*. Eventually, this function of assigning sense or purpose to the world becomes the prerogative of the finite subjectivity. Why? Because the ultimate justification of subjectivity comes not from the subjectivity of the other (in particular, not from the infinite subjectivity) and not even from one's own subjectivity as reflected in and by the other, not mediated by that very justification—but such a justification becomes the *immediate* clear and distinct perception of myself. If subjectivity is immediately verified by and through the self-awareness, then the other's subjectivity, both infinite and finite, has to be established from my own, finite one, so that the distinction between the infinite and the finite easily evaporates and appears to be just imaginary.

As the finite subjectivity gradually emancipates itself from the infinite one and understands itself as autonomous and sufficient, starting from the *cogito*, it

---

[313] Descartes. Disc. III, AT VI 25.
[314] Schramm 1985, 70-77 et passim.

becomes difficult to retain a necessary distinction between reason and will. Since the finite subjectivity is opposed as its other to extended material things or geometrical objects, the infinite subjectivity appears then not as the radical other to the "ego" but becomes the intimate same. The subjectivity of the self-awareness of the "I" thus becomes divine and the other finite *ego* can only be assumed to be intersubjective, but is never directly accessible to the "I". One of the most important methodological requirements of modernity becomes that the "I" should be capable of knowing something other than itself definitively and as true only if this other is completely destitute of any inner subjectivity—of any capacity of producing and ascribing purposes of its own to the world. Indeed, that which is able to set purposes has to be free, that is, not limited in its choice by anything else; such is (or at least historically becomes) only the finite subjectivity, which liberates itself even from its infinite source, the infinite divine subjectivity. Inevitably there arises a *sui generis* circle. The finite subjectivity rather contingently assigns purposes to the world, but then in making decisions, subjectivity has to take those purposes into consideration; it becomes enslaved, as it were, to itself by itself through unconditional purpose-making.

Among the constructed and reconstructed objects of knowledge are mathematical entities, represented in Descartes by abstract algebraic objects, easily reducible to geometrical figures, to which physical things are eventually reduced (see 2.2.1). But since even the physical object is considered geometrically structured, the very activity of construction cannot be that of physical production, because if the mathematical (the geometrical) is constructed under the pattern of the physical, nothing can guarantee mathematical precision, for the physical is not precise *per se*.

Every powerful weapon and instrument may turn self-destructive if not properly used. Of course, the notion of "proper use" is a teleological one: only if there is a certain objective purpose can there be a proper use. When the objective teleology is intentionally destroyed and subsequently abandoned in favor of the subjective one, the constructive capacity of the imagination has to inevitably turn against itself; that is, everything has to be considered as a free, or arbitrary (not teleologically oriented) construction. Descartes, however, still retains the *res extensa* as produced by the infinite mind and thus as capable only of being *re*produced by the finite subjectivity.

Descartes faces the task of reconstructing the whole world, although he himself modestly takes it to be only *a* possible reconstruction that, most importantly, takes place in *imaginary* spaces.[315] In the newly created world, the finite (mental) imagination extends as far as it can—indefinitely, it is *as if* infinite, just as the sea is only seemingly infinite. Human subjectivity is thus separated from the divine by the barrier of infinity and not of substantiality: essentially both are the same, which is why the human mind is assigned an astonishing capacity to create and recreate things and their rules and thus to know them. Illusion or seemingness plays an important role in the constitution of the new world, which is

---

[315] Descartes. The World, AT XI 31-32.

both physical and imaginary, for it should represent the "real" world not existentially but only essentially.[316]

An important question then is whether this imaginable and imaginary recreation of the world is an act or a process. The divine or "real" creation, considered an act (or, at least, a number of consecutive acts[317]), is understood by Descartes in terms of the scholastic doctrine of the constant recreation of the world. This doctrine is further supported by Descartes' observation that the contents of the mind at each particular moment of time are completely independent of the previous momentary mental contents, which finds its expression in the mutual independence of the moments of time. But what can be said about recreation in the imagination? Such a recreation can be considered both momentary and continuous. It is momentary insofar as the primary constituent, the whole of the extension or matter of the new world, can be conceived all at once, in a single and indivisible act of imagination. On the other hand, since this new world has to undergo a certain development in order to present the whole variety of visible bodily things in their heterogeneity, the recreation has to be continuous. The difference between the "real" and the "as if" creation (or between creation and recreation) lies again in the distinction of the *infini* and the *indéfini*: the imagination cannot grasp and clearly represent the infinite or even a substantially large magnitude (a chiliagon). The difference between the finite reason and the finite imagination consists then in that both are limited in a different way. Reason is limited only in its ability to know actual infinity, *l'infini*, while the imagination is limited in its cognition also of the indefinitely large.[318] In other words, reason fails to know actual infinity (in its essence, although not in its existence), the infinite of the divine reason. But imagination fails to represent even potential infinity (for example, the number of particles in the newly (re)construced world), although the process that constitutes potential infinity, that of making another step, is itself perfectly imaginable. One might say that the difference between actual infinity and potential infinity is that the former presupposes an act, while the latter, a process. This distinction is applicable to the construction of a figure that might be considered contemplated when it, first, is constructed by and in the imagination (that is, produced in a process) and, second, is retained in the mind and imagination as wholly and completely present as a single entity (in an act).

The act of imaginary construction thus really belongs to the infinite divine reason, whereas the process of the consecutive engendering of a thing in imagination is accomplished by the finite human mind. In Descartes' example of the chiliagon, the finite mind cannot clearly imagine the figure all at once (in an *act*) although it can easily imagine the *process* of the production of the chiliagon, side by side, according to the rules that describe such a production. The finite mind is able to co-imagine, as it were, only the simplest geometrical entities (circles, spheres, triangles, squares, cubes, and so on) with the divine mind; in doing so the

---

[316] On the connection of illusion, deformation and projective geometry see: Gaidenko 1997, 54-68.
[317] Cp. Gen. 1:1 sqq.
[318] Descartes. Conversation with Burman, AT V 163. Cp. First Set of Objections, AT VII 96; First Set of Replies, AT VII 113-114.

finite mind shares functions of the demiurg to some extent. These simplest—clearly and distinctly imaginable—geometrical figures can be then considered elementary "bricks" of the "grand mathematical book" of the universe. Once again, imagination appears to be fundamentally ambiguous. It is capable both of representing an extended entity (be it a geometrical figure or physical body) as given all at once in a single moment of "now", and of conceiving it as constructed continuously step by step, as becoming in time.

In "The Passions of the Soul" Descartes subdivides all thoughts into actions and passions.[319] Actions are volitions—those thoughts that are completely in our disposition; passions are perceptions of two kinds, caused by the soul itself and caused by the body. Now, where does the imagination belong together with its products, imaginings? Since, as we have seen, imagination is ambiguous in its nature, Descartes cannot place imaginings only in the mental or only in the bodily. But because he does not recognize any intermediate entities, he has to split the imagination into mental and corporeal, which now seem to reappear under the guise of active voluntary imaginings and passive bodily imaginings. The latter do not immediately depend on the nerve structures of our brain, because "they arise simply from the fact that the spirits, being agitated in various different ways and coming upon the traces of various impressions which have preceded them in the brain, make their way by chance through certain pores rather than others".[320] These imaginings just happen to us, without any ostensible inclination of the will; we are not capable of voluntarily constructing them. Active imaginings are, however, purely mental, the imaginings of intellect and the imaginings of will: the latter can be guided by volition when the soul imagines something non-existent, for example, a chimera or a centaur.[321] The constructive active capacity is thus primarily connected with the imagination, because it can imagine whatever it wants and wills without any restrictions whatsoever. Restrictions, of course, appear when the mental (active) imagination imagines geometrical figures and the new world as well,[322] because the final products have to coincide with the "real" ones. Here imagination is bounded by the non-imaginary, by only thinkable (divine produced) properties of figures and physical bodies: for instance, the finite mind cannot imagine a triangle with two right angles, and even if it can, the figure simply is not a triangle in Euclidean geometry.

Thus both the imagination and the mind appear to be constructive. But then how do they, supposedly different, share their constructive capacities? This is a question Descartes does not directly address. One might suggest that the constructive ability of imagination extends only to the construction (or, possibly, the voluntary distortion) of geometrical figures and that it is the mind as cognitive power that determines all the different modes of cognition, including imagination. But then, since imagination is itself determined by reason, it can be said that it is the reason that in the last instance constructs figures through and in the imagination. There is still a difference, however, between the two: reason is the

---

[319] Descartes. The Passions of the Soul I 17-26, AT XI 342 sqq.
[320] Descartes. The Passions of the Soul I 21, AT XII 344-345.
[321] Descartes. The Passions of the Soul I 20, AT XII 344.
[322] Cp. Descartes. Discourse V, AT VI 42-43.

constitutive principle of the intelligible—of that which is only thought. For Descartes, the constructive principle in the proper sense can only be God as the infinite mind; the finite mind has to arrange its contents and cogitations in due discursive sequence of the right and orderly cognition. Imagination, when it operates with the imaginings of intellect, is essentially reconstructive, for it follows a pattern (for example, a notion or an idea of a geometrical object) given to it by reason (in the last instance, by the infinite reason). On the contrary, when imagination deals with the imaginings of the will, it may spontaneously produce such objects of which no "innate idea" or essence as pre-established can be conceived.

Since, however, Descartes still recognizes innate ideas, which restrict the (in many respects autonomous) activity of the will, not everything can be imagined: Descartes has to acknowledge entities that are "purely intelligible and not imaginable".[323] Whatever is constructible is also imaginable. Everything imaginable can be understood, but not everything that can be understood is imaginable, as the chiliagon example shows. Therefore, if not everything is imaginable, then not everything can be constructed. This is the crucial point in the Cartesian proof of the existence of God from the idea of supreme infinite perfection, for this idea cannot be simply a construction of the finite mind.[324]

Furthermore, while reason represents the truth of being (essentially, not existentially), imagination is the only faculty capable of imagining non-being. Non-being for Descartes is, of course, quite different from the absolute privative non-being of Plato and Plotinus. The Cartesian non-being is, as it were, also not existential but essential: it "is" that which does not exist but could have existed (the most obvious reason for its non-existence is that God does not will it to exist in the actual world). The mental imagination then connects non-being as "as if" being with thoughts as passions: "[w]hen we read of strange adventures in a book, or see them acted on the stage, this sometimes arouses sadness in us, sometimes joy, or love, or hatred, and generally any of the passions, depending on the diversity of the objects which are presented to our imagination."[325] Imagination presents the whole drama of a worldly event on the stage of the new world where physical things and geometrical figures are put into the same extension. Yet the mental imagination has to be a capacity of visualization of an imaginable object in contemplating its image or shape as if it were immediately present to the perception. Contemplation as visualization has to be taken then primarily as an act of imagination, not of reason. The contemplation of the Platonic *noys* has to reveal being that *is* and that is thinkable—that is not constructed and that is not changed by an act of contemplation. The contemplation of the Cartesian imagination, on the contrary, can be considered as inventing being by the very act of visualizing it in mental imagining, which can be directed by the will and in which the imagined extended thing is produced together with all of its properties. In order to preserve the constructed in its existence, however, imagination is necessary but insufficient:

---

[323] Descartes. The Passions of the Soul I, AT XI 344.
[324] Cp. Descartes. Med. III, AT VII 40 sqq.; Second Set of Objections, AT VII 123.
[325] Descartes. The Passions of the Soul, AT XI 441.

the effort of "the surprising mental concentration" is needed, which is attention.[326]

Thus, even though the most divine in us for Descartes is the mind as reason or thinking (which, due to its limitations, is discursive)—for it is purely spiritual and incorporeal and thus co-substantial with infinite thinking—nevertheless the faculty that represents the divine creative power in its spontaneity and versatility is imagination rather than reason. It is (mental) imagination that allows the finite mind to some extent reproduce the productive action of the divine creative power. Modern subjectivity, which is often taken to conceive of itself as the creator of its world and thus to replace the divine infinite subjectivity, becomes demiurgic only because of the potential creativity of imagination. Once the world is considered given, the finite reason may suffice to fully investigate and understand the world. One of the main Cartesian methodological presuppositions, however, is not to take anything for granted until the mind is able to understand it as necessary, that is, as clear and distinct. And if the world is not given, one has to (re)create it—to imagine it. Imagination can operate spontaneously (that is, directed only by the will) and is capable of voluntary and arbitrary interpretations, for example, in visualizing sensual things and in actively constructing their images.[327] In the "Meditations" Descartes seems to restrict the spontaneity of the imagination (which allows it to invent fictions, the *imaginatione effingo*) to the sphere of corporeal images only. But at least within corporeal images the imagination appears to be not only reproductive but productive as well, to be unrestrained and thus capable of acting according to the will: I may will to imagine and thus actually imagine that which does not exist or at least which I have never seen.[328] Thus imagination appears to be the constructive faculty *par excellence* (cp. 3.4.1).

A number of implicit presuppositions underlie the Cartesian consideration of construction and reconstruction. First, even though Descartes wants to avoid using a hylomorphic scheme,[329] he still considers the mind (or the soul) as molding extended objects, although now the mind shapes its material through the mental imagination, which may operate spontaneously, at will, depicting the world anew—the world as it could have been, given the requirement that the phenomenal should not be different from the "real". Descartes thus recreates not only the content of the world (the material, the extended), but also the very notions the mind employs in the reconstruction; in a sense, the mind itself through the imagination, the formal.

Second, one of the main presuppositions of early modern science is that the movement of the universe is organized and orchestrated by God, although opinions may vary on whether he constantly puts the same amount of movement into the world and thus preserves the motion of bodies and matter or whether he does it only once or periodically.[330] Descartes supports this presupposition

---

[326] Descartes. Conversation with Burman, AT V 163.
[327] Descartes. Optics IV, AT VII 113-114; To Elizabeth, 6 October 1645, AT IV 311; cp. Passions of the Soul, AT XI 387; To Chanut, 1 February 1647, AT IV 601.
[328] Descartes. Med. II, AT VII 28-29; Passions I 43, AAT XI 361.
[329] Cp. Aristotle. De an. 412a 27-412b 6.
[330] See Nikulin 1993, 213.

throughout his writings: "I think the only general cause of all the movements in the world is God."[331] Nevertheless, since God always, at every moment, reinfuses motion into the matter he himself creates, when the soul imagines the production of the new world, it follows this pattern, *as if* creating or infusing motion into the world. Since there is no distinction between geometrical and physical extension in Descartes, it also becomes possible for the soul to consider a geometrical entity (for example, a point or a line) moving in the imagination and thus to (re)create a figure (respectively, a line or a plane) by drawing or tracing it in the *plenum* of the imagination *as if* in a certain matter (see 3.4.5).

Third, as it has been mentioned (3.1.4), the mind as reason is considered a merely discursive thinking (not only by Descartes but by most modern and contemporary thinkers).[332] Thus, a proposition present to the mind may be considered true only if it is demonstrated, that is, discursively reconstructed in a number of consecutive steps, possibly using other justified propositions. One might object that the *cogito* itself is not discursive; still, in order to arrive at its clear and distinct understanding, the mind gradually has to suspend and remove everything superfluous. In such a case the discursive mind loses, however, its status of intermediary that it has in Platonism, since the notion of *noys* is completely abandoned, for the *noys* can by no means be clearly and distinctly perceived either in an act of imaginary reduction of the external, or by an introspection of the *cogito*. Thinking of the *noys* rather requires abandoning of the self-awareness and oblivion of the *ego*.

Fourth, the notions or the "ideas" of geometrical objects (as well as innate ideas and truths) are not subject to the imaginings of the will. They can be imagined at will but are not produced by the will (only the infinite divine intellect thinks what it wills and wills what it thinks). Because of this, geometrical truths are known "by the power of our own native intelligence, without any sensory experience".[333] Since all geometrical objects that embody these truths can be constructed accordingly, all their properties may be then discerned in these objects *after* the construction has already taken place. And fifth, the new world appears to be a *possible* world, the possibility of which is actualized by imagination.

In the reconstruction of the world, the opposition between "the old" and "the new" is between that which "really" exists and that which is created by the infinite and the non-created substance. However, epistemologically the old world is not a surely existing world. The new world can be known in its inner structure and underlying principles only because it is recreated by the mind and within the imagination. This statement is in agreement with the *verum factum* principle: in order to know something, the finite mind *qua* mental imagination has to create, or at least recreate, that thing in its properties (not in its real existence, which still is produced and supplied by the infinite mind). In recreating the world, the imagination is able to bring differentiation into the originally uniform extension

---

[331] Descartes. To [the Marquess of Newcastle], October 1645, AT IV 328.

[332] Spinoza accepts the cognition of reason (*ratio*) as discursive, but also recognizes intuitive knowledge (*scientia intuitiva*), which is rather an exception, see: Ethics, Bk. II, Schol. 2 ad Prop. 40. Cp. also: Locke. Essay, Bk. IV, ch. II, § 1.

[333] Descartes. To Voetius, May 1643, AT VIIIB 166-167.

Part III: Reason, Imagination and Construction 223

and split homogeneous matter into different entities constituted by tiny particles of a thin-grained "subtle matter", *matiere subtile*.[334] The newly "created" imaginary and imagined matter is, first, completely formless—that is, homogeneous and uniform. Second, it is also not the Aristotelian "prime matter" that lacks all forms and qualities and thus cannot be clearly and distinctly understood (cp. 1.1.1).[335] The matter needed for the imaginary recreation of the whole world is substance for the simple reason that it is extended. Being an extended *plenum* where various figures can be discerned, matter is continuous, so that, third, it can be "divided into as many parts having as many shapes as we can imagine".[336] Moreover, imagination is able to (re)produce even the laws of motion: "each part is capable of taking on as many motions as we can conceive".[337] And with the production of matter and the laws of its motion the world is complete.[338]

3.4.2 Construction in geometry: Kinematic constructibility in Descartes

An important feature of Cartesian geometry is the reduction of various problems to the solution of problems of a single type. Ancient geometry recognizes a classification of different types of problems corresponding to different types of geometrical figures, by which these problems may be solved. These problems and lines are ordered axiologically according to their simplicity: a straight line and circle, conic sections, more complex lines resulting from complex constructions. Another way of ordering geometrical objects is to consider first plain figures and then three-dimensional objects, as in Euclid's "Elements" where consideration of solids follows at the very end, in books XI-XIII. Descartes retains some traces of the ancient geometrical hierarchy of problems and figures in his "Geometry". He still divides problems into the following categories of solvability: by ruler and compass alone, by means of conic sections and by means of more complex lines. He mentions three kinds of problems distinguished in ancient geometry, namely, plane, solid and linear.[339] Ancient geometers also further distinguish so-called mechanical lines constructed by a rather complex mechanical advice (for example, conchoid and cissoid). Descartes, however, rejects the notion of mechanical lines for the reason that it is not clearly understandable, and that some of the ancient "mechanical" lines (for example, quadratrix) can be described by "two separate

---

[334] Cp. Descartes: To Mersenne, 15 November 1638, AT II 440; December 1638, AT II 465; 9 January 1639, AT II 483 sqq.; To Mersenne, 16 October 1639, AT II 593-594; The World, AT XI 16 sqq. Cp. Morin's discussion of the subtle matter (as it appears in the Cartesian "Meteorology") in his letter to Descartes, 22 February 1638, AT I 544 sqq.
[335] Descartes. The World, AT XI 33.
[336] Descartes. The World, AT XI 34.
[337] Descartes. Ibid. Cp. Schuster 1977, 685-739.
[338] In a rather similar way, in his early work "De gravitatione et aequipondio fluidorum" Newton proposes a recreation or reproduction of the world by imagining that God has made some of the parts of the extension impermeable, as if "closing" them. If the property of movability is added to these parts, the resulting world will by no means be different from the phenomenal one. - Newton 1962, 105-109; see also: Nikulin 1993, 129-130.
[339] Descartes. Geometry I, AT VI 380-381; Geometry II, AT VI 388. Cp. To Beeckman, 26 March 1619, AT X 157.

movements which have no precisely measurable relation to each other".[340] The main reason for the ancient geometrical classification of lines is that every line can be considered produced by a construction that follows a certain algorithm that can represent regular movements, the difference between which thus constitutes the hierarchy of lines and problems. Descartes' intention is to reduce *all* curves involved in the solutions of geometrical problems to two or more simple lines and to present a simple way of their generation or construction. At this point, Descartes follows ancient geometers in accepting movement as the way of engendering new curves (and also surfaces and solids) once simpler lines as primary constituents "can be moved through one another, and that their intersections determine other curves".[341] Yet then the whole ancient geometrical hierarchy becomes obsolete, because *any* line is supposed to be constructible and constructed indiscriminately by the movement of some geometrical object. "[I]t seems to me", says Descartes, "that it is very clear that if (as we do) we understand by 'geometry' that which is precise and exact, and by 'mechanics' that which is not; and if we consider geometry as a science that teaches a general knowledge of the measures of all bodies, we must no more exclude complex lines from it than simple ones, provided that we can conceive them as being described by a continuous movement, or by several continuous movements of which latter are completely determined by those which precede: for by this means, we can always have an exact knowledge of their measure."[342]

The construction of geometrical objects plays a central role in ancient geometry as well.[343] As Mueller argues, constructibility of geometricals is essential for Euclid: "In general, Euclid produces, or imagines produced, the objects he needs for a proof... It seems fair to say then that in the geometry of the *Elements* there is no underlying system of points, straight lines, etc. which Euclid attempts to characterize. Rather, geometric objects are treated as isolated entities about which one reasons by bringing other entities into existence and into relation with the original objects and one another... In the geometry of the *Elements* the existence of one object is always inferred from the existence of another by means of a construction."[344] This claim is largely justifiable in Euclid's "Elements", where at the beginning of the first book postulates are precedent to axioms. A postulate (*aitēma*) is a requirement for the possibility of the existence of an object, where such existence is secured by the procedure of construction. An axiom (*axiōma*, in Euclid, *koinē ennoia*), on the contrary, is a general statement that needs not be proved but has to be accepted by every reasonable human being. Such an understanding of the axiom (which goes back to Aristotle) primarily refers to a process of learning (for *mathēmata* constitute strict knowledge, science that can be *taught*) and not to an abstract system of propositions deduced from a number of

---

[340] Descartes. Geometry II, AT VI 390.
[341] Descartes. Geometry II, AT VI 389; cp. Geometry III, AT VI 476.
[342] Descartes. Geometry II, AT VI 389-390.
[343] Cp. Szabó 1978, 185 sqq.; Lachterman 1989, 67 sqq.
[344] Mueller 1981, 14-15. Cp. Viète 1983, 371 sqq.

self-evident statements.³⁴⁵ The distinction between postulates and axioms parallels that between problems (where a construction is required) and theorems (where one has to determine a certain property of a given object).³⁴⁶ (Although, both are related to each other: according to Proclus, who comments on Euclid, every proposition or theorem contains, as two of its six integral parts, construction (*kataskeyē*) and then proof (*apodeixis*).) ³⁴⁷ A postulate requires the constructibility of an object: unless the object is actually constructed, it cannot be said to exist (even though originally postulates (*aitēmata*) came from dialectic, where they denoted assumptions not accepted without reservation by one of the participants of the dialogue).³⁴⁸ And yet in the Late Academy we find many discussions about whether theorems can be reduced to problems (as Menechmos and Carpus thought) or whether theorems, which presuppose the existence of non-constructible, non-changing entities, are prior to problems (as Speusippus and Geminus argued). Put otherwise, the former maintained that the *quod erat demonstrandum* is always reducible to the *quod erat factum*.³⁴⁹ The latter denied such reducibility, stressing that knowledge, as Plato takes it, reveals those entities that always exist without changing their properties. Those properties are to be discovered through demonstration and not through construction, for construction presupposes movement and change. Theorems therefore refer to being in the first place, the only realm of knowledge for Plato, whereas problems always involve becoming and, as such, can at best provide additional supportive evidence for science.

Thus, for instance, the definition of parallel lines is given by Euclid as a possible construction: when indefinitely extended, such lines do not intersect.³⁵⁰

---

³⁴⁵ "An immediate deductive principle I call a posit (*thesis*) if it cannot be proved but need not be grasped by anyone who is going to learn anything. If it must be grasped by anyone who is going to learn anything whatever, I call it an axiom." - Aristotle. Anal. Post. 72a 14-17. Cp. Met. 1005a 19-23; 1005b 11-17; Top. 101b 38-102a 1 and the definition of an axiom in Theophrastus as quoted by Themistius. In anal. Post. 7.3-4. See also: Mugler 1958, 45, 68; Szabó 1965, 355 sqq.; Heath 1970, 50 sqq.; Schmitz 1997, 316-336. According to Barnes, "P is an axiom for S iff anyone knows any proposition in S, then he knows that P" or, in a more *general* form, "P is an axiom iff anyone who knows anything, knows P"- Barnes 1993, 99.
³⁴⁶ Cp. Plato, RP 530b; Aristotle, Phys. 213b 2; Proclus. In Eucl. 178.1. sqq.; Archimedes. Opera I 6.14-10.28. See also: Dijksterhuis 1956, 143-149.
³⁴⁷ Every proposition or theorem is constituted by six steps: enunciation (*protasis, propositio*), exposition (*ekthesis, expositio*), specification (*diorismos, determinatio*), construction (*kataskeyē, constructio*), proof (*apodeixis, demonstratio*) and conclusion (*symperasma, conclusio*). - Proclus. In Eucl. 206.12 sqq.
³⁴⁸ Cp. Aristotle. Anal. Post. 77a2-3. Szabó argues that in Greek mathematics *axiōma* and *aitēma* were interchangeable expressions in dialectic (Szabó 1978, 268 sqq., esp. 287). See also: Breton 1969, 43 sqq.; Van der Waerden 1977-1978, 343-357; Leszl 1981, 293 sqq. According to Stenius, who supports the constructivist interpretation of Greek geometry, the solution of problems provides proofs of the existence of geometrical objects (Stenius 1978, 255-289). Still, even if the existence is not described by axioms, which primarily display the essence of an object, its existence, at least for Plato and the Platonic thinkers, is not secured by construction, but is provided by the *eidos* of the object.
³⁴⁹ Proclus. In Eucl. 241.18-244.9.
³⁵⁰ Euclid. Elem. I, def. 23.

Before Euclid, the constructive approach is supported by Oenopides and also by Hippocrates.[351] Aristotle takes the properties (*diagrammata*) inherent in geometrical figures to be discovered or shown through activity (*energeiai*): namely, by drawing lines, that is, by constructing these figures.[352] These properties are not, however, invented by construction; they simply are rendered distinguishable and as if visible, already inherent in their subject, that is, in a geometrical figure. In this respect, the construction of a figure may be regarded as a non-temporal process, in which all the parts and stages are already present.[353] In the Pythagorean-Platonic interpretation of mathematics—based on the acceptance of number as the ideal paradigm and of the geometrical figure as intermediate entity (see 2.1 sqq.)—construction is only an auxiliary method of displaying the properties of an entity that does not itself come into being with the act of construction, but may be said to exist ideally, independently of the productive activity of any of the mental faculties.[354]

The above mentioned interpretation by Mueller of Euclidian geometry stresses construction as connected with the absence of unconditioned assertions of the existence of geometrical objects, as is often the case in modern mathematics (for example, in Hilbert). Such an interpretation, however, seems to some extent to be a modernization, since ancient mathematics appears to have different initial premises. First of all, axioms are considered statements to which, as to the first principles, all analytic propositions are ultimately reducible. Axioms are thus not produced by our cognitive activity, but simply articulate the given notions and geometrical entities. In early modern science, on the contrary, axioms are often taken to be constructions of the cognizing mind, for instance, in Leibniz.[355] Also, as it was argued, beginning with Descartes modern mathematics, unlike ancient mathematics, does not accept the notion of the geometrical entity as intermediate and as existing in intelligible matter (cp. 2.3.1; 2.4.2), which is missing in Mueller's presentation. For Euclid and Proclus, the geometrical object exists to the extent of its participation in its own ideal (noetic) paradigm, which can only be rendered visualizable through construction but not produced as such. A geometrical object exists thus only insofar as it represents its ideal notion. Unlike Descartes, Euclid is not an essentialist. Euclid demands the constructibility and the actual construction of geometrical objects because of their intermediateness: geometricals do not exist either necessarily (as intelligibles) or contingently (as physical things). Nevertheless, as said, this very construction only exemplifies the geometrical objects' paradigms, themselves not constructed. And lastly, modern mathematics is based on discursive thinking, whereas ancient geometry not only takes into consideration the discursiveness of the *dianoia* supported by the imagination-*phantasia* capable of constructing figures—but also the intellect-*noys* embracing all the paradigms of geometrical objects (see: 3.1.2; 3.2.2).

Being strict and demonstrable, knowledge of geometrical entities for

---

[351] See: Van der Waerden 1977-1978, 353-355; Szabó 1978, 273-276.
[352] Aristotle. Met. 1051a 21-32.
[353] Cp. Aristotle. De caelo 279b 32-280a 10.
[354] Cp. Pritchard 1995, 172-173. Cp. Plato. Timaeus 53c sqq.
[355] Cp. Gaidenko 1987, 313-319.

Descartes is, on the one hand, certain—almost as certain as the proof of the existence of God.[356] On the other hand, it is knowledge of those objects that can be constructed, that is, whose existence before the construction is not yet assured, which corresponds to Descartes' intention to put the weight of scientific research onto questioning the essence rather than the existence of mathematical and physical entities. On his account, even geometry and arithmetic do not require (unlike physics, astronomy and medicine) the actual existence of their objects; therefore, only the object's essence is to be studied.[357] Therefore, the question of the existential status of geometrical objects is not of primary importance to geometry itself, which has to study essential properties of its objects. But then these objects can be taken as only imaginary. Consequently, one might omit the question of their ontological status and consider geometricals only *as if* existent, which is sufficient for the purpose of the scientific "investigation". The Cartesian geometrical method is that of the reduction of a whole class of problems to one single problem, although one can make such a reduction to "an infinity of other problems...thus solving each of them in an infinity of ways".[358] All geometrical problems, according to Descartes, can be then reduced to the (easily constructible) simplest terms, which are lines.[359]

How does the construction of a geometrical entity have to be understood? Is it an act or a process? As we have already seen, the imaginable (re)construction of the world anew can be considered an act, in its "elementary" initial constituents (imagining the whole undifferentiated primary extension-matter), and a process of consecutive differentiation ("grinding" the matter through movement of its parts). The same can be said about geometrical figures, at least, about simple ones: they can be considered both visualizable in a single act of imagination, and produced in the process of a consecutive delineation of their form and shape by movement in the imagination. Yet Aristotle takes imagination to be capable of causing movement.[360] Descartes understands such causation as mechanical: when ideas of internal passions or of external objects arrive in the common sense, they can be further interpreted by the corporeal imagination, which can "change them in various ways, form them into new ideas, and, by distributing the animal spirits to the muscles, make the parts of this body move" in many different ways.[361] At the same time, as it has been argued (3.3.1), rather complex geometrical entities, like the chiliagon, cannot be clearly and distinctly represented in an act of imagination, although the process of their engendering in a finite number of elementary steps (for example, of drawing an interval), which follows a simple algorithm, can be easily imagined. Every geometrical object and—since an extended physical body can be represented for Descartes by its geometrical

---

[356] Descartes. To Mersenne, 25 November 1630, AT I 182.
[357] Descartes. Med. I, AT VII 20.
[358] Descartes. Geometry III, AT VI 485.
[359] Descartes. Geometry, AT VI 369 sqq; esp. 373 sqq.; 422; 440. According to M. Hyppolite, the whole of the Cartesian "Geometry" began from one single problem of Pappus, solved by Descartes in 1631 (Hyppolite 1952, 169). Cp. Lenoir 1979, 355-379.
[360] Cp. Aristotle. De an. 432a 15 sqq., esp. 433a 9-10; Themistius. In de an. 117.33 sqq.
[361] Descartes. Discourse V, AT VI 55; cp. Description of the Human Body, AT XI 227.

substitute—every extended object can also be considered kinematically produced, that is, generated by the movement of another figure or figures (kinematic construction is widely used in the new science, for example, by Barrow and Desargues; cp. 3.4.5).[362] For this reason, not only polygons but "all curved lines which can be described by some regular motion ought to be included in geometry", although for the construction of a problem the simplest curve should be chosen. By the "simplest", "we must understand not only those that are the easiest to describe, nor those that most facilitate the construction or demonstration of the proposed problem, but principally those that are of the simplest class which can be used to determine the required quantity",[363] those that are themselves easily constructible and also visualizable in an act of imagination. As it has been said (2.2.1), the geometrical object is characterized by its extension and movability. Extension is further specified by three characteristics, namely, by dimension, unity and shape.[364] All of these can in addition be considered as resulting from both the act and the process of construction. Obviously, it is not extension, but rather movability that makes the application of the kinematic construction in geometry possible. For example, a line may be constructed by first determining several of its points and subsequently by tracing a trajectory through those points (for example, a spiral) "by a regular and continuous movement".[365] Otherwise, a geometrical line, surface or body can be traced kinematically by a "flowing motion" of another geometrical entity according to some rationally established rule, realized in a construction.[366]

Thus, geometrical constructibility is primarily kinematic constructibility. The only object that cannot be produced in this way is the point, which therefore has a privileged position among geometrical objects (cp. 2.1.3). The point is the simplest geometrical entity not only because it can be taken as the initial, most simple element for construction, but because (unlike all other geometrical entities) it is not to be kinematically constructed. The essential properties of every geometrical entity are thus exemplified and shown in and through movement, where the elementary moving unit is the point. All the more complex kinematically producing objects are reducible to a line, which itself is engendered by the moving point. In particular, the surface tracing a solid can itself be considered kinematically constructed by a line, and the line—by the point; the point can thus

---

[362] Descartes. Geometry III, AT 479, in which Descartes is followed by I. Barrow, see Nikulin 1993, 61-63. Cp. Descartes' description of the kinematic production of geometrical figures that fall under the scope of imagination, To Beeckman, 26 March 1619, AT X 157. Desargues in his "Rough Draft on Conics" takes the infinity of a straight line to be proved by its extension in and by the imagination: "The understanding feels itself wandering in space, not knowing whether that space continues for ever, or if at some place it ceases to continue. To decide the matter, the understanding may for example reason as follows; Either space continues for ever, or at some place it ceases to continue; if at some place it ceases to continue, wherever that place may be, the imagination can find it in time. Now imagination can never find any place in space at which this space ceases to continue; Therefore space and consequently the straight line continue for ever". - Desargues 1987, 141-142. Cp. 3.4.5.
[363] Descartes. Geometry III, AT VI 442-443.
[364] Descartes. Reg. XIV, AT X 447.
[365] Descartes. Geometry II, AT VI 441-412.
[366] Cp. Descartes. Reg. XIV, AT X 446.

be regarded as the primary constituent in the kinematic construction. The object itself then, the *what* of the geometrical construction, is the kinematically producible and constructible geometrical entity.

But what is the *where* of productive geometrical movement? Here we encounter the same difficulty that Descartes encounters when addressing the question of whether the geometrical figure belongs to the *res extensa* or to the *res cogitans* (cp. 2.2.1; 2.4.2). Indeed, the *where* of the movement-production of a geometrical entity cannot be thinking, for the produced and the producing geometrical object are extended, except for the point. But the production of a geometrical object can hardly take place in the extension of physical bodies either, for physical objects do not have the same measurable mathematical properties as geometrical figures, always representing them with a certain approximation. In fact, the question remains unanswered by Descartes, due to the difficulty of solving the problem of the interaction of two finite substances. It might be conjectured that, since the construction is not real, it might be considered imaginary, thus taking place in the imagination. Imagination itself is split, however, into mental and bodily in Descartes (cp. 3.3.1), and therefore it still remains to be seen whether the construction of geometrical objects has to be considered a mental or a physical imaginary process.

Since all extended objects, both physical and geometrical, are implicitly put by Descartes into the same space, matter or extension (there is no room for intelligible matter), it is body *qua* extended that is considered being in motion and constructed by the movement of a point. It is for this reason that mathematics (specifically, geometry) can be practically applied to the construction of bodies, in particular, of instruments and machines.[367] This is just another formulation of the *verum factum* principle, since every physical property can be satisfactorily explained only insofar as it is constructed or produced in extension by the mind.[368] It means that all mathematical properties and laws embodied in constructible geometrical figures are to be found in physical entities as well. And, on the contrary, the property of movability, originally associated with physical things, has to be extended and ascribed to geometrical objects, bracketing the question of whether motion takes place in physical matter or in the imagination. It is in this way that it becomes possible to describe physical things, their properties and movement, in terms of geometrical entities.

Thus, the method of reduction of a whole class of geometrical entities (in Descartes, of lines) to a single, simpler geometrical object which, except for the point, is kinematically constructible, becomes a powerful instrument in the new science. On the one hand, as it has been argued (2.2.1; 2.2.2), numbers and algebraic signs can be represented through and as functional relations.[369] The latter are further representable as geometrical entities, constructible by the movement of other geometrical entities (in this way, the ancient distinction between number and geometrical magnitude is abandoned). On the other hand, physical and mechanical

---

[367] Cp. Descartes. To Hogelande, 8 February 1640, AT III 724.
[368] Cp. Descartes. To Mersenne, 13 July 1638, AT II 238, where the weight of body is explained by a geometrical construction.
[369] Descartes. Reg. XVI, AT X 456.

things are also reducible to geometrical objects, because both are considered as already existing in the same extension and sharing many of the same properties describable as geometrical properties (thus, Descartes considers a string, *la chorde*, either stable or moving, as represented by an interval, that is, by a geometrical figure moving as well).[370] For that reason it becomes possible to understand constructibility as mechanical: there may exist an infinite number of physical objects represented by geometrical lines that can be constructed mechanically—by an instrument "composed of several rulers".[371] Similarly, there can be an infinite number of descriptions (not different from the construction) of a figure, for instance, of an oval.[372] In other words, physical and geometrical magnitudes are constructed in the same way. Ancient ontological and epistemological hierarchies of objects and cognitive faculties become thus superfluous and obsolete, for both numbers and physical things can be represented in and through geometrical objects (in fact, reduced to them). This allows for the *more geometrico* description of physical moving and changing things, by means of (and in the terms of) mathematics, which is now considered capable of embracing and comprising movement and change.[373]

3.4.3 Imagination and geometry: Imagination as constructive

As we have seen, the major operation of mental imagination for Descartes is forming new figures (3.3.1).[374] One might even say that constructing new figures is a *sui generis* purpose of the imagination. This is, of course, only a faint remnant of the traditional teleology in the consideration of cognitive faculties, when every faculty is supposed to be designed to know certain entities, already existing and independent of that faculty. Since early modernity intends to expel and ban teleology, one has to understand imagination not through its purpose—it hardly has any, at least, from the finite human perspective—but through its virtually unlimited capacity to form new objects, even those that it has never seen.[375] There is a further important distinction within the objects of mental imagination; these objects can be considered to be of two kinds. The first is constituted by the imaginings of those things that we have seen or experienced. These come initially from senses through the corporeal imagination. Here belong the imaginings of physical bodies and geometrical figures, whose imitations can be found in the physical world. These imaginings might be called imaginings of intellect, for although constructed or gathered from "real" parts, they are considered to have prototypes not completely dependent on our volition. Such imaginings embrace both geometrical figures and physical bodies, which are put in the same extension without discrimination. They are constructed by the finite imagination, which only follows the divine infinite

---

[370] Descartes. To Mersenne, 15 April 1630, AT I 143.
[371] Descartes. Geometry II, AT VI 391 sqq.; cp. mechanical construction of an ellipse by movement of a point, ibid., AT VI 428.
[372] Cp. Descartes. Geometry II, AT VI 427-428; III, AT VI 464 sqq.
[373] Cp. Descartes. Geometry II, AT VI 414 sqq.
[374] Cp. Descartes. Reg. XII, AT X 415-416.
[375] Cp. Descartes. The Passions of the Soul, AT XI 361.

construction and produces an imaginary or an "as if" construction. To the second kind belong imaginings of things never seen or not "naturally" existing before they are first produced (e.g., chimeras or sky-scrapers), when the finite subjectivity or mind is not bound by any objective restrictions and is completely free to construct whatever it wishes according to its volition. These might be called imaginings of will. Imaginings of intellect have a higher status for Descartes than those of will, because the former follow the objectively established divine order and the latter are to much extent arbitrary. The distinction between intellection and willing is valid only for the finite mind, whereas in the infinite mind there can be no real distinction between the will and thinking: "In God, willing, understanding and creating are all the same thing without one being prior to the other even conceptually (*ne quidem ratione*)".[376] However, since the finite intellect has to pronounce its judgement about actually existing infinity, which is essentially beyond the grasp, one can only state that there should be no such distinction. That is, such a non-distinction should be there, but in what this non-distinction consists, one cannot really say. All truths then are ultimately grounded in God and are true or possible because God knows and wills them as true or possible (i.e., not necessarily but as necessary). It is thus the infinite mind that constructs both extended and thinkable objects through the acts of will.

The divine infinite intellect produces every truth, "innate idea", geometrical figure, and physical body by a single act of volition, which is not really different from an act of thinking—which, in turn, is not really different from the act of imagination in which the infinite mind is able to momentarily grasp any of its objects (not only a chiliagon but even a figure with an actually infinite number of sides). Therefore, from the Cartesian point of view, there can only be a modal difference between thinking and imagination in God, and the infinite imagination is to be presupposed in the divine mind. In fact, the very act of the divine creation of both *res cogitans* (the finite mind) or *res extensa* (the world) can be considered a voluntary imagining of them according to the immanent laws of the divine mind itself.

As it has been argued, the cognitive faculty that enables the finite mind to be constructive is primarily the imagination (yet Aristotle claims it to be within our power).[377] Imagination may voluntarily combine and mix different images into new ones that do not necessarily correspond to any reality (i.e., they are imaginings of the will, cp. 3.3). Since the outer reality is only inanimate *res extensa*, everything that is thought or imagined may be imposed onto matter, which thus can be shaped, constructed and reconstructed. But Descartes puts corporeal things into the same extension and matter as geometrical figures, for the simple reason that there is no other extension. Geometrical figure can be constructed by the mind

---

[376] Descartes. To Mersenne, 27 May 1630, AT I 153. The origins of modern voluntarism may be found in Augustine, and later in Walter of Brugge, Peter Olivi, Duns Scotus and Ockham, who stress the unlimited autonomy and primacy of the will. Cp. Augustine. De civ. Dei XXI.5; Gaidenko 1997, 33-48. From such point of view, the good is good and true is true because God wills them to be good and true, and not because they are necessarily good and true for God, belonging to his nature (cp. 1.3.4).
[377] Aristotle. De an. 427b 17-18.

according to an image or "idea" the mind has or produces (since Descartes still tries to save the divine infinite intellect, innate ideas themselves can be considered as constructed by the infinite divine mind). Corporeal things may also be considered constructed according to their ideas. The production of such images or ideas is not, of course, thought as completely voluntary (it may be reproduced in the imaginings of reason), since it is not in the power of reason not to think something as true when this something is true for the infinite intellect, and is established by means of a (method-oriented) proof. But since for Descartes reason has to prescribe the best for the will (but not necessarily does, for the will can still act on its own—reason and will, two different "modes of thinking" in the "Principles", can coincide only in the infinite mind), the involuntariness of the true cannot in fact be the criterion of being true.

The content of the mind (even the innate ideas) is easily visualizable in and by the imagination, and the demonstration by (imaginary) construction "is obvious to the eye", that is, the inner eye becomes, as it is in Renaissance painting, a precise instrument for producing construction and making decisions about the constructed.[378] Thus, two important features of imagination in Descartes are (a) its intimate connection with matter *qua* extended and (b) its creativity and constructive capacity. The first feature, (a), has already been discussed: extension is easily imaginable and imagination has corporeal things as its object (3.3.1).[379] Still, the *notion* of extension-matter differs from extension as such. The notion is thought by reason alone and should not necessarily require any representation of and in the imagination, whereas spatiality, the three-dimensionality of extension is represented in and by the imagination. Second (b), imagination plays an important role in the creation of figures. It might be that we cannot know how God first created this world and that we are unable to understand how he maintains two created substances by the constant recreation of them.[380] According to Descartes, one has the reason to understand the necessity of the world's creation, but in order to understand *how* it is created, one has to recreate the world, repeating the steps of the world's production. Since this production takes place in the imagination, it is imagination that becomes the demiurgic mental faculty *par excellence*.

Because of the unique constructive capacity of imagination, the autonomy of reason in Descartes turns out to be to much extent the autonomy of imagination, taken as the constructive faculty. A thin border between *as if*-existence and real existence becomes permeable: imagination, which Descartes still understands to be subordinated to reason, may be thus understood as autonomous and creative. Even though Descartes claims that only our thoughts are within our power, in fact, spontaneity is the distinctive mark of imagination, because imaginings are within our power to evoke, to produce and to reproduce them. Moreover, imagination can be taken as both the productive capacity and (since it is able to visualize the extended) as that very *plenum* where production takes place. In other words,

---

[378] Descartes. Geometry III, AT VI 443.
[379] Descartes. Reg. XIV, AT X 442. Cp. Fifth Set of Replies, AT VII 387; To More, 5 February 1649, AT V 270: "Commonly when people talk of an extended being, they mean something imaginable".
[380] Descartes. Second Set of Replies, AT VII 166.

creative imagination assumes the role of both intellection-*noēsis* and intelligible matter, where intelligible objects-*noēta* are produced.

Imagination as constructive appears to be unbounded and free in its operations, especially in "fashioning this matter as we fancy".[381] As Descartes further explains, "the idea of this matter is included to such an extent in all the ideas that our imagination can form that you must necessarily conceive it or else you can never imagine anything at all... [S]ince everything I propose here can be distinctly imagined, it is certain that even if there were nothing of this sort in the old world, God can nevertheless create it in a new one. For it is certain that he can create everything we can imagine".[382] Imagination thus becomes a most important constructive, as it were, demiurgic faculty, even considered prescriptive to the divine reason. Descartes goes as far as to argue that it is not only the case that we are able to imagine everything God can create (except that he can know ideas and produced things eminently), but also that God can create everything we can imagine.

For this reason Descartes needs to state that such a creation is not only possible, but actual: in "The World" he has to undertake an ambitious attempt to recreate the world anew. In this recreation, however hypothetical the initial presuppositions and the very process of such a recreation may be, the final result (the phenomenal world) cannot be different from the real world, that is, from the world created by the infinite mind. Of course, such a recreation is purely imaginary because, first, we do not really know how the real creation takes place. Second, imaginary creation occurs in imaginary space(s).[383] And third, the true appearance is obtained from the presumably false, or only provisional, principles, which Descartes is reluctant to presuppose in the creation by the infinite intellect.[384] The new world still is not really "real", and the purpose of Descartes is not to explain real things, but to produce a world that, although a fake, phenomenally is not different from the "real" one. Moreover, there could be a different number of various hypothetical descriptions and recreations of the same world. The requirement of real being or existence is weakened and reduced to the requirement of essential coincidence with the observed God-given world, which thus can be substituted by the phenomenal illusionary appearance in a clear and distinct panoptical vision, observing every thing and every event from one single point of the finite *ego*. Descartes does not require that life be real; a theater that imitates life will suffice. In fact, there is no way—unless we know the algorithm, the procedure of construction—to tell which world is the "real" one and which one is merely a phantasm. Both share exactly the same attributes, except that being is produced by God in one case, and by the human imagination in the other. This is very much in accord with Cartesian essentialism: Descartes is not so much interested in the

---

[381] Descartes. The World, AT XI 33.

[382] Descartes. The World, AT XI 35-36.

[383] Descartes. Discourse V, AT VI 42-43.

[384] That a true conclusion can be obtained from a false premise (permissible for the operation of the material implication) is accepted by Descartes: "truths may be often illustrated by a false example". - To Hyperaspistes, August 1641, AT III 429; cp. Princ. III 45, AT VIIIA 99-100.

ontological status of the new world, but much more in what we can "construct into" such a world, so that phenomenally it might coincide with the "real" one.

As it has been argued (3.2.2), imagination, as portrayed by Plotinus, is characterized by the following main features. It has an ability to produce images-*phantasmata*; it is intermediate and ambiguous; it is associated with negativity; and it is tightly connected with quasi-extension. Another important feature that is crucial for our present discussion, however, has been left out: namely, the connection of imagination with the geometrical, which is not so clearly established by Plotinus but is later brought in by Syrianus and further elaborated by Proclus.

In his commentary to "Metaphysics", Syrianus' interpretation is that Plato makes imagination the place for geometrical figures.[385] The intellect immediately knows intelligible objects, which are not extended and indivisible forms. Sensible objects, on the contrary, appear to be extended and divisible and are known through mediation of the sense organs. Imagination, which, as Proclus explains, occupies "the central position in the scale of knowing, is woken up by itself to put forth what it knows, but because it is not outside the body, when it brings what it knows from its undivided life into the divided, extended and having figure. For this reason everything that it thinks is a picture or a shape of the thought (*noēmatos*). It thinks the circle as extended, and although this circle is free of external matter, imagination has intelligible matter in itself. This is why there is more than one circle in the imagination, as there is more than one circle in the sense world, for with extension there appear also the more and the less and a multitude of circles and triangles. ...[T]he formative principle (*logos*) of the circle—or of the triangle or of geometrical figure—is of two kinds, the one in intelligible matter, the other in sensual matter".[386]

We have already seen that imagination is essentially effective and operative in the intermediate sphere. There are, however, two intermediate cognitive faculties that both have to do with geometrical objects; namely, the discursive reasoning-*dianoia* and the imagination-*phantasia*, introduced respectively in the first and second parts of the prologue of Proclus' commentary in Euclid. What is the relation between the two cognitive faculties? On the one hand, as Proclus explains, geometrical figures are present in discursive reasoning-*dianoia* and in the imagination-*phantasia* in a considerably different manner: "the circle in the reasoning (*en dianoiai*) is one and simple and unextended, and magnitude itself is without magnitude there (*to megethos amegethes ekei*), for they are all formative principles devoid of matter, and figure is without shape. But the circle in the imagination is divisible, formed, extended—not one only, but one and many, and not a form (*eidos*) only, but a form in instances (*katatetagmenon eidos*), whereas the circle in sensible things is inferior in precision, infected with straightness, and falls short of the purity of immaterial objects".[387] On the other hand, there is also an important difference between grasping the circle in discursive reasoning and in the intellect. The latter conceives the circle in one single act, all at once with all its properties, whereas the former consecutively establishes the properties of the circle

---

[385] Syrianus. In Met. 186.16-22.
[386] Proclus. In Eucl. 52.20-53.22, trans. with changes.
[387] Proclus. In Eucl. 54.5-13; trans. with changes.

one by one through an argument: "For the discursive reasoning contains the formative principles but being weak (*asthenoysa*) to consider them when they are wrapped up, unfolds and exposes them and presents them to the imagination sitting in the vestibule; and in imagination, or with its aid, it explicates its knowledge of them, happy in their separation from sensible things and finding in the matter of imagination a receptacle (*hypodokhē*) apt for receiving its forms."[388]

Thus, on the one hand, reasoning and imagination are both intermediate between the intellect and the senses, the former closer to the intelligible, the latter closer to the sensual. Imagination plays the role of a receptacle for the formative principles-*logoi* effective in reasoning-*dianoia*, formed under the pattern of intelligible objects-*noēta*. On the other hand, both *dianoia* and *phantasia* appear to be ultimate terms in the cognitive triads of intellect-reasoning-imagination and reasoning-imagination-sensual imagination (sensation). Paradoxically, there appears also a *sui generis* inversion between reasoning and imagination. Reasoning is discursive, whereas imagination is capable of presenting its object both (at least, a simple one) as an immediate whole (as the intellect thinks each of its objects in its entirety and all of them in the unity of *koinōnia*), and also as appearing, arising part by part in the medium of intelligible matter. One might consider the relation between reasoning and imagination as that of form and matter, where the activity of discursive reasoning develops and unfolds in the imagination. However, it is not the form-*eidos* but the formative principle-*logos* that appears in reasoning and, consequently, is ascended to in geometrical considerations and constructions; and it is not physical but intelligible matter that appears as matter of and for imagination. Multiplicity, brought to a unity by science (e.g., in formulation of a theorem for an infinite number of objects satisfying certain requirements), is also present differently in discursive reasoning and in the imagination. In the former, multiplicity appears in and through discursiveness, in only partial understanding at each step. In the latter it appears in and through the multitude of circles that can be imagined, as well as in their potentially infinite divisibility.

One has to conclude therefore that in such an unfolding of the previously concealed, it is discursive reasoning that projects its *logos* (which is itself a projection of the *eidos* of the *noys*) into the geometrical matter of the imagination. As intermediate, both *dianoia* and *phantasia* have their share in the constitution of geometrical entities. First, the *eidos* (or, the notion of a figure) is processed as *logos* in discursive reasoning-*dianoia*, which investigates and represents the properties of a figure in terms of consistent propositions and proofs. The *logos* of partless and immaterial figures (*ayla skhēmata*), itself partless and immaterial, is then projected as if upon the "screen" of imagination, which is able to visualize geometrical entities by reconstructing them under their pattern-*logos* now already as extended (*diastatōs*), and to represent them further in and through a physical image (for example, a triangle or square).[389] That is why, strictly speaking, every geometrical object exists as four-fold: in the *eidos* of *noys* as its paradigm; in the *logos* of *dianoia*; in the *phantasma* of *phantasia*; and, finally, in the representation

---

[388] Proclus. In Eucl. 54.27-55.6, trans. with changes.
[389] Syrianus. In Met. 85.4-5; 98.26 sqq.

of the sensual image perceived by the senses.[390] The geometrical figure thus primarily exists not as abstracted from its sensual imitation, not as an imaginable simulacrum, and not even as an object of discursive thinking (which already includes in itself, as in a subject, all its properties), but as the ideal partless paradigm or form.

Thus, when the imagination conceives a geometrical figure, for example, a circle, it takes the circle's image, *phantasma*, not as abstracted from a number of physical circles (all of which are imperfect), but rather forms a circle as if drawing it according to its ideal form or pattern, which is transmitted from *noys* to *dianoia* and further to *phantasia*. A circle in imagination can be either imperfect (i.e., distorted) or perfect; the imagination can present and produce both. But does imagination itself discern between the perfect and the imperfect? The task of imagination is not to judge whether this particular circle is perfect or not; it has to produce a circle, and if it produces the circle under the pattern of discursive thinking, the circle is exact and perfectly round. If, however, the imagination deviates from the *logos*, and either borrows its construction pattern from sense data or voluntarily changes the perfect figure, the produced circle is inevitably distorted. It is thus up to the judgement of the *dianoia* to decide which circle is perfect.

Not only in Plotinus, but also in Proclus imagination is intermediate between sense-perception and discursive reasoning and plays a central role in the constitution of geometrical entities, which themselves occupy an intermediate position between physical bodies and discursive formative principles. As Proclus explains, when the soul (i.e., the discursive reasoning) is acting cognitively (*kata to gnōstikon energoysa*), it projects the formative principles of figures (*toys tōn skhēmatōn logoys*) upon the mirror of imagination.[391] Imagination then presents the undistorted image of a figure (a perfectly round circle or square with truly equal angles) and thus provides discursive thinking with an opportunity for easier consideration of the figure, immediately and not deductively grasping the properties of a geometrical object.[392] This enables ancient mathematicians to represent (but not to equate) mathematical objects, such as numbers and their proportional relations, as geometrical figures: lines, parallelepipeds, and so on (cp. 2.2.2).

Imagination visualizes the dianoetic formative principle-*logos* (the discursive notion), which itself is a discursive representation, splitting an indivisible noetic form-*eidos* (the intelligible notion). Geometrical figures are thus connected with intelligible objects through the mediation of *logoi*.[393] Indeed, the mentioned properties of imagination are all equally discernible in geometrical figures, which may be considered produced in the imagination by discursive reasoning.[394] Furthermore, geometrical objects are intermediate insofar as, on the one hand, they share similar features with both physical things (as extended and divisible) and with intelligible objects and formative principles (as unchangeable

---

[390] Syrianus. In Met. 50.7.
[391] Proclus. In Eucl. 141.4-9.
[392] Cp. Iamblichus. De comm. math. sci. 34.4-12.
[393] Cp.: *geōmetria de noētōn oysa taktea ekei*, Plotinus. Enn. V.9.11.24-25.
[394] Cp. Plotinus. Enn. III.8.4.7-10; VI.3.16.14-15.

and mutually connected), participating not only in the intelligible forms through rational principles but also displaying the irrational as represented by multiplicity and otherness in divisibility and extension (cp. 2.3.1).[395] An important distinction that needs to be mentioned here is that discursiveness in the *analysis* of geometrical objects (which are considered then in an *act*, as already given) differs from discursiveness in the *construction* of figures (which are considered then in a *process* of their kinematic formation by a uniform and undeviating movement). Proclus has this last procedure in mind when he comments on the first three Euclidean postulates of Book I of the "Elements": "The drawing of a line from any point to any point follows from the conception of the line as the flowing of a point and of the straight line as its uniform and undeviating flowing (*homalēn kai aparegkliton rhysin*)."[396] The act of imagination is discrete, as it were, proceeding in a number of steps from one premise or object to another. The process of construction in the imagination, however, is continuous, following a continuous process of as if drawing a line. Such a distinction can be assigned to the fundamental ambiguity of the geometrical as intermediate between the pure intelligible and the bodily. And lastly, the geometrical figure is characterized primarily not by its size or magnitude, but by its shape (*morphē*) of a certain quality (circular, triangular, and so on).[397] This shape is unique but can be present in many geometrical figures of the same form (as in the case of concentric circles, for example), which is only possible when a geometrical figure is represented in the extension of intelligible matter.

Imagination cannot represent either only divisibility or only indivisibility. If the former were the case, it would not be able to display and preserve the form of its object (of a geometrical figure) as extended. And in the latter case, imagination would not be able to construct its objects, because the indivisible cannot be engendered in and by a process. Therefore, the activity of imagination "should start from what is partless within it, proceed therefrom to project each knowable object that has come to it in concentrated form, and end by giving each object form, shape, and extension".[398] There should be an entity that represents indivisibility more than anything else, an elementary unit by means of which all other geometrical entities may be produced. Such an entity is the geometrical point (see 2.1.3).

The principle-*arkhē* of a mathematical entity has to be generically different from ("transcendent to") that of which it is the principle. (The principle of a number—monad—is not itself a number; the principle of a geometrical figure—point—is not a figure strictly speaking; similarly, in ontology the principle of being is not itself being; cp. 1.2.1; 2.1.1; 2.1.2.) This is because the principle is not a

---

[395] Cp.: "[T]he knower in knowing [one part] brings in all the others by a kind of sequence (*akoloythia*); and the geometer in his analysis makes clear that the one proposition contains all the prior propositions by means of which the analysis is made and the subsequent propositions which are generated from it." - Plotinus. Enn. IV.9.5.23-26. See also: Plotinus. Enn. VI.3.16.20-23; Plato. Phil. 16c-17a, 56a-57d; RP 525a-530d.
[396] Proclus. In Eucl. 185.8-12.
[397] Cp. Plotinus. Enn. VI.3.14.20-24.
[398] Proclus. In Eucl. 95.10-14.

genus for that of which it is the principle.[399] Therefore, the principle may be defined negatively: "negative definitions are appropriate to the first principles."[400] In the ontological order principles are the first, but in the order of cognition they are not the first and are arrived at by negation of the given. Since the point is the elementary constitutive unity for any other geometrical entity, it is only the point that is properly negatively defined by Euclid, whereas line and surface are already defined positively.[401] Quite to the contrary, modern mathematicians tend to begin with the axiomatized first principles in the order of cognition, immanentizing these principles by putting them in similar terms with the principiated (cp. 2.1.2; 2.1.4; 2.2.2).

The geometrical point can be further considered representing the arithmetical unit or monad in intelligible matter. What would represent then the indefinite dyad, the principle of otherness in numbers? Monad and point differ insofar as the monad can be conceived both as the formative, generative principle, and as the material principle in and of numbers. A point, on the contrary, can be considered only as the formative principle of a line and not the material one, because a point added to another point does not ever produce a piece of extension. However, a point is also to be considered as the limit of a line and as its productive unit, by which the line is engendered (is drawn). Since such generation involves becoming radically other to itself (the continuous is produced from the discrete), the point, as Proclus puts it, "secretly" contains the potentiality of the unlimited, of otherness (i.e., of matter). Because of this "minimal" materiality (or inherent otherness), the point, while still being indivisible, is to be considered capable of both generating a continuous entity (a line) and of limiting it. The point is then to be considered located in intelligible matter and in imagination, and is capable of being imaginably moved.[402]

The limit and the unlimited are two primary principles for Proclus, which immediately follow the primary cause of being (see 2.4.2).[403] The limit and the unlimited are present as sameness and otherness in every entity.[404] In particular, they are to be found in geometrical entities: every geometrical figure (except for the point) is limited as having a boundary[405] and can be conceived existing as a whole, in an act of imagination and reasoning. Even if the existence of a geometrical object is not presupposed but is to be established by constructing a problem, the object itself cannot suddenly change into another one. The unlimited, on the other hand, is exemplified in extended geometricals through (and as)

---

[399] Cp. Plato. RP 509b; Plotinus. Enn. VI.9.2.47; Aristotle. Met. 1076b 18-19. Aristotle reports that Plato refused to consider the point a genus (Met. 992a 20-21). Plato seems to stress that the point, as the representative of the unit, is *not* a geometrical entity.

[400] Proclus. In Eucl. 94.10-11; cp. Theol. Plat. II 38.13-39.5. Cp. also: Aristotle. De an. 430b 20-21.

[401] Cp. Euclid. Elem. I, def. 1-5.

[402] Cp. Proclus. In Eucl. 88.2-5.

[403] Proclus. Theol. Plat. II 30.22-26 et al. Cp. Breton 1969, 97-110.

[404] Proclus. In Eucl. 5.25-6.7; cp. In. Tim. I 444.16-19; cp. Plato Phil. 16c sqq.; Iamblichus. De comm. math. sci. 12.18-14.17.

[405] Cp. Euclid. Elem. I, def. 13-14.

divisibility and insofar as they can be considered in the process of becoming, kinematically engendered in the medium of intelligible matter.

Proclus considers circular and rectilinear motions as two primary motions, because they correspond to the figures of the circle and the straight line, which have the simplest, and thus most "perfect", definitions and corresponding constructions. Of these two, the former more represents limit, the latter the unlimited, because the circle and circular motion are always held within the limit of their shape, while the line and rectilinear motion can always potentially go further or change direction.[406] Because actually infinite geometrical figures have no finite boundary, and therefore no corresponding *logos*, they cannot be considered by ancient mathematics.[407] For this reason, the circle and circular motion have privileged positions and are simpler and more perfect than the straight line and rectilinear motion, and the latter are simpler and more perfect than any mixed complicated figures and motions.[408] Limit and the unlimited are present then in all geometrical objects in various degrees. Limit (which represents indivisibility, uniformity, stability and form) takes precedence over the unlimited (which represents divisibility, imprecision, irregularity, change, movement and matter), but both are necessarily present in everything that can be considered existent.[409] It is because of the presence of limit and the unlimited, of sameness and otherness, that geometrical objects "can hold fast to their own origins and yet go out to all things, preserving continuity with their principles and not being separated from them, but ever driven by the all-powerful cause in them to move forth".[410]

Even though Plato may have intended to introduce quanta of continuous length (see 2.1.3), and Damascius—quanta of continuous time,[411] the dualism of point and line is not overcome by ancient mathematics. This is because the indivisible cannot be reduced to the divisible, as form cannot be reduced to matter; unity to duality; and sameness to otherness. Still, ancient geometers find a way to establish a connection between the two: a line can be considered both as existing in an act and as kinematically produced, that is, engendered by movement.

3.4.4 Movement in the intellect according to Plotinus

Let us first consider motion in the intelligible in more detail. In the "Sophist" Plato introduces, together with the categories of sameness and otherness (which also play an important role in other dialogues),[412] two further categories within the intelligible (i.e., pertaining to being): those of rest and movement, discussed by Plotinus in his treatise "On the Kinds of Being" (cp. 3.1.1; 3.1.3).[413] For Plotinus,

---

[406] Proclus. In Eucl. 104.11-16, 187.19-27; cp. Aristotle. Met. 1072a 21-22.
[407] Cp. Aristotle. De caelo 272b 17-24.
[408] Plato. Tim. 34a; Aristotle. Phys. 261b 28-265b 15; De caelo 270b32 sqq.; Plotinus. Enn. V.1.7.7-9 et al.; Proclus. Inst. Phys. II 1.
[409] Proclus. In Eucl. 86.5 sqq.
[410] Proclus. In Eucl. 187.11-15.
[411] See: Pines, Sambursky 1987, 64-92.
[412] Cp. Brisson 1974.
[413] See esp.: Plotinus. Enn. VI.2.7.

motion is not devoid of ambiguity, insofar as it embraces opposites and originates intelligible matter (once indefinite thinking turns to its source, see 1.2.1; 2.4.1; 2.4.2), which itself is inevitably ambiguous and does not "stand still" (*mē menei*),[414] presenting an identical non-identity. As Corrigan argues, since intelligible matter is associated with the *aoristos dyas*, ambiguity is also fundamental for Plotinus' account of matter—particularly, of intelligible matter.[415] Why does Plotinus need the notion of movement at all? In the "Sophist" Plato argues that rest and motion are irreducible to sameness and otherness, because sameness and otherness are necessarily present both in rest and in motion, since otherwise motion would have come to a stop and rest would have moved.[416] Here the categories of rest and motion are not specifically reserved for either paradigmatic or eiconic realms (i.e., they are both applicable to the intelligible and the physical). But Plotinus seeks to delineate further two spheres, in order to justify Plato's division between the eternal and its imitation in the moving image of the "Timaeus".[417] Therefore, on the one hand, Plotinus faces an exegetic task of making a concordance between the five categories-*genera* of the "Sophist" and that of the eternity-time distinction of the "Timaeus". On the other hand, he needs to present his own systematic explanation of the relation of the intellect to eternity. For this purpose, the notions of rest and movement appear to be indispensable for Plotinus.

Since the intellect is being, it is always the same, and everything in it is at rest (*hestōta*, i.e., all intelligible objects are stable).[418] However—this reasoning parallels Plato's argument in the "Sophist"—the intellect cannot be only at rest.[419] Why? Because one single act of thinking a particular object involves not only rest in being identically present in this act, but such an act primarily involves activity and therefore cannot stop at one particular object of thought-*noēton*. In other words, thinking is always present to each and every object of thought. Or, otherwise, there can be no thinking without some kind of movement. The transcendent principle of thinking, the One, is then potentiality of movement and itself is neither in movement nor at rest, because it itself is not thought.[420] Thus, the activity of thinking is represented through the notion of movement (*kinēsis*), as thinking the other and going from one object of thought to the other without really leaving any of them, whereas the sameness and being of the intellect (of both thinking and especially of thought) are represented by rest-*stasis*.[421] Both are connected: in the intelligible, movement is always stable and rest is a stillness that is ever in movement and therefore does not bring change. As Plotinus himself puts it, in the intellect "there could not be thinking without otherness, and also sameness. These then are primary, the intellect, being, otherness, sameness; but

---

[414] Plotinus. Enn. VI.6.3.23.
[415] Corrigan 1986, 167-181.
[416] Plato. Soph. 254e sqq.
[417] Plato. 37d-e.
[418] Plotinus Enn. V.1.4.21-22.
[419] Cp. Plotinus. Enn. V.9.10.7-9.
[420] Plotinus. Enn. III.8.7.1-3.
[421] Cp. Gersh 1973, 103-107.

one must also include motion and rest. One must include movement if there is thought, and rest that it may think the same; and otherness, that there may be thinker and thought; or else, if you take away otherness, it will become one and keep silent; and the objects of thought, also, must have otherness in relation to each other. But one must include sameness, because it is one with itself, and all have some common unity; and the distinctive quality (*diaphora*) of each is otherness".[422]

The multiple complex unity of the intellect can be considered in different ways. As subject or substrate, the intellect is said to be substance; as life—movement; as preserving its identity, unchanging—rest; and as altogether one—both the same and the other (cp. 3.1.1).[423] We may say that the categories of sameness and otherness represent the dynamic structure that constitutes the intellect as the intelligible—as thought. Whereas the categories of rest and movement represent the *noys* in its intellectual aspect—as the eternal activity of thinking. Intellectual movement as pure activity and actuality of thinking has to be different from physical movement, which expresses the measure of a physical thing in approaching its *telos* in passing from the state of potentiality to that of actuality.[424] At this point, Plotinus has to reject implicitly the Aristotelian theory of motion (applicable only to physical things) in favor of the Platonic notion of movement in the "Sophist". However, for Aristotle non-physical matter is also connected with motion, although in celestial bodies: "All things that change have matter, but different things have different kinds; and of eternal things such as are not generable but are movable by locomotion have matter, matter, however, which admits not of generation, but of motion from one place to another" (cp. 1.1.1).[425] Such motion can be considered geometrically, because, unlike the motion of physical perishable things, it is circular eternal motion which is identical and ever the same in its alteration. Still, properly speaking, this motion is not the motion of geometrical or intelligible objects, but of celestial material things. Later Greek mathematics and philosophy reappropriate the non-physical motion of the "Sophist". The movement Plotinus is primarily interested in is not a spatial motion from one place to another, but rather is the sameness considered through otherness—a staying in motion, a paradoxical *status movendi*. The other (the object), which the intellect thinks, is not different from the intellect itself, because it lies within the same *noys*, so that the intellectual movement appears to be a circular, non-spatial motion that fits an always identical form and goes out without ever having really left itself.

Movement and rest have to be present in the intellect because of the intellect's duality or distinction into thinking-*noēsis* and being-*noēta*: the being of the intellect "is that in which thought comes to a stop, though thought is a rest which has no beginning, and from which it starts, though thought is a rest which never started: for movement does not begin from or end in movement. And again

---

[422] Plotinus. Enn. V.1.4.33-41; cp. Enn. VI.2.8.25 sqq.
[423] Plotinus. Enn. III.7.3.7-11.
[424] Cp. Aristotle. Phys. 201a 10-202b 29; 224a 20 sqq.
[425] Aristotle. Met. 1069b 25-27.

the form at rest is the defining limit of the intellect, and the intellect is the movement of the form".[426]

Movement is movement towards an end, *telos*, which in the case of the intellect is a noetic object, the limit of thinking at rest, *en stasei peras*. Thus, rest or *stasis* characterizes the whole of the intelligible cosmos, *ideai* or *noēta*, the realm of being (*on*) and substance (*oysia*), whereas movement, *kinēsis*, represents *noys* as the intellectual activity of thinking-*noēsis*. However, movement and rest in the intellect are not, and cannot be, rigidly separated, because the activity of thinking is always directed to, and comes from, the being of thought (*eis ho; aph' hoy*).[427] Movement thus is neither "under" (*hypo*) nor "over" (*epi*) being, but is *with* (*meta*) being.[428] Since, further, the intellect is also one in its multiplicity, is "double one" (*diployn hen*),[429] all binary distinctions and oppositions within it are not real distinctions and belong only to the conception (*epinoia*) (i.e., are only mental distinctions (cp. 1.1.3)).

Intellectual movement cannot be taken, however, as a predicate of the subject-rest. The notion of rest rather conveys the intellect's perseverance in being, which serves the end (*telos*) for movement—that intellectual movement which does not change being but brings it to perfection of communication and reflectivity.[430] Indeed, the intellect thinks itself in the form(s) of intelligible objects which are not really different from the intellect, so that its intellectual activity is always directed to itself and always returns to itself (see 3.1.1). This self-thinking is thus immediate self-knowledge—always present in the intellect through the activity of the self-movement of *noys* (*aytokinēsis*), which is incessantly "wandering" in itself, as it were (*en haytōi planēthentos*).[431] The intellect in the fullness of its being is completed by returning to itself without ever really having left itself. If the intellect were to be understood only in terms of identity and rest, it would have been inactive (*argei*), it would not have thought at all and would not have known itself. In fact, it would not even have existed.[432] Therefore, there is nothing in the intellect that at the same time is not the other. In its thinking, the intellect is ever present to all its objects as if moving towards all of them and at the same time *already* having moved, as if filling them all.[433]

But why are the two categories of movement and rest insufficient for characterizing the life of the intellect? Because there are also other kinds of movement: discursive movement in reasoning; geometrical movement, associated

---

[426] *Eti de hē men idea en stasei peras oysa noy, ho de noys aytēs hē kinēsis*, Plotinus. Enn. VI.2.8.20-24.
[427] Plotinus. Enn. VI.2.8.14-15.
[428] Plotinus. Enn. VI.2.7.16-17.
[429] Plotinus. Enn. VI.2.7.24; VI.2.17.23-24.
[430] Plotinus. Enn. VI.2.7.24 sqq.
[431] Plotinus. Enn. VI.2.18.8-9; I.1.13.4-5; VI.7.13.30-31.
[432] Plotinus. Enn. VI.7.13.39 sqq.
[433] Plotinus. Enn. VI.7.13.4-16. The intellect "in its movement moves always in the same way and on a single, identical course, but still is not the same one partial thing, but all things" (*noys te kinoymenos kineitai men hōsaytōs kai kata tayta kai homoia aei, oy mentoi tayton kai hen ti en merei, alla panta*, Enn. VI.7.13.4-6).

with the imagination; and physical movement. It is in order to distinguish between these kinds of movement that one has to resort to the other pair of categories, those of sameness and otherness. It is only in the intellect-*noys* that there is a subtle balance between the same and the other in the not dissolvable one-many, so that the life "there" is always equal to itself, remains in perfect quietude, *hēsykhia*, possesses itself and is present to itself without any diminution.[434] Discursive thinking-*dianoia* (the soul) is already unable to hold the equilibrium of the same and the other (which is now dissolved into the separate one *and* many), so that the life of the soul is no longer complete but is weakened, as if there were a "spreading out" (*diastasis*) or a succession (*allēn met' allēn; ephexēs*) of mental states and objects.[435] In this state, thinking becomes necessarily discursive, unable to embrace and to know itself in a single act, and therefore always strives in vain to grasp the fullness of the intellect's life (cp. 3.1.3).[436]

If movement were simply identical with change, it would also change otherness into sameness (i.e., into other than otherness itself), since otherness necessarily presupposes sameness: there is no otherness without sameness and *vice versa*. Similarly, there is no movement without rest and no rest without movement in the intellect, since they mutually presuppose each other.[437] When the initial dyad is brought forth, both otherness and sameness are already there, inseparable from each other, however, not yet defined as sameness and otherness unless there is the first "movement" of the intellect back to its principle which is in "rest" (cp. 1.2.1). Therefore, on the one hand, otherness and movement are not identical, for they express different moments of the relation of the dyad to the One. Otherness is constituted in advancing, *proodos*, whereas primary movement is constituted in returning, *epistrophē* (although, as said, movement is always present in otherness and otherness is present in movement). On the other hand, there is no real distinction between otherness and primary movement, because both represent pure change. For this reason Plotinus brings both otherness and primary movement to characterize indefinite thinking, in which "if you approach any of it [the not yet defined object of the indefinite thinking] as one, it will appear many; and if you say that it is many, you will be wrong again: for each [part] of it is not one, all of them cannot be many. And this nature of it according to one and the other of your

---

[434] Plotinus. Enn. III.7.11.14.
[435] Plotinus. Enn. III.7.11.36-37, 41.
[436] Cp. Themistius. In de an 109.18 sqq. Metaphorically, this unbalanced state of the soul can be described as dominated by an "unquiet power" (*dynamis oykh hēsykhos*) that tends to perform that which it should not and cannot do, by a "restlessly active nature (*physeōs polypragmonos*) which wanted to control itself and be on its own, and chose to seek for more than its present state" (Plotinus. Enn. III.7.11.15-21; cp. VI.3.23.1-5). Instead of eternity, there arises time (Enn. IV.4.15.2-4; cp. III.7.11.1 sqq.). At this point of the dissolution of the one and the many into two independent entities, there appears evil, which consists both in desire and in the inability to retain the whole of the life, thinking and being of the intellect. Observations on the connection of this necessarily deficient state of the soul to the "audacity" (*tolma*), "independence" (*aytexoysion*) and "striving" (*orexis*) see in: Jonas 1962, 315-317; Manchester 1978, 101-136; Strange 1994, 48. Cp. Aristotle. De an. 433a 9-11.
[437] Plotinus. Enn. VI.6.3.26-43.

imaginations is movement, and, according as imagination has arrived at it, rest. And the impossibility of seeing it by itself is movement from intellect and slipping away; but that it cannot run away but is held fast from outside and all around and is not able to go on, this would be its rest; so that one may not say that it is only in motion".[438]

Since, as it has been argued, indefinite primary *noēsis* is exemplified in intelligible matter, which, in turn, is connected with the imagination (see 2.4.2; 3.2.4), primary movement also has to be connected with the imagination.[439] In Enn. III.6 Plotinus argues that imagination is capable of originating movement.[440] Now between intellectual and physical movement we have two other (as if intermediate) movements: that of discursive thinking (of *logos*) and of imagination. How are these two related? Plotinus depicts this relation in the following way: "Now the soul [i.e. the discursive thinking] which holds the forms of real beings, and is itself, too, a form (*eidos*), holds them all gathered together (*homoy panta*), and each individual form is gathered together in itself; and when it sees the forms of things perceived by the senses as it were turning back towards it and approaching it, it does not endure to receive them with their multiplicity, but sees them stripped of their mass; for it cannot become anything else than what it is... So therefore both that which proceeds from the rational principle in the higher world has already a trace (*ikhnos*) of what is going to come into being, for *when the rational principle is moved in a sort of picture-making imagination (en phantasiai eikonikēi kinoymenos ho logos)*, either the movement which comes from it is a division (*merismos*), or if it did remain the same, it would not be moved, but stay as it was; and matter, too, is not able to harbor all things gathered together, as soul is; if it could, it would belong to the higher world; it must certainly receive all things, but not receive them undivided (*mē ameros*)."[441]

Movement in matter represents the appearance of an object "part by part", as it were (i.e., in some sequential order). But this "part by part" embodiment of a thing can take place not only in bodily matter but also in intelligible matter, *hylē noētē*, and it is not a physical body, but the rational formative principle-*logos* that is moving. Since, as it has been pointed out (3.1.2), in discursive reasoning, and even more in the imagination, the simultaneous whole of the communication-*koinōnia* of noetic objects is split, discursive reason also has all forms together, but in separation, which it has to overcome by gathering the *theōrēmata* in establishing their properties as visualized and traced in geometrical objects through the embodiment of *logos* in the *plenum* of intelligible matter by means of imagination. When the discursive formative principle (*logos*) is moved (*kinoymenos*) in the imagination, in its very movement the *logos* brings division and distinction in the previously undivided and undistinguished intelligible matter, as if delineating it into distinct (geometrical) objects. Why is such a construction by movement necessary? Because it is only in the intellect that the form, the noetic object, is always what it is. In the discursive reason, and even more in the imagination, any

---

[438] Plotinus. Enn. VI.6.3.33-43.
[439] Cp. Aristotle. De an 428b 11 sqq.; esp. 429a 1-2.
[440] Plotinus. Enn. III.6.4.43-46. Cp. Fleet 1995, 132.
[441] Plotinus. Enn. III.6.18.24-37; italics added.

object is not already *homoy panta* with all other objects of possible consideration and thus it has to be reestablished in its unity (particularly, through construction of a problem or proving a theorem).[442] Here Plotinus disagrees with Aristotle, who stresses the sameness and non-materiality of the image of imagination.[443] To represent an imaginable object as one single whole, one has to visualize it, producing it through construction by movement in the imagination. In other words, the formative principle, *logos*, can be considered as moving and thus as if "cutting out" its object in intelligible matter by means of the imagination.

3.4.5 Motion and construction in Proclus: Production of a geometrical figure by movement in imagination

An object is constructible if it has parts. Since an extended object has parts, it can be constructed according to its notion in discursive reasoning or in the intellect. However, an extended physical thing is not constructible in ancient science (unlike in Descartes' reconstruction of the physical world), because it is considered either not constructed at all, or constructed by the demiurg, the *noys*. Only an imaginable extended thing—in particular, a geometrical object—can be constructed or reconstructed by and within the finite mind. That which is partless cannot be constructed—it is rather created, for it may either be or not be. Thus, for Proclus the intelligible form-*eidos* is not constructible, because it is simple: it is not movable (*akinēton*), not born (*agenēton*), indivisible (*adiairēton*) and has no substrate (*pantos hypokeimenoy kathareyon*).[444] The substrate that makes an object of consideration divisible, and thus potentially constructible, is intelligible matter—not *qua* the principle of otherness and multiplicity, but *qua* that *plenum* where an object may be considered as a *sui generis* extended. Such an object in the mind is primarily a geometrical figure, as if visually represented in the imagination.

But why does the mind need to construct its object at all? As we have seen, in the Platonic ontology four different constituents of an object of cognition can be discerned (see 3.2.3). In particular, in every geometrical figure there can be distinguished, first, the intelligible notion of the intellect-*noys*, or its form-*eidos* (thought as the intelligible object-*noēton*); second, the formative principle-*logos* (or dianoetic notion) of discursive thinking-*dianoia*, according to which the figure can be constructed (see 3.4.3); third, the image of imagination-*phantasia*; and fourth, the sensually apprehensible image of the figure. Of these four, the first and the second are partless and not extended in any way. The third and the fourth are extended in a way and thus have parts. However, the geometrical figure as represented in the imagination is perfect, whereas its sensual physical imitation is not. For this reason, Proclus has to ascribe a special kind of matter and materiality to geometrical objects, in which a geometrical figure is conceivable as extended

---

[442] Plotinus. Enn. I.8.3.6-9.
[443] "[W]hen we contemplate, we must contemplate the image (*phantasma*) as one (*hama*), for images are like objects of perception except that they lack matter." - Aristotle. De an. 432a 8-10.
[444] Proclus. In Eucl. 56.11-13.

and having parts and as constructible. This matter he calls geometrical matter, *hylē geōmetrikē* (cp.2.4.2; 3.2.2).[445]

As it has been argued, geometrical matter is intelligible matter represented specifically in imagination and in geometrical figures. Intelligible matter is a broader concept: as indefinite dyad, *aoristos dyas*, it is the principle of otherness and multiplicity, present also to *noys* (cp. 2.1.1; 2.1.2; 2.4.1). Geometrical objects are intermediate between dianoetic formative principles and sensual bodies (cp. 2.3.1). As the former, geometricals have no modifiable properties but are precise and unchanging over time, studied by science. As the latter, geometricals exemplify otherness through specific—intelligible or geometrical—materiality. Conceived as necessarily related to intelligible geometrical matter, a geometrical object (again, except for the point) can be conceived as quasi-material or extended (i.e., existing in some kind of (geometrical) extension, *diastatos*), as having parts (*meristos*), as divisible (*diēirēmenos*) and as having shape (*eskhēmatismenos*, i.e., visually representing its formative principle).[446]

Most important is that a geometrical object has only one unique notion and one formative principle, which can be represented in a potentially infinite number of instances. In other words, there can be multiple objects of the same shape. Why are there many representations of one figure in intelligible or geometrical matter? First of all, because of the partiality of discursive reasoning—because of its inability to hold the whole of intelligible objects in their timeless communication and to conceive and grasp them all at once in one single, simple act of comprehension and knowledge. The *dianoia* is capable of understanding a formative principle (e.g., in the construction of a chiliagon), but it cannot immediately know all the properties inherent in its object. The notion-*eidos* is simple, and it is not easy for discursive thinking to discern its inherent properties, which are analytically contained in it as a subject. In order to simplify the consideration, as if to return to itself and to the simplicity of the *noys*, discursive reasoning needs the assistance of imagination, which visualizes the object as extended, in order to subsequently analyze it and to reveal its properties through a number of propositions and constructions.[447] To know the properties of a (geometrical) entity, discursive reason has to externalize that entity, representing it first in the imagination. In order to understand that which the reason already has, it has to alienate its objects (*dianoēta*), as if unfolding them by constructing them as divisible, geometrically shaped or formed. Discursive thinking considers then "the outer" (the extended figures) in order to be aware of "the inner" (the formative principle), and to further ascend to the form or notion of the figure, under the pattern of which the extended geometrical figure is formed *qua* extended. There is a single object of discursive thinking, *dianoēton*, representing one single formative principle, *logos*, which further corresponds to a unique form, *eidos*, or intelligible notion of that object. However, there can be a potentially infinite number of

---

[445] Proclus. In Eucl. 56.23.
[446] Proclus. In Eucl. 50.22-51.2; 54.8-9.
[447] Cp. Syrianus. In Met. 91.25-92.7. Cp. O'Meara 1989, 133-134.

representations of this same geometrical object (e.g., of a circle) in the imagination and in the physical world, because it can be constructed always anew (e.g., a number of concentric circles).

"The true geometer", explains Proclus, "should cultivate such efforts and make it his goal to arouse himself to move from imagination to pure and unalloyed discursive reasoning (*dianoia*), thus rescuing himself from extension and the 'passive intellect' (*pathētikoy noy*, i.e., from imagination) for the discursive, dianoetic activity that will enable him to see all things without parts or intervals— the circle, the diameter, the polygons in the circle, all in all and everything is separately and by itself (*panta en pasin kai hekaston khōris*). For this reason even in our imagination we show circles as inscribed in polygons and polygons as inscribed in circles, in imitation of the proof that the partless formative principles exist in and through one another. And for the sake of this, we describe structure and construction of figures, their divisions, positions and juxtapositions, and we use imagination and the extended images that it brings, because the form (*eidos*) is itself motionless and is not in becoming and is altogether free from being formed. But everything that is concealed in the form is brought into the imagination as extended and divisible and that which projects (such images) is the discursive reasoning (*dianoia*), the source of projection is the form in the discursive reasoning (*to dianoēton eidos*, i.e., the form of the intellect as appropriated and processed by the discursive reasoning), and that which it is projected into is the so-called 'passive intellect' which unfolds itself around (*peri*) the partlessness of the true intellect (*toy alēthois noy*), sets a distance between itself and that unextended pure thinking (*noēseōs*) and shapes itself after the unshaped forms and becomes everything that constitutes the discursive reasoning and the indivisible formative principle (*logos*) in us".[448]

As it has been argued (see 3.2.4), multiple geometrical objects are rendered visualizable in intelligible (geometrical) matter which is not different from the imagination. Intelligible matter and imagination share a number of common properties (see 2.2.4; 3.2.3). In imagination, as well as in geometrical matter, geometrical objects can be considered quasi-extended with the above mentioned properties. But matter, even intelligible matter, always represents otherness as possibility (of division, of multiple appearance of the same object, and so on). Everything that exists in the imagination, exists also in intelligible matter[449] and, on the contrary, everything connected with intelligible matter (i.e., every object of thought, both of the intellect and of discursive reasoning) is imaginable or representable in the imagination. Proclus not only equates *phantasia* with *hylē geōmetrikē*, but also further identifies imagination with the Aristotelian "passive intellect" (*noys pathētikos*), because of its ability to be affected and its intermediate position between the intellect and the senses.[450] We find a similar interpretation of

---

[448] Proclus. In Eucl. 55.23-56.22, trans. with changes.
[449] Proclus. In Eucl. 51.13-20.
[450] Aristotle. De an. 430a 10-25; Proclus. In Eucl. 52.3; 56.17-18; In RP II 107.14-29; In Tim. I 244.20-21; III 158.8-10 et al.; cp. Porphyry. Sent. 16; 43. See also: Chitchaline 1993, 22-31.

imagination in Syrianus, who Proclus might follow in his commentaries.[451] Such an identification appears to be particularly appropriate, because Aristotle portrays (very briefly) the "passive intellect" as a kind of matter for the active intellect (which is the intellect-*noys* in the proper sense): the former becomes everything—it embodies every object that the latter produces in thinking. As intelligible or geometrical matter, *noys pathētikos* receives forms placed in it by the activity of the (productive) intellect. In the active intellect, forms or notions are fully expressed in their actuality, but in the passive *noys* they are still only potential (as forms in matter) and thus need to be actualized. Such an actualization is conceived by Proclus as production of a (primarily geometrical) object in intelligible matter or imagination. Potential knowledge is to be actualized, that is, presented in discursive thinking in a number of (true) propositions and arguments. Once produced, an object represents all its properties that can be strictly, or scientifically, known, gathered by the *dianoia* from partiality and dispersion.

Scientific cognition thus presupposes a construction of its object as a procedure that simplifies the considerations. The most adequate, or precise, object that is both quasi-extended and almost visually represents the properties of the formative principle and the corresponding ideal form, is the geometrical figure. The geometrical figure is then to be considered constructible. But where and how does such a construction take place? The drawing of a straight line cannot take place in physical space, because of the presence of physical matter, which inevitably distorts and corrupts every image and representation. The "where" for Proclus has to be intelligible matter *qua* imagination or *noys pathētikos*. The geometrical figure is thus constructed in the imagination. Imagination, as passive intellect, is that "screen" onto which or into which (*en hōi*) the constructed object, the geometrical figure, is projected or thrown upon (*to proballomenon*). The determining form of the geometrical figure, that which is projected, is its formative principle, or *logos*, from which, and according to which, the geometrical object is originated (*aph' hoy proballetai*) and itself is the discursive representation of the intelligible form (*to dianoēton eidos*). And that which "throws" (*to proballon*) the formative principle is the discursive thinking-*dianoia*. The unextended, non-imaginable and not visualizable intelligible notions are present in this way in the imagination, as in an extension or matter that separates itself (*diistas*) and its objects, alienating them for clearer consideration.[452] Discursive thinking is not immediately reflective. Because of this, in order to understand the formative principle, the *dianoia* has first to estrange the *logos*, to subsequently recognize and investigate the *logos* in the image of a geometrical figure, which is an unfolding of the properties that are already contained ("secretly", *kryphiōs*) in the thinkable form (cp. 3.4.3), thus representing the unextended and shapeless as extended and having shape. The purpose of the imaginable projection is to "release" or "liberate" the *logos*, and, further, the corresponding *eidos*, from materiality (although intelligible matter is still present to both) and to gather the broken and dispersed knowledge into unity.

---

[451] *Kalei gar taytēn en heterois pathētikon noyn*, Syrianus. In Met. 110.32-33.
[452] Proclus. In Eucl. 56.14-22. Cp. Trouillard 1983, 233-234.

The construction of a geometrical figure is then an unwrapping of the *logos*, when the simplicity of the noetic form is represented through an analyzable and structured object. But what constructs geometrical objects in the matter of imagination (*phantastē hylē*)? The underlying construction scheme in Proclus is obviously hylomorphic. Therefore, that which constructs has to be actual and limiting. Proclus takes the activity of discursive thinking (*dianoētikē energeia*) to be depicted in the imagination.[453] The *logos* thus as if lends itself to the imagination taken as imaginable matter. But even if it is discursive thinking that represents actuality in the construction, it is not the fully expressed and gathered actuality of the intellect, but it is weakened (*asthenoysa*) by multiplicity. Imagination is potentiality, both the capacity and the place of construction. The constructive activity is transmitted down to the productive power of the imagination, as it were, which is then able to "unfold" itself (*exelitton heayton*) against the partlessness of the intellect.[454] Imagination can be thus taken as motivated by itself, as if (such "as if"-ness is a distinctive feature of the imagination) woken by itself.[455] Imagination, however, is recreative rather than creative, because imaginable construction is reproduction of its object, which has to represent a formative principle and the corresponding notion-*eidos*. Both formative principle and intelligible notion, the patterns for imaginable reconstruction, are themselves not constructible, being neither arbitrary nor contingent, but simply existing and being what they are. The same might be said not only about imaginary reconstruction of geometrical objects and naturally existing physical things, but also about arbitrary images assembled from parts (e.g., chimeras), to each of which a formative principle can be ascribed.

Proclus' interpretation of the postulate in Euclid explains the way motion can be conceived in geometrical figures. Not only can geometrical figures be kinematically constructed, but they themselves can be considered movable, as in the case of two figures that should mutually overlap in order to be conceived congruent. Because geometricals are intermediate between the thinkable and the sensual, they are to be produced neither by intellectual nor physical movement, but by an intermediate one that takes place in the imagination. As Proclus argues, "[L]et us think of this motion not as bodily, but as imaginary (*mē...sōmatikēn alla phantastikēn*), and admit not that things without parts move with bodily motions, but rather that they are subject to the ways of the imagination. For intellect, though partless, is moved, but not spatially; and imagination has its own kind of motion corresponding to its own partlessness."[456] Since there are objects of different ontological statuses, one has to distinguish different kinds of motions and places where these motions occur, for "the motion of bodies is one thing, the motion of objects conceived in imagination is something else; and the place of extended objects is other than the space of partless beings. We must keep them separate and not confuse them".[457] One might thus distinguish four different kinds of motion: in

---

[453] Proclus. In Eucl. 56.1.
[454] Proclus. In Eucl. 56.18.
[455] Proclus. In Eucl. 52.22.
[456] Proclus. In Eucl. 186.9-14; cp. 51.17-20.
[457] Proclus. In Eucl. 186.25-187.3.

noys, in *dianoia*, in *phantasia* and physical motion, where the first three appear within intelligible matter, and the last one within physical matter. It is only the last two kinds of movement that are subject to construction; only in them can construction be rendered kinematically visualizable. At the same time, such a construction can be precise only in the imaginable, since geometrical figures can be produced only in the imagination and then further studied by discursive reasoning. Geometry as a strict knowledge is thus only about geometricals, not bodies. For Proclus there can be no mathematical science of physical things.

As it has been said, the geometrical figure can be considered either in an act or in a process of construction. In the second part of the prologue to his Euclid commentary, Proclus describes imagination as a faculty that "both by virtue of its formative movement (*dia te tēn morphōtikēn kinēsin*) and because it has existence (*hypostasin*) with and in the body, always produces pictures (*typōn*) that are divisible, have parts and shape, and everything it knows has this kind of existence (*hyparxin*)".[458] Such a movement takes place in the medium of intelligible matter by means of the imagination, governed by the formative principle (or *logos*), which, in turn, represents the corresponding *eidos* (or intelligible object-*noēton*, cp. 3.1.1; 3.1.2). The activity of imagination is then expressed primarily as the "formative movement", by which its objects are produced. In the commentary to the "Republic" Proclus also portrays imagination as the "shape-producing thinking which wants to know the intelligibles (*phantasia noēsis oysa morphōtikē noētōn ethelei gnōsis einai*)".[459] The imagery movement that produces, as if drawing, a figure is then an image of the pure activity of production.

There are many examples of the geometrical kinematic construction in ancient geometry: thus, Archytas solves the problem of doubling the volume of a cube by means of an imaginary movement of a two-dimensional figure around a fixed axis.[460] Apollonius describes the generation of the conic surface by the movement of an indefinitely extendible straight line, fixed in a point and moving along a circumference.[461] And Archimedes, as Heath points out, uses a great variety of words for "drawing a line".[462]

However, not every geometrical entity can be constructed: the point cannot be constructed. Indeed, constructible is that which has parts, but a point, according to Euclid, "has no parts" (see 2.1.3). Therefore, the point has a privileged position among geometrical entities. If a geometrical figure is constructed, as if drawn or kinematically produced in the imagination, what is that which is moving or moved by the *morphōtikē kinēsis*? Is it intelligible form or formative principle? Neither, since both are indivisible, unextended and without an underlying substrate, they are not movable, and only extended entities are considered capable of locomotion, because locomotion implies movement from one place to another. It is by movement of the point that a line is produced, as if drawn in the imagination (and the line further produces a plane, and the plane—a

---

[458] Proclus. In Eucl. 51.20-52.3; trans. with changes.
[459] Proclus. In RP I 235.
[460] Archimedes. Opera III 84-101. Cp. Becker 1957, 76-80.
[461] Apollonius. Con. I, def.1.
[462] Heath 1953, clxxiv-clxxv.

solid, so that each time the dimension increases).[463] The geometrical figure should therefore be constructed by a movement in the imagination of a figure of a dimension less by one. The minimal entity, a geometrical unit, is the simplest in all respects, because it has no parts (which is the definition of the point); the maximal is a three-dimensional solid. (Ancient mathematics does not recognize any dimensions higher than three, because more dimensions cannot be visually represented in the imagination and because, as the Pythagoreans argue, the number three is a complete one, representing the whole and thus the cosmos (*to pan*) in its beginning, middle and end.)[464]

The order of construction may not coincide, however, with the order of analysis: the last in the order of analysis may be (and in mathematics, it usually is, as Aristotle points out) the first in the order of production (*en genesei*, cp. 2.2). Thus, in the order of the kinematic construction of geometrical objects, the point is prior to the plane, as the plane is prior to the solid; but by way of analysis, on the contrary, the solid is prior to the plane and the plane is prior to the point.[465] The reason for this is that construction has to do primarily with postulates that start with the construction of a straight line by the movement of a point (it is in the commentary to the first three postulates that Proclus introduces the notion of the kinematic production of the geometrical figure). When a point is traced as moving uniformly in the simplest way without any deviations (displaying not only sameness, insofar as it stays on the same course and preserves the same form, but also otherness, insofar as it always is not in the same geometrical place as it has just been), then the generative point moves, producing one of the two simplest lines: either a straight line (the first and especially second postulates of Book I of Euclid's "Elements") or a circle (the third postulate of Book I).[466] In fact, it is only in the imagination that the straight line can be drawn by a point "moving uniformly over the shortest path",[467] because in physical matter a straight line cannot be produced. In other words, in order to bring a geometrical entity to existence one must as if visually ascertain in the imagination that the entity thought through its formative principle and its form be actually reproduced in construction, as if by an imaginable drawing (e.g., a line). In this way, postulates are then established and the problems solved. In order to understand the first postulate, namely, to draw a straight line from any point to any point, one must actually draw it, reproduce it in (the) imagination: "If we take a straight line as limited by a point and conceive the point as moving uniformly over the shortest route, the first postulate will have been established by us in a simple thinking procedure."[468] Such uniform movement of a point is an image of pure activity of the discursive reason and of stable movement of the intellect represented in and by the imagination.

---

[463] Cp. Aristotle. De an. 409a 4-6.
[464] As reported by Aristotle. Phys. 268a 6 sqq.
[465] Proclus. In Eucl. 85.8-13; 89.4 sqq.
[466] The first three Euclid postulates of Book I are: "Let the following be postulated: 1. To draw a straight line from any point to any point. 2. To produce a finite straight line continuously in a straight line. 3. To describe a circle with any center and distance."
[467] Proclus. In Eucl. 185.17.
[468] Proclus. In Eucl. 185.12-15.

There are, however, two difficulties that arise once a line is conceived as traced by the point in the imagination. First, if imagination conceives divisible and quasi-extended objects, how can it have any representation of the point? To this Proclus replies that since imagination essentially is not different from intelligible (imaginable, or geometrical) matter, it both exemplifies the same and the other, the limit and the unlimited, the undivided and the divided, as if moving "from the undivided to the divided, from the unformed to what is formed".[469]

The second difficulty is: how is it possible that the point, being partless and therefore indivisible, can move or be moved? Aristotle excludes the possibility of the movement of a point or anything indivisible, because when moving, an object moves to some distance proportional to a finite part of its length. Since the point is indivisible, it can move only to the whole of itself (which has no length). Therefore, a line produced in this way will be the sum total of the points added up, which is impossible, because the continuous does not consist of the discrete and indivisible (cp. 2.1.3).[470] In order to resolve this aporia, Proclus has to admit that the point moves not spatially but only *as if*, which means that it moves by an imaginary movement. Such a movement is described negatively, as distinct from the spatial: it is the other of bodily locomotion and thus does not happen in real space, but in an imaginary one, namely, in geometrical matter. However, the imaginary movement of the point can hardly be positively characterized. Unlike in modern science, there can be no mathematical account of the movement of a point: its trajectory cannot be counted by number, since this trajectory is elusive to thought. The geometrical figure is studied and analyzed by discursive thinking once the figure has already been produced and is considered stable and not moving (as, for instance, in Archytas).[471]

How is it then possible to conceive of imaginary movement? On the one hand, as said, there can be no proper consideration of such movement, because that which is in becoming can hardly be thought (it is for this reason that Proclus refuses to characterize properly imaginary movement). On the other hand, the imaginary construction of a geometrical figure is both necessary and possible in Greek science. It is necessary because discursive reasoning cannot embrace and grasp at once all predicates inherent in the subject of consideration. It therefore must as if alienate them from their notions and formative principles by visualizing them, constructing the object of study as quasi-extended in the imagination. It is also possible because of the inalienable otherness present in both what a figure is constructed in and that which constructs it. That in which a figure is produced is intelligible (or geometrical) matter or imagination, where, as it has been argued, otherness is essentially present. That which produces a figure is primarily the point (in "drawing" a line in the imagination by means of some rule-*logos*, according to which a figure—a straight line, a circle, a conic, a cissoid, a helix, and so on—is produced). And the point "secretly" contains the same and the other, the limit and the unlimited. Even the arithmetic monad (whose geometrical imaginary

---

[469] Proclus. In Eucl. 94.26-95.2.
[470] Aristotle. Phys. 241a 7-14; cp. De gen. Et corr. 337a 25-27. See also: Proclus. Inst. Phys., def. I-XIV ad II.
[471] Thesleff 1965, 6.

representative is the point), since it belongs to and represents being, is not altogether free from the grasp of otherness (cp. 2.1.1; 3.4.3). As representing the limited, the point may be thought as identical (i.e., as a geometrical object with no parts). As representing the unlimited, it cannot be imagined (for it has no place that would embrace it; also, that which has no parts can hardly be imagined). It is the presence of otherness that enables discursive reason to consider the point as "not-point". In other words, the other to the discrete (point) is the continuous (line). The point then only *as if* moves (i.e., not really but by an imaginary movement). It is in fact not the point that moves or is moved, but the continuous entity, which in its "flow"-*rhysis* progresses in the imagination (see 3.4.3).[472] Why does it progress? Because the point, on the one hand, is the limit of the line. On the other hand, this limit itself is always other to itself and thus always reserves the possibility of going over the limit of the continuous. As Plotinus puts it, thought (*ennoia*) prolongs the continuous (*to synekhes*) further, into the extended (*eis to porrōi*).[473] The monad is the principle of number. It itself is not a number, yet in order to form a number the monad has to be associated with the dyad. Similarly, the point is the principle of the continuous, which is itself not continuous but needs to be associated with the dyad as imaginary matter to produce a line. As the monad, the point is indivisible; and as the monad, it also presupposes the other of it, the dyad, now exemplified in the "flowing" continuous geometrical magnitude.[474]

Such a duality explains for Proclus why the indivisible point and the divisible line are two visualizable representatives of the indivisible and the divisible in imagination: "For if the imagination were divisible only, it would be unable to preserve in itself the various impressions of the objects that come to it, since the latter ones would obscure those that preceded them—just as no body can at the same time and in the same place have a series of shapes, for the earlier ones are erased by the later. And if it were indivisible, the imagination would not be inferior to the understanding or to the soul, which views everything as undivided; nor could it exercise form-giving functions (*energeias*). It is necessary therefore that its activity should start from what is partless within it, proceed therefrom to project each knowable object that has come to it in concentrated form, and end by giving each object form, shape, and extension. If, then, it has a nature of this kind, the character of indivisibility is in a certain sense within it, and it is primarily by virtue of this character that we must say it contains the being of the point; and by virtue of the same character the form of line also exists wrapped up within it. Possessing this double character of indivisibility and divisibility, the imagination contains the point in undivided and intervals in divided fashion."[475]

The procedure of construction within the imagination is applicable to the restricted sphere of geometrical problems and figures only, since the formative principle of the geometrical figure is not constructed and is not constructible in the described way because the *logos* represents form-*eidos*, which is not constructible either, but simply is or exists. Such a construction remains thus in the realm of the

---

[472] Cp. Aristotle. De an. 409a 4.
[473] Plotinus. Enn. VI.3.12.10-12. Cp. Aristotle. Top. 108b 26.
[474] Cp. Proclus. Theol. Plat. II 14.18-23.12.
[475] Proclus. In Eucl. 95.2-20.

intermediate, which binds the duality of the indivisible and the divisible within the specific imaginable geometrical materiality. The sphere of noetic forms is thus kept out of reach of kinematic construction—that sphere which stays unalloyed and is still separate from both the geometrical and the physical, the sphere of the ever unchanging and already present being.

Conclusion

Much of the difference in considerations of the relation of geometrical entities to physical things (when the possibility of the application of the former to the cognition and constitution of the latter is either implied or denied) appears to be grounded in a difference in understanding of matter and being. As the first part of the book attempted to show, in his approach to matter Plotinus mostly follows Plato's interpretation of matter as pure receptacle and the seat of forms, yet he also embraces Aristotle's conception of matter as the ultimate substrate, utter potentiality and indefiniteness. In construing the notion of matter (if it has a notion), Plotinus presents matter as non-being, as radical otherness to being, stressing its unlimitedness and paradoxality. Descartes, however—and such an approach might be considered exemplary for modern philosophy and science— takes matter as substance; that is, as primarily and adequately represented in being and thought through its clearly conceivable main attribute, extension. A body is then a shaped or formed part of that extension, defined solely in terms of geometrical characteristics. A physical body is therefore presented in such a way as to be already subject to mathematical considerations.

The Cartesian ontological approach, which places being as a primary phenomenon in the center of consideration, is further contrasted to Plotinus' position, which takes being as a synthesis of sameness and otherness, or of oneness and multitude (dyad), themselves engendered by the first principle, the One. If being is not itself primary, then the One has to be postulated as the definitive cause of being, prior to being (i.e., as properly not being). If, however, matter is equally represented as non-being, the question arises of whether it is possible, and how it is at all possible, to make a distinction between the One (the ultimate source of being) and matter (the complete lack of being). As it was argued, Plotinus has resources to establish such a distinction and thus to characterize matter in definite terms, although such a characterization eventually involves a paradoxical description, since it appeals to that which never is and never will be, that which is inescapably missed by any rational discourse.

Substance is thus introduced by Descartes as that which is, that which exists due only to itself and is conceived univocally in its essence, characterized by a (necessary) essential attribute. Still, his attempt to portray matter as an independent substance involves ambiguity, for on the one hand, matter—as characterized by its essential attribute, extension—has to be considered substance, but on the other hand, matter does not exist due solely to itself and therefore is not properly a substance.

In Plotinus' approach, being has to do not only with a synthetic unity, but with a limit as well, which is also thoroughly stressed by Plato and Aristotle. In the Cartesian ontological approach, being, which is God, is conceived as perfection, tautologically expressed as reality, self-causation, inexhaustible power and, moreover, as infinity: it is infinity and not limit that has to constitute perfection. However, Descartes is reluctant to bring actual infinity into the material world and into the realm of mathematical entities, because, as he argues throughout his writings, in regard to the infinite, we are only able to know that it *is*, and not *what* it is (hence the distinction between cognitive procedures of "knowing" and "grasping"). This further leads him to recognize that the physical and the mathematical has to be indefinite as a whole, rather than infinite, and only as such can both be known. Still, admitting actual infinity inevitably involves paradox, which for Plotinus has to be either avoided or logically resolved, whereas for Descartes paradox rather serves an indicator of a potential growth in philosophical and scientific knowledge, and as such can be fruitful.

The very possibility of the application of mathematics to the study of physical phenomena, as discussed in the second part of the book, is the cornerstone of modern science and is consequently denied in ancient science. Thus, for Plato and for the later Neoplatonic thinkers (in particular, for Plotinus and Proclus), mathematics can give knowledge about those things that cannot be otherwise and therefore has nothing to do with the ever-fluent physical things, about which there can only be a (possibly right) opinion. Aristotle develops a different approach to physics, which he considers *scientia*, but this science is not mathematical (Aristotle's physics remains the only science about the world until its radical mathematics-oriented revision in the late middle ages and early modernity).

Furthermore, ancient Neoplatonic thinkers carefully distinguish between arithmetic and geometry within mathematics itself. A reconstruction of Plotinus' theory of number, which embraces the late Plato's division of numbers into substantial (ideal) and quantitative (monadic, or properly mathematical), shows that numbers are structured and conceived in opposition to geometrical entities. In particular, numbers are constituted as a synthetic unity of indivisible, discrete units, whereas geometrical objects are continuous (except for the point) and do not consist of indivisible parts. This mutual irreducibility of number and geometrical magnitude is overcome in modern science, being canceled in Descartes, who, as it has been argued, considers number not primarily in relation to the finite (a limit), but rather to the infinite. Moreover, a decisive step undertaken by Descartes is the non-discrimination of number and (extended and thus continuous) magnitude: even if they are still formally distinguished, both can be used interchangeably in scientific considerations and are taken to represent each other univocally. Besides, the Cartesian project of the universal scientific method, the very way it is constructed and introduced, presupposes that the method should be equally suitable for both mathematical (geometrical) and physical entities. Geometrical objects are applicable to physical bodies, insofar as both are supposed to be structured according to order and measure. This order and measure is then to be discernible in both geometrical entities (themselves expressible through numbers) and physical things, allowing for the possibility of the application of the former to the latter.

The notion of the intermediary further plays an important role in the development of the argument. In the Neoplatonic reading of Plato, as found in Iamblichus and Proclus, mathematical objects are considered intermediate entities between physical things (bodies) and noetic, merely thinkable, entities (notions). As the previous analysis of Plotinus' teaching on number intended to show, arithmeticals (numbers) should be placed in the same ontological category with ideal forms, or noetic objects. Being distinct from numbers, geometrical figures are to be considered intermediate, insofar as they are in a certain respect similar to both thinkable and physical things and, in another sense, are different from both. As Proclus shows, geometricals on the one hand are divisible and in a certain sense extended, as bodies. On the other hand, like noetic objects, geometricals are precise and do not change their properties over time. Therefore, mathematical entities—numbers, as well as geometricals—are to be conceived differently from physical bodies. Descartes, on the contrary, tends to abolish all the intermediate structures in ontology, epistemology and cosmology, and thus simplifies the picture of being and of the world, to ensure the possibility of the consideration of geometrical figures and physical bodies in similar terms—that is, as merely extended, as subjects to order and measure and by the same cognitive procedures.

The notion of intelligible matter becomes of central importance at this point: introduced by Aristotle as a matter of mathematical objects, it is thoroughly elaborated by Plotinus and Proclus. In Plotinus, intelligible matter is conceived as a universal substrate of multiple thinkable forms. It is further associated with an ineradicable otherness within being (a potentiality for being), and is thus present to all ideal entities and to mathematical objects, including numbers and geometrical figures. Intelligible matter is further interpreted as indefinite thinking, (not yet informed by the objects of thinking) when thinking tends to think its own cause, which is not being and thus cannot be properly conceived or thought, since it is not a particular object of thinking. The indefinite thinking, as dyad, thus inevitably "misses" its origin and is informed, as intelligible matter, only when it comes to think itself in definite terms as, and through, noetic objects. As it was argued, Proclus, in his elaboration of the notion of intelligible matter, takes it to be a specific geometrical matter (i.e., primarily a matter of geometrical objects). Such matter can then be consistently interpreted as imagination, as a *sui generis* extension where geometrical objects can be conceived as divisible, as having parts, as extended and as constructible by the movement of another geometrical object (e.g., the point). It is then intelligible matter that separates the mathematical from the physical and makes the two ontologically and epistemologically incommensurable.

In Cartesian ontology, on the contrary, there is no way to distinguish between different kinds of matter, since there is only one matter (which is extension and substance) that is present as the common matter of all extended objects, in particular, of both geometrical and physical things. This inability to distinguish between specifically geometrical and specifically physical matters allows for the possibility of putting both geometrical entities and physical bodies in one and the same extension, and of applying the same set of rules and procedures to the consideration of both. Because of this, Descartes is capable of expressing bodily properties in the precise language of mathematics. Moreover, since he intends to present arithmetical number and geometrical magnitude as mutually expressible through one another, he can build physics as a mathematical enterprise, which further leads to the substitution of the properly physical by the geometrical. In a sense, the whole physical world is then omitted (or, rather, bracketed) and the laws of geometrical, imaginary construction are imposed onto the physical and eventually expel it as concrete and imprecise from scientific considerations.

The third part of the book portrays the relation of matter (specifically, of intelligible matter) and of geometrical objects to cognitive faculties and to the imagination in particular. In the Platonic tradition, as represented in Plotinus, the intellect, seen through the category of life, is capable of conceiving the first principles. Construed as being and pure actuality, the intellect is further presented through a distinction (which cannot be taken as a real one) between thought as thinking and thought as thinkable, as the objects of thought that exist in an uninterrupted communication. On the contrary, discursive thinking, essentially involved in mathematical and logical argumentation, is incomplete and only partial. Discursive reason carries out its activity in a number of consecutively performed steps, because, unlike the intellect, it is not capable of representing an object of thought in its entirety and unique complexity and thus has to comprehend the object part by part, in a certain (correct) order.

The Cartesian cogitating mind is quite different from the intellect in its structure: the mind is a thinking substance, discursive *par excellence.* Mind is also self-transparent and essentially reflective. Reflectivity is considered proper to the mind alone, whereas its ontologically complementary counterpart, matter, is not reflective. In comparison with the Platonic intellect, the Cartesian mind, which conceives of ideas as any content of thinking, appears to be rather simplistic and deliberately simplified. Such simplification of the mind in its structure, constitution and functioning, undertaken for the sake of clarity of understanding, appears to involve difficulties and ambiguities. In a sense, the simplification of ontological and cosmological structures (e.g., the non-distinction of a specific difference between the geometrical and the physical) can be taken to represent a distinctive feature of modern philosophy and science, which allows modern thinking to become particularly efficient in reconstructing and reconsidering the physical cosmos as knowable in a strict and precise way.

Imagination appears further to play a crucial role in the constitution and understanding of the sphere of the geometrical. Plotinus, Plutarch of Athens, Syrianus, Proclus and Porphyry, who have their predecessors in Plato and Aristotle, present imagination in its capacity to produce mental images different both from thinkable objects and from sense-data. Imagination is portrayed as distinct from the intellect and discursive thinking, on the one hand, and from sense-perception, on the other. Put otherwise, imagination is intermediate; it is as if "in between" sense-perception and discursive thinking, both separating and uniting them. Plotinus compares imagination to a double-sided mirror, reflecting both the sensual and the intelligible, sharing certain features with both, but being neither of them. Furthermore, imagination is intimately connected with some kind of extension and movement, insofar as geometrical objects exist and can be constructed in imagination as geometrical in the proper sense (i.e., as extended, divisible and visualizable), thus exemplifying irrationality and otherness (which brings forth a multiplicity of geometrical figures of the same kind). Moreover, since imagination and intelligible matter appear to share exactly the same features, in Syrianus and Proclus the two are identified with one another. Intelligible matter thus can be taken as geometrical matter—that matter in which geometricals not only exist, but also can be retrieved by kinematic construction (i.e., construction by movement) according to their ideal notion and formative principle.

In Descartes we do not find a consistent "theory" of imagination; his treatment of imagination involves a number of difficulties and ambiguities, particularly due to his hesitation about its ontological status. Imagination, split further into the mental and the corporeal, marks a connection of the finite mind to the body. Unlike the mind-reason, imagination is unable to represent and access the reality or essence of a thing, because reason can think that which imagination cannot represent, namely, the infinite. Imagination (which is not an intermediate faculty for Descartes) submits sense data to the interpretation of the mind, which interprets the objects of imagination as extended things, that is, as physical material things and geometrical objects, insofar as both are extended. Through imagination, geometrically extended figures are brought and constructed into physical things, so that the former appear to become not only semblances, but much more substitutes for the former. Geometrical objects are therefore to be recognized as unchanging patterns (themselves constructed after thinkable essences) of physical things, so that both are to be considered (or even imagined into) the one and same matter and extension.

Modern philosophy and science, as it was argued, accept the *verum factum* principle, according to which an object can be known and does not exist to the extent that, and insofar as, it is and can be produced or constructed. This principle is traced then in Descartes, for whom the physical world in its substantial materiality is still a divine construction. Because of that, Descartes has to confine his efforts to presenting a consistent account of the (imaginary) reconstructed world as an object of scientific consideration. However, in this imaginary recreation of the world, the finite mind easily assumes the role of the demiurg, who knows the world insofar as he himself has created that very world. Only that which is put into the object of cognition by the cognizing subject can be admitted then as knowable in the proper sense, which eventually cancels and destroys all objective teleology.

The discussion of the construction principle was mostly focused on construction in geometry, which is already prominent in antiquity (e.g., in Archimedes and Apollonius), although construction is used mostly in problems and not in theorems (in Euclid), and does not appear to play a central role in theoretical considerations within the Platonic approach to mathematics—where, in general, the (already) existing has a higher ontological status than the produced. The method of the kinematic generation of a geometrical figure by uniform movement becomes especially important in early modern science as the model for consideration of the physical. As Descartes intends to show, the geometrical and the physical are both movable and reproducible in the same way, insofar as everything extended can be considered constructible under a geometrical pattern, precisely describable and easily imaginable. This allows for the establishment of physical material things as represented, constructed and studied in their motion and change by means of mathematics exactly in the same way as geometrical figures are represented, constructed and studied.

Engendering a geometrical figure by movement is found already in Proclus. Imagination, considered a constructive and creative capacity, appears to play a crucial role in producing geometrical entities, intermediate between physical things and noetic objects. Moreover, geometrical figures turn out to be inescapably dual, for they can be considered both as already existing and as originated by movement. For Proclus, imagination represents geometrical intelligible matter and is itself intermediate between discursive thinking and sense-perception. Furthermore, imagination is taken by Syrianus and Proclus to be capable of embodying geometrical figures by tracing them as generated or produced by the movement of another geometrical entity (e.g., a point). The geometrical figure appears to be divisible, formed, multiple (since an indefinite number of figures of the same kind can be constructed) and extended only within the imagination, because the physical representation of the figure is distorted, whereas the formative principle of the figure within discursive reason is unextended and indivisible. The purpose of the construction of a geometrical figure in the imagination for Proclus is then a *sui generis* alienation of the figure, when it is objectified as a constructible image, according to the figure's immanent formative principle, and then studied in all its properties. In this way, the properties are rendered visualizable as imaginable, as if being projected onto the screen of the imagination and into geometrical matter, for better and clearer consideration of and by discursive reason.

The kinematic construction of a geometrical object thus does not properly create the object anew, but rather reproduces it under a non-geometrical and non-physical ideal pattern of the intellect—the noetic form—itself represented through the formative principle in discursive reason. And the ideal form and formative principle are not themselves constructible, in particular, within the imagination. A geometrical object can then be considered existing as four-fold: in its intelligible notion form in the intellect; in its formative principle in discursive thinking; as the geometrical figure properly, conceivable and constructible in the imagination; and as a physical imitation, accessible to sense-perception. All these levels of representation of a geometrical entity are never confused within the Platonic account of geometry, whereas the Cartesian acceptance of the extended as substantial opens the possibility of conceiving the geometrical and the physical in similar terms, and thus of applying mathematical entities and precision to the description of physical things. Once the principle of construction is expanded to all "external" reality (taken as extended substance or matter), and once geometrical entities as intermediate are expelled, then every extended object can be considered imaginable and constructible under a geometrical pattern. Hence the physical becomes reducible to the geometrical, since physical bodies and geometrical figures are considered already (re)constructed in one and the same material extension, being subjects of the imagination. The physical world of modern science and philosophy is thus constructed as (and eventually substituted by) a strictly thinkable, and properly knowable, geometrical world.

Bibliography

ABIAN, A. *The Theory of Sets and Transfinite Arithmetic.* Philadelphia-London, 1965.
ALCINOUS (ALBINUS). *The Handbook of Platonism.* Trans. with an Introduction and Commentary by J. Dillon. Oxford, 1993.
ALEKSANDROV, A. D.; KOLMOGOROV, A. N.; LAVRENT'EV, M. A. (Eds.) *Mathematics: Its Content, Methods, and Meaning.* Trans. T. Gould and T. Bartha. Vol. I-III. Cambridge (Mass.), 1969.
ALEXANDER APHRODISIENSIS. *In Aristotelis Metaphysica commentaria.* Ed. M. Hayduck. Berlin, 1891.
ALGRA, K. *Concepts of Space in Greek Thought.* Leiden-New York-Köln, 1995.
ALLEN, R. E. "The Generation of Numbers in Plato's *Parmenides*". - *Classical Philology*, 65 (1970), 30-34.
ALLISON, H. *Benedict de Spinoza. An Introduction.* Yale, 1987.
AMADO, É. "A propos des nombres nombrés et nombres nombrants chez Plotin". – *Revue philosophique* 78 (1953), 423-425.
ANNAS, J. *Aristotle's Metaphysics. Books M and N.* Oxford, 1976.
ANTON, P. J. (Ed.) *Science and the Sciences in Plato.* New York, 1980.
APOLLONIUS OF PERGA. *Quae graece extant cum commentariis antiquis.* Ed. J. L. Heiberg. Vol. I-II. Stuttgart, 1891-1893.
ARCHIMEDES. *Opera omnia.* Ed. J. L. Heiberg. Vol. I-III. Leipzig, 1880-1881.
—*The Works of Archimedes.* Ed. by T. L. Heath. Cambridge, 1912 (repr. New York, 1953).
ARENDT, H. *The Life of the Mind.* San Diego-New York-London, 1978.
ARIEW, R. "Descartes and Scholasticism: The Intellectual Background to Descartes' Thought". - In: J. Cottingham (Ed.) *The Cambridge Companion to Descartes.* Cambridge, 1992. P. 58-90.
ARIEW, R.; GRENE, M. "Ideas, in and before Descartes." - *Journal of the History of Ideas* 56 (1995), 87-106.
ARISTOTLE. *Opera omnia.* Ed. I. Bekkeri. Addendis instruxit fragmentorum collectionem retractavit O. Gigon. Vol. I-III. Berlin, 1960-1987.
ARMSTRONG, A. H. *The Architecture of the Intelligible Universe in the Philosophy of Plotinus.* Cambridge, 1940.
—(Ed.) *The Cambridge History of the Later Greek and Early Medieval Philosophy.* Cambridge, 1967.
ARNAULD, A. *On True and False Ideas, New Objections to Descartes' Meditations and Descartes' Replies.* Trans. with an Introduction by E. J. Kremer. Lewiston-Queenston-Lampeter, 1990.
—*Logic or the Art of Thinking.* Trans. and Ed. by J.Vance Bursker. Cambridge, 1996.
ARNIM, E. VON. *Stoicorum veterum fragmenta.* (SVF) (Ed.) Vol. I-IV. Leipzig, 1905-1924.
ASHBAUGH, A. F. *Plato's Theory of Explanation. A Study of the Cosmological Account in the Timaeus.* Albany (N. Y.), 1988.
BACON, R. *The New Organon and the Related Writings.* Ed., with an Introduction, by F. H. Anderson. Indianapolis-New York, 1960.
BAINE HARRIS, R. (Ed.) *The Significance of the Neoplatonism.* Norfolk (Virginia), 1976.
—*The Structure of Being. A Neoplatonic Approach.* Norfolk (Virginia), 1982.
BALAUDÉ, J.-F. "Le traitement plotinien de la question du mal: éthique ou ontologique?" – *Cahiers philosophiques de Strasbourg* 8 (1999), 67-85.

BARNES, J. "Proof and Syllogism". - In: E. Berti (Ed.) *Aristotle on Science. The "Posterior Analytics"*. Padova, 1981. P. 17-59.
— Translation with a Commentary of *Aristotle's Posterior Analytics*. Oxford, ^{2}1993 (1st ed. 1975).
— (Ed.) *The Cambridge Companion to Aristotle*. Cambridge, 1995.
BARROW, I. *The Mathematical Works: Lectiones Mathematicae et Lectiones Geometricae.* 2 vols. in 1 vol. Ed. by W. Whewell. Hildesheim-New York, 1973.
BASTID, P. *Proclus et le crépuscule de la pensée grecque*. Paris, 1969.
BAUMGARDT, C. *Johannes Kepler: Life and Letters*. With an Introduction by A. Einstein. London, 1952.
BAUMGARTEN, A. G. *Philosophia generalis*. Halle-Magdeburg, 1770 (repr. Hildesheim, 1968).
— *Metaphysica*. Halle, 1779 (repr. Hildesheim, 1963).
BÄUMKER, C. *Das Problem der Materie in der griechischen Philosophie. Eine historisch-kritische Untersuchung*. Münster, 1890 (repr. Frankfurt am Main, 1963).
BECK, L. J. *The Method of Descartes. A Study of the Regulae*. Oxford, 1952.
BECKER, O. "Die diairetische Erzeugung der platonischen Idealzahlen". - In: *Quellen und Studien zur Geschichte der Mathematik, Astronomie und Physik.* Abt. B, Bd.4, 1938. P. 464-501.
— *Grundlagen der Mathematik in geschichtlicher Entwicklung*. Freiburg-München, 1954.
— *Das mathematische Denken der Antike*. Göttingen, 1957.
— "Versuch einer neuen Interpretation der platonischen Ideenzahlen". - *Archiv für Geschichte der Philosophie* 45 (1963), 119-124.
— (Ed.) *Zur Geschichte der griechischen Mathematik*. Darmstadt, 1965.
BEIERWALTES, W. "Causa Sui. Plotins Begriff des Einen als Ursprung des Gedankens der Selbstursachlichkeit". In J. Cleary (Ed.) *Traditions of Platonism. Essays in Honour of John Dillon*. Aldershot et al., 1999. P. 191-226.
— *Proklos. Grundzüge seiner Metaphysik*. Frankfurt am Main, 1965.
— *Plotin über Ewigkeit und Zeit*. Frankfurt am Main, 1967.
— *Denken des Einen. Studien zur neuplatonischen Philosophie und ihrer Wirkungsgeschichte*. Frankfurt am Main, 1985.
BELAVAL, Y. *Leibniz critique de Descartes*. Paris, 1960.
BENACERRAF, P. "What Numbers Could Not Be". - *Philosophical Review* 74 (1965), 47-73.
BENACERRAF, P.; PUTNAM, H. (Eds.) *Philosophy of Mathematics*. Cambridge (Mass.), ^{2}1983.
BENARDETE, J. A. *Infinity: An Essay in Metaphysics*. Oxford, 1964.
BENNETT, J. *A Study of Spinoza's "Ethics"*. Cambridge, 1984.
— "Analytic-Synthetic".- In: *Proceedings of the Aristotelian Society* 59 (1958-1959), 163-188.
BENZ, H. *"Materie" und Wahrnehmung in der Philosophie Plotins*. Würzburg, 1990.
BERNADETE, S. "Aristotle, De Anima III. 3-5". - *Review of Metaphysics* 28 (1975), 611-622.
BERTI, E. (Ed.) *Aristotle on Science. The "Posterior Analytics"*. Padova, 1981.
BEYSSADE, J.-M. "On the Idea of God: Incomprehensibility or Incompatibilities?" –In: S. H. Voss (Ed.) *Essays on the Philosophy and Science of René Descartes*. New York Oxford, 1993. P. 85-94.

BLUMENBERG, H. *Die Legitimität der Neuzeit.* Frankfurt am Main, 1966.
—*The Genesis of the Copernican World.* Trans. by R. M. Wallace. Cambridge (Mass.), 1987. (Originally published as: *Die Genesis der kopernikanischen Welt.* Frankfurt am Main, 1975.)
—"Selbsterhaltung und Beharrung. Zur Konstitution der neuzeitlichen Rationalität". - In: H. Ebeling (Ed.) *Subjektivität und Selbsterhaltung. Beiträge zur Diagnose der Moderne.* Frankfurt am Main, 1976. P. 144-207.
BLUMENTHAL, H. J. *Plotinus' Psychology. His Doctrines of the Embodied Soul.* The Hague, 1971.
—"Plutarch's *De Anima* and Proclus". - In: *De Jamblique à Proclus. Entretiens sur l'Antiquité Classique*, XXI. Vandoeuvres-Genève, 1975. P. 123-147.
—"Plotinus' Adaptation of Aristotle's Psychology". - In: *The Significance of the Neoplatonism.* Ed. by R. Baine Harris. Norfolk, Virginia, 1976. P. 51-55.
— "Some Neoplatonic Views on Perception and Memory: Similarities, Differences and Motivations".- In: J. Cleary (Ed.) *Traditions of Platonism: Essays in Honour of John Dillon.* Aldershot et al., 1999. P. 319-335.
BOLYAI, J. *Appendix. The Theory of Space.* Ed. F. Kárteszi. Amsterdam et al., 1987.
BOS, H. J. M. "On the Representation of Curves in Descartes' *Géométrie*". - *Archive for History of Exact Sciences* 24 (1981), 295-338.
BOUTROUX, E. *L'imagination et les mathématiques selon Descartes.* Paris, 1900.
BOYER, C. B. "Descartes and the Geometrization of Algebra." - *American Mathematical Monthly* 66 (1959), 390-393.
—*A History of Mathematics.* New York, ²1991.
BRANN, E. T. H. *The World of Imagination. Sum and Substance.* Savage (Maryland), 1991.
BRÉHIER, E. *La philosophie de Plotin.* Paris, 1928.
BRENTANO, F. *The Psychology of Aristotle. In Particular His Doctrine of the Active Intellect.* Ed. and trans. by R. George. Berkeley. et al, 1977.
BRETON, S. *Philosophie et mathématique chez Proclus.* Paris, 1969.
BRISSON, L. *Le même et l'autre dans la structure ontologique du* Timée *de Platon. Un commentaire systématique du* Timée *de Platon.* Paris, 1974.
BROMWICH, T. J. I. *An Introduction to the Theory of Infinite Series.* London, ²1926.
BRONSTEIN, I. N., SEMENDYAEV, K. A. *Spravochnik po matematike (Reference Book in Mathematics).* Leipzig-Moscow, 1980.
BROUWER, L. E. J. "The Unreliability of the Logical Principles". - In: *Collected Works.* Ed. by A. Heyting. Vol. I. New York, 1975. P. 107-111.
—*Cambridge Lectures on Intuitionism.* Ed. by D. van Dalen. Cambridge, 1981.
—"Intuitionism and Formalism". - In: *Philosophy of Mathematics.* Ed. by P. Benacerraf and H. Putnam. Cambridge (Mass.), 1983. P. 77-89.
—*Intuitionismus.* Hrsg. D. van Dalen. Mannheim et al., 1992.
BRUMBAUGH, R. S. *Plato's Mathematical Imagination.* Bloomington (Ind.), 1954.
—"Cantor's Sets and Proclus' Wholes".- In: R. Baine Harris (Ed.) *The Structure of Being. A Neoplatonic Approach.* Norfolk (Virginia), 1982. P. 104-113.
BURKERT, W. *Lore and Science in Ancient Pythagoreanism.* Cambridge (Mass.), 1972.
BURNYEAT, M. F. "Platonism and Mathematics: A Prelude to Discussion".- In: A. Graeser (Ed.) *Mathematics and Metaphysics in Aristotle.* Bern-Stuttgart, 1987. P. 213-240.
BURTT, E. A. *The Metaphysical Foundations of Modern Physical Science: A Historical and*

Critical Essay. London, 1964 (1st ed. 1924).
BUSSANICH, J. *The One and Its Relation to Intellect in Plotinus: A Commentary on Selected Texts*. Leiden: Brill, 1988.
CALCIDIUS. *Timaeus a Calcidio translatus commentarioque instructus*. Ed. J. H. Waszink. London-Leiden, 1962. (Plato Latinus. Ed. R. Klibansky. Vol. IV.)
CANTOR, G. *Grundlagen einer allgemeinen Mannigfaltigkeitslehre. Ein mathematisch philosophisch Versuch in der Lehre des Unendlichen*. Leipzig, 1883.
—*Trudy po teorii mnozhestv*. Ed. by A. N. Kolmogorov, F. A. Medvedev, A. P. Yushkevich. Moscow, 1985.
CAPEK, M. (Ed.) *The Concepts of Space and Time*. Boston, 1976.
CASPAR, M. *Kepler*. Trans. and ed. by C.D. Hellman. London-New York, 1959.
CASSIRER, E. *Substance and Function*. Trans. W. C. Swabey and M. C. Swabey. New York, 1953 (first published: Chicago, 1923).
CAVALIERI, B. *Geometria degli indivisibili*. A cura di L. Lombardo-Radice. Torino, 1966.
CHANGEUX, J.-P.; CONNES, A. *Conversations on Mind, Matter, and Mathematics*. Ed. and trans. by M. B. DeBevoise. Princeton, 1995.
CHAPPELL, V. "The Theory of Ideas". - In: A. Rorty (Ed.) *Essays on Descartes' "Meditations"*. Berkeley-Los Angeles, 1986. P. 177-198.
CHARLES-SAGET, A. *L'architecture du divin. Mathématique et philosophie chez Plotin et Proclus*. Paris, 1982.
CHARLETON, W. *Physiologia Epicuro-Gassendo-Charltoniana, or a Fabrick of Science Natural upon Hypothesis of Atoms*. London, 1654 (repr. London-New York, 1966).
CHARLTON, W. "Aristotle's Potential Infinities". - In: L. Johnson (Ed.) *Aristotle's Physics: A Collection of Essays*. Oxford, 1991. P. 129-149.
CHITCHALINE, I. "L'imagination chez Proclus, Porphyre et Erigène". - *Separata* I 2. Moscow, 1993.
CLAGHORN, G. S. *Aristotle's Criticism of Plato's "Timaeus"*. The Hague, 1954.
CLARKE, D. *Descartes' Philosophy of Science*. Manchester, 1982.
CLEARY, J. *Aristotle and Mathematics. Aporetic Method in Cosmology and Metaphysics*. Leiden, 1995.
— (Ed.) *Traditions of in Platonism. Essays in Honour of John Dillon*. Aldershot, 1999.
COHEN, I. B. *Introduction to Newton's "Principia"*. Cambridge, 1971.
COHEN, S. "Aristotle's Doctrine of the Material Substrate". - *The Philosophical Review* 93 (1984), 171-194.
COOPER, N. "The Importance of *dianoia* in Plato's Theory of Forms". - *Classical Quarterly* 16 (1966), 65-69.
COPLESTON, F. C. *A History of Medieval Philosophy*. Notre Dame-London, 1990.
CORNFORD, F. M. *Plato's Cosmology: The Timaeus of Plato*. London, 1937.
CORRIGAN, K. "Is There More Than One Generation of Matter in the Enneads?" —*Phronesis* 31 (1986), 167-181.
CORRIGAN, K.; O'CLEIRIGH, P. "The Course of Plotinian Scholarship from 1971 to 1986". - In: *Aufstieg und Niedergang der römischen Welt*, Teil II, Bd. 36.1. Berlin-New York, 1987. P. 571-623.
COTTINGHAM, J. *Descartes*. Oxford, 1986.

—"Cartesian Dualism: Theology, Metaphysics and Science". - In: J. Cottingham (Ed.) *The Cambridge Companion to Descartes*. Cambridge, 1992. P. 236-257.
—(Ed.) *The Cambridge Companion to Descartes*. Cambridge, 1992.
—(Ed.) *Reason, Will, and Sensation. Studies in Descartes' Metaphysics*. Oxford, 1994.
COURTINE, J.-F. *Suarez et le système de la métaphysique*. Paris, 1990.
CRAPULLI, G. *Mathesis Universalis: Genesi di una idea nel XVI secolo*. Rome, 1969.
CURLEY, E. "Analysis in the *Meditations*: The Quest for Clear and Distinct Ideas". - In: A. Rorty (Ed.) *Essays on Descartes' Meditations*. Berkeley-Los Angeles, 1986. P. 153-176.
—*Behind the Geometrical Method: A Reading of Spinoza's Ethics*. Princeton, 1988.
DALSGAARD LARSEN, B. *Jamblique de Chalcis. Exégète et philosophe*. Aarhus, 1972.
DAMASCIUS. *De principiis. Traité des premiers principes*. Vol. I-II. Texte établi par L. G. Westerink et traduit par J. Combès. Paris, 1986-1989.
D'ANCONA, C. "Rereading *Ennead* V 1 [10], 7: What is the Scope of Plotinus' Geometrical Analogy in this Passage?" in J. Cleary (Ed.), *Traditions of Platonism. Essays in Honour of John Dillon*. Aldershot, 1999. P. 237-261.
DANCY, R. "On Some of Aristotle's Second Thoughts About Substances: Matter". - *The Philosophical Review* 87 (1978), 372-413.
DARRELL JACKSON, B. "Plotinus and the *Parmenides*". - *Journal of the History of Philosophy* 5 (1967), 315-327.
DAUBEN, J. W. *Georg Cantor. His Mathematics and Philosophy of the Infinite*. Cambridge (Mass.)-London, 1979.
DEDEKIND, R. *Essays on the Theory of Numbers*. New York, 1901.
—*Was sind und was sollen die Zahlen?* Braunschweig, [3]1911.
—*Stetigkeit und die irrationale Zahlen*. Braunschweig, [4]1912.
—*Vorlesung ber Differentialund Integralrechnung. 1861/62*. In einer Mitschrift von H. Bechtold. Bearbeitet von M.-A. Knus und W. Scharlau. Braunschweig-Wiesbaden, 1985.
—*Gesammelte mathematische Werke*. Hrsg. R. Fricke, E. Noether, Ö. Ore. Vol. I-III. Braunschweig, 1930-1932.
DES CHENE, D. *Physiologia. Natural Philosophy in Late Aristotelian and Cartesian Thought*. Ithaca-London, 1996.
DESARGUES, G. *Oeuvres de Desargues réuinies et analysées par M. Poudra*. Vol. I-II. Paris, 1864.
—*L'oeuvre mathématique de G. Desargues*. Textes publiés et commentés avec une introduction biographique et historique par R. Taton. Paris, 1951.
—*The Geometrical Works of Girard Desargues*. Introd. and publ. by J. V. Field and J. J. Gray. New York et al., 1987.
DESCARTES, R. *Correspondance publiée avec une introduction et des notes*. Ed. by Ch. Adam and G. Milhaud. Vol. I-VIII. Paris, 1936-1963.
—*Geometry*. - In: *Discourse on Method, Optics, Geometry, and Meteorology*. Trans. by P. J. Olscamp. Indianapolis, 1965. P. 177-259.
—*Lettres*. Textes choisis par M. Alexandre. Paris, 1954.
—*The Philosophical Writings of Descartes*. Vol. I-II. Trans. by J. Cottingham, R. Stoothoff, D. Murdoch. Vol. III (Letters). Trans. by J. Cottingham, R. Stoothoff,

D. Murdoch., A. Kenny. Cambridge, 1985-1991.
—*Oeuvres de Descartes*. Ed. by Ch. Adam and P. Tannery. Vol. I-XI. 2nd ed. Paris, 1974-1986.
DICKER, G. *Descartes. An Analytical and Historical Introduction.* Oxford, 1993.
DIELS, H., KRANZ, W. *Die Fragmente der Vorsokratiker.* Vol. I-III. Berlin, ^{6}1951-1952.
DIJKSTERHUIS, E. J. *The Mechanization of the World Picture.* Oxford, 1961.
—*Archimedes.* Trans. by C. Dikshoorn. Copenhagen, 1956.
DILLON, J. *The Middle Platonists.* Ithaca (N.Y.), 1996 (revised ed., first publ. 1977).
— "Plotinus on the transcendental imagination". - In: J. P. Mackey (Ed.) *Religious Imagination.* Edinburgh, 1986. P. 55-64.
—"Iamblichus and Henads Again". - In: H. J. Blumenthal, E. G. Clark (Eds.) *The Divine Iamblichus. Philosopher and Man of Gods.* Bristol, 1993. P. 48-54.
DIRICHLET G. L. *Werke.* Vol. I-II. Hrsg. L. Kronecker. Berlin, 1889-1897.
DODDS, E. R. "The *Parmenides* of Plato and the Origin of the Neoplatonic 'One'". - *Classical Quarterly*, 22 (1928), 129-142.
DONEY, W. (Ed.) *Descartes. A Collection of Critical Essays.* Garden City (N. Y.), 1967.
DÖRRIE, H. "Präpositionen und Metaphysik. Wechselwirkung zweier Prinzipienreihen". - *Museum Helveticum* 26 (1969), 217-228.
DRAKE, S. *Discoveries and Opinions of Galileo.* New York, 1957.
DUGAS, R. *Mechanics in the Seventeenth Century.* Neuchâtel, 1958.
DUHEM, P. *The Aim and Structure of Physical Theory.* Trans. by Ph. P. Wiener. Princeton (N.J.), 1954.
DUMMETT, M. *Elements of Intuitionism.* Oxford, 1977.
—*Frege: Philosophy of Mathematics.* Cambridge (Mass.), 1991.
DUNS SCOTUS. *Opera omnia.* Vol. I-XIX. Roma, 1950-1993.
DÜRING, I. *Aristoteles. Darstellung und Interpretation seines Denkens.* Heidelberg, 1966.
EMILSSON, E. K. *Plotinus on Sense-Perception: A Philosophical Study.* Cambridge, 1988.
—"Plotinus on the Objects of Thought". - *Archiv für Geschichte der Philosophie* 77 (1995), 21-41.
— "Remarks on the Relation between the One and Intellect in Plotinus." - In: J. Cleary (Ed.) *Traditions of Platonism. Essays in Honour of John Dillon.* Aldershot, et al., 1999. P. 271-290.
ENGLISCH, B. *Die Artes liberales im frühen Mittelalter (5.-9. Jh.). Das Quadrivium und der Komputus als Indikatoren für Kontinuität und Erneuerung der exakten Wissenschaften zwischen Antike und Mittelalter.* Stuttgart, 1994.
ESLICK, L. J. "The Material Substrate in Plato". - *The Concept of Matter in Greek and Medieval Philosophy.* Ed. by E. McMullin. Notre Dame (Indiana), 1963. P. 39-54.
EUCLID. *Elementa.* Ed. J. L. Heiberg. Vol. I-V. Leipzig, 1883-1888.
—*The Thirteen Books of Euclid's Elements.* Trans. with Intro. and Comm. by Th. L. Heath. Vol. I-III. New York, ^{2}1956.
—*Elementa.* Post J. L. Heiberg (Ed.) E. V. Stamatis. Vol. I-V. Leipzig, 1969-1977.
EUSTACHIO A SANCTO PAULO. *Summa philosophica quadripartita, de rebus Dialecticis, Moralibus, Physicis et Metaphysicis.* Paris, 1609.
EVRARD, E. "*Phantasia* chez Proclus". - In: M. Fattori and M. Bianchi (Eds.) *Phantasia - Imaginatio.* Rome, 1988.

FARRINGTON, B. *Greek Science.* London, ²1953.
FIELD, J. V. *The Invention of Infinity. Mathematics and Art in the Renaissance.* Oxford, 1997.
FINAMORE, J.F. *Iamblichus and the Theory of the Vehicle of the Soul.* Chico (Ca.), 1985.
FINDLAY, J. *Plato: The Written and Unwritten Doctrines.* New York, 1974.
FLEET, B. *Ennead III. 6. On the Impassivity of the Bodies.* Translation and Commentary. Oxford, 1995.
FÓTI, V. "The Cartesian Imagination". - *Philosophy and Phenomenological Research* 46 (1986), 631-642.
FOWLER, D. H. *The Mathematics of Plato's Academy: A New Reconstruction.* Oxford, 1987.
FRAENKEL, A. A., BAR-HILLEL, Y., LEVY, A. *Foundations of Set Theory.* Amsterdam, 1973.
FREDE, M. "Substance in Aristotle's *Metaphysics*". - *Essays in Ancient Philosophy.* Minneapolis, 1987. P. 72-80.
—*Essays in Ancient Philosophy.* Minneapolis, 1987.
FREGE, G. "Funktion und Begriff". - *Kleine Schriften.* (Ed.) I. Agnelelli. Hildesheim, 1967. P. 125-142.
—*Nachgelassene Schriften und Wissenschaftliche Briefwechsel.* Unter Mitwirkung von G. Gabriel und W. Rödding bearbeitet, eingeleitet und mit Anmerkungen versehen von H. Hermes, F. Kambartel, F. Kaulbach. Vol. I. Hamburg, 1969.
—"On Formal Theories of Arithmetic". - *On the Foundations of Geometry and Formal Theories of Arithmetic.* Translated with an Introduction by E.H.W.Kluge. New Haven-London, 1971. P. 141-153.
—*Grundgesetze der Arithmetik.* Vol. I-II. Jena, 1893-1903. (repr. Hildesheim-Zürich-New York, 1998).
—*The Foundations of Arithmetic. A logico-mathematical enquiry into the concept of number.* Trans. J. L. Austin. Oxford, ²1978 (1st ed. 1950).
—*Die Grundlagen der Arithmetik. Eine logisch mathematische Untersuchung über den Begriff der Zahl.* Ed. Ch. Thiel. Hamburg, 1986 (1st ed. Breslau, 1884).
FRENKIAN, A. *Le postulat chez Euclide et chez les modernes.* Paris, 1940.
FROMONDUS, L. *Labirintus sive de Compositione Continui Liber Unus.* Antwerp, 1631.
FUNKENSTEIN, A. "Descartes, Eternal Truths, and the Divine Omnipotence". - *Studies in History and Philosophy of Science* 6 (1975), 185-199.
—*Theology and the Scientific Imagination. From the Middle Ages to the Seventeenth Century.* Princeton, 1986.
GABBEY, A. "Force and Inertia in the Seventeenth Century". - In: S. Gaukroger (Ed.) *Descartes: Philosophy, Mathematics and Physics.* Brighton-Totowa, 1980. P. 230-320.
— "Descartes' Physics and Descartes' Mechanics: Chicken or Egg?" - In: S. H. Voss (Ed.) *Essays on the Philosophy and Science of René Descartes.* New York-Oxford, 1993. P. 311- 323.
GÄBE, L. "La Regle 14. Lien entre géométrie et algebre". - *Archives de philosophie* 46 (1983), P. 654-660.
GADAMER, H.-G. "Concerning Empty and Ful-filled Time". - *Southern Journal of Philosophy,* Winter 1970, 341-353.
GADAMER, H.-G.; SCHADEWALDT, W. (Eds.) *Idee und Zahl.* Heidelberg, 1968.

GAIDENKO, P. *Evolutsiya ponyatiya nauki. Stanovlenie i razvitie pervykh nauchnykh programm.* (Evolution of the Notion of Science) Moscow, 1980.
— *Evolutsiya ponyatiya nauki (XVII-XVII vv.).* Moscow, 1987.
—"Volyuntativnaya metafizika i novoevropeiskaya kul'tura (Metaphysics of Will and the New European Culture)". - In: V. Ivanov (Ed.) *Tri podkhoda k izucheniyu kul'tury.* Moscow, 1997. P. 5-74.

GAISER, K. *Platons ungeschriebene Lehre.* Stuttgart, 1963.

GALILEI, G. *Opere.* Edizione nazionale diretta da A. Favaro. Vol. I-XX. Florence, 1890 - 1909. (repr. 1964-1966).
—*The Assayer.* In: *Discoveries and Opinions of Galileo.* Trans. with an introduction and notes by S. Drake. Garden City, (N. Y.), 1957.
—*Dialogue Concerning the Two Chief World Systems—Ptolemaic and Copernican.* Trans. S. Drake, Foreword by A. Einstein. Berkeley-Los Angeles, 1967.

GALPÉRINE, M.-C. "Le temps intégral selon Damascius". - *Les études philosophiques* 3 (1980), 325-341.

GARBER, D. *Descartes' Metaphysical Physics.* Chicago, 1992.

GARDIES, J.-L. "Eudoxe et Dedekind". - *Revue d'histoire des science* 37 (1984), 111-125.

GARRET, D. (Ed.) *The Cambridge Companion to Spinoza.* Cambridge, 1996.

GASSENDI, P. *Exercitationes paradoxicae adversus Aristoteleos.* Ed. B. Rochot. Paris, 1959.
—*Opera Omnia.* Vol. I-VI. Lyon, 1658.

GAUKROGER, S. (Ed.) *Descartes: Philosophy, Mathematics and Physics.* Brighton-Totowa, N. J., 1980.
—"Descartes' Project for a Mathematical Physics". - In: S. Gaukroger (Ed.) *Descartes: Philosophy, Mathematics and Physics.* Brighton-Totowa, N. J., 1980. P. 97-140.
—*Explanatory Structures. A Study of Concepts of Explanation in Early Physics and Philosophy.* Atlantic Highlands (N.J.), 1978.
—"The Nature of Abstract Reasoning: Philosophical Aspects of Descartes' Work in Algebra". - In: J. Cottingham (Ed.) *The Cambridge Companion to Descartes.* Cambridge, 1992. P. 91-114.
—*Descartes. An* Intellectual Biography. Oxford, 1995.

GERSH, S. *ΚΙΝΗΣΙΣ ΑΚΙΝΗΤΟΣ. A Study of Spiritual Motion in the Philosophy of Proclus.* Leiden, 1973.

GERSON, L. *Plotinus.* London-New York, 1994.
—(Ed.) *The Cambridge Companion to Plotinus.* Cambridge, 1996.

GILSON, E. *Etude sur le rôle de la pensée médiévale dans la formation du système cartésien.* Paris, 1930.
—"Note sur le vocabulaire de l'être". *Mediaeval Studies* 8 (1946), P. 150-158.
—*Index Scolastico-Cartesién.* Paris, 1979.

GLOY, K. "Mechanistisches-organisches Naturkonzept". - In: K. Gloy (Ed.) *Natur- und Technikbegriffe. Historische und systematische Aspekte: von der Antike bis zur ökologischen Krise, von der Physik bis zur Antike.* Bonn, 1996. P. 98-117.

GOCLENIUS, R. *Lexicon philosophicum quo tantum clave philosophiae fores aperiuntur.* Frankfurt, 1613 (repr. Hildesheim, 1964).

GÖDEL, K. "On Formally Undecidable Propositions of *Principia Mathematica* and Related

Systems I". - In: *Collected Works.* Vol. I. P. 144-195.
—*Collected Works.* Ed. by S. Feferman et al. Vol. I-III. New York-Oxford, 1986, 1990, 1995.
GRAESER, A. (Ed.) *Mathematics and Metaphysics in Aristotle.* Bern-Stuttgart, 1987.
GRANT, E., MURDOCH J. E. *Mathematics and its Application to Science and Natural Philosophy in the Middle Ages.* Cambridge, 1987.
GRAY, J. J. "Euclidean and non-Euclidean Geometry". - In: I. Grattan-Guinness, (Ed.) *Companion Encyclopedia of the History and Philosophy of the Mathematical Sciences.* Vol. I-II. New York, 1994. Vol. II, P. 877-886.
—"Projective geometry". - Ibid., P. 897-907.
GRENE, M. *Descartes.* Minneapolis, 1985.
—*Spinoza and the Sciences.* Dordrecht, 1986.
GUÉRARD, C. "Le danger du néant et la négation selon Proclus". - *Revue Philosophique de Louvain* 83 (1985), P. 331-354.
GUÉROULT, M. *Descartes selon l'ordre des raisons.* Vol. I-II. Paris, 1953.
HADOT, P. "Être, vie, pensée chez Plotin et avant Plotin." - *Les sources de Plotin. Entretiens Hardt V.* Vandoevres-Genève, 1960. P. 105-141.
—*Porphyre et Victorinus.* Vol. I-II. Paris, 1968.
—"The Harmony of Plotinus and Aristotle According to Porphyry". - In: R. Sorabji (Ed.) *Aristotle Transformed. The Ancient Commentators and Their Influence.* London, 1990. P. 125-140.
HAGER, F. P. "Die Materie und das Böse im antiken Platonismus". - *Museum Helveticum* 19 (1962), 73-103.
HALFWASSEN, J. *Der Aufstieg zum Einen. Untersuchungen zu Platon und Plotin.* Stuttgart, 1992.
—"Monismus und Dualismus in Platons Prinzipienlehre". - *Bochumer philosophisches Jahrbuch für Antike und Mittelalter* 2 (1997), 1-21.
HAPP, H. *Hyle. Studien zum Aristotelischen Materie-Begriff.* Berlin-New York, 1971.
HARTMANN, E. *Philosophie des Unbewußten. Versuch einer Weltanschauung.* Berlin, 1869.
HARTMANN, N. *Des Proclus Diadochus philosophische Anfangsgründe der Mathematik nach den ersten zwei Büchern des Euklidkommentar.* Gießen, 1909.
HATFIELD, G. "Reason, Nature, and God in Descartes". –In: S. H. Voss (Ed.) *Essays on the Philosophy and Science of René Descartes.* New York-Oxford, 1993. P. 259-287.
HEATH, T. L. *A History of Greek Mathematics.* Vol. I-II. Oxford, 1921. (repr. New York, 1981).
—*Introduction.* In: *The Works of Archimedes.* Ed. by T. L. Heath. Cambridge, 1912 (repr. New York, 1953).
—*Introduction and Commentary.* In: *The Thirteen Books of Euclid's Elements.* Vol. I-III. New York, 1956.
—*Mathematics in Aristotle.* Oxford, 1949 (repr. 1970).
HEGEL, G. W. F. *Werke.* Vol. I-XX. Frankfurt am Main, 1969-1971.
HEIBERG, J. L. *Geschichte der Mathematik und der Naturwissenschaften im Altertum.* München, 1925.
HEIDEGGER, M. *Sein und Zeit.* Tübingen, [17]1993.
HEIMSOETH, H. *The Six Great Themes of Western Metaphysics and the End of Middle Ages.* Trans. by R. I. Betanzos. Detroit, 1994.

HEINZE, R. *Xenokrates*. Leipzig, 1892.
HENRICH, D. *Der ontologische Gottesbeweis: Sein Problem und seine Geschichte in der Neuzeit*. Tübingen, 1960.
HENRY, M. "The Soul According to Descartes". –In: S.H. Voss (Ed.) *Essays on the Philosophy and Science of René Descartes*. New York-Oxford, 1993. P. 40-51.
HENRY, P. *Études plotiniennes, I. Les états du texte de Plotin*. Paris-Bruxelles, 1938.
HERON OF ALEXANDRIA. *Metrica*. Ed. by E. M. Bruins. Leiden, 1964.
—*Opera quae supersunt omnia*. Vol. IV. *Definitiones*. Ed. J. H. Heiberg. Leipzig, 1912.
HEYTING, A. "The Intuitionist Foundations of Mathematics". - In: P. Benacerraf, H. Putnam, (Eds.) *Philosophy of Mathematics*. Cambridge, 1983.
HILBERT, D. "Über das Unendliche". - *Mathematische Annalen*, 95 (1926), 161-190.
—*The Foundations of Geometry*. Authorized translation by E. J. Townsend. La Salle (Ill.), 1950. (repr. from the 1902 edition).
—*Grundlagen der Geometrie*. Mit Revisionen und Ergänzungen von P. Bernays. Stuttgart, ^{10}1968.
—*Zahlentheorie*. Göttingen, 1990.
HINTIKKA, J. *Time and Necessity. Studies in Aristotle's Theory of Modality*. Oxford, 1973.
HINTIKKA, J.; REMES, U. *The Method of Analysis: Its Geometrical Origin and General Significance*. Dordrecht, 1974.
HOBBES, TH. *The English Works of Thomas Hobbes*. Ed. W. Molesworth. Vol. I-XI. London, 1839-1845.
HOFFMANN, PH. "Jamblique éxégète du Pythagoricien Archytas: trois originalités d'une doctrine du temps". - *Les études philosophiques* 3 (1980), 307-323.
HONNEFELDER, L. *Ens inquantum ens. Der Begriff des Seienden als solchen als Gegenstand der Metaphysik nach der Lehre des Johannes Duns Scotus*. Münster, ^{2}1989. (1 st ed. 1979).
HORN, CH. *Plotin über Sein, Zahl und Einheit*. Stuttgart-Leipzig, 1995.
HÖSLE, V. *Wahrheit und Geschichte. Studien zur Struktur der Philosophiegeschichte unter paradigmatischen Analyse der Entwicklung von Parmenides bis Platon*. Stuttgart-Bad Cannstatt, 1984.
—*Die Krise der Gegenwart und die Verantwortung der Philosophie*. München, 1990.
HUFFMAN, C. A. *Philolaus of Croton. Pythagorean and Presocratic. A Commentary on the Fragments and Testimonia with Interpretive Essays*. Cambridge, 1993.
HUGH OF ST. VICTOR. *Hugonis de Sancto Victore Opera Propaedevtica. Practica geometriae. De grammatica. Epitome Dindimi in philosophiam*. Ed. by R. Baron. Notre Dame, 1966.
HUSSEY, E. "Aristotle's Mathematical Physics: A Reconstruction". - In: L. Johnson (Ed.) *Aristotle's Physics: A Collection of Essays*. Oxford, 1991. P. 213-242.
HYPPOLITE, M. "Du sens de la géométrie de Descartes dans son oeuvre". - *Descartes*. Paris, 1952. P. 166-175.
IAMBLICHUS. *De communi mathematica scientia*. Ed. N. Festa. Leipzig, 1891.
—*In Nichomachi arithmeticam introductionem liber*. Ed. H. Pistelli. Leipzig, 1894.
—*Theologumena arithmeticae*. Ed. V. De Falco. Leipzig, 1922.

IRWIN, T. *Aristotle's First Principles*. Oxford, 1988.
ISNARDI PARENTE, M. *Techne. Momenti del pensiero greco da Platone a Epicuro.* Firenze, 1966.
JAMMER, M. *Concepts of Space: A History of Theories of Space in Physics.* Cambridge (Mass.), 1954.
JECH, Th. *Set Theory.* New York-San Francisco-London, 1978.
JOACHIM, H. H. *Aristotle's On Coming-to-be and Passing-away.* A Revised Text with Introduction and Commentary. Oxford, 1922 (repr. Hildesheim, 1982).
—*Descartes's Rules for the Direction of the Mind.* London-New York, 1957.
JOHNSON, L. (Ed.) *Aristotle's Physics: A Collection of Essays.* Oxford, 1991.
JOLLEY, N. *The Light of the Soul. Theories of Ideas in Leibniz, Malebranche, and Descartes.* Oxford, 1990.
JONAS, H. "Plotin über Ewigkeit und Zeit: Interpretation von *Enn.* III.7". - In: A. Dempf, H. Arendt (Eds.) *Politische Ordnung und menschliche Existenz: Festgabe für E. Voegelin.* München, 1962. P. 295-319.
JONES, H. *Pierre Gassendi, 1592-1655: An Intellectual Biography.* Nieuwkoop, 1981.
KAHN, CH. *The Verb "Be" in Ancient Greek.* Dordrecht-Boston, 1973.
KANT, I. *Gesammelte Schriften.* Bd. 1-29. Berlin, 1910-1983.
—*Werke.* Vol. I-XII. Hrsg. W. Weischedel. Frankfurt am Main, 1977.
KENNY, A. *Descartes: A Study of His Philosophy.* New York, 1987 (first publ. 1968).
KEPLER, J. *Gesammelte Werke.* Vol. I-XI,1. Hrsg. M. Caspar. München, 1938-1983.
—*Harmonices Mundi.* Linz, 1619 (repr. Bologna, s. d.)
—*Conversation with Galileo's Sidereal Messenger.* Trans., with Intro. and Notes, by E. Rosen. New York-London, 1965.
—*The Six-Cornered Snowflake.* Oxford, 1966.
—*Somnium. The Dream, or Posthumous Work on Lunar Astronomy.* Trans. with a Commentary by E. Rosen. Madison (Milwaukee)-London, 1967.
—*Mysterium Cosmographicum. The Secret of the Universe.* Trans. by A. M. Duncan. Introduction and Commentary by E. J. Aiton. With a Preface by I. B. Cohen. New York, 1981.
—*New Astronomy.* Trans. by W. H. Donahue. Cambridge, 1992.
KIRK, G. S.; RAVEN, J.; SCHOFIELD, M. (Eds.) *The Presocratic Philosophers.* Cambridge, 1983.
KLEIN, J. *Greek Mathematical Thought and the Origin of Algebra.* Trans. E. Brann. Cambridge (Mass.)-London, 1968.
KNORR, W. R. *The Ancient Tradition of Geometric Problems.* Boston-Basel-Stuttgart, 1986.
KOBUSCH, TH.; MOISISCH, B. (Eds.) *Platon in der abendländischen Geistesgeschichte.* Darmstadt, 1997.
KOSELLECK, R. *Vergangene Zukunft: Zur Semantik geschichtlicher Zeiten.* Frankfurt am Main, 1979.
—"'Neuzeit'. Zur Semantik moderner Bewegungsbegriff". - *Studien zum Beginn der modernen Welt.* Hrsg. R. Koselleck. Stuttgart, 1977. P. 264-299.
KOUROMRENOS, TH. *Aristotle on Mathematical Infinity.* Stuttgart, 1995.
KOYRÉ, A. *The Astronomical Revolution. Copernicus-Kepler-Borelli.* Trans. by R.E.W. Maddison. Paris-London-Ithaca (N.Y.), 1973.
—*Descartes und die Scholastik*, 1923 (repr. Darmstadt, 1971).

—*From the Closed World to the Infinite Universe.* Baltimore, 1957.
—*Metaphysics and Measurement. Essays in Scientific Revolution.* Cambridge (Mass.), 1968.
KRÄMER, H. J. *Arete bei Platon und Aristoteles. Zum Wesen und zum Geschichte der platonischen Ontologie.* Heidelberg, 1959.
—*Der Ursprung der Geistmetaphysik. Untersuchungen zur Geschichte des Platonismus zwischen Platon und Plotin.* Amsterdam, 1964.
—*Platonismus und hellenistische Philosophie.* Berlin-New York, 1971.
—*Plato and the Foundations of Metaphysics.* New York, 1990.
KRETZMANN, N. (Ed.) *Infinity and Continuity in Ancient and Medieval Thought.* Ithaca (N. Y.)-London, 1982.
—"Continuity, Contrariety, Contradiction, and Change". - In: N. Kretzmann (Ed.) *Infinity and Continuity in Ancient and Medieval Thought.* Ithaca (N. Y.)-London, 1982. P. 270-296.
KRETZMANN, N.; KENNY, A.; PINBORG, J. (Eds.) *The Cambridge History of Later Medieval Philosophy. From the Rediscovery of Aristotle to the Disintegration of Scholasticism, 1100-1600.* Cambridge, 1982.
KRONECKER, L. *Werke.* Hrsg. K. Hensel. Leipzig, 1895-1930. Vol. I-V.
KULLMANN, W. "Die Funktion der mathematischen Beispiele in Aristoteles' *Analytica Posteriora*" .- In: E. Berti (Ed.) *Aristotle on Science. The "Posterior Analytics."* Padova, 1981. P. 245-270.
KUNG, J. "Can Substance Be Predicated of Matter?" - *Archiv für Geschichte der Philosophie* 60 (1978), 140-159.
LACHTERMAN, D. R. "*Objectum Purae Matheseos*: Mathematical Construction and the Passage from Essence to Existence". - In: A. Rorty (Ed.) *Essays on Descartes' Meditations.* Berkeley-Los Angeles, 1986. P. 435-458.
—*The Ethics of Geometry. A Genealogy of Modernity.* New York-London, 1989.
LASSERRE, F. *The Birth of Mathematics in the Age of Plato.* London, 1964.
LATHAM, M. L., SMITH, D. E. *The Geometry of René Descartes.* Dover, 1954.
LAUER, H. "Descartes' Concept of Number". - *Studia Cartesiana* 2 (1981), 137-143.
LEE, J.S. "The Doctrine of Reception According to the Capacity of the Recipient v., *Enneads*, vi.4-5". –*Dionysius*, 3 (1979), 79-97.
—"Omnipresence, Participation, and Eidetic Causation in Plotinus". - In: R. Baine Harris (Ed.), *The Structure of Being. A Neoplatonic Approach.* Norfolk (Virginia), 1982. P. 90-103.
LEIBNIZ, G. W. *Leibnitiana Elementa Philosophiae arcanae de summa rerum.* Hrsg. Iagodinsky. Kazan, 1913.
—*Mathematische Schriften.* Hrsg. C. I. Gerhardt. Vol. I-VIII. Halle, 1849-1863.
—*New Essays on Human Understanding.* Trans. and ed. by P. Remnant and J. Bennet. Cambridge, 1996.
—*Philosophische Schriften.* Hrsg. C. I. Gerhardt. Vol. I-VII. Berlin, 1875-1890.
LENOIR, T. "Descartes and the Geometrization of Thought: The Methodological Background of Descartes' *Géométrie*". - *Historia Mathematica* 6 (1979), 355-379.
LESZL, W. "Mathematics, Axiomatization and the Hypotheses". - In: E. Berti (Ed.) *Aristotle on Science. The "Posterior Analytics".* Padova, 1981. P. 271-328.

LEVINAS, E. *Totality and Infinity. An Essay on Exteriority.* Pittsburgh, 1969 (originally published as: *Totalité et infini.* The Hague, 1961).
LLOYD, A. C. *The Anatomy of Neoplatonism.* Oxford, 1990.
—"Plotinus on the Genesis of Thought and Existence". - *Oxford Studies in Ancient Philosophy* 5 (1987), 155-186.
— "The Principle That the Cause Is Greater Than Its Effect". - *Phronesis* 21 (1976), 146-156.
LOBACHEVSKY, N. I. *Pangeometrie.* Leipzig, 1902.
LOCKE, J. *An Essay Concerning Human Understanding.* Ed. with a Foreword and an Introduction by P. N. Nidditch. Oxford, 1975.
LONG, A. A., SEDLEY, D. N. *The Hellenistic Philosophers.* Vol. I-II. Cambridge, 1987.
LOVEJOY, A. O. *The Great Chain of Being: A Study of the History of an Idea.* New York, 1960.
LÖWITH, K. "Vicos Grundsatz: *Verum et factum convertuntur*". - In: *Aufsätze und Vorträge, 1930-1970.* Stuttgart, 1971. P. 157-188.
MACINTYRE, A. "Essence and Existence". - *Encyclopedia of Philosophy.* Vol. II. Ed. By P.Edwards, New York, 1967. P. 58-62.
MAIER, A. *Die Mechanisierung des Weltbildes.* Leipzig, 1938.
MALCOLM, J. *Plato on the Self-Predication of Forms. Early and Middle Dialogues.* Oxford, 1991.
MALEBRANCHE, N. *Oeuvres complètes de Malebranche.* Ed. by A. Robinet et al. Vol. I-XXI. Paris, 1962-1964.
—*The Search after Truth.* Trans. by Th. M. Lennon and P.J. Olscamp. Cambridge, 1997.
MANCHESTER, P. "Time and the Soul in Plotinus, III.7 [45], 11." - *Dionysius* 2 (1978), 101-136.
MANIN, YU. I. *Mathematics and Physics.* Trans. by A. and N. Koblitz. Boston-Basel Stuttgart, 1981.
MARION, J.-L. Generosity and Phenomenology: Remarks on Michel Henry's Interpretation of the Cartesian *Cogito*." - In: S.H. Voss (Ed.) *Essays on the Philosophy and Science of René Descartes.* New York-Oxford, 1993. P. 52-74.
—*L'ontologie grise de Descartes. Science cartésienne et savoir aristotélicien dans les* Regulae. Paris, ²1981 (1st ed. 1975).
—"Cartesian Metaphysics and the Role of Simple Natures". - In: J. Cottingham (Ed.) *The Cambridge Companion to Descartes.* Cambridge, 1992. P. 115-139.
MARKIE, P. "Descartes' Concept of Substance". - In: J. Cottingham (Ed.) *Reason, Will, and Sensation. Studies in Descartes' Metaphysics.* Oxford, 1994. P. 63-88.
MARKOVIC, Z. "Platons Theorie über das Eine und die unbestimmte Zweiheit und ihre Spuren in der griechischen Mathematik". - In: O. Becker (Ed.) *Zur Geschichte der griechischen Mathematik.* Darmstadt, 1965. P. 308-318.
MAU, J; SCHMIDT, E. G. (Eds.) *Isonomia. Studien zur Gleichheitsvorstellung im griechischen Denken.* Berlin, 1964.
MCGUIRE, J. E. "Space, Geometrical Objects and Infinity: Newton and Descartes on Extension". In: W. R. Shea. *Nature Mathematized: Historical and Philosophical Case Studies in Classical Modern Natural Philosophy.* Dordrecht, 1983. P. 69-112.

MCGUIRE, J. E.; TAMNY, M. *Certain Philosophical Questions: Newton's Trinity Notebook.* Cambridge, 1983.
MCMULLIN, E. (Ed.) *The Concept of Matter in Greek and Medieval Philosophy.* Notre Dame, 1963.
MERLAN, PH. *From Platonism to Neoplatonism.* The Hague, 1953.
—"Aristotle, Met. A6, 987b 20-25 and Plotinus, Enn. V 4, 2, 8-9". - *Phronesis* 9 (1964), 45-47.
MICHAEL, E.; MICHAEL, F. S. "Corporeal Ideas in the Seventeenth-Century Psychology". - *Journal for the History of Ideas* 50 (1989), 31-48.
MITTELSTRAß, J. "Die Idee einer *mathesis universalis* bei Descartes." - *Perspektiven der Philosophie* 4 (1978), 177-192.
MOHR, R. D. "The Number Theory in Plato's *Rep. II* and *Philebus*". - *Isis* 72 (1981), 620-627.
MOORE, A. W. *The Infinite.* London-New York, 1990.
MORROW, G. R. *Proclus. A Commentary on the First Book of Euclid's Elements.* Trans. with Introduction and Notes. Princeton, ²1992 (1st ed. 1970).
MOUTSOPOULOS, E. "Dynamic Structuralism in the Plotinian Theory of the Imaginary". - *Diotima* 4 (1976), 11-22.
—*Les structures de l'imaginaire dans la philosophie de Proclus.* Paris, 1985.
MOYAL, G. J. D. (Ed.) *René Descartes. Critical Assessments.* Vol. I-IV. London-New York, 1991.
MUELLER, I. "Aristotle on Geometrical Objects". - *Archiv für Geschichte der Philosophie* 52 (1970), 156-171.
—*Philosophy of Mathematics and Deductive Structure in Euclid's Elements.* Cambridge (Mass.)-London, 1981.
—"Iamblichus' and Proclus' Euclid Commentary". - *Hermes* 115 (1987), 334-348.
—"Mathematics and Philosophy in Proclus' Commentary on Book I of Euclid's Elements". - In: J. Pépin, H. D. Saffrey (Eds.) *Proclus lecteur et interprète des Anciens.* Paris, 1987. P. 305-318.
MUGLER, CH. *Dictionnaire historique de la terminologie géométrique des grecs.* Paris, 1958.
MÜNSTER, G. "The Role of Mathematics in Contemporary Theoretical Physics". - In: E. Rudolf and I. O. Stamatescu (Eds.) *Philosophy, Mathematics and Modern Physics. A Dialogue.* Berlin et al., 1994. P. 205-212.
NARBONNE, J.-M. "Plotin, Descartes et la notion de *causa sui*". –*Archives de philosophie* 56 (1993a), 177-195.
—*Plotin. Les deux matières. [Ennéades II, 4 (12)].* Paris, 1993.
—*La métaphysique de Plotin.* Paris, 1994.
NESSELMANN, G. H. F. *Die Algebra der Griechen.* Berlin, 1842.
NEUGEBAUER, O. *The Exact Sciences in Antiquity.* Copenhagen-London-Princeton, 1951. (2nd ed. Providence (R. I.), 1957).
NEWTON, I. *Unpublished Scientific Papers of Isaac Newton. A Selection from the Portsmouth Collection in the University Library, Cambridge.* Chosen, ed. and trans. by A. R. Hall and M. B. Hall. Cambridge, 1962.
—*The Mathematical Papers of Isaac Newton.* Ed. by D. T. Whitehead. Vol. I-VIII. Cambridge, 1967-1981.

—*Philosophiae naturalis principia mathematica*. The Third edition (1726) with Variant Readings. Assembled and ed. by A. Koyré and I. B. Cohen. Vol. I-II. Cambridge (Mass.), 1972.
NICHOLAS OF CUSA. *Philosophisch-Theologische Schriften*. Hrsg. L. Gabriel. Vol. I-III. Vienna, 1964-1967.
NICOMACHUS OF GERASA. *Introductionis arithmeticae libri II. (Arithmētikē eisagogē)*. Ed. R. Hoche. Leipzig, 1866.
—*Introduction to Arithmetic*. Trans. by M. L. Ooge. London, 1926.
NIJENHUIS, J. "'Ens' Described as 'Being or Existent'". - *American Catholic Philosophical Quarterly* 68 (1994), 1-14.
NIKULIN, D. *Prostranstvo i vremya v metafizike XVII veka (Space and Time in the Metaphysics of the XVIIth Century)*. Novosibirsk, 1993.
—*Metaphysik und Ethik. Theoretische und praktische Philosophie in Antike und Neuzeit*. München, 1996.
—"Intelligible Matter in Plotinus". - *Dionysius* 16 (1998), 85-113.
—"Foundations of Arithmetic in Plotinus: Enn. VI.6 (34) on the Structure and the Constitution of Number", *Methexis* 11 (1998), 85-102.
— "Plotinus on Eternity". - In: A. Neschke-Hentschke (Ed.) *Le Timée de Plateu. Contributions à l'histoire de sa réception*. Louvain-Paris, 2000. P. 15-38.
NUMENIUS. *Studie over den wijsgeer Numenius van Apamea met uitgave der fragmenten door* E.-A. Leemans. Bruxelles, 1937.
—*Fragments*. Texte établi et traduit par E. Des Places. Paris, 1973.
NUSSBAUM, M. C. *Aristotle's De Motu Animalium*. Text with Translation, Commentary, and Interpretive Essay. Princeton, 1978.
O'BRIEN, D. "Plotinus on Evil: A Study of Matter and the Soul in Plotinus' Conception of Human Evil". - In: *Le Néoplatonisme*. Paris, 1971. P. 113-146.
—"Plotinus and the Gnostics on the Generation of Matter." - In: H. J. Blumenthal, R. A. Markus (Eds.) *Neoplatonism and Early Christian Thought. Essays in Honour of A. H. Armstrong*. London, 1981. P. 108-123.
—*Plotinus on the Origin of Matter. An Exercise in the Interpretation of the Enneads*. S. l., 1991.
—*Le Non-Être. Deux études sur le Sophiste de Platon*. Sankt Augustin, 1995.
—"Plotinus on Mater and Evil". - In: L. P. Gerson (Ed.) *The Cambridge Companion to Plotinus*. Cambridge, 1996. P. 171-195.
O'MEARA, D. "The Freedom of the One". –*Phronesis* 37 (1992), 343-349.
—*Les structures hiérarchiques dans la pensée de Plotin*. Leiden, 1975.
—*Pythagoras Revived. Mathematics and Philosophy in Late Antiquity*. Oxford, 1989.
—*Plotinus. An Introduction to the Enneads*. Oxford, 1993.
OCKHAM. *Opera philosophica*. Vol. I-VII. Ed. G. Gál, S. Brown et al. St. Bonaventure (N. Y.), 1974-1988.
—*Opera theologica*. Vol. I-X. Ed. G. Gál, S. Brown et al. St. Bonaventure (N.Y.), 1967-1986.
—*Philosophical Writings*. Ed. and trans. Ph. Boehner. Edinburgh, 1959.
ORIGEN. *Vier Bücher von den Prinzipien*. Ed. H. Görgemanns, H. Karpp. Darmstadt, 1976.

OWENS, J. *The Doctrine of Being in the Aristotelian "Metaphysics". A Study in the Greek Background of Mediaeval Thought.* Toronto, ²1963. (1st ed. 1951).
PAPPUS OF ALEXANDRIA. *Collectionis quae supersunt e libris manuscriptis.* Ed. F. Hultsch. Vol. I-III. Berlin, 1876-1878.
PARMENIDES. *A Text with Translation, Commentary, and Critical Essays by* L. Tarán. Princeton, 1965.
—*The Fragments.* Ed. by D. Sider, H. W. Johnstone, Jr. Bryn Mawr (Pennsylvania), 1986.
PASCAL, B. *Oeuvres complètes.* Ed. par J. Chevalier. Paris, 1954.
—*Pensées.* With an English Translation, Brief Notes and Introduction by H. F. Stewart. New York, 1950.
PATZIG, G. "Theologie und Ontologie in der 'Metaphysik' des Aristoteles". - *Kant-Studien* 52 (1960-1961), 185-205.
PEANO, G. *Arbeiten zur Analysis und zur mathematischen Logik.* Hrsg. und mit einem Nachwort versehen von G. Assen. Leipzig, 1990.
PEIRCE, CH. S. "On Physical Geometry". - In: *The New Elements of Mathematics.* Vol. IV: *Mathematical Philosophy.* Ed. by C. Eisele. The Hague-Paris-Atlantic Highlands (N. J.), 1976. P. 359-362.
PEPERZAK, A. "Life, Science, and Wisdom According to Descartes". - *History of Philosophy Quarterly* 12 (1995), 133-153.
—*To the Other. An Introduction to the Philosophy of Emmanuel Levinas.* West Lafayette (Indiana), 1993.
PÉPIN, J. "Platonisme et antiplatonisme dans le traité de Plotin *Sur les nombres (VI 6 [34])*". - *Phronesis,* 24 (1979), 197-208.
PHILO OF BYZANTIUM. *Pneumatica.* Wiesbaden, 1974.
PHILOPONUS. *In Aristotelis De Anima Libros Commentaria.* Ed. M. Hayduck. Berlin, 1897.
—*In Aristotelis Categorias Commentarium.* Ed. M. Busse. Berlin, 1898.
PINES, S.; SAMBURSKY, S. *The Concept of Time in Late Neoplatonism.* Texts with Translation, Introduction and Notes. Jerusalem, ²1987.
PLATO. *Opera.* Vol. I-V. Ed. I. Burnet. Oxford, 1900-1907.
PLOTINUS. *Plotini opera.* Ed. P. Henry and H. Schwyzer. Vol. I-III. Oxford, 1964-1982.
—*Plotins Schriften.* Übersetzt von R. Harder. Neubearbeitung von R. Beutler und W. Theiler. Vol. I-VI. Hamburg, 1956-1971.
—*Enneads.* Vol. I-VII. Trans. by A. H. Armstrong. Cambridge, Mass.-London, 1966-1988.
—*Traité sur les nombres. (Ennéade VI 6 [34]).* Introduction, texte grec, traduction, commentaire et index grec par J. Bertier, L. Brisson, A. Charles, J. Pépin, H.-D. Saffrey, A.-Ph. Segonds. Paris, 1980.
—*Ennead III. 6. On the Impassivity of the Bodies.* With a Translation and Commentary by B. Fleet. Oxford, 1995.
—*Sochineniya.* Ed. Yu. Shichalin and M. Solopova. St. Petersburg, 1995.
PLUTARCH. *Moralia.* Vol. XII, part I. Cambridge (Mass.), 1976.
POINCARÉ, A. "On the Nature of Mathematical Reasoning". - In: P. Benacerraf, H. Putnam (Eds.), *Philosophy of Mathematics.* Cambridge (Mass.), 1983. P. 394-402.
PORPHYRY. *Kommentar zur Harmonienlehre des Ptolemaios.* Hrsg. I. Düring. Göteborg, 1932.

—Sententiae ad intelligibilia ducentes. Ed. E. Lamberz. Leipzig, 1975.
—Fragmenta. Ed. A. Smith. Stuttgart-Leipzig, 1993.
PRANTL, K. Ed. Aristoteles. *Acht Bücher Physik.* Ed. and Notes. Leipzig, 1854 (repr. Aalen, 1987).
PRITCHARD, P. *Plato's Philosophy of Mathematics.* Sankt Augustin, 1995.
PROCLUS. *Commentarium in Platonis Parmenidem.* Ed. V. Cousin. In: *Procliopera inedita.* Paris, 1864 (repr. Hildesheim, 1980).
—In primum Euclidis Elemetorum librum commentarii. Ed. G. Friedlein. Leipzig, 1873.
—In Platonis Rem Publicam commentarii. Vol. I-II. Ed. G. Kroll. Leipzig, 1899-1901.
— *In Platonis Timaeum commentarii.* Vol. I-III. Ed. E. Diehl. Leipzig, 1903-1906.
—Institutio Physica. Ed. A. Ritzenfeld. Leipzig, 1912.
—The Elements of Theology. A Revised Text with Translation, Introduction and Commentary by E. R. Dodds. Oxford, ²1963.
—Les mystères d'Egypte. Texte établi et traduit par E. des Places. Paris, 1966.
—Théologie Platonicienne. Texte établi et traduit par H. D. Saffrey et L. G. Westerink. Vol. I-VI. Paris, 1968-1997.
—Alcibiades I. A Translation and a Commentary by W. O'Neill. The Hague, ²1971.
—A Commentary on the First Book of Euclid's Elements. Trans. with Introduction and Notes by G. R. Morrow. Princeton, ²1992 (First ed. 1970).
PROSPERI, G. "Mathematics and Physics". - In: E. Agazzi, G. Darvas (Eds.) *Philosophy of Mathematics Today.* Dordrecht et al., 1997. P. 261-267.
REALE, G. *Introduzione a Proclo.* Bari, 1989.
RIEMANN, B. *Über die Hypothesen, welche der Geometrie zu Grunde liegen.* Neu herausgearbeitet und erläutert von H. Weyl. Berlin, ³1923 (1st ed. 1919).
RIST, J. M. "Plotinus on Matter and Evil". - *Phronesis*, 6 (1961), 154-166.
—"The Indefinite Dyad and Intelligible Matter in Plotinus". - *Classical Quarterly* 12 (1962), 99-107.
—"Equals and Intermediaries in Plato". - *Phronesis* 9 (1964), 27-37.
—Stoic Philosophy. Cambridge, 1969.
—The Road to Reality. Cambridge, 1967.
—"The Problem of 'Otherness' in the Enneads". - In: *Le Néoplatonisme.* Paris, 1971. P. 77-87.
ROBIN, L. *La théorie platonicienne des idées et des nombres d'après Aristote.* Paris, 1908.
ROBINSON, A. *Non-Standard Analysis.* Amsterdam, 1966.
RODIS-LEWIS, G. "From Metaphysics to Physics". - In: S. H. Voss (Ed.) *Essays on the Philosophy and Science of René Descartes.* New York-Oxford, 1993. P. 242-258.
RORTY, A. O. (Ed.) *Essays on Descartes' Meditations.* Berkeley-Los Angeles-London, 1986.
ROSS, W. D. *Aristotle.* London-New York, ⁵1949.
—An Introduction and Commentary to Aristotle's Metaphysics. Vol. I-II. Oxford, ²1953. (1st ed. 1924).

ROVANE, C. "God without Cause". - In: J. Cottingham (Ed.) *Reason, Will, and Sensation. Studies in Descartes' Metaphysics.* Oxford, 1994. P. 89-109.
ROY, J. H. *L'imagination selon Descartes.* Paris, 1944.
ROZEMOND, M. "The Role of Intellect in Descartes's Case for the Incorporeity of the Mind". - In: S. H. Voss (ed.) *Essays on the Philosophy and Science of René Descartes.* New York-Oxford, 1993. P. 97-114.
RUNIA, D.T. "A Brief History of the Term *Kosmos Noétos* from Plato to Plotinus". - In: J. Cleary (ed.) *Traditions of Platonism: Essays in Honour of John Dillon.* Aldershot et al., 1999. P. 151-171.
RUSSELL, B. *Introduction to Mathematical Philosophy.* London, 1919.
—"The Problem of Infinity Considered Historically". - In: C. W. Salmon (Ed.) *Zeno's Paradoxes.* Indianapolis-New York, 1970. P. 45-58.
SAFFREY, H. D. *Le PERI FILOSOFIAS d'Aristote et la théorie platonicienne des idées nombres.* Leiden, 1971.
SAFFREY, H. D., WESTERINK, L. G. Commentary. In: Proclus. *Théologie Platonicienne.* Vol. I-IV. Paris, 1968-1987.
SAMBURSKY, S. *Physics of the Stoics.* New York, 1959.
—*The Concept of Place in Late Neoplatonism.* Jerusalem, 1982.
—*The Physical World of Late Antiquity.* Princeton, 1987 (1st ed. London, 1962).
SARTRE, J.-P. *L'imagination.* Paris (^{4}1956).
SCHLETTE, H. R. *Das Eine und das Andere. Studien zur Problematik des Negativen in der Metaphysik Plotins.* München, 1966.
SCHMITZ, M. *Euklids Geometrie und ihre mathematiktheoretische Grundlegung in der neuplatonischen Philosophie des Proklos.* Würzburg, 1997.
SCHOFIELD, M. "Aristotle on the Imagination". - In: G. E. R. Lloyd, G. E. L. Owen (Eds.) *Aristotle on Mind and the Senses.* Cambridge, 1978.
SCHRAMM, M. *Natur ohne Sinn? Das Ende des teleologischen Weltbildes.* Graz-Wien-Köln, 1985.
SCHRENK, L. P. (Ed.) *Aristotle in Late Antiquity.* Washington, 1994.
SCHUSTER, J. A. "Descartes and the Scientific Revolution, 1618-1634". Ph.D. diss., Princeton, 1977.
— "Descartes' Mathesis Universalis: 1619-28". - In: *Descartes. Philosophy, Mathematics and Physics.* Ed. S. Gaukroger. Brighton-Totowa, 1980. P. 41-96.
— "Whatever Should We do with Cartesian Method? Reclaiming Descartes for the History of Science". - In: S. H. Voss (Ed.) *Essays on the Philosophy and Science of René Descartes.* New York-Oxford, 1993. P. 195-223.
SCHWYZER, H.-R. "Plotinos". - *Paulys Real-Encyclopädie der klassischen Altertumswissenschaft.* Bd. XXI.1. Stuttgart-Waldsee, 1951. Col. 471-592.
—"Zu Plotins Deutung der sogennanten platonischen Materie". - *Zetesis.* Antwerpen-Utrecht, 1973. P. 266-280.
SEPPER, D. L. "Descartes and the Eclipse of the Imagination, 1618-1630". - *Journal of the History of Philosophy* 27 (1989), 379-403.
—*Descartes' Imagination. Proportion, Images, and the Activity of Thinking.* Berkeley-Los Angeles-London, 1996.

SÉRIS, M. "Language and Machine in the Philosophy of Descartes". –In: S. H. Voss (Ed.) *Essays on the Philosophy and Science of René Descartes*. New York-Oxford, 1993. P. 177-192.
SERRES, M. (Ed.) *A History of Scientific Thought. Elements of a History of Science*. Oxford, 1995.
SEXTUS EMPIRICUS. *Opera*. Ed. H. Mutschmann. Vol. III. *Adversus Mathematicos*. Ed. J. Mau. Leipzig, 1954.
SIEGMANN, G. *Plotins Philosophie des Guten. Eine Interpretation von Enneade VI 7*. Würzburg, 1990.
SIMPLICIUS. *In libros Aristotelis De Anima commentaria*. Ed. M. Hayduck. Berlin, 1882.
—*In Aristotelis Physicorum libros quattuor priores commentaria*. Ed. H. Diels. Berlin, 1882.
SIORVANES, L. *Proclus. Neo-Platonic Philosophy and Science*. New Haven-London, 1996.
SLEEMAN, J.H., POLLET, G. *Lexicon Plotinianum*. Leiden-Leuven, 1980.
SMITH, A. *Porphyry's Place in the Neoplatonic Tradition. A Study in Post-Plotinian Platonism*. The Hague, 1974.
SOLMSEN, F. *Aristotle's System of the Physical World: A Comparison with His Predecessors*. Ithaca (N. Y.), 1960.
SORABJI, R. *Time, Creation and the Continuum. Theories in Antiquity and the Early Middle Ages*. London, 1983.
—"Simplicius: Prime Matter as Extension". - In: I. Hadot (Ed.) *Simplicius: Sa vie, son oeuvre, sa survie*. Berlin-New York, 1987. P. 148-165.
—*Matter, Space and Motion. Theories in Antiquity and Their Sequel*. Ithaca (N. Y.), 1988.
SORELL, T. "Descartes' Modernity". - In: J. Cottingham (Ed.) *Reason, Will, and Sensation. Studies in Descartes' Metaphysics*. Oxford, 1994. P. 29-45.
SPEUSIPPUS. *Fragmenta*. - In: P. Lang. *De Speusippi Academici scriptis accedunt fragmenta*. Bonn, 1911. P. 48-87.
—*Frammenti*. Edizione, traduzione e commento a cura di M. Isnardi Parente. Precedono testimonianze sull' Academia scelte e originate da M. Gigante. Naples, 1980.
SPINOZA, B. *Opera quotquod reperta sunt*. Vol. I-III. Ed. by J. Van Vloten, J. P. N. Land. The Hague, ³1914.
—*Opera omnia*. Vol. I-IV. Hrsg. C. Gebhardt. Heidelberg, 1925.
—*Earlier Philosophical Writings: The Cartesian Principles and Thoughts on Metaphysics*. Trans. by F. A. Hayes. Introd. by D. Bridney. Indianapolis, 1963.
—*Ethics*. Trans. by E. Curley. Princeton (N. J.), 1994.
STALLMACH, J. *Dynamis und Energeia. Untersuchungen am Werk des Aristoteles zur Problemgeschichte von Möglichkeit und Wirklichkeit*. Meisenheim am Glan, 1959.
STEEL, C. "L'Un et le Bien. Les raisons d'une identification dans la tradition platonicienne". - *Revue des Sciences Philosophiques et Théologiques*, 73 (1989), 69-85.
— "'Negatio Negationis': Proclus on the First Lemma of the First Hypothesis of the Parmenides". - In: J. Cleary (Ed.) *Traditions of Platonism. Essays in Honour of John Dillon*. Aldershot, 1999. P. 351-368.
STENZEL, J. *Zahl und Gestalt bei Platon und Aristoteles*. Darmstadt, ³1959.
STEIN, H. "Eudoxus and Dedekind: On the Ancient Greek Theory of Ratios and Its Relation

to Modern Mathematics". - In: W. Demopoulos (Ed.) *Philosophy of Mathematics.*Cambridge (Mass.)-London, 1995. P. 334-357.
STEINER, M. "Application of Mathematics to Natural Science". - *Journal of Philosophy* 86 (1989), 449-480.
—*Applicability of Mathematics as a Philosophical Problem.* Cambridge (Mass.) - London, 1998.
STENIUS, E. "Foundations of Mathematics: Ancient Greek and Modern". - *Dialectica* 32 (1978), 255-289.
STENZEL, J. *Zahl und Gestalt bei Platon und Aristoteles.* Bad Homburg, ³1959.
STRANGE, S. "Plotinus on the Nature of Eternity and Time." - In: L. P. Schrenk (Ed.) *Aristotle in Late Antiquity.* Washington, 1994. P. 22-53.
SUAREZ, F. *Opera omnia.* Vol. I-XXVI. Paris, 1856-1861.
—*Disputationes Metaphysicae.* Vol. I-II. Paris, 1866 (repr. Hildesheim, 1965).
—*On the Various Kinds of Distinctions. (Disputationes Metaphysicae, Disputatio VII, de variis distinctionum generibus.).* Trans. by C. Vollert. Milwaukee, 1947.
SWEENEY, L. *Divine Infinity in Greek and Medieval Thought.* New York et al., 1992.
SYNESIUS. *Opera quae extant omnia.* PG LXVI. Repr. Turnholti, 1977.
SYRIANUS. *In Metaphysica Commentarii.* Ed. G. Kroll. Berlin, 1902.
SZABÓ, Á. "The Transformation of Mathematics into Deductive Science and the Beginnings of its Foundation on Definitions and Axioms". - *Scripta Mathematica* 27 (1964), 27-48A, 113-139.
—"Anfänge des Euklidischen Axiomensystems." - In: O. Becker (Ed.) *Zur Geschichte der griechischen Mathematik.* Darmstadt, 1965. P. 355-461.
—*Anfänge der griechischen Mathematik.* München-Wien, 1969. (Trans.: *The Beginnings of Greek Mathematics.* Dordrecht-Boston, 1978.)
—*Die Entfaltung der griechischen Mathematik.* Mannheim et al., 1994.
SZLEZÁK, TH. A. *Platon und Aristoteles in der Nuslehre Plotins.* Basel-Stuttgart, 1979.
TARÁN, L. *Speusippus of Athens. A Critical Study with a Collection of the Related texts and Commentary.* Leiden, 1981.
TAYLOR, CH. *Sources of the Self.* Cambridge, 1989.
THEILER, W. *Die Vorbereitung des Neuplatonismus.* Berlin, 1930.
—"Einheit und unbegrenzte Zweiheit von Plato bis Plotin". - In: *Isonomia.* Berlin, 1964. P. 89-109.
THEMISTIUS. *In libros Aristotelis de anima paraphrasis.* Ed. R. Heinze. Berlin, 1899.
—*In Aristotelis Physica paraphrasis.* Ed. H. Schenkel. Berlin, 1900.
—*On Aristole's On the Soul.* Trans. R. B. Todd. Ithaca (N. Y.), 1996.
THEON OF SMYRNA. *Expositio rerum mathematicarum ad legendum Platonem utilium.* Ed. E. Hiller. Leipzig, 1878.
THEOPHRASTUS. *Opera omnia.* Ed. F. Wimmer. Vol. I-III. Leipzig, 1854-1862.
THESLEFF, H. *The Pythagorean Texts of the Hellenistic Period.* Collected and edited by H. Thesleff. Åbo, 1965.
THOMAS AQUINAS. *Opera omnia.* Ed. Leonina. Vol. I-XVI. Romae, 1882-1948.
—*De Principiis naturae.* Fribourg, 1950.
—*The Commentary on the De Anima of Aristotle.* New Haven, 1951.
—*Opusculum de ente et essentia.* Torino, ³1957.

TODD, R. "Themistius and the Traditional Interpretation of Aristotle's Theory of *Phantasia*". - *Acta Classica* 24 (1981), 49-59.
TOEPLITZ, O. "Das Verhältnis von Mathematik und Ideenlehre bei Platon". - *Quellen und Studien zur Geschichte der Mathematik, Astronomie und Physik.* Abt. B, Bd.1, 1931. P. 3-33 (repr. In: O. Becker, ed. *Zur Geschichte der griechischen Mathematik.* Darmstadt, 1965. P.45-75).
TÓTH, I. "Das Parallelenproblem im Corpus Aristotelicum". - *Archive for History of Exact Sciences.* Ed. by C. Truesdell, 3 (1967), 249-422.
TROUILLARD, J. *L'un et l'âme selon Proclus.* Paris, 1972.
—"La puissance secrete du nombre selon Proclus". - *Revue de philosophie ancienne* 1 (1983), 227-241.
TYE, M. *The Imagery Debate.* Cambridge (Mass.), 1991.
UNGURU, S. "On the Need to Rewrite the History of Greek Mathematics." - *Archive for History of Exact Sciences* 15 (1975/ 1976), 67-114.
VAN DER WAERDEN, B. L. *Science Awakening.* New York, 1961.
—"Die Arithmetik der Pythagoreer". - In: O. Becker (Ed.) *Zur Geschichte der griechischen Mathematik.* Darmstadt, 1965. P. 203-234.
—"Die Postulate und Konstruktionen in der frühgriechischen Geometrie". - *Archive for History of Exact Sciences* 18 (1977/ 78), 343-357.
—*Geometry and Algebra in Ancient Civilizations.* Berlin, 1983.
VICO, G. *La scienza nuova seconda, giusta l'edizione del 1744, con le varianti dell'edizione del 1730 e di due redazioni intermedie inedite.* Ed. F. Nicolini. Vol. I-II. Bari, ³1942.
—*Selected Readings.* Ed. and trans. by L. Pompa. Cambridge, 1982.
VIÈTE, F. *Introduction to the Analytical Art.* - In: J. Klein. *Greek Mathematical Thought and the Origin of Algebra.* Cambridge (Mass.)-London, 1968.P. 313-353.
—*The Analytic Art. Nine Studies in Algebra, Geometry, and Trigonometry from the "Opus Restitutiae Mathematicae Analyseos, seu Algebrâ Novâ".* Introd. and trans. by T. R. Witmer. Kent (Ohio), 1983.
VIGO, A. "Apuntes sobre la teoría de la predicación y juicio en Platón y Plotino". - In: G. Grammatico, A. Arbea, X. Ponce de León (Eds.). *Silencio, palabra y acción. Collección Iter: Encuentros.* Santiago de Chile, 1999. P. 109-136.
VINCENT SPADE, P. "Quasi-Aristotelianism". - In: N. Kretzmann (Ed.) *Infinity and Continuity in Ancient and Medieval Thought.* Ithaca (N. Y.)-London, 1982. P. 297-307.
VINOGRADOV, I. M. *Selected Works.* Berlin et al., 1985.
VLASTOS, G. *Platonic Studies.* Princeton, 1973.
VOGEL, C. J. DE. "La théorie de l' chez Platon et dans la tradition platonicienne". - *Revue philosophique de la France et de l'étranger* 84 (1959), 21-39.
VOSS, S. H. (Ed.) *Essays on the Philosophy and Science of René Descartes.* New York-Oxford, 1993.
VUILLEMIN, J. *Mathématiques et métaphysique chez Descartes.* Paris, 1960.
WAGNER, H. *Aritoteles. Physikvorlesung.* Trans. and Notes. Darmstadt, 1967.
WAGNER, M. "Realism and the Foundations of Science in Plotinus". - *Ancient Philosophy* 5 (1985), 269-292.

—"Plotinus' Idealism and the Problem of Matter in *Enneads* vi.4 & 5". - *Dionysius*, 10 (1986), 57-83.
WAHL, J. *Etude sur le Parménide de Platon*. Paris, ²1959 (1st ed. 1926).
WALLIS, J. *Mathesis Universalis*. Oxford, 1695.
WARREN, E. W. "Imagination in Plotinus", *Classical Quarterly* 16 (1966), 277-285.
WATSON, G. *Phantasia in Classical Thought*. Galway, 1988.
—"The Concept of 'Phantasia' from the Late Hellenistic Period to Early Neoplatonism". - In: *Aufstieg und Niedergang der Römischen Welt*, Teil II, Bd.36.7. Berlin-New York, 1994. P. 4565-4810.
WEDBERG, A. *Plato's Philosophy of Mathematics*. Stockholm, 1955.
WEDIN, M. *Mind and Imagination in Aristotle*. New Haven-London, 1988.
WELLS, N. J. "Descartes and the Modal Distinction". - *Modern Schoolman* 43 (1965), 1-22.
WEYL, H. *Philosophy of Mathematics and Natural Science*. Princeton (N. J.), 1949.
WHITE, A. R. *The Language of Imagination*. Oxford, 1990.
WHITE, M. J. *The Continuous and the Discrete. Ancient Physical Theories from a Contemporary Perspective*. Oxford, 1992.
WIGNER, E. P. "The Unreasonable Effectiveness of Mathematics in the Natural Sciences". - In: E. P. Wigner. *Symmetries and Reflections*. Bloomington-London, 1967. P.222-237.
WILLIAMS, B. *Problems of the Self*. Cambridge, 1973.
—*Descartes: The Project of Pure Enquiry*. Atlantic Highlands (N. J.), 1978.
WILSON, A. M. *The Infinite in the Finite*. Oxford, 1995.
WILSON, M. D. *Descartes*. London, 1978.
WIPPEL, J. F. "Essence and Existence". - In: N. Kretzmann, A. Kenny, J. Pinborg (Eds.) *The Cambridge History of Later Medieval Philosophy*. Cambridge, 1982. P. 385-410.
WIPPERN, J. (Ed.) *Das Problem der ungeschriebenen Lehre Platons. Beiträge zur Verständnis der platonischen Prinzipienlehre*. Darmstadt, 1972.
WITT, Ch. *Substance and Essence in Aristotle. An Interpretation of Metaphysics VII-IX*. Ithaca (N. Y.)-London, 1989.
WITTGENSTEIN, L. *Zettel*. Ed. by G. E. M. Anscomb and G. H. von Wright, trans. by G. E. M. Anscomb. Berkeley-Los Angeles, 1967.
—*Philosophische Untersuchungen. Philosophical Investigations*. Translated by G. E. M. Anscomb. Oxford, 1958.
WOLFSON, H. A. *Studies in the History of Philosophy and Religion*. Vol. I-II. Ed. by I.Twersky and G. H. Williams. Cambridge (Mass.)-London, 1973-1977.
WYLLER, E. A. *Platons Parmenides in seinem Zusammenhang mit Symposion und Politeia Interpretationen zur platonischen Henologie*. Oslo, 1960.
—*Der späte Platon*. Hamburg, 1970.
XENOCRATES. *Fragmente*. In: R. Heinze. *Xenokrates. Darstellung der Lehre und Sammlung der Fragmente*. Leipzig, 1892 (repr. Hildesheim, 1965). P. 157-197.
—*Frammenti*. Edizione, traduzione e commento a cura di M. Isnardi Parente. Naples, 1982.
YOLTON, J. "Locke and Malebranche: Two Concepts of Ideas". - In: R. Brandt (Ed.) *John Locke. Symposium Wolfenbüttel 1979*. Berlin-New York, 1981. P. 208-224.
ZEKL, H. G. *Topos. Die aristotelische Lehre vom Raum. Eine Interpretation von Physik) 1-5*. Hamburg, 1990.
ZUBIRI, X. *On Essence*. Translation and Introduction by A. R. Caponigri. Washington, 1980.

Index

abstraction, 7, 18, 24, 40, 18 n. 97, 67 n. 306, 72, 85, 102, 116, 123-4, 133, 215
—as *apophasis*, 24
accident, 2 n. 2, 4, 11-3, 19, 19 n. 98, 23, 29, 29 n. 154, 30 n. 154, 31 n.160, 36, 40-1, 61
—*accidentia propia*, 62, 64, 66
activity, 6, 9, 32, 42, 52 n. 252, 73 n. 13, 74, 91, 113, 123-5, 132, 138 n. 329
—as *energeia*, 146, 148, 153-6, 167, 169, 173, 174 n. 34, 175, 180, 183, 187, 192, 195, 196, 196 n. 242, 196 n. 243, 202, 206, 207, 212, 215, 217, 220, 226, 235, 237, 240-2, 247-9
actuality, 3, 6, 9, 32, 42, 52 n. 252, 74, 74 n. 23, 90, 136, 141, 146, 148, 153-6, 159 n. 70, 167, 241, 248-9, 258
addition (*prothesis*), 12, 35 n. 178, 36, 55 n. 262, 81, 81 n. 66, 81 n. 67, 89-91, 94, 94 n. 139, 97, 103, 124, 202
Albert the Great, 40 n. 206
Alcinous (Albinus), 24, 24 n. 125, 25 n. 132
Alexander of Aphrodisias, 70 n. 4, 73 n. 14, 134, 134 n. 309
algebra, 93 n. 134, 106, 115, 115 n. 219, 122 n. 253, 184 n. 193
algorithm, 224, 227, 233
analogy (see also: analogical) 25, 92, 102, 205-6
analysis, 25, 81, 99, 106, 111, 111 n. 201, 111 n. 204, 112, 112 n. 206, 113, 186, 205, 209, 237, 237 n. 395, 251, 256
—and *synthesis*, 38
Anatolius, 70 n. 1

Anaxagoras, 74 n. 20, 94 n. 138, 155 n. 47
Anselm, St., 41 n. 208,
antitypia, 13
Apollodorus, 121 n. 250
Apollonius, 104, 250, 250 n. 461, 259
apophatic, 22-4
appearance, 11, 11 n. 60, 121, 140, 164, 233, 244, 247
application, applicability, 114 n. 210, 120, 170, 187, 193, 209, 213, 228, 254, 256
—of mathematics to physics, 71, 109, 117, 119, 168, 172, 213
Aquinas, 40 n. 206, 42, 44 n. 226, 60 n. 282, 63 n. 291, 64 n. 294, 83 n. 80, 143 n. 353, 158 n. 62, 174 n. 137, 174 n. 139
Archimedes, 70 n. 1, 95 n. 147, 225 n. 346, 250, 250 n. 460, 259
Archytas, 70 n. 2, 96 n. 150, 250, 252
Aristotle, 2, 2 n. 2, 3, 3 n. 3, 3 n. 4, 3 n. 5, 3 n. 6, 3 n. 7, 3 n. 8, 3 n. 9, 3 n. 10, 4, 4 n. 12, 4 n. 13, 4 n. 14, 4 n. 15, 4 n. 16, 4 n. 18, 4 n. 19, 5, 5 n. 20, 5 n. 21, 5 n. 22, 5 n. 23, 5 n. 24, 5 n. 25, 6-7, 7 n. 37, 8, 8 n. 38, 8 n. 39, 8 n. 40, 8 n. 43, 9, 9 n.46, 10, 10 n. 56, 11, 11 n. 63, 12, 14, 14 n. 76, 24, 24 n. 126, 28-9, 29 n. 149, 20-30 n. 154, 34-5, 35 n. 174, 35 n. 175, 35 n. 176, 35 n. 177, 35 n. 178, 36, 36 n. 180, 36 n. 181, 36 n. 182, 36 n. 183, 36 n. 184, 36 n. 185, 36 n. 186, 36 n. 187, 37 n.188, 38, 48-51, 53, 55, 55 n. 262, 56-7, 59-60, 62, 64, 66, 70 n. 1, 70 n. 3, 70 n. 4, 71, 71 n. 9, 72, 72 n. 10, 73, 73 n. 13, 73 n. 17, 74, 76 n. 35, 78, 78 n. 45, 78 n. 48, 79n. 53, 79 n. 54, 79 n. 55, 79 n. 57, 80 n. 62,

81 n. 66, 81 n. 67, 81 n. 68, 82, 82 n. 74, 82 n. 76, 83 n. 77, 83 n. 80, 86, 86 n. 93, 86 n. 96, 87, 87 n. 99, 88 n. 103, 88 n. 104, 89, 89 n. 109, 89 n. 110, 89 n. 111, 89 n. 112, 90, 90 n. 115, 90 n. 116, 92, 92 n. 123, 92 n. 125, 92 n. 127, 93, 93 n. 131, 93 n. 132, 93 n. 133, 93 n. 135, 93 n. 137, 94 n. 138, 94 n. 139, 94 n. 140, 94 n. 146, 100 n. 160, 100 n. 162, 104 n. 170, 108, 108 n. 190, 110 n. 198, 111, 111 n. 200, 111 n. 202, 116, 116 n. 222, 116 n. 223, 116 n. 224, 117, 117 n. 230, 118, 125 n. 271, 127, 128, 128 n. 283, 128 n. 285, 128 n. 286, 129, 129 n. 291, 129 n. 292, 130 n. 293, 133, 133 n. 300, 133 n. 301, 133 n. 304, 134, 134 n. 306, 134 n. 306, 134 n. 311, 134 n. 313, 135 n. 315, 136 n. 317, 137 n. 324, 137 n. 329, 140 n. 337, 148, 148 n. 11, 151 n. 21, 153, 153 n. 32, 153 n. 38, 156 n. 54, 159 n. 70, 167 n. 104, 171-2, 172 n. 121, 173, 173 n. 125, 173 n. 126, 173 n. 127, 173 n. 128, 173 n. 129, 173 n. 130, 173 n. 131, 174, 174 n. 134, 174 n. 135, 174 n. 137, 175 n. 141, 177, 181, 181 n. 173, 183, 183 n. 188, 184, 184 n. 194, 185 n. 195, 186, 186 n. 200, 186 n. 202, 187, 187 n. 206, 196, 196 n. 242, 210, 221 n. 329, 224, 225 n. 345, 225 n. 346, 225 n. 348, 226, 226 n. 352, 226 n. 353, 227, 227 n. 360, 231, 231 n. 377, 238 n. 399, 238 n. 400, 239 n. 406, 239 n. 407, 239 n. 408, 241, 241 n. 424, 241 n. 425, 243 n. 436, 244 n. 439, 245, 245 n. 443, 247, 247 n. 450, 248, 251, 251 n. 463, 251 n. 464, 252, 252 n. 470, 253 n. 472, 253 n. 473, 255-8
arithmetic, 14, 51, 55, 70, 70 n.1 72-3, 85 n. 88, 90-1, 93-4, 104, 115 n. 219, 116, 122 n. 253, 124-6, 184 n. 193,
205, 207, 227, 253, 256
Arnauld, A., 29 n. 151, 29 n. 153, 30 n. 155, 53 n. 257, 66, 166, 168 n. 108, 193 n. 226
astronomy, 14, 113 n. 209, 114, 114 n. 210, 227
attribute, 8, 10, 24, 28, 33, 46, 63, 123, 130-1, 165-6, 171 n. 114, 233
—accidental, 2 n. 2, 19, 23
—divine, 17, 32, 42
—essential, 2 n. 2, 19, 19 n. 98, 23, 29, 30, 30 n. 154, 58, 61-2, 143, 255
—*omni*-attribute, 42, 42 n. 21, 43, 200
—of substance, 18, 18 n. 97, 29, 30 n. 154, 30 n. 158, 31, 59, 61, 61 n. 285, 62, 157, 159, 171, 198, 255
Augustine, 110
axiom, 13, 20, 33, 98, 109, 111, 113, 114 n. 213, 151, 224-5, 225 n. 345, 225 n. 348, 226

Barrow, I., 228, 228 n. 362
Baumgarten, A., 8, 8 n. 44, 32 n. 136
Beeckman, I., 53 n. 257, 55, 108 n. 187, 124 n. 263, 191, 223 n. 339, 228 n. 362
becoming, 9, 14, 22, 33, 36, 38, 48, 53 n. 254, 56, 70-1, 81, 85, 89, 99 n. 157, 122 n. 253, 127, 129, 140, 144, 210, 211, 219, 225, 238, 239, 247, 252
being, 3-4, 6-8, 10-1, 17, 19, 19 n. 98, 20, 21, 21 n. 110, 22, 23, 23 n. 123, 24-8, 29 n. 149, 30, 31 n. 160, 32-3, 35, 35 n. 178, 37-9, 40, 40 n. 206, 41, 42, 42 n. 214, 43, 44 n. 220, 45-7, 47 n. 233, 48, 52, 55, 59, 62, 64-6, 66 n. 299, 68, 68 n. 309, 70-2, 76-7, 77 n. 41, 78 n. 48, 80, 80 n. 58, 80 n. 62, 81, 83, 83 n. 80, 85, 88-90, 93, 97-8, 100, 104, 108 n. 190, 109-11, 116, 118, 123-4, 127, 132, 135-8, 140, 143-4, 147, 151-5, 159-61,

Index

161 n. 78, 164-6,168-9, 172, 174,
179, 181, 181 n. 175, 182, 201, 205,
211, 215-6, 220, 225-6, 229, 233,
237-9, 243 n. 436, 244, 253, 255,
257, 258
—composite (*syntheton*), 82, 141
—as *epaggellomenon*, 9
—eternal, 37, 146, 154-6, 240,
254
—as *noēton, noēta*, 35, 74-5, 77-
80, 82, 84, 139, 146, 148, 150, 156,
167, 185-6, 240, 247
—as *on*, 6, 20-2, 73, 75, 77-8, 80,
82, 84-5, 87-8, 242
body, 5, 5 n. 21, 6, 9, 13, 14 n. 77,
15 n. 80, 18, 31-33, 36, 39-40, 58-
60, 62, 110, 131-2, 135, 143, 157,
173, 176-7, 179, 183, 187-9, 189 n.
215, 191, 193, 195, 198-9, 206 n.
279, 209 n. 288, 219, 227, 234, 250,
259
—as divisible, 15, 29, 55-7, 116, 130,
199, 253
—and extension, 14, 15, 15 n. 82, 15
n. 83, 29, 59, 117, 121, 134, 171,
189, 190, 197, 199, 208, 227, 229,
255
—geometrical, 16, 116, 117, 120, 197-
8, 228, 229 n. 368
—and location, 15 n. 83, 134
—as movable, 15, 134, 229
—physical, 16, 54, 57, 116-8, 120,
130, 132, 134, 197, 208, 219, 227,
231, 244, 255
—and primary qualities, 16
—and secondary qualities, 16
—and shape, 15 n. 87, 15 n. 97, 116,
189, 253, 255
Boethius, 83 n. 77, 156 n. 54, 174 n. 139
Bolyai, J., 96, 96 n. 150
Bonaventure, 40 n. 206
boundary, 41, 80, 181, 238-9
Brouwer, L. E. J., 53 n. 254, 122, 122
n. 254, 123, 124 n. 261, 213
Burman, 41 n. 210, 47 n. 233, 50 n. 242,
53-4 n. 257, 107, 98 n. 155, 106 n.
176, 108 n. 188, 118 n. 233, 119 n.
240, 144 n. 354, 162 n. 81, 194, 195
n. 235, 2012 n. 263, 203-4 n. 273,
207 n. 285, 218 n. 318, 221 n. 326

Cajetan, 17
Calcidius, 134, 134 n. 307
Cantor, G., 38 n. 192, 45 n. 297, 83 n.
77, 99, 99 n. 157, 99 n. 158, 101, 122
capacity, 6, 42, 76, 103, 107, 137-8,
140, 159 n. 70, 163, 171, 172, 174-
6, 186, 188, 192, 192 n. 226, 195-6,
202, 205, 215-7, 219-20, 230, 232,
249, 258, 260
Carpus, 225
Caterus, 18, 40 n. 206
causa sui, 23 n. 123, 32
causation, cause, 4, 16, 16 n. 87, 19, 22-
3, 25, 27, 32-3, 33 n. 169, 40 n. 206,
42, 47, 49, 60, 64, 66, 77, 104-5, 110,
114, 114 n. 210, 121 n. 245, 129, 158
n. 62, 165, 165 n. 99, 179, 194 n.
234, 202 n. 262, 204 n. 275, 215, 222,
227, 238-9, 255, 257
Cavalieri, B., 53 n. 254, 57 n. 271
change, 7, 9, 19, 37-8, 70, 88-9, 95-6,
103, 130-1, 140, 146, 150, 155-6,
178, 183, 205, 211, 216, 225, 227,
230, 238-43, 257, 259
Chanut, H. –P., 42 n. 215, 49 n. 237, 49 n.
239, 49-50 n. 240, 199 n. 254, 199 n.
255, 221 n. 327
characteristic, 21, 36, 42 n. 214, 71, 83,
108 n. 188, 156, 185, 228, 109, 130,
132, 136, 156 n. 54, 255
—distinctive characteristic
(*idiotēs*), 12
Charleton, W., 57, 57 n. 272
Cleserlier, C., 40 n. 205, 43 n. 218, 44
n. 224, 56 n. 267, 123 n. 259
cogitation, 30, 41, 43, 124, 80 n. 62,
160, 162, 166, 178, 188, 194, 220,
159 n. 69
cogito, 43, 58, 68, 104, 104 n. 174, 105,

111, 158, 167, 170, 172, 172, 196, 202, 215-6, 222
cognition, 9, 32, 48, 51, 55, 58-9, 61-2, 67-8, 92, 108-9, 120, 129, 146, 151, 159, 172, 193, 195, 218, 219, 220, 238, 245, 248, 139 n. 332
cognitive faculty, 51, 112, 125, 129, 131-2, 146, 151, 159-60, 176, 187, 191-3, 195, 198, 209, 219, 226, 230-1, 234-5, 256-8
Colvius, A., 33 n. 171
common sense (*sensus communis, aisthēsis koinē*), 183, 187, 187 n. 206, 190, 192 n. 226, 193, 227
communication (*koinōnia*), 37, 149, 153-4, 156, 169, 191, 242, 244, 258
concept,
—formal, 17-9, 45, 64 n. 214, 101, 161-70, 214
—objective, 47, 64 n. 214, 161-70, 165 n. 98
consciousness, 33, 170, 177, 216, 138
construction, constructibility
—divine, 119, 121, 230-1, 259
—of a geometrical or mathematical object, 57, 73, 81, 90, 92, 97, 101, 106, 115, 119, 124, 131, 191, 203, 205-6, 210-1, 217, 219, 222-9, 229 n. 368, 230, 230 n. 371, 239, 245-9, 252-3, 257, 259-60
—kinematic (by movement), 210, 223-229, 237, 244-5, 250-1, 254, 259-60
—and reconstruction of the world, 119, 210, 213, 221-2, 224, 227, 235-6, 245, 260
continuum, 15 n. 82, 54-5, 57, 122, 127
cosmos, 2 n. 2, 5, 39, 115, 126, 129, 150, 158 n. 62, 211, 251
—intelligible (*kosmos noētos*), 74, 74 n. 22, 75, 80, 90, 135, 148, 151, 157, 242
creation, 34, 64, 174, 212, 214, 218, 231-3
creative power, 37, 42, 49, 139, 171, 174-5, 221, 233, 260

Damascius, 24, 25 n. 132, 100, 100 n. 163, 146 n. 1, 239,
Dante, 174 n. 139
De Beaune, F., 33 n. 169, 120 n. 241
Dedekind, R., 98 n. 156, 125 n. 270, 213, 213 n. 304
deductio, 157, 204 n. 275
deficiency (*elleipsis*), 28, 39, 81, 148
definition, 28, 35-8, 46, 49, 51, 56, 64, 66, 66 n. 303, 99, 100, 109, 137, 140, 114-5 n. 213
—negative, 238
Descartes, 2, 35, 37, 42-51, 53
—and matter, 12-9
—and substance, 28-34, 39-41
Desargues, G., 41, 96, 96 n. 149, 96 n. 151, 228, 228 n. 362
dichotomy, 23, 129, 152, 195, 199, 208
—into inner and outer, 59
dimension, 5 n. 21, 13, 15, 49, 91-2, 108 n. 188, 117, 169, 174, 185-6, 191, 223, 228, 232, 250-1
Dionysius the Areopagite, 24, 53-4 n. 257
discrete, 55, 55 n. 262, 82, 86-7, 89, 92-4, 122, 124-6, 205-7, 237-8, 252-3, 256
discursive reasoning, thinking (*dianoia*), 23, 48 56, 72, 91, 112, 150, 157-8, 158 n. 62, 160, 172-5, 177, 180-2, 184, 186, 204 n. 275, 207, 222, 226, 234-6, 243-50, 252
—as intermediate, 129-31, 151, 153, 258-60
distinction
—conceptual, 15, 16 n. 89, 17-8, 198
—formal, 17-8, 126, 165
—mental, 17, 29, 64, 72, 152, 242
—modal, 15, 17, 18, 18 n. 94, 42, 123, 176, 198
—real, 14, 17, 18, 44, 49, 58, 65, 66 n. 301, 152, 156, 193, 198, 200-1, 204, 231, 242-3
divisibility, division,
—conceptual, 239

—indefinite, 54-7
—infinite, 37 n. 180, 39, 55-6, 95, 100, 202, 215, 235
—mathematical, 36, 81, 124
—of number, 37, 55 n. 262, 81, 81 n. 66, 87, 94 n. 139, 256
—physical, of physical bodies, 15, 184
Dirichlet, G. L., 97 n. 153, 125 n. 270 20 n. 104, 239
dualism, duality, 6, 20 n. 104, 21-6, 26 n. 137, 74, 77, 79, 82, 84, 117, 124, 136, 138, 147, 150-3, 169, 176, 185, 239, 241, 253-4
duration, 18 n. 97, 21, 34, 123, 147, 156, 187 n. 206
Duns Scotus, 17, 17 n. 91, 231 n. 376
dyad (*aoristas dyas*), 6, 26, 26 n. 137, 26 n. 138, 27, 37-8, 74, 77-8, 78 n. 48, 78-9, 79 n. 53, 79 n. 54, 79-80 n. 58, 80-6, 86 n. 93, 89-90, 90 n. 113, 92, 125, 134, 137-42, 148, 168, 176, 179, 185-6, 240, 246, 255, 257
dynamis, dynamei, 3-5, 9, 21, 26, 37, 88, 90, 143, 143 n. 351, 147 n. 5, 157, 172-3, 182, 243 n. 436

Eckhart, M., 63 n. 291
Elizabeth, Princess, 15 n. 84, 42 n. 215, 49 n. 239, 123 n. 255, 194 n. 232, 200 n. 260, 206 n. 279, 221 n. 327
emptiness (*khaos*) 28, 179
end, 35, 78, 89, 111, 139, 146, 155, 172, 175, 206, 238, 251
—as *peras*, 80, 100, 138, 93, 160, 242, 242 n. 426
energy, 254
—and actuality, 53 n. 252
entity, 8, 18, 27, 35-7, 41, 45, 55, 57-8, 72, 91-3, 97-8, 98 n. 155, 99, 99 n. 157, 102, 108, 111-2, 122, 123, 131-2, 134, 140, 165 n. 97, 166, 202, 207 n. 285, 208, 208 n. 285, 219, 222, 226-7, 229, 238, 238 n. 399, 239, 247, 249, 251-3, 260

—corporeal, 2 n. 2, 18
essence, 2, 4, 12, 13, 16, 18, 19 n. 97, 19 n. 98, 21 n. 110, 29, 34, 36, 40, 40 n. 206, 41, 58, 62, 66 n. 298, 83 n. 80, 160, 167, 169, 186, 188-9, 197-8, 201-2, 202, 204, 207-8, 216, 220, 255, 259
—and existence, 21-2, 45-6, 48, 63-5, 66 n. 301, 67, 67 n. 303, 68, 68 n. 306, 105, 118, 121, 135, 158, 161, 163, 169, 218, 227, 225 n. 348
—divine, 43-49, 59, 62, 64, 102
—including existence, 22, 32, 45-6, 48, 105, 154
eternal, eternity, 14, 31, 21, 39, 68, 95, 127, 129, 141, 147, 154-6, 201, 207, 215, 240, 241-2, 156 n. 54, 201 n. 262, 243 n. 436
—vs. sempiternal, 5 n. 26, 11 n. 61
Euclid, 25 n. 133, 77 n. 41, 82 n. 77, 91, 91 n. 122, 92, 92 n. 130, 93 n. 132, 93 n. 134, 94, 94 n. 140, 94 n. 141, 94 n. 143, 94 n. 144, 94 n. 145, 94 n. 146, 96, 104, 109, 112, 112 n. 206, 114 n. 211, 122, 125-6, 128, 141-2, 151, 220, 224-5, 226 n. 350, 227, 235, 237-8, 239 n. 405, 250-2, 252 n. 466, 259
Eudoxus, 82 n. 77, 91, 96 n. 150, 125
evil, 8, 8 n. 42, 9 n. 53, 11 n. 61, 28, 39, 135, 140, 243 n. 436
existence, 8, 19 n. 97, 21-2, 28, 30-1, 31 n. 159, 36, 36 n. 169, 36 n. 180, 40 n. 204, 42-5, 45 n. 226, 46, 48, 49 n. 238, 51, 54, 54 n. 257, 59, 61 n. 284, 63, 63 n. 289, 64, 64 n. 281, 65, 65 n. 296, 66, 66 n. 298, 67, 67 n. 305, 68, 68 n. 306, 68 n. 308, 68 n. 309, 73, 76, 85, 97, 98 n. 155, 99, 102-5, 105 n. 176, 106 n. 179, 108-9, 112, 118, 128, 132, 135, 140, 142, 143 n. 353, 146-7, 154, 158, 161, 164, 166, 169, 182, 198, 200-3, 203 n. 270, 208, 211, 213, 216, 218, 220-1, 223-5, 225 n. 348,

226-7, 233-4, 239, 250, 252
extension, 50-1, 59, 93, 95-8, 102, 117, 117 n. 227, 127, 132, 134 n. 310, 143 n. 353, 156-7, 159, 168, 171, 175, 179, 183-6, 194, 199-200, 203-4, 207-8, 216, 221-3, 227-8, 230, 234, 237-8
—and body, 12-4, 15 n. 83, 16-9, 29, 60, 63, 63 n. 289, 67, 143, 190, 209, 229, 231, 257-60
—continuous, 15 n. 82, 56-7, 209, 218
—as *diastasis*, 134, 155, 246, 249
—spatial, 12-9, 49, 202, 209, 229

Fermat, 101-2
Ferrier, J., 122 n. 251
figure, 5 n. 21, 6, 9, 193, 232
—geometrical figure, 16, 51, 54, 70, 86, 91-3, 93 n. 134, 95-8, 106, 108 n. 188, 111 n. 204, 115-6, 117 n. 227, 118-22, 125-7, 127 n. 279, 130-1, 134, 134 n. 310, 135, 141-2, 143 n. 353, 151, 160, 178, 181, 183, 185-6, 189 n. 214, 198, 200, 203-4, 204 n. 273, 205-10, 212, 212 n. 301, 217, 219-20, 222-3, 226-8, 228 n. 362, 229-31, 234, 236-9, 245-6, 248-53, 256-60
—immaterial, 235
finitude, 34, 39-40, 43, 47, 50-1, 54, 101-2, 105, 108, 215
form, 3, 9 n. 53, 11 n. 6, 12, 26, 28, 34, 36-7, 47, 54-5, 81, 95, 106, 108, 119, 124, 128, 131, 146-8, 190, 206, 208-9, 211, 216, 237, 241
—as *eidos*, 2 n. 2, 3 n. 10, 4, 5 n. 21, 6-9, 80, 125, 133-8, 140-1, 143 n. 353, 149-50, 162, 169, 178, 181-2, 184-6, 234-6, 239, 242, 244-7
—as *endeēs*, 9
—not born (*agenēton*), 207
—as thinkable or intelligible, 15, 170, 179, 182, 184-7, 197, 242, 244
formless, 6, 7, 26, 136, 223
Frege, G., 53 n. 254, 72, 72 n. 11, 73, 73 n. 12, 77 n. 41, 99 n. 157
Fromondus, L., 57, 57 n. 270, 63 n. 289, 120 n. 242

Galilei, Galileo, 16, 13, 115 n. 215
Gassendi, P., 33, 46, 34 n. 173, 56 n. 269, 105 n. 176, 118, 118 n. 235, 127 n. 279, 162-3 n. 84, 165 n. 97, 188 n. 209, 190, 197 n. 244, 204 n. 275
Geminus, 124 n. 266, 225
generation, 42, 11 n. 61, 139, 224, 238, 241, 250
—kinematic, 85, 85 n. 88, 90,
geometrization, 13, 116, 116 n. 221, 120, 122 n. 253, 132
geometry, 14, 41, 48, 51, 55, 70-1, 91, 93-4, 96, 96 n. 150, 103, 103 n. 168, 104, 106, 106 n. 182, 110-1, 113, 115, 115 n. 213, 115 n. 217, 115 n. 219, 115, 220, 116-9, 119 n. 238, 120-1, 122 n. 253, 124-6, 126 n. 274, 126 n. 275, 126 n. 276, 126 n. 277, 126 n. 278, 130, 142, 142 n. 345, 184, 184 n. 193, 204 n.273, 205-7, 209, 209 n. 290, 210, 212-3, 213 n. 304, 214 n. 307, 218 n. 316, 219, 223, 223 n. 339, 224, 225 n. 348, 227 n. 359, 259-60
—non-Euclidean, 96
geometrical figure, object (*see also*: figure)
—chiliagon, 195 n. 238, 203, 204 n. 273, 204 n. 275, 218, 220, 227, 231, 246
—circumference, 250
—circle, 96, 134, 131, 160, 178-9, 182, 184, 210, 217-8, 223, 234-8, 247, 251, n. 466, 252
—corporeal, 2 n. 2, 14, 15 n. 83, 18 n. 97, 47 n. 233, 60 n. 281, 111 n. 204, 119, 127, 127 n. 279, 187, 189, 190-1, 191 n. 223, 192, 194, 200, 203, 205-6, 208-9, 227, 230-1
—divisible (*diērēmenos*), 54, 92 n. 127, 93, 116-7, 130-1, 142, 178,

182-5, 199, 234, 236, 239, 245-7, 250, 252-4, 256-8, 260
—extended, 14, 15 n. 83, 93, 95, 116-7, 134 n. 310, 135, 142, 157, 178, 182-5, 199 206-9, 234, 236, 247, 252, 257-60
—four-fold, 235, 260
—having parts, 116, 130-1, 142, 180, 250, 256-7
—line, 14, 92 n. 127, 96, 125, 131, 160, 223, 238, 253
—polygon, 51, 96-7, 198, 228, 247
—as having shape (*eskhēmatsimenos*), 246
—triangle, 45, 71, 95, 113, 119, 119 n. 240, 158, 163, 203, 204 n. 273, 210-1, 218-9, 234-5
Gibieuf, G., 14 n. 78, 56 n. 266, 60 n. 284, 188, 188 n. 209, 196 n. 242
Goclenius, R., 164, 165 n. 95, 165 n. 98
God, 18 n. 97, 23 n. 123, 30, 33 n. 169, 35 n. 178, 40 n. 206, 41 n. 213, 42 n. 216, 43 n. 219, 44, 44 n. 226, 46 n. 232, 49 n. 238, 50 n. 241, 53, 54 n. 257, 56-61, 61 n. 284, 64, 65, 65 n. 296, 66-8, 68 n. 308, 68 n. 309
—attributes of (*omni*-attributes), 17, 30, 42-3
—as being, infinite being, 40 n. 206, 47 n. 233, 53-5, 146, 255
—as *ens necessarium*, 41 n. 208
—as *ens perfectissimum*
—supremely perfect, 41, 53, 66 n. 299
—as infinite mind, 33, 45, 49, 56-7, 68, 158, 161, 163-5, 167, 171, 199, 200-1, 201 n. 262, 204, 214-5, 217, 220, 222, 231-3
—omnipotent, 53
—as substance, infinite substance, 29 n. 149, 39, 50 48-9, 58-62, 64-6, 101, 105, 110-1, 166, 199-200
good (*agatnon*) goodness, 20, 21 n. 110, 22-3, 26-7, 27 n. 142, 104, 138, 139-40, 153, 177-8, 185, 212, 231 n. 376

harmony, 115
Hegel, G.W.F., 24, 53, 147 n. 8
henad, 77, 81-4, 84 n. 85, 85-6, 86 n. 93, 87-8, 88 n. 102, 89-95
henology, 19, 20-1, 23, 25 n. 132, 27, 66
Henry of Ghent, 40 n. 206
Heron, 70 n. 1
Hilbert, D., 70, 83, 83 n. 78, 96 n. 150, 101, 123, 226
Hippocrates, 226
Hobbes, Th., 24 n. 52, 158, 158 n. 65, 162, 197 n. 244, 212, 212 n. 298
Hogelande, C., 106, 107 n. 184, 122 n. 252, 214, 214 n. 308, 229 n. 367
Hooke, R., 114 n. 213, 115 n. 214
Huygens, C., 105 n. 176, 122 n. 251
hylomorphic structure, 4
Hyperaspistes, 33 n. 169, 41 n. 221, 44 n. 224, 61 n. 284, 65 n. 298, 123 n. 256, 163 n. 86, 233 n. 384
hypothesis, 21, 24-5, 70, 74, 81-2, 92, 135, 147, 147 n. 7, 148, 150, 177, 199

Iamblichus, 20 n. 104, 24, 26 n. 138, 77, 77 n. 39, 77 n. 41, 83 n. 77, 85 n. 86, 92 n. 122, 94, 94 n. 140, 125 n. 272, 129, 129 n. 288, 130, 134 n. 305, 137 n. 325, 142, 142 n. 349, 146 n. 1, 182, 182 n. 177, 182 n. 181, 182 n. 182, 182 n. 183, 182 n. 184, 183, 236 n. 392, 238 n. 404, 256
idea, 2 n. 2, 4, 9, 13, 15, 27 n. 143, 28 n. 145, 33-4, 40-1, 42, 42 n. 214, 43-4, 44 n. 220, 45-7, 55, 55n. 254, 60, 63 n. 289, 64, 66 n. 299, 67 n. 289, 68 n. 309, 80, 97-8, 99 n. 158, 100, 102-3, 114 n. 211, 119, 119 n. 240, 123-4, 126-7, 131, 141, 143, 143 n. 352, 144 n. 354, 149, 160-1, 161 n. 76, 162, 162 n. 79, 162 n. 82, 162 n. 84, 163, 163 n. 84, 164-5, 165 n. 97, 165 n. 98, 165 n. 99,

166, 168-70, 178, 181-2, 184, 188 n. 209, 190, 190 n. 221, 191, 196, 198, 202, 205, 212-4, 220, 225 n. 348, 231-6, 242 n. 426, 245-50, 253
image, 7, 11, 14, 26-7, 34, 73, 75, 79, 138, 150, 155, 157, 160-3, 172-4, 174 n. 135, 175-8, 178 n. 161, 179-80, 186, 188 n. 209, 190-1, 192 n. 226, 195-6, 198, 200, 203-6, 208, 212, 220, 232, 235-6, 240, 245, 245 n. 443, 248, 250-1, 260
—of imagination (*phantasma*, *phantasmata*), 182
imagination, 14-5, 15 n. 82, 21, 34, 47, 49, 60-1, 57-8, 63, 68, 72, 93, 96, 106, 123, 125, 127 n. 279, 131, 137-8, 141-2, 152, 159-62, 164, 171-4, 174 n. 135, 175, 175 n. 141, 176, 176 n. 151, 177-8, 178 n. 162, 179, 179 n. 166, 180, 180 n. 170, 181, 181 n. 175, 182-4, 184 n. 193, 185-7, 187 n. 204, 188, 188 n. 209, 189, 189 n. 212, 190, 190 n. 220, 191, 191 n. 223, 192, 192 n. 225, 192 n. 226, 193-4, 194 n. 233, 194 n. 234, 195-6, 196 n. 242, 196 n. 243, 197-203, 203-4 n. 273, 204 n. 275, 205-6, 206 n. 279, 207, 207 n. 285, 208-10, 217-23, 227-8, 228 n. 362, 229-39, 243-53, 257-60
immutability, 70, 211
impassibility, 6 n. 28, 135, 187
impenetrability, 13, 15
imperfection, 37, 39-41, 50-1, 53-4, 54 n. 257, 61 n. 284
inalterability, 6 n. 28, 9, 12
incommensurability, incommensurable, 92 n. 127, 125
—of geometrical magnitudes, 95
indefiniteness (*apeiron*), 3, 5, 9, 26, 35 n. 175, 37-9, 79, 81, 88 n. 105, 99 n. 158, 137, 139, 157, 167, 186, 202, 255
independence, 39-41, 71, 75, 215, 218, 243 n. 436
—and being in itself (*kath' hayto*),

36, 64, 108, 127, 157, 174 n. 139, 175-80, 183, 184 n. 214, 186, 191, 191 n. 223, 208, 222, 256-60
—geometrical objects as, 128-32, 144, 160, 181, 211
intuitus, 157-8, 204 n. 275
irrationality, 135, 173, 175, 179, 182, 186, 196, 258
—as inexpressible (*arrhēton*), 94-5

John Damascene, 40 n. 206, 157 n. 57
John of Gent, 17
judgement, 12 23, 27, 49, 103-4, 151, 159, 163, 168-9, 177 n. 157, 180, 194 n. 233, 213, 231, 236
—as *hypolēpsis*, 173

Kant, 62, 62 n. 287, 123, 164, 168, 173 n. 132, 174, 213 n. 305
Kepler, 113, 113 n. 209, 114 n. 210, 114 n. 211, 114 n. 212, 114 n. 213, 115 n. 214, 115 n. 215, 158 n. 62, 212, 212 n. 301, 212 n. 302, 213 n. 303
knowledge, 7, 14, 40-1, 43, 43 n. 219, 44-6, 51-2, 52 n. 250, 61, 61 n. 285, 62, 66-7, 67 n. 305, 100, 104-5, 105 n. 176, 106-7, 107 n. 185, 109-11, 111 n. 200, 157, 159 n. 69, 159 n. 70, 160-1, 170, 194 n. 233, 197, 199, 203, 212, 214, 222 n. 332, 248, 256
—analogical knowledge, 8
—as *epistēmē*, 70-1, 78, 116, 151, 173, 213, 224
—knowing vs. grasping, 246
—objects of (*mathēmata*), 217, 224-7, 235, 246, 250

Leibniz, G.W., 99 n. 157, 165 n. 98, 170, 170 n. 113, 189, 212, 226
life (*zōē*), 152, 156 n. 54, 182, 233-4
—and being, 74, 74 n. 21, 75, 96, 153-4, 156-7, 243 n. 436
—and intellect, 38 n. 195, 74-6, 153-4, 155, 155 n. 44, 156, 241-2, 243, 243 n. 436, 258

—and *noēta*, 74-5, 153-4
limit, 7, 23, 35-8, 40-1, 49-51, 54-5, 55 n. 262, 88, 90, 92, 92 n. 127, 93-4, 97, 99, 103, 109, 134, 142-3, 156 n. 54, 157, 181, 238-9, 252-3, 255-6
—as *peras*, 80, 100, 160, 242
—as *horiston*, 26, 80
line, 14, 54, 85, 85 n. 92, 92, 92 n. 127, 93, 95-6, 96 150, 100, 116-7, 117, 117 n. 227, 118-9, 125-6, 128, 131, 134, 142, 155, 160, 177, 206-7, 222-4, 228, 228 n. 362, 237-9, 248, 250-1, 251 n. 466, 252-3
Lobachevsky, N., 96, 96 n. 150
Locke, J., 40 n. 207, 50 n. 241, 62, 62 n. 287, 63 n. 291, 203, 272, 212, 212 n. 297, 222 n. 332
logos, 100, 154
—as discursive thinking, 178, 181, 184, 235, 244
—as relation, 36, 75, 92 n. 122, 94, 126
—as speech, 37, 49, 64, 66 n. 303, 154
—as formative principle, 136, 234-6, 239, 244-8, 250
—as rule of construction, 235, 244, 249, 252

machine, 121, 122 n. 251
magnitude, 9, 36 n. 180, 44, 57, 94 n. 138, 229
—as continuous, 51, 55, 55 n. 262, 56, 94, 122, 125-6, 191, 207, 253, 256
—as geometrical figure, 206, 237, 253
—as *megethos*, 36, 71 n. 7, 92, 234
—and multitude, 82, 91, 122
Malanbranche, N., 4 n. 17, 119 n. 238, 143 n. 352
many (*polla*), 9, 21-3, 25-6, 26 n. 137, 28 n. 147, 38, 43, 53, 55 n. 262, 60, 74, 76, 76 n. 36, 77, 80 n. 58, 81, 84-6, 90, 128, 136-8, 142, 146-7, 147 n. 7, 147 n. 8, 148-50, 157, 202, 223, 234, 237, 243, 243 n. 436, 246

mass, 2, 244
mathematics, 2, 44, 53, 53, n. 254, 55, 59, 70 n. 1, 71, 83, 90, 91, 93 n. 134. 95, 97-9, 100-5, 105 n. 176, 106-7, 107 n. 183, 108-9, 111-6, 116 n. 220, 117, 117 n. 229, 117 n. 230, 118-20, 122, 122 n. 253, 124-5, 125 n. 270, 126-8, 133, 143 n. 53, 161, 184 n. 193, 194 n. 234, 204-6, 206 n. 279, 207, 207 n. 285, 209-10, 213, 213 n. 305, 214, 225 n. 348, 226, 229, 230, 239, 241, 251, 257, 259
—and physics, 14, 70, 168, 256
mathematization of the world, 117, 211
mathesis universalis, 106-7, 107 n. 185, 108-9
matter
—and actuality, 3, 6, 9, 32
—bodily, 9, 63 n. 289
—as bulk, 2
—and extension, 12, 19, 49, 259
—and *hypostasis*, 8
—idea of, 13, 63 n. 289
—intelligible, 3, 9, 27, 37-8, 85 n. 36, 93, 126, 132-4, 134 n. 310, 134 n. 313, 135-43, 143 n. 353, 146, 148, 160, 166, 168, 179, 183-7, 208, 210, 226, 229, 233-5, 237-41, 244-8, 250, 257-8, 260
—knowledge of, 62
—and mass, 2
—and negativity, 8-9, 17, 19, 24, 26, 45, 50
—as non-being, 2, 4, 6, 7-8, 22-4, 26-7, 29 n. 149, 37, 39, 41-2, 51-3, 63 n. 289
—and otherness, 2, 6-7, 11, 11 n. 60 12, 21-3, 25-6, 26 n. 137, 26 n. 139, 27-8, 34, 37- 8, 43, 52, 58-9
—particles of, 58
—and potentiality, 4-5, 7, 9, 11, 26, 28, 36, 42, 60, 67, 67 n. 305
—and predication, 7, 39, 52, 64
—prime, *materia prima*, 5, 5 n. 21, 57
—and receptacle, 5 n. 20, 6, 39, 142,

185, 235, 255
—as substance, 2 n. 2, 29 n. 149, 143 n. 252, 255
—subtle, 223, 223 n. 334
—two matters, 13, 140-2, 143 n. 352
measure, 11, 38-9, 57, 72, 81, 83 n. 80, 88-9, 92 n. 127, 94-5, 106, 107, 107 n. 185, 109-10, 124-6, 151, 185, 204 n. 275, 210, 224, 241, 256-7
mechanics, 114-5, 120, 224
memory, 159, 171, 186, 191, 192 n. 226, 193, 199,
mental faculty, 181, 195, 203, 232
Menechmos, 225
Mersenne, M., 15 n. 82, 16 n. 86, 29 n. 152, 40 n. 204, 43 n. 219, 44 n. 221, 44 n. 224, 44, 45 n. 229, 46 n. 232, 47 n. 234, 47 n. 235, 48 n. 236, 54 n. 260, 58 n. 274, 63 n. 289, 67 n. 306, 68 n. 308, 97, 55 n. 264, 97 n. 153, 98 n. 154, 104 n. 175, 105 n. 176, 106 n. 179, 111 n. 199, 113, 113 n. 207, 115 n. 217, 115 n. 119, 115 n. 220, 117 n. 229, 122 n. 252, 137 n. 328, 149 n. 15, 160, 160 n. 74, 162, 162 n. 80, 162 n. 83, 163, 163 n. 90, 187 n. 205, 190 n. 219, 190 n. 221, 192 n. 226, 193 n. 228, 194 n. 234, 196 n. 242, 198 n. 251, 201 n. 261, 202, 202 n. 268, 203 n. 269, 203 n. 271, 223 n. 334, 223 n. 356, 229 n. 368, 230 n. 370, 231 n. 376
Mesland, D., 44 n. 233, 53 n. 256, 54 n. 259, 54 n. 261, 56 n. 266, 192 n. 226, 200 n. 260, 200 n. 261
metaphysics, 4 n. 17, 13, 36, 48, 59, 68, 76 n. 33, 86, 103-5, 105 n. 176, 106 n. 179, 108-11, 117 n. 230, 204
method, 25 n. 132, 101-4, 106-8, 109, 109 n. 193, 112 n. 206, 113, 116-7, 120, 122, 124, 126-7, 204 n. 275, 209, 143, 226-7, 229, 232, 256, 259
mind, *mens*, 60
—attentive, 30, 157

—divine, 33, 47, 101, 104-5, 144, 158, 160, 171, 200, 204, 212, 214, 218, 231-2
—finite, 30-3, 40-6, 46 n. 232, 49, 51-7, 62, 66-8, 95-9, 101-2, 105, 109, 111, 113, 119-20, 157-8, 164-9, 171, 188, 199-201, 207, 212-5, 218-22, 231, 245, 259
—infinite, 33, 45, 49, 56-7, 68, 99, 101, 105, 119, 144, 157-8, 161, 163-5, 167, 171, 199-201, 201 n. 262, 204, 214-5, 217, 220, 222, 231-33
mode, *modus*, 4, 14 n. 77, 15, 17-9, 19 n. 98, 29, 41-2, 63, 123-4, 127, 135, 187, 198
Moderatus, 9
monad, 77-8, 78 n. 48, 79, 79 n. 54, 80 n. 62, 81-5, 89, 91-3, 131, 237-8, 252-3
monism, 20 n. 104
More, H., 13, 13 n. 73, 14 n. 77, 15, 15 n. 83, 42 n. 215, 49 n. 238, 49 n. 239, 50 n. 240, 55 n. 263, 65 n. 297, 121 n. 245, 198, 198 n. 249, 199, 199 n. 254, 208 n. 286, 232 n. 379
Morin, J.-B., 16 n. 86, 223 n. 334
motion, movement, 5, 29, 15 n. 83, 16 n. 87, 18 n. 97, 63 n. 289, 71, 71 n. 7, 78, 78 n. 48, 79-81, 85, 85 n. 92, 86-7, 92, 113, 114 n. 211, 115, 116, 120-1, 121 n. 245, 124, 129, 130 n. 293, 131, 133, 140, 144, 147 n. 8, 152-5, 155 n. 44, 156 n. 54, 157, 163, 173-5, 181, 187 n. 206, 190, 206 n. 279, 212, 221-5, 227-30, 230 n. 371, 237, 239-41, 242 n. 433, 243-5, 247, 249-53, 257-60
—and "flow" (*rhysis*), 228, 237, 253
—intellectual, 154-5, 241-2
—as *kinēsis*, 78 n. 48, 139, 153-5, 240, 242, 242 n. 426, 250
—and locomotion, 130, 241, 250, 252
—physical, 241, 243-4, 249-50

Index

—primary movement, 78, 139, 140 n. 338, 239, 243-4
—self-movement (*aytokinēsis*), 153, 242
multiplicity, multitude (see also: many), 20, 22-6, 26 n. 137, 27, 71-2, 74-6, 78, 79 n. 53, 80, 82, 84, 86-8, 92, 94, 137-9, 142, 147-8, 152-3, 157, 177, 179, 184, 186, 234-5, 237, 242, 244-6, 249, 255, 258

natural light (*lumen naturale*), 30, 45, 67, 105, 114, 168, 200
nature, 2, 9 n. 53, 10, 10 n. 57, 12-4, 16, 16 n. 87, 31, 42, 46, 47 n. 233, 61 n. 285, 62, 85-6, 103, 113, 114 n. 210, 120, 127-8, 138, 140, 143 n. 352, 153, 159, 163, 179, 187, 187 n. 206, 192 n. 226, 204 n. 275, 207, 207 n. 285, 209 n. 288, 219, 231 n. 376, 243, 243 n. 436, 253
—of body, 16
—corporeal, 109, 115, 118 n. 234, 157
—composite, 141, 170
—of extension, 116, 197
—intelligible, 154
—material, of matter, 13, 140
—of the mind, 62
—simple, 157
—universal, 17
negation (*negatio negationis*), 8-10, 16, 23-4, 24 n. 130, 5, 27, 41, 43, 58, 79, 119, 147, 147 n. 8, 163, 167, 188, 238
—as *aphairesis*, 24, 58
negativity, 9, 17, 12, 24, 45, 50, 78, 138, 147 n. 8, 173, 175, 178-9, 182, 194, 196, 234
—of matter, 8, 19, 26
Neoplatonists, 20, 70, 175, 179, 196
Newton, I., 16, 24, 57, 96 n. 151, 115, 115 n. 213, 134, 223, 223 n. 338
Nicholas of Cusa, 24, 53, 63, 212
nihil, 187
—*nihil privativum*, 17, 40, 50

—*nihil negativum*, 8-9, 11-12, 24, 26, 140
non-being, 10, 22, 23, 24, 26-7, 29 n. 149, 37, 39, 41, 42, 51-3, 90, 94, 120, 131, 138, 156, 172, 182, 185-6, 220, 255
—as *mē on*, 6, 20, 63 n. 289, 76
non-existence, 22, 28, 63
—as nothingness, 2, 6, 132
—as privation, 4, 7, 76
non-contradiction,
—the principle of, 4, 10, 12, 14, 43, 52-4, 127
number,
—addition in numbers, 94, 94 n. 139, 124
—commensurable, 89, 94-5, 126
—as composite unity, 90
—discrete, 86, 125
—division in numbers, 81, 81 n. 64, 81 n. 67, 94 n. 139, 100, 124
—essential or substantial (*oysiōdēs*), 73, 75-7, 80, 81-2, 84-91
—ideal, 38, 38 n. 192, 73, 81, 88 n. 103, 89-90
—infinite, 38, 45, 54, 56, 59, 88, 88 n. 103, 96 n. 150, 97-102, 126, 142, 171 n. 114, 197, 204, 230-1, 235, 246
—mathematical, 91
—monadic, or quantitative (*monadikos, toy posoy*), 73, 77, 83, 87-91
—numbering, 83, 85, 89-91, 100, 124
—transfinite, 38, 38 n. 192, 99, 102
—zero, 90, 97, 140
Numenius, 79 n. 54, 137 n. 324

object
—geometrical, 34, 72, 93, 95, 96, 97, 116-8, 120, 122, 124, 126, 128, 130-4, 134 n. 313, 135, 141-4, 146, 168, 178, 184, 185-6, 189, 192, 206, 208-9, 214, 217, 220, 222-4, 225 n. 348, 226-30, 234-40, 244-9, 251, 253, 256-60
—intelligible, 11 n. 60, 28, 38, 75,

78, 84, 87, 130-1, 137-8, 140, 148-50, 152, 155-7, 164, 178, 180-2, 184-6, 233-6, 240-2, 245, 246, 250
—mathematical, 45, 47, 57, 67, 95, 97, 101-2, 104, 113, 126-7, 130, 132, 135, 138, 205, 207, 210-2, 236, 256-7
—material, 13, 113
—physical, 14, 57, 71-2, 109, 113, 115, 118-120, 128-9, 161, 177-8, 205-6, 210, 217, 229-30
—of thinking, of thought (*noēton, noēta*), 74-5, 78, 80, 82, 84, 87, 148, 150-4, 156, 158, 160-1, 164, 166-7, 178, 180-2, 184-7, 188 n. 209, 233, 235, 240-1, 242, 245, 247, 250, 257-8
Ockham, 17, 66, 66 n. 301, 231 n. 376
Oenopides, 226
One, 9, 20, 20 n. 104, 21, 21 n. 109, 21 n. 110, 22-3, 23 n. 123, 24, 24 n. 130, 25, 25 n. 132, 26, 26 n. 137, 27-8, 28 n. 147, 37-8, 38 n. 195, 38 n. 197, 39, 51 n. 248, 52, 52 n. 252, 72, 74-7, 77 n. 41, 78, 78 n. 48, 79-80, 80 n. 58, 83-4, 85 n. 90, 88-90, 92, 100, 134, 136-40, 143, 147, 147 n. 5, 147 n. 7, 147 n. 8, 148, 150, 152, 154, 176-7, 179, 185, 240, 243, 255
ontology, ontological, 5, 8, 19, 20-1, 28, 30, 30 n. 154, 32, 34-5, 35 n. 178, 43-4, 49-50, 53, 58-9, 66, 68, 70, 72, 74-7, 81-5, 97, 99, 105, 108, 114, 124-5, 129-31, 152, 156, 174, 176, 178, 188-9, 191, 192, 199, 200, 207-8, 210, 227, 230, 234, 237, 238, 245, 249, 255-9
opinion (*doxa*), 45, 13, 71, 105, 131, 150, 151, 172-3, 176, 180, 180 n. 170, 181, 181 n. 175, 256
opposite, 3-5, 10-1, 11 n. 60, 23-4, 29 n. 149, 32, 39, 50-1, 53-5, 58, 74, 76, 79, 111, 112 n. 206, 127, 130-1, 137, 147, 180, 240
order, 27, 39, 54, 79 n. 58 60, 68, 75,

84, 87, 88 n. 103, 91, 97-8, 104-5, 105 n. 176, 107, 107 n. 135, 107 n. 137, 109-11, 112 n. 206, 114, 123-6, 129, 135, 143 n. 352, 150-1, 159, 168, 181, 184, 191, 204 n. 274, 204 n. 275, 206, 206 n. 281, 207, 211-2, 212 n. 301, 220, 223, 231, 238, 244, 251, 256-8
Origen, 54, 54 n. 258
otherness (*heterotēs, thateron*), the other, 11 n. 60, 12, 19, 21, 22-3, 25, 25 n. 135, 26, 26 n. 137, 26 n. 139, 28, 29 n. 150, 34, 37-8, 43, 52, 58-9, 62, 78, 78 n. 48, 79-81, 85, 85 n. 87, 86 n. 93, 89, 120, 124-6, 138-40, 140 n. 338, 142, 146-8, 150-3, 155, 159-60, 175, 182, 184, 187, 211, 237, 239-41, 243, 247, 251-3, 255, 257-8
—principle of otherness, 2, 6, 7, 11, 27, 77, 120, 142, 238, 245-6

Pappus, 104, 112, 112 n. 206, 227 n. 359
paradigm, 39, 67, 86, 88-90, 105, 109, 135, 146, 148, 150, 155, 161, 172, 182, 211, 214, 226, 235-6, 240
paradox, 6-7, 9-12, 22, 26-7, 49 n. 238, 51-3, 53 n. 254, 54, 54 n. 257, 55, 83, 92 n. 127, 96, 101, 132, 139, 141, 215,-6, 235, 241, 255-6
Parmenides, 22 n. 117, 131, 146, 146 n. 1, 167, 167 n. 105
"Parmenides", 21, 24-5, 74, 82, 92, 100, 127, 131, 137, 147, 147 n. 7
participation (*methexis, metokhē, metalēpsis*), 20 n. 104, 25, 73, 76 n. 36, 77, 78 n. 48, 81, 83, 88, 90, 185, 226
Pascal, B., 35 n. 178, 67 n. 305
Peano, G., 90, 90 n. 114, 98 n. 156
perception, 16, 23, 30, 33, 46 n. 232, 72, 93, 124, 157, 159, 162-4, 165 n. 97, 166, 168-9, 169 n. 110, 170, 170 n. 113, 172-6, 176 n. 151, 177, 177 n. 157-8, 180, 180 n. 183, 186-8, 192-

Index 295

8, 200, 204, 213, 216, 219, 220, 236, 245 n. 443, 258, 260
perfection, 5, 29, 30, 35 n. 178, 37, 40, 40 n. 206, 41, 41 n. 213, 42-3, 45-7, 47 n. 233, 50 n. 241, 54 n. 257, 61 n. 285, 65, 98-9, 103, 114, 123, 161 n. 78, 165 n. 99, 166, 199, 220, 242, 255
Peter Olivi, 231 n. 376
Philo, 24
Philo of Byzantium, 121 n. 250
Philolaus, 6 n. 30, 143 n. 352
Philoponus, 5 n. 21, 181, 181 n. 174, 182 n. 178, 182 n. 179
physics, 3 n. 2, 13-4, 14 n. 76, 15-6, 48, 51, 59, 63 n. 289, 70-1, 71 n. 7, 91, 95, 105-6, 106 n. 179, 108-9, 113-4, 114 n. 210, 115, 115 n. 217, 116-7, 117 n. 227, 117 n. 230, 118, 120, 128, 144, 161, 168, 208 n. 285, 210-1, 213, 213 n. 305, 214 n. 305, 227, 256-7
place, 2 n. 2, 5, 6, 13, 21 n. 109, 30, 38, 34, 44, 51, 58, 63 n. 289, 72, 83, 90, 96, 110, 128, 132, 134, 144, 158, 179, 187, 197 n. 243, 199, 218-9, 228 n. 362, 229-30, 233-4, 241-2, 245, 248, 249-51, 253-4
—imaginary place, 185-6
plane, 36, 92, 96, 125, 131, 134, 158, 222, 224, 251
Plato, 2-3, 3 n. 7, 6, 6 n. 28, 6 n. 29, 7, 7 n. 32, 7 n. 35, 8 n. 41, 9, 10 n. 55, 14, 14 n. 76, 21, 21 n. 109, 22 n. 111, 22 n. 117, 23 n. 123, 25 n. 132, 26 n. 135, 29 n. 149, 37, 38 n. 194, 43, 48, 52 n. 248, 53 n. 253, 62, 66 n. 301, 67, 71, 71 n. 8, 73, 73 n. 13, 73 n. 17, 74, 74 n. 21, 74 n. 22, 76 n. 37, 71 n. 41, 71 n. 43, 79 n. 53, 79 n. 54, 80 n. 62, 81, 81 n. 66, 81 n. 67, 81 n. 70, 82 n. 71, 82 n. 74, 85 n. 88, 87, 88 n. 102, 88 n. 103, 88 n. 104, 89, 91 n. 121, 92, 92 n. 127, 94 n. 139, 96 n. 150, 99, 100, 100 n. 160,

105, 108 n. 189, 111, 114 n. 211, 116, 116 n. 222, 117 n. 228, 118, 118 n. 237, 125 n. 271, 127, 127 n. 282, 128, 128 n. 283, 129, 129 n. 289, 129 n. 290, 130, 130 n. 293, 132, 133 n. 299, 133 n. 304, 135,138 n. 329, 138 n. 330, 140 n, 338, 143 n. 352, 146, 147 n. 4, 147 n. 6, 147 n. 7, 148, 148 n. 11, 149, 149 n. 13, 149 n. 15, 150, 150 n. 16, 150 n. 20, 151, 151 n. 21, 152, 152 n. 27, 153 n. 31, 153 n. 37, 153 n. 38, 154, 154 n. 39, 156 n. 54, 157 n. 56, 158 n. 62, 160 n. 71, 164, 164 n. 93, 165 n. 99, 167, 171 n. 115, 171 n. 116, 172 n. 117, 172 n. 118, 172 n. 119, 172 n. 120, 175, 175 n. 141, 178 n. 161, 178, 178 n. 163, 180-1, 181 n. 175, 183, 183 n. 188, 184 n. 192, 184 n. 193, 185, 185 n. 197, 207, 207 n. 282, 208, 210, 211, 211 n. 210 292, 211 n. 293, 213, 213 n. 306, 214 n. 310, 220, 225, 225 n. 346, 225 n. 348, 226 n. 354, 234, 237 n. 395, 238 n. 399, 238 n. 404, 239, 239 n. 408, 240, 240 n. 416, 240 n. 417, 255-6, 258
Plempius, V.P., 57 n. 271, 63 n. 289, 120 n. 242
Plotinus, 2 n. 2, 3, 4 n. 17, 6, 6 n. 27, 6 n. 28, 6 n. 29, 7 n. 32, 7 n. 34, 7 n. 35, 7 n. 36, 8,8 n. 40, 8 n. 42, 8 n. 43, 8 n. 44, 9 n. 45, 9 n. 47, 9 n. 48, 9 n. 49, 9 n. 51, 9 n. 52, 9 n. 53, 10, 10 n. 54, 10 n. 55, 10 n. 58, 10 n. 59, 11 n. 61, 11 n. 63, 12, 12 n. 65, 12 n. 66, 12 n. 67, 12 n. 68, 15, 19-20, 20 n. 100, 20 n. 101, 20 n. 102, 20 n. 103, 20 n. 104, 20 n. 105, 21, 21 n. 106, 21 n. 107, 21 n. 108, 21 n. 109, 21 n. 110, 21 n. 111, 22, 22 n. 112, 22 n. 113, 22 n. 115, 22 n. 116, 23, 23 n. 121, 23 n. 122, 23 n. 123, 24, 24 n. 127, 24 n. 130, 24 n. 131, 25 n. 132, 25 n. 134, 25 n. 135, 26, 26 n.136, 26 n. 139, 26 n. 140, 27 n. 141, 27 n. 142, 27 n.

143, 27 n. 144, 28, 28 n. 145, 28 n. 146, 28 n. 147, 29 n. 149, 34, 35 n. 178, 37, 37 n. 191, 38, 38 n. 194, 38 n. 195, 38 n. 196, 39, 39 n. 198, 39 n. 199, 39 n. 200, 42, 48, 51, 51 n. 245, 52, 52 n. 249, 52 n. 250, 52 n. 251, 52 n. 252, 54-5, 57-8, 66, 71 n. 7, 72-3, 73 n. 12, 73 n. 13, 73 n. 15, 73 n. 16, 73 n. 17, 73 n. 18, 74, 74 n. 19, 74 n. 21, 74 n. 22, 74 n. 23, 74 n. 24, 75, 75 n. 26, 75 n. 27, 75 n. 28, 75 n. 31, 75 n. 36, 76, 76 n. 33, 76 n. 34, 76 n. 36, 76 n. 37, 76 n. 38, 77, 77 n. 41, 77 n. 42, 78, 78 n. 44, 78 n. 46, 78 n. 47, 78 n. 48, 78 n. 49, 78 n. 50, 78 n. 51, 79 n. 53, 79 n. 54, 79 n. 55, 79 n. 56, 79 n. 58, 80, 80 n. 59, 80 n. 60, 80 n. 61, 80 n. 62, 80 n. 63, 81 n. 64, 81 n. 65, 81 n. 66, 81. 68, 81 n. 69, 82, 82 n. 70, 82 n. 72, 82 n. 73, 82 n. 75, 83, 83 n. 80, 83 n. 81, 84 n. 82, 84 n. 83, 84 n. 85, 85, 85 n. 86, 85 n. 87, 85 n. 88, 85 n. 89, 85 n. 90, 85 n. 91, 86, 86 n. 94, 86 n. 95, 86 n. 97, 86 n. 93, 87, 87 n. 100, 87 n. 101, 88, 88 n. 104, 88 n. 105, 88 n. 106, 88 n. 107, 89, 89 n. 108, 90, 90 n. 115, 91 n. 117, 91 n. 118, 91 n. 119, 91 n. 120, 99 n. 121, 92, 92 n. 125, 93 n. 132, 96 n. 152, 100, 100 n. 161, 100 n. 162, 125 n. 271, 131-2, 132 n. 297, 132 n. 293, 134, 135 n. 314, 136 n. 316, 136 n. 319, 136 n. 320, 136 n. 321, 136 n. 322, 136 n. 323, 137 n. 324, 137 n. 325, 137 n. 326, 137 n. 329, 138, 138 n. 330, 139, 139 n. 335, 139 n. 336, 140, 140 n. 337, 140 n. 338, 140 n. 339, 140 n. 340, 141, 141 n. 341, 142, 146, 146 n. 1, 146 n. 2, 146 n. 3, 147, 147 n. 4, 147 n. 5, 147 n. 7, 147 n. 8, 148, 148 n. 9, 148 n. 10, 148 n. 11, 149, 149 n. 14, 149 n. 15, 150, 150 n. 16, 150 n. 17, 150 n. 18, 150 n. 18, 151 n. 22, 152, 152 n. 26, 152 n. 27, 152 n. 28, 153 n. 29, 152 n. 33, 153 n. 34, 153 n. 35, 152 n. 36, 153 n. 37, 154 n. 39, 154 n. 40, 154 n. 41, 155, 155 n. 43, 155 n. 44, 155 n. 45, 155 n. 46, 155 n. 47, 155 n. 48, 155 n. 49, 156 n. 50, 156 n. 51, 156 n. 52, 156 n. 53, 156 n. 54, 157 n. 55, 157 n. 56, 164, 167, 167 n. 105, 171, 175, 175 n. 142, 175 n. 143, 175 n. 145, 176, 176 n. 147, 176 n. 148, 176 n. 149, 176 n. 150, 177, 177 n. 153, 177 n. 154, 177 n. 155, 177 n. 156, 177 n. 157, 177 n. 158, 177 n. 159, 177 n. 160, 178, 178 n. 161, 178 n. 162, 178 n. 163, 179 n. 164, 179 n. 165, 180, 183-5, 185 n. 196, 185 n. 198, 186, 186 n. 200, 186 n. 201, 187, 187 n. 203, 196, 208, 220, 234, 236, 236 n. 393, 236 n. 394, 237 n. 395, 237 n. 397, 238 n. 399, 239, 239 n. 408, 239 n. 413, 240, 240 n. 414, 240 n. 418, 240 n. 419, 240 n. 420, 241, 241 n. 422, 241 n. 423, 242, 242 n. 426, 242 n. 427, 242 n. 428, 242 n. 429, 242 n. 430, 242 n. 431, 242 n. 432, 242 n. 433, 243, 243 n. 434, 243 n. 435, 243 n. 436, 243 n. 437, 244, 244 n. 438, 244 n. 440, 244 n. 441, 245, 245 n. 442, 253, 253 n. 473, 255-8

Plutarch, 70 n. 1, 90, 90 n. 113, 129 n. 290, 153 n. 31, 181-2, 182 n. 179
Plutarch of Athens, 258
point, 56, 63, 85 n. 92, 86, 86 n. 93, 92 n. 127, 91-3, 96, 96 n. 150, 101, 108, 109, 113, 118, 120, 125, 128, 131, 132, 142, 155, 184, 205, 222, 228, 229, 230 n. 371, 237-8, 238 n. 399, 239, 246, 250-1, 251 n. 466, 252-3, 256-7, 260
Pollot, A., 59, 59 n. 278
Porphyry, 6 n. 28, 6 n. 29, 9, 20, 29 n. 154, 81 n. 66, 111, 114 n. 211, 132 n. 297, 142, 146 n. 1, 180 n. 170,

179, 182 n. 181, 182 n. 183, 183, 183 n. 189, 184 n. 194, 247 n. 450, 258
position, 5, 13, 39, 47, 86 n. 93, 93, 172, 175, 177, 186, 190, 210, 234, 236, 247
positivity, 8, 50,
possibility, 3, 4, 6, 8-9, 35, 42, 52, 67-8, 75, 99, 111, 116 n. 220, 120, 138-9, 154, 163, 167, 171, 185, 192, 196, 200-1, 213, 222, 224, 247, 253, 255
postulate (*aitēma*), 224-5, 225 n. 328
potency, 3, 21, 26, 28, 37, 81, 139, 143-4, 147 n. 5, 157, 175, 186
—negative potency, 8, 28
potentiality, 4-5, 7, 9, 11, 26, 28, 36, 42, 60, 67, 67 n. 305, 90-1, 122, 136-7, 139-41, 143, 148, 154, 185-6, 213, 238, 240-1, 249, 255, 257
praxis, 212
predicate, 3-4, 6-8, 12, 22-26, 29, 43, 51-2, 55, 60, 64, 71, 76, 78, 81-2, 106, 140, 242, 252
principle
—of being, 43, 52, 75-7, 131, 167, 237
—limiting principle (*horizon*), 26, 93
—of number, 76, 98, 93, 253
—of otherness, 2, 6, 11, 27, 83 n. 80, 77, 120, 142, 238, 245-6
—productive principle, 9, 143
—of sameness, 77, 140
privation (*sterēsis*), 4, 6-9, 17, 24-5, 27-8, 40-1, 63 n. 289, 76, 138, 143-4, 144 n. 354
Proclus, 4 n. 17, 5 n. 26, 8 n. 40, 14 n. 76, 23, 23 n. 124, 24, 25 n. 132, 37, 37 n. 189, 39, 39 n. 201, 42 n. 216, 55, 57, 70 n. 2, 72, 75, 75 n. 27, 75 n. 29, 76 n. 33, 77, 77 n. 40, 77 n. 41, 79 n. 58, 83 n. 77, 85, 85 n. 92, 86 n. 93, 91 n. 121, 92, 92 n. 122, 92 n. 124, 92 n. 125, 92 n. 126, 92 n. 128, 93 n. 131, 93 n. 134, 93 n. 135, 93 n. 136, 93 n. 137, 94 n. 142, 96 n. 150, 100 n. 160, 106, 109, 111, 111 n. 202, 112 n. 205, 114, 114 n. 211, 117 n. 228, 124 n. 266, 125, 125 n. 268, 126 n. 273, 128, 128 n. 287, 129 n. 288, 130, 131 n. 294, 137 n. 394, 141, n. 342, 142, 142 n. 343, 143 n. 351, 143 n. 352, 146 n. 1, 148 n. 10, 151 n. 23, 152, 152 n. 25, 153, 153 n. 30, 164, 167, 171, 179-80, 180 n. 167, 180 n. 168, 180 n. 170, 180 n. 171, 180 n. 172, 182 n. 177, 182 n, 180, 183, 183 n. 186, 183 n. 186, 183 n. 190, 184, 184 n. 193, 184 n. 194, 207 n. 283, 208, 215 n. 311, 225, 225 n. 346, 226, 234, 234 n. 386, 234 n. 387, 235 n. 388, 236 n. 391, 237 n. 396, 237 n. 398, 238 n. 400, 238 n. 402, 238 n. 403, 238 n. 404, 239 n. 406, 239 n. 409, 239 n. 410, 245, 245 n. 444, 246 n. 445, 246 n. 446, 247, 247 n. 448, 247 n. 449, 247 n. 450, 248 n. 452, 249 n. 453, 249 n. 454, 249 n. 455, 249 n. 456, 249 n. 457, 450, 450 n. 458, 251, 251 n. 465, 251 n.467, 251 n. 468, 252, 252 n. 469, 253, 253 n. 474, 253 n. 475, 256-8, 260
production, 11 n. 61, 28, 33-4, 38 n. 197, 47, 82, 113, 119, 141, 143, 147 n. 8, 157, 180, 198, 213-15, 218, 222-3, 228 n. 362, 232
—kinematic production of a geometrical figure, 85-8, 185, 222-3, 232, 229, 245-251
property, 13, 34, 93, 101, 151, 223 n. 338, 225, 229
—accidental, 11
—essential, 11
proof, 40-1, 44, 105, 111, 111 n. 200, 181, 184, 213, 232, 235
—as *apodeixis*, 225, 225 n. 347, 205
proportion, 25, 94-5, 108 n. 188, 117, 117 n. 228, 125-6, 141
purpose, 4, 22, 188, 230, 248,

—as *telos*, 35, 213, 216-7
Pythagoras, 26 n. 138
Pythagoreans, 26, 36, 70, 77, 77 n. 41, 89-90, 93, 125, 143 n. 352, 251

quality, qualities, 6, 9, 12, 14, 19, 24, 31, 40, 72, 114 n. 210, 118, 133, 143 n. 353, 159, 190, 223, 237, 241
—bodily, 16
—elementary 2 n. 2
—primary, 16
—secondary, 16
quantity, 9, 15 n. 80, 16, 16 n. 89, 17, 29, 35-6, 49, 55, 49 n, 238, 73, 86, 94, 99, 107, 113, 114 n. 210, 121 n. 245, 123, 143 n. 353, 202, 210, 228
quidditas, 17

ratio, 70 n. 6, 91, 94-5, 157 n. 57, 158 n. 62, 194 n. 233, 212, 222 n. 332
reality, 17-19, 29-30, 41-2, 49 n. 238, 64, 80 n. 62, 98, 104, 130, 136, 161 n. 78, 165, 165 n. 97, 165 n. 99, 166, 174, 176, 194, 203, 206, 231, 255, 259-60
—physical reality, 117-8, 150
reason, 14-5, 17, 30, 35 n. 178, 43-4, 46, 50, 61 n. 284, 63, 72, 77, 97, 101, 103-4, 106, 114, 121, 123, 125, 146, 157-8, 160, 162, 167, 168, 171-2, 176 n. 151, 184-5, 189-90, 190 n. 22, 191, 191 n. 223, 193-4, 194 n. 233, 194 n. 234, 195-6, 196 n. 243, 197-8, 200, 202, 203 n. 273, 204-5, 208-10, 216-22, 222 n. 332, 232-3, 244, 246, 251, 253, 258-60
receptivity, 9, 143
reflectivity, 10-1, 11 n. 61, 167, 169-71, 177, 196, 242, 258
relation, 3, 4 n. 17, 7-8, 12, 19, 23, 25, 37, 44-5, 60, 75, 81, 81 n. 68, 92 n. 122, 94-5, 106-7, 107 n. 185, 117-8, 122-8, 140-1, 192, 204 n. 275, 205, 209, 212 n. 301, 229, 236
—of equivalence, 30

—"from which", *ex hoy*, 4
—"into which", *eis ho*, 4, 242
res, 33, 48, 64, 66, 105, 201 n. 262
—*res extensa*, 30, 49, 50, 62, 68, 117, 123, 126-7, 132, 143, 166, 198, 200, 205, 209-10, 216-7, 229, 231
—*res cogitans*, 30, 44, 50, 62, 68, 113, 117, 123, 126-7, 132, 143, 166, 198, 205, 207, 215, 216, 229, 231
"Regulae", 15, 106-7, 115 n. 219, 124, 157-8, 189-90, 190 n. 220, 191-2, 201 n. 262, 205-7
rest (*stasis*), 240, 242

sameness, the same (*tayton*), 10, 12, 16, 25-6, 37, 52, 77-80, 94, 138, 140, 142, 146-8, 152-3, 157, 238-41, 243, 245, 251, 255
scholasticism, 17, 31, 40
science, 2, 4 n. 17, 5, 12, 14, 16, 19, 35-6, 53 n. 254, 55, 57, 59, 70, 70 n. 1, 71, 73 n. 12, 83, 91, 94, 97, 103-7, 107 n. 135, 108, 108 n. 190, 109-10, 112-3, 116-7, 119-22, 124, 127, 131, 152, 161, 184-5, 195, 201, 204, 209-10, 213, 213 n. 305, 204, 221, 224-6, 228-9, 235, 245-6, 250, 252, 255-6, 258-60
self-awareness, 30, 43, 45, 104, 170, 216-7, 222,
self-causation, 42, 255
sense-perception, sensation (*aisthēsis*), 21, 33, 93, 176 n. 151, 177, 177 n. 157, 180 n. 170, 181, 183, 187 n. 206, 258, 260
separability, separable (*khōriston*), 3, 5

Sextus Empiricus, 75 n. 27, 79 n. 53, 81 n. 66, 174
shape, 15, 15 n. 33, 16, 16 n. 37, 18 n. 97, 33 n., 108 n. 188, 169, 72, 113, 127, 132, 141-2, 157, 179, 181-2, 187, 189, 198-9, 220, 227-8, 234, 239, 246, 248, 250, 253
—as *morphē*, 136, 237

simplicity, 2, 25, 29, 30, 42 n. 216, 60, 106, 115, 126, 130, 159, 170, 223, 246, 249
Simplicius, 9, 6 n. 28, 6 n. 29, 8 n. 40, 38 n. 196, 70 n. 4, 72 n. 10, 76 n. 33, 81 n. 64, 81 n. 66, 94 n. 138, 129, 180 n. 168, 183
size, 15 n. 83, 18 n. 97, 19 n. 97, 49 n. 238, 94-5, 126, 187 n. 206, 190, 202, 210
soul (*anima*) (see also: mind), 11 n. 61, 18, 43, 59, 60 n. 281, 68, 78 n. 48, 79 n. 54, 85, 104, 110-1, 114 n. 210, 115 n. 213, 129-31, 136, 139, 147 n. 7, 155, 157 n. 57, 167 n. 104, 171-3, 175-6, 176 n. 151, 177, 179, 183 n. 137, 188, 190, 192, 199, 203, 206 n. 279, 212, 214, 219, 221, 236, 243 n. 436, 244, 253
space
—and corporeal substance, 13
—empty, 49, 185-6
—as extension, 13, 209
—idea of, 13
—imaginary, 49, 51, 202, 217, 233
—real, 51, 185, 202, 252
Spinoza, 30 n. 158, 31 n. 163, 32, 32 n. 165, 35 n. 178, 59, 59 n. 780, 60 n. 781, 65, 65 n. 705, 110, 146 n. 78, 165 n. 97, 165 n. 99, 171 n. 114, 222 n. 332
Stampioen, 124 n. 265
status movendi, 241
Suarez, F., 17, 17 n. 90, 18, 40 n. 206, 63 n. 291
subject,
—finite, 113
—and predicate, 51
—and substrate (*hypokeimenon*), 3, 53, 21 n. 110, 79 n. 34, 135-6
subjectivity
—finite, 34, 103, 110, 164, 214-7, 231
—infinite, 47, 113, 132, 211, 214-7, 221

substance
—corporeal, 13, 18, 18 n. 97, 117, 188
—created, 33, 170-1, 222, 232
—and essence, 58, 108, 127
—extended, 15, 29, 50, 59, 194, 260
—finite, 29, 29 n. 129, 30-34, 36, 39-42, 48-9, 58-60, 62, 64-8, 98, 105, 155, 166
—immaterial, 33
—knowledge of, 61 n. 285, 62
—notion of, 28, 31-2, 39, 40, 58, 65, 123
—as *oysia* 2 n. 2, 3 n. 10, 21 n. 110, 4, 8, 28, 73, 117, 242
—spiritual, thinking, 13, 30, 34, 41, 58-61, 61 n. 284, 62, 66, 157, 159, 161, 166-7, 188, 199, 207, 215, 258
—as subject, 30 n. 154
Synesius, 182, 182 n. 185
synthesis, 38, 74, 82, 92, 110-2, 112 n. 206, 115, 139, 147, 147 n. 8, 150, 191, 255
Syrianus, 73 n. 14, 73 n. 17, 77 n. 41, 142 n. 349, 151 n. 24, 171, 179, 180 n. 168, 181 n. 176, 183-4, 184 n. 190, 234, 234 n. 285, 235 n. 389, 236 n. 390, 246 n. 447, 248, 248 n. 451, 258, 260

telos, 35, 146, 155, 213, 216, 241-2
Thales, 83 n. 78
Themistius, 70 n. 3, 92 n. 125, 137 n. 324, 146 n. 2, 156 n. 54, 186 n. 202 187 n. 206, 225 n. 305, 227 n. 359, 243 n. 436
Theophrastus, 70 n. 4, 225 n. 345
thing,
—as *ti*, 4
—as *tode ti*, 3
thinking (see: discursive reasoning or thinking, *dianoia*, intellect, *noys*, and spiritual or thinking substance)
time, 10, 20-1, 85, 89, 124, 131, 139, 150,

155, 239, 257
Toletus, 143 n. 253
trajectory, 228, 252
transcendence, 49, 62, 216
truth, 6, 30, 34, 48, 56, 58, 60, 65, 68, 103-22, 162-3, 168, 170-1, 194, 196, 199, 203-4, 212-3, 220, 231

unit (*monas*), 55 n. 262, 77, 89
—in number (numeric unit), 77
unity, 4, 10, 12, 15-7, 23, 25, 43, 72, 74-8, 78 n.48, 79-80, 80 n. 58, 82-3, 83 n. 80, 86, 88-9, 90 n. 113, 91, 99 n. 158, 108 n. 188, 99 n. 138, 136-9, 146-7, 147 n. 8, 148-55, 170, 174, 177, 184, 187 n. 206, 191, 228, 235, 238-9, 241, 245, 248, 255-6
unlimited, 9, 11, 26, 37, 40 n. 206, 76, 80, 80 n. 58, 81, 88, 90 n. 113, 92, 122, 125, 142-3, 143 n. 352, 147, 180, 204, 215, 230, 231 n. 376, 238-9, 252-3, 255

Vatier, A., 161 n. 78

Vegetius, 121 n. 250
verum factum principle, 210-3, 222, 229, 259
via negativa, 22-4, 46
via positiva, 23
Vico, G., 211 n. 296
Ville-Bressieu, E. de, 122 n. 251
Voetius, G., 117 n. 226, 222 n. 333
Vorstius, A., 55 n. 265, 113 n. 207

Walter of Brugge, 231 n. 376
whole, 11, 19-21, 35 n. 178, 37-41, 50, 68, 77-8, 97, 98, 99 n. 158, 100, 102, 122, 149-50, 152, 196, 235, 238, 244-5, 251-2, 256
—*holon*, 35
Wittgenstein, L., 169 n. 110, 173 n. 133

Xenocrates, 73 n. 14, 73 n. 17, 79 n. 54, 89, 92, 92 n. 127, 134

Zeno, 3 n. 2, 92 n. 127